FLINDERS PETRIE

FLINDERS PETRIE

A Life in Archaeology

by

MARGARET S. DROWER

LONDON
VICTOR GOLLANCZ LTD
1985

First published in Great Britain 1985
by Victor Gollancz Ltd,
14 Henrietta Street, London WC2E 8QJ

ACKNOWLEDGEMENT

Quotations from *The Letters of T. E. Lawrence*, edited by David Garnett, are reproduced by permission of The Letters of T. E. Lawrence Trust, the Editor, and Jonathan Cape Ltd; a short quotation from *Pioneer to the Past* by Charles Breasted is copyright 1943 Charles Breasted, copyright renewed © 1971, reprinted with the permission of Charles Scribner's Sons.

British Library Cataloguing in Publication Data
Drower, Margaret S.
Flinders Petrie: a life in archaeology.
Great Britain—Biography
I. Title
930.1'092'4 CC115.P4

ISBN 0-575-03667-2

Photoset in Great Britain by
Rowland Phototypesetting Ltd, Bury St Edmunds, Suffolk
and printed by St Edmundsbury Press, Bury St Edmunds, Suffolk
Illustrations originated and printed by Thomas Campone, Southampton

To Ann
in gratitude for her help,
and her patience

NOTE

Alternative spellings of some Egyptian place-names will be found both in the text and index. Uniformity has proved impossible, since the orthography current in Petrie's time differs from that in common use today. Where possible, the spelling in Baines and Málek, *Atlas of Ancient Egypt* (1978) has been adopted.

CONTENTS

LIST OF ILLUSTRATIONS

Black and white plates following page 58

Colour plates following page 90

Black and white plates following page 218

Black and white plates following page 282

Colour plates following page 314

Black and white plates following page 378

Black and white illustrations in text

SOURCES AND ACKNOWLEDGEMENTS

A biography of Sir Flinders Petrie, one of the remarkable personalities of his time, and a figure familiar to all archaeologists as one of the founders of their science, is long overdue. Less than ten years after his death, his widow was approached by a writer of popular books on archaeology with the request that he might write a life of the great excavator; his proposal was accepted, and a large amount of papers and letters were handed over to him; he talked many times to her, and also to others who had known her husband—Dr Margaret Murray, Mrs Crowfoot and G. L. Wainwright among them—making rough notes of the interviews. Little more seems to have been done; in 1972 he reluctantly decided that he would never be able to write the biography, and the files were returned to Sir Flinders' daughter Ann. When I was asked to take over the task, he was already in poor health and could make little of his notes, and those to whom he had talked were no longer living.

The sources on which the present biography is mainly based may be briefly enumerated. First, there is his autobiography, *Seventy Years in Archaeology*, published in 1931. It follows a chronological arrangement, and reference to the relevant chapters of it will be given in the Notes under the abbreviation *70 Years*. *PP* are the Petrie Papers, now presented by his daughter to the Petrie Museum, University College London; a large collection of family correspondence, letters addressed to Petrie, press cuttings and miscellaneous documents, and his pocket diaries covering almost every year from 1880 to 1940, in which he briefly noted the main event or activity of each day, often with a list of those to whom he had written letters, and sometimes the weather or the state of his health. His father's diaries, much more detailed, cover (though with many volumes missing) the years between 1850 and 1910, and together with private correspondence, are in the possession of Miss Lisette Petrie.

An early diary of Flinders Petrie during the years 1876–1883, closely written on large sheets of foolscap (two or even three weeks to a page) is also in the Petrie Museum; this is part of the archive referred to here as *UCL* Petrie MSS, which also contains many letters written to Petrie at various times during his life, some juvenilia, and a number of letters from Petrie to his friend Flaxman Spurrell, which were returned to him by the latter's widow at the time when he was writing his autobiography. (Other letters to Spurrell are now in the possession of the Norwich Museum, and are quoted by kind permission of the Librarian.) The Petrie Museum also preserves rough distribution lists of his finds, tomb cards from a number of sites, and 150 small notebooks, usually about 5″ × 3″, containing the excavator's field notes and those of his assistants; these record measurements and angle observations for plans, diagrams of tomb contents, rough copies of inscriptions, lists of names of workmen, with wages and *bakhshish* credited to them daily and weekly lists of antiquities bought, or (for *bakhshish* purposes) prices asked by local dealers; these are also sometimes found in the diaries. The Museum has also a large collection of photographs, from which I have been privileged to choose illustrations for this book.

Tomb cards, several field notebooks, and photographs of Petrie's excavations in Palestine are in the Institute of Archaeology, University of London, along with his collection of Palestinian antiquities.

Petrie's *Journals*, presented to the Griffith Institute, Ashmolean Museum, Oxford (there are copies in University College London) were serial letters sent, usually every week, sometimes more often, by post to a select number of his friends and family in England: each instalment was read by the first recipient and quickly passed on. These letters describe day-to-day events and discoveries in the field, with sometimes a description of an adventure or an amusing experience, and are fullest during the early years before his marriage, when he was often alone in the field; thereafter his wife sometimes wrote them in his stead, or supplemented them with her own. Extracts from the *Journals* are frequent in Petrie's autobiography, and I have not hesitated to quote extensively from them, since they convey, better than his formal excavation reports, both the excitement of discovery and the personality of the writer. The Griffith Institute also holds in its archives letters from Petrie to Newberry, Griffith and Gardiner (referred to in the notes here as *GI/ Griffith* etc.).

The archives of the Egypt Exploration Society (*EES*) contain much that is relevant to Petrie's career in the early days, especially during the years when he was employed by the Society (then called the Egypt Exploration Fund). Here too are private letters written by him to Miss Amelia Edwards, which were donated to the Fund after her death.

In expressing my gratitude to those who have helped me in the course of my research, I must first thank the Provost and Committee of University College London, for permitting me to use and quote from the College archives; I am especially indebted to the staff of the Department of Egyptology and the Petrie Museum, in particular to Dr David Dixon for his help in the selection of photographs, and to Mrs Barbara Adams and Miss Rosalind Hall for their unfailing and patient help in putting the Petrie archives at my disposal; above all, I am grateful to the Edwards Professor, Harry S. Smith, who has from the beginning given me his constant support and encouragement; unsparing of his time, he has read nearly all the manuscript and given me valuable advice and criticism. For what errors remain, I am alone responsible. My thanks are due to those who have given me facilities in other countries: to Mrs Crystal Bennett, who tirelessly drove me about to see sites in Palestine which Petrie had dug, and to Canon Wilkinson, her successor as Director of the British School of Archaeology in Jerusalem, to Ms Zita

Whitfield, and to the Director of the Department of Antiquities in Jerusalem for permitting a search in the archives of the Rockefeller Museum and allowing me to quote from the substance of them. I am grateful to the staff of the Boston Museum of Fine Arts, and in particular to Edward Brovarski and Sue d'Auria, for permitting me to consult the archives in their library; and to Dr Akasha, the acting Director of the National Museum in Khartoum, Dr Khidhr Issa, Inspector of Antiquities, and Mrs Awatif, the Librarian, for kindly allowing me to look at the books from Petrie's library (many of them annotated by him) now in the Library of the Department of Antiquities. Dr Rosalie David and the Keeper of the Manchester Museum kindly enabled me to look through the correspondence between the Petries and Miss Crompton, and gave me permission to use several photographs; Dr J. Málek and the staff of the Griffith Institute gave me every assistance.

I am grateful to the Chairman and Committee of the Egypt Exploration Society for permitting me the extensive use of their archives and allowing me to quote from them, and to Miss Mary Crawford, Mrs Shirley Strong and Dr Patricia Spencer, successive Secretaries of the Society, for their help on many occasions. The Palestine Exploration Fund kindly allowed me to peruse their archives in connection with Petrie's Tell el Hesy excavation, and I have to thank Mr Peter Brown for permission to see, at the British Academy, correspondence relating to the Joint Archaeological Committee and the Librarian of the Society of Antiquaries for showing me Petrie's plans. To Mr T. G. H. James and the staff of his Department at the British Museum I am indebted, as always, for help and advice on matters Egyptological, and also for several photographs; for permission to consult correspondence in the Archives of the Western Asiatic Department I am indebted to the Keeper. Mr Peter Parr, in the Institute of Archaeology, very kindly read through the chapters on Palestine and made some very helpful suggestions for which I am grateful. To the Leverhulme Trust I am indebted for the grant of an Emeritus Fellowship. Robert Morkot, who typed most of my manuscript, deserves my special thanks.

I have had the privilege of talking with a number of people who worked with Petrie in the field; some of them, sadly, are no longer living: Richmond Brown, Gerald Harding, John Waechter and Lady Burton and Dr G. Caton Thompson. Robert Hamilton, Dr Veronica Seton-Williams, and Messrs Jack Ellis and Carl Pape have given me the benefit of their reminiscences and most kindly answered my questions; above all, Miss Olga Tufnell has done me the great kindness of reading through my chapters on Palestine and corrected me on some matters of fact; she has published her own still vivid memories of life in a Petrie camp. Lady Thornton (Miss Bonar) and Mrs Robert Jacobs regaled me with reminiscences of their years as secretaries in London to the British School of Archaeology in Egypt, Mrs Joan Crowfoot Payne and Professor Dorothy Hodgkin O.M. with childhood memories; the late Dame Kathleen Kenyon talked to me about Petrie's work, and Sir Mortimer Wheeler allowed me to quote from his own memories.

The debt which I owe to Miss Ann Petrie will be apparent throughout this book; without her generosity in putting all her father's papers at my disposal, and giving me the benefit of her clear recollections and balanced judgment, this book would never have been written. Finally, I would like to thank my husband for his unfailing patience and support.

M.S.D.
1985

PROLOGUE

ON 17 JUNE 1953 University College London celebrated the centenary of the birth of one of their most distinguished professors, Sir William Matthew Flinders Petrie, K.B.E., F.R.S., F.B.A. At first planned for his actual birthday, 3 June, the celebrations had to be postponed to avoid coinciding with the coronation on 2 June of Queen Elizabeth II. The occasion was an important one for the College and the celebrations were attended by a large number of those who had been Petrie's friends, colleagues and students. His widow, Lady Petrie, leaning on a stick, her white hair straight-cut in a fringed bob above a face lined and bronzed by the sun of countless summers, was the guest of honour; John and Ann Petrie, his son and daughter, were there, with John's wife and small daughter Lisette, the only grandchild. Dr Alexander Petrie, a specialist in psychological medicine (who had been launched on his career through the kindness of his cousin Flinders) and his son Robert were the only other members of the family present. There were representatives of the principal archaeological societies and Schools, and of many of the museums whose collections had been enriched by his discoveries over the years, among them the British Museum, the Ashmolean Museum of Oxford, the Fitzwilliam in Cambridge, the Museums of Manchester and Liverpool, the Boston Museum of Fine Arts, the University Museum of Philadelphia and the Oriental Institute of Chicago. Several, including the Ashmolean, the British Museum and the Royal Ontario Museum in Toronto, mounted small exhibitions in honour of the centenary; one or two booksellers had commemorative displays of his books.

In London, the Institute of Archaeology in St John's Lodge, Regent's Park, had a special display of the antiquities brought back by Sir Flinders from his excavations in Palestinian sites; these had formed the nucleus of the teaching collection in the institute which had owed its foundation in part to his vision and generosity, twenty years previously. At University College itself, the Petrie Collection, the fruit of his long labours and the foundation of his teaching since its beginnings in

1892, was open to visitors; sadly, not in the long galleries above the south wing of the main building which had been its home since the beginning—these had been totally destroyed during the Blitz in 1941—but in a makeshift museum over the boiler-house in Foster Court, at the side of the College, where space was restricted. At that time, only part of the collection had been unpacked from the cases in which the antiquities had been stored in the country during the war, and was being arranged by Dr A. J. Arkell and his assistants. An appeal was to be launched for the re-housing of this valuable collection; today, more than thirty years later, costs of building have escalated and it has still not been possible to remove it from its temporary and unsuitable refuge.

The festivities on this afternoon began with tea, at which several hundred people were present; old friends met and reminisced about the days before the war, their experiences in camp with "the Prof.", or memories of lectures in the Twenties and Thirties which had usually been crowded with those anxious to hear about his latest finds. After tea Professor Stephen Glanville, Provost of King's College Cambridge, who had succeeded Petrie as Edwards Professor of Egyptology at University College, gave the Centenary lecture. He spoke of the remarkable career of this great archaeologist and teacher, of the "driving force which held him unflagging to so arduous a course during almost three quarters of a century of constant labour in the field". He spoke briefly of Flinders' early education at home by his unusually gifted parents, of the rapid growth of his independence and, in the face of precarious health and considerable obstacles, of his determination and his courage—"two of his most attractive qualities, which if they sometimes had a nuisance value for others, were indispensable for the success of his work".

He reviewed briefly the main phases of the development of his career in Egypt. He quoted a number of short extracts from Petrie's letters and writings, some amusing, others illustrating the generosity or illuminating the ingenuity of his mind, and he ended by expressing the debt owed by all Egyptologists to Petrie's teaching and example, in the Chair founded by Miss Amelia Edwards and held by Petrie for so long. The Museum, he said, was already in 1925 the best Egyptological teaching collection in the world, and the College was now "the recognized training ground for all who intend to take up Egyptian Archaeology; in the last sixty years there has hardly been a British Egyptologist who made his career in the subject, who did not come under Petrie's aegis at one time or another".

At the close of the lecture a short film was shown, made by one of the de Laszlo family in the garden of their house at the time when Petrie was sitting for his portrait. For some of us who were present, it was curiously moving to see once more the handsome, white-bearded old man moving about the garden and seated in animated conversation at the tea-table—one could almost hear his light voice and characteristic, high-pitched laugh.

After the lecture, eighty people sat down to dinner in the refectory, under the portrait that so vividly portrays the venerable figure as we knew him in the College, in his academic robes, leaning forward a little and eager to talk, perhaps about the little statuette of an Egyptian goddess which he holds in his long, sensitive fingers. The Provost of University College, Dr Ifor Evans, made a short speech; Dr Margaret Murray spoke of his gifts as a teacher; Professor W. B. Emery, at that time the Edwards Professor, proposed a toast, and Lady Petrie replied; at the end of her talk she presented to the College a cheque for £100, to start subscriptions for a Flinders Petrie Scholarship, to be awarded to students for travel and study in Egypt; the fund was later augmented by money transferred to the College by the British School of Egyptian Archaeology, then in process of being wound up.

Sir Flinders Petrie had died in Palestine during the Second World War, in his ninetieth year. At the time, the world was preoccupied with other events, and news of his death received scant notice by the Press; obituaries appeared sporadically during the following years in various learned journals, but the centenary afforded an opportunity for leading articles in daily newspapers, and a commemorative programme was devised by the B.B.C. in its television service, under the chairmanship of Dr Glyn Daniel; during the programme objects from the Petrie Collection were displayed and commented upon by Dr Margaret Murray, Petrie's erstwhile assistant and colleague, who was herself ninety years of age. Not long after, a plaque was affixed to the house in Hampstead, No. 5, Cannon Place, where Petrie had last lived. He is, I believe, the only archaeologist to be so honoured in London.

Flinders Petrie's output was extraordinary, his energy unflagging. He was responsible for over a hundred books, and more than a thousand articles and reviews. His research into Egypt's past, begun in 1880, continued almost without a break until a year or two before his death; he dug over fifty different sites, in the Delta and the Nile Valley, in Sinai and in the south of Palestine; he also, from time to time during his life, continued his surveys of British hill figures and stone circles which had first occupied him as a young man, before ever he went to Egypt. His restless and inventive mind was forever pondering fresh notions, and finding practical solutions to the problems he encountered, whether archaeological, mechanical or social. His scientific training, his extraordinary visual memory and his acute powers of observation led him to revolutionize excavation methods. He found archaeology in Egypt a treasure hunt; he left it a science. When he began work, the ancient temples were being ransacked for statues and inscriptions, the tombs for their furniture and jewels. Petrie was the first to emphasize the value of pottery and small objects, and the importance of recording meticulously everything found, and every trace in the ground, whether or not its significance is at the time apparent. His methods, imperfect as they were at first, influenced both Schliemann in his later work and Arthur Evans at Knossos, and though in his final years Petrie was overtaken by more modern techniques and many of his ideas were superseded, the basic principles of excavation laid down by him have been followed by archaeologists all over the world. He insisted on the importance of training students, and he was always on the lookout for possible talent. His assistants were encouraged to work on their own and take responsibility, and by observing him and following his advice they learned his methods. Those who dug with him were agreed that he had an almost uncanny "flair", when confronted with the new and unexpected, for making the right decision or finding the right answer. All to whom I have talked emphasized his ability to inspire everyone on the "dig" with his own enthusiasm, the mark of a great teacher.

No book about Flinders Petrie would be complete without anecdotes of his eccentricities, and of the hazards, hardships and humour of life in a Petrie camp. Many of them have grown mightily in the telling, no doubt, and some are probably apocryphal, but anyone who has dug in Egypt will have heard them—they have become part of the Petrie legend.

FLINDERS PETRIE

CHAPTER I

The Flinders and the Petries

MEMBERS OF THE Mutual Information Society cannot have been surprised when they heard the news that Mr William Petrie was to marry Miss Anne Flinders. They were both active members of the Society, she as Secretary and he in constant attendance at meetings to which he often contributed a paper; for several years he had been a frequent visitor to the house where she lived with her aunt and her invalid mother. Their friends may not have been unaware of the precarious financial circumstance which had hitherto deterred him from proposing marriage; they may have realized that she was somewhat older than he; but the similarity of their tastes and interests, their involvement in charitable activities and their absorption in the study of the Bible must have marked them out as likely partners.

William Petrie could trace his descent in direct line from Dr Alexander Petrie, an eminent eighteenth-century Scottish divine; his father and grandfather had both had distinguished careers as Commissaries General in the army. Martin Petrie had been responsible for supplies during the Napoleonic campaigns and had died in Lisbon in 1805 during the Peninsular War. His son, William, had been sent out to Brussels in 1817 to wind up the accounts after Waterloo; he had married Margaret, the daughter of a prominent City banker, Henry Mitton, and for a few years they lived at King's Langley in Hertfordshire, where between 1820 and 1823 a daughter, Margaret, and two sons, William and Martin, were born; then the family were stationed for a time in Portugal and in 1829 they moved to the Cape of Good Hope, where Commissioner Petrie was put in charge of supplies for the Kaffir War. As a boy William rode to school every day with his brother Martin across the desert into Cape Town, an experience which gave him "a hot-country disregard of English habits", later passed on to his son. In South Africa the birth of two more sons, Francis and Alfred, completed the family.[1]*

* References begin on p. 439.

In due course William and Martin entered the South African College in Cape Town; they showed a great interest in chemistry and magnetism, an interest which was encouraged by their father; Sir John Herschel, who was their near neighbour, invited them into his laboratory and talked to them about crystallography, astronomy and chemical matters, and saw that William was given the free use of the laboratory of the South African public library, where he was encouraged to experiment with electricity, still in its infancy. He also met Herschel's assistant, Piazzi Smyth, and the children of the two families became friends. When he was not yet sixteen he started to study medicine at the Cape Town Hospital, but his father was recalled to London in the following year, and William continued his education first with a private tutor, and then under Professor Daniells at King's College London; he had already decided to abandon medicine and specialize in chemistry. At the age of nineteen he followed an intensive course on electricity and magnetism at the University of Frankfurt am Main; the first results of original experiments carried out by him there were published in 1841 on his return from Germany, and in 1846 he read his first paper at a meeting of the British Association for the Advancement of Science, describing a method which he had discovered of hardening steel and producing thinner and stronger magnets. His ingenious mind was constantly devising new and better ways of doing things; one of his first mechanical devices, invented while he was still in Germany, was a simplified form of differential gearing for use in windlasses and cranes; another was a novel magneto-electric device which he was later to put to use.[2]

On William's return to England, he worked for a time as a surveyor on the network of railways then under construction; when in London, he and his brothers were frequent visitors at No. 3 Cheyne Walk, Chelsea, where the Piazzi Smyths now lived. A brief romance ensued. Flinders Petrie in his autobiography tells the story: "Amid the many friends who went to and from there, it did not escape the eye of Mrs Smyth that her eldest daughter Henrietta and young William Petrie were very intimate. Now she was a very careful mother and knew her duties. She felt that my father had not that amount of worldly wisdom which she desired for her daughter's success, so Henrietta was promptly taken to Cambridge, and soon after married the sexagenarian Professor Baden-Powell." It was a source of amusement to their son, Robert, the founder of the Boy Scout movement, and to Flinders who later became his friend, that both their destinies should have been thus shaped by Mrs Smyth.[3] As for William, though for a time he was furious with "Mrs S." and stricken with grief at the whisking away of his Henrietta, he soon became increasingly interested in another of the Smyth's constant visitors: Anne Flinders was often invited to the house of the man whose father, William Henry Smyth the astronomer and antiquary, had been her father's old friend. For Anne was the daughter of Captain Matthew Flinders, the navigator and explorer who had charted the coasts of Australia some forty years before. She did not remember her father—he had died when she was only two—but her mother spoke often of him with love and pride, and Anne was deeply conscious of her heritage.

Matthew Flinders was born on 16 March 1774 at Donington, a small market town in the Lincolnshire fens. His life and career, well known to most Australian schoolchildren, must be briefly told.[4] The family tradition was that the Flinders, or Flanders, had come over to Nottinghamshire as stocking-weavers from the Low Countries in the reign of Queen Elizabeth. Matthew's great-grandfather moved to Donington in about 1700; his grandfather and father were both surgeon-apothecaries, and Matthew was destined to follow in the family practice. At school the boy showed an aptitude for mathematics, as well as for Greek and Latin; in his early teens he read Robinson Crusoe, then and there determined to go to sea to seek adventure; he studied on his own navigation and Euclid; at the age of fifteen he went to sea, serving as midshipman on the *Bellerophon* (on which he later saw action against the French off Ushant), and sailed with Captain Bligh on an adventurous journey to the Antipodes; his quick mastery of the techniques of surveying and chart-making brought him to the attention of the Admiralty, and in 1795 he was sent with the new Governor of New South Wales to Port Jackson (Sydney); while there, he made several adventurous voyages along the coast of Queensland. His report of his discoveries—for Australia was very little known—led to further exploration: he was given command of the *Investigator*, in which he was to make a scientific investigation of the coastline of the continent. Among his ship's company were to be his brother Samuel and his stepmother's nephew, John Franklin. Before he set out, he married the handsome and talented girl with whom he had had an understanding since he was seventeen. Ann Chappell was of Huguenot stock; her great-grandfather had been a ship-owner named Chappelle, who had fled for his life at the time of the Revocation of the Edict of Nantes and had settled in Hull, where his son Benjamin also became a ship-owner. Ann's father died at sea; she had been brought up by her mother and her stepfather, the Revd William Tyler of

Partney. In July 1801 she prepared to sail with her husband, but at the last minute the Admiral forbade him to take her. She was not to see him again for nine years.

Beginning from Cape Leeuwin, Matthew Flinders gradually explored the south coast, then sailed northwards, charting the Great Barrier Reefs, as far as the Gulf of Carpentaria; but his ship started to leak and in June 1803 he was forced to abandon further survey work, though he completed the circumnavigation of the continent; on his return to Port Jackson the *Investigator* was condemned as incapable of repair. In attempting to return to England, fortune altogether deserted him: his first ship was wrecked and he and his crew had to row 700 miles in an open boat. At last he was given a small schooner, the *Cumberland*, but she was so unseaworthy that he decided to put into harbour at the French-controlled island of Mauritius. It was an unfortunate decision: France and England were still at war, and the governor of the island, De Caen, suspecting him of spying, held him prisoner. He remained in custody for nearly seven years, first in close confinement, then on parole as the guest of a Frenchwoman, in whose house he enjoyed moderate comfort and opportunity to read, study and play the flute. He also wrote a treatise on magnetism: he had made the important discovery that the iron in ships attracted the compass needle and caused serious errors in the reading of bearings. The Flinders Bar on a modern ship's compass, which compensates for magnetic deviations, is named after him.

Negotiations were started with the French Government to secure his repatriation and in 1807 an order of release was sent out, but it was not until 1810 that De Caen finally let him go.

Home in England at last, he settled down to write his report for the Admiralty and resume his life with Ann after long separation. After two years a daughter was born to them; they named her Anne (the name is spelt with, or without, a final e in alternate generations of the family). He was tired and ill; the Admiralty, unable to employ him in an active capacity, put him on half-pay. The couple moved to London, where he worked steadily on the narrative of his voyage in the *Investigator*, based on his journals and charts. While writing it he was often in great pain from kidney disease, originating in the long privations of his life at sea, and aggravated by his imprisonment; he died, aged forty, on 19 July 1814, only a few days before the publication of his book.[5]

The house where Matthew Flinders was born has long since been pulled down, but Donington Church is a place of pilgrimage for

Australians; statues of him stand in several Australian cities, and a number of places in that continent, including a river, an island, and a range of mountains, bear his name. Flinders University of South Australia has recently celebrated the bicentenary of his birth.[6] Flinders Petrie was very conscious of the debt he owed to his remarkable grandfather, many of whose qualities of courage, resource and ingenuity he himself inherited. The family link with Australia, too, was important to him: not only his grandfather's explorations, and those of that other distinguished explorer Sir John Franklin, who was later to be Governor of Tasmania before losing his life seeking the North-West Passage; Franklin's sister Sarah Sellwood was the mother of Emily, the wife of Alfred Lord Tennyson, whose son, Hallam Tennyson, became Governor-General of Australia in 1902. There were other family ties also: Matthew Flinders' sister Susannah had thirteen children of whom the eldest, Susanna, married John Pilgrim and emigrated with him to Australia in 1849, and another, Eliza Jackson, followed them in the same year. Flinders Petrie corresponded with members of both families until late in his life, and he presented most of the Flinders papers in his possession to the Mitchell Library in Sydney.

During Ann's long years of waiting for her husband's return from captivity she obeyed his instructions to learn French; in a letter before their marriage he had urged her, "Study geography and astronomy and even metaphysics, sooner than leave thy mind unoccupied. Soar, my Annette—aspire to the heights of science. Write a good deal, work with thy kneedle a great deal and read every book that comes thy way save trifling novels."[7] She was an accomplished artist—two volumes of flower paintings survive*—and she determined that Matthew's daughter, too, should soar. Her stepsister, Miss Isabella Tyler, settled down to live with them and to help in the education and upbringing of little Anne, "our dear baby", doubly precious because of the circumstances of her birth; between them they gave her a remarkable education. She was very quick to learn. "I well remember her delight," wrote her aunt later, "at the success of her first attempt to spell out a sentence in Robinson Crusoe. The *Encyclopaedia Britannica* was a great favourite with her, when the volume was almost bigger than herself."[8] She went to school for a short time to learn German and Italian, but as she grew older she taught herself Hebrew and Greek, Spanish and Portuguese; she read books on astronomy and geology, and browsed voraciously in the classics of literature. Like her father

* At present on loan to Lincoln Cathedral.

she loved music and musical theory. Undoubtedly she drove herself too hard, and once suffered a breakdown; she was always delicate, and was to suffer all her life from nervous headaches, and she confessed herself "subject to strange dreams, sometimes allegorically prophetical".[9] Living always with her mother and aunt, and meeting few people socially, her horizon must have been a limited one. They lived for a time in Reading; when she was considered, in her thirties, to be adult enough to travel on her own, she would sometimes come up to London for meetings of learned societies or to stay with the Smyths or her friend Anne Marston. In the 1840s she published, anonymously under her own name, novels, poems and short stories with religious themes,[10] and under the pseudonym Philomathes, a treatise, *The Connection between Revelation and Mythology illustrated and vindicated*, in which she attempted to show that the mythologies of all ancient nations—Egyptian, Persian, Indian, Phoenician, Chinese, Scandinavian and classical Greek—all reflect a single body of tradition derived from the Old Testament, which she held to contain the primaeval truth, "the earliest facts of Sacred History". The book shows the width of her reading; her copy of Cory's *Ancient Fragments*, which survives,[11] is heavily annotated.

In 1845 Anne and Miss Marston founded a private association, the Mutual Information Society, the members of which met regularly in the house of one or another of them and often in the Flinders' home in Plumstead. At these evening gatherings, one or another of the members would read a paper on some religious, literary or scientific topic, which was then thrown open to discussion by the group. Anne's duty as secretary was to circulate to members beforehand the subject chosen for the next meeting, so that they might prepare their comments and questions. Anne's mother, while generally disapproving of her daughter's advanced views, made no objection and Miss Tyler was sometimes present at the meetings. Among the founding members were the Piazzi Smyth family of Cheyne Walk, William Petrie and his brother Martin; and their sister Marge, or Margaret, sometimes came to meetings. By October 1846 William Petrie was a frequent visitor in the Plumstead house. In February 1847 we find him being entertained to luncheon by Miss Tyler and Miss Flinders; at the meeting afterwards Anne read a paper of his ("she was a little *nervous* while reading it, I perceived"), and the subject, whatever it was, provoked interest and discussion. "I [also] exhibited my new design for a spinning top . . . tell Alfred [his youngest brother, still a boy] it spins for at least *25 minutes*! They asked me to stay to tea with them but I declined, after borrowing a *very* clever book of them, which Miss F. showed me, on moral and religious matters and getting another work that they have long promised."[12] The exchange of books led to a regular correspondence between William and Anne, and in September of that year Aunt Isabella thought fit to write seriously to the young man. She was aware, she said, of the nature of his feelings towards her niece, and thought he should know something of her family history. She gave him an account of Anne's childhood and upbringing: "from her childhood she has never been parted from her mother and myself, except on occasional visits to her friends." They have never been anxious, she said, for her to marry, but hinted that they would not oppose the approach of an amiable and intelligent suitor. As for her financial position, she had a small property of her own, enough to provide for her comfort *as a single woman.*[13]

It was a friendly and encouraging letter, but William was in no position to marry; his inventions had so far brought him nothing but debts, and he was living on a small monthly allowance from his mother. His most recent invention, which he called an "apostadometer", an improved form of surveying instrument designed to take offsets from a line by a single sight and thus enabling measurements to be made of the distance to inaccessible objects, had been shown at a meeting of the British Association that summer, but he had not the financial backing to market his patent, and it was pirated by a Frenchman soon after. He then turned his inventive imagination to the development of electrical apparatus, with which he had already experimented in Frankfurt eight years earlier. In collaboration with an engineer named W. E. Staite, he devised a new and ingenious self-regulating lamp worked from a large battery and so powerful that when it was demonstrated in November 1848, hanging from the portico of the National Gallery, it emitted a flood of light equal to 900 candle power, "which paled the gas lamps not only in the square, but for some distance down Whitehall," as the *Morning Chronicle* reported next day.[14]

A number of patents were taken out and Staite toured the country demonstrating the invention; in October 1851 they arranged a display on the terrace at Worsley Hall near Manchester on the occasion of a visit of Queen Victoria; the papers next day described how the floodlighting of the fountains and jets in the gardens had delighted and amazed Her Majesty. Yet the lamp proved to be no more than a nine days' wonder; neither Petrie nor Staite had the capital to market their invention, and Staite's health was not equal to the strain. A company, the Patent Electric Light Co., was formed but it was hopelessly mismanaged and soon foundered; Petrie never made a penny for his part in the discovery and Staite died in poverty three years later.

By May 1850, when his diaries begin, William Petrie was seeing a great deal of Anne Flinders and sometimes went for long walks with her, over Plumstead Common or in Greenwich Park. In July 1850 he went up to Edinburgh for a meeting of the British Association; the two papers he read were well received and Piazzi Smyth, now Astronomer Royal for Scotland, introduced him to a number of influential people; but he had decided to turn his back on electric light and concentrate on another aspect of his versatile talent: chemical engineering. He had already designed a magnetic spindle "for obtaining and applying electric currents applicable to refining metals", and this discovery, for which he later took out a patent, he offered to introduce into the chemical works of Thomas Farmer in Kennington, as an improvement in the manufacture of sulphuric acid in platinum boilers; in May 1851 he was engaged to work for Farmer on a half-time basis, for the small salary of £2.10.0 a week. At last he could think about marriage.

His letter to his mother announcing Miss Flinders' acceptance of his proposal was sent on 18 June 1851; it would not, he thought, come as a surprise to her since he often mentioned Miss F. in his letters; he was pleased to find that she had an income of several hundred pounds a year, which with his own salary and allowance would be enough for them to live on; she had recently bought a pair of small houses at Charlton, in Maryon Road, "in a remarkably aristocratic situation in the neighbourhood of Woolwich", so that there would be no problem about where to live. He had a deep admiration for Miss Flinders and was sure that his mother would welcome this important decision and wish him to be happy.[15] Her hostility, expressed in her reply to this letter, surprised them; she made it clear that she would no longer send him an allowance. They had planned a conventional wedding with bridesmaids; in the event, there was no formal engagement and they were married quietly in St Thomas' Church, Charlton, on 2 August by special licence. Margaret Petrie was the only member of his family present; they walked to church, but returned in style in the carriage of a mutual friend, Major Little, who had given the bride away.

They made a handsome couple: Anne, short and slender, with her father's large brown eyes and pale complexion, her hair falling in dark ringlets; William of average height, stoutly built, with dark hair, blue eyes, a broad brow and a wide, mobile mouth. Anne was at this time forty, nine years older than her husband. They had much in common: intellectual interests, profound religious faith and a frugal lifestyle; but he was a strict vegetarian and a recent and enthusiastic convert to homoeopathy, and whereas Anne was a member of the established Church, he belonged to a fundamentalist sect akin to that of the Exclusive Brethren.[16] On a Sunday morning she would go to St Thomas' Church, just along the road, while he attended a meeting of the Brethren; on Mondays she would sometimes accompany him to a Bible study gathering in a private house, occasionally their own.

After the wedding breakfast they went by train to Reigate; Anne waited at the station with their luggage till William found lodgings. After only four days they returned to Ecclesbourne Cottage; here they made their home, while Miss Tyler with Mrs Flinders occupied Ashby Cottage next door. William continued, as he had done before his marriage, to list every halfpenny of expenditure in his diary. They both contributed to the household expenses; when in late August they were able to go to the Isle of Wight for a proper honeymoon Anne paid the cost of food and lodging, William all travel and extras. In September they saw the Great Exhibition which they found very tiring and rather disappointing: William, writing of it to his mother, complained that it was full of examples of "wasted childish feats of skill, in using materials particularly unsuited to produce the result" —such as pictures woven in human hair, and flowers made of shells. It contained none of his own inventions, not even the electric light bulb.

Life was not easy for the newly wed couple. Nettie (William's name for Anne) suffered from frequent migraines. William had to be at the factory early, which meant getting up at half-past three in the morning on Tuesdays, Wednesdays and Thursdays and walking over seven miles to work; he would come home tired and sometimes affected by chemical fumes and was seldom in bed much before midnight. Farmer suggested they come and live nearby, but William refused to do this: it was Nettie's house, and he could not ask her to let it and live in furnished rooms; besides, there was her mother to think of; the old lady was ailing and nearly blind. Eventually Farmer agreed to pay William a small allowance to enable him to take a room in Kennington for three nights a week. In February 1852 Mrs Flinders died; she was buried in St Thomas', and Miss Tyler had a tablet put up in the church in her memory, and also one in memory of Matthew Flinders, whose original tombstone in St James', Hampstead Road, had been destroyed by neglect.

In September of that year William and Anne enjoyed a fortnight's holiday at St Peter's Port, in Guernsey. That winter she was in poor health, and in January William was able to tell his mother that they were expecting a child.

CHAPTER II

The Making of an Archaeologist
(1853–80)

THE CHILD WAS born in the evening of 3 June 1853, after a long and very difficult labour; his mother, being slight and delicate and already forty-three, suffered greatly; she was attended throughout by a nurse and two doctors, who repeatedly tried the new chloroform, which Queen Victoria had used for the birth of her seventh and youngest child, Prince Leopold, only two months earlier; she had found it most satisfactory, but in Anne's case it was of little use since it reduced the mother's strength in labour too much before it alleviated pain. At times they despaired of saving her; as William afterwards told his mother "My poor Anne was remarkably collected and calm in mind, through all the bodily exhaustion and agony, and praying continuously in a most submissive and patient spirit; one nurse though strong and very experienced was frequently overcome by the circumstances." William was in constant attendance on his wife; not a mouthful of food, he said, had passed his lips for two days. The baby "has pretty, regular features, with beautiful large dark eyes like its mother, and they say is very like myself in other respects. Nurse and doctors say it is of an unusually fine size and weight, and its head and shoulders are very *fully* proportioned to the rest of it." It also had a pair of very fine lungs which it exercised to the full. For several days Anne's life hung in the balance; then she began to gain strength, but a wet-nurse had to be engaged for the baby and as soon as its mother was strong enough to travel William took her off to Hastings to recuperate leaving Isabella to cope with the household for a month. Before they went the child was registered at Charlton in the name of William Matthew Flinders. A small depression in his temple caused at birth soon disappeared. William's mother wrote congratulating him on the birth of his son, but could not refrain from expressing her surprise at his having been present with his wife during labour; it is not, she said, an English custom "An occasional kind visit being all any wife expects or at any rate *receives*."[1]

One of the relatives to whom William wrote to tell him of the birth was his father's cousin, Samuel Petrie of Ebury Street, the eldest son of a linen merchant, Samuel Petrie of Cricklade; the latter's courageous efforts to secure justice in the celebrated "Cricklade case" in the late eighteenth century had involved him in no less than nineteen lawsuits and a duel with Lord Porchester, and had taken him to the House of Lords: he had accused his opponents of corruption and bribery during successive Parliamentary elections in which he had been the unsuccessful candidate.[2] His son Samuel (who in the family tradition had been a Commissary General) was a bachelor, now retired and comfortably off. He liked William, wrote a cordial letter[3] congratulating him, and set up a trust on behalf of the child, to be administered by his mother till he was twenty-one.

While they were in Hastings, Isabella wrote frequent bulletins of the baby's progress and after they returned she frequently took charge of him.[4] When the monthly nurse had gone, a nursemaid, Harris, was engaged who stayed with them for the next fifteen years, but it was Isabella who gave Willie (as they called him) his early lessons. He was a sturdy and cheerful child, large for his age and quick to learn. According to his mother "he was able to understand maps and his father's engineering plans even before he was able to speak plainly: 'Him go on dere,' he would say, pointing to several parts of a drawing."[5] His parents and his aunt encouraged his precocity, showing him pictures and reading him stories, and he learnt to read very early. His enquiring mind sought always for explanations: "What is this for?—*tell me!*" he would cry. As soon as Willie knew his numbers his father set him measuring things . . . the diameter of his plate, the length of his book, the rise of mercury in the thermometer, the weight of an apple. From time to time, to amuse the little boy and one or two other children, his father let off home-made fireworks or fired a little brass cannon in the garden.

William taught his son the Scriptures and brought him up in his own austere faith; he insisted on the strict observance of the Sabbath ("Wrote a letter to Robins next door, on keeping their Parrot quiet on Sundays" is a diary entry), and on that day he would study the literal interpretation of the Scriptures with Willie; sometimes he went round delivering religious tracts, or else distributing pamphlets on homoeopathy, the little boy trotting at his side; but though he was a strict vegetarian, Anne was not, and she seems to have insisted that Willie ate like the rest of the household. The sect to which William belonged did not approve of infant baptism; when Willie was two, with the connivance of Miss Tyler, Anne took the opportunity of her husband's short absence in Cornwall to have him christened in St Thomas' church. William was understandably displeased, and lectured Anne on the sad errors and failures of the Established Church, but their devotion to each other weathered this storm and as time went on, Willie would accompany his father to the Brethren's prayer meeting on Sunday mornings, and his mother to the parish church on Sunday evenings; later, he played the harmonium for them.

An unhoped-for windfall improved their financial position a little in 1853: Anne was granted a pension of £100 by the government of New South Wales; in acknowledging the gift, Anne wrote that she gladly accepted it in order to educate her son "in a manner worthy of the name he bears". When he reached the age of four, he fell seriously ill and for a few days his life was despaired of. After an expedition to visit his godmother Miss Marston in Chelsea, he had fallen asleep in the back of an omnibus and caught cold; the cold turned to bronchitis and croup and for some days he struggled for breath and was plied with hot water bottles, linseed poultices and hot flannels night and day.[6] The illness abated, but it left him with a serious chest weakness; he caught cold very easily, so that he had to be confined indoors in winter for days or weeks on end, and was prone to frightening attacks of asthma and cramp. All thought of sending him to school had to be abandoned and he was forbidden by the doctor to take part in outdoor games with other children. Instead of football and cricket, chess and draughts and music were his amusements; sometimes the children of neighbours came in to play with him,—one particular friend, Minnie Goldsmith, was often asked to tea; her death when he was five was his earliest experience of bereavement—but usually he was in the company of adults, and it was his great-aunt Isabella who undertook to give him regular lessons, in reading and writing, Scripture, grammar and arithmetic, since his father was frequently away from home and his mother, when she was not ill, was busy with charitable works; she gave Hebrew and Greek lessons privately, and was secretary to the District Visiting Society. She often read to him in the evenings, however, and when he was ill, she would bring him boxes of minerals and coins from her own collection to look at; once, when at a loss for something new to amuse him in bed, she brought him Spineto's *Lectures on Hieroglyphics*, and he spent happy hours copying and learning the signs; she believed that this early interest had sowed the seeds of his future career.[7]

When Willie was six Isabella Tyler, who was now in her mid-seventies, began to find the boisterous and wilful little boy too much for her. It was decided to engage a governess: a friend of Anne's named Miss Cortis came to take over his formal education. Willie was very fond of her and enjoyed her lessons but she was delicate and she found it difficult to control him; she left after two years for an easier post. Miss Jackson, who took her place, was to teach a small group of neighbours' children, who were to come in to share his lessons. The experiment was a disaster; she was a Colonel's daughter, a strict disciplinarian, and she stuffed his head, as he afterwards remembered, with "English, French, Latin and Greek grammars all together". When his mother returned from the country, she found the child quite changed: very subdued, in great dread of his governess, and complaining of constant headache. The doctor, fearing a breakdown, banned lessons for a year or so, and to the whole family's relief Miss Jackson, whom nobody liked, was sent packing.

William was now no longer working in Kennington; he had at last broken his connection with Thomas Farmer, who had not only proved a hard taskmaster, but had attempted to claim the patent of William's improved design for platinum boilers. He now accepted commissions from time to time designing boilers for the manufacture of sulphuric acid;[8] a boiler designed in collaboration with George Matthey was shown in the Paris Exhibition of 1855. In 1859 he began work on a new design of a chemical plant in a factory owned by a Mr Dixon at Warsash, near Netley on Southampton Water; he rented a cottage near the factory and would go down there for weeks at a time; Anne would often join him for a short while, and occasionally Willie came with Harris, though he preferred the sandy beach at Hastings. One night on the eve of his seventh birthday there was a severe gale which threatened to blow down the factory chimney; Willie caught cold in the draughty cottage, and had a bad asthma attack. His parents were at their wits' end; there was no doctor within miles, and William next day had to walk twenty-four miles to Fareham and back to send a letter to Dr Rowbotham asking his advice. When he was better, as Anne wrote to her aunt, "Poor Willy asked what birthday present I would give him. I said the trip to Warsash was my present. 'Then I'll tell you what, your present proved a *mistake*; for it has made me very ill, and given you a good deal of misery.' Nobody could have put the case more clearly."[9] William Petrie completed his chemical plant to Dixon's satisfaction and was employed by him to run it for a time; after his contract ran out he still made frequent visits to Warsash; he had made many friends there and had founded a new community of the Brethren, and he much enjoyed attending their Sunday meetings, at which he would expound the Scriptures and lead the small congregation in long extempore prayers, sometimes several times during the day. He also, out of generosity, spent a great deal of time rebuilding the schoolhouse, superintending the bricklayers and doing most of the carpentry and painting himself, for which purpose he often went down for a few days; he taught his son how to use tools and gave him his own hammer and chisel and workbench.

The boy was now left to his own devices as far as education was concerned, though his great-aunt read a little French with him, fearing he would forget all he had learned. He had no gift for languages; his father sometimes tried to teach him Latin grammar, making out lists of declensions, but it was in the scientific subjects that he found him quick and eager to learn. As he wrote to his mother, when the child was not yet ten: "He continues most energetically studying, for amusement, chemicals and minerals. He has begged as a favour to be allowed to take my largest chemical work (1,000 pages octavo)—Turner—to read it in bed before he dresses in the morning and he tells Mama that it is 'most interesting'. We have given him a bit of garden ground to cultivate, to induce him not to spend too long a time in reading his chemical books and making—considering his age—very deep arithmetical calculations about it, to construct tables of specific gravities, specific heat, atomic weights, atomic values &c. &c."[10] Anne had a collection of minerals and fossils, and these Willie handled till he knew them all by name, and scoured the countryside for fresh specimens. He was also collecting coins; his mother's small collection had fired his interest, and when quite young he would search the shops in Woolwich, "thus beginning archaeology when still accompanied by my nurse at eight, and triumphing in finding an Allectus". His mother bought him Humphreys' *The Coin Collector's Manual* and he would spend his small pocket money on random piles of coins, taking them home to sort and identify. William encouraged these interests as much as he dared; when he was ten he took the boy to the Geological Museum in Jermyn Street, where "he was delighted, and named the specimens as he saw them, with very creditable proficiency. I was amused to see that he was most interested not in the striking or large or brilliant things (as an ignorant person would be) but with things of which the chemical composition and crystallization was curious or unusual."[11] They then went on to see the Panorama of Athens, which led William to expatiate on the city's role in history at the time of St Paul and its future Scriptural destiny as the place from which Antichrist would arise to subdue the whole world; Willie lapped all this up (his father frequently filled his head with such eschatological teachings) and their day ended happily with apricots and strawberries at Covent Garden and a ride in a river steamer.

Charlton was not a very healthy place and they were anxious to move; exhalations from the Plumstead Marshes caused much fever among the inhabitants of the Woolwich area until they were finally drained in the 1870s. In the spring of 1864 there was an epidemic of typhus and Miss Tyler rented a cottage at Welling at the foot of Shooter's Hill and took Flinders and Harris there for three months. They enjoyed the rural surroundings but the boy was suddenly taken ill with what Dr Rowbotham, summoned from Charlton, pronounced to be a heart spasm. Anne herself caught the fever at Charlton and was for a time very seriously ill.

William Petrie's life now alternated between periods of idleness and bouts of intense concentration when he was working to a deadline; he was sometimes commissioned by Johnson, Matthey and Company to design a platinum boiler for the particular requirements of some client; one of them, shown at the Paris Exhibition of 1867, was able to treat as much as eight tons a day. On one occasion he went to Belgium on such an assignment, but he came back after a short time far from well, having been robbed of a portmanteau containing most of his papers; thereafter he refused to take on work if it meant travelling abroad. Money was very tight, and once or twice he had to borrow from Miss Tyler or Miss Marston to tide him over. His restless ingenuity was forever thinking up new devices which he seldom carried through to completion. He had also his pastoral duties; once when he went to Liverpool, he preached to 250 "attentive listeners" at Birkenhead. He had once been offered a post as lecturer in mathematics and natural philosophy at New College in the Finchley Road, but he turned it down on the grounds that it would need too much preparation.

The problem of Willie's education became more pressing; a tutor would have been engaged had they been able to find one who subscribed to William's own beliefs, "but as such would be rare to find, and a constant flow of fresh matter filled my father's attention, the tutor never appeared." Indeed the only formal education he had was when, at the age of twenty-four, he took a University Extension course on Wednesday evenings in algebra and trigonometry; he had already discovered Euclid for himself, when he was fifteen, when he "feasted on a book a day with full delight, skipping all the propositions which were already axiomatic to me, and satisfied if I could visualise the reality of those demonstrations which were not self-evident."[12] His grandfather, Matthew Flinders, had also, at about the same age, taught himself geometry.

In 1866, when Flinders was thirteen, they decided to move from Charlton into furnished lodgings and let the cottage; after some weeks of househunting they found temporary accommodation in Blackheath. This meant joining a new circle of Brethren; William found a group who met in a private house in Lewisham; at the first meeting he attended, he gave them a sermon on Railway Preaching—it was his custom to engage fellow passengers in railway carriages in conversation, and turn the topic to religious matters, sometimes doling out tracts or copies of his favourite weeklies *Precious Truth* and *The Voice on the Mountains.* After two months, unable to let the cottages, they moved back to Charlton. It was while they were at Blackheath that Willie made a friend who was to be a great influence on his life. N. T. Riley kept an antique shop, "the Curiosity and Antiquity and Mechanic Shop", just off the High Road at Lee; he had crammed it with old furniture, scientific instruments, books, coins and miscellaneous bric-à-brac picked up at London sales. He had a reputation locally as a great "character"; he was entirely self-educated but could talk with considerable knowledge and insight on music and painting. Flinders first made his acquaintance when he and his mother stopped outside the shop one day to look at a pile of Greek copper coins for sale; he invited them into the shop and when they could not make up their minds which to buy, he poured the lot into a bag and told them to take them home and choose at their leisure. "That opened a friendship with an extraordinary man. His influence on all who knew him was remarkable. Above all, he taught one human nature, in a rather Socratic manner, with wits sharpened by all the shady practices of life in dealing and cheating, for which he had a withering contempt; he was the most absolutely honest and straight man that I ever met."[13] Henceforward he used frequently to visit Riley's shop, walking over alone from Charlton and happy to spend hours watching his friend at work at the back of the shop; sometimes he was allowed to use his lathe. Then Riley began to take him with him to auction sales in London, and encouraged him to go to the British Museum to identify what he had bought; finding that the boy sometimes brought in coins that the national collection lacked, the staff of the Department of Coins and Medals encouraged him to buy for them. He developed a sharp eye for forgeries and his experience in this field was to stand him in good stead all his life. "I found that any large mixed lot [of coins] which had not been picked over closely, would contain enough prizes to pay for the lot." The surplus he would hand over to Riley, or keep for his own collection. Visits to the British Museum grew more frequent, and the boy would wander round the galleries till he knew their contents almost by heart; when he was twenty-one and qualified for a Reader's ticket, the Museum Reading Room became his university and he browsed at will.

The lonely boy's progress in home education can be traced during these years only by random entries in his father's diaries: (aged fourteen) "Willie has got an old quadrant from Reilly; I examined it and showed him how a double glass reflector in various ways allows motion of it not to shake the reflection. I long arranging reflectors to illustrate it. He studying it to make a sextant of his own contrivance." "New Year's gift from Martin came: the Trinominal Cube. A physical illustration of Algebra. I explained it to Willie." (Aged fifteen) "Willie has taken to calculating the distance a body falls in 1″ by rule $\pi \times$ t of ½ pendulum, I assisting and encouraging him at it." (Aged seventeen) "Set Flinders to prepare experiment in condensing water by a glass balloon in open air." He browsed among his mother's books, read the classics in translation, and Gibbon from cover to cover, and enjoyed poetry, especially that of the seventeenth century—George Herbert being his favourite. As he grew older he occasionally went to concerts on his own, and frequently spent an hour or so in the National Gallery on his way from the British Museum to Waterloo. One of his great pleasures was to visit his cousins the Harveys in Puttenham, near Guildford. There were four sisters, of whom the youngest, Susan, was his favourite; she was ten years older than he, but they had a great deal in common and when she came to stay with the Petries, they would go for long walks and talk about all manner of things. Later they moved to Milford, a few miles away, where their house was to become a second home to the young man, and a refuge from London whenever he needed rest or comfort. With plenty of books to read, long country walks and games of badminton, bagatelle, backgammon, and chess, the days there passed very happily.

Miss Tyler died in 1867, after a long and paralysing illness; she left a small sum in trust to her great-nephew when he came of age. She was buried in Charlton churchyard by the side of her stepsister Ann Chappell. Three years later the family moved to Bromley in Kent, first to a house in Palace Road, and in the following autumn to 8, Crescent Road, to the house which was to be home for William and Anne for the rest of their lives. The house, now pulled down, had a large garden well-stocked with fruit-trees, strawberry-beds and a grape vine, but the interior had dry rot and a good deal of carpentry was needed; Flinders was kept busy making shelves and cupboards, repairing furniture and replacing drains and water-pipes. The Charlton cottages were let for three years more, and finally sold.

Flinders had now grown to his full height, about five foot nine inches. He had inherited his black hair and dark-brown eyes from his mother and his maternal grandfather, and his father's great physical energy and stamina. His mother described him as having "strong feelings, much self-control, quiet pride, very just and exact".[14] There seems to have been little discussion of his future except for a suggestion, when he was nineteen, that he might keep a homoeopathic chemist's shop. He had plenty of enthusiasms to occupy his time and the problem of finding a career does not seem to have bothered him very much. For one thing, he had embarked upon a record of the earthworks, tumuli and other ancient remains in which Kent is particularly rich. It had all begun with the home-made box-sextant; when he was fourteen, he began surveying earthworks near his home, in Charlton Park quite close to the cottages, and on Blackheath Common and in Greenwich Park. Then he moved further afield; Bromley was a better centre for expeditions and in his late teens he would go off on all-day forays on his own, armed with the sextant, a steel dibble, a bundle of surveying rods and a tape or chain. Like his father (who on one occasion covered the thirty-four miles from Brighton to Bognor in eight hours and on a walking tour in Cornwall had averaged thirty-seven miles a day), he was an indefatigable walker. He was much stronger physically now, though he still caught cold very easily and one or two of his outings ended with a spell in bed.

His father let him use his own sextant and showed him a much more accurate method of surveying, the nautical "three-point" method, taking angle readings from three fixed points and measuring the distance between two of them—a method which was quick and well-suited to surveying over broken ground, and by one person alone. "This mode of plotting," he wrote in later years, "gives the fullest accuracy, such as is never possible with the use of station-positions . . . a field of 40 stations can be easily calculated in an hour, and plotted in a couple of hours more."[15] For levelling, he used a simple home-made device consisting of a short rigid pendulum with a mirror attached to it; and placed in a glass tube to shelter it from the wind. "The reflection of the eye back to itself is then a truly horizontal line, and can be sighted on any distance"—readings could be taken "to an inch in 100 feet, and this is sufficient accuracy for most archaeological work".

Enquiring in the Map Room of the British Museum, he discovered that they had no recent plans of even England's best-known stone circles and earthworks. He resolved to remedy that defect. In 1874, he and his father spent a few days at Amesbury and began plotting the greatest monument of all—Stonehenge, which had many times been planned but never accurately surveyed and measured. It was a task greater than they could then complete, but they had made a beginning, and Flinders was strengthened in his resolution to continue what his father was evidently not willing to undertake with him: a record of the prehistoric monuments of Southern England. In September of the following year, having carefully planned his itinerary and searched in the Reading Room for the records of antiquaries such as Camden, Stukeley and Cunnington, he set off for Dorset; he was away for nearly three weeks and returned with plans of some two dozen earthworks and standing stones, among them Lambert's Castle, Cerne Abbas, Plush, Bincombe Down, Winterbourne Abbas, and Tarrant Hinton, and ending in Dorchester (Maiden Castle he found too big an undertaking, especially since that day he was suffering from blistered heels). This was the first of ten such expeditions undertaken between the years 1875 and 1880. He would set out by train with a knapsack containing his maps and surveying instruments and a telescope, and a portmanteau containing his personal belongings; the bag he would despatch by carrier or by railway to the station down the line where he expected to spend the night; he would then set off on foot, and expect to cover ten, fifteen or sometimes twenty miles a day, depending on how many monuments he surveyed. Travelling always third class, and spending on an average 1/- or 1/6 for his lodging, it was an economical trip; he reckoned to spend five shillings and sixpence on food every week. His breakfast was usually bread and cheese; for his midday dinner, usually eaten at the top of a high encampment, he would fish a couple of apples or some biscuits out of his pocket; supper was usually again biscuits and apples or plums, for which the villagers often refused payment. In the evening, having collected his bag at the station (the railway never seems to have sent it astray) he would enquire in the village—generally at the post office—for a modest but clean room in a cottage or a temperance inn. When thirsty he would ask for a jug of water, refusing the proffered cider, for his upbringing had been strictly teetotal. At each village he would enquire for the local landmarks, cromlechs and barrows, mounds and ridges, checking these with the ancient remains on the Ordnance map; occasionally he came upon clear traces of earthworks not recorded by the Survey. His letters home (written partly for the benefit of his mother, who followed his progress with great interest and never ceased to hope that his socks were dry, and partly as a day-to-day record for his own future use), contain many amusing anecdotes of small adventures on the way, the quaint dialect of the West Country folk, descriptions of memorable views from hilltops; his humbler lodgings were seldom free from "animalcules" and at the end of one fortnight's trip he counted more than seventy bites on various parts of his person; sometimes he found his bedroom window hermetically shut, and once or twice he had to share a bedroom with another lodger. He never surveyed or travelled on a Sunday, having been brought up in strict observance of the Sabbath; his comments on the quality of the sermons in church ("a good flow of words and to the point", or "rather high and very dry") indicate his preference; finding himself in Dorchester on a Sunday he joined a meeting of the Brethren: "Found it not very large, 12 communicants and about 18 others. *Very* exclusive in countenance, and speaking uncommonly like a section of an Exclusive book." That same evening he attended the parish church and was pleased to find the preacher "very excellently low".

The survey of Stonehenge was resumed in June 1877; Flinders went ahead and booked a room; he walked over to Stonehenge early next morning but his father did not arrive till the afternoon; next morning "Woke at 3¾, at 4.20 went to call my father who was very valiant overnight about being off early, but though he was not asleep he did not like stirring." It was ten before he appeared on the site and Flinders resigned himself to doing most of the work, planning his surveys so that operations in which two people were indispensable were left for late in the day.

In six days the survey was finished. Their surveying chain was a new one 1,000 inches long, devised and made by Flinders, with lozenge-shaped links of steel wire and so contrived that tension could be maintained by a spring with a catch in one of the handles; it proved much lighter and more accurate than the one they had used before, and made their task much easier. Later that year they returned, borrowed a ladder, measured the lintels and took observations from the tops of the trilithons with a theodolite. One final visit to Stonehenge, on the eve of midsummer day in 1880, was needed to make observations of the sunrise, without which they felt the publication would not be complete. They started from Amesbury soon after midnight, set up the theodolite, and took observations on the Pole Star before it was quite light, "then on several stones to fix the azimuth of stone circle. Then we thought it was so foggy there was no chance of the sun rising, mistaking the horizon for a bank of cloud . . . at last up came the sun, and I secured three observations of it . . . there were about 30 people there; and I heard that on the night before, there were 40 conveyances besides foot travellers; Whitcombe the photographer rigged up table and coffee and did a good trade, and the place was rather a bear garden." Soon after sunrise they had all gone, and William went too, but Flinders stayed on surveying the tumuli on the opposite hill; he did not finish till half-past eight in the evening, having been on his feet for eighteen and a half hours. Flinders Petrie's plan of Stonehenge was more accurate than any previously drawn, being measured to the nearest one-tenth of an inch; he claimed that the photolithographed plan was "accurate to $\frac{1}{2000}''$", somewhat overrating the abilities of the printer.[16]

The experience gained by Flinders Petrie in these field excursions was immeasurably valuable to him in his later career. Familiarity with surveying techniques, the ability to measure quickly and accurately and to gauge distances by eye, and visual memory were all developed in him to an unusual degree. When excavating he habitually carried a two-metre staff, a notebook, and a pencil five inches long. His student, Wainwright, remembered that a surveyor, aghast at Petrie's method, went over the same measurements with conventional instruments; then exclaimed "By Jove, they're all right!" It is related of his later years that a student holding the other end of the tape for him on a *tell*, ventured to point out to the Professor that the wind was blowing the tape in a curve and the measurement would not therefore be accurate—Petrie replied that he had already made the necessary mathematical adjustment. He had an extraordinary visual memory. Francis Galton, the geneticist, considered him a mathematical phenomenon; he could, he says, work out sums "by means of an imaginary sliding scale which he set in the desired way" and then read off mentally. "This is one of the most striking cases of accurate visualising power it is possible to imagine."[17] (See Appendix.) He read books on geology, chemistry and astronomy, and wrote a treatise on the history of magnetism, intended as an appendix to a projected biography, by an Australian author, of his grandfather Matthew Flinders; the book was never written.

In 1877 Flinders Petrie deposited a portfolio containing some forty plans of earthworks and stone monuments in the Map Room of the

British Museum. In June he was invited by the council of the Royal Archaeological Institute to read a paper on Metrology at one of their meetings; to illustrate his talk he made fair copies of fifteen of his plans, tinted with crayons, and put them up around the lecture hall. His talk was well received and aroused great interest; "About sixty were present, the first time I ever spoke to a dozen people in my life, but I did not hitch though I much feared that I should. Had a chat to Col. Lane Fox afterwards, he was the only person there I suspect who really knew anything much on the subject, or knew anything of surveying, and he did not know the box sextant, but had only used prismatic compass." Petrie had already used tracings of the Colonel's plans in his Sussex surveys, and checking them with his own, had found them little different. This was his first meeting with the man who above all others influenced and inspired his work when he began excavating: by his careful record of finds and stratigraphy, Lane Fox was setting a new standard for excavation reporting. It was at this meeting also that he first encountered one of the Committee members, who was to become one of his closest friends, "almost the only man with whom I was ever familiar".

Flaxman Spurrell was somewhat older than Petrie; he had trained as a doctor but did not practise medicine, preferring to live with his parents at Belvedere in Kent and pursue his researches into the antiquities of the region, his special interests being flints and mineralogy. Flinders, delighted to find a fellow enthusiast, sent him plans and drawings, and they arranged to meet; their first attempt to do so was a failure: they made a rendezvous at Kits Coty House when Flinders was in the Canterbury area, but though he rose early and waited there all day, Spurrell never turned up. He was curiously erratic and self-effacing, but they became fast friends; Spurrell invited him to a meeting of the Kent Archaeological Society and arranged that he should speak on the pits he had explored and planned—now called Dane-holes—and Flinders again put up plans to illustrate his lecture; Spurrell spoke impromptu on other pits at Crayford and Eltham. It was a two-day meeting, with excursions to places of archaeological interest; Flinders refused Spurrell's offer of a lift: "I preferred to take my way quietly home over the old pit villages, enjoying the deliciously ironical sight of carriage loads of archaeologists unconsciously driving through the unique remains of the district, with the comfortable idea that they were *doing* the antiquities. But where ignorance is bliss etc. etc. Why should not all the *workers* of each society form a *working* association (on the same basis as the Royal Society) for the discussion *in situ* of remains, and be quit for the time of the task of instructing a swarm of dilettanti, luncheon-seeking fashionables?"[18] But Spurrell defended the luncheon-hunters: they were well-intentioned and willing to learn, he said, and could be of valuable assistance to the archaeologist when it comes to needing facilities for digging.[19] Flinders was to discover before long the importance of cultivating the interest and support of laymen.

As well as planning ancient earthworks and henges, Flinders Petrie was measuring monuments, old crosses in churchyards, and the dimensions of churches and castles and other ancient buildings; his purpose was twofold: to make an accurate record, and also to gather data for a book which he planned as a study of ancient metrology. The idea had come to him when reading an essay of Sir Isaac Newton, *A Dissertation on Cubits*. Ancient peoples, he argued, had their own standards of measurement, based on the dimensions of natural occurrence such as the cubit—the length of the forearm—or the length of the foot. To compile a series of accurate measurements of man-made objects such as buildings and monuments, statues, coffins and sarcophagi belonging to a certain civilization at a particular age, should make it possible to determine the standard unit or units used by that people at that time, since the dimensions of their artefacts were likely to be multiples of the unit employed. He therefore paid particular attention to the height and width of doorways in churches, the length and breadth of ancient buildings, and of such parts as towers, buttresses and porches.

When he was not away on one of his survey trips he took measurements in the British Museum, starting with the Egyptian collection where Dr Birch allowed him to spend many hours with notebook and tape measure; C. T. Newton in the Department of Classical Antiquities admitted him behind the scenes in the basement to measure Greek and Roman monuments, and he measured Assyrian monuments and those of Phoenicia and Asia Minor, and Oriental antiquities in South Kensington. In the Reading Room he consulted as many books as he could find which gave the dimensions of ancient buildings in countries he had not visited—the palaces of Persepolis described by Flandin and Coste, for instance, and travellers' accounts of Baalbek and Palmyra, but he regarded these as probably lacking in accuracy and used them with caution. His book *Inductive Metrology, or the Recovery of Ancient Measurements from the Monuments* which came out in 1877 and made a considerable impression at the time, is still often cited as a standard work; it is one of the most important books he ever wrote. At the end of the Introduction, in a passage indicative of his attitude towards evidence in general, he stressed that in all dubious matters, the uncertainty had been acknowledged and discussed. "No attempt has been made to try and obtain the acquiescence of others by ignoring uncertainties. It has been well said that 'the reader is easily held captive by a writer who has no hesitation'; but this stolen consent is an agreement that snaps with the first shock; whereas, when difficulties and uncertainties have been faced from the beginning, they are not reckoned at more than true value."[20] *Inductive Metrology* was by no means the first time his name had appeared in print; since his mid-teens his father had encouraged him to contribute scientific observations of his own to a popular weekly journal called *The English Mechanic*, and several short articles in *Nature* on mathematical and chemical subjects had come out in the previous year, including two on Metachromism; his first book, which appeared when he was twenty-two, was on quite a different subject.

In 1866 father and son had discovered a new enthusiasm; Flinders brought home one day a book he had found on a bookstall; it was by their old friend Piazzi Smyth, and it was called *Our Inheritance in the Great Pyramid*. William read it eagerly, sitting up late night after night till he finished it. The eminent astronomer, who was a Fellow of the Royal Society and had made important contributions to meteorology and spectrological research, had a startling theory to put forward. It was not, in the main, his own; his book was based on that of his friend John Taylor of Gower Street, whose book *The Great Pyramid—Why was it built and Who built it?* had come out in 1859. Though it was generally accepted that the pyramids of Egypt were royal tombs, Taylor was not the first to entertain speculations about their supernatural origin, but he concentrated on the largest of the Giza group, the Great Pyramid attributed by Herodotus to Cheops, which, he argued, was so perfect in its dimensions, so perfectly oriented to the points of the compass and so nearly exactly placed on latitude 30° that it could not possibly have been built by man—if the world was created in 4004 BC, as Archbishop Usher had established, it was impossible that mankind could have reached so advanced a stage of technological progress only 1,600 years later (the currently accepted date of the pyramid's construction being 2400 BC). It must therefore have been built, not by the idolatrous Egyptians, but under divine guidance. He suggested that the strangers whom the historian Manetho had recorded as entering Egypt and subduing the country without a battle were really people chosen by God before the time of Abraham, and that they converted Cheops (in Greek tradition hated by the Egyptians) though not his idolatrous subjects. The pyramid was therefore not a tomb, but a gigantic chronicle of man's history, past, present and future; if read aright, the orientation of the building and its dimensions would convey God's message to mankind.

Taylor's most striking observation was that the vertical height of the pyramid (as calculated by the slope of the casing stones discovered by Col Vyse and his assistant Perring in 1835) bore the same relationship to the perimeter as the diameter of a circle does to its circumference—that is to say, it exactly expressed the value π, or 3.14159. Thus the ancient problem of squaring the circle, only arrived at by modern man, had been solved by divine prescience. To suit his calculations, he postulated a sacred cubit akin to the Hebrew, made up of 25 hypothetical "pyramid inches", each 1.001 of a British inch. All Piazzi Smyth's theories rested on this imaginary measure. He pointed out that 5,000,000,000 of these inches—and *not* standard British inches—was the measure of the earth's axis of rotation as recently determined by the Ordnance Survey. As a fervent British Israelite, who believed that the British were the lost ten tribes of Israel, it was doubly significant to Smyth that the pyramid's standard of measurement had been inches rather than metres or any other barbarous measure. (The discrepancy between the pyramid inch and that in current use in Great Britain could be explained by supposing that the inch had lost a fraction, not more than half a hair's breadth, in transmission from early times.)

On the basis of the pyramid inch Piazzi Smyth's imagination set to work to decipher the hidden message of the Great Pyramid. The ascending and descending passages, he declared, symbolized the progress of civilization from the earliest Biblical times, year by year; major interruptions in the passages, such as steps, or changes of slope, denoted events in man's history, the transition from the ascending passage to the Grand Gallery being the beginning of the Christian era; Smyth's many followers were soon to elaborate this idea and read in the pyramid Messianic prophecies and predictions of the Millennium. Moreover, maintained Smyth, the Great Pyramid contains within its structure the standards of length, weight, and capacity currently in use in Britain, which would one day be adopted by all mankind: the granite coffer in the King's Chamber was not a sarcophagus, but a standard of capacity from which all later measures were derived, its dimensions being those of the Ark of the Covenant.

William Petrie read this book with mounting interest. Like many devout Victorians he was deeply perturbed by recent developments in the world of science. *The Origin of Species* had come out in 1859, and many scientists found themselves perplexed by the conflicting claims of faith and reason; for fundamentalists like the Brethren, the literal interpretation of the Bible story of creation precluded belief in evolution. Now he had discovered a means of reconciling scientific observation with Biblical authority; he wrote at once to Piazzi Smyth expressing great interest in the book and making various criticisms and suggestions. Since his book had been published in 1864, Smyth had been to Egypt to see for himself; he had spent four months at the Great Pyramid with his wife, measuring and observing, and the results had served to reinforce his beliefs and elaborate his theories; his second book, *Life and Work at the Great Pyramid of Egypt*, came out in three volumes in 1867. By that time he was in constant correspondence with William Petrie, whom he regarded as one of his chief and most inspired disciples. It was William who had pointed out that the mean distance of the sun from the earth was exactly 10^9 times the vertical height of the pyramid (both 10 and 9 being, in his view, highly significant numbers); this Smyth took to be a remarkable confirmation of his own theory of the pyramid's divine inspiration.[21]

More and more obsessed with the Pyramid, William planned to write his own book, "to be proceeded with after my more pressing engagements". A typical theme of his sermons now was "The Great Pyramid; showing reasons for its sanctity in God's sight and why it is not mentioned expressly as well as implicitly in Scripture". He went to the British Museum, where Dr Birch showed him the casing stones and Vyse's original letters on the subject. He chatted to people in trains about Smyth's latest book and induced the local bookseller to stock it. The pyramid theories all rested upon linear measurements; it was clear that more of these were desirable and indeed necessary—Piazzi's had been rather those of an astronomer than of a professional surveyor. William made plans to go out with Piazzi Smyth to Egypt in January 1872; in December he had assembled his instruments, ordered suitable leggings and even designed a travelling case for his false teeth; but an innate reluctance to come to decisions, and perhaps also dread of travel into the unknown, gave him pause. Family commitments intervened to postpone his going: Samuel Petrie had died in the previous March and William found himself an executor and residuary legatee under the old man's will; his co-executor was a solicitor whom he distrusted, and he resolved to see to the legal formalities himself; the house in Ebury Street had to be disposed of—there was much to do.

Piazzi Smyth's books attracted many adherents, but the intellectual public remained unconvinced; the *Academy*, a leading literary weekly, refused to print William Petrie's letters and Dr Birch, as President of the Society for Biblical Archaeology, vetoed discussion of a short paper on the subject at one of their open meetings. When Piazzi Smyth proposed to lecture to the Royal Society in 1874, his paper was denied a reading, and he resigned his Fellowship. Only in Presbyterian Scotland, where he still held the post of Astronomer Royal, did his theories receive a favourable hearing; his book *The Antiquity of Intellectual Man*, in which William's contributions featured prominently, was awarded the Keith prize of the Royal Society of Edinburgh, and William was invited to lecture to them.

Anne Petrie appears to have been little affected by these enthusiasms, and Miss Marston had considered *Our Inheritance* "a wild and foolish book", but it is not surprising that Flinders, by the time he was sixteen or seventeen, was deeply involved and had embarked on his own calculations. With youthful self-assurance he wrote in 1870 to the *English Mechanic and World of Science*, defending the Pyramid theory against its critics, and thereafter became a regular correspondent, ranging himself firmly with the Biblical literalists, in opposition to the new science; the Great Pyramid he referred to as "the grandest writing on earth".[22] He too was now reckoned among Piazzi's chief companions in theoretical research; he made calculations which disclosed the presence of π in the inner chambers of the Pyramid.

His first book, *Researches on the Great Pyramid*, was published in April 1874; the sub-title read "A preliminary notice of some facts (heretofore unperceived) which will be shewn to aggregate into certain *Cosmic and Metric Systems in the Great Pyramid* . . .". These observations, he claimed, "confirm those distinctive principles of its design and construction, first announced by the sagacity of John Taylor and Professor Piazzi Smyth." Ingenuity and coincidence had produced some bizarre results: the Coffer he claimed to be a model for the dimensions of the Pyramid in height, circuit, angle and measure of contents; the total length of the ascending passage equalled 150 units in the King's Chamber; the north-east diagonal of the pyramid pointed straight towards Mount Ararat, the resting place of the Ark, and so on.

In one important respect Flinders, and probably also William, disagreed strongly with Piazzi Smyth and some of his followers: he was not a British Israelite. Some of the Petries' friends in Bromley were enthusiasts for this doctrine, and Flinders was asked to speak more than once on the subject; in April 1877 he had a large chart printed which bore on its title-page "*A Diagram of the great Pyramid* to show that the Great Pyramid's Passages are *not* chronological or not as taught in the so-called time-passage theory". This chart he sent to all prominent Anglo-Israelites, and received one or two furious letters in reply. A few weeks later he published a booklet, copies of which, knowing the storm it would raise, he sent to his friends in advance of publication; it was a compilation of passages from the Old Testament in which the return of every tribe to their home in Palestine is predicted. "We may gather undoubtedly," he concluded, "that Judah and Israel will return together *by the way they went.*" Though there are still some, in tented bondage, who have not yet returned, particularly in the area of the old Assyrian empire, there were never any tribes in the west, and the English could not be amongst them.[23]

After this Piazzi Smyth's friendship appears to have cooled very considerably; more and more the Petries were convinced that they must act independently, and secure more reliable measurements for themselves. William had written in 1872 to the young engineer, Waynman Dixon, who was sent out to Egypt to encase Cleopatra's Needle for its voyage to England, asking him, while he was there, to secure certain measurements; Dixon spent a short while at the Pyramid and discovered the air passages to the Queen's Chamber, and in the following year William and Flinders went to see him and hear of his experiences, and what it was like to live there. They made the acquaintance of Sydney Hall, a portrait painter whose interest in Pyramid theories seemed free from Anglo-Israelite bias; he too had been to Giza and made measurements, and he now corresponded regularly with Flinders and sent him papers and diagrams of his own; it was he who introduced him to David Gill, an astronomer who was in Egypt in 1874 with an expedition to observe the Transit of Venus, and had made a triangulation of the pyramid base; Gill handed over his figures to Flinders before he left for the Cape of Good Hope in 1878, where he was to become Astronomer Royal; before he went he suggested that Flinders might come out and work with him on a geodetic survey which he planned to make of the South African colonies. Flinders was tempted, but he set the idea aside. He now had a sense of mission: he must find out the truth.

He and his father decided to go to Egypt. They took stock of their surveying equipment and decided that more would be needed. Flinders did most of the work. All through 1878 he was busy making new instruments and testing and re-testing the old; he scoured the shops for the best available materials, chose an alt-azimuth and the latest type of theodolite; marked and divided his own measuring rods, testing their accuracy against the public standard in Trafalgar Square; he designed a scale, a hundred inches long, and had it made of steel by instrument makers in London "on a new principle, employing the stiffness of a tube to maintain the straightness of a strip".[24] Special octohedral stands for the theodolites were of his own devising—even the plumb-bobs were made to his improved design. In fitting the spider lines in the theodolites he substituted for a single thread two parallel lines crossed by one horizontal for levelling. The spider's web had to be carefully chosen: "Spider's web is useless, as it is covered with sticky globules to catch small flies . . . the best way of all is to catch a very small spider, and make it spin to reach the ground, winding up the thread as fast as it spins out, dangling in mid-air."[25] Cases and boxes had to be made for all this equipment; he did his own carpentry, and constructed his own rope-ladders. Meanwhile he was making frequent visits to the British Museum, copying plans of monuments, making lists of Egyptian kings, learning the forms of the hieroglyphs, compiling a vocabulary of Arabic words and reading as many books as he could find on the history and geography of the country. Occasionally he allowed himself a little time off, when Marianne or Fanny or Susan Harvey came up to town and he took them to the National Gallery to look at the Turners, or stand in admiration in front of his favourite Masaccio; then he might take his guest to Gatti's for chocolate, before seeing her off at Waterloo Station. In January 1878 he went to see the exhibition of Schliemann's recent Trojan discoveries: "Carefully examined them all, and measured some. There are some puzzles of workmanship among them." On 5 July of that year he watched Cleopatra's Needle being erected on the Embankment; later that month he went to the Crystal Palace and saw Edison's new phonograph. In the summer of 1879 he took five days off for a surveying trip to the Isle of Wight, and afterwards Spurrell came down to stay at Warsash, and they surveyed and planned what they took to be a mediaeval dam system, and dug around a large stone on the heath which had first been excavated by Flinders when he was eighteen (it had been his first "dig"); they decided it was probably natural.

With all these varied occupations he was very busy, but he filled his few spare hours with reading to a purpose: he was writing slips for a new English Dictionary, a task for which he had volunteered in response to an appeal to the public made by the editor, Dr James

Murray (later Sir James), on behalf of the Philological Society;[26] from among the list of authors whose works needed to be searched for unusual words and phrases, Flinders chose to begin with Ruskin's *Seven Lamps of Architecture*; then he embarked on the travels of George Sandys. Sometimes he would write as many as a hundred slips in a day; from time to time he would send off a fresh batch of them to Murray.

In December 1879 Flinders Petrie took stock of all his pyramid equipment: everything was ready and all the packing cases made; on 23 December he enquired about passages for Alexandria. But for some reason they did not go—perhaps William had found some pressing reason for postponing the journey. So for another year Flinders waited, reading, studying as before; he took on Dampier's *Voyages* for the Dictionary* and in the summer he spent nearly two weeks in Cornwall, surveying and measuring megaliths and stone huts and circles from Land's End to Penzance; after midsummer observations at Stonehenge he tramped about Wiltshire for a few days more; he made further day excursions with Spurrell, fair-copied plans, made a set of improved levelling rods, bought a pith hat and made a blanket box. At last he decided that he would wait no longer. On 25 November the Ocean Express carriers came to collect the boxes, and he went to town for a passport and a Turkish visa, both of which he obtained promptly; he then deposited a portfolio containing forty-one sheets of plans of earthworks with the British Museum (later these were bound together in one volume with the ones he had already given them).[27] Next day he came up again to say goodbye to his grandmother and Uncle Francis and his godmother Miss Marston; he was not to see his grandmother again, for she died in the following spring while he was still in Egypt. On Monday he was off; William promised to follow in a week or so. The great adventure had begun at last.

* In all, 2,450 slips are recorded under Flinders Petrie's name, and his mother is also mentioned as a contributor in Murray's Letter Book. From such slips, sent in by more than 1,000 readers, the *Oxford English Dictionary* was born.[28]

CHAPTER III

The Pyramid Survey
(1880–82)

IT WAS RAINING when Flinters Petrie went on board the S.S. *Nephthys* at Liverpool, and next morning they were not far out of harbour when it started to blow hard. The vessel pitched heavily and he suffered his first experience of sea-sickness, an affliction which was to make travel to Egypt an ordeal in future. In the evening he could not face the stuffiness of the cabin, but found a warm spot on the grating of the engine room on which to sleep as best he could. By the third day the sea was calmer and he had got used to the ship's motion; the novelty of shipboard, his fellow passengers, the first sight of porpoises, near views of the coast of Portugal, a fiery sunset, all delighted him and he wrote daily descriptions to his parents. At Gibraltar, where they went ashore, he made a bee-line for a permit to visit the galleries on the summit of the Rock, then strolled through the streets admiring the gaily coloured sashes and Spanish mantillas of the townspeople. One of their fellow passengers, a Moroccan trader, left the boat here; Flinders had been able to practise his small Arabic vocabulary on him, but "beyond a few stray remarks on route, weather etc., our mutual goodwill was expressed by nods, smiles and indications". A few hours on shore at Algiers allowed him no time to make contacts or excursions, but when they docked at Valletta he at once raced off to try and find some prehistoric tombs marked on the map; after sunset he was forced to turn back without locating them. The ship reached Alexandria on 14 December; finding that his nineteen boxes would not be unloaded till later he went ashore, booked into a hotel and set out to explore the town. Next day the English Director General of Customs agreed to pass all his boxes, but they had not yet been unloaded, so he set out after lunch for the catacombs; with his "handy little twelve-foot tape" he made 140 measurements in a little over two hours, and established that the workmanship in some had been accurate to a tenth of an inch.

All next morning he waited impatiently at Customs for an official to come and inspect his boxes, but nobody came; Flinders was experiencing for the first time the leisurely ways of the Orient. When at last he got his baggage through Customs, after interminable arguments during which the Director General had twice to be appealed to, it was past sunset and he had to spend a third night at Alexandria before at last setting off on the morning train for Cairo. Travelling second class —third, he decided, was too dirty—he found his companions friendly and was enchanted by the watery Delta landscape: palms and acacias were reflected in the still lakes; at every station there were hawkers selling oranges, hard-boiled eggs and bread rolls, little girls selling bottles of water, and old men with water-skins; the water he did not dare to sample, but the oranges were cheap and delicious. When the train reached Cairo, he left his boxes to be collected later, and refusing porters and donkey-boys, set off with his portmanteaux on foot to the Hôtel du Nil, which had been recommended to him as clean and reasonable; it was conveniently situated near the Muski, the principal street and centre of commerce, and for the next eleven years he stayed there whenever he was in Cairo; there was a modest Franco-Greek restaurant round the corner where he could dine cheaply and he usually bought fruit for his lunch.

That first afternoon he wandered about Cairo absorbing the sights and sounds and smells; he walked out to Windmill Hill, by the Tombs of the Caliphs, and was "dumbfounded" at the vast accumulation of pottery that composed the mound on which he stood; after dinner he struck out along Shubra Avenue towards the country, between large country houses and pleasant gardens, returning in the moonlight as it grew late. Next morning he went straight to the Bulaq Museum where the antiquities discovered by Mariette and his assistants were displayed, finding it as he had expected full of beautiful and exciting things: the "Hyksos" statues from Tanis, the seated painted figures of man and wife from Meydum and the wooden panels from the tomb of Hesy-Rê' at Saqqara excited his particular admiration.

The administration of the Museum, and indeed of all matters concerned with Egypt's antiquities was in the hands of the Frenchman Auguste Mariette. He had first come out in 1850, when he discovered the Serapeum at Saqqara and opened some of the *mastaba* tombs of the Old Kingdom nearby; the treasures found in these excavations had gone to the Louvre, in which he was for a time Assistant Keeper of Egyptian Antiquities. In 1857, with the encouragement and support of the influential De Lesseps, he was appointed by the Khedive Said Pasha to be in charge of the excavation and conservation of ancient monuments in the Nile Valley, many of which were gravely in danger of destruction. He persuaded the Khedive to give him a large workforce for excavation, and a building in Cairo, at Bulaq on the bank of the Nile, in which to create a museum for the treasures he found. With extraordinary energy and dedication he embarked on a vast programme of exploration in most of the temples and major sites in Egypt; in all, he excavated at no less than thirty-five different places and employed nearly three thousand workmen annually. Inevitably, he could exercise little or no direct supervision over these operations, but used overseers who reported to him; he would visit the scene of an excavation perhaps once or twice a season, and make notes, but little of what he found was adequately published, and many of his papers were destroyed when his house and the museum were flooded in 1878. In order to stem the flow of antiquities leaving the country, he forbade anyone but himself to excavate; he attempted to prevent vandalism by tourists and destruction by local treasure-hunters and the peasants who dug ancient sites for fertilizing earth (*sebakh*) or broke up temple stone for the lime kilns, and he set up workshops on the main sites; he had cleared away the villages which choked some of the temples, so that temples like Edfu, Karnak and Dendara could be seen in something like their ancient grandeur. All this had been very costly, and as Mariette grew older he was increasingly hampered by lack of funds; Said's successor, the Khedive Ismail, during his short reign plunged Egypt so deeply into debt that only the year before Petrie's arrival, he had been deposed by the Sultan of Turkey, and British and French administrators had been called in; stringent measures were needed to rescue the bankrupt economy, and there could be little priority for archaeology.

Mariette's health was failing and he saw his dreams for the rediscovery of Egypt's past fading; in 1879 he had addressed a meeting of the Académie des Inscriptions et Belles-Lettres in Paris, on the urgent work which needed to be done in Egypt, in order to complete the record of Egypt's past—work which he realized he himself would never be able to undertake. The lecture was referred to later by Egyptologists as "Mariette's will". Now he was back in Egypt but lay seriously ill. In the Boulaq Museum his assistant Émile Brugsch was deputizing for him. He was the younger brother of Mariette's friend, the distinguished German Egyptologist Heinrich Brugsch. Though not himself a scholar, he was a competent photographer and lithographer and had made himself useful in the Museum and conducted excavations; Ismail Pasha had showed his favour and married him to a member of his hareem. He was heartily disliked by many of the European community in Cairo and was believed to be making a handsome income from the antiquities he handled for the Museum.

Petrie had an invitation to luncheon from Dr Grant, on whom he had called the previous day with an introduction from Sydney Hall; the doctor and his American wife were most cordial; he already knew of Petrie's *Stonehenge*, which had been receiving good notices in England, and Flinders resolved to give him a copy. Dr James Grant, Physician to the Khedive, had lived in Cairo for many years and knew Piazzi Smyth well, but he regarded his theories with tolerant scepticism and laughed at the time passage theory, though he occasionally made measurements himself at night in the Pyramid. He and his wife kept open house for visiting Englishmen and at their Wednesday evening soirées they welcomed *savants* of all nationalities. He showed Flinders Petrie his collection of Egyptian antiquities, of which he was very proud; it was particularly rich in scarabs of all periods. The Grants were to be very good to Petrie; he often came to the doctor for help and advice, and he was always welcome at their table. Dr Grant now promised to send word, through the grapevine, to 'Ali Gabri, the Arab who had been Piazzi Smyth's assistant in 1864 (Smyth called him Ali Dobree) and had also helped Waynman Dixon and David Gill; he was honest, Dr Grant said, and would prove very useful. He also advised Flinders to obtain, through the English Vice-Consul, a letter from Riaz Pasha the Prime Minister requesting the protection of the local sheikh. It was not advisable, he said, to try to see Mariette Pasha—he was too ill, and in any case no permission was needed from the Antiquities Department to occupy a tomb at Giza.

Next day was Sunday, and Flinders attended the English Church morning and evening, though he found the tone of the sermons "very broad". On Monday he made formal application through Mr Borg, the Vice-Consul, and then went on to the Citadel to look for General Stone, the Prefect of Police, to whom Gill had given him an introduction. 'Ali Gabri appeared in the afternoon and Flinders liked him at once. His "pleasant and trustworthy face" and straightforward manner confirmed the truth of the excellent references given by his former employers. Together they went to Dr Grant's and with his help settled the terms of 'Ali's employment; Mrs Grant gave Flinders advice on diet and health, and they both pressed him to spend Christmas with them in five days' time; they could not have been kinder. 'Ali went with him to the station, loaded the precious boxes on to carts, and spent the night guarding them. He turned up with them early the next morning and found Flinders a donkey to ride (tourists usually went out to the pyramids in a carriage, but this cost 25 piastres—5/-—far more than Petrie was prepared to spend). The donkey was very uncomfortable at first but he soon found it was better to gallop than to trot; they covered the ten miles to the pyramids in about two hours. Flinders planned to occupy the tomb Waynman Dixon had lived in, for which 'Ali had the key; it proved to be three small tombs, with the walls between them broken away, and he decided it would do very well; 'Ali got fresh sand put on the floors and all was ready when the carts arrived and the boxes unloaded and carried up the hill, each by a single man, Arab fashion, with a rope round the forehead. The first thing to do was to unpack the stove, brew coffee and eat a meal of herrings and chocolate; then Flinders set to work to make himself a bedstead of wood, a simple plank frame with two long uprights to which he suspended his hammock; upended, the bed turned into a tolerable easy chair. In the evening 'Ali went down to his village, leaving his negro slave, Muhammad, to sleep as guard in the adjoining tomb.

The next few weeks passed quickly. Flinders set to work exploring the pyramid and its surroundings and then began measuring the interior; he got used to the nauseous smell of bats, but the heat inside the galleries was oppressive and he found it best to do most of his work at night, free of constant interruptions from tourists, and when 'Ali was not there, dispensing with boots, shirt and trousers. During the day, with 'Ali's help, he explored very thoroughly the surrounding area, measuring open tombs and combing the rubbish mounds. He did not go to the Grants for Christmas: that festival had never been observed in the Petrie household, since the Brethren held it to be without Scriptural authority. On the first Sunday, cutting church probably for the first time since his childhood, he went for a long walk in the desert.

The climate agreed with him and he relished freedom from the restraints of conventional dress; he often went barefoot, and he ate, worked and slept as and when the occasion offered. As he wrote happily to Spurrell: "Life here is really comfortable, without many of the encumbrances of regular hours: bells, collars and cuffs, blacking, tablecloths or many others of the unnecessaries of Civilisation."[1] His food was of the simplest; he had a kettle, a frying pan and a primus stove and could boil himself rice and fry up tomatoes and eggs; an occasional tin of pilchards, or cheese bought in Cairo, varied this diet and he had brought out a store of hard ship's biscuits which he crumbled into the eggs or ate dry; for dessert he had oranges, which were plentiful and cheap. 'Ali, marvelling at the rocky hardness of the biscuits, brought him some native bread from the village, but this Flinders could not bring himself to eat. "It is a trial to one's stomach to have a supply of bread brought, each pat with the sign and countersign of Mrs. Ali's two hands, and all bundled up in a cloth in which untold generations of fleas appear to have resided; the Arabic odour of the cloth is not of so much consequence, as the bread smells singularly to begin with." In later years he was not to be so fastidious.

There were other drawbacks to life in a tomb: sleep was apt to be interrupted by a variety of sounds. Sometimes it was the howling of jackals; more often the village dogs would carry on their noctural feuds on the hillside just below. Usually he managed to ignore them, but when he was not well, sleep was elusive; recovering from a feverish cold, he chronicled the night's alarms:

> Did not get any sleep till 11 or 12, and then broken by (1st) trap down, big rat, killed and reset. (2nd) mouse about trap for long, thought bait must be eaten, got up to see; (3rd) Fleas. (4th) mouse let trap down without going in; got up, reset it; (5th) mouse got in, got up, killed him, reset trap; (6th) Fleas; (7th) Dog set up protracted conversational barking (just by my door) with sundry neighbours in adjacent villages; went out and pelted him off. (8th) woke in heavy perspiration, had to change night shirt, & take off sheet. If this is *not* the way to get over a fever-cold I cannot help it.

He went into Cairo seldom, and chiefly to get money from the bank and pick up his mail at the post office; the postal service was surprisingly good: letters from England took less than a week. His mother sent him copies of *Academy*, *Nature* and the weekly journal *Public Opinion*, which kept him informed of current events at home. But time was precious and the journey uncomfortable: he was ruefully conscious of the ludicrous figure he cut on a donkey:

> Behold me! on a small donkey whose only furniture is an old saddle (the leather hump on the front of which has all burst in front) & a double piece of rope round his neck; hugging a canvas bag stuffed with oranges before me, & a check blue handkerchief also full of oranges in my hand, regaling myself with them as I go along . . . the

> consequences of that saddle without any support to my feet, for 17 miles today, may be imagined but not described.

Eventually he managed to buy a saddle with stirrups, which lessened his discomfort, but he never took to donkey riding and preferred to walk wherever possible. On his rare visits to Cairo he always called on the Grants and usually had dinner with them; one day they told him about an earnest Pyramid-measurer who had been seen by the Doctor taking out a saw-file and trying to reduce the granite boss to "the exact size which he wanted for his Inspiration theories!!!"

On 21 January came the news that Mariette was dead; speculation as to his successor gave rise to many rumours; the Khedive, it was said, had promised Brugsch that he should be the next Director, but the Consul General of France, backed by the British, insisted (according to Charles Wilbour, the American Egyptologist, who was in Cairo at the time) "that the place of a Frenchman should be filled by a Frenchman",[2] and a distinguished young scholar from Paris, Gaston Maspero, who had arrived only a few weeks before to be head of the new French Institute in Cairo, was appointed within ten days of Mariette's death.

One day Mrs Grant came out to the pyramids with a Mr Chester whom she introduced to Flinders as an old friend. This was the Revd Greville Chester, an elderly antiquarian and collector who came often to Egypt to buy antiquities, which he usually sold in London; he also had a large private collection of his own. He had a deep knowledge of Egypt as well as a shrewd eye for a good bargain—many fine things bought by him had already been acquired by the British Museum;[3] he told Petrie he was on his thirty-eighth trip. They were to become good friends, and Petrie benefited much, during the next few years, from Chester's experience and his discriminating eye. Another visitor was Mr Loftie, an old friend of Spurrell's, also a clergyman who wintered regularly in Egypt for his health and like Chester was a very knowledgeable collector of scarabs and other antiquities. Both pressed Flinders to call on them whenever he was in Cairo, an invitation of which he took advantage on several occasions in the months to come. Then one day a bearded traveller arrived and began to take observations at the Great Pyramid; perceiving Flinders adjusting a signal, he said: "We seem to be doing the same thing", and started chatting; it turned out to be General Lane Fox who, having come into an inheritance and a large country estate in Dorset, had changed his name by deed poll to Pitt-Rivers; in these altered surroundings, and less conventionally dressed, neither had recognized the other, and they laughed heartily at the incident. He was on his way up the Nile, but promised to call in again on his way back; he was delighted, he said, that somebody was at last undertaking a proper survey of the pyramids. Flinders was very glad to have such visitors, whom he could call upon "as witnesses of some things which I should not get people in England to believe very readily perhaps if only on single testimony". He was preparing for the storm which might greet him when he demonstrated that many of Piazzi Smyth's measurements were inaccurate; in the interior of the Pyramid the unevenness of the floor, and incrustations of salt on the walls, had led to an accumulative error which Petrie, with his superior methods and better instruments, was able to correct. He wrote to him from time to time, and also to Waynman Dixon and Sydney Hall; at length a letter came from Smyth, "politely peculiar as usual", obliquely indicating that he was not prepared to accept any modification of his base measurement. This, however, Petrie was not yet able to make to his satisfaction: clearance of the rubble at the corners was necessary, and he had no permit to excavate.

The triangulation of the exterior was a long and arduous business, and occupied Flinders for most of the season. He searched the plateau for Gill's bronze station marks and found a few of them, but most had been damaged or removed. His own were holes drilled in the rock and filled with blue plaster; in some, for greater accuracy, he sank a pencil lead into the plaster. A cairn by each marked its position. The triangulation was planned to cover all nine of the pyramids of Giza, three large and six small (see p. 54). Two of the stations had to be positioned so that each was visible from fifteen other points: "it requires a good deal of dodging about, and trying first one site and then another, to get all the places visible from behind the loose stones and heaps of rubble and hillocks which cover the ground."

The signal rods had to be centred every day, and taken home in the evening lest roving Beduin should remove them. Some angles were read as many as fourteen times; the long base line was measured over and over again to ensure complete accuracy. Flinders longed for a competent assistant who would save time by checking readings, or writing down the observations; 'Ali was willing and helpful, but was apt to go off at odd times to perform his devotions, which Flinders considered occupied somewhat more time than was required by the dictates of religion. Sometimes a gust of wind would blow over his markers or clouds of dust obscure his view and heat haze sometimes caused the point of observation to shimmer. In the evenings, by candlelight, he would reduce the day's figures by trigonometry, carefully checking each set of measurements to ensure that the instrument had not shifted at all.

Carters arrived to carry off stone from around the Great Pyramid for road mending; to Petrie's delight they uncovered one of Vyse's casing stones, for which he had been searching in vain. Then the men started carting off larger blocks to build a wall. They had to be closely watched lest they removed something of importance or smashed it with a hammer; Petrie promised them *bakhshish* for stones with a worked face, and set 'Ali to watch over them when he was not there. One day he went off to Abu Rawash, five miles to the north of Giza; he examined the huge chamber in the heart of the pyramid which was all that remained, and came to the over-hasty conclusion that the pyramid had once been finished but later destroyed. (It is now known that it was never completed.)[4] The monument was being quarried for stone—he was told that while the Nile was high, three hundred camel-loads a day would be carted off.

As Flinders worked he would observe with some amusement the behaviour of visitors to the Pyramids: a party of Egyptians with their wives, "plucky little Fatimahs sprawling and slipping about and laughing heartily at their tumbles", or Greek priests "with enormous flowing beards and wide hats, and long black gowns, careering across the plain on frisky donkeys". Dr Grant arrived by carriage for a night of measurement; he insisted on going down the well between the ascending passage and the Grand Gallery; they both went down by rope ladder and while Flinders investigated a hole in the "grotto" at one side, the doctor went on down with a candle on his own, only to find the narrow passage blocked eighty-seven feet further down. When Flinders eventually descended to join him, through a thick haze of dust, he was alarmed to find him in a state of collapse, "moaning and breathing hard and quick, and hardly able to speak". He was a large man, and it took 'Ali and Flinders a long time, hauling and pushing, to get him up to the grotto again; there he slowly ate a sandwich and drank a little from his flask of tea, and at last "mustered strength for the mainly vertical pull up into the Grand Gallery. I followed close behind him, pushing and lifting wherever I could, but the prospect of about 15 stone, half fainting, scrambling just over your head in a place where the holding is poor at best, made me quake at his possible slipping." By the time he had rested, he was able to walk shakily down to his waiting coach, and Flinders got to bed at half-past six in the morning, worried about his ladders which he had had to leave in the pyramid.

Maspero and Brugsch came out one day with other Museum officials to inspect a tomb which had recently been excavated; this must have been Petrie's first sight of either of them, but it was a brief encounter and they did not speak. Desultory excavations were being carried on by the Department of Antiquities all the time in nearby tombs. Petrie wrote of his horror at the destruction of monuments:

> The savage indifference of the Arabs, who have even stripped the alabaster off the granite temple since Mariette uncovered it, and who are not at all watched here, is only surpassed by a most barbaric sort of regard for the monuments by those in power. Nothing seems to be done with any uniform and regular plan; work is begun and left unfinished . . . the very rough and rudely cut tomb interiors which had puzzled me, were it seems all lined with finely carved stone, which has all been ripped out for building and for limestone . . . It is sickening to see the rate at which everything is being destroyed, and the little regard paid to its preservation; if allotments all over the hill were made to the different European Government museums, with free leave to clear and take all they liked, and power to preserve it here, something more satisfactory might be done. Anything would be better than leaving things to be destroyed wholesale; better spoil half in preserving the other half, than leave the whole to be smashed.

Shortly before Flinders Petrie left England, he had gone to see Dr Birch at the British Museum and talked over with him what he should do. The Keeper, who had never himself been to Egypt, suggested that Petrie should bring back some specimens of pottery. No such collection had ever been made in Egypt before; it was generally regarded by collectors as rubbish. There were a few pots from Egypt in the Museum, it was true, but nobody there would have ventured to put a date to them, least of all Birch himself,[5] and it is to his credit that he accepted what Petrie brought home, and even offered him £5 to cover the expense of transportation. By carefully marking on every pot or sherd the spot where it was found, and noting what beads or other man-made objects there were in the same context, Petrie was able to suggest a late date—Ptolemaic or Roman—for many of the wares formerly thought to be early, and to identify a handsome sealing-wax red ceramic as the fine pottery of the Pyramid Age.[6] He also collected samples of every sort of stone implement and an ample number of specimens of the casing stones of the different pyramids, as well as discarded cores from stone drills and pieces which showed the marks made by metal saws, to illustrate ancient methods of stone-working. He expected that Birch's Department would select what they wanted and let him keep the rest for his friends. The flints he set aside hoping that General Pitt-Rivers would keep his promise and visit him again, but in this he was disappointed. Dr Birch had also asked him to copy inscriptions whenever he had an opportunity. Many tombs in Giza stood open and whenever the wind blew so hard that work outside was impossible, Flinders would take a picnic lunch into one of them and settle down snugly for three or four hours' copying. Though his knowledge of hieroglyphics was still elementary and his drawing of them clumsy he had an accurate eye for detail and Birch was delighted with his copies.

On a fine March morning now, he preferred to walk the six or seven miles into Cairo. The road ran between fields intersected by canals; small white egrets picked their way through the cultivation and in the distance, two mudbrick villages broke the skyline. "It was a lovely day, a cool slight North wind sweet with all the flowering crops, and the shepherd-boys a-piping in the meadows among the clover to their cows and goats." The description reads strangely to those who know the Pyramid road today, choked with traffic and flanked by night-clubs, hotels and high-rise apartment blocks.

At the end of March, taking 'Ali and his son with him and a few provisions on a donkey, Petrie set off for Saqqara, ten miles south of Giza, where he intended to spend a few days, sleeping at night on a table in Mariette's old house near the Serapeum (which was sometimes made available to tourists) and exploring by day the labyrinthine tombs and passages of that extraordinary city of the dead.

Leaving 'Ali asleep on the second day, he walked south over the desert to the pyramids of Dahshur, reaching them in the noonday heat; he had with him only three measuring rods, a bit of candle in his pocket and a few matches tucked into his notebook. Clambering up to the entrance of the first pyramid, he descended the long corridor into the large chamber; then, proceeding further, "while measuring, I heard the stones knocking about at one end, and as I was unaware of the number and nature of the beasts, and had nothing but thin measuring rods, and no-one within two miles, I beat a retreat without investigating the cause; it is probably a jackal's lair but might be a hyena or a runaway slave." Walking on to the so-called Bent Pyramid, he was rewarded by finding the doorway intact; he noted holes near the top of the side walls which suggested to him an outer flap door of stone with metal hinges, and an inner wooden door pivoting normally. Three quarters of the passage was choked with sand and stones, so that he had to slide and wriggle down feet first, narrowly missed by a pair of alarmed owls.

Petrie had hoped to find other tombs to investigate "not knowing Brugsch and Mariette's passion for *exclusiveness.*" There was evidence of recent work, he noticed on the way back to Saqqara, two pyramids recently opened by Brugsch; both had been blocked, but the burial chamber of one had been broken into from the roof and he decided to defy the ban and see what was inside; letting himself down from the top on a rope ladder next day with 'Ali's assistance, he was delighted to find that this was one of the two inscribed pyramids, the discovery of which had recently been rumoured in Cairo. Mariette had always maintained that no pyramid ever contained an inscription; news of the opening by Brugsch of two of the smaller pyramids of the Old Kingdom at Saqqara whose walls within were covered with religious texts, had been brought to him as he lay on his deathbed; Maspero, new in office, was eager to open more. The hieroglyphs which covered the walls, Petrie found, were only partly visible through fallen débris and stone blocks, but one end wall was almost completely exposed, the hieroglyphs, coloured green, "beautifully sharply cut in the white limestone". He could see by the cartouches enclosing the royal name, which occurred again and again in the text, that the pyramid had been that of King Pepy Merenre' (Pepy I). For hours he copied without stopping, till dusk put an end to the work. This would be enough, he thought, "to shew the character of it, and for Dr. Birch and Dr. Wiedemann to work on".

'Ali meanwhile was becoming increasingly nervous lest they be caught in the act by the *reis* in charge of the area, for they both well knew that "pirating" such a discovery might lead them into serious trouble with the Antiquities Service. As soon as he got back to Giza Petrie sent off his copy of the text to the British Museum with an accompanying description of the tomb, and also gave Mr Loftie an account for *The Athenaeum.*[7] Petrie had urged Birch to keep the identity of his informant secret; he felt himself justified, "because it is well known that Brugsch wishes to keep all to himself, but he has behaved so shabbily in covering up everything, inscribed or not, that I rather relish *doing* him in a small way."

But Maspero, who had superintended the opening of another

pyramid, that of Unas, only three weeks earlier, had announced his intention of publishing all these pyramid texts himself, and when Birch's article came out,[8] with a transcription and translation of the Pepy text, he was naturally incensed, not so much on his own behalf, as he told his friend Miss Amelia Edwards, the novelist and journalist who regularly reported Egyptological news in the *Academy*, but because Birch had robbed the dead Mariette of the credit; his punishment would be to have been responsible for a copy which was incomplete and not without mistakes.[9] He guessed who the copyist had been, but he does not appear to have held it against him, perhaps putting the indiscretion down to inexperience.

Flinders had already decided that he would have to spend another winter at work in the pyramid field; there were measurements still to be taken and without excavation a complete survey was not possible. Perhaps next year his father would come, at least for part of the time, and make his task easier. He had fully expected him to follow within a few days of his first arrival but William had delayed, on one pretext or another: in March he wrote[10] explaining that Marge was not well, and that the garden fence had blown down . . . it must by that time have been clear to Flinders that he was not coming; he thought somewhat ruefully of the carefully stocked chest of medicines his father was to have brought out, though he had found a homoeopathic chemist in Cairo who stocked all that he needed. Now William talked about going out next year, and sent his son advice about the safe bestowal of his instruments and gear in the meantime. An entry in his diary at this time makes it evident that he still adhered to the theory of the Pyramid's divine origin: he was trying to convince his sister (who belonged to the Exclusive Brethren and often disagreed with him on religious matters) of "the symbolic meaning of the Pyramid in regard to Christ's Life and the Heavenly Jerusalem".[11] On 14 May, not long before Flinders was due to return, William was summoned by his brother Francis to Gloucester Terrace in London, where his mother had been taken seriously ill; she died that night and William found himself again an executor, and as head of the family, having to arbitrate in a quarrel between the brothers Francis and Martin about their share of the inheritance.

It was getting very hot now, and the discomforts of Flinders' cave were increased by invasions of ants and flies; he killed a snake, and found that the Arabs were terrified of them, assuming all to be poisonous. Working in the pyramids at night, he would strip completely, and outside, when he was on his own, he worked in no more than vest and underpants; as he later wrote, "if pink, they kept the tourist at bay, as the creature seemed to him too queer for inspection." There must have been rumours going round Cairo concerning strange goings-on at the pyramids.

One day in April Flinders woke up with a sore throat; after a few days it was worse and a soaring temperature sent him into Cairo to consult Dr Grant, who diagnosed pharyngitis and put him straight to bed. He stayed there for over a week, tended by Mrs Grant and the little German maid. To repay their kindness—for the Doctor would accept no payment—Flinders resolved to find out what books he needed, and bring them out next winter.

The tourist season was ending, and the dealers who had swarmed round visitors to the pyramids were now prepared to let their wares go cheaply. Flinders Petrie bought a number of bronzes, coins and scarabs, reckoning that he could more than recoup the cost by selling to collectors and to his friends in England. His knowledge of coins enabled him to secure several valuable prizes for very little, and he was learning to detect forgeries, particularly of scarabs, of which there was already a flourishing industry in Luxor; the German Consul there, he was told, was selling fake scarabs at "a rattling price: £5 to £10 each". Some of Petrie's purchases were bought by Loftie and Greville Chester; others he brought home to sell and some he kept for himself, for he was beginning to form a collection of the things that interested him, especially scarabs of historical interest with royal names, or the titles of officials.

By mid-May the heat had become so uncomfortable that Petrie decided to stop working; by 23 May he had packed up, locked his cave, and was off to Cairo with his instruments, to leave them in Dr Grant's safe-keeping; he had not booked a passage in advance, and found that he would have to wait ten days before leaving Alexandria. He bought presents: sweetmeats in the Muski for the family, and photographs by the dozen for his friends. Before he left Alexandria he wrote to Karl Baedeker pointing out a number of mistakes in his Guide. On the way home he went ashore again in Malta, and tried to walk to the temple of Hagiar Qim, but once more he was overtaken by dusk and had to give up; he concluded that the guide-book must be misleading.

On 22 June he caught the overnight train from Liverpool and was home to breakfast the next morning. During the next few days he unpacked and arranged his treasures; then he went up to the British Museum to see Birch and show him the bronzes, and to the Coin

Room with his purchases, some of which they bought on the spot. He called on Loftie and sold or exchanged some of his finds with him, and on Greville Chester who showed him his collection of Phoenician antiquities. Dr Birch came down to Bromley one day to see the pottery and stone fragments, and selected some pottery for the Museum, and Mr Franks, of the Department of Prehistoric Antiquities, came to pick out some of the flints. Dr Grant, home on leave, stayed with the Petries for a night or so and Flinders took him to see Rochester Cathedral.

All August he was working through his notes, reducing the triangulations around the pyramids, checking his observations and plotting his results. He decided to add photography to the record; never having owned or used a camera in his life, he set to work to design one. It was essentially a box of japanned tin about the size and shape of a biscuit tin; the lens had two apertures, drilled in a sheet of tin, and the drop-shutter was also of tin, strengthened by a slip of wood; there was a sleeve of opaque material into which he could insert his hand to remove and replace successive plates, exposed and unexposed plates being separated by a slip of cardboard; reflectors of tin were stored in a separate box.[12] The tripod stand, too, he designed himself. This simple camera, or later variants of it, he used all his life for photographs of objects: for these he would use very slow film, especially made for him by Kodak, and might leave the shutter open as long as half an hour; he developed his plates at night, and usually left the fixing and printing of his photographs till he got back to England. Once, in 1897, he was invited by the Camera Club to talk about his camera, which he had been using for sixteen years; the members agreed that some of the pictures he had taken with it were "as good as any they had seen". Some early plate glass negatives which have survived are admirably clear and show minute detail. When he got to Giza he experimented with interior candlelight shots of the King's Chamber and galleries, and took some quick action shots, and long exposures in dim evening light.

This year, he decided, he would go much earlier to Egypt and return before the onset of the summer heat. Travelling by way of Venice, he reached Alexandria on 13 October 1881 and Cairo the following day. He called at once on Maspero in his houseboat moored next to the Museum in Bulaq. He found him cordial and anxious to help; no mention was made of the Saqqara pyramid. It would be best, said he, if Petrie were to excavate as his employee, as a temporary official of the Museum, thus avoiding the necessity, and possible difficulty, of obtaining a *firman* from the Khedive; one of the Museum staff would be sent to work with him. This Petrie understood to mean that he would be under surveillance; he hoped that the man would at any rate be useful (in this he was to be disappointed). He sat down in his hotel to draft an application: "to uncover some of the points of original construction which are requisite for the completion of the subject", listing separately the various points he wished to examine, in and around the pyramids. If there were time, he would like to explore, in the neighbourhood of Giza, "likely sites for primaeval settlements".[13] When he returned to the Museum Maspero was not well and Brugsch had been left to draw up the permit; it allowed work on only two of the three pyramids, so that he would have to apply again later on for the third. Flinders was sure this was not what Maspero had intended but he judged it prudent to leave the matter thus.

The Grants received him warmly; he met a young man called Corbett, a friend of the Lofties who was tutor to the Khedive's sons, and liked him at once. Loftie and Chester were yet to arrive. After church on Sunday, Petrie took an afternoon walk in the area of the Tombs of the Caliphs; to his fury he was roughly accosted by some soldiers and robbed of his wallet containing £40. Two passers-by in a carriage, a Greek and a Copt, had witnessed the incident, and he determined to bring his assailants to justice and recover his money; he therefore went straight to the British Consul, and also wrote an account of the incident for *The Times* and *The Globe* in England, both of which newspapers published the item: the more publicity given to the affair, he thought, the greater the likelihood that he would get restitution, since the Egyptian Government would be anxious "to avoid scaring travellers away just as the season is beginning".[14] Alas, he had a lot to learn about Egypt. At an identification parade next day he picked out his attackers, but they denied the accusation; the Greek, who promised to testify for him, later withdrew his testimony, and the Copt was nowhere to be found; the trial, some days later, was a farce, since the officer prompted his men in a stage whisper whenever their statements disagreed. Eventually, through an interpreter, Petrie declared in exasperation that it was useless to expect justice from such a court, and abandoned the case. He never saw his money but he was the richer for the experience. The army were getting out of hand and there had been a number of such robberies, his friends told him. In the pyramid area, where he was among friends, he felt safe but he kept very little money in his tomb and concealed it well.

He was warmly welcomed by 'Ali and the other Arabs at Giza,

much to the astonishment of the Museum official whom Brugsch had detailed to accompany him. He was a young man who spoke English, but it soon became clear that he had no experience of excavation, nor any intention of acquiring any. He tried to persuade Petrie to live in a house in the village—it had, he said, a bed with a fine canopy, and a beautiful mirror—and was uncomprehending of his insistence that he preferred his tomb, and only needed "bread, dates and water"; "I am *ibn el beled*, a son of the country," Petrie explained, "all the Arabs are my friends and I know them all." He began at once to excavate the lower passage of the Great Pyramid, starting with one man to dig and five boys to clear the debris; the Museum man at first stood by, but later contented himself with making an occasional appearance from the village to pass the time of day. Flinders was told later by 'Ali that of the ten piastres (2/-) a week that he was required to pay this official, the lion's share went into Brugsch's pocket.

The view from his tomb now was very different from that of the previous winter: on either side of the road the waters of the inundation formed a lake which stretched as far as the edge of the escarpment; clusters of palm trees here and there stood with their feet in the water, and the villages and isolated farmhouses stood on little islands, linked by paths running along earthen causeways. The inundation had reached its height in late summer and had flooded the whole valley from cliff to cliff; now the waters were just beginning to subside, and in another month, in November, the fields would emerge, wetly muddy, and ploughing and sowing would begin. From his tomb Petrie photographed the scene one evening (**6**): the tawny orange ball of the full moon hung low above the horizon and the needle-like minarets of the mosque of Muhammad 'Ali on the distant Citadel were silhouetted against it; in the foreground a broad sheen of yellow light gleamed on the water. One night the moon was in eclipse, and a hullaballoo came from the village as drums were beaten, tin cans rattled and guns fired off to frighten away the evil spirit that was devouring the moon.

Friends sometimes came out from Cairo to sleep in his spare bed or in a neighbouring tomb: Corbett would come on a Thursday evening, for a day's shooting on Friday, his day of leisure. Petrie himself did no work on Sundays, but seldom went into Cairo to church, since he enjoyed the "general feeling of nothing to do", and a seventeen-mile donkey ride there and back, after getting up at half-past six, was anything but restful.

The excavation of the corners of the pyramid base had enabled him to make a preliminary measurement of the length of the actual base below the "sockets"; though it was not accurate enough for his final survey, it amply confirmed his belief that there was no such unit as the "pyramid inch", thereby destroying Smyth's whole theory. Two Americans arrived to be showed around; one was a clergyman named Dennis, whose wife was a Great Pyramid enthusiast; "After seeing and hearing all, he said he felt 'as if he had been at a funeral', being grievously *disenchanted*, as dear Sydney Hall was." Loftie urged him to write a preliminary account of his work for *The Academy*, "to save somebody perhaps from becoming a Piazzi-ite." He did so, announcing at the same time his discovery that the long galleries of brickwork to the west of the second pyramid had been barracks, each about a hundred feet long, which he assumed to have been constructed for some two to three thousand workmen building the pyramid.[15]

In Cairo in November he saw Maspero again, who readily granted him permission to excavate at the Third Pyramid but advised him not to make a formal complaint of the Museum official's idleness since it might cause trouble with Brugsch; the Director was evidently walking very carefully in his relations with that well-established member of his staff.

In December Flinders put aside his surveying instruments, locked his tomb and with a handbag, rode into Cairo for the start of a journey he had long wanted to make: a voyage up the Nile. The previous summer Loftie had invited him to join a party he and his wife were making up, which was to include the Revd Professor Archibald Sayce, his friend Professor Percival, and one or two others. They were to hire a *dhahabiya* and travel as slowly as they pleased, stopping to look at ancient sites. The complete trip, including seven days in Nubia, would cost £90; Petrie could, if he wished, leave the boat at Luxor and find someone to replace him for the last week. This seemed too good an opportunity to miss. His father had urged him to go and had given him the money;[16] though it might mean an interruption of his work at the pyramids, it would be good to be in the dry and healthy climate of Upper Egypt and above all, he might have a chance to see and measure the pyramid at Meydum, the "missing link" in his record of early pyramids, which had recently been opened by Maspero.

He had met Sayce in Oxford during the summer and liked him at once. He was an Orientalist with a wide range of interests: his enthusiasms included Hebraic studies and Assyriology, he delighted in the decipherment of rare scripts and was one of the pioneers of Hittite studies.[17] A bachelor of independent means, forced by delicate health to winter in a warm climate, he ranged the Middle East visiting archaeological sites and sending to the editor of *The Academy* frequent reports of recent discoveries. Sayce and Flinders Petrie were to be friends for forty years. Percival turned out to be "a pleasant, lively little man, without any pride or pomposity".

To sail on the Nile in a privately-hired *dhahabiya* was a leisurely and delightful way of seeing Egypt.[18] Some of these craft were very small, but usually they carried as many as eight or ten passengers; there were sleeping cabins, a dining saloon, and an observation lounge, and quarters for the servants and crew. Some had bathrooms; all were comfortably furnished. A huge triangular sail in front, and a smaller one behind, caught the breeze and the boats had a very shallow draught to avoid grounding on sandbanks. It was a little more expensive to travel this way than to take a passage on one of Thomas Cook's steamers, which left Cairo once a fortnight and did the trip to Luxor in eight days,[19] but those made few scheduled stops and when tourists were set ashore at ancient sites, little attempt was made by the dragoman to explain what they saw. On a private charter, the captain of a *dhahabiya* was under orders to stop wherever and for as long as his passengers desired; with several eager archaeologists on board, this would be an ideal way of seeing Egypt. The drawbacks of the sailing craft were later to be made plain.

Their boat was of moderate size; the complement of passengers was made up by an artist named Tristram Ellis, and two other Englishmen who were keen sportsmen and hoped to get some shooting; when they moored near an ancient site, Mrs Loftie usually stayed on board, Ellis sketched, and Flinders, Sayce and Percival, and occasionally Loftie, would rush ashore and explore, Sayce and Petrie making hasty copies of whatever inscriptions they found, and Petrie, wherever he could, taking measurements. On their first day's sailing they passed the elegant steamer of the Khedive, who ordered his band to play "God Save the Queen" as a compliment to the Englishmen. Flinders had been unfortunate at the start; the day before the boat sailed he had been stricken with another bout of pharyngitis and was running a temperature; Dr Grant had cauterized his throat and stocked him up with medicines, but for the first week of the trip he felt very unwell and his throat did not completely heal for a fortnight. In spite of an ague fever, he went ashore with the rest near Bedrashein and took Sayce to Saqqara to see the Pepy pyramid; then they walked to Abusir and Sayce copied hieroglyphs while Flinders dropped down a shaft to explore some ibis galleries.

They had hoped to find Maspero at Meydum, which they reached on the fifth day after a long donkey ride; but he had not yet arrived and the *reis* would not let Flinders take any measurements at the pyramid; he had to be content with taking notes in the *mastaba* tombs excavated by Mariette. After a day in the Fayum, where the sportsmen got some shooting, they went back to Meydum, again being carried over the wide canal on the shoulders of two men wading thigh-high. Flinders took some photographs of the pyramid but was prevented from photographing the entrance; in vain he pulled out his *firman* for excavating, with the Director's signature upon it: the *reis* could read, and declared it to be valid only for Giza. They decided to give up waiting for Maspero, and returned to the *dhahabiya* but the wind had dropped; for another day they lay becalmed, waiting for a breeze; on the third day it came suddenly, the boat swung out into midstream, hit a sandbank, and broke her rudder post and stern spar. Another wasted day was spent in repairing the damage and at lunch time Maspero passed in his steam launch, hurrying south to Luxor; he did not even see them.

Twelve days later, they had made very little progress against contrary winds and had only managed to visit one major site: the walled town of el-Hiba, where they explored for several hours and found a tomb "stuffed with sarcophagi", some of them unopened. At Kom el Ahmar next day Sayce, Loftie and Petrie spent several hours copying inscriptions in the rock tombs high in the cliff; on the ancient mound they could see the walls of houses still standing and in good condition, and they viewed with astonishment the thousands of whitewashed domes of the cemetery of Mina—a modern City of the Dead. At Beni Hasan they clambered up to the painted tombs of the Middle Kingdom; while Sayce copied the texts, Petrie made over three hundred measurements. At el-Till opposite Deir Mawas they picked up quantities of the blue-painted pottery which abounded on the surface of the site of el 'Amarna, ancient Akhetaten, and next morning in fog went out to look at the tombs in the cliff face—the others on donkeys, Petrie striding along so fast that he easily kept pace with them. Sailing on to the southern end of the ancient city they bargained for *antikas* and bought "a quantity of good beads".

Now they had to take stock: they had been travelling for four weeks, and had only managed to cover 190 miles; some were fretting at the delay, and the boat manager needed medical attention. Several passengers decided to disembark at Assiut. Flinders, Sayce and Loftie elected to stay on board, but make what speed they could, abandoning

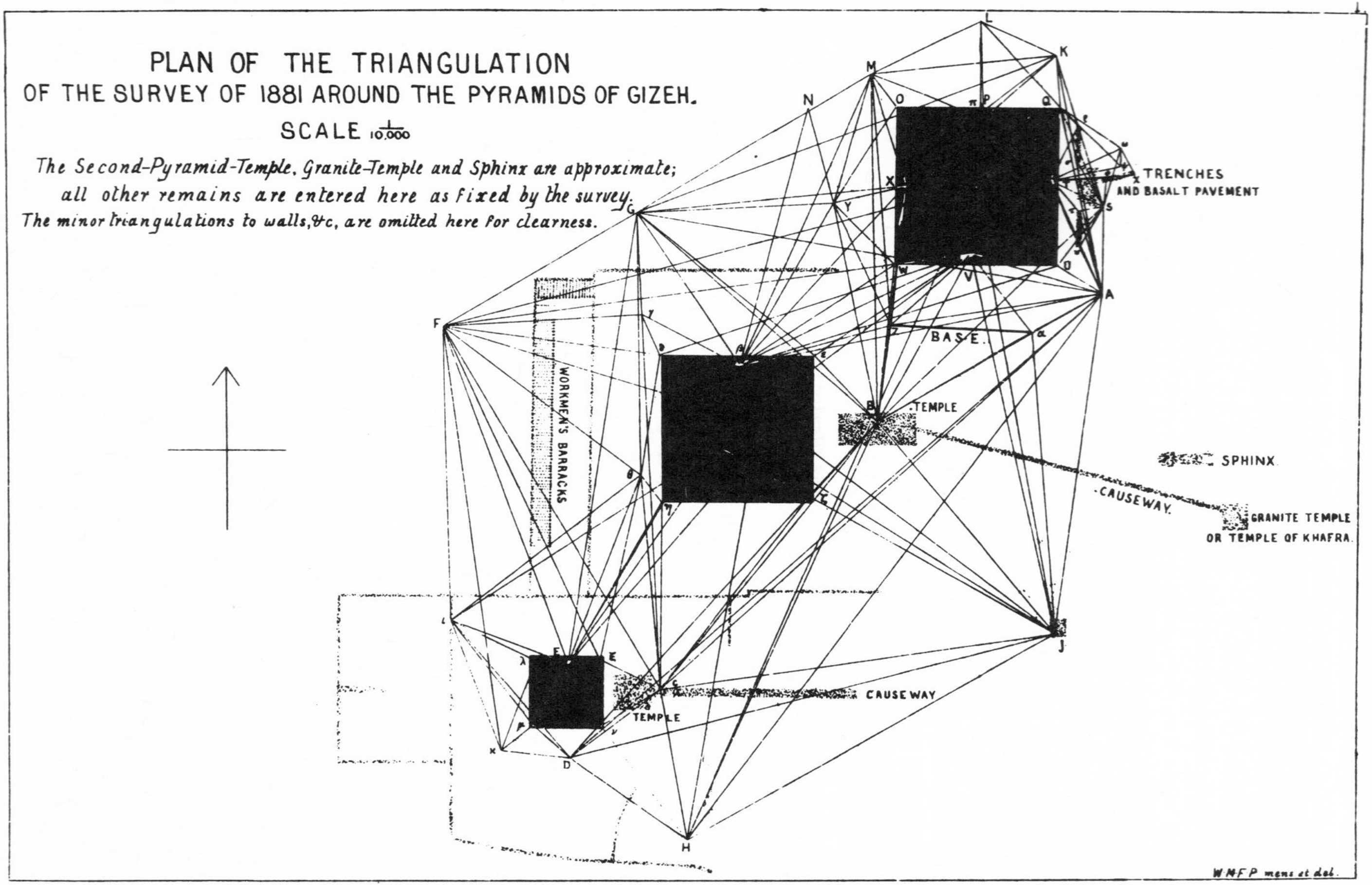
PLAN OF THE TRIANGULATION
OF THE SURVEY OF 1881 AROUND THE PYRAMIDS OF GIZEH.
SCALE 1/10,000
The Second-Pyramid-Temple, Granite-Temple and Sphinx are approximate;
all other remains are entered here as fixed by the survey.
The minor triangulations to walls, &c, are omitted here for clearness.
TRENCHES
AND BASALT PAVEMENT
BASE
TEMPLE
SPHINX
CAUSEWAY
GRANITE TEMPLE
OR TEMPLE OF KHAFRA
WORKMEN'S BARRACKS
CAUSEWAY
TEMPLE
W.M.F.P. mens et del.

A. *The Pyramid Survey, 1880–1882.* A base-line (a–z) south of the Great Pyramid was very carefully
measured, and observation points, A K L M, etc., were established in relation to this line by

any hope of stopping at sites they had planned to see. They were once more becalmed; Flinders decided a *dhahabiya* must be "a lesson in laziness" and made the best of it by reading, and playing backgammon; he managed to find time to explore the temple of Dendara; finally, once more stuck on a sandbank north of Luxor, on 17 January they decided to abandon ship, and reached their destination by *felucca*. The trip had taken forty days. Sayce, in his account of it for *The Academy*,[20] declared his belief that a *dhahabiya* was not, after all, the best way of seeing the remains of ancient Egypt. Nevertheless, he continued to use this mode of travel in future winters, and eight years later he bought his own large houseboat (which he named after the Babylonian goddess *Ishtar*), filled her with books and lived in her all winter long, using her as a base for his annual visits to Petrie's excavations, and a *pied à terre* when he was in Cairo.

Surrendering his cabin to a tourist who wished to take over the rest of his boat ticket, Flinders took his bag across the river to join Tristram Ellis in his tent on the west bank, by the Ramesseum; Ellis, who had been there some days sketching, had acquired a palm-stick bedstead, but Flinders was content to sleep on a mat on the ground, rolled in a blanket (**79**). There was much to see; each morning he left, usually on his own, to explore the "tombs of the nobles", where among the wall paintings he recognized many old friends familiar to him from John Gardner Wilkinson's publications, though many of them he found "sadly defaced" since Wilkinson had drawn them more than sixty years earlier. In the temple of Hatshepsut at Deir el Bahari he was able to see the wall relief showing the Queen's fleet of boats; part of the temple had already been excavated by Mariette and others before him, and most recently by Maspero, but the upper terraces were still partly hidden under huge mounds of brick and stone débris and a Coptic monastery concealed the southern end.

One morning Petrie walked up past the temple of Medinet Habu to explore the hills behind. "I had a splendid climb to the top of a peak of the Theban range, about a thousand feet; from there I saw all over the Theban range on the one hand, with blue Nile winding and doubling in the green valley, and on the other hand the wild and parched rocks of the Valley of the Tombs of the Kings. . . ." All day he clambered among the cliffs and rocky gorges, following the ancient paths. On subsequent days he explored the Royal Tombs: "The path goes down a cleft in the rock with merely footholes in many places to step on, & I found it rather awkward with a camera and measuring rods." Of course he was taking measurements wherever he went. Belzoni's

Tomb (the tomb of Sethos I) he found impressive and awe-inspiring: as he clambered down and down vast serpents folded their green bodies along the walls. "It is more like a realised nightmare than anything you ever saw; and to go alone, without anything to distract you and only one candle just showing group by group, leaving the vastness of it to be felt in darkness, adds strength to the marvel of it." Visitors to the tomb today, pushing their way in dozens down wooden staircases and crowding into the brightly-lit chambers, can have little notion of the awesome impression it once made on the solitary visitor peering with his guttering candle through the gloom.

Flinders spent a whole day measuring in the royal tombs, engaging a boy to hold a candle for him. On the seventh day, after a morning photographing in the temple of Medinet Habu, he packed up his treasures in an old pair of trousers and he and Ellis struck camp, loaded tent and baggage on to a donkey and set off back over the river to Luxor. Petrie had been buying antiquities daily from the dealers that haunted the west bank; he reckoned that he had now about sixteen thousand beads. Finding a modest hotel, Petrie that evening set about developing some of the photographs he had taken; for the next few nights he worked till the small hours. Unfortunately the lid of his plate box had a tendency to fall off, and some of his plates had been spoilt, but most had come out well, and he had a long list of people in Luxor who were anxious for copies when he could get them printed in England; it was not easy to buy photographs in Luxor in those days, and few travellers yet possessed cameras of their own.

On 27 January Petrie went to see Maspero on his steamboat moored near Karnak; he wanted permission to enter the pyramid at Meydum. Maspero was amiable but firm: he regretted that the pyramid was to be shut, on his orders, on 1 February; if M. Petrie was unable to be there before that date, he would be happy to supply him with plans and measurements. With this Petrie had to be content. He asked about the brick tunnels he had seen behind the Ramesseum: the Director, he found, agreed with him in supposing that they were barracks for the garrison at Thebes in Ramesside times. "I suggested that excavation might be useful, and M. immediately said that if I would like to do it I was quite welcome; I thanked him but said that I had no time here for such work. . . . He is now freely accessible, very polite, & as obliging as he can be." Fourteen years later, Petrie was to live in those tunnels and excavate the brick buildings of which they were part (p. 219): they proved to be temple storerooms and the houses of priests.

Maspero introduced Petrie to his friend M. Edouard Naville, a

Swiss Egyptologist who was staying with him; the two were planning to go upriver to El Kula to investigate a small stone pyramid; they were also discussing the English plan to excavate in the Delta, of which Petrie had already been made aware by Professor Sayce, who was involved in the negotiations. The idea had originated with the novelist and journalist Miss Amelia Edwards, whose happy winter on the Nile in a *dhahabiya* in 1873–4 had kindled in her an enthusiasm for the history, the religion and the art of ancient Egypt. Her book *A Thousand Miles up the Nile*, illustrated by her own sketches, came out in 1877 and was an immediate best-seller. In it she expressed her concern for the ancient monuments which she saw everywhere being ruined by neglect or by wanton destruction. She had herself discovered a small chapel in the temple of Abu Simbel in Nubia. She wrote:

> I am told that the wall-paintings which we had the happiness of admiring in all their beauty and freshness, are already much injured. Such is the fate of every Egyptian monument, great or small. The tourist carves it over with names and dates, and in some instances with caricatures. The student of Egyptology, by taking wet paper "squeezes" sponges away every vestige of the original colour. The "Collector" buys and carries off everything of value that he can, and the Arab steals it for him. The work of destruction, meanwhile goes on apace. There is no one to prevent it, there is no one to discourage it. Every day more inscriptions are mutilated—more tombs are rifled—more paintings and sculptures are defaced. The Louvre contains a full-length portrait of Seti I, cut bodily from the walls of his sepulchre in the Valley of the Tombs of the Kings. The Museums of Berlin, of Turin, of Florence are rich in spoils which tell their lamentable tale. When science leads the way, is it wonderful that ignorance should follow?[21]

On her own initiative, and with the encouragement of a few of her friends who were interested in Egyptology, she had written to Mariette some two years earlier suggesting that a fund might be raised by subscription in England, to finance the excavation of some site for scientific ends only. Mariette had shown interest in this idea but he was already a sick man; after his death Miss Edwards had written to his successor, M. Maspero, with whom she was already in cordial correspondence (he had given her much help with her hieroglyphic studies in preparation for her book). He seemed to be in favour of the plan, but felt that the time was not yet ripe. The political situation in

Egypt was delicate, the army restive, Anglo-French relations had been strained under the Dual Control; he advised her to wait. She had bided her time, and meanwhile sought the support of several like-minded enthusiasts among her friends: Reginald Stuart Poole, Keeper of Coins and Medals in the British Museum, though an Egyptologist at heart; Professor Sayce; a scholarly clergyman named Tomkins; and, not least, Sir Erasmus Wilson, the eminent surgeon and dermatologist whose fortune, amassed by judicious speculation on the Stock Exchange, had been spent on charitable enterprises the most notable of which had been the transport from Egypt, and erection in London, of Cleopatra's Needle. Naville was a friend of Poole's, and a frequent visitor to London; he too was enthusiastic about the scheme, and had offered to sound Maspero. The Director was encouraging: a year had passed and he now felt more firmly in control; he was confident, he told Naville, that no obstacle would now be put in the way of an English excavation. He suggested that Naville should look in the Delta for likely sites with an Old Testament connection, since any search for archaeological proof of the literal truth of the Biblical narrative would attract support from church and synagogue alike. Tanis, the city called Zoan in the Bible where Mariette had found impressive monuments, was a likely site, he suggested, for further work.[22]

Petrie remained a few more days at Luxor; he walked a long way into the desert to the east of the town, without finding any site of interest; he spent a day searching behind the Valley of the Tombs of the Kings, picked up a few palaeolithic hand-axes and identified the site where Pitt-Rivers had found flint artefacts deep in the breccia in which the tombs had been cut. Though there was enough to keep him in Thebes for many weeks, he decided he had better get back to Giza to finish his survey before the weather became too hot. On 3 February he took a cabin on the rapid postal steamer, and reached Assiut in two days; thence he was able to catch the evening train back to Cairo, finding himself in the second class with a large party of officers who, to his great amusement, swathed themselves like mummies at night in quilts and blankets. Next morning he collected his mail and hastened back to Giza. The English papers, he found, were full of gloomy reports about the situation in Egypt.

> I see there is much excitement in England about Egyptian matters, but I do not see here anything extraordinary; everything in Cairo seems just as usual. . . . As far as I have had to do with natives I find

Left **(1)**: William Petrie (1821–1908) about the time of his marriage; *right* **(2)**: Captain Matthew Flinders R.N., explorer and cartographer (1774–1814). From a miniature

Below left **(3)**: Anne Petrie with her son Flinders (Willie) aged eight; *right* **(4)**: Ann, widow of Matthew Flinders, with her daughter Anne and (*r.*) her step-sister Isabella Tyler. About 1830. (Watercolour in possession of the family)

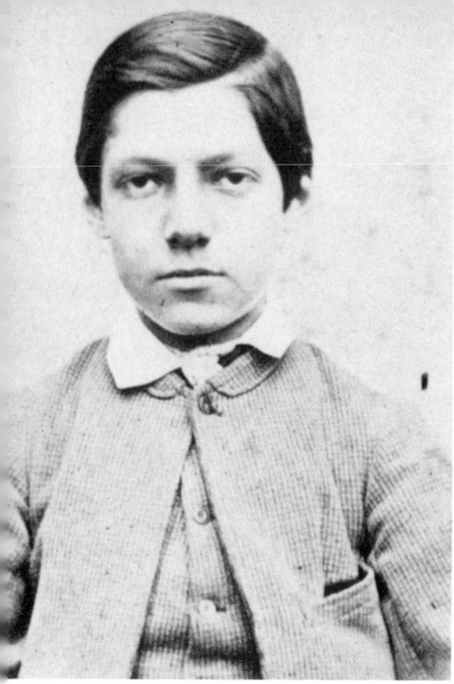

Left **(5)**: William Matthew Flinders Petrie, about twelve years old, *c.* 1865; *right* **(6)**: The view from the tomb, looking east over the inundation flood in October 1881; *below* **(7)**: Flinders Petrie at Giza in 1880, outside the rock-tomb in which he lived for two winters

Left **(8)**: Reginald Stuart Poole (1832–1895), keeper of Coins and Medals in the British Museum 1870–1893; *right* **(9)**: Miss Amelia Edwards (1831–1892)

10 The *dhahabiya* in which Petrie and the Amoses explored the eastern Delta

Above **(11)**: After the great rainstorm, Tanis, May 1884; *below* **(12)**: Brother and sister: children in Petrie's workforce at Tanis

13 Some of the contents of the cellar of the house of Asha-Ikhet ("Bak-akhiu") in Tanis (British Museum)

Early experiments in archaeological photography: *above* **(14)**: the "Carian" figurine that led Petrie to the site of Naucratis. He has attempted, by using a mirror, to show both the back and the front. *Right* **(15)**: foundation deposit from the temple of Ptolemy II at Naucratis

16 Market scene

17 The limestone quarries at Tura

18 Francis Galton

19 Flinders Petrie, *c.* 1886

20 The Valley of the Tombs of the Kings as it was in 1886

21 King Sesostris I at his jubilee, running before Min, the god of fertility; from Coptos, 1894 (Petrie Museum)

23 (*right*) Ebony figure of a Nubian servant-girl, bought from a dealer in 1897 (Petrie Museum)

22 (*below*) Captive Philistines: plaster casts of paper squeezes taken by Petrie at Medinet Habu (see pl. 28) and mounted for display. Some are still on exhibition at the British Museum

> that, though desperate beggars to strangers, yet if they once find you perfectly firm & yet kindly, & jocular, they immediately settle down as good friends, & never bother you again. I am simply disgusted with the brutal tone I have seen adopted towards them by travellers. . . . The smallest entering into their ways pleases them immensely; only sit squat, return the proper replies to the salutations, catch their tricks of manner, imitate their voice, they will laugh heartily and pat you on the back with delight. Of course in all this I am writing of the country people with whom I mainly have to do. The army is a different question altogether; in case of any attack on Europeans I should feel quite safe if in the country away from the soldiers who are looked on as the natural enemies of the fellahin. . . .

Privately he had resolved that if, as some of the European colony in Cairo feared, the nationalists got out of hand and it became necessary to flee to Alexandria, he could walk there in a week by way of the desert edge, travelling at night, with 'Ali to forage for supplies in the Delta villages during the day.

By the end of February, in spite of high winds, he had completed his measurement of the courses of the first pyramid; now he had urgent need of an assistant. Tristram Ellis, who had set up a studio in Cairo, agreed to come out to Giza for a week. Impecunious as most young artists, he was grateful for the daily fee which Flinders, at his father's suggestion, paid him. With 'Ali's help they measured the exact thickness of the sides and base of the 'coffer' in the King's Chamber; first they raised the massive sarcophagus a few inches with crowbars, using an anvil for a fulcrum; putting stones and blocks of wood beneath, and lying on his stomach, Petrie could then, by theodolite, take offsets every six inches from the base to a horizontal plane. Before lowering the coffer once more he wrote in chalk his name and the date. Ellis added his to the floor beneath; they are presumably there still. (It was the only time in his life that Flinders left his name on a monument.) Then the theodolite was raised and corresponding measurements were taken of the floor inside. This operation took nearly all night and he spent the next two days reducing the measures, inside and outside, to determine the exact thickness of the stone; it proved to be very uneven. Then he made a frame of wood to lie on top of the coffer; a plumb bob suspended from this frame first outside, then inside, gave perfect vertical planes from which offsets could be taken to determine the profile of each side. The two men then made a final check on the length of the survey base, measuring very carefully by chain, then twice by tape. Finally they levelled the Great Pyramid stage by stage, beginning at the south-west corner at eight a.m. and getting to the top at noon, then in the afternoon going down by the north-east corner.*

On the afternoon of 20 March Petrie had a visitor: an American lawyer whom he already knew of as something of a crank, "the man who thinks the pyramids were built for water". Cope Whitehouse was a tall, good-looking man of forty; of independent means, he had been educated in Europe and had spent many years travelling in England and Europe.[23] For the past three years his whole interest had centred on the civilization of ancient Egypt, on which he had highly unorthodox theories of his own: one concerned Lake Moeris, the larger precursor of the Birket Karun in the Fayum basin, and the Wady Rayan to the south of it which he maintained had been in ancient times a great reservoir for the waters of the Nile; he also envisaged the pyramids of Giza as surrounded by gardens supplied by some lost aqueduct or reservoir. A steady stream of articles and lectures on these subjects had already led to his name being abbreviated to Copious. Petrie was wary of his eccentricities but liked him well enough: "When 'my theory' does not come in (as it does like King Charles' head) he is—barring a habit of talking torrentially—a pleasant and gentlemanly American." He was later to prove less gentlemanly; but that afternoon he made himself agreeable and even useful with the theodolite, and he offered to take Petrie and Tristram Ellis next day on a surveying trip to the Fayum. Ellis declined, but Petrie was very tempted to take the opportunity of desert exploration, with camels and dragomans and tents all provided; only the consideration that the following week would be the best for "Polaris azimuths for which I have been waiting" kept him from accepting the proposal. Whitehouse then suggested a compromise: they could go for just two days,

* The final dimensions of the Great Pyramid, arrived at after long calculations back in Bromley, may be found in Petrie's book *The Pyramids and Temples of Giza* (1883). At the request of Professor Borchardt, who was engaged on a refutation of "Zahlenmystik" theories, its "vital statistics" were again measured, with the most modern instruments, by J. H. Cole in 1925 for the Survey of Egypt. His results tallied remarkably closely with those of Petrie, the mean difference in the two sets of linear measurements being no more than .6 of an inch (though the difference on one side—the north—was as much as 4.3 inches). Further excavation of the pavement by Borchardt enabled the slope of the sides to be determined with greater accuracy by azimuth readings taken with a micrometer theodolite, whereas Petrie's had had to be computed from a hypothetical square with its corners lying on the diagonals of the sockets.

and on the evening of the second he would deposit him at Dahshur, handy for the Saqqara pyramid field which Flinders had promised to show to Ellis.

Flinders was very glad that he had decided to go. It was his first experience of the real desert, and his first camel trip. As they journeyed they stopped from time to time to take "azimuths and dips" on a roughly measured base; they followed a wady southwards to its head on the second day, and established that it could never have communicated with the Nile. Returning by way of Saqqara Petrie took the opportunity of another day at Dahshur, this time with his camera, before returning to Giza. The next few evenings were ideal for his Polaris observations; then he was ready for a longer "chase with the American wild goose"; for as he said, if a man insisted on taking him over interesting country, with more than a chance of finding the Labyrinth, why not let him? Taking the train to Medinet el Fayum, he found that Whitehouse had business in the town before starting, so Flinders took the opportunity of a free day to explore and to walk out in a dust storm to Biahmu to see the "pyramids" there, known locally as the "thrones of Pharaoh". He decided that they were probably seats for the enormous statues described by Herodotus, and that if ever he had the opportunity, this would be a site to investigate (see Chapter 6).

Blinding rain hindered their departure for another day. Whitehouse took Flinders to meet the local Copts; they were entertained with rosewater and thick coffee, and taken round their school by the boys. An unprecedented rainstorm had turned the streets to liquid mud and people were wading barefoot, carrying their shoes. Next morning it had cleared, and being Palm Sunday, they went to the Coptic church. The congregation were all busy during the service plaiting their own palm leaf crosses and then the tiny half-dark church was filled with rustling palm branches, excitedly waved. The music Flinders found very curious: "the men and boys antiphonally, in strange meandering pointless quaverings, not unlike the character of the old Saxon church music." He had been greatly interested in the songs and tunes he had heard in the village at Giza, and had sent Spurrell the musical notation of a wailing chant he had heard at a funeral and a bugle song played for marching soldiers, and had described to him the monotonous songs of the children as they worked, and the ecstatic piping of the negro Muhammad on his flute, outside his tomb at night.[24]

Next day they were off early on camels but after two days' travelling were still, they were told, only half-way to the oasis of

Wady Rayan; the camel men, afraid of the unknown desert, refused to go further. Whitehouse admitted defeat and agreed to turn back; they returned to Fayum next day, Flinders making an eighteen-mile detour on foot to make barometer readings.[25] Striking east, they made for Kalamsha and on the following day walked to the convent at Gebel Sedment, said to be the most ancient in the Fayum; thence crossing the Bahr Yusuf canal by ferry, they lunched at Hawara and afterwards Petrie made a careful examination of the area round the pyramid, coming to the conclusion that the building at its foot looked much more like the Labyrinth than the brick buildings so identified by Lepsius; in this he was one day to be proved correct. In the evening (Whitehouse by this time on a donkey, Flinders still on foot) they got back to Medinet el Fayum, and next day returned by train to Cairo.

By mid-April, his observations almost complete, Flinders Petrie began to think about going home. Scrambling over rough stones, and donkey-riding, had reduced his boots and trousers to a precarious condition—they would not last much longer; ants and clouds of flies in his tomb made life uncomfortable. One matter remained however: he wanted to examine the limestone quarries at Tura and Ma'sara near Helwan; opportunity came when Tristram Ellis decided to paint there; Petrie joined him for a few nights in his tent near the village of Sheikh Othman on the west bank. Going over the Nile by ferry he found the quarries very impressive, a series of huge halls sometimes fifty feet high, with pillars thirty feet square, and a labyrinth of galleries branching and joining; here, he decided, and not in the Mokattam hills had the fine limestone been cut for the mastabas and the casing of the pyramids. Crossing the Nile for the last time on the third day he narrowly escaped disaster when the small felucca in which he was crossing almost capsized in a sudden storm. Then he went off for a day to the site of ancient Memphis, a series of mounds among groves of palm trees; once there, he set off "to settle the age of the various mounds by the character of the pottery". No other visitor to that great and still impressive site could till then have ventured to suppose such a thing possible. On one mound he found "very good houses of the Ramesside period. Some of the houses are three floors high, the holes for the beams showing plainly: their bricks are very fine and in good condition." Little of this remained visible when he eventually came to dig at Memphis twenty-six years later.

Ellis returned to Cairo by boat next day and Flinders went back to Giza for a last check of the south passage and a very awkward survey, crawling and wriggling flat, in "Vyse's chamber" deep in the rock below the pyramid, which was nearly choked with stones. The air was bad and gave him a headache, and next day, after checking levels once more in the passages, he felt ill and feverish. It was time to pack up and leave. Moreover, news had reached him of a meeting recently held in London, at which Miss Amelia Edwards and Mr Poole had been appointed Honorary Secretaries of a newly formed Society for the Promotion of Excavation in the Delta of the Nile; Sir Erasmus Wilson was named as Treasurer, and contributions were invited towards the first excavation.[26] Flinders had written at once to Sayce, who had first told him of the project and who, as Flinders knew, had been negotiating in Egypt on the Fund's behalf; he also wrote to Dr Birch, whose name he was surprised not to see on the new society's manifesto. He was reluctant to write to Poole, whom he hardly knew; he and his assistant in the Coin Room, Barclay Head, as well as Franks, Loftie and others could put in a word for him as soon as he got home. He would hurry back, he decided, without stopping for a week, as he had planned, to measure the Maltese monuments.

Dosed with quinine, he made last checks in the pyramid; sure now that he would return to Egypt, he left his less valuable gear locked in the tomb; Dr Grant would again take care of his boxes of instruments. For his numerous boxes of pottery and stone fragments, and the small antiquities which he had bought during the winter, he realized that he must obtain an export permit. Maspero, he believed, would make no objection to his taking them home: when they met in Luxor, the Director had declared his intention that all the antiquities found by the projected Delta expedition should go to the British Museum, only keeping casts for Bulaq. "This is really allowing the English public to dig for, and carry off, what they like for the British Museum," was Petrie's surprised comment at the time. Since then, however, Maspero had had to reconsider this rash promise. The founders and organizers of the society in London (already known as the Egypt—or Delta—Exploration Fund) wrote to seek confirmation of what they understood from Sayce and Naville to be Maspero's liberal intention, and were met with a flat denial; it was against the law, he declared, to allow any antiquity to leave the country; the best he could suggest was that he might be able to persuade the Khedive to make a "*don gracieux*" of some object which would be a tangible reward to the subscribers in England for their endeavours.

When, therefore, Flinders Petrie called on Maspero, ready to show him the *antikas*—scarabs, figurines, pieces of glass and faience, and coins and weights—which he wanted to take home, Maspero recommended him not to declare them at Customs.

> He recommended me to carry the little things away in my pockets. . . . I think that he has none of the somewhat brutal force of character of Mariette; and being a Frenchman is included in the dislike of the National Party; and is accordingly snubbed and thwarted at their mercy. . . . He decidedly recommended me to run the cargo as well as I could; and if things were seized and sent to him, he must take one or two little things for form's sake, to say that he had taken what he wanted, and return the rest; I mention this as it illustrates the disorganisation existing here now.

In future years Petrie appears to have been scrupulous in submitting everything that he found to the Museum and obtaining export permits; he was condemnatory of those, like Wallis Budge, who boasted that they had smuggled out of the country what they would not have been permitted to take legally.

Tristram Ellis planned to go home by British India from Suez; it was cheaper than P. & O. or Orient, and landed at London Docks rather than Liverpool. Flinders decided to go with him. He spent the last few days at the Grants', classified the Doctor's coin collection for him, and saw for the first time, in the Bulaq Museum, the royal mummies found in the previous year in the *cache* at Deir el Bahari. At Suez they had to wait a week for a boat; Ellis spent the time sketching but Flinders, unlike his usual self, did little but eat and sleep; it was the measure of his exhaustion. Nevertheless he had made a firm resolve; his future lay in Egypt. Whatever happened, he must somehow come back, for he had work to do which no one else could do. Egypt was like a house on fire. "My duty was that of a salvage man, to get all I could quickly gathered in."[27]

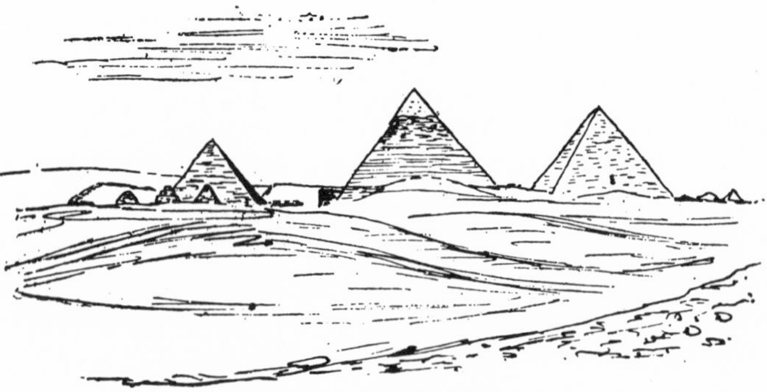

The pyramids of Giza

CHAPTER IV

"Father of Pots": Delta Explorations
(1883–6)

As soon as Flinders got back to London, he went to see R. S. Poole and his assistant, Barclay Head, in the British Museum; they were interested in his coin collection, particularly in a hitherto unknown gold Claudius, and they bought some of his specimens. He asked about the "Delta Society" and was told that nothing could be done for the moment; the political situation in Egypt was tense and they had been advised by Maspero to wait. Dr Birch whom he also called upon was sceptical; he had refused from the beginning to take any part in the negotiations with Maspero, being opposed, as he said, to "sentimental archaeology" which had not as its primary aim the procuring of objects for the Museum.[1] Poole and Head, however, were enthusiastic; Amelia Edwards, from her home in Bristol, was energetically engaged in writing letters asking for support from the prominent and wealthy; they had enrolled their colleagues A. S. Murray, of the Department of Greek and Roman Antiquities, and his chief Charles Newton, the excavator of Halicarnassus, and also the classical archaeologist Percy Gardner in Oxford; Professor Sayce and an Irish M.P. named Villiers Stuart who frequently visited Egypt, were to be the Fund's liaison there. Many eminent personalities had lent their names as sponsors. In the newspaper announcement of the formation of the society, it had been stated that its chief aim would be the exploration of the Delta, where "the documents of a lost period of Biblical history must lie concealed".[2]

The Academy gave further details.[3] It was hoped that records of the Hebrew sojourn in Egypt might be found on a mound identified as the capital of the Land of Goshen and in the ruins of the Cities of the Oppression, Pithom and Raamses. Exploration at Naucratis, could the site of that Greek emporium be identified, would illuminate an obscure period of Greek art. The Delta was rich in mounds of famous cities such as Sân and Xoïs—"this last being the capital of an early dynasty (the XIVth) which is as yet wholly without written history." If sufficient money could be raised, both Goshen and Naucratis could be simultaneously explored; otherwise Goshen would have preference.

Who would dig for them? The first person to be approached had been Heinrich Schliemann, who responded enthusiastically to the suggestion that he should excavate Naucratis. This proposal was vetoed at once by Maspero: Schliemann would never do: he was tactless and quarrelsome, sought only publicity for himself and would alienate the authorities. If the Committee had no better suggestion to make, he, Maspero, was willing to dig himself on their behalf during the months when he was not engaged in excavations for the Antiquities Department. Further, if they could find a young Englishman, ready to learn and with some qualification in Oriental studies, he offered to train him so that in time he could take over the direction of the Fund's work and publish in his own name.[4] No such person occurred to the sub-committee; instead, Petrie discovered, they had approached Edouard Naville. He was a distinguished scholar with an international reputation; (at the age of forty he was engaged on a comprehensive edition of the Egyptian funerary texts known as the Book of the Dead), but so far as Petrie knew, he had no experience of excavating, apart from watching Maspero's men tearing apart the Kula pyramid the previous year. For M. Naville, archaeology had only one aim: to discover new texts, fresh inscriptions which might throw light on the language, the history or the religion of the ancient Egyptians. An intensely religious man, he was particularly involved in the controversy aroused by recent German studies of the ancient geography of the Delta in relation to the narrative in the Book of Exodus of the captivity of the Israelites in Egypt[5] and their expulsion. When it was suggested to him that he might go to look for epigraphic evidence in the mounds which had been suggested as the sites of Pithom and Raamses, he had jumped at the opportunity.

For the time being, however, any idea of an expedition was out of the question. Matters were moving to a crisis in Egypt: the unpopularity of the Dual Control under whose stern régime drastic economies had had to be made, the vacillations of the Khedive in the face of a nationalist movement headed by 'Arabi Pasha, the unwillingness of the Sultan of Turkey to interfere, all contributed to a deteriorating situation. Only a few days after Petrie had left Port Said a squadron of French and English gunboats sailed into Alexandria harbour; early in June rioting broke out in that city and 'Arabi prepared to defend it against attack; foreigners were advised to leave Cairo and most of them did so; shops were shut and there was looting in the streets. Only Maspero, afraid for his Museum (for there were rumours—probably quite untrue—that 'Arabi planned to sell the contents to some foreign government in return for arms) stayed on in his houseboat at Bulaq, until, in the heat of midsummer, his wife's ill-health forced him to return to France. On 11 July, after the French and the Turks had refused to act, the British fleet bombarded Alexandria and a week or so later a considerable army under the command of Sir Garnet Wolseley landed at Port Said, took control of the Suez Canal and advanced towards Cairo along the Sweet Water Canal; the British army were engaged by 'Arabi's forces at Tell el Kebir on 13 September and routed them. 'Arabi fled, the British occupied Cairo, the Khedive returned: the war was over. Lord Dufferin was brought from India to take temporary charge of the administration, Maspero came back from Paris and the foreign community returned to their homes in Cairo. As soon as things appeared normal Stuart Poole and Miss Edwards approached Maspero again; he wrote enthusiastically, welcoming his old friend Naville as their excavator and promising to do all in his powers to help the Fund. Lord Dufferin sent his approval and Sir Erasmus Wilson headed the subscription list with the princely sum of £500. Naville was go to out in January 1883 to search for Pithom.

Petrie possessed his soul in patience, for Sayce assured him that in future years the Fund might well be in a position to offer him employment. He had much to do meanwhile: in his study at Bromley he worked on the pyramid survey, plotting and checking his observations to obtain the maximum accuracy. "It was a matter of thirty-six simultaneous equations, which I worked in triplicate, one version with half values of co-efficients, the other with double values; by comparing these at each stage, any error was easily detected." In order to obtain absolute conformity of angle from his twenty observation centres he devised an ingenious method of seeing through twenty sheets of paper at once, by making small windows of transparent mica over the vital points. When all was done, he could say with confidence that there was "seldom a tenth of an inch of uncertainty in the final results".[6]

He came to London occasionally to copy scarabs in Dr Birch's department, to use the Reading Room, to attend sales at Sotheby's or to call on Loftie, Greville Chester and other friends. At clubs and dinner parties he met, among others, Herbert Spencer, Andrew Lang (who wanted him to write on Mythology for the *Encyclopaedia*

Britannica) and Lady Anne Blunt. He plotted the desert survey he had done for Cope Whitehouse, and somewhat unwillingly attended a long-winded lecture given by him at the Archaeological Institute. He himself gave several talks. One of the things that had most interested him at the pyramids had been the examples he found of ancient technology. As he had written to Spurrell in 1881: "I am paying special attention to the methods of workmanship here, and trying as far as possible to get into the minds of the old people; for that is the only way to realise what they intended, and how they looked at things."[7]

On some unfinished casing blocks he had found a projecting boss left for lifting; evidently the casing had been smoothed and polished *in situ*. In March of the following year he lectured to the Anthropological Institute on the mechanical methods of the Pyramid builders, illustrating his talk with slides and with specimens spread out on a table; as Spurrell had once advised him: "you must give people something to *finger*, if you wish to stick anything into their minds."

He also gave a talk to the Archaeological Institute on "The Domestic Remains of the Ancient Egyptians", and another on Egyptian pottery,[8] in each case presenting an entirely new view of what had hitherto been disregarded as rubbish by those who had excavated in Egypt. He was making a study of ancient weights and measures and had been permitted to weigh all those in the British Museum. After one of his lectures he dined with Hilton Price the banker and antiquary, one of his staunch supporters in years to come.

On the 2 May he had finished faircopying the manuscript of his book;[9] the publication was to be financed by a grant of £100 from the Royal Society at the recommendation of Francis Galton, the geneticist; this sum had been earmarked for a survey of the pyramid field by the Royal Engineers, but as Petrie himself pointed out when they interviewed him, the work was already done. Galton had been in correspondence with him as early as 1880, on the subject of mental faculties, and had been greatly impressed by his unusual capacities. (See p. 24 and Appendix)

Having deposited his manuscript with the publishers, Flinders was at last free to take one of his solitary walking holidays; this year it was in Devonshire and Cornwall. He pressed Spurrell to come with him, but his friend had urgent business with palaeoliths in a chalk pit and would not come. Walking up the Dart Valley from Ashburton, he explored Dartmoor from temperance inns at Postbridge and Princeton, plotting Grimspound and a number of other stone circles, picking his way precariously over shaking bogs, his day-long sustenance a pound of raisins, and getting sunburnt "to a shade betwixt lobster and mahogany". Then he moved on to Bodmin Moor, where he planned more stone circles, four of them in a single day. In all he was away for three weeks; it was the last of such expeditions for many years. A fortnight's visit to Paris in July gave him a chance to study the rich Egyptian collections at the Louvre. He sold his gold Claudius to a dealer for 800 francs, which probably more than paid for his trip.

Not long after, Poole asked him to the Museum for a talk. M. Naville had been successful in finding, at Tell el Maskhuta in the Wady Tumilat, near the still-strewn battlefield of Tell el Kebir, what he regarded as documentary proof that the ruins were indeed those of Pithom, or *Per Atum*, a domain of the god Atum, in Ramesside times.[10] He had been allowed by Maspero to bring back two statues as a personal gift from the Khedive to Sir Erasmus Wilson, as President of the Fund; they were to be donated to the British Museum. This augured well for the future: new subscribers were enrolled, and Miss Edwards was in touch with a clergyman in the United States, the Reverend William Copley Winslow, who had started an energetic campaign in the American press for "Spades for Zoan"—for San (Tanis) must be the next objective. If enough money for a second expedition came in, Poole asked Petrie, would he consider going? Flinders Petrie had only one reservation: he was determined not to go out as Naville's assistant; their methods and their whole approach to archaeology were totally different. In August he wrote a memorandum which he sent to Poole and Sayce, outlining his own proposals for work with a rough estimate of the time he thought it would take to finish each task.[11] In Saqqara, he would examine the peribolus wall of the Step Pyramid to see if it threw light on the date of the pyramid; this would take a week. He would like to excavate the pyramid of Pepi I entirely, for "much has been wholly lost already by neglect"; this he thought might take six men about a month. To clear and survey the bases of other pyramids would need "only a few days to each". At Beni Hasan he would spend a week emptying the tomb shafts, and at el 'Amarna the tombs should all be cleared out and copied, and fresh tombs searched for; this might take three or four months (the recording of these tombs, more than twenty years later, took some fifty months, spread over six years). Last, but by no means least, he wanted to examine the debris along the whole length of the Valley of the Kings in Thebes, searching for undiscovered royal tombs. A letter from Naville settled the matter: he wrote from Geneva that he would not, alas, be able to go out that winter since he was very busy finishing his *Book of the Dead*; he hoped the Committee would be able to find someone to take his place. The suspicion may have occurred to one or two that Naville, who liked to live comfortably, was apprehensive at the prospect of tackling so desolate and unhealthy a spot as San el Hagar.[12]

The Pyramids and Temples of Giza came out early in September 1883; Flinders took copies to the British Museum for Birch and Poole, who were greatly impressed; Poole consulted members of the Committee of the Fund suggesting that Petrie go out to Egypt in place of Naville. Miss Edwards needed a little persuading—she thought that Maspero might have reservations about the young man[13]—but when she saw the Pyramid book, which had been sent to her for review, and realized the grounds for Poole's enthusiasm, she wrote expressing her pleasure that he would be the Fund's Explorer. Maspero wrote encouragingly, Naville declared his satisfaction, Sir Erasmus Wilson promised £1,000, and the matter was settled.

Reviews of Petrie's book were enthusiastic; *The Times* praised the author's originality and ingenuity, other papers his scientific objectivity and accuracy. "All future theorizers," said *The Saturday Review*, "will be obliged to grapple with a series of incontrovertible facts." Miss Edwards, writing in *The Academy* at some length, concluded: "There can be no second opinion as to the special importance both of the work that Mr Flinders Petrie has done and of the book he has written; yet the latter is so unostentatious that readers may well fail to realise the extent of the services he has rendered to history and to science."[14]

From this time on she was to prove his loyal ally, and soon, a personal friend. Piazzi Smyth's review of the book came out after Petrie left England and was sent on to him by his father; entitled "New Measures of the Great Pyramid by a New Measurer", it appeared in *The Banner of Israel*, the weekly organ of the British Israelites. Its tone was surprisingly mild: yes, there may well have been differences between his own measurements and those of the "smart young scientist", but it made no difference; allowance had to be made for earthquakes, and also for the errors of the ancient builders, who were unwilling workers and idolaters—accuracy could not be expected from them![15] Petrie smiled when he read this nonsense; it was useless to suppose that such people could be cured of their hallucinations, since their theories were more precious to them than facts.

Throughout October Petrie was getting together his excavating gear, making improvements to his camera, buying and boxing tinned stores and large supplies of ships' biscuits, preparing maps of the Delta and cutting them into strips for easy use. It was decided that he should be given £250 a month for excavation, and his personal expenses. One thing remained to be settled: he was adamant that he must be allowed to continue to buy small antiquities found by his workmen on the dig, or offered to him there by local dealers. Naville, having no interest in such things, had brought back hardly any from his excavation, and was to publish none. Yet these, for Petrie, were the stuff of history. It was impossible to keep constant watch on a hundred or so workmen, and when one of them turned up an object with his *turia*, he could easily conceal it in the pocket of his baggy cotton trousers and sell it to one of the dealers who lurked nearby; the provenance of such objects would be lost and their value as historical evidence destroyed. He proposed to offer himself to Maspero as an agent of the Bulaq Museum, authorized to purchase antiquities on their behalf; at the end of the season he would submit everything to Maspero, who would keep what he wanted for the Museum and let Petrie take the rest. Objects found on the site, if allowed to come to England, would be the property of the Fund and could be given to local and colonial museums "with a hint that donations are very acceptable to the Fund", if the British Museum did not want them. Things found elsewhere he would pay for himself, and if not wanted by Maspero, they would be his property.[16] Poole was at first alarmed by this proposal, fearing that it might jeopardize the Fund's good standing with the Egyptian authorities; but the sub-committee decided that if Maspero were to approve, all would be well; Petrie was required to call on the Director in Paris on his way out to Egypt, and obtain from him a written agreement.

Accordingly Flinders' first stop on his journey to Egypt in November was Maspero's house in Paris; they had a most cordial conversation and the Frenchman expressed himself willing to appoint Petrie as the Museum's agent, only stipulating that the agreement between them be kept private until he, Maspero, returned to Cairo at the end of the year, lest it should be misconstrued by the authorities. A document signed by them both was posted to Poole,[17] and Petrie went on to Italy, stopping for a few hours at Geneva on the way, to call on Naville at his house in Malagny as a matter of courtesy, and a few days in Turin, where Signor Lanzone made him welcome in his museum and gave him free access to the scarabs. Major Prescott, the Chief of Police in Cairo, his fellow passenger on the voyage from Venice, helped him with the passage of his voluminous baggage at Port Said, and he reached Cairo by train on the evening of 23 November.

The Egyptian Delta spreads like a half-opened fan, between two major branches of the Nile, the eastern branch debouching at Damietta, the western at Alexandria; numerous smaller waterways criss-cross the flat green landscape, and salty marshes and lakes fringe the northern coast. San el-Hagar, the ancient Tanis, was the most northerly city on the eastern side; a few miles beyond its ruins lies Lake Manzala. To the east of the Delta, about half-way along the Suez Canal, is the town of Ismailiya. Here ends the Sweet Water Canal, first cut in late Pharaonic times, which runs through a depression called the Wady Tumilât, generally supposed to be the Land of Goshen, the route by which from time immemorial travellers from Palestine and Hither Asia had reached the Land of Egypt. Petrie's plan was to hire a small *dhahabiya* and travel up the Mu'izz Canal as far as Zagazig, thence to Fakus, where a small canal led directly to San. While he was waiting for Maspero to arrive and write his permit, he would explore sites in the northern part of the Delta, perhaps as far west as Kafr esh Sheikh, in the neighbourhood of which the ancient Xoïs was reputed to lie.

He enquired at Thomas Cook's for boats; it proved difficult to find one small enough for his slender budget, but luck was with him: at Corbett's suggestion he called on Professor Sheldon Amos and his wife, and found that they were planning a short holiday and would like to come with him. Amos had been a Professor of Jurisprudence at University College, London, and was now a judge in the Court of Appeal in Cairo. Flinders found him "a quiet thinking, satirical man"; he proved to be connected by marriage with Petrie's cousins, the Hensleys. His wife was "an utterly unconventional, active, sensible woman, a great manager, with her own opinion and ideas on most subjects, siding with Octavia Hill and Dr. Barnardo." The arrangement would suit Flinders admirably, for they would share expenses, and she was prepared to do most of the cooking. They were to start in four days' time. Meanwhile, Petrie went out to Giza and saw 'Ali Gabri, Muhammad and his other old friends, who greeted him warmly: one of them came up with some *antikas*, and Petrie bought a few, one of which interested him particularly: it was a small figure of a warrior in alabaster, finely carved (**14**), and from the helmet and the general appearance he took it to be Greek rather than Egyptian —perhaps, he thought, a Carian mercenary. He asked where it had been found, and was told that it had come from the Delta, from Nerib near Kafr Dowar. He resolved he must follow up this clue.

The *Philitis* (**10**) had a crew of nine; in addition Flinders took a donkey-boy, Ibrahîm, accustomed because of his trade to long walking, who accompanied them whenever they stopped to look for ruins. Petrie noted Tell el Yehudiya as a likely site for future exploration. They branched from the Nile at Benha into a canal leading to Zagazig, and then sailed slowly eastwards along the Sweet Water Canal; Petrie walked about in the Wady Tumilât, finding a promising mound, Tell el Retâba. He explored the region around Tell el Kebîr, plunging knee-deep in the salty marshland, but he found no trace of tombs. The outworks of 'Arabi's camp were everywhere fresh as the day they were thrown up, and quantities of ammunition, some still unexploded, lay about on the battlefield. He also visited Tell el Maskhuta, the site which Naville had dug the previous year, and was somewhat astonished to find in the spoil-heaps a number of small antiquities, including fragments of an iron grille, and pieces of a gilded relief of Nectanebos II which had apparently been overlooked or disregarded by the excavator. He mentioned this only in a private letter to Poole, and not in the Journal he was sending to his parents and friends. At Ismailiya he met M. Jaillon, the contractor who had shifted earth for Naville, and found him unfriendly, perhaps sensing Petrie's unspoken criticism of the work for which he had been partly responsible.

Meanwhile things were not going according to plan. The boat met with a mishap due to a careless lock-keeper; then they found that it was impossible to get to San by *dhahabiya*—there was a stone bridge at Zagazig which nobody had warned them about. The Amoses returned by train to Cairo and Petrie hired a donkey for the day to look at Tell Muqdâm, about twelve miles away; the mounds there were high and wide but appeared to be of late date. Another day was spent at Tell Basta, the site of ancient Bubastis, where huge monuments lay around. Meanwhile the boat had been repaired; he left Zagazig on Christmas Day to return to Cairo. He was in a hurry, for time was getting on, he had to get the boat back and every day the water was going down. But in Egypt nothing is predictable: at Mit Radi, where the canal joined the Nile, a barrage was closed and would not be open again for some days. Accordingly he too left the stranded boat, and returned by train, to stay with the Amoses till news should come through that the dam was open. Meanwhile he was not idle: he made the acquaintance of Col Scott-Moncrieff, the head of the Irrigation and Canal Department, who was soon, he found, to be made Under Secretary of the Department of Public Works, the British official under whom (though nominally under an Egyptian minister) the general direction of the Bulaq Museum and the Department of Antiquities would come: he found him friendly and helpful, and in general very well disposed towards Petrie's projected work. Maspero was back in Cairo now, and promised to furnish him with the necessary papers; he also offered to lend him a soldier, one of the Museum guards, as a protection, but this Petrie declined, believing that he would do better by avoiding any appearance of officialdom. He went out to Giza and engaged 'Ali Gabri to come with him to San; he had proved himself a capable foreman, and Petrie was convinced of his honesty and good sense.

Hearing from Moncrieff that there was now water in the canal, Petrie went back to retrieve the *dhahabiya*; contrary winds made the journey maddeningly slow, though he was able to take advantage of a day becalmed near Benha to visit Tell Atrîb, the ancient city of Athribis, and there, with a little help from Khalil, the brightest of the crew, dug out several inscribed blocks and copied them.

Back in Cairo he had to reconsider his plans: should he go to Xoïs at all, or should he proceed straight to Sân? He had written to Poole for advice, but received no reply. He decided to leave the boat and take the train for a short reconnaissance only—he could not resist the temptation to find out where the "Carian" warrior had come from. In spite of a heavy cold he set off, with Ibrahim the donkeyman and Khalil, and spent the first night in the station waiting-room at Teh el Barûd, then moved on to Damanhur, pitching his tent on waste ground near the station. Enquiring the next morning for Nerib, he found there was no such place; it must, he though, be Nebeira, nearer to Teh el Barûd than to Damanhur. There was nothing for it but to walk. When he reached the spot, he was delighted to find two "pyramid Arabs" from Giza, one an old friend, 'Ali's brother Sheikh Ruhuma. Bringing out the little alabaster figure, he asked to be shown where it had been found; they led him straight to the spot and offered him two other figures.

> Oh what a feast of pottery! The whole ground thick with early Greek pottery, and it seemed almost sacrilege to walk over the heaps with the fine black lustrous ware crunching under one's boots. Pieces with fret pattern, honeysuckle pattern, heads, arms, legs of figures, horses, and such like lovely things were soon picked up; both in black figures on an orange ground, and red figures on a black ground, mostly with incised outlines. It seemed as if I was wandering in the smashings of the Museum vase-rooms. Such a half-hour I never had before.

He realized the importance of his discovery, and in writing the Journal implored his friends to keep it a dead secret; not only was this a Greek settlement, and a wealthy one, but it would enable him to date pottery he had found at other sites and thought to be Ptolemaic—it must be much earlier. He told Ruhuma he would probably come back to work here, and promised him money if he kept silence about it.

Flinders got back to his tent after nightfall, hungry and tired after his twenty-three mile walk, but triumphant; in spite of a high fever next morning he set off for Dessuk, near which, on the authority of Herodotus and Strabo, most authorities had hitherto located Naucratis. There he hunted about and made enquiries, and soon found that there was no ancient mound in the neighbourhood; this puzzled him—he does not seem to have realized yet that in Nebeira he had already found Naucratis. Sakha was his last objective; he found little on the surface there except a Roman inscription which Maspero, he was told, had already copied; it confirmed that this had been the city of Xoïs.

Back in Cairo next day, Mrs Amos insisted on his taking to bed and Dr Grant dosed him with quinine; thereby he missed seeing "Chinese Gordon" coming through Cairo on his way to Khartoum. When he was better, he went on Sunday to church, and met many of the British community after the service.

> It is most interesting to be here at the present time, and see all the people who are here to reconstruct Egypt—Scott Moncrieff, Edgar Vincent, Sir Evelyn Baring etc. The great point, which no one is yet agreed on, is how to set about it. Col. Gibbons says very sensibly that he believes it should be done by splitting the country up into independent little states, each under the absolute autocracy of an Englishman who would be only responsible to the Khedive; and that after setting matters to rights there they might get on afterwards.

At last he had recovered sufficiently to make a start; unloading his boxes from the *dhahabiya* and transferring them on a horse and cart through slippery, muddy streets in the rain to the station was a feat not easily accomplished, but at last they were off; and reached Fakus by evening. 'Ali's nephew and adopted son, Mahmoud, had come with them, and also Mursi, another Giza lad. Flinders found he was getting used to sleeping in a tent in spite of the howls of wolves on the outskirts of the town and the excited barking of the dogs. Fakus was a considerable market town; next morning they bought stores—candles, sugar, soap, paraffin—at a Greek grocer's shop before starting out. This was to be Petrie's base for supplies for the next five months.

The small San canal was navigable; he found a fisherman who had brought his catch up to Fakous and was returning empty; he would take Petrie and his men and baggage to San. The twenty-mile boat trip took all day; the smell of fish was unbearable, but had to be borne. Next morning he inspected the huge site, and decided that he must build his house on the enclosure wall by the entrance to the temple area; the temple itself was deep in mud, and the great blocks excavated by Lepsius and Mariette lay in confusion in pools of water. Naville had been right in his description of the surroundings as "*affreux*". As far as the eye could see there was nothing but desolate marshland.

> The flat expanse, as level as the sea, covered with slowly drying salt pools, may be crossed for miles, with only the dreary changes of dust, black mud, water, and black mud again . . . the only objects which break the flatness of the barren horizon are the low mounds of the cities of the dead; these alone remain to show that this region was once a living land, whose people prospered on the earth. . . . The miserable Arab huts of San first meet the eye . . . huddled together without any plan or order in the most unhealthy flat, with on the one side a muddy stream into which they throw their dead buffaloes, and from which they drink, and on the other a swamp full of rotting graves and filth. But the high mounds which rise behind this sickening mass of dead fish and live babies, bowls and flies are the remains of Roman and Greek Tanis, a city well built and ordered, whose inhabitants show no small taste in their native pottery and their imported marbles, their statuettes, their delicate glass mosaics and their fine metal work. . . ."[18]

He wrote these words with the hindsight of his discoveries, describing too the glories of the splendid city of earlier ages, the city of Ramesses II, the city of the "bearded Hyksos, the fishy people", to whom were ascribed the strange granite figures found by Mariette.

He pitched his tent in a heavy rainstorm and the first few days had to be spent in constructing a temporary wooden shelter for himself and his men; it was a week before the rain abated a little and he could start building a house. By then he had taken on about seventy men, boys and girls and was engaged in cleaning and planning the temple area as best he could for the mud. The local people, he found, were still wary of the English, and rumours flew: ten thousand soldiers were coming, and he was there to build barracks for them—he had twenty-two *khawagas* (Englishmen) with him—he was a Government surveyor for the land tax—his money was counterfeit. One by one the rumours died down, as villagers were taken on for work at a proper wage and well-treated.

An old *reis* of Mariette's turned up, who had worked at San and knew the site well, and exactly where things had been found; he was a formidable old man, who always wore a black cloak and huge black goggles, and leant on a long staff.

> . . . ready to smite the wicked. The people were scared at seeing him come up to inspect, as they remembered his former doings under Mariette, but Ali assured them that he would not be allowed to go on in that way now. . . . It is very well to have such a man here, he will serve as a ferocious sheepdog, who would bite if he dared; the Arabs will appreciate mild treatment all the more. . . . He can not do harm so long as engagements, dismissals, and the money-bag, are all in my hands, and anyone can complain to me at once. . . .

His own method of supervising and paying his men worked very well. Every morning he went round allotting each man his task; each one's name was entered in a notebook, and towards the end of the day he went round inspecting what they had done; those who wished were paid daily, others preferred to receive their wages for the week on Saturdays. At sunset he blew a whistle to end the work.

> Thus there is no chance of impersonation or question of identity as each is paid or checked while at work, and as it is done while I inspect the work there is the least amount of time lost. Sayce writes to me that Schliemann spent over an hour every night in paying his 161 men; but by this way work is going on while they are being paid, so that they don't sit idle.

Once a week a trusted lad was sent to Fakous to fetch money, which by arrangement with the management in Cairo, the Fisheries Board supplied. Payday was by no means a simple affair:

> Firstly, I cannot get enough change here, and have to persuade the workers to group themselves so that I can give a dollar, half a napoleon or sovereign, or even a whole sovereign. Most of them I have to pay with parisis. . . . These coins . . . were all struck in Paris for the Egyptian government, and profess to be 10 piastres; but of course there is some trickery or jobbery about the business, and their value is anything you please according to the locality. One of the greatest blessings to daily business in this country would be a reformed coinage. When you come to deal with parisis, worth 19/8ths of a piastre, the odd value must be evened by means of copper currency worth 1/7th of its nominal value: there is a mess of accounts to be squared at every payment!

He had a scale of rewards (*bakhshish*) for small finds and found that the men seldom attempted to "plant" an antiquity from outside the work; he could always tell when they did. He was getting used to the broad dialect of the Delta and beginning to understand the mentality and the capabilities and limitations of his men. They were moving huge stones, to get at the inscriptions concealed on the under side; Petrie found them singularly inept at such work and had to supervise them constantly to prevent them undermining some huge block and bringing it down on top of themselves. His intention was to record and copy every inscribed piece, photograph everything, and plan the position of every stone in the temple area.

Storms and heavy rains continued through February; his corrugated iron roofing was waiting at Suez, but Poole had not yet sent the bill of lading so it could not be forwarded; at last it came, and the house could be finished. It had several rooms round a small courtyard, and Petrie planned to make furniture for a guest-room. The village sheikhs —there were five of them—would come up to drink coffee and he deemed it wise to entertain them, though he refused their invitations to eat in their own houses; a lavish gift of coffee and sugar, half-way through the season, ensured their continuing co-operation. For his friends at home, Petrie described his house:

> In the first place you cannot lose your way . . . you have only to go ahead until you reach what you want in either the European or the Arab quarter. The dining-hall, or the sitting-room, as I have modestly called it, might perhaps be stigmatised by cynics as kitchen, scullery and bathroom all in one. The first thing you see on entering is a telescope lying on a couple of nails over the

windows ready drawn out; with this I continually watch how things are going on down in the workings whilst I am up at breakfast. I only now wish for a telescopic voice to hit the offenders. Along the walls are sundry boxes, and piles of biscuit tins, and behind the door on a box is a paraffin stove. My easy chair is a box which contains tins of paraffin, and here again I claim an advantage over stereotyped civilisation; whoever had a chair which they could vary to two or three different heights according as they may want to sit up in dignity, to put out a platter on their knees, or to work on the floor? Yet all these benefits I have just by turning my seat over. The next room I intend for my bedroom and for *photografia* and other matters, but at present I sleep in the end room. . . . After a month of reposing on a deal box I fear that I shall become quite sybaritical now that I enjoy the softness of a sand floor on which to lay my pile of blankets. . . .

Early in April a tragedy occurred; he reported it privately to Poole:

The side of a cutting which was supposed to be quite sound, suddenly gave way; the slip buried two boys, of whom one was recovered uninjured, but the other one was found to be dead. I cannot tell you all the misery this has been to me, it has undone me altogether, I have not the heart to do anything, and only the necessity of seeing that the work suffered as little as possible has kept me going on. I cannot write about it. I have not mentioned the whole affair in the journal, as so many persons see that and I thought that you might not wish it talked about at present.[19]

Soldiers and an officer had arrived with a doctor; there had been an official enquiry, evidence was taken and the verdict had been that the death was an Act of God. Nobody appeared to blame Petrie; he would of course compensate the family. The cutting had only been eight feet deep; and the soil had seemed solid and hard; nevertheless he was going to attempt no more cuttings for the present. As far as is known, this was the only fatal accident ever to occur on Petrie's work. As he grew more experienced, he would watch very carefully to make sure that there was no danger of earth-slide or the collapse of a wall. Margaret Murray, who worked in one of the deepest of his excavations, at Abydos in 1902, used to say that he never allowed any of his workmen to take a risk, or do what he himself would not do.

The Journal letters he was sending home, which in the first place were intended for his family and immediate friends, went also now to Poole, to keep the Committee informed about the progress of the dig, and at her request to Miss Edwards, who used them as material for short articles in *The Times*. At the end of his first season, she wrote to him:

> I know you so intimately now, through your journals, that I feel we are old friends—at all events on one side, and I address you accordingly. I wish to tell you again with what deep interest I follow you in these records of your daily life and arduous work: and how heartily I appreciate your courage, your endurance, your wonderful pursuit of good humour under difficulties, and your thoroughgoing style of work in whatever you do or undertake. In adapting your material to journalistic purposes, I beg you to believe that I take a hearty pleasure and pride in the task of making your manner of work known to the public, and I feel that you are setting a splendid example of scientific excavation to all Europe . . . I tell Mrs. Petrie that there is but one W.F.P. and that I am his prophet. I am delighted to be his prophet.[20]

She credited him with half the fees paid by *The Times* for her articles.

Petrie was making a record of every inscribed monument, every statue and obelisk and block and pillar in the temple area as they were exposed; those excavated and reburied by Mariette he left untouched. Some of the statues had been very thoroughly smashed, by human agency or by earthquake; there were many fragments of a red granite colossus which, by the dimensions of the toes, Petrie calculated must have been at least ninety-two feet high—probably, he thought, the largest statue ever carved. More than the large objects, however, it was the small things that held his interest and of these there were plenty—glazed amulets, beads and pottery were everywhere strewn about the site, and in houses of the Ptolemaic period built on or against the great wall of the temple a number of domestic objects, ornaments of terracotta and glass, and bronze and ivory furnishings were found. In a street of houses on the eastern side of the temple enclosure there were the ruins of wealthy houses of the Roman period which appeared to have been destroyed in a conflagration—Petrie guessed it to have been at a time of political disturbance which he dated, on the evidence of the coins, to the revolt of AD 174. From one of them, the house of a lawyer whose name he read as Bak-akhuiu,* a number of important papyri were disengaged, as well as large numbers of pots, glass and glazed ware, fragments of plaster moulding, figurines and lamps, iron implements and the bronze ornaments of furniture (**13**):

> A find which is invaluable to us, as showing contemporaneous examples of bronzework, figures of deities, glazed ware, pottery &c. at a period of which we can probably fix the close to a single year. The possessions of Bak-akhuiu give us a key whereby to settle the age of a large part of the Roman remains so abundantly found over the whole of Egypt.

It was the beginning of a new era in Egyptian archaeology; in years to come, Flinders Petrie would find many such assemblages of artefacts of different periods and with the aid of careful records, and his own extraordinary visual memory, would be able to anchor them in time.

The papyri, here and elsewhere in the rooms and cellars of houses, were extremely brittle and required delicate handling:

> Monday (March 10th) was an interesting day: in a house of Ptolemaic date (or rather earlier) the boy who was digging turned out a quantity of burnt papyri. They had been in a wooden case, with the reeds, and all had been burnt with the house. The case was broken up, and most of the rolls broken; but I carefully gathered up and examined whatever could be of value. One roll shows no trace of writing, but another shows the demotic writing clearly on its glossy surface of carbon. Another little roll about ½ inch diameter and 2½ long I got perfect with the strings still round it. The three larger rolls are unhappily all broken, but the legible one is a very long one, making a roll about 1½ inches diameter, and I have some hopes of this when it is laid out on gummed paper. Besides these there were quantities of burnt garments of different textures, of which the carbonised threads held together sufficiently for me to collect pieces: also a quantity of green eyes and statuettes, and two or three larger statuettes in porcelain [*sic*] 4 or 5 inches high, of very fine work. Pieces of a large brown vessel and the neck and handle of a bronze jug were all got, broken anciently in the fire: and several bronze stapler-rings which had been inserted in wooden boxes, an

* The Demotic name is now more correctly read as Asha-ikhet.

> armlet, a kohl pot in alabaster with bronze stick, and other small objects. I shall now sift over all the earth taken out of that room.

Only when sudden disaster brings domestic life to an end is such an assemblage of its daily chattels preserved together for posterity.

Occasionally, on a suq (market) day, he would go off with a donkey boy and a tent to explore the neighbourhood for likely sites. At nearby Tell es Suelin, an island of sand in the marshes, a Roman cemetery was uncovered; some of the dead had been buried in stone sarcophagi and there were large numbers of blue-glazed eye amulets.

Like many other Europeans in a similar situation, Petrie found it difficult to remember the names of some of his workpeople; so often they were combinations of the most usual: 'Ali Hassan, Hassan Muhammad, Muhammad 'Ali, Ibrahîm Ahmad, Ahmad Hassan, and so on; but others had less usual patronyms to distinguish them, and his memory was good; by the end of March he could put a face to every one of the 183 names on his payroll. The children's pranks were a constant source of amusement: several of the girls who were too frisky with the men were sent off to work with the most senile. "After a few days of this bondage they all escaped again to more congenial companions, but even before this, Khadijah had tried to bribe the inexorable ancient with the promise of a kiss if he would let her go back."

When engaging his workpeople, Petrie refused to listen to the recommendation of a *reis* or a fellow worker, but relied on his own reading of character by appearance alone. Discipline had to be maintained. "To keep up a proper activity in the work it is needful to hold the dread of dismissal before them continually. If a man is caught standing still he is noted, and after any further laziness is informed some morning that his services are no longer required. But if he is caught sitting down it is all up with him. . . ."

Difficult decisions had sometimes to be made. Towards the end of the season he found out that Reis Muhammad's brother, a "very respectful and respectable old man", was a dealer, and not averse to treating with the diggers and even doing a little clandestine tomb-digging on his own when no one was about. Petrie considered reporting him to the police, but decided to leave matters as they were, since in any event, as soon as he left San, the tombs were sure to be looted. He had found out from 'Ali what used to go on behind the scenes in Mariette's work: the *reises* the Frenchman employed (he seldom visited the site himself) used to make a handsome profit by levying two hundred men, and then excusing a hundred of them from work, on payment of a monthly sum; when the finds were so meagre as to excite suspicion, they would buy from dealers in Cairo enough to keep up Mariette's interest in the place. "Thus the great boast of Bulak, that they are certain of the locality and genuineness of everything there, is rather a dubious one." Petrie tended to turn a blind eye to occasional misdemeanours, confident that for the most part, his system of paying *bakhshish* was working well.

Letters arrived from home at irregular intervals, with newspapers to keep him informed of what was happening in the Sudan.

> All my news comes from England; Baker Pasha's defeat and Graham's victories both came to me from here, and I suppose some of my Cairo friends will remember to send me word when the Mahdi comes there. . . . Probably settlers 500 miles up in the Australian bush, or in the heart of the Canadian backwoods, know the affairs of this country before I do, although all the news goes almost within the sight of my house.

He was finding difficulty in getting tinned stores from Cairo; sometimes someone in the village would send him up a plate of rice, but try as he would, he could not get used to Arab cookery. He dosed himself daily with quinine and strychnine to ward off the marsh fevers, and found that under his strenuous regime he kept surprisingly well: it was too hard a life for most people, but it suited him.

One day in May there was a storm of remarkable ferocity which lasted for several hours; in the torrential rain, the courtyard of Petrie's house became a pond and the walls began to disintegrate, the mud mortar being washed from between the stones and the brickwork dissolving into mud. For two hours it thundered incessantly, and he reckoned that nearly two inches of rain had fallen. In the plain below the house a rushing torrent dashed over obstacles, "roaring like a Dartmoor river". The temple was a lake, out of which rose heads of sphinxes, and shoulders of statues; all the smaller figures were covered, and in front of the pylon the water was six feet deep. He went out to photograph the effects of the storm (**11**); it halted work for several days to come, and the villagers' wheat and barley already harvested and laid out for threshing, were ruined.

> Here I have been for two hours patching up the effects of the storm on my roof. I have become quite an artist in mud—the national cement for everything from governments downwards. I suppose

it's because I was not allowed full swing for mud pies when small, that I still want to gratify that taste; it is nice, and it is not naughty here. Behold me; perched on the top of two tottering boxes, so as to reach well over the roof; said boxes being held in place by one damsel (who occasionally relieves the tedium by the amusement of fingering the *khawaga*'s toes (such a novelty) while another bullion-bearing damsel hands up neatly patted handfuls of mud, with which I relay on rows of bricks a-top.

It was now June and becoming extremely hot. Petrie had hoped to be able to take his larger finds by boat to Suez and so directly home, but Maspero wrote that everything must be brought to the Bulaq Museum for inspection: he therefore decided to leave the larger things and the pottery, boxed up, until next year; the smaller objects and all his personal belongings had to go by camel to Fakous, since the canal was now too low for a boat, and thence by rail to Cairo. He dismissed most of his workmen, and spent some days on the final survey of the site, starting before five in the morning and resting in the noonday heat and making his own boxes; on 23 June he left early, caught the noon train and was in Cairo by evening. Again the Amoses insisted on his staying with them. It seemed strange to get back to civilization. "First I got my hair cut, which had gone its own way for five months and hung out like the brim of a flop hat all round my head; Mrs. A. said that I looked like Robinson Crusoe, and her daughters confided to her that I looked like a bear." He had been alone for twenty-one weeks.

Maspero and Brugsch looked over his finds and allowed him to take the large pieces, but he was disappointed that they took so many small objects for the Museum, ruefully imagining that Brugsch would add them to the stock of the Museum shop for sale to tourists. Nevertheless they allowed him to keep the small statue of Bak-akhuiu together with the whole contents of his house, and all the papyri. Although Maspero was most cordial, Petrie regretted letting the Museum have anything, since his precious small finds would be likely to be swamped among all the unlabelled clutter of the cases: the rearrangement and cataloguing of the collections had scarcely yet begun.

On arrival in Venice on his way home, Petrie was detained on the boat for a day or so by quarantine regulations: there had been plague in Egypt. He spent some time in Turin, finishing the copying of all the scarabs, and was back in London by 17 July. He had written to Poole suggesting that the Fund might hold a small exhibition of his finds; the Archaeological Institute offered space in their rooms at

Oxford Mansion, in Oxford Circus. Meanwhile, until the arrival of his boxes, he immediately started to work on his records for the publication of his results, which would appear as the Fund's Second Memoir. He was very anxious that *Tanis* should appear quickly, since he held that speed in publication was a duty owed by the scientist to the public: not till discoveries were made known did they have any value. This ideal he kept before him for the rest of his life: no archaeologist has equalled him in the promptness of his excavation reports. A second edition of the Pyramid book was planned; designed for the general public, it omitted many mathematical and technical details which would only interest the specialist.[21]

Towards the end of August his boxes arrived and he set about arranging the exhibition with Spurrell's help; Riley came up to act as doorkeeper when it opened to the public. One whole display table was devoted to the things he had picked up at Tell el Maskhuta and Tell el Yehudiya. Then came the task of allocating the finds; Miss Edwards was insistent that the American contributors should be well rewarded, and the Museum of Fine Arts in Boston was made a major beneficiary, though the best and most important finds went to the British Museum.

It was generally assumed that Petrie would be going out again for the Fund in the winter of 1884–5. He told Poole he would welcome an assistant, if an intelligent volunteer could be found. Not long after, he received a letter from Francis Llewellyn Griffith, the youngest son of a country parson, who had been recommended by Professor Amos to write to him; he had been studying the Egyptian language on his own, since at Oxford he could find nobody to teach him, and had attained some proficiency in hieroglyphics and hieratic; he wished to know if there were any possibility of his going to Egypt for the Fund. Unfortunately he was without financial support, and would have to accept an offer of employment in some other field if Petrie could not help him.[22] Flinders Petrie liked the sound of the young man; he wrote to Amelia Edwards and asked her if the Fund would consider employing him; he would be glad to have company, and hoped that he might find a disciple to whom he could hand on the experience and the skills he had himself developed in the field. She at once consulted Poole; after interviewing Griffith they decided to launch a special appeal to endow a scholarship. Two donors, one a wealthy friend of the family, came forward: £250 was guaranteed for three years. It would be enough. Petrie met the bespectacled young man for the first time only five days before their departure for Egypt and found him "a quiet, intelligent, tolerably firm and pleasing fellow", eager to start.

On 29 October, in the theatre of the Royal Institution, Flinders lectured on his discoveries to the Second Annual General Meeting of the Egypt Exploration Fund. Summarizing the results of his survey of some twenty mounds, he pointed out that negative results too were valuable: sites that had always been supposed to be important sometimes proved to be negligible, or very late in date. To counter-balance these there had been unexpected and exciting discoveries: he described, without locating it, his Greek site "never before visited by a European so far as is known", secondly, the site of "a royal mausoleum" where an immense sarcophagus stood on end on a pavement of granite; and third, in a field, part of a magnificent gateway of Amenemhat I, the founder of the twelfth dynasty. All these sites, he said, the society hoped to dig during the coming season. He described the main results of his season at Tanis; on the table in front of him, in the well of the lecture theatre, he had displayed all the contents of "Bak-akhuiu's" house except the pottery (which would be brought home next year).

> Altogether such a collection has never hitherto been obtained from any single house; and in this, as in the other antiquities I have brought, the value consists more in the knowledge of the exact age and locality of everything obtained, than in the rarity of the objects themselves, though many of them are unique.[23]

One cloud hung over the meeting: Sir Erasmus Wilson, the Fund's President and munificent benefactor, had died during the summer; his loss was the more grievous since in spite of his expressed intention to do so, he had not changed his will, and had not left them a single penny. Henceforward the Fund must depend solely on the number and generosity of their subscribers.

Naville was to go out separately, to continue his exploration of sites along the Sweet Water Canal; he would join Petrie for a few days at San to check some of the latter's copies of hieroglyphic inscriptions, which he complained were inaccurate.

During the last weeks before Petrie's departure on 8 November, the hitherto cordial relations between himself and the Committee were clouded by impatience on his part, and Poole's dilatory and unbusiness-like conduct of affairs. The matter at issue concerned the money to be given to Petrie for expenses. The previous year he had asked for £200, which was what Naville had been given; having lived with his usual frugality he had not spent nearly so much and some had been returned. This year he felt that in equity he should ask for the same sum, and he proposed to the Committee that whatever was left over should be put to some specific purpose, for the benefit of the Fund. Poole lost or forgot about his letter and two months later, when Petrie pressed for an answer, the Committee hummed and ha-ed and Poole sent a vague letter which he took to be acceptance of his scheme, but he noted in his diary "All in confusion . . . no clear and business-like disposal of matters; & self much annoyed, at the absurd distrust shewn (though not intended) by various parties. If they cannot trust me at all after what I have done for them, the less we have to do together the better."[24] It was a distant rumble of thunder, presaging the storm one day to break.

Sailing from Liverpool, Flinders Petrie was glad to find that he had Greville Chester as a fellow passenger. When they stopped for a day in Malta, he was able at last to see Hagiar Qim and the nearby temple of Mnajdra; in torrential rain he studied the details of the stone working and decided that the builders were not, as was generally supposed, Phoenicians—there was no sign of the use of bronze implements, and no trace of an inscription. They had perhaps, he thought, some connection with the builders of Stonehenge. In Alexandria Chester introduced him to some of the dealers he patronized, and at one shop Flinders bought a fine series of Greek leaden weights to add to his collection. The Amoses in Cairo insisted on his staying with them again; one evening they gave a dinner party at which Sir Evelyn and Lady Baring were the guests of honour. Flinders was not impressed with the Consul General: he seemed "rather drowned in his work" and "had not much else to him". In Giza he found that 'Ali Gabri was unwilling to go with him to the Delta—it was sowing time, and he had his crops to look after—but he offered to send his son, who being able to read and write Arabic would be very useful; two other of the pyramid men also volunteered to come to Nebeira.

Flinders bought his stores, saw Maspero and made preparations for his deaprture to the Delta. (Griffith was to come by the shorter sea route and would arrive later.) On 1 December he took the train to Teh al Barud, hired two camels and reached Nebeira by nightfall. In spite of Maspero's official letter it took some days to establish his identity with the local sheikhs; meanwhile, while the matter was being referred back to Cairo, he explored the neighbourhood. Not very far from the *tell* a large farmhouse stood partly empty; he was offered rooms on the ground floor for a very reasonable rent; later in the season they were able to move upstairs and were much more comfortable.

First gleanings on the mound, which was very much cut about by *sebbakhîn* digging for fertile mud for their fields, were encouraging: he and his men picked up Greek sherds by the dozen, and handles of jars of Rhodian were stamped with short Greek inscriptions; he was to find many hundreds of these stamps during the course of the season. Then, in the gateway of the house he was staying in, he noticed a broken grey stone which had served as a door pivot; on it was an inscription which began with the words Η ΠΟΛΙΣ Η ΝΑΥΚΡΑΤΙΤ. . . . So this was the city of Naucratis! He managed to conceal his excitement (for he planned to buy the stone, later in the season, by offering "a trifle in an off-hand way") but he telegraphed straight away to Poole that he had found Naucratis, and sent him a copy of the inscription by the next mail. He was disappointed to find later that the cautious Poole had not published the discovery, preferring to wait for further proof.

Petrie let it be known that he was interested in buying antiques, and many were brought in, including to his pleasure a large number of weights. When a more satisfactory official letter had been obtained from the Museum, he was able to start work, but at first there were hardly any volunteers: it was the maize harvest. Sheikh Ruhuma turned up, and Petrie promised him "gold *bakhshish*" if he would stay away from the dig till the end of the season and keep off other Giza dealers who would be sure to swarm around at news of any big discovery. While he waited for his workers to turn up, he explored on foot south and west of the village; Kom Afrîn, he thought, looked promising; later he bought a fine bronze there, probably a figure head from a sacred boat. As soon as Griffith arrived they went on a three-day trip with a donkey up to Sa el-Hagar, the site of the city of Sais, stopping at nightfall with the sheikhs of villages they passed through. Back in Nebeira, and still waiting for the *durra* harvest to finish, they had visitors who helped them in "grubbing about" in the mound: first Mrs Amos with her young son Maurice who found it so delightful an occupation that she let him stay on for a few days, and then Professor Sayce; together he and Flinders stood on a high mass of brickwork and came to the simultaneous conclusion that they must be on the great altar of the Hellenion, the principal temple and municipal centre which Herodotus describes. They were told that within living memory it had been surrounded by great walls, no doubt the temenos or sacred enclosure.*

* Later excavations proved them wrong. The Hellenion was in the northern part of the city: this was a fort in the Egyptian quarter.

Workmen and children were beginning to come forward and he set them to work in the town; they came upon what was evidently a large scarab factory (there were hundreds of moulds with the glaze paste still sticking to them) and the ruins of houses; under some of these a white layer puzzled Petrie till he realized that there were traces of streets running between the houses: limestone dust had been used to mend the road surfaces, and the thicker patches showed "the puddles of Old Naukratis". By the gateway of the great enclosure a building had been entirely removed in later times, but the foundation deposits laid down by the Ptolemaic builder remained (**15**): it was the first time such things had been found *in situ*.

> The first was found by chance, and then at each corner we dug down carefully through some ten feet of earth which had accumulated since the building was destroyed. Coming to the thin line of white sand which had been placed beneath the wall, that was scraped away carefully, and then a small rectangular patch of white sand showed plainly in the dark earth around it. That was the top of a sort of box-shaped hollow filled with sand, which had been poured in over the models. Brushing it aside tenderly with the side of the hand, first a model mortar, then a model hoe, a chisel, an adze, a sacrificial vase or some other little delicate object would be seen; all the sand as it was removed had to be lifted up in handsful, and rubbed through the fingers, for there were also buried in it chips of the precious stones which were used in adorning the building; scrap by scrap these chips were picked out, obsidian, jasper, turquoise and lapis-lazuli. All this sort of work is beyond any native care, and such results can only be got by rigorous European supervision. To hack about in an irregular hole and look for gold, with some trifling attention to bronzes, is the Arab's notion of excavating for antiquities.

The brick mass in the great Temenos proved to contain a number of chambers, some of them domed and probably used as cellars; Petrie decided that the further exploration of these would have to wait for another year. He dug deeply in the area of a temple identified by its votive dedications as that of Apollo, and produced a diagram of the relative depth of the ceramic remains found in it, in effect the first stratified section ever made on an Egyptian excavation.[25] The characteristic pottery, with striking Orientalizing designs on a white ground, became known as Naukratite.* By the dedications on some of the sherds Petrie deduced that temples of Hera, Aphrodite and the Dioskuroi must also be there to be discovered, but the site was too large to attempt a complete clearance.

Flinders' description of the race home after the whistle went at the end of a long day shows a happy man on terms of ease and sympathy with his workmen:

> The work over, then comes the saturnalia of the day: a shouting, joking, merry crew of men, and girls, and boys all speed homeward as fast as they can. I lead off at a brisk rate, and away we all go together; a man begins to race me in walking, and we spin along at well over five miles an hour until he makes a spring to keep up, and then he is laughed down for running. A little imp dances along in front, to try to tantalise me into catching him; he tries it once too boldly, a dash, and he is caught, and crows of delight come from his fellow imps behind as they see him tossed aloft. On we sweep to the crazy old bridge, everyone tries to seize the inside of the curve round the canal, to be first on the planks; and then, some one way, some another, they file off in the orange twilight to their huts. Many, however, come on to my house, the girls bearing the baskets on their heads full of pottery and small antiquities, and many a child with some scrap, for which he or she hopes to realise the value of a chop of sugar-cane.[26]

Naville, meanwhile, was installed, with a cook and a servant, in the house of a Greek at Khataana, a site which Petrie had recommended; his wife and children were staying not far away, at Jemila near Fakous, where Naville's cousin had an estate. He invited Petrie to visit him; it was a tedious journey involving several changes of train, but Petrie went over twice; on the first visit Naville bemoaned the fact that he had found so little at Khataana in the way of inscriptions; on the second, he was at Saft el Hinna, and happier; he had a beautiful shrine covered with religious inscriptions to keep him busy, but he agreed to go up with Flinders to San for a couple of days, to check his copies of inscriptions. Petrie, in no way offended, welcomed his help; he was warmly greeted at San, and spent some days after Naville had left making boxes for some of the sphinxes and statues which, by arrange-

* It has since been found in Chios and other East Greek sites and is no longer supposed to have been locally made in Egypt.

24 Beni Hasan: the Nile, the cemetery and the village from the cliff tombs

25 Tanis: Ramesside blocks in the temple

26 Thebes: Temple of Karnak from the top of the first pylon

27 Foreigners portrayed on the walls of Theban temples: Hittites in the Ramesseum

28 Philistines at Medinet Habu

29 Libyans at Medinet Habu

30 Gebel Silsila: quarries and rock shrines

31 Aswan: inscriptions on rocks in the Cataract region

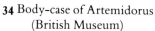

34 Body-case of Artemidorus (British Museum)

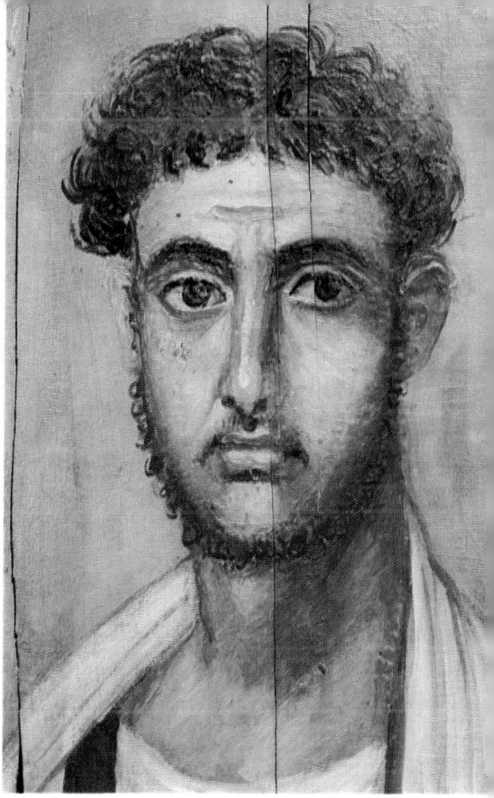

From the tombs of the 2nd century AD, Hawara: *above, right* **(32)**: Encaustic portrait of an unknown man; *right* **(33)**: Gilded cartonnage of a woman (both Manchester Museum)

35 The Pyramid of Meydum

36 The pyramid temple at Meydum as Petrie first uncovered it (from his water-colour sketch)

37 Meydum: Mastaba 17. Petrie failed to find an entrance in 1891, but in January 1910 found the burial of an unknown prince

38 Excavating a tomb shaft, water-colour by Petrie.

39 Fragment of wall fresco from a palace at el 'Amarna: two little daughters of Akhenaten at the feet of their parents (from a water-colour copy by Mrs N. de G. Davies by courtesy of the Egypt Exploration Society. The fresco is in the Ashmolean Museum, Oxford)

40 Veterinary papyrus from Kahun: the text relates to the treatment of illnesses in cattle (Petrie Museum)

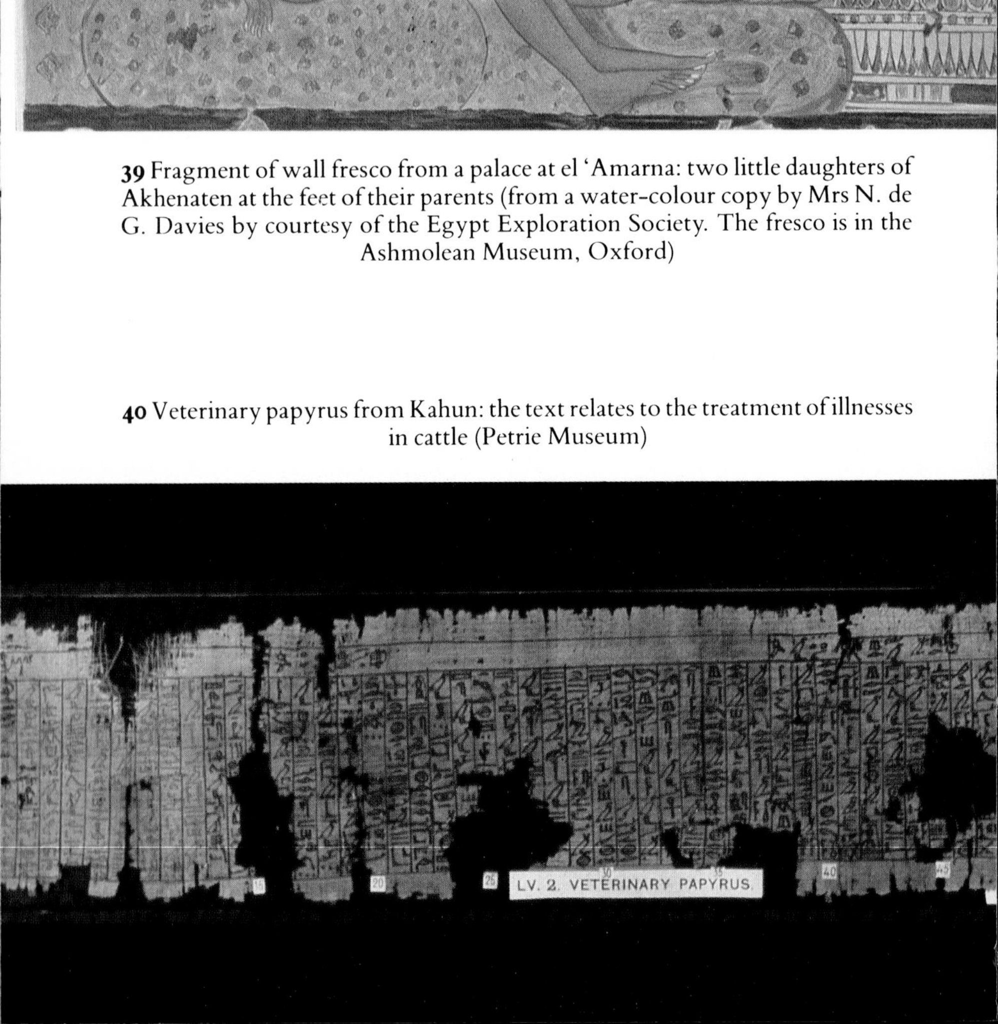

ment with Maspero, he was to send direct to Port Said for shipment to England; Maspero had been generous about these larger antiquities, only stipulating that he should have a complete set of pottery for the Museum, a proviso which had Petrie's wholehearted approval. The rest went with the stonework by boat to Port Said. "When all my 19 cases of pottery are unpacked, I think folks in England will agree in the Arab nickname for me, 'Abu Bagousheh', *father of pots.* Griffith's name is 'Abu Shukf', *father of potsherds.*"

Griffith had been carrying on in his absence with the excavation of the temple area: he was gaining in confidence and learning Arabic, and his health was better: at first he had been plagued with sore throats and bouts of influenza which had sent him more than once into Mrs Amos' care in Cairo. While he watched the men on the *tell*, and recorded the hundreds of sherds of votive Greek pottery which were found in the rubbish heaps of the temples, Petrie filled the roles of "paymaster, photographer, cook, doctor and chaser of *Gizawiya*"—the dealers from Giza who in spite of all his precautions were haunting the fringes of the excavation since the discovery by an illicit digger of a large hoard of votive bronzes. Petrie evidently enjoyed these "steeple-chases" in spite of his anger at the intruders:

> The way is to walk straight at any suspicious character, openly and ostentatiously; he moves off, you follow; he quickens; you quicken; he doubles; you cross to cut him off; then he fairly bolts; and off you go, with perhaps a furlong between, across fields, jumping canals, doubling, hiding behind bushes and so forth; if he once gains a village it is useless to look for him in the houses; so the way is to keep him out in the open for as much time as you can spare for the game; two to four miles is a fair run. This exercise is valuable morally and physically; the rascals are always laughed at by my diggers for running away, so their habit of flight is worth cultivating.[27]

He bought wood at Teh al Barud for boxes; by now it was late in May and getting very hot: "We have a storeroom downstairs, so retreating there I work away much like Brady's Japanese carpenter who had nothing on but a pair of spectacles, except that I do not need any spectacles." They stopped work at the end of May and then camel-loads of boxes went to the railhead for Cairo. Both of them were having trouble with their eyes, and Griffith was forced to lie for two weeks in a darkened room in Alexandria with ophthalmia before leaving. Though Petrie liked him personally, he had been somewhat of a disappointment on the dig: he was hopelessly impractical and singularly unable to look after his own health; he was always forgetting and losing things, and was very slow and absent-minded (he had exasperated the Amos family, with whom he had spent Christmas). Still, he was undoubtedly a gifted philologist and he was learning more than the rudiments of archaeological practice; one day he might yet make an "explorer".

When Petrie started unpacking his boxes, he again enlisted the help of Riley and Spurrell, and also an enthusiastic schoolboy named Percy Newberry, to whom Poole had introduced him; he let him draw some of the plates for the Naucratis volume. Two members of the British Museum staff contributed to the publication: Barclay Head for the coins and Cecil Smith on the subject of the Greek pottery; the inscriptions were translated by Ernest, the young brother of Professor Percy Gardner, a recent graduate in classical archaeology, twenty-three years of age, who was keen to go out with Petrie in the following season. Flinders liked him at once; they were to be lifelong friends and, later, close colleagues.

Over one hundred people attended the first day of the exhibition; the discovery of Naucratis had been sensational news and in America, in particular, had done a good deal to rectify the harm done by the hostility and spite of Cope Whitehouse; that eccentric had protested to Poole and Miss Edwards that Naville could not have found Pithom, since he himself had certain proof that the Land of Goshen in which the Israelites had dwelt in bondage had been near Memphis, at the mouth of the Fayum.[28] In the American press and at the Fund's General Meeting he even hinted that inscriptions found by Naville at Tell el Maskhuta were forgeries planted by Jaillon with Naville's connivance.[29]

An anonymous review of Naville's book in *The Athenaeum*, and reproduced in *The Egyptian Gazette*, depicted Naville as a laughing-stock and the Fund discredited among scholars.[30] Naville decided to ignore the calumny; he knew that Maspero and most Egyptologists regarded "Copious" as a crank and an ignoramus. Petrie resolved to avoid his company in the future.

Tanis. Part I came out in October; it was in the same large format as Naville's *The Store City of Pithom*, had eighteen plates and two fold-out plans, and was the first of a long series of publications, in the same size and general lay-out, which Petrie was to produce annually for the next fifty years. It had cost 3*s.* 1*d.* a copy to print, and every subscriber to the Fund of £1 or more was entitled to receive a copy. He finished the manuscript of his Naucratis book on 19 November, before starting for Egypt again. His lecture to the members at their autumn meeting had been well reported; he decided not to read a paper—to speak from notes, he felt, had more life, and one could better gauge the mood and interest of one's audience. Miss Edwards was full of his praise; she wrote to his mother:

> Our brave explorer—he must have been overdriven. Is it possible that he has really finished Naucratis? It is miraculous. His lecture was admirable—picturesque, profoundly interesting, with touches of delightful humour. . . . The more I see of him, the more interest and affection I feel for him. His self-denial—not merely his unselfishness, but his *self-denial*—his generosity, his largeness of soul, are most delightful. And I can assure you the Museum appreciates him more than ever. . . .[31]

She had a particular reason to be grateful to him, for he had promised her that he would buy a few *antikas* privately for her—nothing extravagant, for she could not afford expensive treasures, but certain things that she particularly wanted for her own collection, her "modest little museum", as she called it, at her home in Westbury-on-Trym. Ever since her visit to Egypt she had been building up this collection; she longed to have time to catalogue it, and enough money to house it properly.

> Stowed away in all kinds of nooks and corners, in upstairs cupboards, in boxes, drawers and cases innumerable . . . are hundreds, nay thousands, of those fascinating objects. . . . Here for instance . . . packed side by side like figs in a box, are all the gods of Egypt—fantastic little porcelain figures plumed and horned, bird-headed and animal-headed. . . . Rings, necklaces, bracelets, ear-rings, amulets, mirrors, and toilet objects, once the delight of dusky beauties long since embalmed and forgotten; funerary statuettes, scarabs, rolls of mummy cloth and the like are laid by "in a sacred gloom". . . .[32]

Such things could be obtained very cheaply still in Egypt, and she could rely on Flinders to buy at the right price. On his return next summer she wrote to him:

> I feel much excited about the arrival of your boxes, & much covetous & avaricious & commandment-breaking as to their contents . . . if you have any duplicate scarabs you know how grateful I

shall be to be allowed to buy them from you. I do not want you to let me have anything at the bare price you paid—but at the price you would part from them to Mr. Hilton Price or the Museum. I do not want to take advantage of your friendship in *any* way; for I know of course that you must repay yourself the cost of your delay & trouble in getting things.[33]

He insisted on first showing everything he had bought—even those pieces he most coveted himself—to the British Museum; Amelia protested that this was not fair, but he was adamant that the national collection must have priority of choice, and this she accepted.

Gardner and Petrie travelled out together that winter, and Griffith joined them at Nebeira a little later; Petrie intended to stay only long enough to initiate Gardner, who had no experience of excavating and had never before been to Egypt; he engaged a Berber cook for him and was able to negotiate for his greater comfort the lease of the whole farmhouse; two of 'Ali Gabri's sons were to be his *reises*. The temples of Aphrodite and the Dioskuroi were soon identified, and Gardner found in the cemetery the coffins of Greek settlers, buried with their jewellery and toilet objects to accompany them to the next world.[34]

Early in January they left Gardner on his own. It was hoped that his friend Arthur Smith, another young classical scholar, might join him, but his health was not equal to the life of an excavator and he left Gardner after a week. In Cairo Flinders found Mrs Grant very ill, and he heard with sorrow of the death, in Alexandria, of Professor Amos. He and Griffith stayed in a hotel and made preparations for their next venture, buying stores, accumulating a large stock of the scarce small copper coins and finding a cook for Griffith, who was going to be left on his own for part of the season.

Their new site, Tell Nabesha between Faqous and San, was also called Tell Far'un, the Hill of Pharaoh, after the great stone "sentry-box" which crowned it; Petrie had assumed this to be a royal sarcophagus: it turned out to be part of a shrine. The site, an island of sand in the marshy swamp, had once been a place of some importance, but little was left of the town save scanty remains of two temples, and a number of tombs. The sheikh of the place, an old man of eighty-five, was delighted to have their company and put part of his house at their disposal; the accommodation was primitive: there were two rooms, but only one was roofed (Petrie sent over to San to fetch some corrugated iron sheets from the house) and they were infested with flies and white ants, or termites, which ate their paper and their blankets; large rats ran across the ceiling, and cats stole their food. The old sheikh himself was a problem: garrulous and embarrassingly affectionate, he never left them alone. He had in his younger days been a great sheikh of the Beduin in the eastern desert around Esna; he had fought with Ibrahim Pasha and Abbas Pasha, and was said to have had forty-six wives, but now he had been pensioned off with a few hundred acres of desolate marshland and a handful of retainers. He was delighted to have someone to whom he could retail his past adventures and would come in to gossip at all hours; he drank a bottle of their precious mineral water every day, and took a fancy to their enamelled iron saucepans. They promised him a set of four of these treasures, as soon as they could be sent from Cairo.

The excavation of Nabesha produced some fine monuments—a colossal statue of Ramesses II, nearly seven feet high and "only a little knocked about the face", and several other fine blocks from the main temple, which proved to have a history going back at least to the Twelfth Dynasty. The identification of the site with the city Am, or Imet, the capital of the nineteenth nome of Lower Egypt was soon confirmed by finding the name in several inscriptions. "Whitehouse will probably say I forged them," Petrie wrote to Poole, "I wish he would try and forge something, just to show how easy it is to do! Challenge him to make a stele with a new inscription!"[35] There appeared to have been two temples; Griffith did not think to look for foundation deposits, but Petrie, groping under the sand into the subsoil water with his toes, found under the corners of one of them a number of faience plaques, and others of gold, silver, copper and lead, all with the cartouches of Amasis, showing that the temple had been built in the twenty-sixth dynasty. Some of the shaft tombs appeared to have been built for foreigners: they contained spear-heads and other curious implements which Petrie took to be fish-spears; later he realized they were spear-butts. He suggested that these were the graves of Cypriote or Lykaonian mercenaries and dated them to the Saite period; they are now known to be Western Asiatic and much earlier. Imet was on the extreme edge of the Delta, and open to influences from Egypt's eastern neighbours. Other tombs contained large sarcophagi; one, finely carved in basalt, was among the monuments brought to London by the Fund several years later and presented to the British Museum; the Boston Museum of Fine Arts had several other of the best pieces, including the colossus of Ramesses II, and a granite column surmounted by a figure of a hawk.

In February Petrie left Griffith in charge of Nabesha with his most trusted *reis* Muhammad, 'Ali Gabri's eldest son, and went off on a three-week tenting trip in the Delta; he called at Nebeira on the way and found that Gardner was managing very well on his own; the cemetery had been cleared and the Temple of Aphrodite, he was able to report, "really looks an imposing building now". He gave Gardner advice about packing his pottery: eighty petroleum boxes would be needed, and a great deal of straw. Then he went off with a tent and two men, one of them a tall negro, and a donkey, to explore the Delta for likely sites for excavation in the future. The great mounds of Tell el Fara'in, east of Dessuk, were just where, from his study of the Geography of Ptolemy, he expected the ancient city of Buto to be. The village nearby, Ubtu, still kept the ancient name, if proof were needed. Between the mounds he noticed a great square enclosure where the temple had once been. "Two or three hours here to plan the place, and I turned my back on Buto *for the present*." It was to be nearly twenty years before he returned. The town of Sanhûr stood on part of what had evidently been a large Graeco-Roman city: he had no hesitation in identifying it with the Kabasa of Ptolemy. "Why these cities should not hitherto have been sought where Ptolemy places them, on the riverside road northwards from Sais, seems strange . . . there are no other remains to rival their claims."

Moving eastwards from Kafr ez Zayat to Mansura by train, he found impressive remains of a temple at Behbeit al Hagar, but little of the town remaining; Thmuis, too, looked promising, but they were systematically carrying away the Roman town—the donkeys had special wooden crate-panniers to carry the bricks. Several large camps aroused his particular curiosity and one of them, Tell el Na'ûs, he longed to dig. But by now he had been nearly three weeks on the road, and the sight of his little caravan—the bearded, shabbily dressed Englishman (his boots had given out and he was wearing Arab shoes), his two lads and the laden donkey, were beginning to excite comment in the countryside; once they were taken for gypsies, and the police were summoned during the night.

When they got back to Nabesha, Petrie found that Griffith had moved to a small mound three miles away, Tell el Gumayima; he was camping there with a few men, and the cook brought over his dinner every day. Here, too, there was a temple, and here, too, Griffith had forgotten to look for the foundation deposits (Petrie found them at once, but they lacked the founder's name); he had also failed to preserve all but a small portion of a wooden shrine decorated with glass mosaic—"a unique and priceless piece of decoration"; Petrie was displeased, and wrote a confidential report on his protégé to Poole, complaining that he was curiously slow to grasp the implications of what he was finding. Nevertheless, he encouraged Griffith to go off later in the season, alone on a camel, to explore the region of Qantara, on the Suez Canal, and the young man made several enterprising forays into the desert around Pelusium, in the great heat of the approaching summer.

In the meantime, leaving him back at Nabesha, Petrie moved again, with Muhammad and some forty of his workpeople; the second site he planned to excavate was Tell Defenna, or Defna, in a remote part of the eastern Delta near the Sinai border. A brackish canal ran nearby, but there were no villages and all supplies had to come from a distance.

Tell Defenna turned out to be, as had been supposed from its position and from its name, the site of another important Greek settlement: the fortress of Daphnae mentioned by Herodotus as having been founded by Psammetichus I for his Carian and Greek mercenaries; it lies on an ancient trade route about ten miles west of Qantara. The citadel of the fortress stood high; it was solidly built and under the corners, to clinch the identification, were the foundation deposits of Psammetichus; moreover, in the main mound a great deal of early Greek painted pottery was found as well as iron tools, and weapons, amulets and beads and seals with the names of Saite kings.[36] The citadel mound, he was told, was known to the Arabs as *Qasr Bint el Yehudi*, "The Castle of the Jew's daughter", and he remembered that Tahpanhes, in the Book of Jeremiah, had been a place of refuge for Jeremiah and the remnant of the Jewish people who had fled from the Babylonians after the capture of Jerusalem by Nebuchadnezzar, with "all the officers and the king's daughters". As the first place on the road to Egypt, it would have been a likely place for fugitives. Petrie believed that the large building was not only a fortress but a palace, a kind of hunting lodge perhaps for the Egyptian kings, and that Jeremiah's reference to the brickwork of Pharaoh's house at Tahpanhes, where Nebuchadnezzar was to pitch his royal tent, was the platform in front of the fort; he was a little disappointed to find no stones in the brickwork which might conceivably be those put there by Jeremiah, but honesty compelled him to admit that he could find none.[36] Nevertheless it was a rich and important site; the Greek pottery was of a different and more striking type, and slightly earlier, than that found at Naucratis, and there was a good deal of jewellery in the town, and many small weights—so many, in fact, that he suspected there had been a jewellers' quarter in the town. Some were scattered far from the *tell*, and about twenty of the local Beduin spent their days scouring the desert for them. No less than 79 were brought in in one day; even old women, delighted with the reward they got, joined in the search. In the end Petrie had something over 1,400 weights from Daphnae: "I believe that with Layard's Assyrian weights, Burgon's Athenian, and now two such wholly unprecedented hauls as Naucratis and Defenneh, the Brit. Mus. will always stand as the supreme collection of weights."

Maurice Amos came up for a few days, and on a day of *khamasin* in April, Sayce came riding over from Qantara. It was noon; the thermometer stood at 120°, and Petrie was nowhere to be seen. On asking where he was, Sayce was told "*yistanna fil moya*" (he is standing in the water); "and there in the canal I found him standing like a buffalo with water up to his neck and an umbrella over his head."[37]

The canal served also to soak the salt from the larger pots; a complete range of Egyptian pottery of the Saite period was, in Petrie's eyes, as great a prize as the Greek wares.

Petrie was supremely happy:

> I never spent two months more smoothly than while heading our desert camp. Yet the people had not much to content them: they came without any shelter, and nothing but what they wore; they had dry bread to eat, and brackish water to drink; and they worked for sixpence a day, most of them but five days in the week, as they had to walk twenty-five to forty miles to fetch their food. . . . Their shelter they made up, partly by digging a hole in the sand mounds, partly by booths of thin tamarisk bushes. . . . A merry party they were; excepting one or two older men, there was hardly a lad over twenty or a girl over fifteen in the whole lot. Each night a blazing row of camp fires flickered their yellow flames up into the starlight, all along the line of booths which skirted the canal banks; mounds of sand tufted over with tamarisk bushes backed the line, while the distant ruins of the *kasr* showed dimly on one side, and the gleam of the sluggish canal on the other.

Led by a visiting dervish, the men would occasionally gather in the dark for a *zikr*, "howling and groaning in set phrases, *ya há-ah-há, ya há-ah-há* as it sounds (probably *ya.allahu*) repeated hoarsely, hundreds of times, quicker and quicker, until they break down, one by one, the combined noise sounding most like a great engine puffing hoarsely, with the noise of a snarling dog for its sound." Elsewhere would be parties of girls singing and clapping hands, and boys playing games in the dark starlight,

> and not another sound within ten miles of us, nothing but sand and tamarisks, and marsh, and water and desolation. But I like it better than most civilised places; one lives with the people more; and the ever-fresh desert air and living in a tent, doubles one's contentment and peace of mind. Neither Gardner nor Griffith would appreciate it, I fear; they neither of them like having to do with the people, and would prefer an immense excavating machine to do their work. To me all their bye-play, and jokes, and songs and wills and ways, give a colour and an interest to life here, which no one will ever reach in staid, school-boarded England.

It was nearly the end of May, and time to pack and go home; after many difficulties with the railway, Petrie got his boxes back to Cairo and Maspero inspected what he had found; he took some of the jewellery, one or two fine scarabs and a steatite figure of Isis, one of the best finds from Gumayemi, but refused to look at two of Petrie's greatest prizes lest Brugsch's covetous eye fall on them: a little gold figure of the god Horus, in its silver box, and the gold handle of a tray with a palmetto design. He asked for the return from England, after they had been studied, of some of the Greek pottery and a complete set of weights for the Museum, and he gave no inkling to Petrie of what was to be announced only a few days later—his resignation and imminent return to France. Nobody knew the reason, and speculation was rife: had he perhaps been sacked? The truth was made known in a week or so: it was because of his wife's health, for she could not support the climate of Egypt.

Before leaving, the Director had named his successor; he was M. Eugène Grébaut, his sometime student and the head of the French Archaeological Mission in Cairo. The appointment had come as a surprise to some; there were rumours that Maspero would have preferred Naville, and Petrie's name also (as he later learned) had been put forward, perhaps by Scott-Moncrieff. But Grébaut was a Frenchman and this decided the matter: at any rate Brugsch was excluded, to the general relief.

Petrie's letters to Poole during the years 1885 and 1886 reflect his growing impatience with the muddle at home. He complained that he frequently received conflicting instructions from his two employers; uncertainty wasted both time and money. Sometimes their requests were unreasonable and ill-considered: the year before, when he was at

Nebeira, Miss Edwards had written to him asking him to bring back a thousand bricks from Tell el Maskhuta, for distribution to subscribers; they would, she felt sure, treasure a genuine brick, made, as the Book of Exodus relates, without straw, by an Israelite in bondage. Poole, more realistically, asked for twenty or thirty. Petrie wrote in reply: "This would imply a large number of cases, as they are too heavy to go more than two in a box. If I or Griffith were to attend to it now, it would keep us at least a week longer in the country."[38] Moreover Naville had told him he disliked the idea of "trading in relics". They must remember that one Egyptian brick was very much like another, and frequently made without straw. Evidently the Honorary Secretaries thought better of the matter, and it was not mentioned again.

In August, Petrie wrote to Poole on the "unpleasant subject" of handbills for which he had again received contrary instructions. At Miss Edwards' request he had drafted leaflets for distribution at his exhibition, but the text had been arbitrarily altered by Poole without consulting him; his emendations, he said, had only caused confusion and led to time-wasting correspondence.[39] Petrie's mother made things no easier by complaining to Poole that the Committee were putting too heavy a burden on her son; Flinders had spent long hours unaided at the exhibition, she said, and had worked often until midnight sorting and cataloguing the weights. Poole's reply was not very sympathetic; her son had undertaken these labours, he said, of his own free will; his friends would do well to avoid attacking the administration.[40]

The truth was that both Stuart Poole and Miss Edwards were gravely overworked. Between them, they had the whole responsibility for the day-to-day running of the Fund, the collection of subscriptions, recruiting new members, correspondence with the Press, lecturing to the public and dealing with enquiries and complaints. Neither of them could afford a secretary; before the era of telephones and typewriters everything had to be written by hand. Their letters to each other often complain of tiredness and lack of sleep. Their respective duties were not well-defined and they sometimes disagreed on matters of policy; though they were old friends, a note of reproach sometimes creeps into their correspondence. Neither was able to delegate responsibility and the distance between them—he in London and she in Bristol—made frequent misunderstandings inevitable. The General Committee met but once or twice a year, and except on the day of the Annual General Meeting was usually attended by members of the Sub-Committee only. In consequence, policy decisions of importance were usually made by the latter, often without even consulting Miss Edwards; they met in Poole's room at the British Museum—Newton as Chairman, Poole and Head, and sometimes Professor Gardner—and they decided who was to be sent out to Egypt to excavate, and where, and how much they might spend, the distribution of antiquities and the details of publication. Petrie frequently protested to Miss Edwards, and privately to his friends, at this concentration of power in the hands of what was virtually a British Museum triumvirate (for Head supported his Keeper in matters of dispute) and at the general inefficiency of the administration.

During the winter there had been irritating delays: photographic supplies urgently needed had not been sent, proofs had failed to arrive. When at last page proofs of *Naucratis. Part I* reached Petrie, he was on his donkey trip; he sat down in his tent, read them and did the index in six hours, and sent them back the next morning, but when he returned to England in the summer he found that Poole wanted to delay publication till the following year, so that subscribers should not be presented with more than one volume in a single year. Petrie protested vehemently: *Naucratis. Part II*, then, would be "two years stale" and subsequent volumes even more out of date. He proposed to publish *Tanis. Part II, Nebesheh and Defenneh* in one volume entirely out of the unspent balance of his expense account. At the same meeting of the Sub-Committee at which this offer was turned down, other complaints of Petrie's were considered: one was the high cost of the plates of Naucratis: no attempt, it seems, had been made to obtain estimates from other lithographers. The other concerned a collection of pottery and small objects from Naucratis and San, carefully sorted and labelled by Spurrell and himself in the shed of the British Museum after the previous year's exhibition, ready for despatch to various museums, which he found six months later still undistributed, and scattered in hopeless disarray, many of them smashed. He was told that it could not have been helped—that "nobody was responsible": the objects had suffered damage when a man had fallen through a window into the shed; fortunately he had not been killed. The Committee could give no promise about the future disposal of antiquities.

The Sub-Committee then decided to reappoint M. Naville as their "explorer" for the coming season; neither the Committee nor Miss Edwards were consulted and when she heard of it she was greatly displeased:

> I do not see the use of my giving up everything—earnings, health and home duties—if I do not have the least confidence reposed in me by the Committee and am only told of things when they are done. . . . Not to send out Mr. Petrie would be very unjust; he has worked harder than Naville ever worked, and has brought home richer results. Naville in his last letter to me describes the excavation of Tahpanhes as a "coup de maître". If *he* had done it, we should have had no results for Museums at all.

During August and September she and Flinders wrote frequently to each other and at great length, almost as if they were thinking aloud; he called it "conversation by letter".[41] They agreed to be frank with each other. Both were certain that the management of the Society must change, and soon, but where could they find someone with the right scholarly qualifications and the self-sacrificing enthusiasm necessary for such voluntary work? If reforms could not be brought about peaceably, Petrie declared, there were only two courses open to him: either to denounce the Committee publicly, calling attention to the waste and mismanagement, or to resign and leave the field to Naville and Griffith. Miss Edwards begged him to do neither: his resignation would be a grievous loss to the Fund and to Science: "it would mean the loss of the greatest explorer in the world and of the greater part of the portable objects." Yet to denounce the executive would be disastrous: it would mean the end of the Fund and the destruction of all they had built up. Eminent scholars must not be publicly disgraced. Perhaps a businessman added to the Committee, and a salaried clerk to run the day-to-day work of the society, might help to remedy the situation.[42]

Petrie had already suggested several possible additions to the Committee and he at once followed up the suggestion of paid assistance; the Archaeological Institute, he knew, had a room to spare and a part-time secretary, Hellier Gosselin, who would be willing to do routine secretarial work for the Fund.

Miss Edwards convened a meeting of the full Committee for the day when she would be passing through London on her way to represent the Fund at the Fifth Congress of Orientalists in Vienna. At the meeting, it was agreed that the office be rented and Gosselin engaged. Amelia had asked Petrie to attend and he came armed with a statement which he read out. It contained proposals for a new set of rules: the full Committee should meet at least quarterly, the Secretary should send out every month a statement of authorized business concluded, petty cash expended, and all suggestions or questions sent in by subscribers; each member of the Committee would ratify such transactions by signing the monthly report and returning it. The plan had its imperfections, but it would have ruled out arbitrary decisions made by the Medal Room alone. The chairman, Newton, refused to allow discussion of these proposals but agreed that they be printed and circulated to Committee members before the next meeting.

On 6 October the Sub-Committee met for the last time and at Miss Edwards' insistence, resigned in a body; they recommended that the whole Committee meet once a fortnight. Since there was no provision for a quorum, this would in effect mean the continuation of the triumvirate. Neither Poole nor Newton, wrote Petrie to Amelia, showed any signs of relinquishing control; and Newton, for all his promises, had suppressed his memorandum.

> I consider his action a declaration of war . . . this clinches my determination never to cooperate in any way with Mr. Newton in future. His autocratic arrogance is simply unbearable. I would rather forswear Egypt altogether, and go into chemistry, than to have anything further to do with Mr. Newton; this is final on my part.[43]

On 16 October Miss Edwards reluctantly read to the Committee Mr Petrie's letter of resignation from the Fund; he preferred, he said, to give no reasons, either to them or at the General Meeting.[44] No mention was made of the rules, but the Committee determined to codify existing rules and to propose others at the coming General Meeting. In sending him an account of these proceedings, Amelia assured Flinders "They were all horribly confounded and shocked at your resignation—and they all refused to believe that you would not be induced to reconsider it."[45] It may be doubted whether Poole, had he been present, would have shared their consternation; in his letters to Petrie during the past year the changes in his mode of address—"Dear Petrie", then "Dear Mr. Petrie", then "Dear Sir" and finally, "Sir", —are a falling barometer of his feelings towards his correspondent.

One tiresome matter remained to be settled before the sorry chapter could be closed; it concerned the sum of £268. 9s. 7d which Petrie claimed the fund owed him: in the published annual accounts the full expense allowance of £200 had been credited to him, whereas he had not drawn it all from the Treasurer. Anxious that the money should not be swallowed up in the day-to-day expenditure of the Fund, or perhaps on Naville's extravagant operations in the field, he asked the

Committee to invest it as a Trust. Poole at first denied that any money was owing to him, but the matter was referred to a lawyer on the Committee, who gave his opinion that Petrie was entitled to his surplus. After some argument they sent Petrie a cheque for the amount to do what he liked with. Petrie promptly invested it in 3% India Stock in the name of Amelia Edwards, asking her to devote the money to "work which I may undertake in the future in connection with the Egypt Exploration Fund". She could not but accept the trust, though she urged him to spend the money on his own behalf in Egypt: "Remember, M. Naville ate and drank and cooked all his allowance," she reminded him. If his too-delicate sense of honour forbids this, he must arrange "that your formal trustee may bequeathe it in yoŭr name to University College, London, to swell the modest amount which I have promised them. Thus it wd. go to the lasting service of Egyptology, and benefit Englishmen for ever."[46] She was referring to a plan about which she had told him some time before: she intended to leave her collection of antiquities and her books to the College in her will, together with a modest bequest to endow a Chair in Egyptian Archaeology. It was a scheme which was one day to alter the course of Petrie's life and the whole future of Egyptological studies in Great Britain.

In the end, the Committee were spared the embarrassment of a valedictory speech from Petrie at the Annual General Meeting of the Egypt Exploration Fund. Learning that it was to be on 8 December, he decided to leave England before that date, leaving his report on Nebesha and Defenna to be read for him by Miss Edwards. The meeting might still prove an uncomfortable occasion; as Honorary Secretary she could not herself query his resignation, but she hoped that when it was announced someone—perhaps Hilton Price or Sayce—might pluck up courage to do so; Petrie could then be asked to write giving his reasons and his answer could be printed and circulated to subscribers, and the Committee would have to resign *en bloc*. That, however, she admitted was pure fantasy, and she was now resigned to his going. "Goodbye," she ended her letter, "good luck, and God bless you. Ever your faithful friend, A. B. Edwards."[47]

Sherd from Naukratis

CHAPTER V

Up the Nile
(1886–7)

FLINDERS PETRIE WAS now in a dilemma. Without the Fund, and with no private resources, it would be impossible to continue excavating in Egypt. Nor could he now contemplate working for the British Museum. In November Le Page Renouf, Birch's successor, had written very curtly to Miss Edwards, complaining that the antiquities donated to the Museum by the Fund were valueless: Nothing that Budge had chosen for the Museum had been delivered: he could not recommend the Trustees to accept "a vast quantity of pottery and small objects which from our point of view are worthless".[1] She, furious at the tone of the letter and the slur on the Fund's reputation, indignantly repudiated the accusation; unless Renouf apologized and retracted, she declared, nothing should go to the Museum.[2] Further investigation showed that there had been a stupid misunderstanding: Budge had misinterpreted or misheard what Griffith had said; in fact, the objects he had chosen were awaiting transfer from the exhibition.[3] Renouf did not reply for a month; his grudging apology, when it came, restored amicable relations with the Committee and the Trustees got their treasures,[4] but Petrie could not exonerate Budge, whom he rightly suspected of having been responsible for Renouf's first letter (the draft of which, preserved in the archives of the Oriental Department, is in Budge's writing),[5] and he could not forgive the word "worthless". "[Renouf] has thus cut me out of the last refuge I hoped to work in for Egyptian doings," he wrote to Amelia. "The false statements of that letter, and the gross ignorance it shewed of genuine and scientific archaeology, bar me from having anything to do with that quarter again."[6] His estrangement from the British Museum, and strained relations or open hostility between himself and Wallis Budge, were to last the rest of their lives.

Yet Petrie was reluctant to abandon archaeology for some other profession. The experience of the last six years had been arduous, but infinitely rewarding. "I work," he had written to Spurrell, "because I can do what I am doing, better than I can do anything else, in comparison with the way other people do things. I enjoy it because I know that my time produces more result than in any other, and I am aware that such work is what I am best fitted for." If all else failed, he was considering going to the Congo; "Arabic, surveying, organization and management would all be of value there, and there I would have ground enough for any amount of work and *action* I liked to put into it."[7]

But first he had a commission to carry out. The geneticist Francis Galton, for his studies on the skull measurements of racial types, needed photographs of the heads of different enemies and allies —Libyans, Hittites, Syrians, Nubians and Beduin—depicted on the walls of temples and tombs in Egypt; visiting Egypt many years before, he had noted the acute observation shown by the ancient sculptors of these portraits. He had written to the Fund in the summer, and Poole had recommended Petrie, who accepted at once since, once in Egypt on Fund business, he would thereby have an opportunity to see Upper Egypt again, at more leisure than on the last hasty visit. But now matters were different; the grant of £20 provided by the British Association for the Advancement of Science for this project would barely suffice to get him to Egypt; his own means were slender and he was too proud to accept more from his father, or call on Miss Edwards' trust fund. There was one possibility: Frank Griffith would be free until the spring, when, at Miss Edwards' insistence, he was to accompany Naville to the Delta, with a watching brief for small antiquities and for unexpected walls. His studentship had one more year to run, and by the terms of it he was required to spend part of the year studying in Egypt; he had never been south of Saqqara. Petrie liked him and was used to his slow ways, and he would be invaluable when it came to recording inscriptions. If he would share the expense of a trip up-river, a season in Upper Egypt—perhaps Petrie's last —became a possibility. Griffith found it hard to make up his mind; it was a splendid opportunity and he would learn a great deal, but perhaps his past experience of the Spartan life with Petrie gave him pause.

At length Petrie decided to go whatever happened, and on 27 November he set off on a ship from Liverpool, choosing the cheapest possible route. At Algiers he found in the museum "some curious native weights and measures"; in Malta he hunted in vain for a "Phoenician temple", walking about sixteen miles without finding anything worth seeing. Meanwhile, urged by Miss Edwards to go, Griffith had left for Egypt by the shorter route overland to Marseilles. He and Petrie met at Alexandria and travelled together to Cairo, where they stayed with Dr Grant, now a widower (for his wife had died in the spring). It took several days to find M. Grébaut, the new Director of Antiquities, and obtain from him the necessary permit to take squeezes, and it was 19 December before they set off. At Minya they managed to hire a small boat with a cabin about twelve feet long built over the stern half, "quite new, as it was done for the accommodation of a bride brought up from Tanta". As befitted a bride, it was painted pale lavender. The services of *reis* (captain) and a crew of two boys were included in the hire price, ten francs a day. Petrie and Griffith brought with them also two men from the Naucratis work, Said and Muhammad el Gabri, whom they knew well and could trust; the former could cook a little (they had decided they could not afford a professional cook). In the narrow confines of the cabin Petrie and Griffith ate, talked and worked whenever they were on board; on the side benches, made wider by their boxes of stores, they slept at night, while the crew curled up on the bank. Across the prow of the boat "a fold of coarse canvas is nailed up from side to side to hold our bread store." (Egyptians away from home bake a large batch at one time, to last for weeks; when needed a loaf is soaked in water to soften it.) The space between the benches being too narrow, a table for dining and working was a problem, until Petrie hit on the solution of suspending the lid of a large box, by loops of string, from nails driven into the roofing.

The arrangement worked splendidly; the boat was snug and comfortable enough, and small enough to tow when the wind dropped; it was cheap, and it was available for as long as they wanted it. Every day they went ashore, and walked inland from the river, looking for tombs and archaeological sites—partly for Griffith's benefit, since this was his first visit, and also in the hope of finding something new. Petrie had intended to photograph the already famous group of visiting Asiatic nomads in the tomb of Khnumhotep at Beni Hasan, but on climbing the cliff, found that it was partly obscured by a film of dirt; with difficulty he resisted the temptation to give the walls a good washing down with water. They were in excellent spirits: "G. is enjoying himself very much, and so am I, in this sort of working holiday," Petrie wrote to his mother and father, "and we look forward to a delightful six weeks or so ahead, going where we like, and clear of civilisation."

Two days before Christmas they reached Roda and walked westwards some five miles to Eshmunein, the site of the ancient city of Hermopolis. No organized excavation had yet been carried out there, but granite columns still standing showed the presence of a handsome late Roman building, now known to be a basilica. "The place is being ransacked over by a dealer Arab, in the interests of Bulak." At El Bersha they saw, still undamaged, the celebrated relief depicting the transport of a colossal statue. In a tomb of the Old Kingdom at Esbeyda, Petrie scratched off some later, Coptic plaster to reveal some curious paintings, including the head of a unicorn with a large horn.[8] A two-day visit to Tell el 'Amarna (one day for the tombs, and two half-days for the town) whetted his appetite for further exploration; five years later he was to make one of his most successful excavations there. None too soon, for the villagers were already digging: "any quantity of little things are found there, and I bought up a good deal, nearly all of Khuenaten."

Then a long and heavy thunderstorm, followed by torrential rain, demonstrated to them that their fine wooden cabin roof was by no means watertight. After an uncomfortable night, the quarries of Gebel Abu Foda rewarded their exploration by two masons' working drawings of capitals: "All the construction lines are marked out, the latter design (of a head of Hathor, the cow-goddess) being filled into a net of squares of half a cubit each. These throw great light on the design of complex and curved forms." Near Manfalut on the next stage of their journey, they found some unrecorded tombs in the mountain behind Beni Muhammad, at a place called Deir el Gebrawi; though the tombs had been partially cleared, the inscriptions were still hidden by whitewash. Excitedly they began to copy whatever they could uncover, but it became evident that there was work here for several days at least, and so they reluctantly decided to leave the tombs until some later opportunity. (When these tombs were finally copied in 1899[9] the tracing of these scenes and inscriptions took seven weeks to complete.)

Petrie was now suffering from a streaming cold and rheumatic pains, brought on by sleeping in wet blankets, but by the time they reached Baliana on the west bank of the Nile he felt ready for another sortie; leaving the boat moored to the embankment of the town, he and Griffith walked through the town and seven miles through fields on a country road towards the hills, to El 'Araba el Madfûna, the ancient town of Abydos. They explored far and wide in this huge site, which stretches for miles along the edge of the desert; it was to be the scene of some of Petrie's most important discoveries. They wandered through the chief tourist attraction, the great funerary temple of the Pharaoh Sethos (Sety) I with its delicately carved reliefs; characteristically, Petrie's Journal does not wax enthusiastic about the sculpture, which he considered to be "not anything like equal to that of the Old Kingdom", but he describes with admiration subtleties of architectural design in the fluting of columns, the rounding of door jambs, the jointing of roof slabs and the way in which limestone walls which bore weight were reinforced by incorporating sandstone pillars into their thickness.

Four days becalmed, or battling against headwinds, left them irritable and frustrated; How or Hu, where one day Petrie was to make important discoveries, proved disappointing and Chenoboskion held little for them. Returning tired and hungry at twilight after a long walk through fields of maize they had dinner and then brewed coffee on their stove in the cabin as usual; Griffith had taken a good sip before he discovered that the boy had filled the kettle with paraffin instead of water.[10]

The temple of Dendara, which is Ptolemaic in date "and very wretched as to the art of it", nevertheless occupied their attention for many hours; Petrie was fascinated by the intricate details of its construction; he explored with glee the secret chambers and passages in the thickness of the walls, noting the ingenious way in which the entrance to a lower chamber was concealed by a sliding slab of stone, sculptured to make it appear part of the wall either side; it was possible that there might be other passages as yet unopened, and he resolved to come back one day to hunt for them. Quft, the ancient Coptos, was the next port of call, and here Petrie's appetite was whetted when his sharp eyes noticed, among the ruins of one of the Roman temples, a column with the cartouche of Tuthmosis III. He was to find even older remains at Koptos (in 1894) as well as in Dendara (1897). Proceeding to Shenhur, they found there a small Roman temple "almost perfect, but of wretchedly bad work, and sculptured in coarse nummulitic limestone". Here Petrie observed that it was some way below the surrounding ground level; he concluded that since the temple must have been built a couple of feet at least above the level of the inundation, the ground must since that time have risen some six or seven feet.

On reaching Thebes, they landed somewhat to the north of Qurna on the west bank of the Nile, to avoid tourists, and moved cautiously into the Valley of the Tombs of the Kings; they were fortunate to have the less-frequented western valley to themselves for the rest of the day. In those days the royal tombs were not closed by doors, and among the rubble they found "quantities of pieces of funeral woodwork (coffins, ornaments etc.) and pieces of alabaster vases". These they hid away for further study when they should return. Griffith "copied entirely" the tomb of Ay. Then they walked back, up the steep hillside and along the cliff top to the Northern Monastery, the Deir el Bahari, and thence towards the cultivated land, past the Ramesseum, back to the river, and picking up their boat, crossed over to Luxor.

As soon as they got near the shore they heard Greville Chester's voice hailing them, and saying that they were to dine with Mustafa Agha. He was the British consul, the same picturesque character who had lavishly entertained Amelia Edwards and her friends twelve years before.[11] They "dined round a vast tray, native fashion, tearing up an excellent turkey, and dipping into various dishes which came on in turn." On the following day Chester took them shopping among the dealers of Luxor; one of these, Todros (who in another capacity acted as German Consul), offered them a set of foundation deposits of Tuthmosis III—little bronze models of tools inscribed with the king's name, which had once been buried under the corners of some building in Thebes—it was useless to wonder which. Petrie considered the asking price, £25, too much, and left his friend Chester to negotiate for less. Then they dined with him in his hotel, looking briefly on their way at the Luxor temple which was still being cleared, on Maspero's orders, from the mass of houses that almost buried it. The temple of Karnak they left for their return. After dinner Petrie sat in the little cabin of the boat till the small hours of the morning, reading by candlelight the letters that had been awaiting him in Luxor, and answering some of them.

The post had brought him four eyewitness reports of the General Meeting of 8 December: from Amelia Edwards, who had promised to tell him what had passed;[12] from Petrie's father, almost illegible and full of underlinings;[13] from Spurrell, sarcastic at the Committee's expense,[14] and from Mrs Benest, whose account was the fullest and the most amusing:[15] she described young Ernest Gardner reading his report on Naucratis in an almost inaudible voice: "on the whole, one felt glad when he sat down—he seemed to stand with much difficulty and be much embarrassed by his hands and feet." Griffith's report came next and then Miss Edwards was called upon for Mr Petrie's report. "She said it was with *deep regret* that she had to announce that *for the present* your invaluable services did not belong to the Fund." She had read his report "most beautifully, with intelligence, point and expression". Mr Fowler had then voiced his deep admiration of Mr Petrie's work; the fund deeply regretted the loss of his services. Mr Newton, the Chairman, then "seemed struck by a happy thought" and launched into a short eulogy of Petrie's work, and "finished up by challenging *Mr. Poole* to second the vote of thanks. Mr. Poole struggled to his feet with something approaching a gasp, and observed that it gave him the greatest pleasure to rise. He had had a good deal to do with you and could testify to your industry and great powers of endurance (and he ought to be judge of this!) Really you had injured your health and it was a wise and most necessary arrangement that you should have comparative rest this season. Your absence, he said, was only temporary for two or three years." Finally, Poole had been elected Honorary Vice-President, and thanked for the fatigues he had undergone in the service of the Fund. Miss Edwards and Spurrell had waited in vain for one of Petrie's supporters to rise and demand to know the reasons for his resignation; no such occasion, said Spurrell, had arisen and he did not think that any of them had been there. Newton had, moreover, so skilfully arranged proceedings that nobody could, in politeness, have edged in a word. Amelia Edwards assured Petrie that she had been waiting for someone to get up and ask questions, but nobody had: "It was very strange—I cannot understand it." Now there was nothing more to be done.

Later in her letter she expressed her own nostalgia for Egypt, which she longed to see again. "I am heartsick—literally heartsick, sometimes, with the infinite yearning that one has for the palms, and the sands, and the wide rushing river. How wonderful the daybreak is—and how beautiful the commonest things are under that pure sky! I remember some white woodbine that grew by the path side, on the way to the Ramesseum, and the little white butterflies circling round the blossom—it seemed quite fairy-like there, yet here one would not even notice them."[16]

One matter to which she refers in this and subsequent letters is a task which he had undertaken for her, and with which he had occupied himself on the voyage out, and by candlelight on the river: in a rash moment, she had undertaken to translate into English her friend M. Maspero's book, *L'Archéologie égyptienne*, which was soon to appear. She had begun the task but found it took far too much of her time: to relieve her of worry, Petrie had offered to do the translation for her. By the time the boat reached Luxor his task was complete; she wrote to him of her gratitude: she could finish the second half herself, she said—"but for your great kindness, I could not have got through at all."[16] She did not think it would be tactful to incorporate the notes Petrie had made correcting the author on certain points of fact, but she would send Maspero the notes in the hope that he might like to use them as *addenda* at the end of the book: she could then translate them back for the English version. She begged him let her pay for his work, but he refused; nor would he consent to have his name on the translation, except in the unlikely event of Maspero's accepting all his emendations.[17]

Meanwhile the travellers had moved on southwards stopping briefly at Armant which they found disappointing, only seeing remains of a "Roman church" (they do not appear to have found the blocks of Ptolemaic temples scattered around the town). On the opposite bank of the Nile they tramped the desert fruitlessly for some miles before returning to the river bank; at Gebelên next day they discovered a shrine or chapel cut in the rock and copied "a good deal of a very indistinct inscription"; Griffith's skill in decipherment was proving invaluable. Griffith, for his own purposes, was collecting skulls and animal bones: "our cupboard I now call Golgotha," wrote Petrie to Spurrell.[18] At Esna he measured three Roman quays at the river's edge: "The middle quay is still perfect to the top and has two or three feet of wall above it remaining, and the doorway which closed the quay buildings." None of this now remains. They admired the great columns in the dim hall of the temple, and Petrie took a photograph by long exposure "showing more than could be seen up in the dark roof, cobwebs and all". They walked eight or nine miles out from Esna to the nearest cliff, but found no tombs or buildings there; but for Petrie the trip was after all worth while, for he picked up a palaeolith, a hand-axe "which might have come from Abbeville or Cambridgeshire by its form". It was, he noted, river-worn but lay on a hilltop between two stream beds, so that it must have been of very great antiquity—in fact, he concluded, he must be holding in his hand the oldest man-made object so far found in Egypt.

At el Kula, they saw the "barbarously mangled remains" of the small pyramid which Maspero and Naville had tried in vain to enter; it was, he noted, a sad example of how *not* to dig a pyramid. "The deeds of the Bulak Department in Egypt remind me of that blackbird in our garden who used to pick off all the finest bunches of currants, eat one, and leave the rest to rot on the ground." Five miles further on, on the west bank of the river facing el Kab, they spent some time exploring the extensive ruins of Kom el Ahmar, the Red Mound, once the city of the hawk-god, Hierakonpolis. Petrie at once realized that here was a site of the first importance, flint flakes lay about everywhere, and they filled their pockets with arrowheads and scrapers; but the greatest prize of all, a perfect lance-head—"the finest piece (but one) of flintwork that I have ever seen in Egypt" dropped out of his pocket as they walked back to the boat after dark, and next morning retracing their steps, they hunted for it in vain. Much of the pottery and stone fragments were completely strange to him; this must have been his first encounter with remains of the age of the earliest kings, and he was unable to put a date to them: "it is unlike my Delta pottery, so I am quite at a loss." In fact this site, the ancient Nekhen, was one of the most important of all the cities of Egypt in the period before dynastic history, and may have been a predynastic capital; excavations here between 1897 and 1899, carried out not by Petrie himself but by two young archaeologists[19] under his direction, were to uncover carved ceremonial mace-heads and slate palettes, the first royal monuments of the Archaic age.

Visiting the tombs cut in the cliff, they decided to copy only one of them; then, crossing the river to el Kab and the eastern bank, they walked through the great town enclosure with its massive surrounding wall; a bitterly cold wind was blowing as they passed through a gap in the rampart on the further side and walked on to examine three small temples in a bay of the hills; one of them, the little *naos* of Amenophis III Petrie considered "one of the freshest and most beautiful works I have seen of that age". Dozens of early graffiti were noted, mostly of the Old Kingdom, and also drawings of animals "which are far more weathered by the side of them, looking twice as old at least". In the tombs of the princes of el Kab on the hillside Petrie copied part of an inscription which had not before been recorded, and which gave the names of the members of the family and servants of the deceased: "I washed them down carefully, and copied 70 names, mostly with titles; they are invaluable as a collection of one period to shew what was in fashion then." Dozens of other names were noted, from tombs of the early New Kingdom—"all are curious for the dozens of relations, out to 'son of brother of mother of mother' and in one tomb the *nurse* of each child is drawn as well, with her name."

January 27th found them at Edfu, admiring the completeness and imposing size of the Ptolemaic temple of Horus; but the endless repetition of figures on every available space on the walls and columns and roof they found "wondrous and wearisome", and the execution of the sculpture "clumsy and wooden, and bare of all artistic and historic interest. . . . The immense figures of the Ptolemy on the pylon smiting his enemies are comically bad; he looks as if he were just going to topple over and could only save himself by getting a grip of the lump of enemies in front, while to add to the effect his crown is cut away and seems as if it would snap across in the middle with his majesty's lurch."

Near the village of El Hôsh, where boulders of sandstone begin to strew the river bank, Griffith and Petrie found themselves in a region of graffiti, left as mementoes of their visits by ancient travellers and quarrymen from the Middle Kingdom onwards. Clad in greatcoats and with folded blankets over their heads as a protection against the strong north wind, they spent the whole of one day copying as many as they could, reaching the "Valley of Seven Men", the main object of their search, in the late afternoon. They were there until dark, and most of the next day, copying and photographing; noting also Greek inscriptions and one Phoenician traveller's name; moreover, "all over the rocks are animals cut in all periods, but most *very* interesting, being usually far darker than the oldest graffiti. . . . These animal figures are, I believe, the oldest things in Egypt, and I wonder no one has described them before." Tracing the inscriptions up the valley, they concluded that they were following an ancient trade route which by-passed the rocky barrier of the Gebel Silsila, to which they next came; here cliffs of fine sandstone fringe the Nile and ancient quarries bite into the hills on either side (**30**); handcopies were made of accessible carvings and inscriptions left by the quarrymen in the little shrines along the west bank and Petrie studied the methods used by the ancient stonecutters wherever they overhung the river, punting the boat beneath them and climbing up from the cabin roof by ledges and handholds in the rock.

"I very specially examined all evidence for or against the theory of the bursting or breaking down of the rock barrier of the Nile here in the XIIth dynasty, which has been much named. I completely disbelieve it. No doubt such a ridge of rock has been worn through, and the Nile has fallen above this point in consequence, but I think that was more like 40,000 than 4,000 years ago."

From a little south of Kom Ombo, where they explored the temple and noted that much colour was still left on the reliefs, Petrie walked most of the way to Assuan, a distance of about twenty-five miles. It was high time they reached a town, for they had run out of lentils, eggs and bread, and were eating the hard loaves of the crew, dipped in the river. This last does not seem to have bothered them; they had become used to drinking Nile water, without boiling it, but only ensuring that their jar was filled when they were well clear of a town or village. Finally, taking their boat past Assuan, they landed their stores and pitched their tents south of the town beyond the Cataract Hotel; the boatmen were paid off and the boat dismissed. This was the end of the journey for them, and Petrie and Griffith were not sorry after all to be alone with their own two men again.

> Assuan is a strange mixture: it is approached through one of the most lovely parts of the Nile valley, thick with trees of all sorts and fertile with beautiful crops of many coloured peas. But here all is bare rock; granite below, sandstone above. Clambering over rocks, while a band plays below, seems like Tunbridge Wells or some watering place, while the crowd of redcoats reminds one of Woolwich—the steep rock paths, of Gibraltar,—the black population shews one is nearly in to the tropics,—and the rock inscriptions towering above some Greek wine shanty or facing "Thos. Cook & Son" are such as one would only find in the deserts of the Thebaid or the wilds of the eastern desert.

Suspecting that many of these inscriptions on the granite boulders had never been recorded, the two friends set about copying as many as they could find (**31**). Early every morning they would set out with a rope ladder, a basket and a roll of squeeze paper for making wet paper impressions; they would work all day, returning at dusk to their tent for an evening meal, having eaten nothing all day; every moment was precious, there was so much to record. In the main street of the village on the island of Elephantine, they were excited to find part of an Old Kingdom inscription half-buried in the roadway; on clearing it with the help of two villagers, under Muhammad's direction, they found that it was what Petrie called a "royal register", containing the names of a number of Pharaohs not previously recorded for the region, and therefore a discovery of considerable historical importance. This was not the only discovery to be made by their sharp eyes: "there is still something to do," wrote Petrie in glee, "in a place which every Egyptologist has visited."

Crossing by felucca to the west bank of the river to visit the tombs of the early nomarchs or governors of Assuan cut in the cliff facing the town, they had an unexpected encounter: Wallis Budge was there, copying one of the tomb inscriptions recently uncovered by the excavations of Sir Francis Grenfell, the Sirdar in charge of the Egyptian garrison. "He was very cordial and pleasant and having been informed by Chester of the content of that B. M. letter, at once opened the matter by assuring me that he had nothing to do with it, and did not know of it before it was sent. So I could but accept what he said."

During the second week of February they walked the wild and rocky valleys between Assuan and Shellal, finding dozens of inscriptions; some they knew had been recorded by Lepsius and his party forty-four years earlier, but to be on the safe side they copied them all. Altogether they got about eighty inscriptions from the Assuan region; they were interested again in the proper names and the family relationships recorded in these rock memorials. The inscriptions of Sehel island they omitted, assuming (incorrectly) that Mariette had recorded them all, but the island of Konosso yielded some fine examples and a rocky valley within sight of Philae provided an "enormous crop" which took them several days to finish.

The temple of Isis at Philae, in its island setting of rocks and pools and palm trees, pleased them better than the other late temples they had seen on their trip. "From the smallness of its proportions—compared with Dendara or Edfu—and the freshness of colour, it may be described as pretty." Faint praise perhaps, but the memory of the delicate reliefs at Abydos and the grandeurs of Luxor temple were still fresh in their minds. The colour, alas, was to be washed from Philae's walls and columns when the temples were drowned by the raising of the Assuan Dam. In the granite quarries to the south-east of Assuan, Petrie noted the method of cutting the stone and picked up some "hornstone hammers"—the lumps of dolerite which are everywhere to be found among the workings—and speculated by what method the smooth surface of the granite blocks might have been dressed before polishing. One of his students, in later years, was to make a thorough study of the techniques employed in cutting the great blocks used for statues, shrines and obelisks.[20]

Their work done, the two friends decided to return to Luxor where Petrie's main task awaited him. An inspection of the second-class cabins on the government steamer filled them with distaste; moreover, they wished to economize; so they decided to travel third or deck class at a fare of only six shillings. The journey took a day and a night; it was far from comfortable, for they had to share the deck with sixty conscript Egyptian soldiers and their packs, and found great difficulty in securing a corner in which to sit by day and to sleep, rolled in blankets. In spite of the miseries of their journey, Petrie and Griffith had great sympathy for their fellow-passengers:

> Poor fellows, they had been conscripted and marched up to Assuan; stationed there for 3 years, and were now hoping to see their homes once more. Often when the boat came near a man's village he would begin shouting out the names of his brothers in the hope of seeing one of them on the bank; and as we neared Esneh a boy on shore caught sight of his brother on board, and ran along beside the steamer screaming "Hassan, Hassan". Some of them were from the pyramid neighbourhood, and fraternized with our men; one was from Zagazig. All day they sat mending clothes, brushing up, reading, and overhauling their bags. I only wish that I may never have worse travelling companions. . . .

Good news awaited Petrie at Luxor, for Greville Chester told him that a considerable sum had been placed at his disposal by an anonymous donor for excavating. Miss Edwards' letter, which was awaiting him at the post office, further explained the matter. "I have come to know, through correspondence only, a very wealthy and intelligent man (merchant class) who has travelled in Egypt & is enthusiastically fond of Egyptian antiquities. The acquaintance is quite recent—since you left England—but I think from what I have learned of him in this short time that he is a sort of Sir Erasmus Wilson". At the time she wrote this, she had not already broached the subject to him: "if you like the matter, I will begin tunnelling my mines and laying my gunpowder."[21] Three days later, she wrote again: this "good and enlightened man" had said he was willing to place £300 at Petrie's immediate disposal "for the purpose of exploring the Western Valley of Biban el Moloök or *for any object that you (A.B.E.) and he may think desirable in the way of Egyptian research*. . . . I would even go so far as to make the amount £500; but I must ask my name not to be mentioned."[22] The money, she told Petrie, could be had direct from Chester, from whom the gentleman in question had acquired, through her, a very special and very costly object which he, Chester, had finally obtained after two years' bargaining, for much less than the price originally demanded. Petrie knew what this mysterious object was: Greville Chester had been for long negotiating secretly for the purchase of a throne thought to be part of the funerary furniture of Queen Hatshepsut:[23] he was about to leave Luxor hoping to smuggle his prize out of Egypt as he often did in those unscrupulous days. The anonymous benefactor, Miss Edwards said, would leave Petrie's hands quite free and had no desire to acquire ordinary antiquities such as a mummy, though he would be delighted if Petrie were to find an intact royal tomb.

Petrie's hopes were soon to be dashed; they had reckoned without M. Grébaut. The Director happened to be in Luxor at the time, and Petrie went straight to him to ask permission to dig for a week or two in Western Thebes. He was met with a blank refusal: everything in the Theban area, he was told, was reserved for the Museum. So were Saqqara and Akhmim. The English already had plenty of scope for excavation in the Delta and in Assuan; with these they must be content. In vain Petrie protested that he had now no connection with either the Egypt Exploration Fund or the British Museum; it made no difference—the refusal was definite and final. Petrie felt himself entirely blocked; he did not wish to dig in the Delta in rivalry with the Fund; Budge was in Assuan. "So I must do as I intended, survey Dahshur, and go home. The money is here, the worker is here, but—*the dog is in the manger* and has a nice warm bed in the hay, and does not want it disturbed." The situation was the more ironical since native dealers were being allowed to dig in Thebes unsupervised, provided they handed over half their finds to the Museum.

So Griffith and Petrie moved into the temple precinct and pitched their tent under the shadow of the great colonnade of the temple of Luxor. They bade farewell to Greville Chester, who was continuing on the same boat, and next day procured camels and moved their belongings to Karnak, where they camped beneath trees near one of the pylons. "Three hundred Tommy Atkinses were all marched over to see the place; drawn up in line, addressed, then dispersed for an hour's ramble over the temple, then re-formed, and marched back to their boat at Luxor with band playing."

The walls of the various temples that form the Karnak complex produced a rich harvest of heads: here were the enemies of Egypt at the height of her empire—Hittites, Syrians, Libyans, Nubians mown down by Pharaoh's chariot or held by the hair in one improbable bunch to be despatched with his scimitar. After experimenting with photography, Petrie decided it would be far more satisfactory to make wet squeezes of the carvings; a box of such paper impressions weighing only a few pounds could be brought home to England and a cast made of each separate head. This was a complete success; the squeezes were eventually waxed before a plaster cast was taken, and the photographs obtained from the casts were far clearer than if they had been made from the "stained and darkened sculptures". To reach some of the reliefs, Petrie hung from a rope ladder slung over the wall;

by hooking his left arm through the ladder he could hold the paper sheet in place, while with his other hand he beat the surface with a wetted brush.[24]

Griffith stayed for a few days, and then with some reluctance went off to join Naville at Tell el Yehudiya as he had promised. He had greatly enjoyed his two months with Flinders Petrie; as he wrote to Poole from Assuan, he would never regret having taken the trip.[25] After seeing him off by the weekly steamer, Flinders moved his tents back to Luxor and spent a few days taking impressions of the heads in the battle scenes on the outer walls of the temple; he left unrecorded the Hittite warriors on the great pylon, to reach which would have needed a twenty-foot ladder. An American missionary, the Revd Chauncey Murch, invited him to dinner; he was a keen collector of antiquities, and also a dealer—not always, it was said, a very scrupulous one[26]. Short and extremely stout, he was not at first a prepossessing figure, but Petrie found that he improved on acquaintance, and his wife was charming and intelligent.

Crossing next to the west bank, Petrie and his men camped by the Ramesseum. The second pylon of that temple had not yet been rebuilt; among the piles of overturned blocks he found some fine chariot groups of the Hittites with their long skulls (**27**). Some reliefs, on which colour still remained, Petrie photographed rather than risk damaging them. The temple of Medinet Habu also yielded some splendid examples of foreign types, in particular the Libyans (**29**) with their heads shaved but for one side-lock, and the "Peoples of the Sea" (**28**) with their curious topknots. By the time he had finished, he had between two and three hundred squeezes on double sheets of paper. He bought a number of small objects from dealers and from the swarms of persistent villagers who lived in and around the rabbit-warren of ancient tombs in the cliffs behind the temples. He wandered around the necropolis area, keeping his eyes open for likely spots for excavation, and found what he believed to be an untouched and undiscovered tomb. He could not resist taking Amelia Edwards into his confidence: the tomb, he wrote, was of the great Viceroy of Nubia, Mer-mose.[27] Several pottery cones bearing the name of this important man had been brought to him, and he made a small boy show him the heap of limestone chips whence they had come—for a row of such cones were often affixed as a frieze over the entrance to the tomb of an official, proclaiming the name and rank of the owner. "I would not let Grébaut know for a thousand pounds," he wrote gleefully. "It is evident that these cones ought to be all trucked up and mapped, as keys to unopened tombs all over the place. That would be my first step in a campaign here."

While he was working on the West Bank, the comings and goings of a constant stream of tourists afforded Petrie entertainment.

> One of the amusements of Thebes is seeing the visitors, who come here in most comical style; it is here fairly warm, but the sun is not at all overpowering, for I still go about in a black cap; but up ride tourists swathed up in all the clothes for an English spring, kid gloves, &c., and protected about their heads by pith hats, veils over them, puggerees over them, and umbrellas to shelter the whole. Their bodies are dressed for Christmas and their heads for the tropics.

Good pictures of foreign types could be found in one or two of the royal tombs; these he photographed by magnetized flash. The private tombs, though full of good examples, were less easy to record since "they are in such a state of dirt and damage that I can scarcely get anything from them. . . . There is nothing wanted now so much as careful cleaning up, but I dare not undertake such work on well known and valued paintings, for fear of a row."

At length on 6 March, his task accomplished, Petrie packed up the cones, ostraka, lead figures and other small antiquities he had bought and crossed the river again; leaving his tents and baggage on the landing stage he went to call on the Coptic dealer Todros, to make arrangements for the packing and despatch of a fine mummy which Miss Edwards had asked him to buy for a friend of hers. The mummy, complete with cartonnage and case, was not difficult to come by and cost but £20; in those days, as Amelia said, mummies were as plentiful as blackberries.

The steamer was not due to sail, he found, till late evening; the intervening hours were pleasantly spent dining in civilized comfort with Wilbour and his wife aboard the *Seven Hathors*. In contrast his accommodation aboard the Nile packet was even worse than before; no cabin was available, and Petrie and his two men were forced to share the deck space not only with soldiers but also with a contingent of condemned prisoners under guard, on their way to prison, each wearing a heavy iron collar, & linked by a heavy iron chain to his fellow. The first night it was impossible to find any space to lay his blankets on deck, but the second night he managed to grab a position on top of the paddlebox, which was somewhat public but at least big enough to stretch out on. He was glad to find that his friend A. S. Murray was on board with his wife, taking the opportunity of a visit to Greece to see a little of Egypt as well, "so nearly half my time was spent on the narrow barrier of respectability which separates the 1st from the 3rd class deck." Another passenger, a stone merchant, was about to go off on an expedition to the eastern desert to look at the porphyry quarries of the Gebel Dokhan; Petrie was sorely tempted to go with him, but decided not to disrupt his own plans.

Disembarking at Assiut, he took his boxes up to the station. Here he met with the usual difficulties: his order, signed as was necessary by Grébaut, authorized "two or three" boxes to be transported by rail. Having been able to get only smaller boxes, he had five. This presented an insuperable problem; there was nothing to be done but camp in a tent near the railway till a new permit could be obtained by telegram from Grébaut. The tedious two days' wait was alleviated by the friendly hospitality of Major King, the town's commanding officer, two of his fellow officers, and an English doctor. "Luckily I have some elements of respectability with me, though my only hat blew overboard, with a precious collar and tie inside it. How I have nursed that specimen! tying it up with a handkerchief and carrying it by hand to save it (for I never wear aught but a cap), & it was too bad for it to desert me after all." No answer came from Grébaut, so at last after much searching and bargaining two large boxes were found into which the contents of the five could be packed, and the boxes despatched to Cairo.

Flinders Petrie now continued his explorations. At Badrashên he hired a man with a donkey for four days, to carry his baggage while he walked. Crossing the river, he tramped about the desert on the eastern side noting several Roman and Arab mounds and the large brick enclosure of Atfih, which he estimated to be thirtieth dynasty or Persian; in the cliffs behind Helwan he noted the similarity between ancient and modern quarrying methods. Muhammad, home in Giza for a few days' leave, had sent his elder brother 'Abdel Wahid in his stead, "as quiet and pleasant as the rest of the family". It was some days before he told Petrie of his recent misfortunes: he and another man had been wrongly named by a slave dealer as being his accomplices, and had been kept sixty-five days in prison without trial. At length, two of the slaves were asked to identify their oppressors: they picked out the slave-dealer but denied ever having seen 'Abdel Wahid. So at last he was free, "having had all his agricultural affairs spoiled by his detention; his only fear now is that the police will come every few weeks and threaten to take him again in order to screw more out of him. Such is Egypt."

Catching an early train to Cairo, Petrie was able to breakfast with Dr Grant, meet Muhammad at the station, hand over the boxes to him to take back to his house in Giza, do some shopping and lunch with the Grants; then he walked back to the station and returned to Badrashên. Next morning early, Muhammad and another brother, Talba, met Petrie, who had come with a camel and his tent and stores, at a rendezvous in Saqqara, and together they set off over the desert towards Dahshur; they arrived at sunset and pitched the tent in a grove of trees, with a lean-to annexe "rigged up with canvas and boxes" for the men. During the next few days, in spite of rain and bitter winds, Petrie set about surveying both the great stone pyramids, noting what he considered must be the site of the temple attached to each; from the heaps of limestone chips and plentiful fragments of red and grey granite, alabaster and basalt, he concluded: "This would be a grand place to work at, perhaps a parallel to the granite temple of Gizeh. But I do not expect that Grébaut would allow me. No one has touched it; nor so far as I know noticed it before."[28] One day when the wind was too fierce for work, he went up with Muhammad to do some measuring inside the pyramids. "The chambers in the north one are open, and we scared the owls; one flew out and the other was very helpless; it would let me noggle its bill with the edge of the candlestick, and only flopped off on being stroked. Muhammad caught it to have a look at it, the plumage was lovely. Griffith would joyfully have sacrificed it to his collection, but we left it to look after its eggs in peace." In the last three days of March the wind dropped and the triangulation could be completed as far as possible; but to complete the survey he needed to excavate down to uncover the corners of the pyramid at ground level, as Maspero had allowed him to do at Giza; he had long ago written to Grébaut for permission, but no answer had come.

Meanwhile the place was far from lonely: within a day or so they had noticed the remains of two bodies, unmistakably human and unmistakably recent, not far away from their camp; the police were reluctantly summoned by the sheikh of the village, and the place soon swarmed with police and guards:

> There are fifteen men loitering, slumbering and dawdling about in a chronically thirsty state at the foot of the pyramid. I improve the opportunity by getting on with my work while there is such a

strength of respectability there, for it relieves one of the Nehemiah-like feeling produced by working with a revolver always at hand and scanning the country every few minutes to see if anyone is about. It is an ill wind that blows nobody any good, and this absurd parade over the remains of these two unlucky wights will make the place safer than it has ever been before, just now while we are here. But they *do* smell.

Not long after this there was another excitement: Petrie witnessed from afar the interception of five stolen buffaloes by the police: shots were fired, and the smugglers escaped. Two night watchmen were set to guard the camp, but to Petrie's relief they slept soundly all night, instead of keeping him awake with their talking. One night Muhammad saw a hyena creep up to the tent and sniff longingly at the guards' toes; he scared the hungry beast off—its hideous whining woke Petrie—but the guards went on snoring peacefully.

A few days were spent in surveying the desert road from Saqqara to the Fayum—not for the benefit of Cope Whitehouse but for Major Fox, the army officer in charge of the survey; the road was marked, Petrie discovered, by Roman milestones, a large tablet at each *schoenus* (four miles) and a smaller upright block at distances of a third of a mile (1,000 cubits). On 15 April, having still heard nothing from Grébaut, he went up to Cairo by an early train and went to see Col Scott-Moncrieff, who promised to see what he could do. When at last the permit came, it was almost too late, for the local men were almost all off harvesting their corn and maize; during the second week in May Petrie managed to complete the survey of the southern pyramid, but was forced to leave the northern one unfinished, since all the pavement about the corners had been destroyed and much excavation would have been needed to establish the plan.

Back in Cairo, Petrie found Naville and Griffith at the Museum, their season at Tell Yehudiya and Tukh el Karamus at an end. Naville was all apologies for an unfortunate incident which had greatly angered Petrie: during the winter, two of Naville's staff, George Cowan and Count Riamo D'Hulst, went to Cairo on the instructions of the Committee to make an inventory of the Fund's stores in the warehouse of a storekeeper named Large, with whom Petrie usually left his boxes until they were wanted. They found a number of boxes there, some labelled with the name of Petrie or Griffith; instead of leaving these alone, they foolishly opened everything, and then repacked them, filling up half-empty boxes at random. Petrie, who carefully planned his stores so that each box held a fortnight's supply of tinned foods, soups and biscuits, was furious to find, when he opened them at Dahshur, that they had been tampered with: one, carelessly packed, was soaked with citric acid from a broken bottle, some of the contents were Griffith's or Gardner's, and to add insult to injury, his tins of Huntley and Palmer's mixed biscuits—"a little luxury I do indulge in out here"—had been replaced by "a lot of the cheap and nasty rubbish to which no maker ventures to put his name". He had written a furious letter to Griffith, and another to Mr Gosselin in London,[29] and Naville had to send D'Hulst over to Dahshur to explain and apologize; Petrie, somewhat mollified, decided to leave it at that; but he came to the reluctant conclusion that it would be wiser not to accept Naville's invitation to visit Tukh el Karamus: "I think it much better to avoid all remarks or misunderstandings," he wrote home, "by keeping strictly clear of the Fund work and Fund doings."

One other matter which had caused Petrie anger and anxiety was more serious. It had been brought to his notice by Miss Edwards in a letter received in early April: Wallis Budge, she told him, had written to her telling her that rumours were "widely circulating" in Cairo that he, Petrie, the previous spring had smuggled out of Egypt seventy-five cases of antiquities from Nabesha and Defenna; Grébaut, Budge had said, was inclined to believe the accusation. What malicious person had circulated this rumour she had no idea—she was inclined to suspect Cope Whitehouse, or Emile Brugsch, or both—but she advised Petrie, when he saw Grébaut next, to clear himself of the charge; she herself would write to Maspero in Paris.[30] In her next letter she told him that on getting her letter M. Maspero had at once written to Grébaut to put the matter right; his own suspicion was that Brugsch was responsible: "he says that Brugsch always opposed any concession of antiquities and that Brugsch hates *you* and mistrusts you." Col Moncrieff, she said, was convinced of Petrie's innocence and M. Grébaut, who disliked Brugsch, would be fully aware of the situation. "I am quite elated," she wrote three weeks later, "at the results of our little row and of Maspero's intervention. It has enormously bettered your position in Egypt. It has made Grébaut agreeable and put you on a first-rate footing with Col. S. Moncrieff. . . ."[31] Fortunately she was right: in Cairo he found Grébaut most cordial. He passed Mr Wicksteed's mummy for export without asking for the case to be opened, scanned Petrie's list of the contents of his boxes and only asked to see one tablet from Naucratis; he also offered to collect for Petrie scarabs with such royal names as were missing from his collection. He invited him to his house and gave him two handsome volumes of the recent publications of the French Archaeological Mission. "Nothing could be more completely confiding, agreeable and thoroughly friendly than his manner and his actions. He plainly wished to shew that the false reports were completely set aside, and he wished to be on the best of terms with me." His failure to reply to his letters was, Petrie felt sure, due to nothing more sinister than laziness and procrastination. "What passes under him will be as much—or more—open to misrepresentation than [under] Maspero's régime." In this Petrie was unfortunately to be proved correct. Brugsch's guarded politeness gave nothing away.

It is possible that Grébaut had already become aware of the shameless way in which Wallis Budge had recently smuggled antiquities out of Egypt for the British Museum. This shocked Petrie when he heard of it. He had written to Miss Edwards from Dahshur:

> When Grébaut knows how the Bugbear [their nickname for Budge] has acted, he will be riled. That sweet 'un took 6 cases and passed them at Bulak, but left *17* others to be dealt with as military baggage, to the confoundment of his military friends. After he left, those 17 came down the Nile, and had to be sent out; one was a block of ¾ ton, and as no packing could be had for it, they had, at Assuan, boxed it in railway sleepers spiked together with 6 inch nails! This was a tough morsel for military baggage; but Major Bagnold (who told me) had it cased in canvas, painted all over and a fine formal direction painted on it, and so it *went.*[32]

After the usual difficulties with the railway—caused, as he was assured, by his refusal to give the expected *bakhshish*—Petrie's sixteen boxes of antiquities and squeezes were safely brought to Alexandria and on 27 May or thereabouts he was off on a slow boat for Liverpool. Griffith stayed in Egypt; he had decided to take Petrie's advice and return to Assiut with a telescope and a ladder, to copy the inscriptions in the tombs at Deir Rifa.

CHAPTER VI

Pyramids and Portraits
(1887–9)

THE IDENTITY OF Flinders Petrie's prospective benefactor was made known to him by Miss Edwards before he came home: he was Jesse Haworth, a wealthy Manchester businessman who had once visited Egypt, *A Thousand Miles up the Nile* in his hand, and had become enamoured of the country and its antiquities. Though he had no wish to form a collection himself, he intended to present the Hatshepsut furniture, and some gaming pieces from the same source, to the British Museum after they had been exhibited in Manchester. His money would be put at Petrie's disposal without any reservation, to do as he liked with it in the cause of science. "He is a religious man, and if you could throw any light on the Bible as at Tahpanhes, he would be gratified. But he does not want plunder and he wishes to keep quite out of sight, and not be mentioned in any way."[1]

She herself had another plan for Petrie: she hoped he might be considered for a position in the Cairo Museum, perhaps as Brugsch's successor. She had had some correspondence about this with General Grenfell, the Sirdar (Commander-in-Chief) of the Egyptian army, and he had seemed "much taken" with her suggestion and had promised to do what he could. The possibility had already been suggested to Petrie in Cairo, but he felt he could only accept if Brugsch were gone, and if he were given considerable freedom of action in minor matters. If the English were to take over the administration he would be happy to be Director of Excavations, but he would be reluctant to accept a purely administrative post; "I hate officialism and all pertaining to it . . . all I want is liberty to work where, when and how I like, means to work with, and no interference of anyone else in my business nor in the distribution of my finds: that is my ideal." The laborious task ahead, of transferring the whole contents of the Museum from Bulak to its destined home in a derelict palace in Giza, he would detest above all.[2]

He arrived home on 9 June, to find the corrected proofs of his book on Nabesha and Defenna still not sent to the printer; important changes had been made in the draft without consulting him, and a whole chapter omitted; manuscript and proofs lay forgotten in drawers at the British Museum; there seemed to be no prospect of Poole or Newton giving up their management of the Fund. The antiquities Petrie had brought home were divided; about a third, including the scarabs and most of the weights, he kept for his own collection, a third he divided, at cost price, between Miss Edwards and his other friends; the rest he sold at Sotheby's at about double the purchase price, thus covering his expenses. In two months he completed the proofs of *Tanis II* and prepared text and plates for the report of his Nile journey, which he intended to publish as a volume the same size as the Fund's Excavation Memoirs, but with a red spine to distinguish it from the black of the Memoirs. The final plates were not ready for the printers until a few days before he left England in December. It took until mid-August to finish making plaster casts of all his squeezes (**22**). Then they had to be photographed; the resulting publication took the form of a box folder with 190 photographs, of which a very limited edition was issued[3]. He allowed himself little rest, and at times suffered from stomach pains. In August he went up to Manchester for a meeting of the British Association, at which his photographs and casts were displayed; he took the opportunity to meet the Haworths, whom he found to be genial hosts; he stayed with them two nights at the Grange, Altrincham, before moving to old friends, the Dodgsons. Meanwhile, a chance introduction in London had found him another financial backer, a businessman named Martyn Kennard who unlike Mr Haworth was an avid collector, and was prepared to contribute to Petrie's enterprises on the understanding that a proportion of the antiquities brought home would be his.

There remained the choice of a site for the coming season. Before he left Cairo in May he had obtained the assurance of Col Scott-Moncrieff that he would receive special consideration when it came to making an application for a permit to dig; his list of priorities then had been headed by the pyramid field of Meydum (already a happy hunting ground for illicit diggers); Abydos, with a chance of finding "the early temple" came next; then Ahnas el Medineh, an imposing heap of ruins near the entrance to the Fayum, known to cover the ancient city of Herakleiopolis: this site Maspero had urged the Fund to dig and Naville was known to be interested in it (though his immediate intention was to continue at Bubastis). So also, Petrie had heard, was Cope Whitehouse, and it was in order to prevent either of them wrecking what promised to be a site of great historical interest that he put Ahnas high on his list of preferences. Dahshur he longed to continue investigating, but felt fairly certain it would be denied him by Grébaut; but Illahun and Hawara, the probable site of the Labyrinth, were other tempting possibilities.

He wrote to Miss Edwards for advice; her answer was long and carefully considered: Ahnas would indeed be a prize but Naville would have to be consulted and it was unlikely that he would yield it up without protest. He was, "so amiable, gentlemanly and courteous, that I am particularly anxious he should not feel hurt"; but if Naville did not want it himself, he would certainly prefer Petrie to dig there rather than Cope Whitehouse.[4] She had still not given up hope of luring him back into the Fund; in September she urged him once more to reconsider his attitude: they would shortly be asking him back—Mr Poole was very unwell, he must soon resign. Petrie's answer, written as he said "with all full and constant friendship", made it clear that it was not merely the attitude of Poole and Newton that he found impossible, but the incompetent and—yes—dishonest way in which matters were run by the Committee: "fudge" was the word he used for the papering over of mistakes and the misapplication of funds[5]. After that letter, she made no more attempts to lure him back. She was deeply grieved, for her loyalties were hopelessly divided.

> If Mr. Poole were not really a dear friend, & if I was not sincerely attached to Mrs. Poole & the children, I should do all you point out without hesitation—namely write round to the Committee & expose all the shortcomings of the executive. But I confess I cannot bring myself to this heroic sacrifice of the friendship of a family . . . with whom I enjoy such close & delightful intercourse whenever I am in London. . . . I am getting on towards the evening of life—I cannot take new people into my heart—and I cling to the few—the very few—friends I have. This is a very selfish way of putting it—but it is the truth[6].

In October Petrie found time to visit her in Westbury-on-Trym, as she had long been urging him to do, for she longed to show him her collection of Egyptian *antikas*, particularly her scarabs. He stayed one night, looked them over carefully and gave her advice about mounting her treasures.

Petrie wrote to Grébaut early in October for permission to dig, but received no answer. After a month, unable to book a passage or purchase stores, he cabled Scott-Moncrieff, and received the reply "Nothing settled". A friendly letter followed: M. Grébaut was on leave; before he went he had got a new law passed stopping all private excavations. Nevertheless Moncrieff advised Petrie to come, confident that he could put matters right—"I have got a Museum committee organised," he wrote, "that will, I hope, exercise a good effect."[7] It turned out that Grébaut had lost Petrie's letter in France —"he seems to lose three for every one he gets"—and that he was willing to make an exception to the law in Petrie's case and grant him a permit for both Illahun and Hawara.

This settled the matter, and Petrie made his last preparations and did his last-minute shopping: Fronts, 5 @ 5½d; 6 socks 12/-; 6 shirts £12.11.0; 2 scarves 2/-; 2 caps 2/-; 6 towels 2/4½; 9½ yards calico for Muhammed 8/6 and (expensive but necessary item) insect powder 4/-. On the morning of 5 December he wrote his paper for the British Association, before packing his bags and setting off for Liverpool by a late-afternoon train.

His boat left from Liverpool in a gale, which did not abate for several days; after the misery of the Atlantic, he enjoyed a few days in Algiers and Malta before crossing on a calm sea to Egypt. At church in Cairo on Christmas Day he saw many of his English friends; Cope Whitehouse was affable, talked at length about his own intentions to excavate, and tried in vain to pump him about his plans. Grébaut, once he could be found, was affable and put no obstacle in the way of his working: the Fayum, he said, needed protection from illicit diggers and he then and there appointed Petrie an accredited agent of the Museum—at which Brugsch barely concealed his disapproval. News of Petrie's arrival spread by the grapevine, and Muhammad turned up; Petrie bought stores and a small tent, and despatched his baggage in advance. That evening, his last in Cairo, Dr Grant held one of his soirées; Griffith and D'Hulst turned up, Grébaut and Greville Chester were there, and Petrie met for the first time an elderly Norwegian Egyptologist named Lieblein, "a quiet and very pleasant, unassuming man". And he had the pleasure of denying, in public, Cope Whitehouse's reiterated accusation that Naville or Jaillon had forged the Roman milestone at Tell el Maskhuta.

Next morning he was off early to the Fayum with Muhammad and his little cousin Omar. The railway terminus at Medinet el Fayum is not far from the site of the ancient capital of the nome, Arsinoë or

Crocodilopolis; having in the afternoon prospected the site and determined the location of the temple, he returned to the station and pitched his tent nearby. Next morning early he was visited by Murad Pasha, the *mudir* (district governor), a "fine-looking elderly man", well-liked in the province; later he met the Inspector of Irrigation Mr Hewart, whose kindness and occasional companionship were to lighten Petrie's burden during the next two years.

Moving his camp to the further side of the mound about a mile and a half from the town, by a water mill near the canal, he began taking on men and work started. He did not expect to find much, for the temple site was nearly all under cultivation; the excavation was to be a practice exercise for his later work at Hawara. Lazy workers were summarily dismissed, and the best trained for delicate work to come.

By 14 January he had finished all that he wanted to do: the pylon had yielded no inscriptions, the temple not a single stone *in situ* and no foundation deposits. He was not sorry to leave the place, for digging in clouds of foul-smelling *sebakh* dust from ancient rubbish heaps had not been pleasant and his quarters were too cramped for comfort.

> I dare say many folks think it is a very pleasant and easy sort of life in a tent; and so it would be if room was unlimited. Imagine an ordinary bedstead 6½ ft. long, & a space for—say—one's bed and nothing else. But besides bed, I have 9 boxes in it; stores of all kinds, basin, cooking stove and crockery, tripod stand (serving as a clothes stand) bag and portmanteau, and some *antikas*; and in this I have to live, to sleep, to wash & to receive visitors. The consequence is that if by any chance merely a few things get out of place, the whole affair seems choked, and it is only by rigorously shoving everything out of the way the moment it is done with, that I can get on at all.

When Miss Edwards read this, she wrote offering to send him her own camping tent; he thanked her but refused on the grounds that such a tent would be too heavy and cumbersome to transport and erect; that round tents with a central pole were not well adapted to accommodate piles of boxes; and thirdly, "I am so much happier in a square hole than in a round one, that I would sooner join up two square tents than live in a round one. The sense of direction is to me a great deal, and I feel almost as much at a loss when I do not know how everthing stands around me as I do in the dark."[8]

Flinders Petrie's next objective was four miles away in the village of Biahmu. Here there were the remains of two stone platforms side by side, which Lepsius had taken to be the twin pyramids which Herodotus says that he saw in the middle of Lake Moeris, surmounted by statues of the king who created the lake.[9] This Petrie had always doubted: pyramids were not built to support statues; in his book *The Pyramids and Temples of Gizeh* he had suggested sloping parapets surrounding open courts as a possible explanation. He determined to find out.

> The first day I saw much red granite, & sandstone about, besides fine limestone chips. So I took samples of the stones in my hands & showed them round to all the people, telling them to set aside every bit of such stones. As they knew that meant bakhshish they all looked out diligently, & I had to reject pounds' weight of useless scraps. But a piece of red granite was found with delicate low relief panelling on it; & as I was watching an old man dunce of a fellow cutting down some stuff I caught sight of a cartouche, & jumping down, read off the name of Amenemhat III, the king of Lake Moeris, & therefore the very person to whom Herodotus assigns these buildings. This was a splendid result so soon in our work here.

Better was to follow on the afternoon of the second day:

> As I was just strolling over to the fellow building, which we had not begun on yet, I saw two boys lugging a stone over to show me, and it glittered in the sunshine, the polish was so bright. They laid it down, and I puzzled what it was: could it be the paw of a sphinx, battered about? No, it was the *nose* of the colossus. This then was the thing that was most wanted, to prove that these were the thrones of colossi, & not pyramids. The very piece which clinched the matter. Here was a nose all but a foot wide; and hence there must have been a statue about eight times lifesize, or about 36 feet high, seated. And what work! The rough-grained sandstone was polished until after all these ages it still reflected like glass. I have never seen such polish on any sandstone before. That the colossi were seated on piles of masonry we found the evidence of by the multitude of pieces of the fellow colossus in the ground all around the central pile. Some of these pieces bore large hieroglyphs, finely cut. Once given the king's name and the colossi, & the history and meaning of these so-called pyramids of Biahmu is now settled.

Herodotus was vindicated; his "pyramids" were statue bases, magnified in size by being seen over the shallow waters of the inundation. Lieblein, visiting the excavations with a party of friends the next day, was able to share in the excitement of the discovery.

At the end of the week, his excavations at Biahmu at an end, Petrie moved his camp with fifty-two men and boys to Hawara, a distance of only four miles as the crow flies, but double that distance because a canal had to be crossed by the only bridge. The canal ran close to the great mudbrick pyramid of Hawara which was their destination; the men built shelters with loose bricks against the canal bank to keep the wind off their sleeping quarters. "They seem to like it very well, and there is a constant tootling of pipes, singing, clapping, shouting and general jollity going on."

Work began at once on clearing the loose brickwork round the pyramid in the hope of finding the entrance, and digging trial holes on the southern side where a jumble of brick rubble, pieces of columns and scraps of inscribed architrave showed where a huge monumental building had once stood. A surprise rewarded Petrie on the north side: here, he found, there had been a huge cemetery of Roman date, with brick tomb chambers still containing the bodies of their owners. Disappointed at first with the late date of these burials—he had hoped for Middle Kingdom tombs contemporary with the pyramid—on the second day he was about to move his men elsewhere when a mummy was found on whose face, on a wooden panel, was a painted portrait, "a beautifully drawn head of a girl, in soft grey tints, entirely classical in its style and mode". This exciting discovery luckily coincided with the arrival from Cairo of Martyn Kennard equipped with tents, an English manservant, a dragoman, a cook, two donkey boys and two hangers-on, to watch the progress of the work towards which he had contributed. He was enthusiastic and determined to stay a week at least. (Petrie, forewarned of his coming, had just time to build a makeshift plank bridge over the canal near the camp.)

Then another portrait was found, this time of "a young married woman of about 25; of a sweet but dignified expression, with beautiful features and a fine complexion. She wears pearl earrings and a gold necklace." As her mummy was not well preserved, he retained only her skull, realizing the importance, to anthropologists as well as to art historians, of being able to match the portrait with the actual cranial measurements of the subject. From then on, three or four of these portraits were found every week, and sometimes more than one in a single day. The value of the discovery was evident to Kennard as well as Petrie, for very few such paintings had ever been found before—the

British Museum had but a couple—and they fetched high prices on the market. Altogether sixty were found in this cemetery, "some much decayed and worthless, others as fresh as the day they were painted". Their importance for the history of ancient painting was immense. Their immediate, on-the-spot preservation caused Petrie much anxiety; in the end he found that the careful application of a fresh coating of beeswax—or even in some cases, gently melting the original wax surface with a lighted candle—was enough to bring up the colours fresh and clean (**32**). On those flaking portraits which did not respond to this treatment he used rice water to apply a thin sheet of paper to the surface.

So many mummies had now turned up that he had had to build a special store to shelter them from the rain. He was kept very busy. "Time passes very quickly here. I have to saw up and make all the boxes for my mummies. I wash out all the embroidered clothes, besides copying and drawing the big sarcophagus as I may have to leave it at Bulak. Generally, when I am not after the men, they are after me. Sometimes 5 at once claim me, in different directions. Altogether, the *rag and bone* business—as cemetery work may be called—keeps one employed." Mr Hewat's offer to house the precious boxes was gratefully accepted. News of the find spread to Cairo, and more visitors started to arrive. Lieblein, arriving with his son, was occupied by texts painted on a great sarcophagus; Griffith had already been sent a copy of these and had pronounced them to be late, but of unusual interest, being full of information on the geography and administration of the Moeris district. The British consul at Alexandria came with Hewat and Professor Sayce, the latter particularly excited by the quantity of fragments of demotic and Greek papyri, mostly letters and accounts, which were turning up in the cemetery. While they were walking round "a whole pitfull of Roman period mummies were turned out, all with gay gilt & painted face coverings, but so crushed and cracked up that very little could be preserved. They were—strange to say—all stacked on end in the top of a filled-up square rock well, some feet uppermost, apparently jammed in anyhow to get them out of the way. From the way in which two or three mummies are found in one grave often, I had suspected that the mummies—especially those with portraits—were kept above ground in the house, for perhaps years, and then finally interred. A large number found thus jammed in a hole confirms this view. No thieves would have taken them out of tombs to rebury them, and they were not broken open to rifle them. They must have been a household of mummies cleared out some day, & sent over to the cemetery by an undertaker. There the first convenient tomb well, standing partly empty, was utilized, & all the family thrust in; 'No room for all the shoulders above,' cries the mate. 'Then turn some upside down,' replies the undertaker. And thus we found them in all their finery."

The personalities behind the portraits intrigued him; a young lady he describes as "tolerably good looking, and evidently thought herself more so"; a rather plain young man "looks as if he would have made a very conscientious hard-working curate, with a tendency to pulpit hysterics".

Many small objects of interest and value were found with the mummies: small glass vessels, part of a white kid slipper, a set of leather-workers' tools tied in a bundle; dolls and children's toys, and a great number of coins, some of which enabled Petrie to assign approximate dates to the burials.

Meanwhile work on the site south of the pyramid had come to an end. Clearing away the ruins of the brick houses that Lepsius had wrongly taken to be the remains of the Labyrinth, Petrie had made soundings over a large area in every direction, and had found nothing but thick layers of stone chips and below them, a smooth bed of plaster in which pavements had once been laid. No trace of walls had been left by those who had robbed the site of limestone for the kilns, and of granite for the railway embankment more recently. Petrie calculated that they must have stretched for a thousand feet by eight hundred feet at least: "On that space could be erected . . . all of the temples on the east of Thebes and one of the largest on the west bank." Classical authors had described the enormous extent of the ancient labyrinth: its buildings, said Herodotus, exceeded in vastness all of the temples of the Greeks put together, and even surpassed the pyramids. Petrie's tentative reconstruction of the plan owed something to his imagination, and much to the vague descriptions of halls and courts in the works of Diodorus, Pliny, and Strabo.[10] Some scholars have recently disputed whether the Labyrinth was indeed a palace, or a huge mortuary temple, and indeed whether Petrie was excavating one building, or a complex of different structures.[11] Whatever it had been, within the limited resources at his disposal he could do no more.

The pyramid was another matter; he was determined to find the burial chamber in the heart of it. Since no trace of an entrance was visible on the north side, he decided to tunnel straight through the brick core.

> This work was very troublesome, as the large bricks were laid in sand, and rather widely spaced; hence as soon as any were removed, the sand was liable to pour out of the joints, and to loosen all the surrounding parts. The removal of each brick was therefore done as quietly as possible, and I had to go in three times a day and insert more roofing boards, a matter which needed more skill and care than a native workman would use.

But this was the sort of work Petrie really enjoyed: the Roman tombs were all very well, they meant *bakhshish* and excitement for the workmen, and would "make both ends meet or rather overlap", but the possibility, however remote, of finding a royal burial at the unknown heart of a pyramid was the quintessence of exploration.

The preservation of his finds occupied Petrie every evening. The textiles in particular needed careful treatment. "A bag full of bits of embroidered cloth comes in; and if I can clean ten pieces in an hour I have done well. Each bit requires soaking, soaping very carefully, rubbing it between the palms of the hands, and then many rinsings. In this way I clean pieces which are half rotten and all in a tattered state."

One day a great prize came to light: under the head of a nameless woman buried in plain ground, a thick scroll of papyrus had been placed. It was partially destroyed, but without being able to unroll much of what remained, Petrie could read, in beautiful Greek uncials, the words "Agamennon", "Achaeans", "Corinth", and the numbers twelve and eighty; he realized that this must be a manuscript of Homer, perhaps part of the Catalogue of Ships. When Sayce came next time, he confirmed that this was indeed part of the second book of the *Iliad*; as he hoped, Sayce was later asked to write the commentary in Petrie's publication, and at his request the manuscript was presented by Mr Haworth to the Ashmolean Museum in Oxford.

Petrie's tent was now surrounded by headless bodies, for he had given up the attempt to preserve the mummies complete with their portraits, taking only the heads, except in very few cases where the painted and gilt cartonnage (**33**) was worth keeping. Familiarity breeds contempt, and in these grisly surroundings the little boy Omar, sitting on a couple of mummies for a bench, "plays at counters with the gilt buttons from mummy wrappings on the top of a coffin".

March brought the *khamasîn*, the fierce dusty wind from the desert; the temperature soared to the nineties, then topped a hundred. To walk the sixteen miles to Medinet el Fayum and back for the weekly wages-bag, he started off at four in the morning on Sundays, dropped in on Hewat for breakfast, and was back by half-past ten, before the worst of the heat. Even in the comparative cool of the skullery it was over ninety. He went over to Tell Gurob to prospect: "It was a day which reduced all dogmas about drinking boiled water to mere philosophic abstractions, which had no point of contact with the realities of life. A day when one thought not of glasses, or jugs, or pails of water, but of nothing short of canals and rivers, and when a whole lake might have barely satisfied the imagination. Happily the Bahr Yusuf is about as respectable a source of water as the Nile, and it was at hand all day." He was rewarded by what he found at Gurob: the mounds marking the town and cemetery were strewn with pottery, and much of it was similar to what he had seen in Tell el 'Amarna the previous winter. "This alone is a valuable result as it carries the styles of that pottery down to middle Egypt, and shews that they belonged to that period, and not to a place only." This, he resolved, was where he would work next year. By the end of the month the temperature had soared to 106°—"it seemed as if the world had caught fire"—and Petrie found himself dealing with cases of heatstroke among the workmen; he himself was suffering from the effects of dust in the pyramid, which irritated the membranes in his nose and made them bleed. It was cooler in the tunnel, but that had two disadvantages: "it is too narrow now to do anything in but sit still, and it swarms with fleas from the workmen so that I have to sit with a big pot of insect powder open at hand to rub in continually." They were near the centre of the pyramid now, the rock floor started to slope downwards; they came to a solid brick wall, and turned to the west, following it. Petrie felt he must be very near the burial chamber: he set three men to work in round-the-clock shifts, "with great consumption of candles", and promised ten shillings to the first one who came upon masonry.

April 3rd was a red-letter day. It had got cooler. Early in the morning a note came over by messenger; Petrie was to have visitors. Soon they arrived: Heinrich Schliemann himself, "short, round-headed, round-faced, round-hatted, great round goggle-eyed, spectacled, cheeriest of beings; dogmatic, but always ready for facts." With him were Rudolf Virchow, a "calm, sweetfaced man with a beautiful grey beard", who had excavated with him at Troy, and Schweinfurth, "a bronzed bony fellow of uncertain age, an infatuated botanist", who was delighted with the large boxful Petrie showed him of wreaths of red roses and other flowers from the tombs, which he intended to bring home for identification. He was also "incredulously pleased" that Petrie could put a date to any potsherd he picked up; he assured

Petrie that "it was very important to know the age of pottery—it was the key to archaeology, and so on, and he hoped I would make a collection of pieces to show as types; I replied that I had not only collected pieces but I had taken home collections of perfect examples all dated, and the British Museum practically rejected them. He howled at their folly and assured me that Allemand would be only too thankful in Berlin to receive my dated collection of pottery." Schliemann, who was very excited about the *Iliad* papyrus, also showed interest in the pottery,—since coming to Egypt he had made a collection for his museum of some 300 pots bought from dealers[12] —but he appears to have concealed a degree of scepticism about Petrie's dating, for when he and Virchow visited Tell Basta four days later, he expressed himself, according to Naville, "in the strongest terms on the utter impossibility of establishing anything like a chronology of Egyptian pottery". (Naville, gleefully reporting this conversation to Poole in a letter the next day, commented: "I should have liked Griffith to hear him.")[13] As for Virchow, he was delighted with the skulls and asked Petrie to keep fifty at least for him.[14]

Over lunch they talked about England's involvement in Egypt, and the iniquities of the latest Liberal Government. "Schliemann says it is a shame & disgrace to Englishmen that they have not hung Gladstone long ago. Bravo!" wrote Petrie to Amelia Edwards in his next letter.

"Then a report of another mummy, and by the time they have lunched a procession of three gilt mummies is seen coming across the mounds glittering in the sun." One of them was a great prize: the case is still one of the finest in the British Museum, to which Martyn Kennard presented it. The portrait is a speaking likeness, a young man in a wreath of olives; the red plaster mummy case is adorned with scenes of Egyptian mythology in gilt relief; across his breast are the words "O Artemidorus, farewell" (**34**).

The three visitors went away impressed; had they stayed another half-hour, they would have seen one more notable discovery: part of an ivory casket was brought in, with a cover decorated with incised figures; a pair of woollen socks with a separately knitted piece for the big toe to allow for the sandal strap; patterned clothing, sandals, papyrus and a pretty glass flask. These were only some of the things found in one busy day.

Next day there was fresh excitement: the men in the pyramid tunnel came to the springing of a brick arch, and soon after midnight on the following night one of the boys came running: "the stone has appeared! the room is here!" The stone proved to be one of the

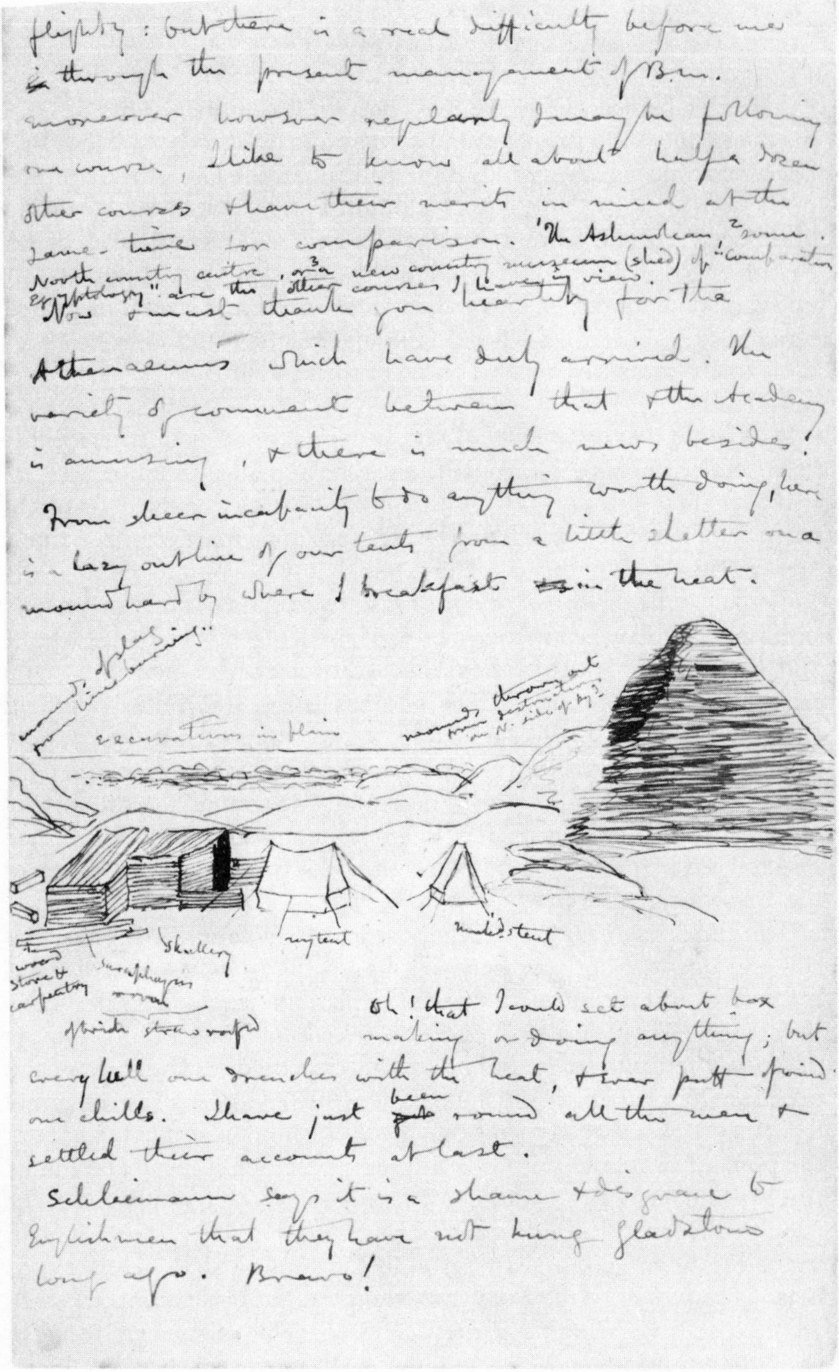
flighty: but there is a real difficulty before me in through the present management of B.M. moreover howsoever regularly I may be following one course, I like to know all about half a dozen other courses & have their merits in mind at the same time for comparison. '1 The Ashmolean, 2 some North country centre, or 3 a new country museum (shed) of "Comparative Egyptology" are the other courses I have in view. Now I must thank you heartily for the Athenaeums which have duly arrived. The variety of comment between that & the Academy is amusing, & there is much news besides! From sheer incapacity to do anything worth doing, here is a lazy outline of our tents from a little shelter on a mound hard by where I breakfast in the heat.

Oh! that I could set about box making or doing anything; but every walk one drenches with the heat, & every puff of wind one chills. I have just been round all the men & settled their accounts at last.

Schliemann says it is a shame & disgrace to Englishmen that they have not hung Gladstone long ago. Bravo!

B. *A page from one of Petrie's letters to Miss Edwards*: from Hawara in April 1888. He discusses his possible future career '(1) The Ashmolean, (2) some North Country centre or (3) a new country museum (shed) of "Comparative Egyptology" '; he complains of the intense heat and quotes Schliemann on Gladstone.

vaulting slabs above the roof of the burial chamber. This posed a problem. In the pyramid of Pepy I at Saqqara there had been three layers of stone vaulting, in all about fifteen feet thick—far too much to tunnel through; the only hope, thought Petrie, would be to find the joint between the sloping roof slabs and the vertical wall of the chamber; but he soon discovered that the side walls were built directly up against the solid rock into which the chamber had been sunk. There remained the end walls, where in the angle of the vaulting stones, they were likely to be thinner. So on went the tunnel, along the length of the chamber.

A severe cold kept Petrie miserably in bed for a day or so; he had to leave Muhammad to distribute to the men a small amount on account towards their weekly pay, which could not be collected from the bank. When he felt a little better, he started some men digging in a new area north-west of the cemetery which turned out to be an early Ptolemaic village; some of the houses (of which he unfortunately published no plans) contained a litter of small objects, many little pots, and "a vast number of little bags of sawdust tied up", some with a faint resinous aroma—scent satchels perhaps? suggested Petrie. Perhaps the inhabitants of the village had lived by selling such trifles to those who came to visit the tombs. And on the north-east of the cemetery, during the last week, a crocodile necropolis was found: the animals "of all sizes from monsters 15 feet long, to infants and even eggs," had been buried by priests of Sobek in vaults, for the pious worshippers of the crocodile god.

The time was near when he must leave Hawara: his money was running out, the hot weather was approaching, and he had an intermittent fever. Having still a stock of citric acid, he slaked his perpetual thirst with lemonade and struggled on. Making boxes occupied more time than he could spare, but he had his own theories about them and no carpenter could have satisfied his demands. Almost all the mummy cemetery was now clear, but one more splendid example turned up, the portrait bordered with gilt and semi-precious stones. The tunnel reached the end of the wall and turned—alas, the end proved to be even thicker than the side walls. The only thing left, Petrie decided, was after all to sink a shaft through the roofing slabs. He set four masons to work, two by day and two by night under contract: they were to receive a bonus if they cut two cubic metres or more in twenty-four hours; in this way he was confident that they would get through before the end of April, when he had determined to leave. But after a few days' work the men had got nowhere, and it became obvious that the final penetration of the pyramid of Hawara would have to wait till next season.

The last days were occupied with the final survey, the packing of boxes, burying spare timber and surplus stores, and walling up the pyramid tunnel. On the last page of his Journal Petrie wrote: "And now my friends, don't abuse me too heartily for deserting a pyramid in an interesting condition, and exchanging May work for November. Wait till *you* have had a week at 109°." In Cairo, chafing at delay, Petrie had to wait two days for the boxes to arrive and two more for Grébaut. There was a heavy rainstorm and his precious boxes were left standing in the courtyard of the Bulaq Museum in a pool of water. For this "hideous misfortune" Petrie blamed the Museum officials: he wrote an official letter of complaint to Scott-Moncrieff, pointing out that the sum charged for sealing the cases alone would have been sufficient to provide a shelter. To unpack everything was impossible: all that could be done was to raise the boxes on boards and hope that they would dry out slowly. When it came to the division, Grébaut went out of his way to be polite and co-operative; he chose for the Museum, to Petrie's disappointment, a dozen of the finest portraits, but this was less than a third of the whole; he also took the great painted sarcophagus, a complete duplicate set of the finest embroideries, and most of the glass vessels; but he left Petrie all the papyri including the *Iliad* roll, and a unique cut-glass vase; all the plant remains, and almost all the small objects, toys and clothing and the Biahmu fragments. On the whole, it was a satisfactory division, and Petrie wrote to *The Egyptian Gazette* pointing out how much the Museum had benefited from allowing him to dig.

Meanwhile in England, Martyn Kennard eagerly awaited his treasures. In order to exhibit the portraits as befitted their unique interest and spectacular appeal, he had hired for two months a large hall in that most apt of exhibition centres, the Egyptian Hall in Piccadilly, with its façade covered in hieroglyphs and decorated in the style of a Pharaonic temple. The room in which Petrie's discoveries were to be shown was the same in which Belzoni, sixty-seven years before, had displayed his replica of the tomb of Sety I—one very old man could remember the event. Petrie reached Liverpool on the last day of May, and having next morning passed his boxes through customs, deposited them in Piccadilly that afternoon. There was no time to take even a day's holiday: Riley, Spurrell and Griffith all helped him unpack, and he set to work arranging his antiquities on tables, writing labels and preparing the catalogue as he went along. His father had already, at his request, ordered wooden frames for forty of the best portraits; these duly arrived, and Petrie mounted and framed each picture. Each evening he came home late, exhausted but jubilant: his portraits had not suffered from their soaking, and even the textiles appeared unaffected. Sundays, as ever, he devoted to his parents: dutifully he still went with his mother to church in Bromley in the morning, and with his father to the meeting of the Brethren in the evening.

On Monday 18 June the exhibition opened. The portraits caused a sensation in the Press, and London flocked to see them. Petrie was in the hall every day; when he was not taking people round, he took the opportunity to unroll another papyrus, or draw some of the small objects for his publication. Jesse Haworth came up to see the exhibition; he and Martyn Kennard and Petrie agreed on an equitable division of the antiquities: they were henceforward to operate as a syndicate, each taking a third of what Petrie brought home. After the exhibition closed, Kennard presented Artemidorus and various other outstanding pieces from his share to the British Museum, while the Manchester Museum was the ultimate recipient of most of Jesse Haworth's. One or two of Petrie's choicest portraits were taken by Sir Frederick Burton, the Director of the National Gallery, for the national collection; there was particular interest among painters, and Petrie got to know some of them, in particular Alma Tadema, Edward Poynter and Holman Hunt; after two weeks of hard work dismantling, sorting and packing at the close of the exhibition, the entry for 31 July in his diary reads: "Finished packing: all out by six. Dined Holman Hunts."

During August he spent a few pleasant days in Oxford, staying with Sayce and mounting the papyri destined for the Ashmolean Museum. He managed to snatch a couple of weekends with his cousins the Harveys at Milford, spent two days with the Haworths, and then went on to Manchester: in his suitcase were boxes of textiles from Hawara which Miss Edwards' friend, Miss Kate Bradbury, had promised to treat and clean for him; these he took over to Riversvale, her home in Ashton under Lyne, where he dined with the family. For the rest of August and September he was at home most of the time writing his report on the season's work and completing a book on scarabs he had long been compiling. He finished the latter on 20 October and delivered it to the printer the same day.[15]

Two days later Petrie was off for his second winter in the Fayum. At Marseilles he was able to spend a pleasant morning in the museum of the Château Borély, where he saw the collection of Egyptian antiquities made by the surgeon and antiquary Clot Bey, before going aboard his Messageries boat. A calm voyage was made even more pleasant by the company of Sir Charles Cookson of Alexandria, "as amiable, as mild, and as literary as ever". He had been acting consul at the time of the 'Arabi riots and had narrowly escaped death at the hands of the mob. Most of the other passengers were French, "good little boys reading their Télémaque, naughty papas with yellow covered novels, and discreet mamas with more orthologic literature." One lady in particular fascinated him by her outline as she lay in an easy chair on deck: "on her back of course, for any other position would imperil the whole fabric too much, as the natural strength of material would scarcely bear the strain of a less stable position. On this support her nose—with its appendant head—is first to be discerned for certain, and then there rises her person wave after wave in incomprehensible exuberances to a vast altitude, which at last gently declines toward the feet. Between her knees reposes her little white dog, like some peaceful hamlet with its white walls nestling in the ravine of some great mountainside."

At Dr Grant's he was welcome as ever. The poor man had suffered during the summer the loss of many of his antiquities by burglary; a house boy had set fire to the drawing-room and stolen cash and about £100 worth of gold objects from his collection. Petrie had a present for him: a coin cabinet which he had made himself. He was furious to learn that Grébaut had given an Arab dealer, Farag, permission to dig at Hawara during the summer; according to Muhammad, he had found four or five portraits and a number of gilt masks. The unique painted sarcophagus, which Petrie had spent so long preserving, had been left on the verandah at Bulaq exposed to sun and damp—"exactly the way to ruin it." (It eventually disappeared from the Museum; when Petrie enquired, he was told it had dropped to pieces.)

Back in Medinet el Fayum, Hewat again allowed him to dump his baggage, and put him up for the night. He was planning a visit to the further side of the lake (Birket Karun) and suggested that Petrie should accompany him; they crossed the lake in the curious shallow, high-prowed boats of the region, rowed by four men perched high, two to an oar. "They roll to a touch, and seem always to be going over, but never go." On the further side they pitched a tent on an island, and then climbed up to Dimay, the site of the ruined city of Soknopaiou Nesos, the wall of which still stood forty feet high in places; they explored the ruins of streets and houses and Petrie took photographs.

At Hawara he found a few of his walls still intact, and spent the day digging up boards and roofing the store room next to his tent. Next day he was joined by Maurice Amos, now seventeen, who was taking a holiday before going to College. He was clearly marked out for a legal career (he later became a judge in the Cairo courts, then Judicial Adviser to the Government of Egypt), but although Flinders Petrie had little hope of converting him to archaeology, he welcomed his company and found him a willing and competent assistant. Maurice pitched his tent next door, and joined Petrie at dinner every evening.

The pyramid of Hawara was naturally Petrie's first concern; by hook or by crook he must enter the chamber. Twenty-two men were put on to work; but when seven new tunnels into the brickwork on the south and west sides proved fruitless he decided that the entrance must lie somewhere outside the pyramid altogether; nothing remained but to cut through the roof as he had at first planned. Last year's tunnel had therefore to be re-opened and re-boarded; to fill in time for the rest of the workmen and keep them happily rewarded with *bakhshish*, he decided to go back to the Roman cemetery area, where he could rely on a few more coffins and portraits, and perhaps some wreaths and gravegoods.

Now came bad news: a German dealer named Kruger had recently come into the area, with a permit from Grébaut to dig; he had shown himself to be totally ignorant and only out for pillage, having abandoned excavation at Medinet Maadi because he had found no silver or gold; but he had told Hewat that he intended to try digging at Illahun and at Gurob—both sites in Petrie's concession, and already chosen by him for his main work during the winter; he decided to move into occupation. Accordingly, he brought over Muhammad and a handful of men, and installed them in the storeroom of Hewat's inspection house near Illahun, at the mouth of the Bahr Yusuf canal, while three more of his best men were set to dig at Gurob (Tell Medinet Ghurab), a few miles away on the south side of the canal, near the desert edge. Not liking to leave Maurice Amos on his own, he decided he would have to walk over twice a week to see how the work progressed, in spite of the waste of time (it was sixteen miles there and back). The idea that relatively untrained men could be set to work without supervision strikes the reader of today with dismay; but allowance has to be made for the urgency of the situation (Petrie dared not risk being forestalled), and it must be remembered that in Egypt in those days, Arab dealers who were agents of the Antiquities Service were usually left to carry on by themselves for weeks on end, or even work for a whole season without inspection.

In Hawara, meanwhile, work progressed slowly: three fine Greek papyri were found in a jar, and enough in the way of portraits, Petrie said, to pay for the less profitable side of the season's work. The discovery of underground catacombs approached by a sloping passage, with signs that mummified crocodiles had been buried in them, led Petrie to write excitedly in his Journal, "If only they buried these sacred crocs decently and in order, we ought to get fine sarcophagi and a series of tablets like the Serapeum find. Don't you wish it!" But archaeology is full of disappointments, and the tombs proved to have been several times plundered and re-used, and at some time completely ravaged.

Early on 8 January, after three weeks' work, the specialist masons brought from Cairo finally broke through the roofing blocks in the pyramid. Petrie, still in his flannel nightgown and nightcap, hurried to the spot, and squeezed in through the narrow hole and down through a roof chamber below, then through a crack peered into another "all of sandstone, polished and plain". He was hanging upside down, and could see little; they dragged him out by the feet, and a slender boy with a candle was sent down on a rope ladder; he reported that there were three feet of water in the chamber and two sarcophagi, rifled and empty, their lids pushed aside. The masons were set to enlarge the hole somewhat, and next morning, were paid generously and sent back to Cairo. The task of finding the real entrance to the burial chamber occupied several days and was wet, muddy and sometimes dangerous work. A hole led northwards to another chamber, filled with stones and earth.

> I was afraid of their going further with it, as they were foolhardy; so I took it in hand myself, having my shirt off as well as my coat for the heat of the place. I pegged and pegged for half an hour or more at the mass of blocks and earth filling this chamber, not daring to work in too close for fear of being caught by them when they fell into our passage. I got one big block down, and turning it over kept one foot on it, ready to spring up on it, the moment a rush should come. At last the rush came, and I sprang back squat on my islet, while a heap of blocks came bowling down in wild confusion. When they had settled I crawled over them and looking up saw the chamber open above; so I at once went up with Abder Rahim [the thin boy] and Ahmed [his brother] following. In one corner of this is a well, which I think must lead to the proper entrance to the sepulchral chamber: it is half full of broken potsherds.

The passage led to another with a sliding trapdoor, and this to yet another, in a different direction; the pyramid had been planned with a labyrinthine entrance, to baffle would-be plunderers. The passages were mostly blocked with mud and stones: "in many parts the only way along them was by lying flat and sliding along the mud, pushed by fingers and toes." Candles were constantly going out, and a boy had to be sent for fresh light. " 'Why did you not carry matches?' asks an impatient reader. Because we none of us had aught but trousers or drawers on, and they were soaked with mud or sweat. No matches would survive."

Eventually, slithering, crawling and wading, they reached a sloping passage which Petrie decided must lead to the entrance; by measuring back the way they had come, he could reckon its approximate position, in the ground outside the pyramid as he had surmised . . . but on the south side. "This," he wrote "is about the last place I should have looked for it; and so my roof cutting is amply justified." On further examination the burial chamber proved to be carved from a monolithic block of quartzite; there was not a trace of an inscription on its walls, but boys were set groping underwater for the stone fragments which littered the floor, and promised *bakhshish* for every hieroglyphic fragment found. The search was soon rewarded: the name of King Amenemhat (Amenemmes) III was found on part of an alabaster vase; later the name of his daughter, Neferu-Ptah, was discovered on a fine table of offerings; she must have died during her father's lifetime and been the occupant of the second sarcophagus. Inside both sarcophagi were fragments of burnt bones and charcoal, and scraps of inlay from the coffins, which must have been burnt after the ancient plunderers, whoever they had been, had stripped the royal dead of their regalia.

While the search went on for the entrance, Petrie embarked on one of the most difficult operations of his whole career: the exploration and clearing of a great twenty-sixth dynasty tomb in the cemetery. It involved working in the dark for much of the time, stripped naked, and in filthy brackish water. This was the family vault of a man named Horuta;* "first one swings down a rope ladder for 25 feet, then squeezes through the top of a doorway nearly choked, and at once slides down the slope inside into the water. The whole of the walls are pitch black, owing to some deposit or growth when the water has filled the chambers. So it is very dark, and the candle only just shews

* Or Harwoz.

you where you collide with floating coffins or some skulls that go bobbing around. One wades in carefully, the ground being strewn with slippery sodden wood, bones and mud; in the outer chamber are two recesses, one with a sarcophagus and some wooden coffins; and in the inner chamber are the other two stone sarcophagi. . . ." The first find was a quantity of magnificent amulets, then some hundreds of splendid *ushabti* figures. Petrie was delighted, for these little green glaze figures were exceptionally fine: "exquisite work, the faces elaborated to shew the dimples and muscles, and the details of the pick and hoe and basket all standing out in high relief. . . ." The removal of the lids of the sarcophagi and the clearance of the tomb were to take several months.

At the end of January Petrie had an unpleasant surprise: he discovered by accident that his trusted *reis* Muhammad, who had been with him for eight years, was compelling the workmen to hand over to him twenty-five per cent of all the *bakhshish* they received. Petrie's reaction was characteristic of him: "It is very abominable of him, especially after his continuous pious comments and moral reflections that he used to indulge in. At the same time one must not view it like a theft or such offence; it is no crime in Arab morality, and I must not forget the really good service that he has done." He held an enquiry, and found that the rake-off had been regularly extorted since the work began the previous year; moreover, he had been over-charging on the stores that he bought for the camp. Realizing that he must go, Petrie sent Maurice over to Illahun with a list of the men's claims against him; Muhammad accepted his dismissal philosophically and deposited a lump sum from which at least some of his creditors could be recompensed. Petrie had learned his lesson: he never again employed a *reis* on his digs.

Petrie now decided to move over into Major Hewat's house at Illahun; his baggage and supplies went along the canal by boat. Here he and Maurice were able to make themselves very comfortable; their neighbours were two amiable employees of the Irrigation Department who looked after the regulator sluices controlling the inflow of water to the Fayum, and they were waited on by a little boy they called the Cherub. At Petrie's request, Maurice Amos had brought a bicycle with him; they had both had to learn to ride it, for Maurice had only had a tricycle previously, and Petrie had never ridden a bicycle in his life. At Hawara the ground was too soft for them to be able to make much use of it, but now they could bump along on the "knubbly" surface of the dyke road—somewhat precariously, for there was a sheer drop on either side into the water. When in mid-March Maurice left, Petrie let him take the bicycle; he found that the rough jolting made his bones ache, and it was not a good way to convey objects of a delicate nature. He never used a bicycle again.

One of his objectives now was the pyramid at Illahun, another huge mud-brick pile but differing from that at Hawara and all others in that it is hewn from the natural rock up to a height of about forty feet. For the rest of the season, a team of workmen cleared the ground all round the rock base, searching for the entrance. Exploration of the area where the mortuary temple had once been produced stone fragments with the cartouches of Sesostris II, to whom Petrie could with confidence now ascribe the pyramid. Late tombs were turning up in the cemetery at Illahun, some with beadwork over the mummy; careful application of melted beeswax, spoonful by spoonful, just before it hardened secured the beads in a single sheet so that the elaborate patterns could be preserved and the beads later restrung. After this successful experiment, Petrie always used the wax method to secure beads as they were found.

Beyond the temple, on the north side, Petrie had discovered an area which had clearly been residential—the town, he assumed, in which the workmen had lived while they were building the pyramid; the pottery scattered on the surface resembled the twelfth-dynasty sherds he had found in Hawara. If so, he realized, "it will be a prize to work for historical interest of dated objects." On asking the name of the site, an old man told him "Medinet el-Kahun" which he mis-heard as "el-Kahun". Later he realized his mistake, but the name was distinctive and useful, and so as Kahun the site was known ever after. It was indeed a prize: here, virtually untouched since the day it was abandoned, was a compact walled town of the Middle Kingdom with regular streets of back-to-back houses; in the rubble, above and below the floors, were the domestic paraphernalia of the community: pottery of course, and tools and implements of all kinds, ropes, fishing nets, sickles, hoes and rakes; games and dolls, sandals, pieces of furniture, toilet objects. . . . Petrie decided to clear the town systematically, forming the workmen into a line along the outermost street. The first line of rooms was cleared, turning the débris into the street behind; then the next row of rooms, and so on. "Every chamber as it is cleared is measured and planned, and we can see the exact scheme of the architect and where he expanded the town as time went on." Scraps of papyrus in Middle Kingdom hieratic, of which very few examples had ever been found, began to turn up; when Griffith subsequently studied these precious documents he found them to be wills and deeds of sale, letters and accounts, a medical treatise on gynaecology, part of a veterinary papyrus (**40**) and a hymn of praise to Pharaoh.[16]

Gurob too was yielding treasures: in one of the nineteenth dynasty tombs had been found two charming little wooden statuettes, one of a priestess clasping a sistrum (rattle), the other a spoon in the form of a swimming girl reaching forward to touch a duck. These Ramesside tombs, however, held a greater surprise, for some of the pottery found in them was quite un-Egyptian: Flinders Petrie at once recognized it as Greek—"Achaean" was the word he subsequently used. Schliemann had found this pottery in abundance in Mycenae twelve years before, and it was now turning up on other Greek sites. Petrie was uncertain whether to ascribe its presence in Gurob to traders or to foreign settlers; he inclined to the latter: the name of one of the tomb owners, which he read as Tursha, suggested a possible Etruscan.* Moreover, some of the weights he found were not of the normal Egyptian standard, and some of the pottery had curious marks which he took to be alphabetic, again suggesting the presence of foreign traders.

He wrote excitedly at the end of March: "It really seems as if we had got here one of the great prizes that we have been waiting for, the contemporary remains of the Western races in their earliest contacts with Egypt; an historical plum, verily! In quality, though not in quantity, it beats Naukratis and Defenneh. How strange that three such places for the earliest Greek archaeology should have fallen to me, unsought for, and just in receding order." In one small cemetery at Gurob, in tombs of the Ptolemaic period, Petrie was excited to discover what he had never noticed before—that the cartonnage around the heads of the mummies was composed of layers of compressed papyri, waste paper used as papier-mâché by the undertakers, and covered with plaster. "By soaking them the layers of papyri can be separated easily none the worse for their pasting and plastering. I shall in this way get a quantity of Ptolemaic papyri, in pieces as large as one's hand. This is somewhat like picking out early MSS from mediaeval bindings." One or two of the texts appeared to Petrie to be royal decrees; others were later identified by A. H. Sayce as private letters, wills and receipts, the accounts of tax-collectors, and one a letter from Ptolemy's gooseherds saying that they were unable to supply twelve geese for the royal festival. One or two turned out to be literary: fragments of the *Phaedo* of Plato, and portions of a lost play of Euripides.

* The identity (*Tyrsenoi*) had been proposed by Egyptologists for the TRŠ, one of the Sea Peoples who had attacked Egypt about 1200 BC.

On 30 April Naville and D'Hulst came over, having finished their season at Bubastis; with them was Dr Farley Goddard of Boston, a young American on a travelling scholarship subscribed for by members of the Egypt Exploration Fund in the United States. Amelia Edwards had hoped he would go to Petrie, where he would learn the true way to excavate; Petrie was perfectly willing to take him, but in the end he preferred the comparative comfort of Naville's camp and elected to remain the whole season at Bubastis. Two more visitors stayed in the house at Illahun: one was Sayce, who was very excited about the Greek pottery and the papyri; he copied the "alphabetic" signs, expressing the opinion that they were more likely to be Greek or Cypriot than Etruscan. The other was a cheerful young man called George Willoughby Fraser, whose parents Petrie had met in Cairo; he was a civil engineer, working as a volunteer in the Irrigation Department, and he came over from Minya anxious to help. His arrival was opportune, for the lid of the sarcophagus of Horuta had at last been drawn aside and the coffin lay ready for the final assault. Together, Fraser and Petrie went over to Hawara, "donned their 'cutty breeks'", and plunged in; screwing bolts into the sides of the coffin and attaching ropes to either end, they signalled to the men to pull: "Hauling and howling, slowly, bit by bit it rose under the water, until at last up it came altogether, a brown mass 'as big as a buffalo', as they said, and amid yells of frantic delight, Horuta was really within our reach and handling, after months of labour. No wonder the Arabs yelled after all they had done, week after week, to get at it." Sliding off the coffin lid, an inner coffin was revealed, and in that, the mummy itself.

> Tenderly we towed him out to the bottom of the entrance pit, handling him with the same loving care as Izaak his worms. Then came the last, and longed-for scene, for which our months of toil had whetted our appetites—the unwrapping of Horuta. Bit by bit the layers of pitch and cloth were loosened, and row after row of magnificent amulets were disclosed, just as they were laid on in the distant past. The gold ring on the finger which bore his name and titles, the exquisitely inlaid gold birds, the chased gold figures, the lazuli statuettes delicately wrought, the polished lazuli and beryl and carnelian amulets finely engraved, all the wealth of talismanic armoury, rewarded our eyes with a sight which had never been surpassed to archaeological gaze. No such complete and rich a series of amulets has been seen intact before; and as one by one they were

removed all their positions were recorded, and they may now be seen lying in their original order in the Ghizeh Museum.

Petrie was not present at the opening of the Tomb of Tutankhamun, but the sense of achievement, and of wonder, with which he gazed on this panoply cannot have been far short of Howard Carter's, thirty-three years later.

George Fraser, greatly excited by this initiation into archaeology, agreed willingly to Petrie's suggestion that he should spend the three months of his summer holiday at Illahun, taking care of the site and perhaps doing a little digging on his own; he was untrained, but had "the estimable quality of making very full notes of all he sees and finds, with sketches of things". When he had left, Petrie continued at Kahun; at the end of April the *khamasîn* blew hot and dust-laden, and Petrie, temporarily blinded by ophthalmia, considered closing down the work, but he cured himself with quinine, and went on digging a few weeks more; every day he found something new to interest or puzzle him. In the Gurob tombs the men were working on their own now; they would bring their finds across at the end of the day, and Petrie accepted their assurances that the Greek pottery they continued to find indeed came from the tombs . . . corroborating what he already knew. He dared not leave Kahun, and if he stopped the work at Gurob, it would mean losing everything to the dealers. At Kahun now a few sherds of quite different, but equally alien pottery were turning up, in contexts which could not be later than the Middle Kingdom —on Petrie's chronology, about 2600–2000 BC. Petrie had never seen anything like this delicate, polychrome ware, but with extraordinary intuition he at once recognized it for what it was: Aegean ("I cannot call it *Greek* at this age"). Those to whom his Journal was sent—his parents, Miss Edwards, Haworth and Kennard, Griffith and Spurrell —were urged to keep the matter dark; it was vital to avoid a leak to the Press, lest the precious potsherds might not be allowed back to England for study.

George Fraser came back on 11 June, ready to take over; by that time Petrie had almost finished packing and was anxious to be off. Grébaut had originally offered to come down to Illahun and inspect the season's finds, to save unpacking at Bulaq, but indolent as ever, he failed to answer three consecutive letters, and it became clear that he would not come. So Petrie's 101 boxes went off by canal, were carted to the railhead, and dispatched by train to Cairo; after several days' delay, Grébaut at last made his division. He took most of the most spectacular and most valuable things for the Museum; this Petrie had expected, but he was sad to lose the amulets of Horuta, the finest coffins and sarcophagi, the wooden statuettes from Gurob and the altar from the Hawara pyramid. However, he realized his good fortune in being left not only the fine alabaster canopic jars from Horuta's burial, but better still, all the papyri and almost all the finds from Kahun and the pottery, in which Grébaut was not interested. At Dr Grant's soirée he gave an hour's informal talk on his finds to a large audience which included Wilbour, General Grenfell and Scott-Moncrieff and a number of British officers; never, he said, had he seen more attentive listeners. On 22 June he sailed from Alexandria; he had been nearly eight months in the field.

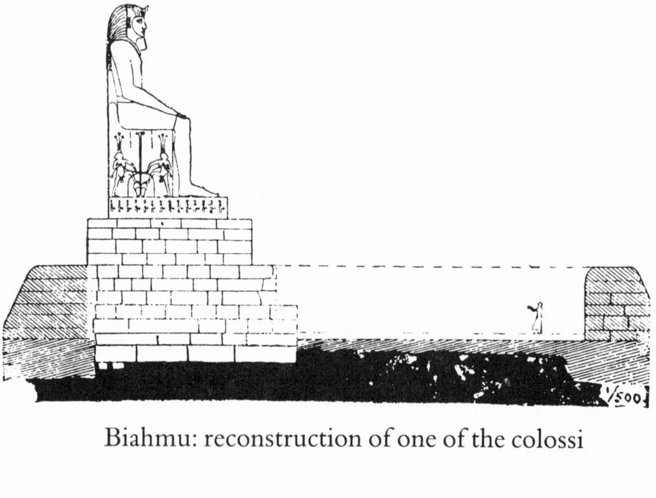

Biahmu: reconstruction of one of the colossi

CHAPTER VII

Interlude in Palestine
(1889–90)

JULY AND AUGUST 1889 were very busy months for Flinders Petrie: boxes had to be unpacked and the precious contents treated, textiles and papyri mounted and hundreds of drawings made; plans and sections of the pyramid of Hawara, and of the cemetery area, had to be completed, and the first volume of the final report prepared for the press.[1] His friend Spurrell helped him with many of these tasks and he also contributed a chapter on the flintwork, his special interest. Young Newberry, in his last year at the University, had taken over the task of identifying the plant remains of wreaths and funerary bouquets, and the fruits and seeds from the formal repasts of the dead. His chapter for the book was based on a report which he had read at a meeting of the British Association, and again when he displayed some specimens at the Royal Society. Very few ancient plant remains had been subjected to analysis before (with the exception of Dr Schweinfurth's report on the garlands found in the royal *cache* of mummies at Deir el Bahari), and Newberry's little exhibition had aroused much interest. Some of the plants were remarkably well-preserved: rosebuds, when immersed in warm water, had opened their petals, myrtle and sweet marjoram retained a faint aroma, the Rose-of-Heaven campion its colour, the woody nightshade its red berries; there were seeds of castor-oil and flax, twigs of henna and peach stones, shrivelled pomegranates and grapes, and little heaps of wheat and barley. Petrie had experimented at Hawara with grains of the corn, in order to test the theory that "mummy wheat" found in tombs would sprout; neither grains of wheat nor grape-pips, carefully planted and watered, had germinated.

Petrie's annual exhibition had to be postponed until mid-September in order that the hundreds of exhibits could be unpacked and prepared for display at Oxford Mansion, for the cases sent by long sea did not arrive in Liverpool till the end of July. He was busy fourteen hours a day, working against time, for it was vital to get back to Illahun before Fraser his *locum tenens* was due to leave. On 12 September he wrote the catalogue in a single day, and took it to the printers; next day he wrote and sent 110 postcards of invitation to the exhibition, and gave a preview to newspaper men, and on the sixteenth the doors opened to the public. Ten days later he left England, and arriving in Cairo in the early morning by the overnight train from Alexandria, was at Illahun by half-past two in the afternoon . . . a record seven days and nine hours from door to door. Fraser, to his relief, was still there. The ever-helpful Spurrell would close the exhibition and pack up the antiquities after his departure—a kindness for which Petrie expressed his great gratitude. He had been near the end of his tether: "when I got to Illahun, I slept nearly—or quite—twelve hours a day for the first two or three weeks."

Mr Hewat had been replaced as Inspector in the Fayum by Major Brown, who was equally hospitable in allowing the use of his house, and just as glad of the opportunity to come over for an occasional chat. George Fraser had seen to it that no intruders were permitted on the sites at Gurob or Kahun. During the summer he had succeeded in entering the pyramid of Illahun: as Petrie had suggested, had investigated a deep well-shaft in the pavement and at a depth of forty feet had come upon an ascending passage leading into the pyramid. It was in fact a secondary entrance, made for the workmen before the chamber was finished; a wider passage was found later. A red granite chamber in the centre contained the sarcophagus "one of the finest products of mechanical skill," wrote Petrie, "that is known from ancient times". Delighting as he did in precision craftsmanship, he measured it very carefully, finding that it erred from absolute flatness, not more than the thickness of a visiting card, and that the accuracy of each dimension fluctuated by only $\frac{1}{1000}$. It was, he said, the most superb example of stone-cutting he had ever seen. No trace was found of the coffin or the sarcophagus lid . . . the ancient robbers had been very thorough in their plunder.

The work at Kahun went on; they were finding larger houses now, some with a large central hall with wooden pillars around a central impluvium like a Roman house. More "Mediterranean" painted pottery was found, again "in good positions", by which Petrie meant well-dated, undoubtedly twelfth-dynasty context. Then a large and important tomb came to light, the shaft of which had been sunk in the cellar of a Middle Kingdom house. Twelve coffins in all were found, some of them with the remains of several bodies, the wrappings reduced to black sooty dust. "I stripped for the work, and for hours was occupied in opening coffin after coffin, carefully searching the dust inside each, cataloguing everything as I found it, overhauling the pottery and stone vases heaped in the chambers and handing everything out to the one native lad whom I took down to help me. At last I finished the place, and came out much like a coal-heaver or a sweep, so that I had to go to the nearest pond to wash all over." It appeared to be a family tomb, used for generation after generation; the richest coffin bore the name of the lady Maket. Among the grave goods were a number of pots of Cypriot and "Greek" (Mycenaean) ware. The date of the tomb puzzled Petrie, because some of the scarabs bore the name of Tuthmosis III of the mid-eighteenth dynasty, yet many of the beads were like those in the Ramesside tombs at Gurob; he came to the conclusion that the early scarabs must have been heirlooms. More recent studies of the tomb, based on the careful details recorded in the field notebooks as he toiled in the dust, have shown that the burials may have spanned at least two centuries.[2]

On 1 November a new assistant arrived to join him. W. O. Hughes-Hughes was a prospective pupil whom Petrie hoped to train; when interviewed in London he had seemed keen and eager to learn, but it soon became evident that this young man was very different from the willing, eager Maurice and that cheerful young extrovert, George Fraser. At first Petrie put his bad temper down to inability to sleep; he disliked being corrected and would not accept instruction, even on archaeological matters. Worse still, as Petrie explained in a private letter to Spurrell, he had no notion of how to treat the workmen: "he thinks the Arabs ought to learn somewhat of our manners when they deal with us, whereas I always take them on their own basis. He has no approximation to the easy-going, off-hand, joking, rub-shoulders way that softens the inexorableness of laying down the law. If kind—as he wishes to be—there is so much condescension and superiority in his tone that I—as an Arab—should feel ribbed." He soon gave up trying to give him advice or correct him, and decided to let him work at Gurob entirely on his own. "The worst of it is that I have not in the least succeeded in my object in having him here, namely to raise another explorer; he protests that he shall never think of coming out again."[3]

There is no denying that this unhappy situation led to a grievous loss of archaeological information. No plan of the site could be published; many objects in the Petrie collection and elsewhere are known to have come from Gurob, but their exact provenance is unknown. Hughes-

Hughes' notebooks, if he kept any, have not survived. Petrie acknowledged his contribution to the publication in somewhat guarded terms; he met him on three occasions in London next summer but never saw him again. As Petrie had predicted, the *sebbakhîn* moved in and ravaged the site as soon as it was abandoned, yet subsequent soundings in the area, some by Petrie's students (see p. 275) and the evidence of papyri published later, show that Gurob was Mi-Wer, a royal harîm of the New Kingdom Pharaohs, with a great temple and a town of artisans and servitors.[4] Petrie's deduction that foreigners had lived there may have been right, since every royal harîm had its complement of alien ladies with their retinues; musicians, cooks and weavers, and perhaps some high officials could well have come from overseas.

February and March were months of frustration and inactivity. Going to Cairo for a few days after Hughes-Hughes left, to get an injury to his leg treated, he caught influenza from Corbett, struggled back to his house at Illahun and for weeks lay helpless with a high temperature, eating very little, and tended by the Cherub. To occupy himself—for even in illness he was never idle—he began a book which Spurrell had long been urging him to write: a popular account of his discoveries of the past ten years, designed for a wider public than his reports. "Your journals", Spurrell had written, "show yourself. The way you work. The reasons for working. The spirit which animates you (and your friends, for *your following* is a power); the labours, privations, the cleanness and certainty of your methods and conclusions and the *swiftness* with which you act and *reason*, are all exposed." A small book was the result of these promptings; he continued it in the summer, and finished it in 1891, illustrated by his own sketches; the last chapter, entitled "The art of excavating" gave the general reader, probably for the first time, an answer to the perennial question "How do you know where to dig?"[5]

In April, as soon as he felt better, he decided to pack up and leave Gurob. He had urgent business elsewhere: during the previous July he had been approached by the Committee of the Palestine Exploration Fund through their Chairman, Walter Besant, on the possibility of excavating a site for them.[6] Their survey of the country, east of the Jordan as well as west, was complete, and they felt the time had come for some archaeological work, but knew nobody with the experience, and the time, to undertake it; if Petrie would go, at the end of his season in Egypt, he could put in a few weeks in the cooler climate of Judaea before the hot weather set in. Petrie agreed in principle, and a formal invitation was sent to him: the Fund would pay the costs of labour and Petrie's personal expenses for outfit, travel and food, and an honorarium to be agreed. Petrie was very tempted by this offer: it would give him an opportunity to search for links between the objects with a "foreign look" which he was coming across in Egypt, and one of the regions from which they might be expected to have come. He consulted Sayce, who knew Palestine well, as to likely sites; Sayce suggested 'Ajlan, and Tell ez Zeita which was thought to have been the ancient Lachish. The Fund sent a formal application through the Foreign Office to the Sultan of Turkey, for a *firman* was required for any archaeological work to be done in Syria (in which Palestine was included). In February 1890 Besant had sent Petrie maps and a formal contract to which Petrie readily agreed: the estimate should be ample. "I am never afraid of spending money freely, if I see that it is needful and will give results; but I think I always make every pound go as far as possible." He was not surprised that no *firman* had yet been sent: "I heard somewhat of the German way of proceeding from Count D'Hulst, who was told by the minister at Berlin. They do not get a firman, but only a less formal *permission*, on which they are now excavating at Carchemish. And when things are found the Emperor makes a personal request for them as a favour to himself from the Sultan, which is always granted." He doubted, however, whether Queen Victoria or the Foreign Office would descend to such "high-handed and undiplomatic ways".

He decided to go to Jerusalem and wait there for his permit to come. Grébaut, after some delay, refused to make the division, saying that the Antiquities Committee must see the contents of the boxes. Petrie could wait no longer; he decided to leave his boxes, some opened, and leave money with Brugsch to forward them to him when they were released and the Museum had taken its pick. Scott-Moncrieff was indignant at the way he had been treated but could not override Grébaut. A storm in the Mediterranean delayed his arrival in Palestine; they rolled miserably at anchor outside the harbour at Jaffa for a day and a half, before the sailors would venture to row them ashore. Prostrate with seasickness, Flinders found refuge at the house of a missionary, the Reverend J. L. Hall, to whom he had an introduction; Mr Hall was in Jerusalem but his wife, their four children and a governess made him at home. Having arranged on Monday for his boxes to be passed through customs and kept in store for him, he booked a seat in a carriage going up to Jerusalem next day.

First impressions of the Judaean hills were not favourable: after the golden sunshine of Egypt, everything here was grey—grey limestone hills, grey stone houses, grey olive groves. But higher up there were wild flowers, crimson poppies and pale-purple orchids, and almond trees in blossom. They reached Jerusalem at sunset. The hotels were crowded with tourists. In the inn he finally settled in he was glad to find Hayter Lewis, an old friend; he located Mr Hall, and was introduced to a Dr Zeller, who "tells me that the Turks have a fixed idea that the English want to take Syria, not from a wish for conquest, but to hinder the French and Russians from advancing there; hence exploration in some parts is jealously watched." But Reshad Pasha, the Governor of Palestine, he was told, was an educated man, who would not be likely to be suspicious of genuine research; moreover, he was on excellent terms with the British Consul upon whom Petrie next called, finding him encouraging and helpful. In the company of Herr Schick, an elderly antiquary whose knowledge of Jerusalem's antiquities was unrivalled, and Professor Hayter Lewis, who was an authority on Islamic architecture, Petrie enjoyed the enforced idleness of the next two or three days, exploring the old city and the circuit of the walls, and taking measurements in the tombs in the Kedron valley; he went on sightseeing excursions to Bethlehem and Hebron. He was advised never to walk alone more than a mile outside the walls; "we were told that someone had ventured three miles and only his skull remained to tell the tale." Petrie had been forewarned that his mission might not be without danger: a few years before, two young officers surveying for the Fund had been attacked and wounded in the Safad region and had barely escaped with their lives.[7] One was Lieut Conder, the other Lieut H. H. Kitchener of the Royal Engineers; it had been a rough introduction to the Levant for the future Sirdar of Egypt. Such was Palestine under Turkish rule.

At last the *firman* came and Petrie and the Consul called upon the Pasha to receive it. The terms were harsh: everything found was to be the property of the Museum in Constantinople, and a Turkish official must always be present on the site to take charge of everything as it was found; his salary was to be paid by the Fund. Though he disliked the idea of being thus supervised, Petrie was bound to acquiesce; he asked only that the official seconded to him might be Arabic-speaking rather than a Turk with whom he could have no communication. Ibrahim Effendi, who was eventually sent to him, was a relative of one of the Jerusalem notables.

Flinders Petrie went back to Jaffa and was met by Muhammad, who was to be his personal servant and companion for the next two months; he had brought a donkey for the baggage and helped load up the stores. Two camels and a driver were hired and on 3 April they set off down the coastal road, the Halls and their children waving till the little caravan passed out of sight. The first night they pitched by moonlight in the flat green cornfields; rolling sand dunes lay between them and the seashore. Next day they journeyed past Ashdod and south-eastwards inland to Bureyr, camping in a field outside the town. An intruder in the night, intent on theft, was scared off by shots from Petrie's revolver. The next day he strode around the countryside prospecting for likely sites. Neither Umm Lakis, which he had suspected from its name might be the site of ancient Lachish, nor Ajlan looked promising; there was very little pottery on the surface and what there was appeared to be Roman. He decided he must look elsewhere in the neighbourhood for Lachish. First however he thought it prudent to pay a call on the paramount Sheikh of the district.

> I found him a pleasant fellow, sitting under an enormous flat tent with a number of his following. I did a deal of silence, for that is orthodox; and in the interval stated my business. Soon after I arrived, there was a chorus of dogs, and a man came up bearing a wide wooden bowl on his head, with the midday meal. It was set before us, and we gathered round, about half a dozen at once. The mixture was bread in sour curds, and plenty of butter melted amongst it, with a layer of pieces of fat mutton on the top. I smelt the sourness, and judiciously grabbed a good bit of plain meat, which kept me in play as long as the others. It was amusing to see them grasping handfuls of the fearful mixture, and stuffing it into their mouths. . . . After coffee I bid goodbye, slipping a napoleon into the Sheikh's hand, as a smoother for future business.

During the next few days Petrie looked at several more *tells*; Tell el Hesy seemed to him the most likely to have been the great city fortified by Hezekiah and besieged by Sennacherib and Nebuchadnezzar: it was a huge mound, and none of the surface pottery was Roman. He made two excursions to the town of Gaza, twelve miles away, where he was received kindly at the home of a medical missionary; it was reassuring to find that he had a fully equipped dispensary, so that Petrie felt more "within humanity's reach" than he had in the Fayum. The Kaimmakam or District Governor of Gaza he found to be "much Europeanized in ways and feelings", having spent much of his life in Berlin and Vienna. Until now there had been no word of Ibrahim

Effendi, without whom Petrie could not start digging. Then he sent word that he was in Gaza at the office of the Kaimmakam—would Petrie come and discuss the matter? When they met it was plain that he hated the idea of living in discomfort and was looking for any excuse to avoid coming: he had brought neither tent nor bedstead, and expected Petrie to provide them: he could not eat the local bread, he needed a man to cook for him, a horse—he was not used to walking, and so forth. Petrie reluctantly agreed to let him have a bed and one of his two tents, and when he still made difficulties, threatened to write to the Pasha in Jerusalem asking for someone else to be sent; "this soon brought him down, and he offered to come on Monday early."

A couple of days' digging at Umm Lakis confirmed Petrie's first impression that the site was Roman and Arab; so he decided to excavate Tell el Hesy. He moved camp and pitched at the foot of the *tell*. This was Beduin country: not a house in sight, only straggling groups of brown tents. The Effendi (sometimes referred to as the FND in the Journal) insisted on negotiating with all the local sheikhs himself. Because of the lawless and unsettled state of the countryside they needed four guards: two from Bureyr, one from the nearest settlement, and one appointed by the big sheikh of the district: "so everybody is responsible for us". It was very different from working in Egypt; the townsfolk who made up his labour force were poor workers at the best of times, and he dreaded the approach of Ramadan. The Beduin did not come to work but lounged about on the fringes of the excavation; Petrie got on well enough with them: "they are pleasant and civil enough when not out for plunder. A few small jokes, and especially a little mimicry of any peculiar manner or ways, will set them all laughing and make us good friends for the time, and probably less touchy afterwards."

Work was started on the sloping sides of the *tell* and on the eastern face where the scouring of the stream, the Wady Hesy, had cut deep into the mound leaving the successive levels visible, like the layers of a cake sliced through. Diggers were put on at each level, and the pottery, flints and other objects they found were carefully marked and kept together. The height of the top of the mound was taken from the Fund's previous survey and from there he levelled up and down the site; as the men excavated, walls and floors came to light. His section through the mound (Fig. C) is not the first archaeological section —General Pitt-Rivers drew cross-sections of the barrows and earthworks he excavated, and Schliemann had published sections through the great mound at Hissarlik—but here for the first time the relationship of the pottery to the stratigraphy of the site was recorded; the earliest wares (coarse pottery with a combed face, spouted jars, thick-brimmed bowls such as he had never seen before) he named "Amorite", from the period before the Hebrew invasion of Palestine; he dated it to between 1600 and 1000 BC. (We now know it to be much older, and classify it as Early Bronze and Middle Bronze.) His "Phoenician" pottery had similarities with the juglets and bowls he had found in the New Kingdom tombs in Illahun and Gurob; here too were the "Aegean" wares, the black-painted vessels we know as Mycenaean. One precious fragment of a bowl bore a few scrawled letters in an early alphabetic script;[8] this was the earliest occasion on which a "proto-Canaanite" inscription was found in a datable context, though the discovery appears to have gone without comment at the time. Part of the city wall was found, and a tower and part of the glacis, or sloped fortification, which is now known to be characteristic of the period Petrie in his later excavations called Hyksos; after the destruction of this fortified city Petrie discerned a long gap and then a period when the town was rebuilt after the tenth century; the pottery in this level he called Jewish. Above that there were early Greek wares which he recognized from his work at Naucratis, and at the top of the mound, a few sherds of pottery of the black-figured classical Greek type.

Petrie's short season at what he was convinced was ancient Lachish* laid the foundation of all future work in Palestine;[9] he was well aware of the importance of what he was doing there, he wrote, he had "an ideal place for determining the history of pottery in Palestine". This was worth all the discomforts that he encountered: black scorpions, deadly in summer, were plentiful; he killed a large tarantula in his tent one day. Water was a problem: they got their only potable supply from a deep well at Bureyr six miles away, stagnant and very green and salt; "though I boil it well, yet the colour and taste of it is almost too much for me. When boiled it is three courses in one, soup, fish and greens."

The Effendi was now proving more amenable, even affable. Conversation was sometimes difficult, but Petrie found he could keep him interested by reading out to him from *Whitaker's Almanack* the salaries of government officials in England. At first he had insisted that everything should go to Istanbul; later, realizing that no great treasures were going to be unearthed, he decided a few pots would suffice;

* Now proved to have been further north, at Tell el Duweir.

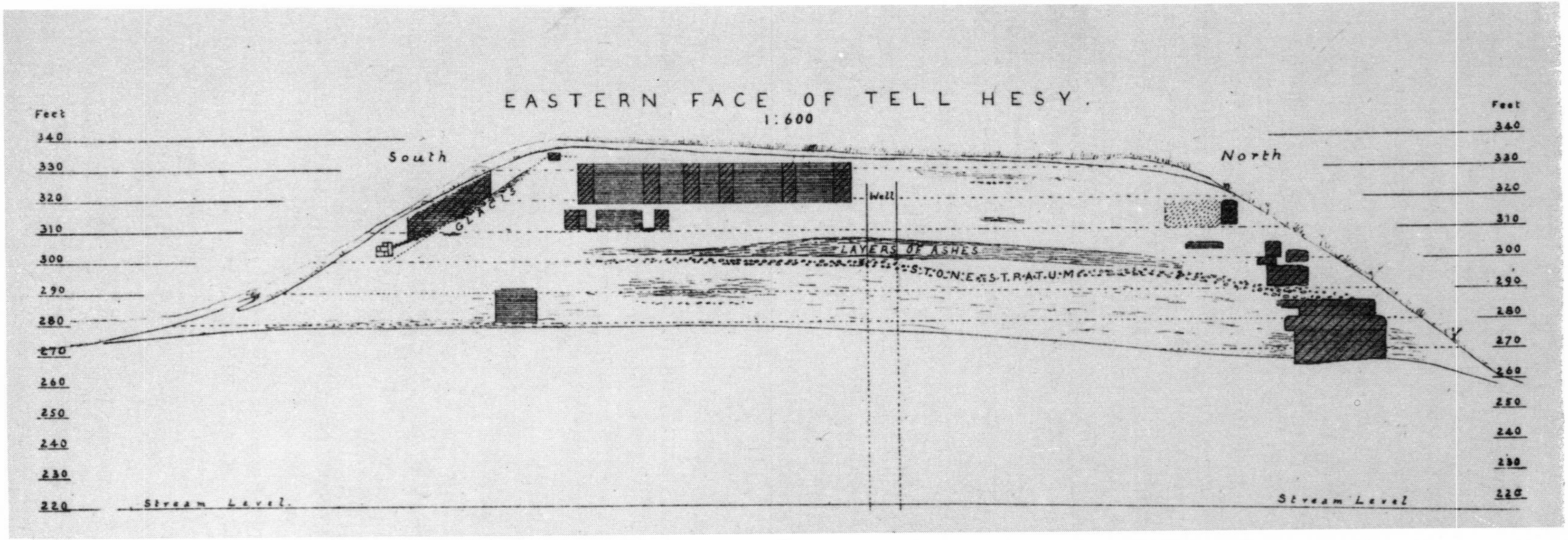

C. *Cross-section through the mound at Tell el Hesy, 1890*. The first attempt at stratification on a Near Eastern site. Walls of buildings are plotted at various levels on the mound, and a layer of ash indicates a conflagration.

Petrie could keep duplicates and as many sherds as he wished, since of course broken pottery was quite useless. This suited Petrie very well; as he said, "there is great scope for mending up sherds, as my friends know." On the denuded face of the *tell* he could now distinguish nine successive levels; a layer in which there were no walls, above the Amorite pottery, he supposed to be of the period of the Judges; a fairly thick wall, that of Rehoboam; four smaller walls represented successive rebuildings by Kings of Judah, and a thin and hasty wall was perhaps built by Josiah to stay the Egyptian army in 610 BC. Two masonry blocks with voluted decoration were found—a discovery, as he realized, of considerable importance for the history of Jewish art; he took paper casts of the mouldings.

Naville and Count D'Hulst paid him a visit one day, on their way through to Jerusalem, and a Dr Cobern, whom he had met and liked in Cairo, stayed for five days; these interludes were doubly appreciated since Petrie found himself out of sympathy with his Beduin neighbours; they were, he said, total barbarians, ignorant and feckless; he could not help contrasting them with his industrious fellahin.

> I urged on the sheikh that if they would only dam the deep watercourse and hold up the winter rains (which all run down to the seas at present) they would have good water and could cultivate as they liked with it instead of being dependent on showers. He only said that no one had a head to do that and they did not care to cultivate (beyond the interminable barley) as they might go anywhere at any time. So the sooner they are moved off the better. They pay £5,000 a year to the Govt. for what might bring in 5 million in proper hands.

At last the misery of Ramadan was over: "people venture to use salt again, which they dare not do when they must not drink all day." The FND was anxious for the work to go on into June, for then he could claim a whole month's pay, even for a few days; by cheese-paring he had already managed to save most of his £15 a month—a salary, observed Petrie, equal to that of the Governor of Gaza; he had hired a horse for a time but gave it up and used Petrie's donkey instead; he had dismissed his cook and got the guards to cook for him. But Petrie was determined to finish before the hot weather, and to his relief, Ibrahim Effendi went off to Gaza and did not return.

Having brought the work to an end: Petrie packed his gear and decided to set off on a ten-day exploratory walk around the countryside prospecting for possible sites. His workers had already melted away for harvesting, and the guards refused to accompany him into the dangerous uplands. In the end, Petrie sent off his camel man alone to Jaffa with the baggage, including a large sum in gold hidden at the bottom of a tin box full of photographic plates, while he himself set off with Muhammad and the second camel, a tent and a minimum of stores, eastwards into the hills. On the second day they took a rough path over the hills towards Dhaheriyeh; when they had gone some way Petrie, striding ahead with the camel, was ambushed by four men armed with swords and a pistol, handkerchiefs tied over their faces below the eyes. With presence of mind, he backed up the slope, leaving them to plunder the baggage, and was able to drop his purse and a bag of coins into some bushes, leaving only small change in his pocket, "so when all four armed men closed in on me and grabbed my windpipe, breaking its top ring, I went limp and let them rummage." Having turned out his pockets and taken his revolver, they took a suit and a couple of shirts from his suitcase; they then let him go, returning to give him his watch (which had an identification number) his measure and his handkerchief, as well as his precious notebook. "Altogether I think the business was conducted as pleasantly as such affairs ever are." When they had gone "I dropped in the grass and bewailed my losses while I grubbed about for my purse and gold, put them in my pocket and we went on." His throat never quite recovered from the injury, to which he subsequently attributed a slight hoarseness of voice. He wrote a full account of the affair that evening and sent it to the consul at Jerusalem, but Mr Moore was on leave and the acting consul, while protesting his intention to make a strong representation to the Kaimmakam of Hebron, did nothing effective and Petrie never got redress.

The country round Dhaheriyeh proved to have little of interest; he found the inhabitants of the town hostile in their attitude, and buried his gold for safety; they demanded payment even for water. Three days' prospecting produced no sites earlier than Roman or Herodian; it was very hot, and he began to think about going home. He had had several enquiries from the villagers: when was he thinking of going? on which day? He was on his guard, for he did not want his baggage "overhauled" again; so he decided to leave suddenly, and to go with an escort. The local sheikh provided him with four men; he packed, struck camp very quickly and departed, reaching Hebron in the early afternoon. Next morning he was sorely tempted to go inside the great Haram, the mosque said to contain the tombs of Abraham and Sarah, which in those days was strictly prohibited to infidels; it would have been as much as his life was worth, he decided, and he had to be contented with Muhammad's description of the interior.

Petrie left for Jaffa on 14 June; on the way he noticed a promising site at Tell Sandehanna, a high *tell* in which he saw pre-Seleucid pottery. Part of the site was called Khirbet Marash, and this, and the size of the mound, suggested an identification with the ancient city Mareshah; the identification has been upheld by later excavation. Other *tells* he thought might be the Philistine cities Ekron and Gath. On the 17th, with Muhammad and the camel still plodding behind he reached Jaffa and for the first time in eleven weeks was able to enjoy the luxury of a proper bed and a bath, and a quiet night's rest; one of his greatest deprivations had been lack of sleep at night.

There remained two things to settle before leaving. When in Jerusalem he had begun to photograph Syrian (i.e. Palestinian) racial types, particularly among the boys at Bishop Gobat's orphanage school, where he had noticed two "decided Hittites" who came, he was told, from east of Jordan. Mr Hall had promised to collect more of such photographs, and he now made arrangements that sets should be sent to six English residents in different parts of the country, from Dr Torrance in Tiberias to Dr Elliot in Gaza, all of whom were keen photographers, asking them to take similar racial portraits. "If (this) succeeds," wrote Petrie, "we may learn a great deal as to the distribution of the Amorite, Hittite, Hyksos and other races in Palestine." Whether anything came of this project is not recorded. The other problem was to get his boxes through the customs; a mild greasing of palms was arranged for, and his pottery got safely to London.

The whole pots and the pilasters, which he had no hope of bringing, he had photographed carefully. "As I generally take two plates in case of accidents I shift the camera slightly between them so that the two serve as stereoscopic views; most of the objects therefore will do for the stereoscope as well as for the lantern. These double views are very desirable as such will often clear up and explain details which are all confused in an ordinary single photograph. I exaggerate the distance of the eyes from distant objects, so as not to give merely a natural solidity, but an exaggerated solidity in order to throw out the relief more fully."

According to the terms of the contract, the Effendi had taken perfect pots for the museum at Constantinople. There remained a huge collection of sherds. Those which looked as if they would make up into whole vessels were packed together; they were all destined for the

P.E.F. The rest were sorted into ten sets, each representing as far as possible every form and variety of pottery found on the site; three of the best sets were for the Fund, one for the British Museum, one for the Berlin Museum, and one for Petrie himself; other sets had been distributed in Palestine to Dr Hall, his host in Jaffa; to Baron d'Ustinov of Jaffa whose collection of antiquities was the best in the country, visited by all archaeologists;[10] to Herr Schick in Jerusalem, and to a Mr Clark, of Thos. Cook and Son, who travelled a good deal about the country and would, Petrie hoped, keep his eye open for likely sites. All these people, he hoped, would be able to use their collection intelligently. It was a novel idea; nothing hitherto had been known about Palestinian pottery. "Once settle the pottery of the country, and the key is in our hands for all future explorations. A single glance at a mound of ruins, even without dismounting, will show as much to anyone who knows the style of the pottery as weeks of work may reveal to a beginner." In his report to *The Academy* that month he was able to say "Pottery is now pretty completely known, and we shall be able in future to date the ages of towns at a glance, as I can in Egypt."[11]

The Committee of the Palestine Exploration Fund, to whom he made his report two days after his return on 1 July 1890, begged Petrie to consider returning to Palestine the following year, but he had already made up his mind. His life's work was in Egypt. He had refused a similar offer during the previous summer, to work in Cyprus. All he could do was to promise to give whomsoever they might find to take over from him every assistance in his power.

Petrie's report on Tell el Hesy was not without its critics. Conder doubted his conclusions: "deductions from pottery," he wrote, "are apt to mislead." Petrie's reply was prompt: he had examined, he said, about fifty thousand pieces of pottery in Palestine; in Egypt, some three million. "If after such searching during the last nine years I have never yet seen any distinctive pottery of any age which I could mistake for that of any other known period, though I was always searching and looking for exceptions—or anything which disagreed with the conclusions which I was forming—I think it justifiable to say that deductions from pottery are not misleading. No excavations can yield their proper fruits without using this main key to understanding them."[12]

His exhibition opened in mid-September. Meanwhile he went down to Bristol to see Miss Edwards, bringing her various small *antikas* for her collection. He found her in a sorry state; she had returned from her strenuous tour of the United States in March, tired and far from well: in Columbus, Ohio, she had fallen on a stairway but in spite of a compound fracture of her arm she had insisted on carrying on with her strenuous programme of lecturing; on the way home she had been thrown against her cabin wall in a gale and a third fall on her return caused a splinter of bone to pierce an artery; she had almost lost the use of her hand and arm. She was delighted with what he brought her; she had secured for him a grant of some hundreds of dollars from the Archaeological Association of the University of Pennsylvania, who were starting a museum; they would welcome antiquities. Petrie promised that they should have some of his finds from the Fayum. Her American lectures were going to be published and she insisted that he should be paid for the use of his photographs in the book.

By the end of October the exhibition had closed, all the exhibits had been packed up and sent to their destinations, the proofs of *Tell el Hesy* corrected and despatched to the publishers, and an article written for *The Journal of Hellenic Studies* that was to make history.

Tell el Hesy: alphabetic signs

CHAPTER VIII

Tussles with M. Grébaut

(1890–2)

In spite of his dislike and distrust of committees, Petrie had been drawn into membership of one which appears to have been formed, if not at his instigation, at least as a result of conversations he had with prominent members of the artistic and intellectual life of London. On 8 August 1888 he was invited to Edward Poynter's studio, to a gathering which included the painters Alma Tadema, Frank Dillon and Henry Wallis, and the Director of the National Gallery, Sir Frederick Burton; Wallis Budge was the only other Egyptologist present. The theme of their discussion was the rapidly deteriorating state of the temples and tombs in Egypt, for the safety of which, it was felt, Britain bore the ultimate responsibility. The comparative security brought to Egypt by the British military occupation had produced its own problems; tourism was on the increase, and with it vandalism and destruction. Tombs had become quarries; paintings and reliefs were being hacked out, for souvenirs or for sale, and whole blocks removed from the walls. In some areas new construction projects had created a demand for building stone and limestone for the kilns, and local authorities did not enquire from what source these materials were so readily provided. British officials in the Egyptian administration had neither the time nor the money to spend on protecting the monuments and many of them, it was felt, were not greatly concerned to do so. After some discussion it was decided to form a Committee (later Society) for the Preservation of the Monuments of Ancient Egypt; its objects would be to aid the Egyptian government in preserving their antiquities and protecting them from further damage "by means of doors and enclosures, and by the appointment of responsible guardians and inspectors; and, where possible, by works calculated to resist and neutralize the encroachments of the Nile."[1] Poynter and Henry Wallis were to be Joint Secretaries. Among those invited to be the first members of the Society were Amelia Edwards, Sayce,

Holman Hunt, Burne-Jones, G. F. Watts and Sir Henry Layard.

They decided to meet again in October. In a rash moment, hearing that Cope Whitehouse was in London, Poynter wrote inviting him to come to the meeting and join the Committee. The answer must have surprised him: it was an attack on the Fund—"The appeal to *protect* ancient monuments scarcely comes with a good grace from those who are asking money to *rob* Egypt of the valuable stones at Bubastis. . . ." and continued with a personal attack upon Petrie: "Schweinfurth told me that Virchow said to him that the horrors of Königsgratz (*sic*) had not prepared him for the revolting sight of Petrie's mangled remains at Hawara." The "gentle-faced" Virchow, to whose hotel Petrie had taken the trouble to deliver three boxes of skulls he had asked for, had evidently repaid this kindness by spiteful gossip. Wallis sent the letter to Petrie, who replied that he was not at all surprised; Whitehouse should be told "that not a single bone or piece of mummy was left unburied at the close of my work at Hawara. Why does no one complain of the thousands of bones lying on the hill of Gizeh which is visited by every traveller?" Wallis framed his reply accordingly, but Poynter appears to have made no effort to stop Whitehouse from coming to speak at the meeting; The latter arrived with the American naval attaché; his way was barred by Wallis, there was a scuffle, high words were exchanged and the Americans were forced to leave. Poynter later wrote to apologize to Whitehouse but did not again invite him to join the Society.[2]

As a result, it would seem, of pressure exercised by Poynter and his friends that winter through the Foreign Office, a preliminary report on the state of the monuments was drawn up and the authorities of the Antiquities Service agreed to devote the money raised by a tax of 100 piastres on every tourist, admission charges to the Museum and the sale of antiquities in the Museum shop, to the repair and maintenance of several of the Theban temples and for doors to be affixed to the Tombs of the Kings. In April Sir Colin Scott-Moncrieff was able to tell Poynter that £1,000 had been raised; this was, at any rate, a beginning. Then the Committee protested to Lord Salisbury, the Minister of State for Foreign Affairs, against the removal of the contents of the Bulaq Museum to the derelict palace at Giza, which they regarded as totally unsuitable: it was far too large, inaccessible to tourists (that is to say, too long a drive from Shepheard's Hotel) and a grave fire hazard, as well as being very damp. Sir Colin Scott-Moncrieff tried to block the sending of this memorandum; the new museum was in many ways an excellent building, he said, and they were very lucky to get it; there was no money to build a new museum, and it had become essential to move from the Bulaq building, which was far too small and right on the river bank where it was in annual danger of flooding. The petition was forwarded to Sir Evelyn Baring in Cairo but little notice was taken of it and the transfer to Giza went ahead.

The next objective of Poynter and his committee was to press for the appointment of an English inspector to watch over the monuments, report damage and recommend prompt remedial action. As a result of some agitation in the Press, Lord Salisbury promised them in December 1889 that Sir Evelyn Baring would be required to put a proposal to the Egyptian Government that "if the S.P.M.A.E. will devote its available funds towards placing the temples and other monuments in a proper state of repair the Egyptian Government will appoint and pay an English officer, with sufficient staff, as Inspector of Temples and Superintendent of Guardians."[3] The urgency of the matter became apparent in February 1890; Greville Chester wrote from Egypt reporting serious deterioration of the monuments. The previous day he had visited El Bersheh; the wall-relief showing the transport of the colossus had recently been wantonly, irretrievably, hacked about and the tombs of Beni Hasan had also suffered defacement. "All this destruction," he said "must have taken a *very long time* and the use of appropriate *tools* if not ladders." He suspected a foreigner, if not a gang at work. George Fraser, writing from Minya, confirmed the story of damage, and offered himself to Poynter as their Inspector; he had had experience of digging, he said, he knew Arabic and some Egyptology and was young and used to summer heat. Angry letters appeared in *The Academy* from Lieut Col Ross, the Inspector General of Irrigation, and Professor Sayce,[4] reiterating the sorry tale of destruction; not a farthing of the money raised by the Antiquities tax on tourists, said Sayce, had been spent on the protection of the monuments. "It is evident that whatever inscriptions there are above ground in Egypt must be copied at once, if they are to be copied at all." At the second annual meeting of the S.P.M.A.E. it was decided to ask Sir Evelyn Baring once again to press the government of Egypt for the appointment of Arab guardians for the tombs and temples and for an effective inspector to be appointed, who should be an Englishman, and not a Frenchman "who would not command the confidence of the English public".[5]

Baring was in a quandary. He was particularly anxious not to offend the French government at a time when there was still great ill feeling in France against the British over the matter of the Conversion of the

Debt. All public expenditure had to be sanctioned by the Caisse de la Dette, and France was one of Egypt's main creditors. It had recently been agreed by a Convention that in return for certain financial concessions on their part, the French should be allowed a free hand in the Antiquities Department; they would certainly not tolerate the appointment of an Englishman to interfere in what they had always regarded as a purely French sphere of influence. Yet agitation in England was growing and the recent reports of damage had aggravated public concern.

This was the situation when Petrie returned from Syria. At the Society's July meeting he proposed that, since it was evidently "hopeless to expect any benefit from the government", they should themselves pay an independent inspector, some young English engineer of their own choice, not necessarily an Egyptologist, who would scour the country and rush from one point to another when there was the slightest suspicion of anything requiring to be examined; he knew of one young man who might be suitable (he was thinking of Fraser).[6] The suggestion met with some support but in the end it was decided to abandon the question of the inspectorate and devote the money instead to the rescue of the temple of Karnak from damage by salt-infiltration. Petrie in disgust resigned from the Committee, but resolved to carry on the battle for an English inspector by himself; he had the support of Henry Wallis and one or two others.

Meanwhile, the Egypt Exploration Fund had been roused into action. They decided to embark on a new venture, one which was in part Petrie's brainchild: an Archaeological Survey of Egypt. The scheme was first made public in a letter written by Miss Edwards to *The Times*;[7] they planned, she said "to map, plan, photograph and copy all the most important sites, sculptures, and paintings and inscriptions yet extant, so as to preserve at least a faithful record of those fast-perishing monuments". She invited contributions from all lovers of ancient art and history towards this new and important undertaking. Francis Llewellyn Griffith was to be entrusted with the task of organizing and editing the work of the survey. He must have discussed the need for such an undertaking with Petrie during their journey up the Nile four years before. He envisaged at first a complete survey of all the monuments of Egypt: two scholars should be commissioned to scour the country from end to end "verifying the accounts of travellers, collecting placenames, searching out new monuments and describing the order and condition of those already known." He himself was now an employee of the British Museum and could not go: he chose George Fraser, whose knowledge of Egypt and training with Petrie would be valuable, and Percy Newberry, who had been studying Egyptology at Petrie's suggestion, and was a competent draughtsman; he was now twenty-two. They proposed initially to survey that part of Egypt that Fraser knew best—the area from Minia to Asyut; they would begin with the district of Beni Hasan and the region immediately to the south. To copy the tomb paintings at Beni Hasan alone, they reckoned, would entail studying and tracing twelve thousand square feet of paintings. It was a formidable task on which to embark without previous experience.

When Petrie heard that they were going, he was full of helpful advice.[8] It would be necessary to record accurately the position in the cliffs of every inscription which they copied; the best way to do this would be to devise a system of decimal numeration, simple but capable of accurately defining the location. Rule your map of the area, he suggested, into latitude miles and divide it into districts; then Derut 3 will mean a certain mile, Derut 32 defines a certain stade, Derut 326 a certain chain, and Derut 3264 a certain fathom; for longitudinal position the cliff could be divided into twenty levels, judged by eye; so Derut 3264 F would mean a tomb in that particular latitude, in that fathom strip, and fairly near the top. The end of a line of tombs could be fixed by compass bearings from landmarks such as distant villages. In another long letter Petrie sent him detailed advice about the stores and provisions he should take, and how to get them out to Egypt. Blankets are the best kind of bedding: a pile of six folded will serve as mattress and bedding in one. A petroleum stove, kettle, saucepan and frying-pan and a large enamelled basin are all the hardware they will need; a dozen penknives are useful for presents. Their stores should include packet soups, tins of peas, tinned meat and fish, jams (Petrie had a sweet tooth and reckoned on eating three quarters of a pound of jam a day), dried fruits, tins of biscuits ("good for native company") tea, loaf sugar ("good for presents"), salt, carbolic soap and insect powder.[9]

Petrie enjoyed introducing Percy Newberry to Egypt; they travelled together from Paris (Henry Wallis was also on the boat) and on the way from Alexandria stopped a few hours at Naucratis. In Cairo they called on the Grants; the doctor had married again, and Petrie was glad to find that the young woman had been well received in Cairo society and got on well with her stepdaughter. He introduced Newberry to various of his friends, showed him the museum, took him to the pyramids at Giza and out to the Tombs of the Caliphs, and went with him round the dealers; they met Fraser and the three of them saw General Grenfell and talked over with him their proposed work and their need for permits.

Flinders had decided the year before what he wanted to do. The great stone pyramid of Meydum stands like a sentinel on the desert edge looking over the wide green Fayum depression. The Arabs call it the "False Pyramid", for its walls rise tower-like from a mound of stone chips at the base and the sloping outer case has quite gone. Its builder was unknown, but it was attributed by most Egyptologists to Snoferu, the father of Khufu, the builder of the Great Pyramid; if this were indeed so, Meydum might hold the key to a civilization earlier than that of Giza—"Could we there see the incipient stages, or at least their traces? Could we learn how conventional forms and ideas had arisen? Could we find Egypt not yet fully grown, still in its childhood?"[10] It was a tempting possibility. The pyramid (**35**) had been entered by Maspero in 1882 but nothing had been done to clear the débris around or to investigate the surrounding structures.

Grébaut, as usual, was away. Col Ross, who was deputizing for Scott-Moncrieff, was most helpful; Newberry and Fraser were given permission to start copying at once, but a permit to dig at Meydum had to come from Grébaut and all Petrie could do was wait till he came. Meanwhile he made some satisfactory purchases in Cairo, lunched with Sir Francis Grenfell, and had a not altogether unrewarding interview with the Consul General, Sir Evelyn Baring, on the subject of the need for an inspector for the protection of the monuments. Henry Wallis went with him to Old Cairo and encouraged him to try his hand at watercolour sketching. He walked out to Heliopolis, where he determined to dig one day. At last, when he had been more than a fortnight in Cairo, Grébaut turned up; he gave Petrie permission to begin at Meydum, clearing and copying the tombs opened by Mariette and his assistant Danino twenty years before; the permit for the pyramid, he promised, would follow. Leaving at once for Lisht, Petrie packed up the stores he had left in the Irrigation house, collected a dozen of his best workmen from the year before, and the same afternoon set off on foot for Meydum eighteen miles away. On arrival at the site, half a mile north of the pyramid, he set up a tent, which he intended to use for cooking and for working; he would sleep in one of the tombs, where he would be quiet and warmer at night. A canal on the edge of the cultivation at the foot of the hill would provide drinking water and there was a village not far away from which he would be able, when the time came, to recruit labour.

It was, and still is, a delightful place. Below the escarpment, the wide green carpet of the Nile valley, patterned with fields and palm groves and little mud villages, spreads towards the distant eastern cliffs; westwards stretches the flat and limitless desert.

> Here I am once more in peace in this land, and the relief of getting back here I never felt so much before. The real tranquillity and room for quiet thought in this sort of life is refreshing. I here *live*, and do not scramble to fit myself to the requirements of others. In a narrow tomb with the figure of Nefermaat standing on each side of me—as he has stood through all that we know as human history—I have just room for my bed, and a row of good reading in which I can take my pleasure when I retire to the blankets after dinner. Behind me is that Great Peace, the Desert. It is an entity—a power—just as the sea is. No wonder men fled to it from the turmoil of the ancient world.
>
> It would do many a modern more good than anything else, both for mind and body, just to come and live in a cave, and cultivate a little bean plot like an ancient eremite, for half the year, and then return to the jangle of Europe. Every time I come back to England I am more and more disgusted with the merciless rush, and the turmoil of strife for money . . . the writhing and wriggling of this maggoty world is loathsome. . . . It is delightful to have done with the degradation of having always a lacquey—or still worse a woman—helping you when you don't need it; degradation to you, because degradation to them. When I see an obsequious waiter, I can hardly help begging his pardon for being accessory to a condition which so unmans him.[11]

Mariette's publication of the tombs of Nefermaat and of Rahotep (in which he had found the remarkable lifesize painted statues of the owner and his wife Nefert, still amongst the greatest treasures of the Cairo Museum) had been perfunctory;[12] not a quarter of the area of wall painting had been copied, and the hieroglyphs had been very inaccurately drawn. The tombs had not been properly closed again and vandals had destroyed or disfigured the delicate paintings. "As these are probably the oldest tombs known in Egypt they are among the most important, and yet they have been wholly neglected for twenty years." To make full-sized copies of the reliefs and inscriptions, by dry-squeezing—pressing a thin sheet of paper over the outline with the tips of the fingers and then transferring it to a drawing board—he reckoned would take three weeks. The sheets of paper he intended to join into rolls; some of the figures were over five foot high. Six colours were used; these he noted carefully. In one tomb the figures had been hollowed out and filled out with coloured paste; the experiment had not been very successful, for much of the paste had fallen out. Elsewhere, where the reliefs were surface-painted, Mariette or one of his helpers had removed most of the colour by wet-squeezing. Petrie set great store by the accuracy of his copies; "when I started such copying a plate was actually cancelled by Poole as being incorrect forms, and was redrawn in a pretty and orthodox way by Madame Naville." When Newberry wrote to him reporting progress, Petrie sent him a detailed exposition of the art of exact facsimile drawing: the smallest change in the line of the lips, he said (illustrating his point with pencil sketches) alters the expression of a face. It might be possible at Beni Hasan to distinguish the work of different artists by noting tiny variations in the form of hieroglyphs and figures, so he urged Newberry to "tabulate all variables". The hieroglyphic signs at Meydum were of especial interest, since they were the earliest forms known, and it was sometimes possible to see, from the detailed drawing of a sign, what object it had originally represented before it became stereotyped in the conventional repertory of a later age. Above all, he urged Newberry and Fraser to copy *everything* they saw on the walls.[13] Unfortunately, though they followed his advice (as did the trained artist Marcus Blackden who joined them in the spring), in the final publication of the Beni Hasan paintings, for reasons of economy, too small a scale was chosen, with the result that much of the detail of these unique paintings, so carefully observed, was lost in the reproduction.[14]

Petrie also sent Fraser advice on surveying and planning the tombs; he urged him to measure every dimension, and in particular, opposite and symmetrical parts, in order to ascertain how small or great an error the craftsmen had made. If opposite dimensions are the same to 1/10 inch, they should be measured to 1/100 inch. Interpreting the people's mistakes, he said, tells a great deal, and careful observation of the errors made in dressing the walls of the tomb chamber and in cutting and fluting the columns will throw light on the methods of the ancient stonemasons. "In short, try to understand exactly *what* the workman aimed at, *how* he tried to do it, and *where* he fell short of his intentions." He concluded with a wise piece of advice born of his own long experience: "Do not take a mass of figures and leave them undigested; work out the results, and what they point to, as soon as possible." The letter ended with an invitation to Newberry to visit him at Meydum; he should leave the train at Rikka station, walk three miles to a point opposite the camp, "howl at the canal just below us, and the men will carry you over."

Newberry and Fraser did come, later in the season; it was on an exciting day when the workmen had got almost to the bottom of the unopened well of the tomb of Rahotep. They decided to stay till next morning. Newberry was not feeling well, but Fraser helped Petrie lever away the great stone portcullis closing the passage to the burial chamber, and to clear the masonry blocking behind it, so that he could crawl in. The body was there, but it had been disturbed by the ancient plunderers who had removed all the ornaments and the funeral furniture, leaving only the mummy, "marvellously plumped out and modelled, in pitch and resin, and coated with the most exquisitely fine linen, like that of Pepi and Mentuemsaf of the VIth dynasty." This one, of course, was much earlier; indeed it was, and remained one of the most ancient of all known mummies; it went, with other human remains from these Meydum tombs, to the Royal College of Surgeons in London; but unfortunately all were destroyed when the museum of the College received a direct hit during the Second World War.

After Petrie had been in Meydum for nearly three weeks, Grébaut's permit arrived; but it contained one proviso which threw him into despair: "*Il y aura partage des antiquités après prélèvement des pièces uniques au profit du Musée.*" "Unique pieces"? Practically everything found in Egypt could be said to be unique, if the Antiquities Department chose to think it so. He decided to cut short his season and abandon his plan to dig; he sat down at once to write numerous letters: to Col Ross in protest, to Naville and D'Hulst warning them of the new rule, to Jesse Haworth and Martyn Kennard, who had a right to know of the frustration of their prospects, and to Henry Wallis who was still in Egypt; he also drafted an angry letter to *The Times*, but forbore for the moment to send it.[15] Henry Wallis at once wrote to Sir Evelyn Baring warning him that Petrie was preparing to raise a storm in England; Baring, anxious to avoid criticism of his failure to support archaeologists, wrote and telegraphed Petrie and finally asked him to come to Cairo to discuss his complaints. On 3 January, Flinders Petrie attended a meeting with the Consul General, Grenfell, Ross, and Palmer, the head of finance; it was the Armenian ministers, Tigran Pasha and Artin Pasha, he understood, who had been against him, as an Englishman and an outspoken critic of the administration; one of them had been heard to say "Mr Petrie must be made to understand that there is no room for him in Egypt."[16] After several days of discussion a new formula was worked out for the Council of Ministers that satisfied everybody: the Museum was to keep objects *sans pareil*—that is to say, outstanding treasures such as had always been prevented from leaving the country—and no more; the excavator was to guarantee to present at least half of what remained to museums, and to publish the results of his finds within two years; disputes would go for arbitration to the Public Works Department, not to the Museum.

Petrie was satisfied, not least because Grébaut had been discomfited; the Director was also in hot water, people said, about his accounts, which had not been presented for several years and were reputed to be in fearful disarray. Artin Pasha, who was the Minister for Education, now went out of his way to be amiable; rather surprisingly he suggested that Petrie might write an elementary geography for use in the country schools; Petrie was tempted. As he wrote to Spurrell: "What I am going to try is to write a word for word translation into English . . . of what I would say to a fellah boy in Arabic about the various countries. . . . I doubt if there are any English here who know the fellah understandings more than I do." Yet he had admitted that he found it impossible to see the world as the fellah sees it; "after living the most part of ten years among the fellahin, and being accused of having gone some way toward them, I yet feel the gulf between their nature and my own as impassable as ever."[17] For some reason the geography book was never written: Artin Pasha seems to have withdrawn his proposal, and Petrie let the matter drop.

As soon as he got back to Meydum he took on men from the village and started to work in the area round the pyramid. They uncovered the south-eastern cornerstone and part of the pavement; there was no sign of a temple to the east of the pyramid, yet here, as in all known pyramids elsewhere, there should be one; Petrie concluded that it must lie deep under the huge mass of rubble and chips and sand surrounding the base of the pyramid. He marked out a space "which would have held two or three London houses", and set the men to clear away the débris. It took several weeks, and proved difficult and sometimes dangerous work; under the surface there were huge blocks, fallen from the casings of the pyramid; some were too big to shift and had to be cut up, others slipped and rolled down, starting a small avalanche. High winds raised stinging clouds of sand and dislodged loose stones from the sides of the pit; one great fall "came near to burying us at the bottom of the work". The men worked hard: they were paid by the cubic metre, and although this was considerably less than the current government rate, as Petrie gleefully pointed out to Ross when he came they earned far more by their efforts than the average daily government wage.

At last they came upon the pyramid temple, a small limestone building with a tiny courtyard behind it in which there stood two tall slabs of stone with rounded tops, devoid of inscriptions (**36**); when the roofed chamber and passage in front of the stelae were cleared, the walls were seen to have been scribbled on by ancient visitors who had come in the eighteenth dynasty, a thousand years later, to admire "the beautiful temple of King Snoferu". Petrie was just able to make out the royal names in these hieratic graffiti; he now had proof of the date of his pyramid. The strange little building had an importance out of all proportion to its size and lack of decoration: it was, in those days, the earliest temple ever to have been found in Egypt. Petrie studied the construction of the pyramid itself and was able to establish that it had first been built as a mastaba, then enlarged by successive layers or coats of masonry, each wrapped around it so as to increase the width and height, till the final sloping outer cladding of polished stone gave it the final pyramid form. It had been remarkably like its larger successor, the Great Pyramid of Khufu, being almost identical both in the angle of the slope and in the ratio of height to base: "theories will have to be recast a bit," he wrote, "though I suppose nothing will be too tough for C.P.S. to explain away" (Piazzi Smyth's book had recently been reissued for the fifth time).

During these weeks he had a number of visitors. The Wilbours arrived with their two young daughters from the *Seven Hathors*, moored near Wasta. The girls were much impressed by the strange bearded figure in his careless, dusty clothes; he had eyes, they said, like an eagle's.[18] The next day Frederick Bliss arrived. He was a young American, the son of Daniel Bliss the founder of the American College in Beirut, who had been engaged by the Palestine Exploration Fund to carry on Petrie's work at Tell el Hesy; Petrie had offered to brief him, and to give him what we should nowadays call a crash course in archaeology. He stayed at Meydum for nearly three weeks, learning the basic principles of digging under Petrie's critical eye. "My first impression of Petrie," he wrote to his father "was very pleasant—a clear intelligent eye—black hair and beard—and a pleasant but very decided quiet manner."[19] To begin with he found life on a dig strenuous and rather alarming. "Three to four hours this morning and three to four hours this afternoon I have rushed after the rapid Petrie from gang to gang. His knowledge is marvellous. He manages his men like a good despot—he has an iron will and evidently good judgement. He expects me to eat with him—cooks himself and I take my tins and anything I may have cooked [he had brought a Berber servant] and we share . . . I am very comfortable and astonishingly well . . . P.S. He wears no stockings!"

This flouting of the conventions seems to have worried his sister, who in a later letter had to be assured that Petrie defended his socklessness on grounds of hygiene. Bliss was still there when Newberry and Fraser came. Together he and Fraser were initiated into the mysteries of surveying; to begin with they both found it very difficult to follow Petrie's instructions, but Bliss persevered, practising with a prismatic compass, and then trying his hand at levelling, pretending that the mound covering one of the larger mastabas was a Palestinian *tell*. He was also shown how to develop photographs. When he left on 7 February, bound for his new life as an archaeologist, Petrie could say approvingly: "He has industry, and conscience for his work, and may I hope do well. He intends to aim at the fullest results, and will certainly not fail for want of will and understanding." A month later he had a letter from him: all was well, he had begun work, he was getting on well with the Effendi.[20] Petrie felt he could now abdicate responsibility for Palestine with a clear conscience.

The tug-of-war in the Antiquities Department went on. It was decided to appoint two inspectors; at Sir Evelyn Baring's instigation, and with recommendations from Petrie and Naville, the Prime Minister Riaz Pasha invited Count D'Hulst to be one of them; as a German national it was hoped he might be acceptable, but there was an immediate outcry in the French community in Cairo, and the French Consul went so far as to write to M. Naville asking him to withdraw his testimonial; the appointment was not confirmed. Meanwhile M. Grébaut had telegraphed from Assuan that he could not recognize the recent decision of the Council of Ministers on the division of antiquities. "If the English officials over here were not so supine and ignorant," wrote Petrie to his friends at home, "there would be a clean sweep of this confusion, I expect. The French Consul *will go to any length to keep things in French hands*."

As the season went on, he did not lack for company. His visitors included Robertson Smith, the Biblical anthropologist, several friends of Miss Edwards, Capt. Lyons of the Royal Engineers, and J. J. Tylor, just returned from copying tomb paintings at Thebes and anxious to see Petrie's technique. Naville and D'Hulst came, the former much interested in the hieratic graffiti but in too much of a hurry to check Petrie's copies for him. Canon Rawnsley of Keswick, on a tour of Egypt, arrived late one day and had to crave hospitality for the night; he wrote a book about his experiences and describes in amusing detail his reception by the "brave explorer"; they had supper together in the tiny tent, and Petrie "set his lamp a-going and gave me of his store a supper fit for Sneferu; lent me his own pocket knife to eat my feast, shared his single teaspoon with me, and finished piling on his desert courtesy with a bit of crystallized ginger such as Sneferu and Nefermaat never knew. I proffered my English bread in return; he haughtily refused it. What was English bread to a man who can get Arab bread thrice a week from Wasta? I suggested that fowl recently killed and cooked would be a pleasant addition to his supper. He fiercely refused to believe me; had he not potted pilchards in abundance . . . that were better than all the fowls of the Nile valley?"

Taken next morning to see the pyramid temple, the Canon felt a little apprehensive: "Here, above our heads as we talked, hung the chip-sealing, a single gun-shot fired, and all would be re-buried again!" He was astonished at the friendly relationship existing between Petrie and his workmen. "I had seen them labouring with their palm-baskets and adze-shaped hoes till after sundown. Mr. Petrie had been late in taking observations, and so had not given his usual signal of a whistle for the men to cease work, but they did not cease, and I soon found that there had been established such relations between employed and employer as made the day's work not slaves' labour, but the work of men who wished to serve their master in love to the uttermost." He contrasts this easy relationship with what he had seen at Luxor and Karnak, where men and children were lashed with the *kurbash* by their overseers. "*Mafeesh kurbash, shoghul mafeesh*" ("Without the kurbash, there's no work"), he was told. But here in Meydum, he found workmen labouring with pleasure and with pride for the Khawaga Engleezi—the English gentleman. ". . . a light was in their faces, and a smile on their lips, for they toiled for honest bread at honest price, and their master was a friend!" He quotes from a letter Petrie wrote to him subsequently on the same subject. "I have never found occasion to strike a man or child that was in my pay, during ten years' work. This is not from any sentimental reason (for I heartily believe in the kurbash as a penal measure) but simply that no one is worth employing who needs punishing. . . . My workmen always form my natural guards and friends, and I have never known them steal anything. On the contrary, they will often dispute an account against their own interest, and if accidentally paid too much in error, they will bring back the money and go over it."[21]

Petrie had "solved Meydum" by finding the temple, but there was still much work to be done in the cemeteries north and south of the pyramid. One very large mastaba, No. 17 (**37** also p. 312), defied his attempts to find the tomb chamber, but afforded a quite unexpected insight into the methods used by the ancient architects in constructing the building: they had constructed short brick walls at right angles outside each of the corners and on the white-plastered inner surface of each, they had drawn lines sloping at the correct angle from bedrock to ground level; by sighting from one line to the other at the opposite end of each side in turn, they could ensure the correct angle of slope for the brickwork of the *mastaba*.[22] Such technical matters delighted Flinders Petrie. The early history of technology was illustrated too in the hieroglyphs: several kinds of pillar, for instance, were drawn in careful detail, showing that before the age of the pyramids of Giza, fluted columns and papyrus capitals were already features of what he called the "lost architecture" of the earliest buildings. In the tombs there was plenty of the polished bright-red pottery which he had found ten years earlier at Giza and already then attributed to the fourth dynasty; this fine tableware of the nobility is usually known as "Meydum ware". In smaller tombs in the cemetery, complete skeletons were found in a crouched position, lying on their left side, and without grave goods. Since the bodies found in the *mastabas* were buried outstretched, with ample equipment for the afterlife, Petrie deduced a fundamental difference of tradition and belief, and postulated the arrival of a "dynastic race" imposing their rule on the indigenous population.

It was getting very hot but he felt unusually well; this year he had not suffered, he told Spurrell, from the cramps and palpitations that usually plagued him. "It is the drive and worry of England that knocks my circulation over; it is part of a long-standing affair and one that mainly needs the quiet I get here. . . . If I am to avoid evil causes I must keep away from Committees and troublesome people, keep my work as simple as possible, in my own hands, and as clear of other people as may be. These are good resolutions; don't you wish I may keep them!"[23]

By 14 April the packing was finished; Flinders deposited his gear with Major Hewat at Wasta and the next day went down to Cairo with his boxes of antiquities. Grébaut was somewhere up the Nile—nobody knew where, as he never wrote letters—but Brugsch dealt competently and, to Petrie's relief, generously with the division, and took none of the painted fragments or the alabaster dishes. After a few days, having seen to the despatch of his boxes, Petrie moved to Alexandria where Sir Charles Cookson had "booked" him to give a lecture at the new Athenaeum Club. Next day he boarded a steamer for the Piraeus.

He had long wanted to visit Greece; now the reason was pressing. The full report of his discoveries at Kahun and Gurob during the previous two years had not yet been published—one or two contributors had been slow with their chapters—but during the previous summer, at the instigation of Ernest Gardner (with whom he had discussed the matter at length) he had contributed an article to a classical journal with the challenging title "The Egyptian Bases of Greek History".[24] In it he had set out his evidence for the second millennium dating of the "Aegean" pottery he had found. As he had expected, the conclusions reached in this short article had excited great interest among classical scholars, and some disbelief. Pottery like that which Schliemann had found at Mycenae in 1876 and had dated vaguely to the Heroic Age was turning up on other Greek sites; many thought it later than the Dorian invasion. Heinrich Schliemann himself may have read the article, but he was already a sick man, and he died at Naples just after Christmas. None of the treasures of Mycenae had been allowed to leave Greece; Petrie resolved that he must now see them for himself.

Ernest Gardner was now the Director of the British School at Athens, and he and his wife received Flinders cordially in their house on the outskirts of the city and took him straight off to the Polytechnikon to see the material from Schliemann's excavations at Mycenae in 1876 and those more recently carried out by Tsountas; he planned to spend three weeks in this museum and others, drawing and taking notes. He was happy in Athens: the fitful sunshine and rolling clouds and the thyme-scented air were a delightful contrast to the hot, windy, dusty Egypt he had left, and the "high civilization" of Mycenae surprised and enchanted him. Dining at the Gardners, he found there an old friend, Walter Leaf, the Homeric scholar, who had worked in England on his *Iliad* papyrus; he was going, he said, to the Peloponnese: would Petrie care to come with him? This was a great stroke of luck. They were joined by an American professor of Greek named Maclean, and for three days they lodged at an inn in Nauplion, and visited the great Mycenaean sites: at Tiryns Petrie noted particularly the methods used in cutting the great stones (the saws, he remarked, had been over 4½ feet long); at Mycenae he espied rows of nails and nail-holes in the dome of the great *tholos* tomb called the Treasury of Atreus which he concluded from their position to have been for cloth draperies, rather than for rosettes or bronze ornaments of some kind (the idea does not seem to have found favour subsequently). He returned to Athens and moved up to the Gardners' house to stay, his head buzzing with ideas; after another week's work at the Polytechnikon, he spent a day setting down his conclusions: "From a study of the Mykenaean and other things I came to a different view as to their relative history to what is generally held; and much of my ground was from Egyptian comparisons which I could make. Gardner encouraged me, but referred to my 'heresy' for some days. When at last I put down all that I had to say in order, and he read it, he said that he could not but agree with me throughout; and he considered that I had 'done more in a week than the Germans had done in ten years to clear up the matter' from my Egyptian basis."

This second article appeared a month later;[25] it was to create considerable excitement and much controversy among classical scholars in England as well as in Germany. Relying on his remarkable visual memory, Petrie compared the finds from Mycenae with various fragments of glass and glaze, alabaster dishes and other objects from Gurob which he could date closely; on the basis of these he dated the tombs to be between 1400 and 1200 BC. He refuted Professor Ramsay's theory that the Lion Gate at Mycenae was derived from Phrygian prototypes and could not be earlier than the eighth century BC: lions, he pointed out, were a popular feature of architectural decoration in Egypt during the New Kingdom. Various other motifs which he enumerated were also, he claimed, derived from the valley of the Nile; familiarity with Egypt argued an Aegean presence in Egypt from about 1500 BC—not merely trade. Other details such as the Baltic amber, and drapery in tombs, he held to show "a Northern intercourse".

His paper safely posted, Petrie was able to enjoy the archaic sculptures in the museum on the Acropolis. He had been nearly six weeks in Greece, and he decided he would leave with Walter Leaf for Italy; he had no particular plans but he was not in a particular hurry to get home, and for the first time, had enough leisure and enough money in his pocket to see some of the places he had always wanted to visit. A young American archaeologist named Pickard who travelled with them invited Petrie to stay at his *pensione* in Naples: he spent six days in the Naples Museum, drawing the rich collection of tools from Pompeii; he wandered at will around the ruins of Pompeii on a student's free ticket, and found it delightful, though the much-vaunted paintings were poor stuff, he thought, compared with his Hawara portraits. As the Museum shut at four, he had plenty of time to wander around the countryside. Then he moved on to Rome, joining Pickard in lodgings near the Forum. He was to visit Rome many times in the future, and would come to know it as well as he knew London; now, like anyone making first acquaintance with that great and bewildering city, he had to restrain his sightseeing to those places which held the greatest interest for him. He saw the bronzes and sculptures of the Vatican Museums ("a wilderness of mediocrity"); he spent hours in the Capitoline Museum, where, in his view, there were some of the best things, "all the statues from later excavations exactly as they were found, without the abominable scraping and polishing and patching which has been done in the Vatican". Best of all, he thought, was the Kircherian Museum in the Collegio Romano with its fine Etruscan collection; the anthropological and prehistoric sections seemed to him to be "far in advance of any other museum in management." The other collection of Etruscan antiquities, in the Villa Giulia, which he was to study closely in years to come, had not yet been catalogued or arranged; Professor Peterson, whom he met there, on being told that he had been working in Egypt, asked him if he had been helping a Mr Petrie. The ensuing laughter began a lasting friendship.

Here in Rome museums shut even earlier, so Flinders' afternoons were spent roaming the city. In the first week of June he moved on with Pickard; they went to Chiusi, Perugia, Cortona; in each town they made straight for the museum and Petrie made copious notes and sketches of early pottery, weapons and tools. In Florence Egyptian and Etruscan antiquities occupied most of his time, though he did allow himself a day looking at the Botticellis and Fra Angelicos. Then, Bologna: the richness of the Etruscan and Umbrian collection here surprised him; wherever groups of objects had been found together they had been carefully reassembled in the museum, "moved bodily on the block of earth into the building." This met with his entire approval: he was constantly insisting on the importance of keeping groups of objects together as they were found and he was delighted to see the "Room of the Foundry" where thousands of tools, found in a bronze foundry, were displayed. Finally he visited Ravenna, which made a very deep impression on him. "Every other place almost has died; Pompeii is dead; the Egyptian temples are dead; even the Pantheon is in a new guise. But here are the churches as Honorius or

Theodoric built them, brick for brick. . . . Ravenna, from its vitality and its perfection, is a far more moving sight than Rome—perhaps the most impressive place I have ever seen."

Stopping briefly at Milan to admire the "icy mountain of the cathedral, the inside perhaps the grandest effect I have seen after the Pantheon", Flinders travelled through the night and reached home on the evening of 15 June; "and so ends about the most instructive two months I ever spent".

His article appeared that summer, and the "pre-Dorian" date of the Mycenaean civilization was at once accepted by the majority of classical scholars. Georg Steindorff in Germany reinforced his argument by pointing out that foreigners depicted on the walls of Theban tombs of certain officials of Tuthmosis III and his successor in the fifteenth century BC carried gifts of goblets and cups very similar in shape to those found by Schliemann and Tsountas at Mycenae and Vapheio.[26] Leaf declared in *The Classical Review* that Petrie's second article "must form the foundation of all the chronology of the Mykenaean period".[27] Yet in the following year A. S. Murray of the British Museum published in 1892 a *Handbook of Greek Archaeology* in which he claimed that the antiquity of the Mycenaean discoveries had been much exaggerated; he denied that there were parallels between this art and that of Egypt, talked vaguely about a "colonial style" and suggested that Mycenae and Tiryns might have been built by the tyrants of the seventh century BC. Then Cecil Torr, reviewing *Illahun, Kahun and Gurob* (which had come out in the winter of 1891) disputed its findings, concluding "Even if Mr. Petrie has stated the evidence accurately, he has not shown that the evidence necessarily leads to his conclusions; and it is hard to believe that a man who is so inaccurate in his reasoning can be altogether accurate in his statement of the evidence."[28] So offensive an attack could not be allowed to pass, and in June 1892 Petrie was forced to embark on a long and tedious exchange of letters with Torr in the pages of *The Academy*; during the next five months the same accusations had again and again to be refuted, while *The Athenaeum* and *The Times* were drawn into the battle. Finally the editors decided to call a halt to the debate. Thenceforward the antiquity of Petrie's "Aegean" finds was not in doubt, and when in the summer of 1893 a young archaeologist, John Linton Myres, announced that he had found in a cave at Kamarais in Crete pottery identical with Petrie's delicate polychrome sherds from the twelfth-dynasty town at Kahun, the vital link between what was to be known as the Minoan civilization and that of Middle Kingdom Egypt was established; the reign of Sesostris II became a lynchpin for Cretan chronology, and Petrie was triumphantly vindicated.

The publication of *Medum* occupied Petrie all through the summer of 1891; he laboured on the inking-in of his full-sized tracings of the wall paintings in the tombs; the finished sheets, eleven foot high, had to be mounted for photolithography for the book. There were not enough spectacular finds this year to be worth the labour and expense of an exhibition; instead, he rented a small house in Bromley in which he could spread out his drawings; Spurrell helped him mount the pieces of loose fresco he had brought back. The text of *Medum* with its twenty coloured plates was completed, and *Ten Years' Digging* ready for the printers, before he left England in mid-October. He was hard pressed for money to pay for these publications. His fixed income, just £110 a year, was barely enough to pay his expenses of living and travelling; otherwise he depended on the sale of objects from his share of the antiquities divided between the members of the "syndicate" and those which he bought in Cairo—if he could bring himself to part with them—and on the modest royalties from his books. But publishers were slow to pay, and even the British Museum owed him money on *antikas* he had sold them long before.[29]

He did not go down to see Miss Edwards this summer. She had been very ill during the previous winter and in the spring, her companion Kate Bradbury had taken her to Italy at her doctor's orders. The trip evidently did her good; a letter to Petrie that summer expressed her concern at the proposed drowning of Philae, against which she had organized a petition. The affairs of the Fund still occupied her and she was particularly involved in the activities of the Archaeological Survey. Petrie had offered to train a young man for the Fund; the suggestion met with her enthusiastic approval: "Of course I fully appreciate the enormous advantage it would be for us to have an explorer trained in the right way. M. Naville is not growing any younger, his family is growing older. His duties as a father will yearly become more urgent and I foresee that he will not *wish* much longer to spend two or three months per annum in Egypt. . . . Now to dismiss M. Naville would not be possible; and to make things so unpleasant that he could not stay would be a method which none of us would contemplate; but heaven defend us from his trained successor! Therefore, you see, a man of *your* training would be supremely valuable."[30] Blackden's name was suggested; he was to go again to Beni Hasan that winter, and would come over to join Petrie for a time. Another young artist, Howard Carter by name, was also to go out, to help with the colour reproductions of some of the tomb paintings. He was only seventeen.

The site that Flinders Petrie was particularly hoping for this year was Tell el 'Amarna, which he had visited briefly with Griffith in 1886. It was a semi-circular plain some seven miles long at the river's edge, bounded on the east by the low hills of the Arabian Desert. Here in about 1375 BC the Pharaoh Akhenaten, or Ikhnaton—then usually known to Egyptologists as Khuenaton—anxious to found a centre for the worship of his patron deity, the sun-god Aton, had built a new capital. After living there for some years with his queen Nefertiti he had died; the court soon moved back to Thebes, and the city was gradually abandoned, and within a generation, deserted. It was an ideal site in which to dig: no subsequent building had disturbed the ruins and many small pieces of sculpture and brightly coloured "faience", or glazed paste, found from time to time by those who rummaged, showed that excavation would reveal something of the rich decoration of the houses and palaces of one of the wealthiest of all Pharaohs and his court. Moreover, a few months after their visit a peasant woman digging in the decayed mud-brick mounds had found many clay tablets which proved to be letters, in Babylonian cuneiform, from Akhenaten's vassals and fellow-monarchs—a sensational find which added a whole chapter to the diplomatic history of Western Asia; there might be more of these documents.

When Petrie arrived in Cairo at the end of October 1891 he heard on all sides of Grébaut's impossible behaviour. D'Hulst told him that he was appointing unsuitable inspectors from among his friends, and allowing Farag and other dealers to dig; Petrie's permit to excavate had not come through. Muddle and procrastination ruled in the Antiquities Service. Sir Evelyn Baring, upon whom Petrie called, "was quite open and pleasant on the subject, but is evidently not free to take a strong course. 'The whole difficulty is that one man Grébaut', said he again and again, with a fist on the table." After five days the Director General consented to see Petrie, and asked him which site he wanted. Petrie, wary by now, asked first for Saqqara and then for Abydos, both sites which he rightly supposed would be refused. Then he asked for Tell el 'Amarna. The tombs, said Grébaut, were already being worked on, but Petrie could have the town area; when pressed, he refused to name the terms on which he would grant the concession: it must go to a meeting of the Committee; Petrie must report at a stated time next Saturday. He kept the appointment, but was told that Grébaut had proposed exactly the conditions which Petrie had refused to accept the year before. Eventually, when he had been in Cairo for a fortnight, the Committee of Management met again; as Sir Francis Grenfell told him afterwards, "We had a desperate struggle over your body for two and half hours." Grébaut would not budge, and finally the English members—Grenfell, Moncrieff, and Palmer—walked out of the meeting declaring that they would never again sit on any committee over which Grébaut presided. Even Tigran Pasha and Artin Pasha had backed Petrie.[31]

He decided to leave for 'Amarna, and leave the final negotiations for his permit in the hands of Sir Colin Scott-Moncrieff. On the way he stopped in the Fayum to enlist five of the best of the workmen from Illahun who had been with him at Meydum in the previous season. He was surprised and pleased at the eagerness with which they agreed to come. These five were to be the backbone of his workforce at 'Amarna and in years to come. Muhammad Mansur, "one-eyed and split-nosed", a cheerful fellow who never grumbled; Misid, a "cheerful, affectionate lad of about seventeen"; 'Ali es Suefi, "one of the meekest, most conscientiously obliging lads I ever knew", who was to become Petrie's devoted companion and friend; 'Abdullah, who could read and write; and his younger brother Hussain, "a lively little fellow, full of jokes and fun, whose laugh alone is worth 7½d. a day". Going first to Wasta to pick up the gear he had left in Hewat's house, he travelled thence by train to Derut, the nearest station, with his men. Next morning the heavy boxes had to be manhandled to the river and on to the felucca, reaching the village of el-Hagg Qandil an hour before sunset. An excited crowd turned out to greet them; Petrie refused their offer of a house in the village and chose a site for his tent to the north-east, up against a high mudbrick boundary wall. "Of course nearly everybody wanted me to do something different; but I found a curiously effective way of settling objectors; by taking one aside, and in a very slow and low voice imperatively stating that I must do as I intended because of so and so. They are so accustomed to loudness and declamation that the strangeness of it reduces them amazingly. I had the satisfaction after all the to and fro of hearing that 'all his words are good'; which was more than might be expected as I had done exactly as I thought best without heeding anyone."

Building a house was the first task; 3,000 bricks sufficed to construct a bedroom for Petrie, a storage- and guest-room next to it, and a room for the Lahunis. They set about the task with zest, three trampling a huge mud-pie and two handing the bricks to Petrie, who was his own bricklayer. On the second day the contract came by post; Grébaut had signed it, although it did not contain the conditions he had so long insisted upon; Petrie, for the moment, had won his battle. Then, while the men were busy plastering, "I walked over the place, and entered on my heritage."

First impressions were daunting. "It is an overwhelming site to deal with," he wrote. "Imagine setting about exploring the ruins of Brighton, for that is about the size of the town." He soon decided that he could not attempt to plan the whole area; to excavate it all would take a whole lifetime. Accordingly he planned to skim the cream from the site, by digging a selection of the houses, so as to recover a typical house plan; excavating the royal palace, if he could find it; and plotting the layout and, if possible, finding the foundation deposits of the temples. Lepsius had drawn a plan of the ruins as they had been in the 1840s; with a copy of this in his hand, Petrie went over the area trying to identify the various low mounds. He soon located a very large building which, he felt sure, must be the palace. It was oriented to north and south, in contrast to the two temples which ran east and west, and had had a huge pillared hall with emplacements for over 500 columns. Fragments of smashed statues of Akhenaten lay about, and in a complex of buildings to the north of the hall there were many fragments of architectural mouldings with a brilliant green glaze. Deep hollows in one or two of the buildings he took to be lakes or fishponds like those shown in the reliefs on the walls of the tombs; a close study of these scenes, showing the king and queen, Akhenaten and Nefertiti, worshipping the Aton in the temples or riding to or from their palace, had already told Petrie something of what to expect, as they have guided later excavators.

Digging began on 20 November. In the first house excavated, he was delighted to find part of a jar of "Aegean" painted ware. It was to be expected: he had found similar pieces at Gurob, in his eighteenth-dynasty tombs; what surprised him now, as the excavation continued, was the great quantity of it. During the season he counted no less than 1341 pieces, representing not less than 800 vessels. Some were stirrup jars and pilgrim bottles striped with black lustrous paint, now known as Mycenaean wares but known to him as "Rhodian"; others were globular vessels he recognized as Cypriot. The importance of the discovery, in so closely dated a site, for Mediterranean archaeology did not escape him; from the evidence of the dated dockets on wine jars and other objects he was able to show that the city had only been occupied for a little over twenty years. "There are few facts in all archaeology," he wrote in his report, "determined with a more

D. *Painted pavement, Tell el 'Amarna.*

overwhelming amount of evidence than the dating of this earlier stage of Aegean pottery to the beginning of the fourteenth century BC."[32]

Forty workmen were taken on and objects began to turn up; it was obvious that "that brute of a plunderer" the dealer Farag had been there recently and others before him, but plenty remained close to the surface and the villagers also began to bring in scraps of inscriptions and small pieces of sculpture, and the blue-painted pottery common at Gurob. Almost as soon as they started digging in the palace area they began to uncover what Petrie unhesitatingly pronounced to be "the most important discovery artistically that there has been since the Old Kingdom statues of Mariette": a large hall was found to have a painted pavement. It covered an area of about 250 square feet, and was of plaster, painted in bright soft colours: the border was a formal design, bouquets of lotus flowers alternating with dishes of food offerings; on either side of a pathway there was a small lake with fish and water plants, and around the lake, a series of delightful little scenes painted in a naturalistic style, of pintail ducks flying up from clumps of reeds and papyrus, and spotted calves gambolling among bushes.* On the pathway there were bound captives, alternately Negro and Asiatic, to be trodden underfoot. Two adjoining rooms proved to have similar floors. Petrie decided that all must be preserved from damage; he wrote at once asking if the Office of Works would pay the cost of roofing it in. The letter was passed to Grébaut, and nothing happened. Meanwhile, anticipating a rush of visitors, Petrie designed and built a walkway of planking nine inches above the pavement, supported on posts driven into the ground at intervals where columns had been, so that they could make the whole circuit of the paintings without damaging the surface. The first callers to see them were Newberry, Carter and Fraser, over from El Bersha just eight miles away where, with Blackden, they were now copying tombs.

The expedition house was complete; after the *durra* harvest, the wooden roof could be covered with a thatch of maize stalks, warm in winter and cool in the summer to come. At first Petrie had been kept awake by the incessant barking of dogs; neither protestations nor threats could induce their owners to silence them. He resorted to a typically "Petriean" ruse: announcing one morning that there would be no work that day—he was too tired—he repaired to the ruins and there slept most of the day through. The workmen whose pockets were affected by this "lockout" were "all indignant with the dogs, and

* See opposite.

next night dogs were chased and hunted away diligently, and if a stray dog is found about in the evening he is ignominiously taken to his owner to be tied up".

Newberry and Carter came several times before Christmas and Petrie went off with them on long and arduous walks over the *gebel* looking for the numerous rock inscriptions or stelae with which Akhenaton had marked out the limits of his domain. There was another private reason for their desert searches: it was rumoured in Cairo that the lost tomb of Akhenaton, concealed somewhere in the desert behind el 'Amarna, had been found and plundered by some Arabs years before, but that its whereabouts was now known to the Museum authorities. Grébaut, thought Petrie, was keeping the secret in reserve "to float his reputation at the last gasp" by claiming the discovery as his own. Newberry and Carter were very anxious to find the tomb. So, it transpired, were others.

Early in January Petrie and Newberry were walking across the plain towards the entrance to the central *wady* when, as Petrie wrote, "I sighted a print of a *boot* in the sand, and a boot in an out-of-the-way desert is as much as the footprint to Robinson Crusoe. There was a wild hope that it was some official going to look after the tomb of Khuenaten . . . we anxiously tracked 'Boot' who was accompanied by a native 'Barefoot', up and down little ravines. Boot went in the most headlong way, and after a couple of miles or so came some confusion, and Boot struck away from the mountain. I hunted closer and found that Barefoot had led Boot up to see a natural pit in the rock produced by water action, which would never have been adopted for a tomb. Then Boot went down and soon mounted a donkey that was waiting for him, joined a camel and so returned." Carter came over, and the mystery of Boot and Barefoot was out: it was Fraser and Blackden, intent on forestalling Newberry; but the Arabs told Newberry, and they had to confess to the whole story. "The affair does not leave a pleasant taste in the mouth," was Petrie's comment.[33] Newberry was understandably furious; he had already had cause to complain of Fraser's work and the camp at El Bersha was unhappily divided; he wrote straight off to Amelia Edwards sending his resignation and vowing never to come back to Egypt.[34] Petrie tried to dissuade him, for he was the only one of the four young men with enough education to be an archaeologist: it was essential that the Fund should not lose him. But Newberry had stormed off to Cairo, where, before he sailed for England, news appeared in the local press announcing that M. Grébaut had found the tomb of Akhenaten. The English papers picked up the story. Newberry, feeling that there was nothing to lose, wrote a letter to *The Academy* attacking the French officials in the Museum for withholding the truth for more than two years, and implying that M. Grébaut was falsely claiming credit for the discovery.[35] The Fund hastily disassociated themselves from Newberry's "astonishing and mischievous letter"; but Petrie wrote gleefully: "I hear that M. Grébaut is stated, in English papers, to have discovered the tomb of Khuenaten; I can however add to Mr. Newberry's letter . . . by saying that so far from having discovered the tomb, the Director has not yet seen it."[36]

The truth about the tomb's discovery remains obscure. Alexander Barsanti, an Italian technician employed as a salesman in the Cairo Museum, who came to el 'Amarna with orders to fit the tombs in the cliffs with iron doors, claimed to have found the Royal Tomb himself on 30 December. He took Petrie to see it, in company with M. Daressy of the Service des Antiquités, Professor Sayce, and two other visitors. Petrie, racing on ahead, could claim at any rate that he was the first Englishman to see this much-sought tomb. It had by then been "raked over" by Barsanti's men with very little supervision; one of the men muttered to Petrie that they had been clearing it for four months. Petrie, powerless to interfere since he had been forbidden to touch the tombs, could only deplore the loss of vital evidence concerning the burial, and perhaps the fate, of the most controversial figure in Egyptian history.

Sayce's visit gave him pleasure; he dined with his old friend on the *dhahabiya Ishtar* and was able to show him some of his finds, in particular the pavement and another gem of painting recently discovered: this was a mere fragment, the lowest part of a large painted group on the wall of a room; it showed two small children, two of the little princesses, playing at the feet of their mother (**39**); "an exquisite Group . . . about 6 inches high, painted so closely, like good Indian miniatures, that I was startled". To detach this little masterpiece on its plaster from the crumbly mud wall, riddled by white ants, and to give it a firm backing that would not soak through and stain the picture taxed both his ingenuity and his patience. In the end his gridiron of wooden slats, backed with fresh mud plaster, held the fragile slab firmly and it reached England intact, to find a permanent home in the Ashmolean Museum in Oxford.

There were two of them now: Howard Carter, instead of Blackden, had come over to Petrie to learn something of his methods. His expenses were paid by the wealthy Thyssen-Amherst M.P. (later Lord

Amherst of Hackney), who hoped to acquire pieces for his already large collection. Carter was accordingly given his own part of the site to work on, the area of the great temple. In view of his later fame as the discoverer of the tomb of Tutankhamun for another patron, it is interesting to read Petrie's first impression of him: "Mr. Carter is a good-natured lad whose interest is entirely in painting and natural history: he only takes on this digging as being on the spot and convenient to Mr. Amherst, and it is of no use to me to work him up as an excavator."

Every day fresh scraps of evidence were turning up concerning the identity and relationships of members of the royal family, in particular tiny objects such as amulets and scarabs and the bezels of faience rings. Glass was plentiful and two large factories were found where the brilliant multi-coloured glazes were made that had adorned the palace. The discovery of workshops enabled Petrie to study the processes of manufacture from the crushing of quartz pebbles to the final decoration of the delicate glass vessels and the brilliant tiles and inlays that had adorned columns and walls. He kept samples of everything, particularly crucibles, lumps of frit and rods of glass, and pottery moulds for inlays and amulets—a collection of the greatest value for the history of technology. Then one day a rough, life-size plaster face was brought in; it seemed to be a cast, and Carter, who had studied sculpture at art school, pointed out that it must have been taken from a dead person, since the eyes were half open and there was no sign of breathing holes at the nostrils or mouth. Petrie concluded that he had the actual death-mask of King Akhenaten; if that were so, it was a unique and priceless find which the Cairo Museum would and should retain; he therefore made from a paper mould a number of casts of it for other museums.[37]

The discovery of the pavement had had a not altogether welcome effect on Petrie's daily routine. The news spread quickly and visitors began to arrive on *dhahabiyas* and steamers; usually they stayed a day or so, and almost all invited Petrie to dinner on board. Never before had he eaten so well and lived so social a life in the wilderness; never again was he to do so. Officials of the administration came with their wives: Col and Mrs Ross of Irrigation, Milner the Finance Secretary (later Lord Milner), Lord Waterford and the Gaskells; after Sayce came other old friends: the Dodgsons from Liverpool with Miss Oldroyd, Greville Chester, still shaky after a serious illness, and Wilbour on the *Seven Hathors* with his wife and daughters. At each visit he was obliged to set his own work aside and accompany them on a guided tour of the pavement; some, like Wilbour, he felt obliged to take to the Royal Wady, though the tomb was now closed. When Sayce came for a second time, he was able to show him an important new find: the hoped-for cuneiform tablets had turned up; these, found in rubbish holes under the floor of a room which Petrie dubbed the Foreign Office, were the first to be recorded *in situ*, where the original find had been made. There were eighteen fragments, including, as Sayce was delighted to see, part of a large dictionary or vocabulary of Akkadian and Sumerian for the use of the Babylonian scribes; he made preliminary copies of them all, and was later entrusted with their publication.[38]

There was another "lockout": two hammers were missing, and the culprits were not found. Petrie stopped work for four days and took the opportunity for a long walk into the hills surrounding the plain. Mapping the ancient road system and scouring the cliffs on either side of the river for the rock inscriptions with which Akhenaten had delimited the boundaries of his domain, occupied a number of days from time to time. He found all the known boundary stelae and several not previously known; only one escaped his vigilant eye. Of the largest, Stele S, he took a squeeze; a cast of this was later exhibited and kept in the collection at University College. Davies, who kept Petrie's numbering and made use of his notes and sketches when publishing the texts years later, was astonished at the energy and the accuracy with which Petrie had "beaten the bounds" of Akhetaten.[39] His triangulation of the area employed visible eminences in the surrounding hills; from these, using a compass, he paced out the distances up each valley "counting steps all day" and going from twenty to twenty-six miles on different days. Three days were spent on the further bank; he crossed with 'Ali es Suefi, the boy Hussain and a donkey, walking from Tuna el Gebel to Bawit. On 27 February he wrote to Sir Colin Moncrieff asking for permission to open tombs on the western side of the river, and to restore and preserve a little painted Coptic chapel at Bawit which he felt was in danger of destruction; he also asked for a permit to excavate three unopened tombs which he was sure he had observed in the eastern hills. He was seeking, he said "a little more ground, as this place [el 'Amarna] proves to have been so ransacked that I have got very little and am almost ready to close work here. The only prizes are the pavements and a cast of Khuenaten's face taken after his death; both these treasures of course will remain in Egypt."[40] He was presumably refused the permits he sought; what is surprising is that he should have asked for them. The clue lies in his last sentence: although the historical information he had obtained from his excavation was of the greatest importance to Petrie, he was nevertheless disappointed that he would have so few objects of intrinsic value to bring home to his patrons, on whom he depended for support. Broken pieces of sculpture, scraps of faience and fragments of cuneiform tablets, whatever their value to the historian and the student of technology, were not *objets d'art*; an unopened tomb would have supplied Haworth, and particularly Kennard, with their hoped-for "loot".

Petrie's letter ends: "I hear of a delightful clearance, but is M. de Morgan going to play Rehoboam and must he revolt? or is there to be a decent policy in future?" News had recently come through that Grébaut had been replaced, on what grounds was not known. Was it over the affair of the royal tomb? There was much speculation. As was to be expected, his successor was another Frenchman: Jacques de Morgan was a young engineer who knew nothing of Egypt but had had archaeological experience in the Caucasus and at Susa in Khuzistan. The removal of Grébaut should have given Petrie cause to rejoice, but he had misgivings: before Grébaut left, his new regulations had been passed by Khedival decree. Briefly they were as follows: everything found in an excavation belongs to the State; nevertheless, in consideration of the expenses incurred by the excavator, some part of the finds will be allotted to him. The division is to be conducted as follows: the excavator and the Administration will divide the objects found into two equal parts, by agreement between them; for these they will draw lots. The Administration then has the right to buy back from the excavator any object from his share which it desires for the Museum at a price to be agreed between them.[41]

Looked at from the point of view of today, these provisions appear reasonable, indeed generous, but Petrie's objection was based on practical considerations: if an excavator did not know what he would be able to keep, he would have to draw, photograph and record every single small object on the dig before bringing it to Cairo for division; this would mean shortening the digging season, or prolonging his stay in Egypt until far into the heat of summer. If de Morgan were to be bound by the new law, pressure must be brought to bear on the government by the British; otherwise, Petrie told his friends, he was seriously contemplating taking French or German citizenship in the hope that he might get the diplomatic backing he needed. Alternatively, he might go back to Palestine, or dig in the Bahrein Islands or in Persia. "Naville has weakly given in," he wrote to Griffith, "and asserted that he will not remove anything except small objects—

which he never finds. The Fund will have no more sculptures to distribute, nor anything else so far as I can see."[42] Greville Chester, Griffith and Spurrell all wrote to dissuade him from any rash step.[43] Chester reproached him for lack of patriotism, and Griffith doubted whether a change of nationality would improve Petrie's situation: "It would probably make the English officials hostile, and I have my doubts about the French welcoming you; I believe the French do not in the least appreciate English work, barring Maspero. . . . The French have their own people and their own system—won't they look askance on a newcomer from abroad?"

When Ramadan began at the end of March, Petrie dismissed most of his workmen and regarded his exploration of el 'Amarna as more or less finished. As he told Griffith: "One year of life is enough to give to a single king and his works." There was a lot still to be done on the site, however. After long delay the Antiquities Service sent men to build a roof over the pavement; Petrie himself had to undertake the construction of a railing for the gangways—270 feet of handrails and posts. Unable to trust a local carpenter, he made the whole thing single-handed. To 'Ali es Suefi he entrusted the plastering of the broken edges. Making an outline copy of the part of the pavement,[44] and a full-sized colour reproduction of a small section of it, took Petrie several weeks. With infinite care he covered the whole surface of the plaster with a thin coat of tapioca water, applying it gently with his forefinger; as it dried the glutinous mixture formed a thin protective film over the paint. For some years to come the pavement was a great tourist attraction; Cook's steamers stopped there and the Society for the Preservation of the Monuments of Egypt paid the cost of a proper shed to afford further protection. Its very popularity proved its undoing, for the authorities failed to provide an access path from the landing stage through the cultivation, and one night about twenty years later the pavement was hacked to pieces by the irate villager who owned the trampled fields. Petrie's copies, and the descriptions of those who saw it, are all that is left of one of the masterpieces of the ancient world.

It was getting very hot, and neither Petrie nor Carter was well. Drawing and surveying occupied most of April, and through May they were busy making boxes and packing; on the last day of that month they finally arrived in Cairo with 125 boxes of spoils, and Petrie, a little apprehensive, met M. de Morgan for the first time. He found him reasonable and co-operative, and above all, business-like; it looked as if he would be a welcome change from the dilatory and devious Grébaut. He kept only a few important pieces for the Cairo Museum and was not interested in the tablets or in broken pottery and faience scraps.[45]

In spite of his exhaustion, Petrie could feel well pleased with the accomplishments of the last six months. He had planned the whole area and traced the main outline of the buildings in the central part of the city; he had found examples of every aspect of the craftsmanship of the 'Amarna artists; and from a study of the dockets on wine jars giving the date of the vintage, he could work out, with Griffith's help, a new chronology of the period: the king had died in, or just after, his seventeenth year (not his twelfth as had been thought); he had been succeeded at Akhetaten by Tutankhamun. Much that had been written previously could now be corrected. In spite of his effeminate plumpness and grotesque physique, Khuenaten had been neither a eunuch nor a woman. The key to the naturalism of the 'Amarna style, the depiction of intimate family life and the freedom of plant and animal forms he found in the king's motto "Living in Truth". It was this concept, expressed in five simple hieroglyphic signs, that Petrie chose many years later as his own impress on the cover of his autobiography. Many seasons of work have since been devoted to the site, and the excavations of the Egypt Exploration Society (as the Fund is now called) still continue, yet the basic work accomplished by Petrie in that one season has remained fundamental to all subsequent study. His verdict that "Khuenaten stands out as perhaps the most original thinker that ever lived in Egypt, and one of the great idealists of the world" has been much quoted and is still the view of some, both laymen and scholars, who write on this unique episode in history.

While he was in Cairo, he received a letter asking him to accept the honorary degree of D.C.L. from the University of Oxford. It was his first academic honour, and it came at a very opportune moment, for he was about to take a step which would change his whole life: at the end of April news had come of the death of Amelia Edwards, and he was returning home to take up her bequest to him. It was one of the turning points in his career.

Inundation employment

CHAPTER IX

University College, London
(1892–7)

AMELIA EDWARDS HAD caught cold on a wet October afternoon in 1891, hanging about the Millwall Docks seeing to the despatch of cases of antiquities from the Fund's work at Ehnasya; the cold turned to influenza. In spite of her illness she struggled on with proofs of her last book.[1] It came out in December: she sent a copy to Petrie's mother for him to read when he returned from Egypt. "I am much driven," she wrote to him, "and very poorly—so this must be a brief screed. Please to remember any windfalls of jewellery or duplicate scarabs for the undersigned. Wishing you every success and a glorious victory over the French."[2] She developed bronchitis and her lung became affected, though she rallied a little in February and asked Kate Bradbury to write to Petrie asking him about certain theories concerning the Pharaoh Akhenaten which puzzled her. In reporting the state of her patient's health, Kate explained, "I give you details, not knowing how little of a detail their whole significance is for you—knowing too that Amy had for you a private affection—and she does not love many people for all her seeming geniality. She once enumerated to me the two or three people for whom she 'cared'—and of you she said 'And I am fond of Petrie—though I might just as well be fond of a young obelisk.' "[3] On 15 April she died at Weston-super-Mare. The news reached Petrie at 'Amarna about a week later; he was ill with stomach pains and exhaustion and it was the second bereavement he had suffered that spring, for in early March the news had come of the death, peacefully and without long illness, of his mother. They had been very close, and her passing left a gap in his life which he felt deeply; "thereafter," he later wrote, "my link with Bromley was much less". A coolness had grown up between himself and his father, and it was increased when in the following year William Petrie married again, taking to wife his cousin by marriage, Cecilia Flinders, the granddaughter of Matthew Flinders' brother Samuel, a woman of the same age as Flinders himself. It was, on the face of it, a sensible and a happy marriage for both of them, but Flinders appears to have disapproved of the match and although Cecilia, or Celia as she was often called, lived on until 1924, after her husband's death she does not appear to have kept in touch with her stepson or his family.

Flinders Petrie knew enough of the contents of Amelia Edwards' will to know that his whole future would be affected by it. Instead of stopping, as he had planned, in Sicily, he hurried home, and was at Bromley by 11 June. He felt very ill but had urgent and immediate matters to attend to. He stayed a few days with Sayce at Oxford and was fêted when he received his D.C.L.; he lectured to the Palestine Exploration Fund. Then he was off to Bristol to help Kate Bradbury sort and pack Miss Edwards' collection of antiquities and her Egyptological books. They went together on Sunday to Henbury Church, where she is buried; perhaps there and then they planned the great stone *'ankh*, the hieroglyphic symbol for Life, which lies on her grave. In Bristol, too, he met Miss Emily Paterson, Miss Edwards' part-time secretary, who for the past three years had taken some of the burden of routine work for the Egypt Exploration Fund from her shoulders. She was now to move to London to replace Mr Gosselin as the Fund's General Secretary, a post which she was to occupy for nearly thirty years. Though she had not, Petrie thought, the mental keenness of Miss Bradbury, she would be excellent for her work "clear, decisive, precise, a good shorthand writer and very pleasant. She will be a success for the London office I do not doubt."

By the terms of Miss Edwards' will,[4] a capital endowment sufficient to provide an annual income of £140 was bequeathed to University College London in order to found "a Professorship of Egyptian Archaeology and Philology including the deciphering and reading of Hieroglyphic and other ancient Egyptian scripts or writings". Her Egyptological library and photographs and her collection of Egyptian antiquities were also to go to the College. The Professor would be expected to teach Egyptology "with a view to the expansion of the knowledge of the history, antiquities, literature, philosophy and art of ancient Egypt". His classes should be open to students of either sex (this was her reason for preferring University College—the only academic institution in those days which admitted women students). No name was mentioned but Amelia had seen to it that her wishes in this matter were known to her executors, one of whom was Kate Bradbury; the proviso that "no person holding office in the British Museum be eligible to be elected to the Professorship" effectively eliminated Wallis Budge as a possible candidate. Nor, by the terms of the will, should the appointee be over forty years of age; this ruled out other undesirable possibilities. A further pointer to her wishes was the specific mention of the sum held by her in trust for Petrie; this sum she wished to be added to the endowment; and she desired him to finish the labelling and cataloguing of her collection, for which task an extra £50 was devised. The College was required to provide proper accommodation for the collection in glazed bookcases. The proviso that the Professor on appointment must not be more than forty was added in a codicil dated 8 March 1891, when Petrie was already rising thirty-eight; she must have known that she had not long to live.

The Committee of Management of the College met during the summer and formally appointed Petrie to the Chair. They drew up the terms of his appointment: recognizing that "research work of active exploration" was a necessary part of the Edwards Professor's duties, they stipulated that he should give a course of lectures in the first and third terms, but would be free during the winter months to work in Egypt. At last Petrie had academic status, a fixed income, albeit a small one, and security for his future work; he could look ahead to the time when he would be able to train students to learn his methods and follow in his footsteps.

Returning from Bristol, he worked at home to complete the 'Amarna maps and plans until his boxes arrived from Egypt; then he came up to town on most days building cases for his exhibition at Oxford Mansion and with the help of Riley and Spurrell, Carter and Newberry, arranging the displays of pottery, glass and glazes, the painting of the little princesses, the sculpture and the cuneiform tablets. Feeling worse every day he struggled on until at his anxious friends' insistence he went to a doctor, who diagnosed severe ulceration and haemorrhage of the stomach. With so much to do and so many people to see he still refused to rest; in August he did go down to his cousins at Milford for a few days, but returned to make the cast of the great stela which was to form a startling backdrop to the exhibition. He was anxious to open in September, when many distinguished visitors would be in town, for as luck would have it the Ninth International Congress of Orientalists was due to meet in London that year, at University College. Petrie's was one of the first papers; he lectured on "Recent Discoveries at Tell el 'Amarna" to a packed hall and was very favourably reported in the daily press; the next day he spoke a second time, this time in the Geography section, on "the Causes and Effects of Egyptian Geography"; among other conclusions he pointed out that "the position and nature of Egypt are particularly favourable for the measurement of a geodetic arc of the meridian, and it is to be hoped that the Government might carry out such a work".[5] It was a fortunate chance that the Congress took place when it did; *Biblia*, the journal in which the Revd Copley Winslow regularly gave news of Egyptological happenings, reported that Petrie had been "the man oftenest praised in the Congress", and it must have given his academic career a flying start. But by the time the exhibition opened on 19 September he was almost too ill to attend; with severe back pains, he only managed to struggle up to town once or twice and then left others to carry on while he retired to bed. At the beginning of term he was seriously ill and unable to take up his appointment; some of his friends feared his excavating days were over.

At the end of November, feeling a little better, he moved up to London and took rooms in Margaret Street, near Oxford Mansion, so that he could begin dismantling and packing up the exhibition; in December he was interviewed by a committee of the Faculty of Arts of the College to discuss his prospectus. Fourteen cases of 'Amarna material were despatched to Oxford, some to Philadelphia, and the rest came in crates to University College where it had to remain till Petrie had room to accommodate it. He moved to a room in 32, Torrington Square, close to the College; Griffith, in Doughty Street, was ten minutes' walk away. By the beginning of term he had arranged his books and those of Miss Edwards, and when the Edwards Library was formally opened on 12 January, Lord Cromer (as Sir Evelyn Baring had recently become) was one of its first visitors. Two days later, to an audience of about two hundred, Petrie gave his inaugural lecture. The occasion, he said, marked a landmark in historical research: for the first time in England, provision had been made for the study of ancient Egypt. He outlined the facilities that would be available for students as soon as there was accommodation for them: the reference library, the teaching museum based on Miss Edwards' collection and his own, which he intended to lend to the College, the squeezes and the photographs. He intended, he said, to take students with him to Egypt every spring, and he appealed for funds—£300 or £400 a year, he estimated, would provide the cost of travelling, living and working in Egypt for one excavator for a season. This *Egyptian Research Account* would be quite separate from his own excavations, which would be carried on as before "with private friends".

Petrie then went on to define the directions in which he anticipated that the study of Egyptology, hitherto generally confined to language, could be expanded. It was a forecast of what his own special interests would be. "The religion and law of Egypt is particularly the taste of the French, the language has its greatest exponents in Germany," he said; Wilkinson's work on the artistic and material civilization could well be the speciality of the English. There was need for a *corpus* of drawings and descriptions of each class of object—pottery, scarabs, beads and so forth; and for studies of the development of Egyptian art and architecture, of the history of the hieroglyphic signs from their prehistoric beginnings, of the presence in Egypt of foreign races and their influence on the native Egyptians, and of the scientific bases for ancient chronology. In conclusion he stressed that a subject such as Egyptology could be enriched not only by full-time professional scholars, but by those who could only study part-time. Much important work was done in the stray hours of busy men. He hoped that the College would become a centre for such volunteers. "Here the means of study and research will be provided as far as possible. The future lies with you."[6]

The appeal seems to have borne instant fruit, for a fortnight later some gentleman whom he had once met in Egypt promised to donate a sum for a scholarship, the interest on which would be enough to pay the expenses of a student on alternate years.[7] The rest came more slowly, but the Research Account was thereby launched; it was to be maintained for more than half a century. At least eight students enrolled for his first course of lectures; they were nearly all ladies and two of them were married. One was Miss Emily Paterson, anxious to extend her knowledge of Ancient Egypt now that she was the Fund's Secretary; another was Miss Janet Gourlay, who was one day, with her friend Margaret Benson, to conduct the first all-feminine excavation in Egypt. Dr James Walker, the only male student, was a graduate of the College, whose special interest was in ancient medical texts. His willingness to sit in the library during the hours when it was open and to supervise the students when Petrie was away solved a serious problem, since each Professor was librarian in his own department. During January and February, the new Professor delivered a course of six public lectures on the subject of Egyptian art. For Egyptian history there was no suitable textbook he could recommend to his students . . . the best was Wiedemann's and that was in German and out of date. He decided that writing a new History of Ancient Egypt must be one of his first tasks. Meanwhile he was determined to provide language teaching for his students; the terms of Miss Edwards' will required this, but he did not feel equipped to teach hieroglyphics himself and knew no Coptic, so he proposed to engage Frank Griffith, who now had a position in the Department of British and Mediaeval Antiquities at the British Museum, to teach these subjects. Failing him, he suggested Walter Ewing Crum, a brilliant young Oxford graduate who had been studying in Berlin for the past two years. The Senate considered the matter and refused to authorize the arrangement. It would have cost the College nothing—the fees of students were paid in those days direct to their teachers—but one of his colleagues had vigorously objected: R. S. Poole considered that he, if anybody, should have been asked to teach the language. On Sir Charles Newton's death in 1889 he had been appointed to the handsomely endowed Chair of Classical Archaeology; he had decided to widen the scope of the courses, keeping part of the stipend for himself and paying specialists in other branches of archaeology, from Assyrian to Mediaeval European, to lecture for him, thus enabling him to concentrate on his favourite subjects, numismatics and Egyptology.[8] He had been surprised and bitterly disappointed at Petrie's appointment, but the coolness between them—they had for several years not been on speaking terms—had abated, and in June he had written somewhat grudgingly welcoming Petrie as a colleague; Petrie's reply had been cautious: as he told Spurrell, though he was "not going to fall into his arms exactly", he was anxious to avoid friction within the College. So Griffith held his classes in hieroglyphics on Thursday evenings in Petrie's bed-sitting room in Torrington Square, and Spurrell was one of the first to join the class.

At the end of February the doctors' insistence prevailed and Petrie went off to recuperate in Italy for two months. He tried to persuade Spurrell to come with him, but that strangely irresolute individual would not make up his mind; in the end Petrie went in company with another friend, Jack Borrowman; Griffith moved into the room at Torrington Square, where he was soon teaching a dozen cramped but enthusiastic disciples. To recuperate perhaps, but not to rest: it was not in Petrie's power to be idle, even for a day, and he and Jack embarked on a strenuous tour of museums and ancient sites. From Naples they saw Paestum (noting the differences between the tilt of the columns in the earlier temples and the later) and spent nearly a week at Pompeii, where Petrie took about sixty photographs of details. In Rome he met Professor Mahaffy for the first time; he had corresponded with him before about his papyri, now he found him a delightful companion, an effervescent white-haired Irishman who took him sight-seeing and introduced him to many interesting personalities, among them Rodolfo Lanciani, Professor of the Ancient Topography of Rome, George Dennis, the author of *Cities and Cemeteries of Etruria*, and Barnabei, the excavator of Falerii.

Petrie and Borrowman left Rome on 4 April in company with Mahaffy, Stillman *The Times* archaeological correspondent, and A. S. Murray (the two latter had been in the same *pensione*) for Corneto, Pisa and Florence. In Florence Schiaparelli was cordial and allowed him to have anything he wanted out of the cases to examine and photograph; for five days he copied inscriptions noting with disapproval that although everything was kept clean and in excellent order, hardly anything was labelled. Most useful of all, he found a marble-worker who introduced him to his supplier, with whom Petrie bargained for alabaster mounts for statuettes. "I ordered 600 at once, at 1d. to 2d. each, polished, to be sent on to London; and I can order over whatever I want in future for mounting. This is the cheapest, neatest and quickest way of mounting things." The little alabaster blocks were still used in the Petrie Museum until the collection was re-arranged after the Second World War.

The Director of the museum at Bologna was equally obliging, though some of his showcases were screwed down and could not be opened. Finally Turin, where Lanzone greeted him warmly, and again he was given the free run of the museum. One last day in Paris, spent, of course, in the Louvre, ended his holiday and on 29 April he was home at Bromley, and ready to take up his duties again in the College. He felt better, but still suffered from palpitations and head-aches.

Term had already begun. Back in his room at Torrington Square, he had much to do. He was an astonishingly fast worker: a lecture on "Early Egyptian Art" took him only two days to write, and another day to prepare the slides (he always processed his own lantern slides). On Saturday mornings he gave a course of lectures, discussing in turn various tales from the repertory of ancient Egyptian literature; these formed the basis of a small book illustrated by his friend Tristram Ellis; Frank Griffith, who had moved into another room in the same lodging house, helped him with the translations. Fifty or more people were now coming to his lectures, and publishers were pressing him for books with a popular appeal. He was also completing the publication of *Tell el Amarna*, and writing the first volume of his *History of Egypt*; all these came out before the end of the year. With all this, he was devoting as much time as he could to the organization of his department at the College.

The small collection of books left by Miss Edwards to the College was at first given a temporary home in the North Library; her antiquities had to be left in packing cases until, with the removal of the Engineering Department in May 1893 to new premises, space could be found on the top floor of the College for both books and antiquities. Kate Bradbury, Miss Edwards' residuary legatee, undertook to provide extra showcases for the Professor's own not inconsiderable collection; in August he took several days to pack and move up from Bromley fifty boxes full—no doubt to the relief of his new stepmother. An annual sum was allocated to the upkeep and augmentation of the Edwards Library; some gaps were filled by books from Greville Chester's library, presented by friends in his memory; the old man had died in May of the previous year, soon after his return from Egypt. Other books were acquired by Petrie's own initiative: he persuaded the French Government to give volumes of their archaeological series to the library, and the German Emperor donated the huge and expensive volumes of Richard Lepsius' *Denkmäler aus Aegypten und Aethiopien*, an essential tool for the Egyptologist, for which Petrie designed an ingenious cradle. By 1894 the library already contained some six hundred volumes, and the antiquities were arranged in nine large cases, one of them containing a unique series of Egyptian pottery of all periods, running the length of the room.[9] The premises were somewhat cramped, for the Yates Archaeological Library, also established by a recent bequest, occupied half the width of the floor.

For the unpacking and arrangement of the Museum objects Petrie had several willing helpers: Newberry was busy with his own exhibition, but Spurrell and Griffith came in whenever they could, and there were two who came every day: Dr Walker and a modest, quiet young man named James Quibell, a recent Oxford graduate in Greek and Chemistry (a combination Petrie heartily approved of), who was to accompany the Professor to Egypt in the coming winter as the first recipient of the studentship.

Throughout the autumn Petrie drove himself hard, writing, arranging his museum and preparing his lectures; he still felt very unwell and low in spirits. That summer the sparrows in the great plane trees around Torrington Square had woken him every morning at three; try as he could, he could not get to sleep again. He had tried everything, he told Spurrell, even clipping his ears together with spring clips, which proved both painful and ineffective. "If I leave London, I almost fear I leave the College, and all my prospective work . . . I fear that the sparrows will make an end of all my plans, and drive me to some different line of life altogether."[10] (A less drastic solution to his problem appears to have occurred to him in the following year, when he eventually moved away from the sparrows of central London to the quiet but still accessible suburb of Hampstead.) In the same mood of depression he wrote to his father in August, congratulating him on his remarriage:

> To me life seems such an unsatisfactory experiment (in spite of the many advantages that I am blessed with having) that I always feel the less one has to do with it the better. My own sense of right and wrong in it is summed up in doing as well as I can whatever is put before me to be done—in the course of events uncontrolled by me—day by day and year by year. I have no personal aims or wishes beyond doing what is laid upon me to do as my immediate duty. And I cannot but feel I have been marked out, by very unusual and unexpected circumstances quite beyond my control.[11]

Later in the year, when he had lectured in Manchester, Birmingham and Hull within the space of four days, and was preparing to leave for Egypt, he again wrote to his father:

> You kindly wish—as many people do also—to see me taking some rest. Probably you do not realise therefore that this mental overwork is a *necessity* to me, as a narcotic to deaden the mind to the condition of a solitary life which my circumstances (and still more now my health) have imposed on me. Without work enough to choke my thoughts I should be brooding and wretched. Overpowering work has been a necessity to me; and though I have begun to pay the price of it, and do not expect ever to be strong again, there can be no respite for me until I am relieved of work altogether.

Before Petrie left, he was able to make satisfactory arrangements for his absence: Dr Walker was to see that students could continue to read and borrow books, and Griffith was to be permitted to hold language classes in the Library—since he now had seventeen students, of both sexes, it could scarcely be argued that there was no demand for the subject.

Happy to be back in Egypt, Flinders Petrie seems to have recovered his spirits at once; a trip to the Giza pyramids with his new student was rewarded by a rare find: the dealer Farag showed Petrie a Greek papyrus roll, still in fairly complete condition, so interesting at first sight—Petrie could recognize place-names in Egypt, and some legal phrases—that he was prepared to gamble more on it than he could usually afford. "It may be a great loss to me," he wrote "but is possibly a great prize." It proved to be the latter: the Revenue Papyrus, as it became known, is one of the treasures of the Bodleian Library at Oxford.

De Morgan was affable and asked Petrie to dinner, and he readily granted the site he asked for. Quft, the ancient *Gebtu* (in Greek, Koptos), is a small town north of Luxor, on the east bank of the Nile near where the Wady Hammamat, the nearest and most frequented route to the Red Sea, debouches into the valley. Maspero had done a little digging here on more than one occasion, and remains of ancient buildings were still visible in the triangular space between three villages. It was evident that the ancient town had been extensive and commercially important; it was the ancient centre of the worship of the god of fertility, Min, and Petrie felt sure that it would prove to have been a centre of very early settlement at the dawn of Egypt's history. Quibell was sent ahead to collect 'Ali es Suefi and one or two other men from the previous year's work and pick up Petrie's stores left at Hagg Qandil; they arrived at Quft after dark and set up camp by candlelight. Building their huts against the old city wall, they began to dig on the site of the temple, where Ptolemaic blocks above ground marked the latest phase of building; they soon discovered that there were earlier temples of many periods, blocks and sculptures from which could be recovered below the floors and in pits dug in yellow clay below the Nile mud. A new hazard plagued the work here: the proximity of the place to Luxor brought dealers, some of whom had already been illicitly at work on the site and were anxious to watch the progress of the excavation to see where they could best dig by night; their spies would hang about the fringes of the excavation; several slabs of relief were almost stolen one night and the exasperated excavators had to keep a sharp lookout for any loiterer whose dress proclaimed him to be a townsman rather than a villager. "One man Quibell held down while I walloped him. He swore that he would go to the Consul; that I had broken his leg; I let him crawl off on hands and knees some way, and then, giving a great shout, ran at him, when he made off like a hare." Then they tried a new stratagem, grabbing the headshawl of an intruder as he fled; to go bareheaded was a disgrace, and to get his headshawl back the culprit was forced to give the name of his local sheikh or headman, which he was generally reluctant to do.

Some fine statuary started to appear; first a colossal granite head of Caracalla, and a group, six feet high, of Ramesses II between two goddesses; when this triad had been extracted from the mud and dragged out of the temple area by boatmen with ropes, Petrie was amused to watch a small boy, who thought he was unobserved, carefully spit into the eyes of each of the figures in turn; "the Egyptian boy delights in an insult whenever he can indulge in it *quite* safely!" Henry Wallis came to stay with them for a few days; visitors always bring luck, said Petrie, and sure enough it was while he was with them that the most extraordinary of all their finds was made: three very crude, pillar-like limestone statues of the god Min, the patron of Koptos, which had once presumably stood in his temple; all were badly battered, broken and headless, but when complete two would have been about thirteen feet high and weighed about two tons apiece. The third was rather smaller. A strip hanging from the girdle of each was carved with emblems in low relief: a saw-fish, Red Sea shells, part of an elephant and so on, and above these an object recognizable as the early emblem or fetish of the god Min.[12] Nothing like these figures had been seen before, but Petrie felt they must come from a very early stage of man's development, possibly before the dynastic kings, and he was tempted to suggest that they indicated an early link with the Red Sea and the African people of Punt. They were, he supposed, the oldest sculpture in Egypt: primitive idols of the first settlers in the Nile Valley.

A few days later De Morgan arrived, on a brief tour of inspection; he elected to take for the Ghizeh Museum only the largest objects like the Ramesside triad, and one of the Min statues: these he offered to transport to Cairo at the Museum's expense. (This suited Petrie very well, for he did not wish to bring home large monuments which neither he nor his patrons wanted.) Other early stone sculptures appeared, formed, like the Min figures, by hammering rather than by the use of chisel or of metal tools: a bird, and lions, and fragments of other animals. Petrie and Quibell kept all the pieces; recently work has been resumed on a case of fragments,[13] from which two large limestone lions have been reconstituted. On 16 January they were joined by Bernard Grenfell, a young classical scholar travelling on a Craven Fellowship. He stayed for seven weeks. Many Latin and Greek inscriptions of the late period were coming to light, and to record these was his special care; the publication of them, in Petrie's report, was entrusted to a more experienced classical scholar, D. G. Hogarth, who spent a couple of days in the camp in January. Martyn Kennard too had visitors' luck, when during his visit foundation deposits from the eighteenth-dynasty temple were found intact.

At the end of February Petrie felt that he could safely leave Quibell alone to finish the work and superintend the packing of antiquities; he and Grenfell spent a couple of days in Luxor, where Petrie went round the dealers with Kennard, and they crossed the Nile to Deir el Bahari where Naville was now excavating the temple of Queen Hatshepsut (**42**) with the assistance of Carter and Hogarth and Newberry's architect brother. Back in Cairo he spent a day at Saqqara and walked over to Dahshur. De Morgan had just started work, and he allowed Petrie to enter the newly opened gallery of the brick pyramid. Then, after a couple of days in the Museum, he was off. On his way through Paris he was careful as usual to call on Maspero at his house, feeling no doubt that in case of future difficulties with the French he might count on the Professor as an ally and friend.

Settling into lodgings in Hampstead, he found that term was just ending; the next two weeks were largely taken up with unrolling and mounting the Revenue Papyrus, a task which taxed his ingenuity: it was in so friable a condition that it could not be dampened, and so instead of unrolling the scroll, he had to cut it into hundreds of small strips and mount them on thin paper before securing the whole under sheets of glass.

A new student, he found, had joined the Department during his absence; Margaret Alice Murray had been reading under the guidance of Dr Walker and learning hieroglyphs with Griffith. Plump and fair, and less than five feet tall, with a downright manner and bubbling sense of humour, she had had no formal education of any kind; since her childhood in India the sum total of her experience had been as a district visitor (suitably chaperoned), and a Sunday School teacher. She had joined the classes at University College, so she afterwards declared, solely at her sister's suggestion, because she wanted something to do. In her autobiography she described her first meeting with the black-bearded Professor.[14] It was to change her whole life. He soon recognized her ability; Griffith could testify to her quickness and proficiency in the language and she could draw with a firm stroke and an accurate eye. She volunteered to help Petrie with the inking-in of his drawings that summer and listened intently to his lectures; he was not, she maintained, a good teacher in the ordinary sense of the word, having little time for those "who wished to be taught, and not to learn"; but he gave lectures that "held his audience breathless for the boldness and convincingness of his theories or explanations". More than once she heard an audience burst into applause at the end of a routine class.

Some of the illustrations for *Koptos* which she inked in for him, posed, in that Victorian age, a delicate problem. Min, to whom the temples were dedicated, was a god of fertility and procreation; he is shown in human form, and ithyphallic—that is to say, sexually aroused. How were reliefs depicting him to be published? The problem was solved by omitting to draw the offending part. In some reliefs it was easy to do this—near the edge of a stone slab, the tracing line simply petered out; but in the finest relief of all, which shows King Sesostris I performing a running dance before the god (**21**), Min faces inwards towards the king. Before photographing it, a large descriptive label was stuck on the centre of the scene. In the museum at University College, where the splendid sculpture found its permanent home, this label, in Miss Murray's firm round hand, remained in position to avoid causing embarrassment to visitors, until after she and Petrie had left the College. There is no photograph in the publication of the colossal figures of Min, which had once been similarly endowed —only the reliefs on the girdle are illustrated. These figures were offered by Petrie in the first place to the British Museum, where he felt that, as unique monuments, they should be; his offer was turned down by the authorities on the ground that "they were unhistoric rather than prehistoric"—Petrie clearly suspected Budge as the author of this piece of nonsense—and so they went to the Ashmolean, together with the other early "protohistoric" sculptures; London's loss was Oxford's gain and the Ashmolean became the home of much of Petrie's best early material in subsequent years. Other fine things went to Philadelphia.

But first the Koptos finds were exhibited in the Department in University College. The College authorities allowed the portico doors, usually kept shut, to be used by visitors, making an imposing entrance. Quibell got home at the end of May. The last of the boxes did not arrive from Egypt until 16 July, so that to arrange all, write a catalogue and get it printed and ready for the opening day, 23 July, was no small feat. At the exhibition, Petrie also distributed leaflets announcing the formation of the Egyptian Research Account, which he was determined should henceforward support more than one student. The fund was to be administered by two of Petrie's antiquarian friends: the banker Hilton Price as Treasurer, and A. L. Lewis. "It has long been realised that a British School of Archaeology is greatly needed in Egypt; such an institution has practically begun, though not in name; and as the Research Account develops it may be transformed in the future into a more definite scheme of an archaeological School." It was to be ten years before that scheme became a reality.

With all that he had to do that summer, Petrie was drawn into another time-consuming task: the organization of a petition against the building of the Assuan Dam and the consequent drowning of the island of Philae, which now appeared imminent. In May he conferred with Maunde Thompson, a Vice-President of the E.E.F., who invited him to attend the General Meeting of the Fund in June, but when he found that they were not, after all, intending to send a vigorous protest he would not go. Instead he wrote to De Morgan and also to Maspero in France, Schiaparelli in Italy, Erman in Germany, Hechler in Vienna and Golénischeff in Russia, suggesting that each country simultaneously send a memorandum, on the lines of a draft which he enclosed, to Nubar Pasha in Cairo, protesting against the proposed dam. Sir Edward Poynter circulated a document drafted by Petrie, and obtained signatures from individuals and from learned societies throughout the world. The memorial addressed to the Earl of Kimberley (now Secretary of State for Foreign Affairs) pointed out the beauty and the historical interest of the buildings on the Island of Philae; submitted that to move them would be disastrous, and regarded by the world as an act of vandalism for which Britain would be ultimately responsible; and earnestly entreated that "immediate steps should be taken to press on the Egyptian Government the strong feeling that exists against carrying out the project". "We are unable to believe that it is not within the resources of nineteenth-century Civil Engineers to provide at a reasonable cost a suitable reservoir for the irrigation of Egypt without destroying a series of monuments of absolutely unique interest to historians, archaeologists, architects, painters, and indeed to every educated man."[15] There was in fact such a scheme: Cope Whitehouse's idea of turning the Wady Rayan into a reservoir had been seriously considered by some as a viable alternative.[16] But Sir William Willcocks' plan won the day; Petrie rather bitterly commented later that the economic interests of wealthy landowners such as Sir Ernest Cassell (who had bought a wide tract of land near Assuan) were involved. His own preferred scheme for saving the temples by adopting Sir John Aird's offer to level down one of the higher islands, and transfer the temples block by block, with wire rope haulage, to another island above the level of the flood has only recently, since the building of the Assuan Dam's giant successor, the High Dam, been adopted and carried to a triumphant conclusion, not with wire ropes but with cranes and barges; but the wonderful colour of the painted reliefs has been washed away by the swirling waters of three-quarters of a century's ebb and flow.

The exhibition of the discoveries from Koptos closed on 1 September and on that same day Petrie moved once more, to the reassuring address Lily Lodge, Tranquil Vale,* Hampstead. It was his fourth move that summer, but this time the place suited him very well; it was in the rural surroundings of Hampstead Heath, and only a short walk from the terminus of the horse tram that took him to Gower Street, and he was safe from sparrows. It was to be his home for four years. He was busy finishing the first volume of his *History of Egypt*,[17] which covered the early periods, the Old and Middle Kingdoms; it had a very short introductory chapter entitled "Prehistoric Egypt", containing some information on the geological structure of the Nile Valley, and a tentative discussion of the various racial types he had observed among the representations of men and women on the monuments of Egypt; he cited the Min figures as evidence that the dynastic Egyptians had come up the Red Sea from Pun (i.e. Punt), and were akin to the Punic or Phoenician peoples to whom, he suggested, the Philistines might be related. In the next chapter, "The First Three Dynasties", he was again at a loss; he had to admit that they were "a blank, as far as monuments are concerned", and he debated whether the lists of early kings preserved in fragments from the Ptolemaic history of Manetho and on the walls of Egyptian temples were in fact mythical or literary concepts, rather than historical figures whose monuments would one day be found. He was inclined to think that Zoser and one or two other kings of the third dynasty might have been real personages but that earlier rulers of whom legends had survived had had not more than local authority, or else had been fictional or symbolic figures. Convinced as he was that Koptos had been one of the earliest centres of the dynastic people, he determined to look for their cemeteries; he had sought these in vain near the town: perhaps they lay on the western bank of the Nile? During the previous season he and Quibell had walked about the neighbourhood prospecting for likely sites; at Ballas opposite Quft, and at Naqada a little further south, potsherds and other remains scattered over a wide area proclaimed a very extensive cemetery area and at one point carved blocks indicated the site of a temple. This was where they were going to dig.

* Now the Vale of Health.

Flinders Petrie arrived at Tukh, a village a few miles north of Naqada, on 3 December 1894 and set about building a house near the temple. Quibell was already at Ballas, for he had a number of helpers this year: Quibell had brought his sister Annie and an "invalid" named Hugh Price had come out for his health (though he found his voluntary occupation far from a rest cure). A young clergyman, J. Garrow Duncan, was with them for six weeks and proved "an active and precise observer". Bernard Grenfell came for a week or so, and D. G. Hogarth and Howard Carter visited them from Deir el Bahari. The nucleus of their workforce was the small Fayumi contingent led by 'Ali es Suefi, released from military service by special permission of the Sirdar, Sir Francis Grenfell; most of the other workmen were men from Quft who had proved intelligent, efficient and trustworthy the year before. Some of them were thenceforward employed regularly by Petrie wherever he might be digging; they formed a nucleus of skilled excavators who would train the local pickmen, and undertake the more delicate tasks themselves; their sons and nephews were apprenticed to them as basket boys, and grew up to be the next generation of "Quftis"; some of their descendants of the third and fourth generation are still employed by excavators in Egypt and have a reputation for reliability and honesty which they zealously maintain. The American excavator Reisner employed Quftis of Petrie's training, and took them with him to the Sudan in 1907 for cemetery work; young recruits came at the recommendation of their elders, the family thus holding itself responsible for the good behaviour of its members. The story goes that one young Qufti was caught stealing; his uncles were summoned and asked what they wished to be done with him. "Send him home," was the answer; this disgrace would be punishment enough. Back in his village, however, he was ostracized; nobody would speak to him or give him food, until he could bear it no more, and went out into the desert and killed himself.[18]

The first task was to establish the ancient name of the place; inscribed blocks soon settled the question: the temple had been dedicated to Seth Lord of Nubt, the city known to the Greeks as Ombos. Old Kingdom and twelfth-dynasty remains showed that the town had been occupied, and prosperous, but not very much was left. Petrie turned his attention to the cemetery area. Meanwhile Quibell and his sister had already started to excavate an extensive field of graves at Deir el Ballas. Miss Quibell did most of the drawing of the objects found; she seems to have enjoyed excavating and took very kindly to life in Egypt. Later, when her brother was living in Cairo during the First World War, she kept a dame school for the children of English residents; those who attended it spoke of her with affection and admiration: she was an excellent teacher.[19]

The cemeteries proved to be of the utmost interest. Here were hundreds upon hundreds of graves containing pottery which was quite different from anything previously found in Egypt, with the exception of a few puzzling fragments found the year before at Koptos; it was not wheelmade, some of it was polished and red, with black at the top, and some buff with designs in red paint; both the decoration and the shapes were unfamiliar and so were the grave goods that accompanied the pots in the grave: the ivory combs and pins and little carvings, the slate palettes, the flint knives, beautifully flaked, and the stone mace heads. The bodies were flexed, the knees drawn up in the "embryonic" position, and often lying on a mat of reed. Not a shred of writing was found: these people were clearly illiterate. Nor was there anything in any of their tombs that could be called Egyptian. There was only one explanation, Petrie concluded: these must be the graves of a New Race, who must have conquered the locality, driving out or annihilating the inhabitants. This disaster could only, he supposed, have taken place during the interval between the stable regime of the Old Kingdom and equally strong rule in the Middle Kingdom, during that troubled time known to historians as the First Intermediate Period. Whence the invaders had come he could only surmise; he saw certain similarities between patterns on some of the pottery and the modern ceramics of the Kabyles of Libya, but other characteristics reminded him of the Mediterranean world—Palestine, Malta, even Spain—he was groping in the dark, seeking to explain the inexplicable. In the end he was inclined to plump for Libya.

The truth was far simpler: what he had found was more important by far than the war cemeteries of ephemeral invaders, for here were the predynastic inhabitants of Egypt, the forerunners of the dynastic Egyptians at the dawn of their history. It is odd that this essentially simple fact did not dawn upon Petrie, odder still that for two years, in the face of the scepticism of colleagues and increasing evidence to the contrary, he clung to his belief in the existence of his "New Race"; the explanation must lie in the very ingenuity and self-confidence that had made him what he was. Once he had seized upon a hypothesis it was sometimes difficult for him to envisage that he could be wrong; on matters of chronology and historical interpretation throughout his life he clung to theories of his own, sometimes in the face of disagreement by the consensus of scholars in his field, till overwhelming evidence forced him to admit his mistake. It has been said of him "By his incredible ingenuity, complex problems were liable to be rendered excessively simple and surmountable, simple problems might be tangled into inextricable complexities."[20] It is likely that Quibell guessed the true explanation of their discoveries; if so, he wisely kept his opinion to himself.

From the point of view of the technique this season was one of the most important in the whole of Flinders Petrie's career. Within a few days he had established a system for tomb-digging which was to set a standard for later archaeologists.[21] First the surface of the desert was inspected, and basket boys set to clear likely looking spots where there was a slight depression in the ground. If they found the edges of a grave they cleared the rim, and then men from the village would take over and dig into the tomb pit with their *turias* (hoes) until they touched the tops of pots in position. Immediately the skilled Quftis took over and with knives and brushes would clear the earth and sand from around the grave goods and lay bare the skeleton; and finally 'Ali, the master, with his delicate touch would clear away the last débris and expose the tiniest objects—beads, copper tools, and ivory pins—so that everything could be drawn in position by Petrie or his assistant and meticulously listed. "Thus . . . when we came to register the group everything was clear and visible, even the cage of ribs would be left standing up in the air, unshifted."[22] Everything in the grave, even tiny lumps of minerals, had to be recorded, and the contents of pots noted. Petrie's drawings to scale of the graves and their contents have been called "little masterpieces of archaeological recording".[23] In all, some 2,200 graves were excavated that season. The cost of publishing the complete record would have been prohibitive, so Petrie published details of only 136 burials, and Quibell thirty-two. Records of the rest were kept in notebooks at University College and later used by Petrie in establishing a chronological sequence for these finds (see p. 251). Meanwhile he compiled a *corpus* or catalogue of outlines of the differing shapes of stone and pottery vessels, so that excavators in future could refer to the exact shape of the pots they found without having to draw each one meticulously: B were Black Topped, P Polished Red, and so on, and each category was graded by number so that W1 was the fattest type of Wavy-handled pot, W2, W3 and W4 progressively thinner and taller, and finally W80 a cylindrical, drain-pipe shape. Thirty-six plates were devoted to pottery alone in *Naqada and Ballas*. The buff pottery painted with boats and water-birds (**84**) must, he thought, be of another people, and these he connected with his "Pun-ite" invaders from the Red Sea. Many of the graves had been plundered; in those that appeared to be intact, Petrie noted that the skull was sometimes separate from the body as if decapitated, and that sometimes bones were cracked open, out of place or missing; he concluded that the New Race sometimes cut up their dead, and on occasions even ate them.

Early in February Petrie had important visitors: young James Breasted of Chicago arrived with his bride Frances on their *dhahabiya* the *Olga*. He had recently been studying hieroglyphs with Erman and Ranke in Berlin and this was his first visit to Egypt; he eagerly anticipated meeting Petrie, with whom the University Museum in Chicago was already in correspondence, and Petrie welcomed them warmly; the couple stayed at Naqada for a week and Breasted was greatly impressed by Petrie's excavation technique, and marvelled at his frugality and the simplicity of his life in camp. The portrait of the tatterdemalion excavator which emerges from the biography of Breasted written in 1948 by his son reflects the caricatured image of Petrie later current among Egyptologists, especially those from the United States, who were usually supported by generous grants and lived in comparatively comfortable circumstances. As such, it is worth quoting:

> Petrie was a man of forty-one . . . with a genial face, kindly eyes and the agility of a boy. His clothes confirmed his universal reputation for being not merely careless but deliberately slovenly and dirty. He was thoroughly unkempt, clad in ragged, dirty shirt and trousers, worn-out sandals and no socks. It was one of his numerous idiosyncrasies to prefer that his assistants should emulate his own carelessness, and to pride himself on his own and his staff's Spartan ability to "rough it" in the field. He served a table so excruciatingly bad that only persons of iron constitution could survive it, and even they had been known on occasion stealthily to leave his camp in order to assuage their hunger by sharing the comparatively luxurious beans and unleavened bread of the local fellahin. . . . The fact remains that he not only miraculously survived the consistent practice of what he preached, but with all his eccentricities . . . established in the end a record of maximum results for minimum expenditure which is not likely to be surpassed.[24]

It was to be expected that Frances Breasted, like the American Miss Bliss, should be deeply shocked by his indelicate lack of socks. She liked him nevertheless and the two men got on well; before he left Naqada Petrie suggested to Breasted that they might one day collaborate in an excavation financed in part by the University of Chicago. Breasted, while tempted by the idea, probably realized that so self-sufficient an autocrat would not run easily in harness with a younger and less experienced man. He promised at any rate to try and find money for Petrie's digs, on the understanding that a proportion of the finds should go to Chicago.

Early in March the work was closed, and 70 crates of bones and skulls and 300 boxes packed with New Race pottery and small objects were sent off; De Morgan kept very little, and Petrie was able to allot a complete series to his collection at University College and another to the Ashmolean. A set of wavy-handled pots went to the Berlin Museum, others to Chicago and Philadelphia. That summer Petrie went to Edinburgh to receive the honorary degree of Ll.D. and lecture to the Royal Society; during the summer he finished the second volume of his History and started on the third, wrote a number of articles for Hasting's *Dictionary of the Bible* and wrote up his excavation. The July exhibition no longer had its faithful sentinel: Riley was seriously ill, and died not long afterwards.

During the winter of 1895–6, Petrie decided that he and Quibell would work side by side in Western Thebes, Petrie on behalf of Haworth, Kennard and himself, and Quibell independently for the Research Account. The concession he applied for was not more than three-quarters of a mile in length, along the edge of the desert, but it included the Ramesseum, the great mortuary temple of Ramesses II, and other ruins which had never been properly investigated; during his stay in Thebes in 1887 he must have noted this area as a promising field for excavation, and he was pleased to find that De Morgan offered reasonable terms, stipulating merely that all royal monuments were to be kept by the Museum, and the other finds were to be halved . . . a proviso which Petrie had now to accept as inevitable. To Miss Pirie and Miss Paget, two of his University College students who were skilful artists, he assigned a different task: they were to make facsimile copies of reliefs in the mastaba tombs at Saqqara; rooms in Mariette's house were put at their disposal and they were to have a cook and a servant. Quibell saw them settled in, not a little excited at the prospect of living on their own: Petrie next day started them off on a suitable tomb. He called on Dr Grant, whom he was distressed to find in bed convalescing after serious illness. Next day he started for Luxor with Quibell and Joseph Grafton Milne, who was to be with

Above left **(41)**: 'Ali Muhammad es Suefi; *right* **(42)**: M. Naville directing the excavation of Deir al Bahari in 1892; *below* **(43)**: Tomb-digging at ?Ballas, 1895

Above left **(44)**: Flinders Petrie at about the time of his marriage; *right* **(45)**: The young Hilda Urlin

Below left **(46)**: Hilda Petrie descending a tomb-shaft by rope-ladder, perhaps at Dendera in 1897-8

47 Hilda Petrie outside the expedition h[illegible] Hu, 1899

48 Flinders Petrie and Amy Urlin in the courtyard of the first "dig" house at Abydos, 1901

49 Amy Urlin in the mess room of the Abydos house

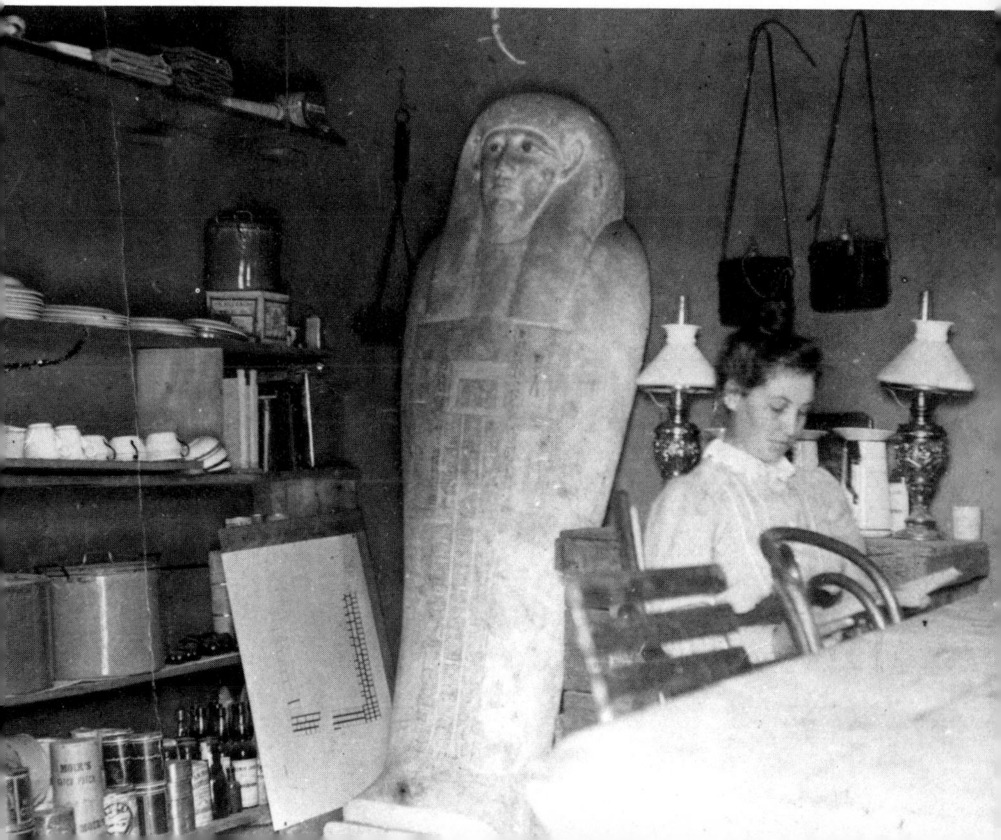

Above left **(50)**: Tiny ivory figure of a first dynasty king in his embroidered jubilee cloak, found at Abydos in 1902 (British Museum); *right* **(51)**: Four bracelets of gold, amethyst, lapis lazuli and turquoise as they were found on a wrist in the tomb of King Zer, Abydos; *below* **(52)**: Hilda Petrie at Abydos

Above left **(53)**: Head from a figurine of Queen Tiy, the mother of Akhenaton, found in the temple of Serabit al Khadem; *right* **(54)**: Tarkhan, 1911-12: rush basket-work and wooden lining of a grave of the Archaic period

55 Hawara, 1911: mummies awaiting transportation

56 Sinai, 1906: the morning walk to work at Serabit al Khadem

57 Sinai, 1906: Hilda on camel back

58 Serabit al Khadem: stelae and pillars of Hathor in the temple

59 Model of the temple at Serabit al Khadem, shown in Petrie's exhibition at University College in July 1906. On the extreme right behind (no. 13) is a figure inscribed with the Sinaitic alphabetic script.

60 Flinders Petrie at Abydos *c.* 1900

61 A chain of basket-boys excavating the Osireion, 1902–3

them for part of the season. He was a young classical scholar who had recently been digging in Greece; he was becoming increasingly interested in the history of Graeco-Roman Egypt and he welcomed the opportunity of so valuable an introduction to Egypt and its antiquities.

In Luxor they met Newberry, and Petrie stayed the first night there with him; he was engaged in cataloguing the tombs of the Theban necropolis and copying in some of them. "He has a sweet garden, and a small native house, and he and his wife have been as kind as they can about all our affairs," wrote Petrie in his first Journal. Howard Carter, still with the Navilles at Deir el Bahari, offered his former teacher the hospitality of his house in Qurna while the quarters Petrie had chosen for the expedition were made ready for occupation; these were a row of vaulted brick magazines at the back of the Ramesseum (**81**), of the same date as the temple and still standing some thirteen feet high; the roofs of some were more or less intact and by clearing the floors and building cross-walls in four of these long galleries, fairly spacious and weather-proof accommodation was provided for the Quibells, Milne and Petrie, for the nine Quftis, and for 'Ali es Suefi, his wife and their new baby. A space was walled in for the storage of the larger finds, and a deep trench dug around the encampment to keep out intruders. The unexpected sight of this settlement, complete with the workers' donkeys and camels, could not fail to astonish tourists visiting the Ramesseum, whose curiosity tempted them to peer over the wall. Another gallery was later prepared for visitors like Amelia Oldroyd, who with her nephew Borwick stayed for ten days; Henry Wallis came over for a couple of days, and painted a romanticized picture of Petrie directing excavations at the Ramesseum (**80**); and later Annie Pirie and Rosalind Paget, having finished their work at Saqqara, arrived to take charge of the colour copying. When the cold winds of January blew, the party shivered in their draughty quarters and Petrie wrote up his diary in bed in the evening with numbed fingers; in spite of this it was a happy camp, enlivened, no doubt, by the presence of three young ladies. Quibell was later to marry Miss Pirie. In view of the undoubted fact that in Petrie's camps one was expected to eat food out of half-empty tins left over from the previous day, it was later rumoured that their friendship had ripened when they were both recovering from a bout of ptomaine poisoning.[25] Situated as they were near Luxor, the party were never without visitors; Carter and Percy Brown used to walk across the hill from Deir el Bahari; Newberry regularly brought their post and sometimes fresh vegetables from his garden. Both Sayce and Wilbour visited them, and Sayce persuaded Petrie to take the old Duke of Cambridge, infirm but indefatigable, round the Ramesseum, and, on a subsequent occasion, to the Valley of the Tombs of the Kings. Very fortunately, too, a young German scholar, Wilhelm Spiegelberg, who had studied under Maspero in Paris and had already made a name for himself as a philologist, was doing epigraphic work nearby. He often came over to help them by making rapid translations of their newly-discovered texts; Petrie got on very well with him—"He is the pleasantest German I know, next to Wiedemann, for absence of their usual bumptiousness"—and decided to hand over to him the publication of all the inscriptions.

Quibell set to work in the Ramesseum and in the brick complex surrounding the temple, using the Quftis whenever he came upon a tomb of later date cut into the Ramesside ruins. Petrie, taking on two hundred men, started to clear the area southwards, where Pharaohs of the New Kingdom had built temples for their mortuary cults. With the exception of the Ramesseum itself little remained of these save mounds of earth and a few blocks of stone; even the identity of some of the builders was unknown; or had been wrongly attributed. Petrie excavated six, in several cases finding little more than foundation deposits; one proved to be of a Queen, Ta-usert, showing that she had reigned in her own right as Pharaoh, and a small chapel yielded the beautiful portrait head of an unnamed princess whom Petrie called the "White Queen" (**86**).

One of the disadvantages of being so near Luxor was the difficulty of preventing theft. The Quftis Petrie could trust, but he had a large local workforce and there were always dealers hanging about, squatting by the well from which the thirsty drew their water, ready to buy whatever they had pocketed; tourists bought avidly and without question from the dealers. Carter and Newberry warned Petrie that objects were being stolen from his work, and although he was offering as much in rewards as the dealers paid, he was unable to stop the pilfering. Only his old friend, the dealer Muhammad Mohassib in Luxor, refused to buy anything stolen from Petrie's work on the ground that "he would not make a profit from the robbery of his friends". In the end he sacked all the local men from Qurna, and relied on his own workers from Quft and Ballas, and on men brought from distant villages.

The largest of the funerary temples, that of Amenophis III, was out of alignment, having been built not on the desert edge, but on land annually flooded by the Nile's inundation; the site was marked only by the Colossi of Memnon, solitary sentinels that once sat by great pylons at the entrance to the temple. This temple De Morgan had reserved for himself, but the building to the north of it, which was also attributed to Amenophis III since only his name appeared on blocks strewn over the site, was in Petrie's concession. Could one king have had two mortuary temples? Petrie dug and soon solved the puzzle: the temple had been built by Merenptah, the son and successor of Ramesses II, almost entirely from stone plundered from the temple of Amenophis III nearby. Statues of the latter had been smashed and the pieces thrown into the foundations; fragments of couchant stone jackals, which must have once formed an imposing avenue approaching the pylon, and broken drums of columns from halls and courts, gave some idea of the splendour of the original temple. A statue of Merenptah himself was found—the first known portrait of this king; Petrie knew that it would be taken for the Ghizeh Museum, but he realized that even a photograph of it would cause interest in England because of its Biblical connotation: since Ramesses II was generally believed to have been the 'Pharaoh of the Oppression' (of the Children of Israel), his successor must surely have been the Pharaoh of the Exodus.

Better was to follow: two splendid stelae were found,[26] both of them usurped on the reverse side by Merenptah, who had turned them face to the wall. One, beautifully carved, showed Amenophis III in battle with Nubians and Syrians; the other, of black granite, was over ten feet high, larger than any stela previously known; the original text commemorated the building achievements of Amenophis and described the beauties and magnificence of the temple in which it had stood. When it could be turned over an inscription of Merenptah recording his triumphs over the Libyans and the Peoples of the Sea was revealed; Spiegelberg came over to read it, and near the end of the text he was puzzled by one, that of a people or tribe whom Merenptah had victoriously smitten—"*I.si.ri.ar?*" It was Petrie whose quick imaginative mind leap to the solution: "Israel!" Spiegelberg agreed that it must be so. "Won't the reverends be pleased?" was his comment. At dinner that evening Petrie prophesied: "This stele will be better known in the world than anything else I have found." It was the first mention of the word "Israel" in any Egyptian text and the news made headlines when it reached the English papers.

In early March, leaving Quibell in charge of the Ramesseum work, Flinders Petrie went home; instead of going first to Bromley, as he had always done in the past, he went straight to Lily Lodge: his ties with his home were weaker now. Reginald Stuart Poole had died in February of the previous year; and Petrie found himself on the committee to appoint a new Professor of Classical Archaeology. Two candidates were shortlisted: one was Miss Jane Harrison, a forceful personality and a leading authority on ancient Greek religion; she had been a strong contestant for the Chair in 1889 when Poole was appointed. The other was Ernest Gardner. Petrie presented a strong case for his friend's election on the grounds that he had had practical experience of excavating; his counsels prevailed, and once more that lady was deprived of the distinction of being the first woman professor in an English University. Petrie and Gardner were to remain friends and colleagues for the rest of their lives; in Hampstead later on they saw much of each other, and Gardner was to be Chairman of the Egyptian Research Account and after the war, as Vice-Chancellor of the University of London, Petrie's constant ally and advocate. At first they sometimes disagreed vehemently on such matters as the ventilation on either side of the partition between the Edwards Library and the Yates Archaeological Library. A. E. Housman, the Professor of Latin, was another of Petrie's friends; others were W. P. Ker, who occupied the Chair of English for over thirty years; Arthur Platt, the Professor of Greek; Karl Pearson, Professor of Applied Mathematics and later the first Galton Professor of Eugenics, who was to be his next-door neighbour in Hampstead and one of his closest friends; and Sir George Thane, the Professor of Anatomy from 1877 to 1919, in whose department Petrie's skeletons from Naqada were examined before they went to the Royal College of Surgeons; among other distinguished colleagues were William (later Sir William) Ramsay, the Professor of Chemistry, and Sir Ambrose Fleming in the Chair of Electrical Engineering. Petrie enjoyed their company at coffee after lunch, though he seldom ate with them, preferring a more frugal meal at the teashop round the corner.

Another change concerned his own department. A few days after his return to England, in March 1896, he had had a serious talk with Frank Griffith, who wished to ask his advice. Since Miss Edwards' death her mantle had to some extent fallen on Kate Bradbury; that capable lady had helped with the arrangement of the library and collection at University College, and she and Griffith had been fellow members of the Committee of the Egypt Exploration Fund, where they had formed a kind of Petrie lobby, with a watching brief for the standards which he had set in excavation and in publication, privately often seeking his advice on matters concerning the running of the Fund; Miss Bradbury would then set forth the argument at the meeting and Frank Griffith would back her up, though he often sat silent, too shy to express his opinion—"Oh, I could shake him!" she once said to Flinders.[27] Now Frank needed his old friend's advice: should he—dared he—ask Miss Bradbury to marry him? She was several years older than he, and wealthy, whereas he had only a small salary in the British Museum and a pittance as Assistant Professor in University College. Flinders Petrie had no doubt what his advice should be: he was very fond of Griffith and had frequently been invited to his home in St Albans where his father and brothers received him cordially; and he thought very highly of Kate. They married that summer, and left London and the British Museum to live at her home in Ashton-under-Lyne; her father, a wealthy mill-owner, and long a widower, welcomed Frank and from then on he had no financial worries and was able to carry on his own researches and build up a library; during the next two years his first task was the study and publication of the Middle Kingdom hieratic papyri which Petrie had found in Kahun.[28] The marriage was a happy one, but sadly short: after only six years Kate died; Frank stayed on at Riversvale, eventually inherited his father-in-law's not inconsiderable fortune; moving to Oxford, he was able generously to endow the study of Egyptology in that University and during the course of a distinguished career of research, launch many young scholars on the path which his letter to Petrie in 1883 had opened to him.

Class teaching had never been the shy Griffith's *forte*: Margaret Murray remembered in her memoirs the bewilderment of beginners at University College as he suggested first one interpretation of a text or grammatical point, then four or five others.[29] Under Petrie's guidance, she had already carried out a creditable piece of research, and now he asked her to take over the teaching of the first-year students, while Dr Walker was to tutor the more advanced students in the second year. W. E. Crum was already teaching Coptic and pursuing his own research in the Department, and one of his students, Herbert Thompson, a convert from the Medical Faculty, was to become a leading authority on Demotic. Miss Edwards would have been delighted no doubt to know that, so few years after her death, the Edwards library was already the centre of "as brilliant a team of scholars in our subject as has ever been found at one time in any single University" (thus S. R. K. Glanville, the second Edwards Professor, in 1953). The other matter which Frank Griffith wished to discuss with Flinders that day in March 1896 was the possibility of his return to the Egypt Exploration Fund.

Flinders Petrie had never intended to leave the Fund for good; his letters to Miss Edwards made that perfectly clear. Griffith had often urged him to come back, and in the spring of 1892 he wrote again, this time at the request of the Committee, "I think that if you were to name terms of almost any description they would agree like a shot."[30] Petrie's reply then made it clear that he was not yet prepared to do so: so long as the Fund was mismanaged by its present committee, he could not submit himself to their control, and he urged on Griffith the need to appoint a full-time Director, a man of organizing ability with some experience of conditions in Egypt, perhaps recently retired from business; he suggested several names.[31] Nothing, of course, was done. But now Poole was dead; the new Honorary Secretary was to be James Cotton, newly retired from the editorship of *The Academy*, whom Petrie had always found courteous and helpful. It might now be possible to form a partnership with the Fund, not on the old terms, but as an established scholar, a professor with academic status similar to Naville's, two honorary degrees* and an international reputation. His letter to Grueber, the Hon. Treasurer, made it clear what he expected. The Committee had just heard from Hogarth, who had been digging in Alexandria and with Grenfell in the Fayum, that he did not intend to work again in Egypt. Petrie volunteered to work for the Fund in Hogarth's place; he would remain Director of the Egyptian Research Account, but would guarantee to devote half of each year to the interests of the Fund in excavating, attending to their exhibition, and publishing results. He insisted on sole control of field operations, "as I do not wish to give myself to supporting work with the method of which I do not agree". He also claimed the right to choose his own staff, and asked for an assurance that typical series of objects, such as pottery, should be kept together.[32] These terms were agreed by the Committee, and Petrie was voted £500 for his coming season; Grenfell, who would go out with him in expectation of papyri, would get £150 of this for his own work. The sum was not over-liberal, particularly since the agreement with Jesse Haworth and Kennard was now at an end (the former continued to be a generous donor to the E.R.A.). Still, Petrie did not expect this season to be very costly in terms of staff or labour—Thebes the previous year had been the most expensive dig of

* D.C.L. (Oxford) and Ll.D. (Edinburgh); his Cambridge Litt.D. came in 1900.

his career, but the £1,000 had been well spent in view of the treasures found.

At the Fund's Annual Meeting on 13 November 1896, Petrie addressed the audience once more as their explorer. The Chairman was tactless enough to refer to him as the returning Prodigal Son (which of them had been prodigal? Petrie wondered, thinking of the Fund's past extravagance and his own frugality). The real reason they wanted him back, he was sure, was that they badly needed objects to distribute to their American supporters; Naville's operations at Deir el Bahari had been singularly unproductive in that respect.

Quibell was already in Egypt: he was to excavate on his own for the E.R.A. at el Kab, a site which Petrie and Griffith had marked out as promising ten years before. Flinders himself set out on a grey winter morning with a new student, Geere; De Morgan was also on the boat and he and Flinders had several friendly talks. The Frenchman was anxious to make it clear that any restrictions he imposed upon excavators were "solely official, and not due to any ill-will". He had been digging a little at Abydos and at Tukh (Naqada) himself since Petrie left the site, and he showed him a copy of his most recent book.[33] Petrie found it very puzzling, for he classified all users of flint implements, including those of the New Race as "Neolithic". The book was beautifully illustrated but Petrie considered it to be completely mistaken; he was glad his own book on Naqada had already come out.

After nearly a week in Cairo, visiting dealers and paying the customary calls (Dr Grant, sadly, was no longer there; he had recently died in Scotland)—Petrie decided not to wait for his permit but to go ahead to his destination. This year he had chosen the mounds of Behnesa, on the desert edge twelve miles west of the town of Beni Mazar, beyond the Bahr Yusuf. Here were the ruins of a city which had once been the capital of a nome; the Greeks had called it Oxyrhynchus and it was known that papyri had been found there. Bernard Grenfell had arranged to join him there, and his friend Arthur Hunt, who had already spent a season papyrus-hunting in the Fayum with him, was to come if the site looked promising. Petrie himself would use the camp as a convenient centre for investigating early remains in the surrounding countryside. He and Geere set about building a house; finding that nobody in the neighbourhood would sell him bricks—people were moving from Behnesa to a village on the other side of the Bahr Yusuf for greater safety from the desert Beduin, and much building was going on—they decided to make their own bricks; this meant making a brick-mould, but the saw which 'Ali es Suefi had brought up from Luxor with the rest of the gear had been damaged the previous year, so "our building began by sharpening the saw, to cut the board, to make the mould, to mould the bricks, to build the huts". The House that Jack Built had its echoes in Egypt, and Flinders Petrie had the versatility of a Jack-of-all-trades. He planned ten rooms ("don't be alarmed by the grandeur of it, the cost will be about £2 or £3"), which would allow for the accommodation of occasional visitors; Sir Francis Grenfell was to spend a night or so, and the intrepid Miss Oldroyd and her nephew would be staying for a time.

'Ali es Suefi came from Luxor with his wife Fatma, and their little son and his younger brother Mahmud. The pleasure Petrie felt at 'Ali's coming was not merely for the arrival of his most skilful and reliable workman; a deep and lasting friendship had grown up between them based on mutual liking and respect.

> It will be a great pleasure to have him with me again, for I feel that all must go well with such a faithful, quiet, unselfish right hand to help. As far as character goes he is really more to me than almost any of my own race. Few men, I believe, have worked harder for me or trusted me more. Perhaps none are sorrier at parting, or gladder when we meet again. A curious link in life but a very real one, as character is at the bottom of it. Kipling's "East and West" is the only expression of such a link that I know.

He was distressed to find that 'Ali, though himself of thrifty habits, was incapable of keeping the money he earned: his family all sponged on him, and he was too good-natured to deny them. At Behnesa he rigged up an oven, and Fatma baked the bread for the camp, crouching for hours on end in front of the blazing fire, tossing each lump of dough on a fan of palm leaves till it spread to almost paper thinness, then slipping the flap into the hot clay dome, where in about a minute it was baked. The expected permit to excavate was long in coming: every day Mahmud was sent to Beni Mazar, twenty-two miles there and back, to look for post; every day he came back empty-handed. Meanwhile Petrie, unable to turn over a spadeful of soil, watched camel loads of stone and rubble being wrenched from the site of the old town and carted away to build the new. The permit finally arrived, brought by an *effendi* in a town suit who was to stay on the dig as a resident inspector at the excavators' expense. Petrie was furious, since De Morgan had promised him that he would not send any such official; the permit, moreover, only referred to the town site and made no mention of excavation in the surrounding countryside which he hoped to explore. Once more an indignant letter went off to Cairo, and the unfortunate inspector was sent back whence he had come.

A few days' digging at Behnesa made it plain that the site was likely to yield little of Pharaonic date, but the rubbish dumps on the edges of the Roman town were already yielding quantities of papyri. Petrie decided to hand the site over to Grenfell and Hunt. It turned out to be a treasure-house; though the tombs were waterlogged, the town heaps were full of papyri, some literary scraps, others the "closed files" of local government offices—administrative documents of the greatest historical interest. On one day alone, so many papyrus rolls were found that it was impossible to find enough baskets to contain them, and the local tinsmith was put to work to make hundreds of boxes for the precious fragments. Oxyrhynchus occupied Grenfell and Hunt for more than ten years; no other site has yielded so many treasures to the papyrologist and the harvest they reaped is still being published, year after year, in the series of volumes initiated by Grenfell and Hunt for the Egypt Exploration Fund.[34]

Leaving Geere with Grenfell, Petrie and 'Ali es Suefi now set off on a five-day camping trip along the desert edge prospecting for sites. It was a journey not without perils; the local Beduin encamped beyond the limits of the cultivation had a reputation for wildness; many of them carried blunderbusses and loaded pistols and the fellahin feared them. Petrie, who was unarmed, found them friendly enough, but he was warned by 'Ali not to make a sound when walking near a village after nightfall. This was a part of Egypt to which no tourists and very few townspeople ever came; the Libyan hills here recede and to Petrie's surprise he found that a series of sand dunes ran parallel to the valley, concealing between them long strips of water; as the lakes dried they became grassy upland valleys on which the Beduin grazed their flocks. To walk barefoot on the dunes and on the short grass was delicious to Petrie. They would rise very early and when 'Ali had brewed coffee, they would send the donkey boy with their gear to the next rendezvous, and go off into the hills; when they sat down to rest, Petrie often pulled out his paintbox and sketched. One day they covered about thirty-four miles, at full speed, mostly on sand, and Petrie was glad to find that he was not too tired at the end of the day. When they rejoined their baggage they pitched the tent and 'Ali made lentil soup for them all. "To have 'domestic providence' . . . always at your elbow, ready for sketches, donkeys, cooking and everything else, and withal one of the pleasantest of friends to be about with, is the luxury of travelling. I have learned more of his ways in these five days, and respect him even more than before." The respect was mutual; in his old age in the 1930s, 'Ali would often speak of the "Basha Betrie" with reverence and affection. He spoke little English, and never learned to read and write, but he developed a sharp eye for a buried site or a hidden cemetery, and Petrie had taught him to distinguish types and shapes of pottery and assign each sherd and each bead to its period. Flinders Petrie's Arabic must have been fluent by now, though it was never accurate, having been learnt solely by ear without any grounding in basic grammatical structure. Some words he always got wrong. There is a story that once Petrie was directing the men in hauling a heavy coffin from the bottom of a tomb shaft; just as they had got it to the top Petrie shouted "Push!"; automatically they all gave a mighty shove, and back the coffin fell to the bottom of the well. 'Ali was heard to say to the men "From now on remember that when the Pasha says 'Push!' he means 'Pull!' "[35]

Sometimes, during their years of companionship, Petrie was reminded of the differences in mental attitude between the fellah and the European; at el'Amarna a glorious sunset over the Nile, which set the whole sky ablaze, evoked no response whatever from 'Ali,[36] and although he would weep when parting from his master, he had no tears for the departure of his faithless wife, enticed back to her family by her ruffianly brother after several angry skirmishes; his only sorrow seemed to be for the loss of his little boy. In rural Egypt, it seemed, marriage was an affair of the purse rather than of the heart.

A search of nearly ninety miles of ground from Minia to Hawara in the Fayum produced little in the way of promising early sites—Petrie was not interested in Roman cemeteries or Coptic monasteries. He finally decided to dig at Deshasha, a little south of Ahnas el Medina, and they moved their equipment down by boat on the Bahr Yusuf. A gale blew, and it was only 'Ali's undaunted manner which kept the boatmen up to towing in the teeth of the storm all day; often he would haul the rope alone. It took them forty-eight hours to travel eighteen miles. Huts were built for Geere and himself; Miss Oldroyd and Borwick followed as soon as there was room for them and stayed long enough to see the first tombs opened. The cemetery here was of fifth-dynasty date. Two of the tombs were rock-cut grottoes of the local aristocracy; the reliefs on the walls of these were badly damaged, but one or two of them were of considerable interest. One unique scene depicted an attack by Egyptian soldiers on a walled village or town, the mining of the walls, the listening defenders within; Petrie could claim it as "the most dramatic, by far the earliest, battle scene known" (see p. 230).

The discoveries at Deshasha contributed greatly to knowledge of Old Kingdom burial customs, hitherto known only from mastaba tombs of the wealthy at Saqqara and Giza. In particular, the burials displayed a new feature: some of the bodies had not only been dismembered, as in some tombs at Naqada and Meydum, but each limb had been separately wrapped in cloth before the body was reassembled in the coffin, and some bones appeared to Petrie to have been defleshed before wrapping.[37] Petrie's discussion of this phenomenon, in an article in *The Contemporary Review*[38] (*The Academy* no longer published archaeological news, having become after Cotton's retirement mainly a literary review) caused a minor sensation, for he suggested that it must be evidence of the practice of ritual cannibalism among the ancient Egyptians. This conclusion was to give rise, years later, to some controversy (see pp. 345f.). Most of the bones were brought back to London, where they were measured and examined by members of the Anatomy Department at University College who were already studying skulls and bones from Meydum and Naqada; in Petrie's publication of the Deshasha tombs, which came out that same year, there are several Roentgen photographs showing disarticulated leg bones beneath the wrappings.[39] As far as is known, this is the first use of X-rays in archaeology; perhaps they were the work of Professor J. N. Collie, who took the first medical X-rays in the College at about this time.

Petrie's notebooks for the winter of 1896–7 contain carefully tabulated measurements of some 187 skulls from late tombs at Behnesa, and nearly as many Old Kingdom crania from Deshasha. One of the conclusions reached by the anatomists was that there was a greater difference in type between the "New Race" skulls from Naqada and those of the fifth dynasty, than between the latter and those, four thousand years later, of the Roman Age. This, claimed Petrie, was a strong argument against the New Race being the prehistoric ancestors of the dynastic Egyptians; he still believed they were a totally different people. To University College also came several bundles of linen from the Deshasha tombs. Nine long shirts were found in a wooden coffin. They were too fragile to be unwrapped, but remained in the Petrie collection till in 1981, modern technology came to the aid of the Museum's curators (see p. 321) and some could be mounted for display (**96**).[40]

Flinders Petrie remained at Deshasha until mid-March; on the voyage home, the steamer ran aground on an island as they were nearing Marseilles; grabbing a lifebelt, he stationed himself on the prow so that he could leap ashore if the ship started to founder. He was determined to preserve not only himself, but the treasure he had wrapped in his pocket handkerchief and slipped into his pocket at the first alarm: it was a little ebony figure of a Nubian servant-girl which he had bought from a dealer in Cairo, for far more than he usually paid. This charming little statuette, "a perfect joy to look at", is one of the treasures of the Petrie Museum (**23**). The night passed without further alarms and passengers were taken off by tug the next morning. On 25 March Petrie arrived in London, his mind in a turmoil of anticipation mingled, no doubt, with some apprehension. During his months in Egypt, his diary had noted from time to time letters written to "H.U." Now he was about to make a proposal of marriage.

Deshasha: siege of a fortified town

CHAPTER X

Hilda
(1896–8)

HILDA MARY ISOBEL Urlin was the youngest daughter of Denny Urlin, a lawyer, and his wife Mary, born Addis. Her father was an Englishman who had spent twenty-six years as a barrister practising in the Fore Courts of Dublin.[1] In 1875, when Hilda was only four he had returned to England to live, and had settled in the Grange, Rustington in Sussex, a comfortable flint house which had been built in 1815 by his wife's grandparents. Finding it difficult to break into the closed circle of English law, he turned to lecturing and writing and to social and church activities: he was for some years a Board School inspector, he was active in parish work and local government and he wrote a short biography of John Wesley and another of Father Reece, his own grandfather, who had been one of Wesley's disciples. He often visited the Continent, accompanied by his wife and one or other of his daughters. Hilda had happy memories of her childhood in Rustington, and Ann remembers vividly her holidays there; after her grandparents' death, the house was finally sold to developers in 1926 and pulled down.

Of Hilda's four sisters the eldest died in infancy. The second sister, Maud, broke away from home early. In her political sympathies she went against the family tradition, voted Liberal and supported the Boers, and she married an Oxford don, Frank Peters; of their two daughters one, Phyllis, was to become a particular favourite with the Petrie children. Ethel, the third sister, was the author of two books: a short *History of Marriage*, and a *History of Dancing*; in her later years she took to frequent travel abroad for health reasons. Amy, the last but one, was six years older than Hilda. She too never married: her life was devoted to charitable works and she had little use for creature comforts.

Deprived of the companionship of brothers and sisters near her own age, Hilda appears to have been an introspective and rather melancholy child; her own memories of early childhood[2] are ceasing in her eighth year to care for dolls, preferring sailing boats, tops and marbles and other boyish games, and having only boys as friends; she wrote little stories under the name of "W. Blade", and perhaps even imagined herself to be a boy. One of her idols as she grew older was Philippa Fawcett, a tall athletic girl destined later to become a Senior Wrangler and a suffragette, who lived in the neighbourhood. School for Hilda was a small group of children at Rustington Rectory, taught by a governness. As she grew older, she began to develop an interest in Gothic architecture, church antiquities and "the more engaging aspects of history"; she read omnivorously, and had a passionate love of nature, studying botany and pressing wild flowers, and collecting geological specimens. She and her friends would cycle about the countryside, daringly clad in the new-fashioned "bloomers", visiting churches armed with rolls of paper and cobblers' heelball, to add to their collection of rubbings of monumental brasses. Life at Rustington in the 1890s was enlivened by tennis parties and theatricals, long walks and picnics; the family went by carriage to picnic on the downs, and walked to the sea, a mile away, to bathe; Hilda remembered as a small child being carried to the sea on his shoulders by Hubert Parry, the composer, who was a near neighbour.

The Urlins also had a London house, 22, Stafford Terrace, Kensington, and there their winters were spent. Hilda resented these interludes away from the country. "I must tell you," she wrote once to Flinders, "that leaving R. has, three times a year, for many, many years been an agony of misery to me. . . . I leave all that I most care about, and return to fogs and dullness and the hideous surroundings you know so well. . . . How I thank God for those oases of 'Pops' and Old Masters, and talks with friends, and visits to Museums, every otherwise dreary winter."[3] As she grew up, she was kept busy enough: she would accompany her father on Board School inspections, and occasionally at a comparatively youthful age took his place; she attended lectures at King's College for Women, including a geology course given by Professor H. G. Seeley, and often went with the other students on field expeditions armed with hammer, specimen bag and notebook; she studied facsimile drawing and attained considerable skill in drawing botanical specimens and copying examples of ecclesiastical ornament. Among her parents' friends was Henry Holiday, the Pre-Raphaelite painter, for whom she was persuaded to sit as a model, duly chaperoned by her elder sister. With her wide heart-shaped face, clear blue eyes and fair hair, she was just the type of beauty he was looking for; he painted her as Aspasia and she was the original of Beatrice in the painting, now in the Leeds Art Gallery, of the meeting between Dante and Beatrice on the Ponte della Trinità in Florence. Finding that she had some skill as a copyist, he asked her to make some drawings for him and it was in University College, in the summer of 1896 when she was visiting Flinders Petrie's July exhibition of the discoveries of his recent season in Thebes, that the Professor caught sight of this beautiful girl whom he "eyed from room to room". Plucking up courage to speak to her, he discovered that she was actually working in the College, making drawings of classical detail for Holiday.

The first approaches were made by him; she was pleased and flattered by the Professor's attention. He encouraged her to come to his Department and help him by drawing scarabs; during the autumn she was a frequent visitor. He lent her books, sent her lecture tickets, and encouraged her professed interest in ancient Egypt; she attended his lectures and began to learn the forms of the hieroglyphs. One day they walked together down Gower Street to the British Museum. On the way, he talked about going to Egypt; she told him that she had always longed to go there. This conversation, underlined in his diary, he regarded later as the turning point in their relationship; it was then that he decided that he would one day ask her to marry him. He was forty-three, and until that time appears to have ruled out the possibility of marriage; no woman, he was convinced, could be asked to share his life of constant toil and discomfort, even danger sometimes. He had almost persuaded himself that he disliked the idea of being shackled by matrimony. Yet the Griffiths' obvious happiness had given him great pleasure and may have been one of the factors in his change of heart. At any rate he went off to Egypt in mid-November leaving Hilda the key of the scarab cases and tracings to ink in for him, and he begged her to write and let him know how she got on with the reading list he had left her. Her name joined the list of recipients of his Journal that winter and he wrote her personal letters from Behnesa and Deshasha encouraging her to persevere with her studies; growing bolder, he had a parcel of books sent to her for Christmas, but received a gentle rebuff: Hilda protested that she could not possibly accept so large a gift from him; she would consider the larger books as a loan, and would keep for herself only the "little Stoic philosophies"—but with the protest "I had rather you had not sent them." One of the Stoics was Flinders' favourite, Epictetus, which he always took with him on his travels.

They continued to exchange letters through January and February, though Hilda confessed that much as she had tried to find time for his scarabs, she was usually too busy at home, helping her father with his work, running errands for him and bicycling or walking with "B.O.", her greatest friend Beatrice Orme; she was attending a weekly choral class, two Greek classes and Wicksteed's lectures on Dante, and reading with her friend *Piers Plowman*, and Dante's *Vita Nuova* in Italian. When Flinders Petrie returned to University College (by the quickest route—no dallying in Italy or Greece)—he had clearly made up his mind to propose. Not finding her at the College, he wrote at once; but she replied that she had influenza and would not be coming to the College before leaving for the country. Relenting a little at the end of her letter she invited him to call at Stafford Terrace with sheets of tracings for her to ink while she was away; he brought them, but had no opportunity to engage her in the serious conversation he had planned. She returned the drawings unfinished after three weeks. She was indeed unwell, for she developed measles in May; Petrie, desperately busy with a number of lectures to prepare and proofs to read, miserably decided she had no use for him; a note in his diary for 27 May reads, "*Down, very; Syria only hope.*" He wrote sending her a ticket for the Greek play in the College, and inviting her and her sister Amy to his exhibition which was to open on 30 June with a *conversazione*. She did not come to either; first she was in the Lake District, then she wrote from the Isle of Man, then from Dublin to promise that she would come to the College on her bicycle (should she leave it at the Porter's Lodge?) on 29 July. What passed between them at that meeting will never be known: Flinders must have declared his feelings for her and been met with a dismayed repudiation: she did not love him—he must never see her again. Next day he wrote her a despairing letter: if he was to her, as she told him, "no more than an ordinary acquaintance" it must mean the end of his life in England. "I cannot again live as I did before I knew you, nor as I have done for a year past with the ceaseless wear of thought, pain and sleeplessness that I have borne. I must look to altogether breaking with England, which is bound up with you at each turn of my surroundings; for since I knew you, and drank in your mind and character last summer, and found your interests all in common with my own, you have lived in every thought of mine, often more present than the people and things around me." He had decided, he said, to go to live in Syria for good. "You may perhaps realise what it is to leave here, with its friendships, ambitions, society, position and means—all that I have gathered and won—and begin to lay out a new form of life. But this is the needful 'price of tranquillity', if I may regain it thus after knowing you. It is but an opiate to deaden that writhing and rending of the whole being, which I hope you may never know or understand." She was the only woman, he assured her, that had ever handled his life, and she had broken up the monastic reserve in which he had always lived. He asked her to confirm that her feelings really were as he supposed; if so, the inevitable step must and would be taken.[4]

Hilda wrote back by return of post, begging him not to take so rash and irrevocable a step. She did not yet know herself—she had never been in love—they must get to know each other better. Before writing, she had showed her mother Flinders' letter and asked her advice. The sensible Mrs Urlin wrote him a tactful note suggesting that he should come down and stay somewhere in the neighbourhood, at Arundel perhaps, or Worthing, from which base it would be easy for him to pay visits to Rustington; this, she felt sure, would give Hilda, who was young and inexperienced, the opportunity to make up her mind. Petrie was greatly relieved; he wrote Hilda a long letter in which he pointed out how little they really knew each other; he had never even seen her laugh. As for himself, he had always walked alone:

> I was an only child never at school, and have a few intimate friends. The greatest blessings I have yet known have been three close friendships with good right-minded women, who have been to me as sisters [he referred of course to the Harveys] but even in the greatest intimacy, without one touch of what you are. . . . I knew that circumstances were against me in my start in life, owing to causes I could not help; and I resolutely avoided any possible entanglement for it would, I always knew, be almost life and death to me to really care about anyone. I drowned my mind in work, and have kept my balance by filling every thought with fresh interests and endeavours, at a cost and a strain which I could hardly live under. Success has come to me far more than I expected; the world has been very kind to me, and I have never failed in any serious work that I have undertaken. Friendships have grown around, and I have long had to deny far the greater part of those I might make because they would fill all my time.[5]

On the first Sunday in August Flinders went down to Littlehampton by an early train, walked the two miles to Rustington and met Hilda after church. He stayed nearby, and met her daily; one day they made an expedition to Bosham to see the Saxon church and watch the little boats bobbing in the harbour. The visit was clearly encouraging to them both, though he confessed he found it difficult to talk freely "when nearly all one's thoughts will not do for the character of the 'ordinary acquaintance'". He spent sleepless nights and for the first time found difficulty in concentrating. On the way back to London he stopped a night at Milford for a long talk with Susan Harvey; it may be imagined that she gave him comfort and encouragement. Hilda wrote to him telling him of her day to day pursuits. Instead of sending her a present he now sent her some of his own books on loan, and as such she was pleased to accept them, though she confessed she was so busy that she had little time for "promiscuous reading". The tone of her letter gave him encouragement, and he "had six hours' sleep that night—the first for more than a month".

Ten days after his first visit he was back at Littlehampton and walking along the beach to Rustington. All Sunday, Monday and Tuesday they talked, pacing up and down the quiet garden of the Urlins' house, and on Tuesday, he proposed to her and was accepted. Joyfully he went back to Milford, and on his return to London on 26 August he wrote—now to "My dearest Hilda" instead of the formal "My dear Miss Urlin"—assuring her of his cousins' wholehearted approval. He signed himself "Yours in all faith and all reverence, Flinders." A few days later he telegraphed his closest friend to come at once to Gower Street; then he was able to tell her that Flaxman Spurrell, too, approved of the step they were taking, and had no doubt that "I had done the very best thing for my future life".

And so indeed it proved. For the next three months they corresponded almost daily, with an ecstatic and almost mystical fervour. At first he found it difficult to believe in her complete capitulation, but her declarations of tenderness and trust reassured him. The floodgates were open and they poured out their feelings in their letters. Flinders looked forward to a happiness he had never known before.

> How we will make this work-a-day world lightsome and gladsome in every turn of it to each other! I am naturally a most light-hearted fellow, who loves to meet everything with jest and ease, and toss difficulties aside, and make the best of everything. But grinding repression has flattened me down, and I cannot escape from a morbid sense of duty. To have this new duty of pleasing you, and making all things as bright as I can for you, will I know be the very best thing for my own life. How we will rake all through Cairo, and raid about that Eastern desert![6]

Hilda had always longed to go to Egypt, she said; she had already begun to plan what she would take with her: for reading, Epictetus and the Bible—though she expected he would be taking those; a psalm book she would find indispensable. Would a geological hammer be too heavy to take? Someone had told her she would need a pistol—surely the desert was not so dangerous? As for clothes, she proposed to take what she would wear on a summer mountaineering expedition. Flinders promised her a list of all she would want. "You did rejoice me by naming that, for I knew that you looked to Egypt with hope and pleasure, and not as a dreadful solitary exile as I had feared from what you said [now for some Beethoven]. . . ." He was working hard, but managed to slip down to Rustington at weekends; they went for long rambles over the downs and on one long-remembered occasion, took their picnic to the top of Chanctonbury Ring and talked all day undisturbed.

Flinders Petrie tried to keep his engagement quiet at University College but the news leaked out and he was warmly congratulated. He met with his lawyer cousin Robert Hensley to draw up a new will in favour of his future wife; he wrote to her that he was ordering stores and seeing about booking passages on the Messageries Maritimes line. He bought her a cane dress-basket, a trunk, a deck-chair and a holdall, and a blotting case for her writing things. As a wedding present he sent her two books: Sowerby's Botany, and a large two-volume work on monumental brasses. He intended them, he said, to explain to her that he wanted her to go on following her own interests in life, as well as taking up new ones. For her adornment he made up a parcel of ancient beads into two necklaces and a matching armlet.

He dined several times at Stafford Terrace and got on well with Hilda's parents and her sisters. He wrote happily "To me how blessed it is . . . that I should meet around you those whom I can gladly accept as giving that sense of a family life which I have never had among my own relatives." It was the more important to him because since the death of his mother and his father's remarriage, a coolness had sprung up between father and son. Earlier that year, while he was in Egypt, Robert Hensley had written to him to tell him that his uncle Alfred, William's youngest brother, who all his life had been an anxiety to his family, had died leaving his wife and son virtually penniless. Some years before he had appointed Flinders and Robert his executors and the trustees of his estate, but what little money there was had been left, it seems, to an illegitimate son. This was a situation in which, Flinders felt strongly, the family must rally round. The boy Alexander, Lexie as he was always called, had stayed with him in Hampstead two years previously when he was eleven, and had impressed him with his intelligence and good manners. He accordingly wrote to the surviving members of the family of that generation, his father, William, his widowed aunt, Margaret Barber, who lived in Wales, and his uncle, Captain Francis Petrie, in Australia, suggesting that they combine to provide Alfred's widow, Edith, with a small annual allowance to enable her to live modestly and to give Lexie a proper education to prepare him for a career in medicine or engineering. He himself volunteered to be a fourth contributor; they should each, he suggested, give Edith an immediate sum of £100, and contribute £25 a year till the boy was earning. William's reply to the letter is a curious document, full of pious platitudes and self-righteous protestations; he has always, he says, helped the Flinders side of the family financially; he suggests that Lexie should seek entry to the Civil Service as a Treasury clerk, but he nowhere offers to contribute to his education or to help his mother. Francis simply declined, saying that he was living on capital. Flinders' pencilled comment on his father's letter tells its own story: "Yet not a soul would help Edith except Mrs Barber by a *legacy*. They left it all on my shoulders."[7] He guaranteed £400 for the boy's education—he read medicine, became a successful doctor and eventually paid back every penny.

In September Flinders went down to Bromley to break the news of his engagement to his father, and was met with less than enthusiasm; nothing in what his son told him convinced the old man that Miss Urlin was "interested in anything beyond mortality", and he spent a sleepless night. Nevertheless he was anxious to meet her and he came to University College for that purpose at the end of October, but was only confirmed in his view that Flinders had not chosen a suitable bride.[8]

On Friday 26 November, in spite of one of his heavy colds and a raging headache, Flinders managed to finish the manuscript of *Syria and Egypt in the Amarna letters*. On the following Monday, at eight o'clock in the morning, they were married in their travelling clothes in the church of St Mary Abbot's, Kensington. The Urlin family were there in force; Flinders had only his friend Flaxman Spurrell, as best man—neither his father nor Cecilia came. By ten minutes to ten the marriage ceremony and the communion service were over, the farewells said, and the couple were off by cab to Victoria Station where they had just time for a glass of milk and a bun at the A.B.C. opposite the station before catching the boat train for Calais. Twelve

Urlins sat down to the wedding breakfast without them, and drank the health of the bride and bridegroom.

The honeymoon did not begin well: the sea was so rough that repeated attempts to dock the ferry-boat at Calais failed and they were forced to return to Dover. It was the worst storm for years, they were told; it was bitterly cold and not till seven in the evening did they find warmth and food in a Dover hotel. Next day however the storm abated and they made a calm crossing and reached Paris and the Hôtel Britannique in time for a brief visit to the Louvre. The train to the south next day was crowded and they had to spend most of the thirteen-hour journey to Marseilles standing in the corridor; but in Marseilles the sun shone and they spent a happy morning exploring the town centre, and took a tram to Flinders' favourite Château Borély. For the first few days the *S.S. Sénégal* rolled and tossed, and Flinders kept to his bunk and ate nothing; Hilda "reeled off and got food whenever there was any". Monday brought fine weather at last and the next day Hilda had her first sight of Africa, as Pompey's Pillar came into view above the harbour of Alexandria. On Wednesday they disembarked.

> And oh! the landing! We took up our stand, with our bags, close to the square hole one emerges from, and there waited, and the whole Arabian Nights poured in upon us, pell-mell, in every wild richness of Oriental dress—porters tumbling in for baggage. . . . Part of Alexandria looks French, and the streets are a strange medley of French, Greek, and Italian, faces, dresses and inscriptions, with a rich glowing admixture of Eastern life. . . . I shall never forget the narrow Arab alleys of tiny shops full of gorgeous stuffs, and scarlet slippers, and red and orange dates and pomegranates, and pottery, and the gorgeous natives at their work, or squatting idly everywhere in picturesque confusion, old men chanting their wares, looking like prophets, women in black, veiled—then towering above them a white minaret and over all, the Egyptian sky.

She never thought, she wrote in the round robin sent to Beatrice Orme and others of her friends a day or so later, that "Egypt could be so Egyptian". It was love at first sight. On the railway journey to Cairo she watched the changing kaleidoscope of rural life in the Delta, the harvesting of the cotton crop, children driving buffaloes down the canal banks fringed with prickly pear, lotus blooms on the surface of the canals, palm groves and pigeon houses. Even the crowds waiting on station platforms fascinated her, and the water boys chanting in "mysterious Arabic" which Flinders translated for her. Cairo did not disappoint her: the antiquities dealers, "prophets in trailing draperies", from whom Flinders bought *antikas*, the bazaars and the Museum where he showed her "his great statues, the Israel stela and his set of amulets". They visited Professor Sayce in his luxurious *dhahabiya* and had tea with a baroness; they made an excursion to the Gebel el Ahmar, where they clambered to the top for "splendid views of the Delta and the Pyramids", and they spent a long and happy day at Giza.

Necessary business had meanwhile to be attended to. Flinders had applied for a concession to dig at Dendara on the east bank of the Nile opposite the town of Qena, about twenty miles downstream from Tukh. This had been the seat of the ancient cult of the goddess Hathor, and on previous visits Petrie had noted the wide area of cemeteries which could be seen from the top of the pylon of the Ptolemaic temple; here perhaps he might find fresh clues in his search for the origins of Egyptian civilization. He was becoming a little unhappy about his own theories now. Griffith, reviewing De Morgan's book, had voiced his own disbelief in the "New Race";[9] moreover, last spring while Petrie was at Deshasha De Morgan had carried out fresh excavations, not this time at Tukh but a little further south at Naqada proper, beyond the limits of his own excavations, and had uncovered, so he had heard, a great *mastaba* containing grave goods very like those which Petrie had found in the largest and richest of burial fields, Cemetery "T": in it were found the names of King Mena who appears as the first of Pharaohs in the ancient lists of kings, and of a queen, Neithhotep.[10] Moreover, a Frenchman named Amélineau had been finding similar objects near Baliana, at the site of the ancient city Abydos, in association with the names of other of the early "legendary" kings of Egypt. If this was true, Petrie would have to abandon his belief in the dynastic date of his Naqada tombs.

Now De Morgan had resigned, and a new Director had been appointed in his place at the head of the Antiquities Service. Victor Loret was a man about Petrie's age; he had been in Cairo as a student of the French Institut with Maspero in the early days, but since then he had pursued an academic career and unlike his predecessor had no experience of excavating; his interests were philological and botanical. In spite of a few grumbles, Petrie had got on tolerably well with De Morgan; it remained to be seen what changes M. Loret would make. He went to the Museum, only to find unexpected difficulties put in his way: by the new rules nothing bearing a royal name might leave the country. "Loret wants to screw me into new and disadvantageous terms," Petrie wrote to his friends; he went to see the Chief Justice, to consult him on the legality of these new regulations, and Scott-Moncrieff's successor, Sir William Garstin, the chairman of the Excavations Committee who had had them drawn up at Loret's request. He was "cordial and understanding, and saw the absurdity of the new terms", and agreed to convene another committee meeting to reconsider the permit. Meanwhile, on another visit to Ghizeh Museum, Petrie was given a private view of De Morgan's finds from the "Tomb of Mena" at Naqada; one look convinced him that his own Naqada finds must be pre- or protohistoric. "Mena's things," he wrote home, "are New Race in several points, and in each point they are *late* and not early New Race." It was unfortunately too late to alter his erroneous conclusions in the publication *Naqada and Ballas*, which had already gone to the printer. An erratum slip had to be added, asking readers to ignore the historical conclusions in chapter eight.

They hung about in Cairo for ten days, waiting for the committee to meet again; Hilda was taken to lunch with Mrs Grant and introduced to other friends of Flinders'. Loret, he found, was "already out of touch and disliked by everyone—Museum people, officials and natives. Brugsch said to an Arab that 'De Morgan was but a small devil, but Loret is twenty devils'. And this has gone the round of the natives." He took Hilda out to Old Cairo, where she spent a happy afternoon rummaging in the mediaeval ruins of Fostât, the oldest of Cairo's cities. "H. was delighted at picking out of the mound a spoon and various pieces of patterned clothing belonging to about the XIIth cent. AD. Late enough, but yet a first taste of the joys of grubbing about for antikas on one's own account."

At last the Committee met and a new permit was drawn up without the offending clause. On the last afternoon they went out to the pyramids again; Flinders was greeted as an old friend and entertained to tea; shaking off the guides and touts he took Hilda to the Third Pyramid where she was proud to find she could read the name of the builder, Menkaure', in hieroglyphs; taking off her skirt, she clambered to the top "without the usual tedious help", "leaping from ledge to ledge"; then they both removed more garments, lit candles and crawled down two passages till they reached the inner sarcophagus chamber.

At last, on 16 December, they were off by the eight o'clock train, travelling south through the day in the company of a young clergyman friend of Kate Griffith, Norman de Garis Davies, who had stopped in Cairo on his way from Australia to England in order to participate in the work at Dendara. On the journey south, Petrie pointed out to them, one after another, the pyramids of Saqqara, Dahshur and Medum on the western skyline, and later, on the left, the distant site of Beni Hasan where Newberry and Carter had worked, and el 'Amarna where Davies himself was destined later to spend many months in solitude copying in the tombs.

At Nag' Hammadi station they came to the end of their thirteen-hour journey, for the train went no further. It was ten o'clock in the evening and the little town boasted no hotel. They were offered primitive accommodation in the courtyard of a wine shop, two rough huts with mud floors and no furniture but bedsteads of palm ribs; fortunately Petrie had bought four blankets in Cairo and they had a little food left over from their picnic lunch in the train. Next morning early they debated how best to proceed. Camels and donkeys, they decided, would never cover the remaining thirty miles over the desert to Dendara in a day—they had better go by river. Flinders accordingly hired a small and rather dirty cargo boat with a crew of four, in which they started at eight in the morning, hoping to be able to tack upstream; but they were too optimistic. A little wind at first helped the flapping sail, but "it dropped to almost nothing at Kasr es Sayd, and we merely crawled after that. . . . As sundown came on it was evident that we should not reach Dendara, nor even Dishneh halfway. And to avoid the chill there was nothing for it but to crawl in under the half deck. So before dark Davies, Hilda and myself all arranged ourselves in the small space with what spare clothes and few blankets we had, and there we made the best of it for twelve hours, anchored in mid-Nile. The deck was only four inches above my nose as I lay down, and each had to crawl in end on as there was no room to turn." Dawn came as a blessed relief from discomfort; the boatmen were roused and two began poling again—for there was still not a breath of wind—while the other two jumped ashore and towed the boat along the bank. Fortunately Flinders had insisted on buying a few provisions at Nag' Hammadi: bread, "little fritters" and some beans and jam, which had sustained them the night before and served for breakfast and lunch; they had all three to share a single knife and one leaky tin mug provided by the boatmen, which they dipped in the Nile. By two they were still about ten miles from Dendara and it was obvious that they would not make it by nightfall. The Petries accordingly left Davies in the boat in charge of the baggage, and set off walking the rest of the way along the river bank and across the desert, arriving at dusk to be greeted by Arthur Mace and 'Ali es Suefi with welcome lamplight in the newly built camp house. Poor Norman Davies did not get there till two o'clock in the morning, guided to the camp by a party of men sent down to meet the boat.

Such was the journey which has gone down in archaeological legend as "the Petries' honeymoon on a coal barge". Hilda seems, at least in retrospect, to have enjoyed every minute of it. "It was all a most delightful adventure," she wrote to her friends "and everything hugely picturesque and strange!"

She took to life in an archaeological camp like a duck to water. Unlike the majority of archaeologists' wives today, she was not expected to concern herself with the domestic arrangements. Flinders had generally left the catering to his cook, only seeing to it from the start that the camp had a regular supply of water, brought up from the Nile by donkey and boiled for drinking, and of the flat loaves of local bread baked by the villagers; otherwise he had always lived out of tins. This suited Hilda well; she was not domesticated by nature and had never been taught to cook. Nor did she have any skill in sewing, which had not been on the Rectory's curriculum: the Professor continued to darn his own socks, or do without.

Relieved of the housekeeping, Hilda spent her days in marking and drawing the many hundreds of small objects that were found in the course of the excavation, in assisting her husband to survey and plan the tombs and in drawing up lists for the catalogue of objects.

"It is a splendid free open life," she wrote to her friends, "this life without the ordinary necessities in so many ways; but rich in sensations of the splendour of the East, width of desert, glow of sky and mountain, and unfolding interest of excavation going daily forward." She described the basic simplicity of their desert home, the row of squat mud huts opening on to a long courtyard, and the stupendous backdrop of cliffs. Flinders has been making furniture for their rooms, she says: in each room a plank hung by ropes from the roof boards by string for a shelf, a great rough table in the dining hut; boxes for cupboards, and a grass mat for each room to serve as a door. "All the things of domestic usage at home which one considers quite indispensable, are suddenly found to be entirely unnecessary here, and life is simplified a hundredfold."

They began excavating in some tunnels behind the huts, which proved to be the catacombs of sacred animals—cats, gazelles, ichneumons, birds and snakes—whose mummies had been burnt at some time in a great holocaust. When these were cleared the tunnels were used as sleeping-quarters for the men from Quft. Meanwhile work had started on the cemetery between their house and the back of the temple enclosure; here a number of large mounds proved to be the superstructures of *mastaba* tombs; others were denuded to ground level, and there were dozens of tomb pits, most of which proved to be of the Old Kingdom or of the "First Intermediate Period" from the sixth to the eleventh Dynasty. Arthur Mace, who worked with Flinders Petrie on these, was a distant cousin, a grandson of Bishop Bromby of Tasmania and a nephew of Anne Mallinson. He had recently graduated at Oxford, and had no immediate prospects in mind, but a hankering for Egypt; he proved a pleasant and helpful member of the team. For Davies also it was his first experience of Egypt; he was an accurate draughtsman and as soon as a painted sarcophagus was found he was set the difficult task of tracing the badly damaged lists of offerings; a wall painting in another tomb later took him several weeks to copy.

Petrie was well aware of the importance of this cemetery; although it contained nothing comparable with the reliefs and paintings at Saqqara and Meydum, the *mastabas* here were of unique value as tombs of local rulers in Upper Egypt; only rock cut tombs of this period had hitherto been found in the south. Some were very large, and in some a row of stone panels were carved with the figures and names and titles of the deceased. A long sloping corridor with an arch of bricks led down to two of them, the tombs of nomarchs of the sixth dynasty. These, Petrie observed, were the oldest brick vaults known (**83**). Another mastaba, slightly later in date, had a brick dome over the well leading to the burial chamber—again, the oldest dome ever found.[11] Such discoveries were of the greatest importance for the history of architecture; so was the somewhat naïve provincial style of the reliefs for the history of Egyptian art; and the clumsy forms of some of the hieroglyphs on the later panels and sarcophagi showed (as Griffith who published them pointed out) that during the dark period between the Old and Middle Kingdoms there had been a great break in tradition and some of the old forms had been forgotten. Nevertheless, as Petrie realized, the cemeteries of Dendera were proof that civil life and art had continued in Upper Egypt more or less unchanged from the Old Kingdom into the Middle Kingdom, "across a time which had hitherto been an entire blank in our knowledge"; there had been no foreign invaders here, no break in civilization, no return to illiteracy—fresh proof that there had been no New Race.

Hilda proved to be a stalwart walker; on the first market day (the day of rest for the workmen), dressed in bloomers, she went off with

Flinders on a fifteen-mile walk into the hills searching for rock-tombs; next week their walk took them further up on to the high plateau; they took food in a saddlebag, an aneroid barometer and a compass and walking sticks. Flinders' sharp eyes picked out the site of a Neolithic flintworker's workshop, surrounded by chips and flakes, and higher up they found palaeoliths and had a magnificent view of the Nile valley and the range of hills beyond . . . in the clear air, hills forty or fifty miles away looked quite close. She and Flinders sometimes took their paintboxes down to the work, and attempted to capture the glowing beauty of the sunsets; once or twice they saw the "green ray", when after a golden sunset a bluish-green light appears for an instant above the disc of the sun before it disappears from sight. It was probably sitting in the cool air after sunset that she caught a chill at the beginning of January: for nearly a month she kept to her bed with a fever; she ate little, and Miss Oldroyd, arriving on her usual visit, stayed on to nurse her and to tempt her appetite with little dishes beyond the competence of Muhammad Osman the cook-boy. Flinders was worried and sent a long telegram to Cairo, to his friend Dr Sandwith, who could make no long-distance diagnosis. Then an English doctor, visiting Dendara as a tourist on the post-boat, of his kindness came out to the huts and diagnosed congestion of the liver due to chills; his medicine soon brought her temperature down and she recovered her strength. "The first day I got her up she was much wrapped up to sit in a chair in my room, but the sight of a revolver worked wonders, and when it came to shooting off went the shawls with 'One can't shoot straight with all these fiddle-faddles.' " His new recruit was showing her mettle. She was learning Arabic, compiling her own vocabulary of the words she heard Flinders use, and she was learning how to handle the sextant, to help him with measuring and surveying. She drew plans of the mastaba tombs, and her skill in copying was needed when a sarcophagus with a very long and important inscription was found in the mastaba of Beb. Flinders reckoned that it contained some twenty thousand hieroglyphs; photography was impossible, and they were therefore both copying at the rate of twelve hundred signs a day, sometimes lying flat on the ground.

One day news was brought to the camp that M. Loret had arrived; Petrie went down at once, to find him looking round the temple in "a very touristical way" with his wife and her brother; he evinced no interest in what the excavator had to tell him and, amazingly, showed no desire to see the work, though it was only a few hundred yards from the temple. Petrie's opinion of the new Director fell still lower.

Several members of the Fund's Committee visited them, including Sayce, the Marquis of Northampton, a keen amateur Egyptologist who arrived wearing Arab clothes and complaining of the heat, and Miss Brodrick, a learned friend of Amelia Edwards, who travelled much in Egypt. The visit of Mrs Sara Yorke Stevenson,[12] the Fund's representative in Philadelphia, early in February was welcome and not unexpected. This forceful American lady, the curator of the Egyptian section of the University Museum of Philadelphia had already been in correspondence with Petrie; she had come out to Egypt to discuss a plan of operation for the newly formed American Exploration Society; a young man named Rosher, sent ahead to negotiate with Loret, had so far proved ineffectual, and she wanted Petrie's advice on her scheme for moving monuments from Tanis, since she knew he had once contemplated such an operation. If the new society would use its funds for this purpose some of the statuary might be given to Philadelphia; M. Loret, however seemed likely to refuse her request. She was now on her way to Assuan to persuade him to change his mind. Meanwhile she had decided that Charles Rosher had better learn something about excavation method, and who better to teach him than the Master? Petrie promised to see that he had every opportunity to learn, but in fact Rosher did not turn up until almost the end of the season; he did not make a very good job of cemetery work, published nothing and left only an amateurish plan of one or two tombs,[13] but Petrie did not greatly concern himself with what happened to a site after he had left it—he gave up hope that it would not be wrecked as soon as his back was turned and the dealers moved in.

In the middle of February another volunteer came to join the team: good-looking and well-mannered, David Randall-MacIver was a welcome addition to the camp; his interest was anthropology, and he spent much of his time measuring bones and skulls. On the feast of Bairam Flinders and Hilda took advantage of a pause in the work to go off together on a four-day tenting trip; they followed the edge of the cultivated land in a westerly direction, for from Dendara to Hu (Hiw), the limit of their concession, the Nile flows west before turning abruptly northwards three miles or so above Nag' Hammadi. 'Ali es Suefi came with them; all three rode white donkeys, and they were followed by a camel laden with bedding and tents. Both the Petries wore the white baggy native trousers which Flinders had found cool and comfortable on such occasions; he wore a cloth cap, she a wide-brimmed hat with a puggeree veil. In the evening they camped in a grove of tamarisk trees; 'Ali cooked his lentil soup to supplement their tins of meat and jam. The sight of this little procession caused some astonishment in the outskirts of villages as they passed; most had never seen a European woman before and once they were followed for several miles by a curious crowd. 'Ali's sharp eyes were quick to pick out ancient remains as they went along, and as usual he proved a tactful diplomatist in their encounters with the local population. From Semaina as far as the village of Sheikh 'Ali, where they spent the second night, there were tombs with "New Race" pottery, and Petrie resolved to begin his work there next year. Around Hu, tombs of all periods could be seen; there was a temple enclosure, and many Roman remains. Tales of a splendid, intact tomb full of inscriptions "like those at Thebes" sent them up a long zigzag path into the hills, but the "tomb" proved to be no more than a hermit's cave, scrawled over with Coptic *graffiti*.

During the last weeks at Dendara Petrie left the direction of the excavations largely to Mace and spent his days recording and making a photographic catalogue of the finds. When the time came to leave, there was no need to take a boat back to Nag' Hammadi; during the winter the rail extension to Luxor had been opened and they were able to travel by train overnight from Qena to Cairo. Davies came with them; Mace stayed on for another month, packing the antiquities, while Rosher and his wife ran their own small excavation. Flinders felt the Committee would be pleased with his season's work: he had discovered new aspects of ancient Egyptian architecture, thrown light on the burial customs of a hitherto little-known period of Egyptian history, and found a great many objects for distribution, some of them in brightly coloured glass and faience, which would delight museums.

The Petries went home on an Italian boat, stopping at Naples and "doing Italian archaeology" in Pompeii and in Rome on the way. On their return they settled in Flinders' old lodging, Lily Lodge in the Vale of Health, where Hilda had no domestic cares. Flinders wrote to Spurrell, urging him to come up and stay nearby, and take meals with them; he assured him that they lived as informally as he had always been accustomed to do. "I should think no man had his externals less changed by his marriage. We call over the banisters 'Dinner for two tonight' and go off to grub at U.C. without another thought about the domus."[14] The arrangement suited them both, and when next summer they had to move, they found convenient board and lodging once more in a small Regency cottage facing Hampstead Heath, at 12, East Heath Road.

College affairs and teaching claimed Petrie once more. Hilda went down for a short holiday to her parents, and spent a few days at Angmering Rectory with her friends the Ormes, and Flinders managed to fit in a week's holiday with her at Rustington before the 238 boxes arrived at the docks in mid-June; Mace helped to unpack them. Quibell's discoveries for the Research Account at Hierakonpolis, which had been particularly sensational that year, were exhibited at the same time, and to some extent stole the limelight. Some of the finest objects—the gold head of a sacred falcon, the copper statues of King Pepy and his son, and the palette of Narmer, the first of kings, had been kept for the Ghizeh Museum, but many treasures of the Archaic period—mace heads, palettes, ivory pieces, had been allowed to come to England and were destined for the Ashmolean Museum.

Hilda came daily to the College to help her husband with the preparation of the plans and drawings for the excavation report, reading through his text and sometimes re-writing whole sentences to make them more intelligible, since, as she once explained, he was in the habit of expressing himself in "a kind of telegraphese". Sometimes they would sit up proof-reading into the early hours of the morning, for Flinders set himself a stern deadline for the completion of each book. One of the chores that devolved upon her was the appeal for donations for the Egyptian Research Account; this task she continued to shoulder for nearly forty years. She wrote personally to each subscriber or potential donor, rounded up defaulters with a gentle reminder, and if that failed, sternly struck them from the list.

In August after a meeting of the British Association in Bristol, the Petries were able to spend a few days together in Wiltshire, where Flinders showed his wife some of his favourite haunts; he took her to call on old General Pitt-Rivers at Rushmore House in Cranbourne Chase, to Salisbury and Stonehenge, and to Bemerton, the home of his beloved George Herbert. After his years of loneliness, it was delightful to have so eager and appreciative a companion; she must share everything with him—his work and his pleasures.[15] Their lifelong partnership had begun under the best of auspices.

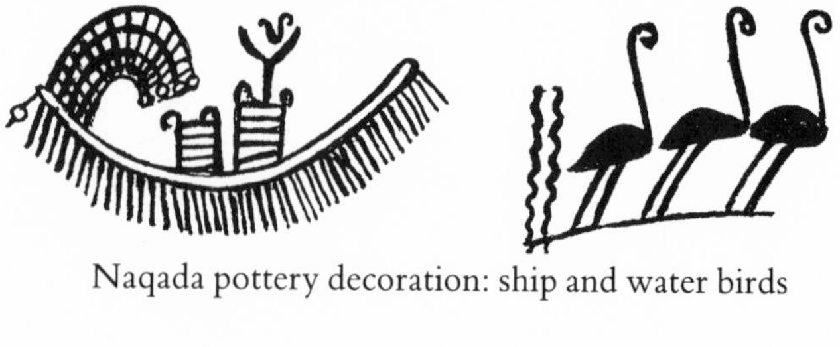

Naqada pottery decoration: ship and water birds

CHAPTER XI

Most Ancient Egypt

(1899–1903)

TERM STARTED AGAIN, and Petrie's time was divided between his students, the publication of his results, editing Quibell's report, and delivering lectures in various parts of England. At the end of October, after Manchester and Liverpool, he crossed to Dublin and for the first time lectured in Trinity College, where his friend Mahaffy, the Professor of Ancient History, was delighted to entertain him. Two weeks later the Petries set out for Egypt. Flinders knew exactly what he had to do: in the desert between Dendara and Hu he would find enough prehistoric material to supplement what had come from the Naqada cemeteries—and enable him to complete his task: "a relative dating of all the prehistoric things into successive periods."[1] He already had his permit; no difficulty was made by Loret about renewing it on the same terms as before. Hilda was to have female company this winter: Beatrice Orme came with them, and Miss Lawes, one of Petrie's students, was to draw the pottery. Mace and MacIver were there again. Their first camp was at Abadîya opposite Dishna; four cemeteries were dug between Semaina and Sheikh 'Ali; the region had been superficially plundered already by the Qurnawi dealers but some hundreds of pots, stone vases and other grave goods were found. On rest days Hilda and Beatrice hired horses and rode into market at Sheikh 'Ali, or out into the desert; every working day they were kept busy marking bones, copying potmarks, and drawing. MacIver again spent much of his time measuring bones and skulls.

After a month they moved over to Hu and built a row of new huts up against the wall of the Roman fort. A hundred cases were by this time already packed and ready for dispatch. Hu (sometimes spelt Huw or Hiw) was once the capital of a nome; its Greek name was Diospolis Parva. Petrie was debarred from digging in the temple area by a local landowner who claimed the land as his; this was clearly untrue—all land containing obvious antiquities was Government property and might not be cultivated or built over—but he found so much of importance in the cemeteries behind and around the town that he was content to concentrate on tomb-digging. The plates of classified pot shapes drawn at Naqada and Ballas four years before were used to "type" the pottery found in Hu and Abadîya; 150 new shapes were added to the original corpus of 750, and fitted into the series. In addition large tomb-groups of dynastic date, from the Old Kingdom to the New, provided a wealth of beads, stone vases and pottery.

Hilda's diary noted little excitements that punctuated the routine of daily work: "two dogs stole turkey"; "Tambourine dances of wailing women like anc. Egyptians"; "glorious fire-colour sunset on pale blue". Mrs Sheldon Amos came to stay for a few days, and in Ramadan the Petries took a short holiday in Luxor with "B.O."; this was the first opportunity Flinders had had of showing his wife the Theban temples and tombs. After he returned to Hu, the two women stayed on a little, seeing more tombs and enjoying the hospitality of Newberry, Spiegelberg and Howard Carter. When they got back they found some excitement in the camp: it seemed as if the soil of Egypt never ceased to yield fresh puzzles. In one or two of the cemeteries shallow pan-like graves were appearing; the pottery in them, sometimes incised with patterns, was not unlike some of the earliest hand-made bowls of red or black-topped ware, but the bodies had been clad in leather, their ornaments were strips of shell, and in or near the graves were the skulls and horns of sheep, goats and cattle, painted as if to hang on a wall. Clearly they were a pastoral people, and clearly they were not predynastic, for among their grave goods were some Egyptian pots and beads of late Middle Kingdom date. Petrie called them the Pangrave People, and concluded that they were semi-nomadic settlers; he supposed them too to be Libyans. Since Petrie's discovery, Pangrave cemeteries have been found elsewhere in Upper Egypt, and excavations in Nubia have thrown light on the origins; since their tombs in Egypt often contain weapons it is thought that they may have been a Nubian warrior people, used as mercenaries during the troubled times following the Middle Kingdom and during the expulsion of the Hyksos invaders. In one of his last books, *The Making of Egypt*, Petrie accepted this explanation.[2]

At the beginning of March Flinders and Hilda went off on another tenting trip with 'Ali; this time they were away six days, and explored the desert edge from Hu northwards to el 'Araba, the site of the ancient city Abydos. The cemetery at el 'Amra, which they passed on the second day, had been recently turned over, they noticed; it had been within the concession of M. Amélineau, the excavator of Abydos, whose work at the site of the Royal Tombs Petrie was anxious to see. He had thought the Frenchman gone; Amélineau was indeed on the eve of departure, but deciding to pay a last visit to el 'Amra, "after having passed the temple of Seti I, I met a small caravan composed of two donkeys: on the first of these docile animals, a lady was riding, and beside her walked, with naked feet in Turkish slippers, a man with an unkempt beard, of very sunburnt complexion, whom I took for a Greek merchant; a servant rode behind them on the second donkey. I attached no importance to this encounter, for I had no suspicion that the travellers I had just met, and whose tent I saw set up further on, opposite the site I had explored that very year, were none other than M. and Mme. Flinders Petrie." On learning who they were, he had that evening sent them a note apologizing that he would not be able to show them round; had he known that they were coming he would have invited them to dinner.[3] Petrie replied, explaining that they were exploring the west bank for tombs, and so could not have forewarned him of their arrival. He had probably recognized Amélineau, whom he had met before, but he would certainly not have been anxious to meet him, since he had already in the previous year made application, through the Fund, for the concession at Abydos which Sayce had assured the Committee the Frenchman had given up.[4]

His examination of the Umm el Qa'âb cemetery next day confirmed his suspicion that the excavation had been scandalously misconducted—indeed it was common knowledge that Amélineau, a Coptic scholar, had no previous experience of digging and no notion of archaeological method; the local sheikh, thinking the Petries tourists, sold them some objects which had obviously come from the digging, and one look at Amélineau's spoil heaps showed Petrie that he had only been interested in recovering intact objects of saleable value. On his way through Cairo he again asked for the concession, but was told by Loret that M. Amélineau's five year permit had two more years to run.

On his return to London—Hilda stayed on in Italy with Beatrice Orme for another ten days—Flinders Petrie started at once on the project which was to occupy him for much of the summer: the ordering of his pottery from Naqada, Hu and Abadîya into a chronological series; he called it Sequence Dating. His method was simple but ingenious: taking the record of nine hundred of the four thousand-odd tombs he had excavated, he cut nine hundred cardboard slips seven inches long, each ruled into sections. On each tomb-slip he entered the number of pots present of each of the nine groups he had distinguished at Naqada, also noting other characteristic grave-goods in the tomb, such as slate palettes and beads. He then set himself a giant game of Patience, shifting the cards about on boards to find likely juxtapositions; perhaps he used trestle tables, or else the glass tops of the waist-level show cases in the museum at University College. Beginning with late forms such as those in the royal tombs at Naqada and Abydos of the first dynasty, and then with the wavy-handled jars in which he saw a long stylistic development from globular to narrow, he applied what statisticians now call the Concentration Principle —the most probable order results from the shortest range of types. In arriving at his final sequence, Petrie made several necessary assumptions: that each of his pottery types had a "life cycle", appearing, flourishing, becoming obsolete and finally disappearing, not to reappear; that graves nearest in time to each other were likely to have most nearly similar contents; and that if one grave was above another, and showed no signs of having been dug through, it must be later than the one beneath—this gave a useful check. No tomb was used unless it had at least five varieties of pot.[5]

When finally the nine hundred tombs had been put into an order which seemed to satisfy all his requirements, Petrie divided the sequence for convenience into equal sections, numbering them from 30 to 80, to allow for the possible future discovery of still earlier types. The discoveries at Badari and Deir Tasa in the 1920s were to show the wisdom of this provision. Petrie's Sequence Dating, which arranges in chronological order though it cannot assign absolute dates, is now termed by statisticians Seriation; Petrie has been regarded as the inventor of the concept, and therefore as one of the founders of modern statistical method; in Cambridge the terms "Petrie Matrix" and "Petriefication" are said to be used. Professor David Kendall has indeed ranked Flinders Petrie as "one of the greatest applied mathematicians of the nineteenth century".[6] In the main, his classification still stands, though some modifications have had to be made . . . for instance, in the sequence of wavy-handled pots which was based on a stylistic assumption the validity of which has been questioned. His division of the whole series into two main periods or phases, the one characterized by red pottery decorated in white paint, the second with buff pottery painted with designs in red, was at once accepted by prehistorians in Germany, who talked about Naqada I and Naqada II; Petrie himself was later to work over the material once more during the war years when a more complete corpus was published.[7]

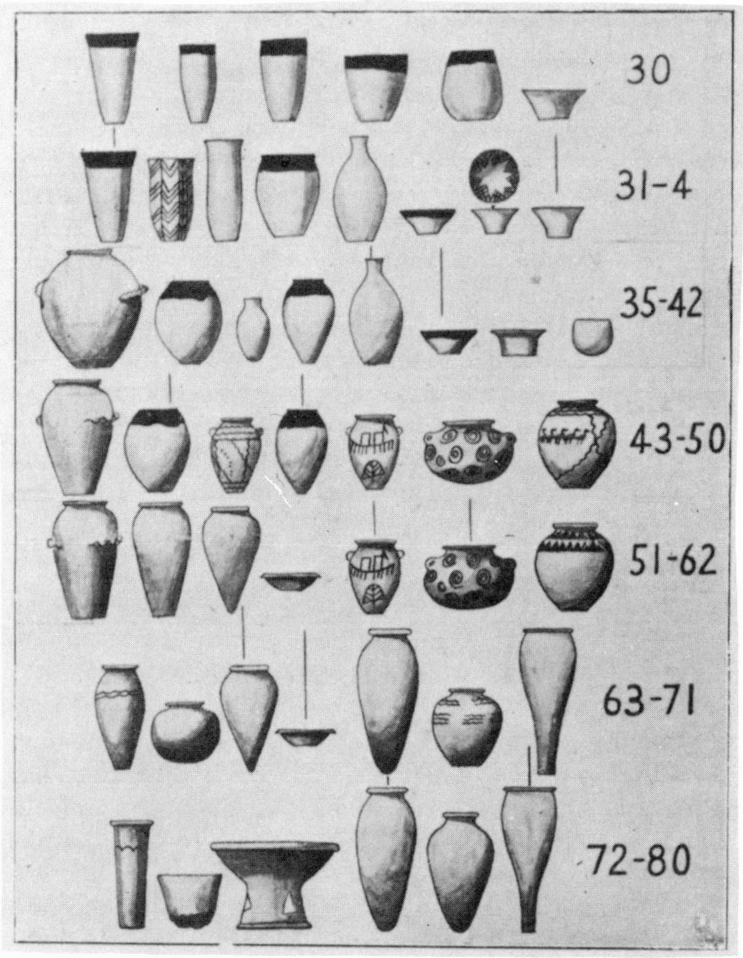

E. *Petrie's original sequence-dating chart for Predynastic pottery*. Seven successive stages are identified, each linked to the one before and after by at least one similar shape; at the left of the five lower rows are the "wavy-handled" pots, ranged by Petrie in a sequence of "degradation"—his clue to the order of the whole series.

At the Annual General Meeting of subscribers to the Egypt Exploration Fund in November, he used a simple analogy to explain his method:

> If in some old country mansion one room after another had been locked up untouched at the death of each successive owner, then on comparing all the contents it would easily be seen which rooms were of consecutive dates; and no one could suppose a Regency room to belong between Mary and Anne, or an Elizabethan room to come between others of George III. The order of rooms could be settled to a certainty on comparing all the furniture and objects. Each would have some links of style in common with those next to it, and much less connection with others which were farther from its period. And we should soon frame the rule that the order of the rooms was that in which each variety or article should have as short a range of date as it could. Any error in arranging the rooms would certainly extend the period of a thing over a longer number of generations. This principle applies to graves as well as rooms, to pottery as well as furniture.[8]

In the summer exhibition, some fine tomb groups of every period from the Old to the New Kingdom were on display. The tombs had contained enough beads, stone vases and pottery to enable Petrie for the first time to trace a properly dated succession of such domestic things. Bit by bit, a connected narrative of the development of Egyptian civilization was emerging. The work of the E.R.A. was also represented. Quibell was now working for the Egyptian Government on the great catalogue of the Museum in Cairo; but the work at Hierakonpolis had been carried on by his assistant F. W. Green; a facsimile copy of his most important discovery, a painted tomb of the Archaic period, was displayed on the walls of the exhibition room as the most ancient wall painting in Egypt.[9]

In November, when Flinders Petrie was again invited to give a series of lectures in Dublin, he and his wife were the guests of the Chief Secretary, Lord Balfour; but Flinders was so prostrated by the crossing that he arrived in a state of near-collapse (never, he vowed, would he cross the Irish Sea again); after struggling through the first two lectures he took to his bed, and Hilda delivered the next for him, managing the lantern slides with complete confidence. In time she became a sought-after lecturer herself, and often spoke to literary societies and women's clubs on her husband's work, as part of their joint effort to raise money for excavation.

Petrie had found a new Research student, John Garstang, a Cambridge graduate in mathematics, but he was uncertain where his next season's work would be. Things seemed to be going from bad to worse in Egypt; George Fraser wrote to him in July that the tombs at Meydum were being wrecked for lime-burning. He had reported the damage but nothing had been done.[10] In the autumn came good news: Loret had resigned, and had been replaced by none other than Professor Gaston Maspero, lured back to his old post by the promise of a large salary and increased authority. Petrie was delighted; at the next General Meeting of the Fund he could say with sincerity, "When I look back more than ten years to the days of his former direction, and remember the perfect confidence with which I could trust his impartial feeling and his wish to help forward research, when I recall our uninterrupted friendship in the years since then, I feel that no change could have been more happy than that which again places at the helm so great a scholar and so true a man."[11] The Committee of the Egypt Exploration Fund, of which Maspero had been for some years an Honorary Vice-President, were equally pleased at his appointment. One of his first acts was to grant Petrie the Abydos concession; Amélineau had declared that there was nothing more to be found there, and in any case the site had been so mauled by his ineptitude that, in Maspero's eyes, he had forfeited any right to continue. Nobody appears to have told Amélineau of this decision; in the third volume of the publication of his results, some years later, he complained that after that casual meeting at el 'Amra he had heard no more until, after another year, he had thought of applying for a fresh permit—and had discovered to his astonishment that Petrie had taken it over.[12]

Abydos (the ancient *Abdu*) lies on the desert edge eight miles from Baliana, the nearest town and railway station. The modern villages on the site are 'Arabah, called el Madfûna, "the buried", and el Khirba (the ruined), a little to the north of it; between and behind them, in a great bay of the Libyan hills, is a vast ancient cemetery containing tens of thousands of burials of every period of ancient Egyptian history from prehistoric till Roman times. It was the burial ground of Thinis, the earliest dynastic capital of Egypt according to Manetho; the two Ramesside temples which Petrie and Griffith had admired on their visit in 1886, and which tourists come to see today, occupy but a fraction of the area which once bristled with tombs and temples, shrines and cenotaphs. Egyptian legend connected Abydos with the gods of the dead; the annual mysteries of Osiris, at which his death and resurrection were enacted, were attended by pilgrims from all over Egypt and it became the ambition of most Egyptians either to be buried in this hallowed spot or at least to be represented by a memorial stone or better still, a shrine or chapel; kings built cenotaphs or funerary temples here irrespective of their real burial places.

The site had been thoroughly dug over by *sebbakhîn* and by dealers over many years and Mariette had set his men to ransack the ground; they had found tombs of every age from the sixth dynasty, and some important pieces of statuary for the Bulaq Museum; Maspero too had dug there for a short while. Since 1895, Amélineau had had the concession; his first two seasons had been largely concentrated on a mound out in the desert to the west of the temple of Sety I, a site known to the Arabs as Umm el Qa'ab, "Mother of Little Pots", because of the heaps of potsherds strewn over the ground. Here he had made his sensational discovery of great tombs of the Archaic Period. He had employed an enormous workforce, whipped on by overseers, and not rewarded for what they found: it was not surprising that he had recovered so little in the way of small antiquities. With trained men, well paid for every inscribed chip of stone, the matter would be very different.

The prospect of excavating at Abydos was exciting to Flinders Petrie. He had repeatedly asked Grébaut for the site, and always met with a refusal. It would have been useless to ask De Morgan, who had himself spent some time excavating with his friend Amélineau. Now at last it was his, and he set about planning a long campaign of work: so huge and complex a site would take some years to dig. The house built for the accommodation of his party was accordingly larger and more solidly built than usual; it had plenty of rooms, for he would have a larger number of helpers than usual and he expected constant visitors. Security was important too: the district had a bad reputation for lawlessness and violence. A few months before they went out in the second year an English resident and his wife were murdered at Baliana; the Fund wrote to Lord Cromer pointing out that since Petrie's party would probably include ladies, they would like assurances that their explorers would receive adequate protection from the police. In fact they had little trouble, except that on one occasion somebody took a pot shot at Hilda as she came out of her bedroom, fortunately missing her. They were asked never to travel abroad after dark without police escort, and they guarded against theft by fixing stout wooden doors to the storerooms which were kept locked. Mace had built the house before they arrived; as soon as they were installed, eight Quftis arrived, and men and boys were quartered in small huts above the house, which had been built against the great mud-brick wall of the town enclosure.

Petrie started work, and almost at once found that what was said of Amélineau was true; indeed the Frenchman had himself boasted that he had smashed into smithereens what he did not carry away: he was only interested in complete stone jars with a marketable value. In one afternoon alone during the first few days, Petrie's workmen found two or three hundredweights of stone fragments, some with royal names; clay sealings with the impressions of royal seals upon them were one of the great prizes which had been overlooked.

Umm el Qa'ab is an impressive place. "The situation is wild and silent, close round it the hills rise high on two sides, a ravine running up into the plateau from the corner where the lines meet. Far away, and below us, stretches the long green valley of the Nile, beyond which for dozens of miles the eastern cliffs recede far into the dim distance." The royal tombs lay close together; each was a large square pit lined with brickwork and surrounded by small chambers ranged in rows, each containing a flexed burial and one or two pots. Petrie supposed these to be the tombs of retainers, members of the royal household; he observed that they had been buried hastily and apparently at one time, because the bricks had been imperfectly dried and in some cases had collapsed in consequence (whereas the brickwork of the main tomb was firm and solid); therefore, he concluded they must have been buried within a day, or a few days, of their master in order to accompany him to the next world. Each of the great tombs had originally had two stone stelae above it carved with the king's name and small tablets belonging to the officials or servants had been ranged around; Amélineau had missed a number of these; he had also failed to find more than a few of the most important contents of the tombs: the small labels or plaques in ivory or wood, inscribed with lines of pictographs which, though they are difficult to interpet, have been hailed as the beginnings of hieroglyphic writing. The names of kings on these tablets, and on stone vessels and jar sealings, enabled Petrie to ascribe the tombs to their royal owners. Amélineau had assumed them to be the "tombs" of divine personages, Osiris, Set and other deities; but Sethe had read the name in the "Tomb of Osiris" as Djer, and another as Merpeba, and had identified them with Manetho's Usaphais and Miebis.[13] Petrie gradually built up a list of the

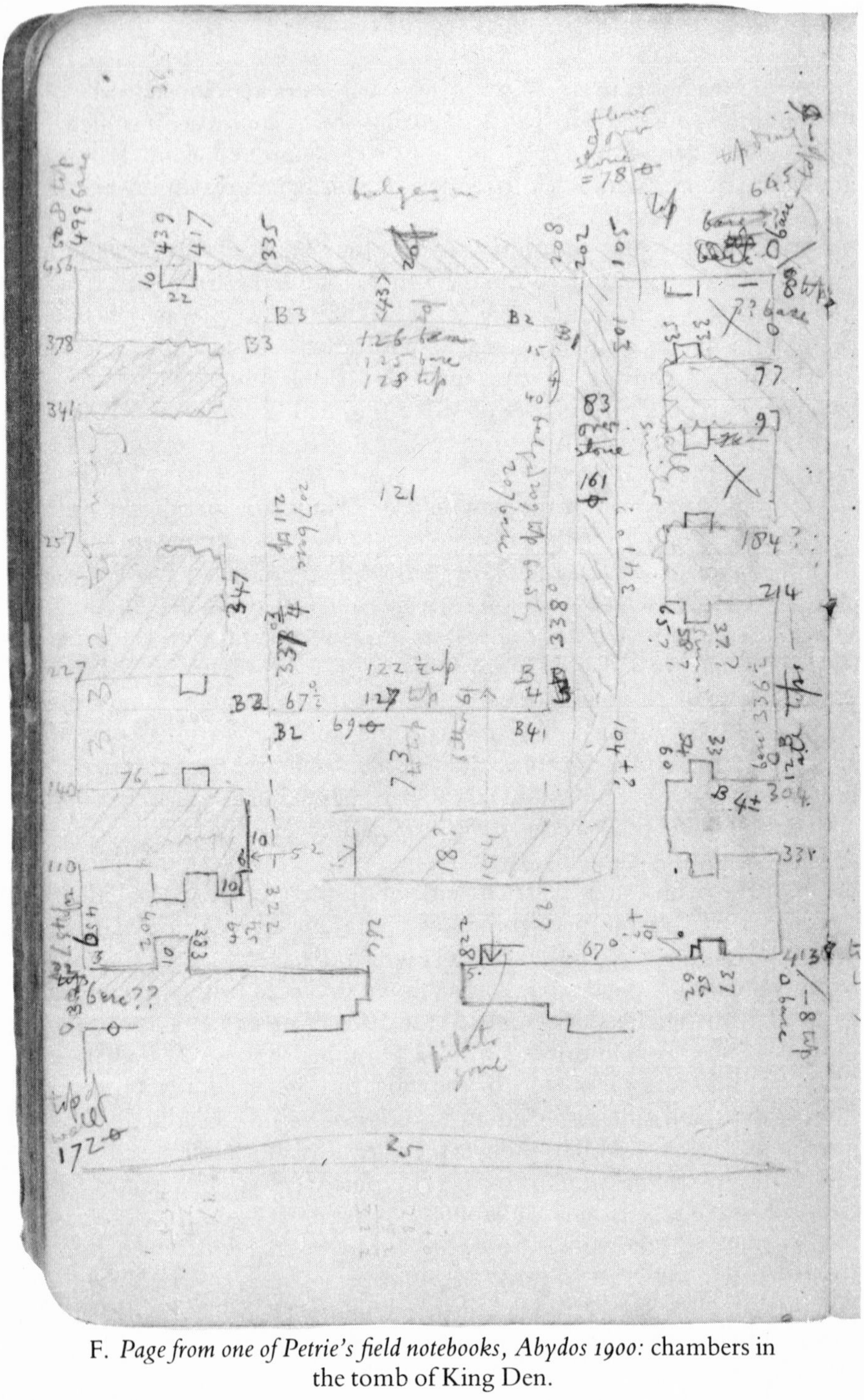

F. *Page from one of Petrie's field notebooks, Abydos 1900:* chambers in the tomb of King Den.

early kings and by means of stylistic differences, and instances where one king had added his name to the grave goods of another, or usurped them, he was able to put them into a historical sequence. Menes —Meni or Mena—had not been a mythical figure, as some had supposed—here was his very tomb! Recipients of Petrie's Journal were enjoined to secrecy; the news must not leak out yet, for if Amélineau knew how much he had missed, he might try to come back and reclaim his concession.

Meanwhile Mace was excavating a late cemetery, and had found several fine burials including that of a princess. Garstang, having served a short apprenticeship with the Professor, was given another cemetery site not far from Mace's to dig for the E.R.A.; while MacIver was on a mound covered with pottery near the royal tombs. Petrie completed his plans and drawings as he went along, for the importance of what he was finding was so great that he determined to get out the first illustrated report as soon as possible; he did in fact manage to produce a fat volume in time for the opening of the exhibition in London at the beginning of July—something of a record for the prompt publication of excavation results.[14] His tomb plans, drawn from hundreds of dimensions recorded on a sketch-plan in his notebook (Fig. F.), were neatly redrawn and inked in by Hilda, who also did much of the drawing of pot-marks and many of the objects, and helped her husband in the time-consuming task of sorting and fitting stone fragments. Many of his evenings were spent on the seal impressions on mud jar-stoppers; the design had to be reconstructed from dozens of repeated scraps of impression, and then drawn as a whole. "If I finish one seal in an evening I am satisfied," he wrote. Another competent artist arrived in the shape of Anthony Wilkin, a young Cambridge graduate anxious to acquire some training in archaeology.

As Petrie had anticipated, they had a constant stream of visitors. News of his discoveries spread quickly to Cairo and Sayce, von Bissing, the Liebleins and the Macalisters of Cambridge were among their guests. Maspero arrived, and professed himself delighted with the work. Then Francis Galton came to stay, with his great-niece Eva. Petrie in inviting him begged him not to bring his own dragoman or donkey-boy from Luxor. As he explained: "We see the cloven hoof in all such and avoid having any outsiders about the place or work. . . . We find the need for keeping our work and discoveries as dark as possible in the country. The dealers—especially at Luxor—stick at nothing if they see a chance of robbery. . . . All our workmen live behind our house, and are forbidden to go to the village on pain of dismissal, so needful is it to keep our business to ourselves."[15] They came without their servant, were met at the station, and thoroughly enjoyed their week in camp. The old man (he was nearly eighty) wrote enthusiastically of his visit: the Petries had been most hospitable; the life was very rough, and the fare frugal, but it had been one of the most interesting experiences of their lives. They had been so cold at night that they had piled all their clothes on top of their blankets and slept in jerseys and stockings.[16]

Leaving Abydos in the middle of March, the Petries hurried home with their sheaves of drawings; a month later all sixty-seven plates were in the hands of the printer. Hilda helped with proof-reading the text and with preparations for the exhibition, then went off on a bicycling holiday with her friends Beatrice Orme and Mrs Ray Hope Pinker, a painter in whose cottage near Godalming she sometimes stayed. Petrie himself spent Whitsun weekend in what appears to have been his first visit to Edward Clodd in Aldeburgh; Holman Hunt was there, and Clement Shorter, and there was much pleasant and stimulating conversation in the comfortable cottage of their host. In June he was in Cambridge to receive an Honorary D.Litt.; he lectured on his recent finds and stayed with Macalister. In September he sat for his portrait to G. F. Watts; the picture—not considered by his family to be a very good likeness—is now in the Ashmolean Museum in Oxford. Meanwhile Hilda and he had decided to rent a house of their own; after several weeks' househunting they found just what they wanted at No. 8, Well Road, Hampstead. It was situated in a quiet, pleasant road, facing an old, walled kitchen garden. They tried to persuade Flaxman Spurrell to share it with them, for the house was too large for them and there were several rooms to spare, but Spurrell could not make up his mind, and the matter had to be dropped, though he occasionally came to stay for a day or so. They kept on their old housekeeper for a time, and sometimes let the house when they were away in the winter, but Petrie had room now for his books and his coins and it was pleasant to have a comfortable home to come back to after their Spartan winters. Galton's successor, Karl Pearson, lived next door, and a lasting friendship developed between the two University College Professors.

The year 1900 was a landmark in the history of the Egyptian antiquities administration. Under the energetic regime of Gaston Maspero control of illicit excavation was tightened and the Public Works Department appointed two Inspectors, one for Middle Egypt as far as Abydos, and the other for the south; the fact that the men chosen—Quibell and Carter—were both Englishmen was indicative of the change of attitude brought about by the new Director. The building of the new Cairo Museum, planned and begun some years before, was pushed ahead; the huge task of removing the collections from Giza was already under way; the catalogue, compiled by an international body of scholars, was coming out volume by volume, and more money was to be spent on the consolidation and preservation of monuments; it was to be the duty of the Inspectors to see that this work was carried out.[17] Maspero's liberal attitude was displayed, too, when he permitted one or two treasures from the Abydos tombs to be taken to England on loan for the summer exhibition, "a precedent speaking well for the new order of things," as Petrie pointed out at the Annual Meeting.

The second season at Abydos was as successful as the first. This year Hilda had with her not only Beatrice Orme, who was to undertake most of the photographic work, but also her sister, Amy, who had never been to Egypt before; Mace and Garstang, MacIver and Wilkin made up a strong team. They stopped at Paris to see the Paris Exhibition, and Amy was taken out to see the pyramids in the new electric tram which now ran as far as Mena House. When the party arrived at Baliana, 'Ali es Suefi was there to meet them, with Hilda's horse, donkeys for Flinders and "B.O.", and four men with a deck chair which they carried as a litter for Amy, who was small and frail and unaccustomed to donkeys. 'Ali, who had lived as caretaker in the house during the summer, had planted a small vegetable garden and a plot of sunflowers, protected by a thorn hedge. Mrs Amos and Professor Sayce visited them; fortunately not when a disastrous rainstorm, lasting an unprecedented thirty hours, soaked bedding, clothes and everything else in the camp (the antiquities, which were quickly covered up, escaped serious damage). There were many treasures this year: in the tomb of Peribsen, which had been previously "cleared" by Daressy for the Museum, a perfect stele carved with the king's name was the greatest prize, and in Khasekhemui's tomb a diorite bowl, two copper cups, a quantity of carnelian beads and what Petrie suggested might have been the king's sceptre—a rod covered with carnelian and gold.[18] Then on 26 February came the most exciting discovery of all: in the tomb of Zer, one of the earliest kings, the bones of a forearm were found in a hole in the wall; "apparently the first plunderers who broke up the royal bodies, had wrenched off the forearm and hidden it in a hole in the wall. There it had lain neglected by Copts and Amélineau and the Museum. Our men saw gold in the wrappings, and brought it down intact; so on cutting through the folds of fine gauze we could see all the jewellery in place, and recover the exact arrangement." Hilda restrung the beads next day (**51**). There were four bracelets, one of little turquoise and gold plaques strung together, one of gold and lapis lazuli beads, one of hour-glass shaped beads of gold and amethyst, and one of gold wire and gold rosettes. These royal ornaments, the oldest found in Egypt, are still among the greatest treasures of the Cairo Museum. They were taken there by Quibell when he came on his tour of inspection, but alas—"Brugsch only cared for display; so from one bracelet he cut away the half that was of plaited gold wire, and he also threw away the arm and the linen. A museum," commented Petrie, "is a dangerous place."[19]

This year MacIver and Wilkin were on their own at el 'Amra, six miles to the south of Abydos. The two were firm friends; during the summer they had gone off together on an adventurous trip into the hinterland of Algeria, inspired by Petrie's conviction, based on likenesses in shape and decoration between some Naqada pottery and that of the Kabyles, that some, at any rate, of the early prehistoric population of Egypt had been Libyans, a desert people who had entered the Nile valley and there adopted a riverine way of life.[20] MacIver and Wilkin went on mules to the Aurès mountains; they drew the pottery and made careful cranial measurements in the villages. Their conclusion, which must have disappointed Petrie, was that these people were in no way related to the ancient Egyptians: any similarities in their material culture must have derived from a common source elsewhere.[21] At el 'Amra they built their own little house and with nearly forty Quftis excavated that part of the cemetery which De Morgan's and Amélineau's men, digging without supervision, had not ransacked. Under Petrie's supervision the two young men uncovered and recorded several hundred graves; then MacIver was sent to investigate a stone protruding from the sand one and a half miles south of Umm el Qa'ab. Suspecting a chapel, he dug; it proved to have been a large and once imposing temple. These excavations, and those of the dynastic tombs dug by Mace, were published in a single volume under the excavators' names;[22] it was Petrie's policy to give his helpers every credit for their work, and the preparation of a volume for publication was part of their archaeological training. During the excavation of the late tombs so many thousands of little *ushabtis* were found that it was decided by the Committee of the Fund to make a free distribution of them to members both in England and in America—a popular move which gained the Fund new members, but which they were never in a position to repeat.

Garstang was sent off to dig a prehistoric settlement of wattle and daub huts which the torrential rain had helped to outline, at Mahasna north of Abydos; he then moved further north to Beit Khallâf, where out in the desert five large mastabas proved to be of third-dynasty date.[23] In February, at Bairam, Flinders and Hilda set off on one of their tenting trips with 'Ali, the donkeys and a camel, she wearing a *galabîya*, the long loose-fitting garment of the fellah. They travelled along the desert edge, first visiting Beit Khallâf, and camped for the night in the desert by the great mastaba that both Petrie and Garstang thought must be the tomb of King Neteri-er-khet Zoser; it is now thought to be one of a group of tombs of important officials of his reign. Next morning the Petries climbed down into the interior of the great mastaba, and also into another with "a perilous descent, 40 ft. down, which it was great fun to scramble down, and we ducked under props into small chambers, and turned corners in the dark, and had to swing ourselves up the sloping shaft with a rope." Archaeology for Hilda was a splendid adventure. They continued to Reqaqna, surprising a party of tomb robbers rifling Coptic graves, and on the third day reached the ruins of Athribis where Flinders copied as many inscriptions as he could. Finally they visited the Coptic communities of the Red and White Convents, near Sohag, and were shown round their ancient churches; thence they rode seven miles across the cultivation to Shendawîn and caught a train back to Baliana.

The July exhibition was crowded: nothing like these little fragments of history, exquisite in their craftsmanship, had been seen before. "Some workmen would spend their whole dinner hour in the room." In a historic address to the members of E. E. F. at their Annual General Meeting in November 1901, he summarized his achievements:

> It is now twenty-one years since I began work in Egypt. Mariette then ruled, and the Fund was as yet unborn. In those days the pyramid of Khufu was our boundary of history; nothing whatever was known of the archaeology of Egypt as a comparative science, and no trace of Europe in Egypt was thought of, earlier than the Ptolemies. The situation is now completely different. The monumental history has been carried back to the very beginning of the written record, which has been entirely confirmed; and beyond all that, the whole course of the prehistoric civilisation has been mapped out for perhaps two thousand years, more completely than

> has been done for such ages in any other land. The archaeology is better known than that of the most familiar countries: not a vase nor a bead, not an ornament or a carving, but what falls into place with known examples, and can be closely dated.
>
> The connection with Europe has been led back to the beginning of Greek records, then to Mycenaean times, next to the XIIIth dynasty and now even to the Ist dynasty, and Egypt is the sounding line for the unmeasured abyss of European history. No such opening of new fields to the mind has come to pass since the days when the Renaissance scholars burst into the world of lost classical authors; even the surprising unfolding of Assyria and Babylonia lacks the historic completeness of the Egyptian record and is still almost untouched in its archaeology and developments.[24]

It was the culmination of all his work: page by page he had unrolled the record of the past; now at last he had linked prehistory to history. The first volume of his *History of Egypt* could be rewritten.

Returning to Abydos in late November they at once started building a new house for the expedition, on the sloping side of a *wâdi* further from the cultivation; the position would be quieter, more private and more convenient for the new work he planned, and the house would be larger (p. 347); it had eleven rooms including one for a policeman who, after Hilda's narrow escape, had been detailed to guard them. A well was sunk deep into the sand to tap seepage water from the Nile. Not long after the house was completed, another heavy rainstorm poured through the roofs and all the sand on the floors had to be taken out and replaced and blankets and clothes hung out to dry. Mace was no longer with them: after four years' work for the Fund he had been offered employment with the American Reisner who was starting work at Naga' ed Dêr on the opposite side of the Nile, not far north of Baliana; the work was financed by the wealthy Mrs Phoebe Hearst and sponsored by the University of California. Mace was to work in the field of American Egyptology for the rest of his life. Reisner had earlier visited Upper Egypt in Quibell's company, and at Quft had been introduced by him to some of the workmen; in his excavation of the early cemetery with Mace he was using Petrie's methods and the Quftis Petrie had trained. Relations between the two dig directors seem at first to have been friendly enough—Reisner offered to store some of Petrie's boxes in a dry cave near his dig at the end of the season—but in later years they were sometimes to find themselves at odds on matters of method or of fact.

There were other changes in Petrie's staff: MacIver was still there but Wilkin was missing: he had gone off at the end of the last season on a trip to the oasis of Kharga and on his return to Cairo in May had fallen ill and died of dysentery. His death must have cast a shadow over the camp, and Garstang dedicated his volume on Beit Khallâf to his memory. Nor would Garstang himself be there; he now held an honorary position as Reader in Egyptian Archaeology at the University College of Liverpool. The Research Account student this year was a young man of twenty-one, an Oxford undergraduate named Arthur Weigall whose lively personality and witty conversation must have made him a welcome addition to the camp. Two volunteers were to work in the Temple of Sethos: Algernon Caulfield, and an artist named Christie.

Petrie's own work was now concentrated in the town; his work at Umm el Qa'ab was done and already published. He had drawn plans of all the tombs, and traced the development of the architecture, and he had identified and ranged in order all the royal names of the first two dynasties of Egyptian history; subsequent work on the site by Naville and by others failed to find any more tombs or add significantly to the results he had obtained. Now it was the turn of the great temple of Osiris, in the central part of the ancient town. Mariette's men had dug here, in the quarter known as Kôm es Sultan, but the random holes which they had made only confused the plan. Petrie dug as systematically as he was able, planning each structure as it was exposed and measuring very carefully the depth of each wall and the position of each large or small antiquity discovered. The earlier buildings in the lower levels of the temple were of mud brick, very difficult to trace in the surrounding mud; fortunately during that year the Nile had been exceptionally low, and the inundation one of the most meagre in living memory;[25] though disastrous for the fellah, it made the task of the archaeologist much easier. Petrie spent two winters digging in this area; he distinguished nine phases of rebuilding from the uppermost temple of the Late Period down to the earliest, First Dynasty shrine. Inevitably, the site gave the appearance of great complexity, as Hilda described it:

> The work in the great temple area has been on a colossal scale. A large body of our Qufti workmen have been digging great pits in the mud, generally down to water, and swarms of local basket boys, taken from neighbouring villages, have been running across long tip-heaps of their own making, and shooting their rubbish into the

> worked-out ground below. The whole area is a mass of narrow walls and pillars of hard mud between pits 15 ft. deep, and as one jumps over the tops of all this, and chambers in between, one sees on the low levels jambs of gateways, stone thresholds, columned halls (only the bases still standing) rude flights of steps and bases of weathered and rotted steles . . . lintels, colossi etc. . . . the whole looks a scene of inextricable confusion, but Flinders seems to know by heart about twenty different levels of the entire area and has been determining, day after day, mud walls almost indistinguishable from the mud around them. . . .

It was probably the most complex excavation he ever attempted in Egypt. Unfortunately he drew no sections, and did not record, as a modern archaeologist would thereby have been able to do, instances in which the foundations of later walls were cut into the floor of the building beneath. Nevertheless his careful plans, and the meticulous measurements recorded in his notebooks, have enabled later archaeologists to reconstruct in large measure the history of the temple from its earliest foundation.[26] One or two early votive objects of faience and ivory were of almost unique artistic value: a tiny ivory figure of a king in his jubilee robe (**50**) is thought to date from the Archaic Period, and a little statuette, only seven centimetres high, of King Khufu enthroned,[27] is the only named portrait of the builder of the greatest of pyramids. The finding of this little figure was a triumph for Petrie's policy of rewarding his workmen: it was broken by a careless pickman, and half—the head—was missing. Petrie set the man to sieve the tip-heap, promising him great reward if he found the missing piece, but nothing for the broken piece if he did not; the man went on patiently sieving day after day until at last he found it.[28]

Young Arthur Weigall was put in sole charge of the excavation of a large cemetery to the south of the Royal Tombs, and he also copied many of the inscriptions from the town area.[29] He proved to be first-rate—"the most capable student we have ever had" was Petrie's verdict; but they were destined to lose him; at the end of the season he accepted a permanent post with Maspero in the Inspectorate. Carter, Quibell, Mace, MacIver, Garstang, Weigall—one by one they were leaving for established positions elsewhere, but Petrie, though sorry to lose them, felt no regret that they should go. This, after all, was what he had set out to accomplish: young men, trained by him in the right principles and methods of scientific archaeology, were going off to fill positions of importance in their chosen field; ancient Egypt would henceforward be in good hands.

Flinders and Hilda came home slowly that year, spending a month travelling through Italy, visiting innumerable sites and museums, of which neither of them seemed to tire, a little sketching, a few restful days at Lake Como before returning to Hampstead and the new term at the College.

A new team had to be chosen for the final season (this it must be) at Abydos. Suitable applicants were not lacking. One was Edward Ayrton, a young man born and partly brought up in China; he had not been to university but his enthusiastic manner and his reputation as a great walker commended him to the Professor (he was to spend the next six years excavating in Egypt, before the Archaeological Survey of India claimed him). Then one day a young Canadian named Charles Currelly arrived at the College with a note of introduction from the British Museum. He had been studying for Holy Orders, but had already decided to make, if possible, a career in archaeology rather than the Church, and had been working on material from Crete. Petrie liked the exuberant enthusiasm of this young man and, as he often did, he asked him to stay for a few days before recommending him to the Committee of the Fund as a suitable member of the Abydos team. In late summer came the news that cholera was raging in Upper Egypt. Petrie decided to call off the expedition; he himself would spend three months in Naples, for the doctor had advised him to avoid the cold and fogs of an English winter. In November, however, they heard that the epidemic was over; the Baliana region had escaped lightly, and though many had died in Quft his own men and Reisner's, trained to take precautions about water, had all avoided infection. Weigall went ahead with Currelly to open up the camp before returning to Cairo to take up his new appointment.[29]

Hugh Stannus, a retired architect who came out for his health, helped Petrie with the temple plans, and took many photographs.[30] Canon Rawnsley, the founder of the National Trust, who had so greatly enjoyed his visit to Petrie at Meydum in 1890, sent his son Noel as a volunteer; he could think of no better way to complete a young man's education than a winter in one of the Professor's excavation camps. There were also to be several women: Miss F. Hansard, who was an accomplished artist, came at her own expense on condition that she had some time free for her own painting and an opportunity to visit Luxor. Lina Eckenstein, a close friend of Hilda's, was of German origin; she had lived many years in England and had published a book on Women in Monasticism which proclaimed both her mediaeval scholarship and her interest in women's rights; she took charge of the registration, mending and storing of objects and helped in the general running of the camp. Finally there was Margaret Murray, who was coming to Egypt for the first time; she was invited because of her knowledge of hieroglyphs and in particular of the funerary texts which Petrie knew awaited a copyist. During the previous season Caulfield had noticed a large oblong depression in the ground behind the Temple of Sethos I; preliminary excavation had come upon the upper end of a long descending passage, on the stone walls of which were texts much like those of a manuscript of the "Book of the Dead". It seemed to be an underground tomb. Petrie called it the Osireion and he determined that the excavation should be directed by his wife. She was to have full control of the workmen, keep the paybook and pay them herself, while Miss Murray would record the inscriptions; she too was sometimes in charge of the workmen and she describes in her autobiography how the Professor "tested" her ability to control her workforce, in spite of her diminutive size and her sex; she was proud that she passed his test.[31] When the passage was cleared down to a depth of over forty feet, Miss Hansard joined them to copy the sculptured figures in a vaulted antechamber and part of the hall beyond which they were able to reach. It was an all-feminine excavation, and not without its difficulties and even dangers: the deep cutting was constantly threatening to cave in and "the whole of the excavation was greatly retarded by heavy falls of sand, the Roman filling being so loose that there were continual rivulets of sand running down the sides; and a big wind would bring down half a ton of sand and stones in one fall. To sit in a deep pit under an irregular but continuous fire of small stones with the chance of a big stone coming down too, is an experience more amusing to look back on than to endure,"[32] wrote Miss Murray in retrospect. In the end the "Osireion" had to be abandoned; years later it was tackled once more by Naville, but he too was defeated by sliding sand and seepage water and it was not until 1925 that Henri Frankfort, on behalf of the E.E.S. (as the Fund had become) finally cleared it with the aid of a gravity railway pulled by water buffaloes, and a steam engine pump.[33] Now once more it lies sanded up and partly under water.

Currelly too had a difficult task: deep beneath the cliffs, an underground tomb had been found and partly excavated by Weigall the previous year. Noel Rawnsley described the site: "a great devil's punchbowl, a hollow whose sides are slopes of treacherous sand, with a simple winding path up which long lines of native boys pass the palm-leaf baskets filled with rubbish. Deep, deep down in the hollow one sees the dark opening of a rock shaft leading to the tomb passage a quarter of a mile into the heart of the cliffs, where gangs of naked men toil and pant and sweat in the hot air . . ." It was no easy assignment for a beginner, and the riddle of the tomb was never fully solved: perhaps, like other tombs in sacred Abydos, it was a cenotaph or duplicate burial place.

Several of the voluntary helpers that winter have left us eye-witness accounts of life in a Petrie camp at the turn of the century: Currelly described his first "dig"; Margaret Murray in her autobiography looked back at what had probably been one of the happiest, and most strenuous few months of her life, and Noel Rawnsley contributed a chapter entitled "Sketches of Life and Labour in the Excavators' camp" to his father's book on Abydos.[34] The camp was built round three sides of a courtyard. At one end were the Petries' rooms and the store rooms, at the other end was the dining-room with the kitchen behind, and along one side were bedrooms—tiny cubicles each with a mat over the doorway "to keep out such night-prowlers as stray animals and bats"; a low wall enclosed the courtyard, in which pottery, bones and skulls were stacked. The whole structure was of grey mud-brick, with plank roofs and straw thatching which kept the rooms warm at night. There was no furniture, except for packing cases and a few deckchairs. Every year a supply of tinned groceries was sent out from London in large wooden cases, each holding a carefully selected supply for a certain number of people for one week; these, full or empty, served as tables and washstands, and supported the wire bedsteads. At the end of the season they served to pack the antiquities. Any tins of food still unused at the end of the season were buried, so it was said; next year they would be exhumed and each tin in turn would be thrown against a wall: if it burst, it was discarded. The floor was of soft clean sand. "As to sanitation, the desert is wide and there are many sheltered hollows," wrote Miss Murray.

Rawnsley describes a typical day's work:

> You are woken very early, and wash in ice-cold water; Muhammad Osman shouts "Breakfast!" and you go to the dining room for strong tea and biscuits; down one side of the room is a rough trestle table on which there are bowls of food and open tins of meat and fish covered with saucers to keep out dust; at one end there is an oil stove, by the other door, shelves for crockery. The windows are

narrow slits. One member of the party is deputed to see to the stores for the day; those who are going out to work forage for their lunch and a bottle of water to take with them. Boys come up to be hired for the work; they wait squatting in the sand beyond the camp in a half-circle, shivering in their blue cotton *galabîyas*, each with his basket. They are chosen by appearance; each gives his name and his village, which are noted in the roll-call, and they stand aside among the chosen few; the selected party is then marched off to the work. The trained workmen dig with *turias*; each boy's basket in turn is filled with loose earth scooped into it at the digger's feet; he shouts "*shîlu*" ("take it away"), the boy grasps one handle of the basket, the man the other, and up goes the basket on to the boy's left shoulder, his right arm, held behind his head, steadies it, and off he goes to the dump. If the slope is very steep, a chain of boys will be stationed at intervals, each passing his basket up to the one above (**61**). Work starts at 7.30 and goes on till noon; the *khawâga* lunches by himself in a shady spot, while the workmen sit in the sun in circles eating little hard buns of maize flour, radishes and onions, one or two fetch water in jars; the boys wrestle and play games. After an hour the whistle goes and the men begin again. The exact position of every find must be recorded in the *khawâga*'s notebook and at the end of the day all work must be carefully measured, for payment is by the cubic metre, and varies according to the nature of the soil: if it is wet mud, the pay is higher. . . .

Let us make friends with the big man in the rough, soiled coat and scarlet neckerchief, the *Khawâga kebir*, who rules this little kingdom. Very hot and tired, he is coming up from his shift in the furthest tomb, a dirty candle in one hand, a measuring tape in the other. A genial smile beams out from behind his spectacles, and up we go to the little hut. It is teatime . . . with a pot of jam, a couple of knives and plates and some biscuits we take our places upon the unmade bed, discussing our meal with true desert appetite, and talk of excavation and the idiosyncrasies of the fellaheen.

At sunset comes the end of the work. A shout goes up, baskets are downed, and off go the village boys "wrapping their heads and tying their garments as they go". The Quftis shoulder their *turias*, twist up their headshawls and return to camp with the baskets. Then comes the time for *bakhshîsh*. Men who have found something during the day's digging line up along the wall of the compound; the lantern is lit, the finds are examined and the value of each is written down in the notebook under the finder's name. When the day's harvest of antiquities has been locked away in the storeroom, it is supper-time; each excavator fetches his own bucket of water from the pump, and having washed, comes to the table; Muhammad, dressed in white, puts bowls and tins on the deal boards of the table; there is a pot of lentil soup on the brazier by the door. The day's work is discussed, and plans made for the morrow.* After dinner there are inscriptions to be copied, photographs to be developed in the dark; the sick and wounded come up to be doctored, damaged hands and feet are bound up. On the weekly pay day, the money store is opened; each site supervisor pays his own men; he sits on his bed, a candle in a bottle by his side, and interviews each workman in turn, making sure that he agrees how much is due to him for each day's work, and for *bakhshîsh* for his finds; the men are paid in English gold, with a few riâls and silver coins to make up small amounts. On market day there is no work. The village boys come for their weekly wage; each group of eight has a sovereign to divide between them. In the camp workroom those who draw are busy, others mend pots, letters are written, clothes are washed and hung out to dry, there are expeditions to the high desert, or visits to the market to buy vegetables or poultry.

Noel Rawnsley foolishly neglected to ask the Professor's permission to publish his description of camp life. Flinders Petrie was angry; the young man was in breach of his contract, and there were passages in the chapter to which he took exception.[35] The Fund's solicitor was put in touch with the Rawnsleys, but it was too late, the book had gone to press. The matter was settled out of court: Noel agreed to insert a correction slip in all unsold copies. The offending passages were not many: the author was required to make it clear that Petrie had never struck any man in his employment; the phrase "we lit our pipes" should read "I lit my pipe"; a somewhat exaggerated description of the chaos in the living hut was to be deleted, and a phrase concerning the "savage joy of destruction" as a wall is demolished, should be replaced by an explanation of why it is sometimes regrettably necessary for a wall to be removed in order to see what lies beneath.

After four years at Abydos, Petrie felt it was time to move elsewhere. There were years of work left on the site, but he had achieved his two main objectives, the Royal Tombs and the Osiris temple, and

* While Mrs Amos was staying with them, the conversation was bound to turn to women's rights; Margaret Murray took note: she was later to become a militant suffragette.

he had not enough resources to finish the Osireion—that must be left to others. There was one particular concession he now desired above all others: Saqqara, that vast necropolis on the cliff above the ancient capital, Memphis, which had already yielded so many treasures to the spade. Two sites in particular he coveted: the area around the Step Pyramid (was this Zoser's tomb, or had he been buried at Beit Khallâf?) and near the Serapeum where he hoped he might find the burials of the earliest sacred Apis bulls, perhaps from the First Dynasty. In his previous applications for sites to Grébaut and De Morgan he had put Saqqara high on his list of priorities, but without success: under Maspero's liberal regime, and in view of his personal friendliness, things might be different. In the autumn of 1902, on his way out to Abydos, he had raised the subject and been encouraged to think that a concession would be granted; next summer he put in an application for the Step Pyramid and its surroundings. The Archaeological Committee in Cairo turned down the request: Saqqara, like royal Thebes, was reserved solely for the excavations of the Museum authorities. Although Maspero professed himself sympathetic to Petrie's request he held out little hope that they would change their minds. Petrie then offered to work at Saqqara as Maspero's agent; he was prepared to waive any claim to objects found, provided only that he might have the direction of the work in the field, and the right to publish the results.[36] Maspero declared himself willing to employ Petrie on those terms, which he thought the Archaeological Committee would accept, provided that the E.E.F. supplied the necessary funds. After some discussion (for the London Committee felt that their members would hesitate before contributing to an excavation which yielded no material results) the President Sir John Evans wrote to Maspero agreeing to his proposal but expressing the hope that they might receive a few duplicates. Maspero replied from Paris: Sir John should make formal application—acknowledging the special and exceptional nature of the request—that M. Petrie be allowed to dig in the Step Pyramid area "in order to complete his Abydos discoveries". At the same time, it might be wise to apply for an alternative concession.[37]

The Archaeological Committee met on 15 November 1903 and refused Petrie permission to dig at Saqqara on any terms whatsoever. Ahnas, the alternative site that had been asked for, was granted. Sir William Garstin wrote apologetically. There was no question, he said, of discrimination against the English—"this may have been the case in the past, but it is certainly not so now"; nor was there personal animosity against Professor Petrie. "We, the English members of the Committee," he assured Sir John, "appreciate to the fullest extent the services which he has rendered to Egyptology."[38] Petrie was not willing to give up easily: next year he again applied, this time asking for "the desert behind the cemetery" (an area which has since been found to be rich in tombs). As he wrote to Grueber, Maspero "seemed well inclined to my fresh application . . . then I saw Lord Cromer, who was very friendly, and said he would see Sir William Garstin on my application. Yet after all it was refused, and I know that Maspero, Garstin, Lyons, Artin & Co. were all against it, and only von Bissing (the German member of the Committee) for it. When I saw Maspero after seeing Cromer his manner was quite different, and he seemed annoyed and full of difficulties. . . . From what I saw I believe Maspero never was inclined, but trusted to throw the refusal on the Committee. . . . The puzzle is why Cromer's open friendliness and intervention has had no effect."[39] He was disappointed and angry, and felt that Maspero had let him down; relations between them were never easy thereafter, and once or twice became distinctly strained.

The reason for Cromer's failure to intervene is not far to seek. That same year, 1904, saw the Anglo-French Declaration by which Britain recognized French Control of Morocco, while the French recognized British control of Egypt. A clause in the agreement provided that for the duration of the Treaty (thirty years) the office of Director General of the Egyptian Antiquities Department (under whom came the administration of the Cairo Museum) should always be held by a Frenchman; this concession, made by the British Government in return for advantages in other (to them more important) matters, confirmed what had already in effect become a *fait accompli*, but it strengthened Maspero's hand and made Cromer more reluctant to interfere in the affairs of the Department. Petrie did not ask again for Saqqara; it remained one of the few major sites in Egypt never to come under his spade. Not until after the Second World War was a site for excavation in Saqqara granted to an agent of the Egypt Exploration Society, in the person of Professor W. B. Emery, who had previously dug there on behalf of the Egyptian Antiquities Service: the privilege of the concession is still enjoyed by the E.E.S. today; but the early Serapeum has yet to be found.

CHAPTER XII

Naville and Petrie: A Clash of Personalities (1903–6)

FLINDERS PETRIE'S DECISION to excavate at Herakleopolis, the modern Ehnasya or Ahnas al Medina, must have surprised the Committee of the Egypt Exploration Fund, for M. Naville had dug there with Count D'Hulst in 1891, hoping to find the remains of the ninth and tenth dynasties when the city had been for a time the capital of Egypt, and had found nothing in the temple area older than the reign of Ramesses II, though there were a few blocks, reused, from the twelfth dynasty; having dug down about eighteen feet to "the original pavement" he had concluded that nothing remained of earlier buildings on the site.[1] Knowing Naville's shortcomings as an excavator, Petrie could not believe this, and in 1897 when he was digging at Deshasha he had taken a few days off to visit the site and make a sounding or two; he saw at once that Naville had only exposed a small part of the great *temenos*, and that deep below the Ramesside pavement much earlier work remained—perhaps even the Old Kingdom temple. He had intended, if he was granted the Saqqara concession, to let Currelly dig at Ahnas; as it was, he found himself committed to the task of proving Naville wrong.

Edward Ayrton was to be with them again, and also Leonard Loat, a zoologist who already knew something of Egypt, having taken part in an ichthyological survey of the Nile. Currelly and Loat were sent off to Sedment, the necropolis of Ahnas where Naville had dug up some coffins; finding the place badly plundered, they went on to Petrie's old site at Gurob where 'Ali es Suefi, whose home was at Illahun, joined them. The Petries and Ayrton built a house on the edge of the cultivation near the main town site; they found it damp, "a shivery snuffly contrast to the dry desert where we have been ten years past; how much we shall do is not clear. The mounds are immense and all disgustingly late." The inundation water was still up to the Ramesside floor and while they waited for it to dry out, they began by clearing

Roman houses in the upper town levels. Mrs Milne, the wife of Grafton Milne and herself a classical archaeologist, stayed for nearly a month, taking charge of the finds from the Roman houses and helping Hilda in such uncongenial domestic tasks as mending sheets. Many Roman lamps were found in association with coins and so, with the pottery, could be closely dated; Petrie purchased many more lamps coming from Fayum sites, and planned a supplementary "corpus" volume which should be of value to all classical students.[2]

Supposing that he would be working at Saqqara, Petrie had promised the previous winter that he would give four lectures in Cairo in aid of charity; though it was very inconvenient and cost him eight days wasted from work, he kept his promise: starting early on the twelve-mile donkey ride to Beni Suef, he would catch the train to Cairo and arrive in the late afternoon, give his lecture, stay the night with his friend Dean Butcher, and return to Ahnas next day. Now the water level was lower and the workmen were able to tackle the temple area, far beyond the "vestibule" which was all that Naville had found; they were much hampered by having to remove his huge rubbish dumps. Almost at once, several feet below his pavement, an important find was made: a gold statuette of the god Herishef, of fine workmanship and unusual size was found in the hard mud by one of the workmen; he reported it at once—a further testimony to Petrie's policy of rewarding the finder—and Ayrton dug it out. The value of this treasure, which Maspero allowed Petrie to take home in exchange for some Abydos jewellery the Museum wanted, was so considerable that the Committee of the Fund, which was in low water financially, decided to make an exception to their usual policy of donating to Museums, and offer it for sale; it was bought by the Boston Museum of Fine Arts.[3]

Below the Ramesside level Petrie planned a temple of the eighteenth dynasty and one of the twelfth; further it was impossible to excavate, but in the town there were ruins from an earlier period.[4] At Gurob Currelly dug a cemetery discovered by the unrivalled flair of 'Ali es Suefi, who noticed that in one place the rock was somewhat softer than the surrounding limestone; on probing it turned out to be a thick incrustation of gypsum covering the sand filling of the tombs. All proved to have been rifled in antiquity, but pottery coffins and fragments of Mycenaean false-necked vases and Cypriot base-ring ware confirmed Petrie's supposition that Gurob had been a foreign settlement. (see p. 156.) Just south of the temple area, to Loat's delight, a cemetery was found in which oxen and large numbers of sacred fish, the great Nile perch, had been buried. Loat published this discovery in a volume shared with Margaret Murray[5] who, with Miss Hansard and another woman artist, spent several months at Saqqara copying tomb reliefs for the Research Account. Ayrton stayed with them the first week, helping them to make their Spartan living quarters habitable; Mariette's old *reis*, Rubi, was still living and able to indicate to his son Khalifa the exact whereabouts of the tombs to be reopened.[6] During their stay in Saqqara they must have met a recently appointed Inspector of Antiquities, Cecil Firth, who had come to Cairo as a lawyer but had been captivated by ancient Egypt; he and Miss Hansard were married the following year and they lived in Cairo for nearly thirty years. The Firths were among the Petries' greatest friends in Egypt and Flinders often visited them when later, as Inspector of Antiquities at Saqqara, Firth had the task, which Petrie had so greatly coveted, of excavating the Step Pyramid.

Petrie had long wanted to dig at Tell el Fara'in in the Delta, which he had identified as the site of Buto, the sacred city which had been the capital of a predynastic kingdom (p. 96). Now he determined to see what could be done. Currelly was sent ahead with a few Quftis to reconnoitre,[7] and the Petries arrived at the end of February. For once their carefully laid plans had miscarried, for the boxes containing their bedding, workaday clothes and supplies were sent on by the railway to Alexandria by mistake and they were left with "evening dress and a camera with no plates".[8] Frantic messages up the line had no effect, so they made the best of it with one small tent pitched on an embankment above the marshes, getting what supplies they could from Dessuk, the nearest town; the local sheikh asked them several times to sup with him, and they were entertained at Dessuk on the last day by an English official, George Hornblower, an enthusiast for archaeology, who came out to see what they were doing. The lower levels of the site proved to be waterlogged beyond hope of recovery; Petrie noticed, as he planned the site, that limestone blocks had been sawn up, and an ancient lime-kiln showed where many may have ended. Scattered fragments of first-dynasty pottery were tantalizing witness to what might lie deep under the mud; the Delta has been steadily sinking, and any hope of recovering the early city must be abandoned. After five days they returned to Cairo. It was now that Flinders made his last attempt to obtain the concession for Saqqara; the Committee met on 9 March and gave him his final refusal. That afternoon the Petries left for Alexandria; next morning they were off for a three-week tour of Sicily.

This was one of their happiest holidays. In long walks over the hills they forgot the vexations and disappointments of the past winter. Hilda wrote almost daily[9] to her family and to her friends Lina Eckenstein, Ray Pinker and Beatrice Orme (now Mrs Eustace), describing the profusion of wild flowers seen from the train from Messina to Taormina, the picturesque dresses of the peasants, the snowfields below Etna. They explored Syracuse, Flinders noting that the methods of ancient stoneworking in the quarries were similar to the Egyptian; at Girgenti they found men at work with long picks, still extracting the blocks in the old way. Hilda collected fossils, and Flinders took a great many photographs of the temples, and in the churches of Palermo. He had his new swan's necked camera with him, made to his own ingenious design especially for the photography of high buildings without distortion of the natural perspective; with a flexible bellows he could tilt the lens up to forty degrees, the plate being held in a plane parallel with the façade of the building.[10] In the museum at Palermo he studied the "Palermo Stone", a lump of diorite containing part of the annals of the first kings of Egypt; one or two other fragments of this important monument, or other copies of it, found their way into the Cairo Museum. Petrie was later to be offered a small piece by a dealer at Memphis; recognizing at once what it was, he bought it. It is now in the Petrie Museum in London (**95**).[11]

The Egypt Exploration Fund's summer exhibition that year included Petrie's finds at Ehnasya, those of Naville and his assistant, Sidney Hall's son Harry (who now held a junior position in the British Museum under Budge), at Deir el Bahari, and more papyri from that inexhaustible fount of manuscripts, Oxyrhynchus. Loat's work and the Saqqara tracings were also included. If Naville found the display, at University College, of what he ought to have found embarrassing, he did not betray his feelings.

Flinders Petrie's friends now urged him to make available in the form of a book the wisdom and experience he had accumulated during more than twenty years of excavating: to write a kind of manual of archaeological practice. He was not reluctant to do so. *Methods and Aims in Archaeology* is still read by those who work in the field and find it full of useful and practical advice, though some of the methods recommended are now outmoded and new materials and fresh techniques have greatly increased the resources of the modern archaeologist. The book abounds in practical suggestions born of the writer's inventive mind and long experience: how to take impressions of objects by dry- or wet-squeezing, or by means of tinfoil backed by wax; how to move heavy stones; the best way to pack pottery; alternative methods for preserving fragile objects of wood or ivory; the proper treatment of beadwork, stucco, corroded silver, bronze; the simplest way to draw up a pay-slip and the quickest and most accurate way to plot a building. In the section on drawing objects, he describes a simple but ingenious apparatus which he devised himself in the second year at Abydos, whereby stone bowls could be drawn when only small fragments of rim and base remained: the rim was moved about on a card of concentric circles until it exactly fitted the curve of one of them; the base was attached above it by beeswax to a moving rod centred on the card: by sliding the rod up and down the axis until the curves of rim and base fell into line, the height could be determined and the dimensions read off the scale; the shape of the whole pot could then be accurately drawn to scale.[12]

Petrie's experience in organizing his workforce is crystallized in two chapters. He chooses his workmen by their appearance, by the eyes, which show honesty, and by a fresh and open bearing. Young lads are the best; only a few can be employed after forty. He argues the advantages of piece-work as against daily wages: men keep their basket-boys at work if they are being paid for the amount of work done; otherwise the gang is apt to idle and has to be constantly watched. Gang overseers, or *reises*, are undesirable (he had learnt this to his cost at Hawara).

> Each well-trained man should have half-a-dozen new hands placed near him, and he can be ordered to see that they follow instructions. . . . Thus every man is directly under the master, all instruction is given at first hand, and every one is in close touch, and not fenced off by intermediate intriguers. Doubtless, two or three men will come to the front by their ability and character; but though full use should be made of them, yet they should always be kept nominally on the same terms and work as every one else. Their reward consists in being given all the more promising places, where things are likely to be found, so that they may reap more profit than the others.[13]

He enumerates the qualities needed to make a good archaeologist: an education combining the scholar and the engineer; a strong historical sense; an ability to organize; acute powers of observation and an accurate visual memory. "The master should be able to go over the whole site, and every man at work on it, entirely from memory; he should be able to realise at once, on seeing the place next day, exactly how every one of fifty holes looked the day before; and know at once how the work stood, and what has been done since, so as to measure it up without depending on any statements by the workmen. . . . Of all inherent mental qualifications there is perhaps none more essential to a digger than this permanent picture of a site in mind."[14]

Your archaeologist should be able to draw accurately, have some knowledge of the written language or languages of the ancient civilization with which he is dealing, and of the spoken language of the modern inhabitants; he should be physically robust and ready to work long hours in the most uncomfortable circumstances; the pick and the knife should be in his hands every day, and his readiness should be shown "by the shortness of his fingernails and the toughness of his skin." His clothes must suit the work: "the man who cannot enjoy his work without regard to appearances, who will not strip and go into water, or slither on slimy mud through unknown passages, had better not profess to excavate. Alongside of his men he must live, in work hours and out; every workman should come to him at all times for help and advice. His courtyard must be the pay office and the court of appeal for everyone; and continual attention should be freely given to the many little troubles of those who are to be kept properly in hand. To suppose that work can be controlled from a distant hotel, where the master lives in state and luxury completely out of touch with his men . . . may be amusing, but it is not business."[15]

Petrie's chapter on the ethics of archaeology is as relevant today as it was in 1904. In seeking to recover the past, the archaeologist must destroy the past; his responsibility is therefore the greater.

> Conservation must be his first duty, and where needful even destruction of the less important in order to conserve the more important. To uncover a monument, and leave it to perish by exposure or by plundering, to destroy thus what had lasted for thousands of years and might last for thousands to come, is a crime. Yet it is the incessant failing of the thoughtless amateur, who knows nothing of the business; and far too often also the inexcusable malpractice of those who know better.

He emphasized the importance of the written record; even objects preserved in museums have a limited expectation of life, but books can be reprinted, knowledge of a discovery can be handed on indefinitely by means of the published report. The excavator must also be technically competent.

> To undertake excavating and so take the responsibilities for preserving a multitude of delicate and valuable things, unless one is prepared to deal with them efficiently, both mechanically and chemically, is like undertaking a surgical operation in ignorance of anatomy. . . . To suppose that excavating—one of the affairs which needs the widest knowledge—can be taken up by persons who are ignorant of most or all of the technical requirements, is a fatuity which has led, and still leads, to the most miserable catastrophes.[16]

Few of Petrie's friends would have been in any doubt that the ideal archaeologist Petrie described was a portrait of what he himself was, or strove to be, and that in his portrayal of the incompetent excavator, destroying evidence and incapable of conserving what he found, M. Naville was foremost among those he had in mind. For years now, within the Fund and outside it, he had been openly critical of his fellow excavator and had repeatedly warned the Committee of his shortcomings. "Archaeology," it has been said, "is not a science, but a vendetta." The same might be said of other disciplines to which men devote their lives and in which they are passionately and single-mindedly involved. The long feud between Flinders Petrie and Edouard Naville, the Egypt Exploration Fund's first excavator and for thirty years until his retirement in 1914 their chief representative in the field, was inevitable from the first, for it arose from widely differing temperaments and a totally separate approach to their profession. Naville was an Egyptologist of the old school, deeply learned in the language of the hieroglyphs and a leading authority on Egyptian religion.[17] He regarded excavation as a means of uncovering new monuments, and in particular inscriptions which might throw fresh light on the history and mythology of the ancient Egyptians; to dig a site without large monuments was for him a waste of time. He did not consider it necessary to be constantly on the site, but would remain in the house deciphering inscriptions, or sometimes spend a few days in Cairo, leaving a contractor to shift earth at so much a square yard, or an assistant to supervise the workmen. At Saft el Hinna in 1884 Jaillon had excavated a large square area marked out for him by Naville, and in doing so completely dug away a solid wall which ran across it.[18] When moving blocks in the temple at Bubastis, D'Hulst had neglected to note their positions. Naville's own inadequacies as an excavator were revealed in the publication of his first season's work in the field: his plan of the massive complex of brick walls which he identified as the "store chambers" built by the Israelites in bondage lacked doorways; apart from inscribed blocks and one or two statues not a single object found was illustrated or even mentioned in the text: such things as pottery, beads, figurines and metal tools did not interest the philologist. Petrie, describing the fragments of gilded relief which he had picked up on the site, commented to Poole: "How it is possible for workmen to pass over shining surfaces of gold several square inches each it is hard to imagine!"[19] Villiers Stuart, who had visited the site while Naville was digging, had noted other important discoveries made by the workmen:

> Among the articles which I saw in the store chambers was a beautifully made bronze brazier for holding fire: soon after its discovery, however, it fell to pieces from the action of the air. . . . In one of the chambers near the river M. Naville showed me an immense collection of bones of various quadrupeds, birds and even fish; they were fragile with age and we could not account for their presence. I saw also, in another chamber close by, masses of a species of gum or resin; the mark of the sacks in which it had been contained was still stamped on the outside, although the sacks themselves had long since fallen to dust. I took some of this away with me, and on setting fire to it, found that it burned with a strong aromatic perfume. It had, in fact, been frankincense and was no doubt stored there for the use of the temple.[20]

These matters had had no mention in Naville's reports; Miss Edwards in her review of Villiers Stuart's book remarked rather tartly that this was the first time she or Mr Poole had heard of them.[21] Her doubts about Naville's competence as an excavator were reinforced by what Petrie told her, but she was unable to convince Poole and the other members of the E.E.F. Committee; year after year they asked him to go out for them again, and though she realized the mistake they were making she was unable or unwilling to protest; she opposed, but could not prevent, their acquiescence when Naville announced, after Petrie's departure from the Fund, that he no longer intended to give *bakhshish* for objects found.[22] He was an expensive luxury, too: he drew a salary three times the size of Petrie's expense account and unlike Petrie in the early days, surrounded himself with assistants. As Amelia Edwards wrote in sarcastic vein:

> My dear Mr. Petrie, I regretfully discover that after all your experiences in Egypt, you do not yet know the right way of

> excavating. It takes *five* to do a digging in the true high and mighty style. At Bubastis, for instance, there was M. Naville to preside (in his tent, bien entendu) where he probably spent his days in writing to Madame and the children; there was Mr. Macgregor to take photographs; Mr. Goddard to spend American dollars and curl his hair and moustachios; Mr. Griffith to rescue a few small objects, and Count D'Hulst to talk Arabic and pay the men.[23]

Nevertheless at the Annual General Meeting in 1889, Spurrell was angered by hearing Naville's praises sung even by Miss Edwards herself; she had spoken of his wonderful capacity for exploration; his latest excavation at Bubastis had been a marvel: "not a stone has been left unturned, not an inscription uncopied"; there was nothing left for the future, nor any speck for the Arabs to collect in the sand; the place was *done*.[24]

Then came the disaster of the Library of Mendes. In the winter of 1892, Naville explored several sites in the Delta, one of which was Timai el Amdid, the site of the ancient city of Mendes. Here he hoped for new inscriptions which might "throw light on those parts of Egyptian history which are still in nearly complete darkness". In this he was disappointed, but in the Roman area of the mound he made trial excavations and uncovered a series of rooms filled with Greek papyri; in his report to the Egypt Exploration Fund he described numbers of large rolls, most of them carbonized and so fragile that very few could be extracted, and these were "nothing but crumbs of charcoal and ashes" when they reached London. "What treasures we probably have lost," he ended, "by the destruction of the library of Mendes."[25] What indeed! Petrie was horrified when he read the report of this lecture in *The Times*; he wrote at once to *The Academy*. The Fund, he said, had a site of the highest possible value in their hands, and it was essential that a properly skilled worker be sent out to rescue what had not already been destroyed by the finder in cleaning the chambers of the library; he had seen some of these rolls in a dealer's shop in Cairo; they seemed to be in much better condition than the ones he, Petrie, had found at Tanis; yet those had been saved, without appreciable loss.[26]

M. Naville was deeply affronted by this attack. "It is not the first time that Petrie expresses his contempt for my work, I know that he never did it so openly as this time." He denied having used the word "cleaning"; it was a misprint for "clearing". "However low his esti-

62 Memphis, 1908: in the Ptah Temple

63 Flinders and Hilda Petrie, 1903

64 Petrie with the artist Holman Hunt, *c.* 1905

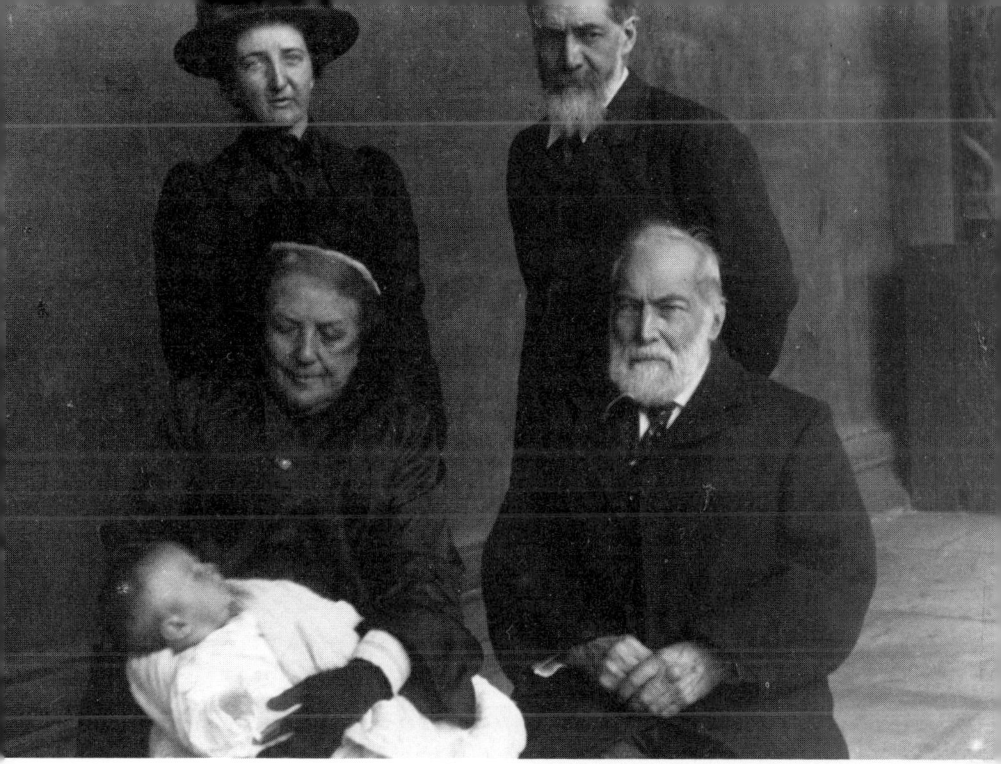

65 On the portico of University College, September 1907: Mrs Urlin and William Petrie in London for the christening of their grandson John; Hilda and Flinders stand behind

66 Hilda with John, 1908

67 Digging below the water-table in the Ptah temple, 1910 (*Memphis III*, pl. XXX)

68 Excavating the temple of Ptah, Memphis, in 1908. The village of Mit Rahina is in the background (*Memphis I*, pl. XXI)

69 Terracotta heads from the "foreign quarter" at Memphis

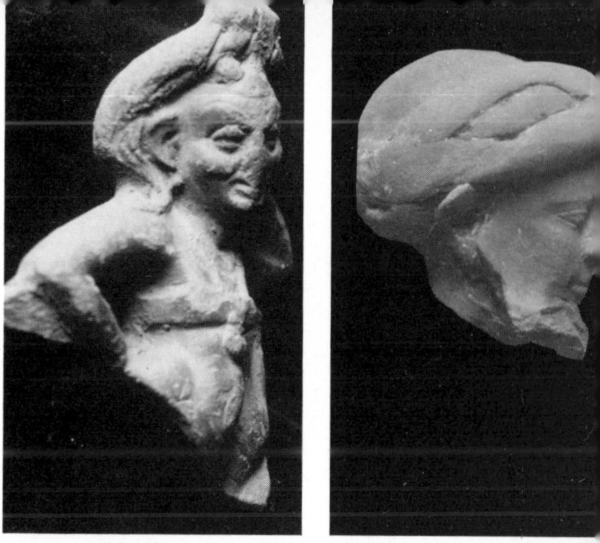

70 Lintel from the temple of Ptah, Memphis: a court official does homage before the name of King Si-Amun. The block is now in the Museum of the University of Pennsylvania, Philadelphia (Petrie: *Memphis II*, pl. XXIV)

71 Mit Rahina (Memphis): massive brickwork of the palace of Apries

72 Excavating Silbury Hill, Wiltshire, in August 1922. Petrie, in a cloth cap, can be seen in the centre of the picture

73 (*below*) Vigorous at 69, Petrie strides across the desert at Abydos in 1922; G.W.H. Walker follows him

74 Flinders Petrie in his museum at University College, London; the figure of Meryrehashtef, found in January 1921 at Sedment, was subsequently bought for the British Museum by the National Art Collections Fund

75 (*below*) Tomb at Qau used as a living room

76 J. L. Starkey

77 Karl Pearson

78 Petrie in his study at Well Road *c.* 1916

mate of my work may be, I have not yet gone down to the level of being a mere sweep." Petrie's wish that every document should have its position recorded he considered mere nonsense: "you might as well make a plan of the position of raisins in a plum pudding. . . . That I should be accused of having practised wholesale destruction by my clumsiness and brutality in 'cleaning' the rooms is not only unjust, since it rests only on Petrie's fancy, it is mean; and it is a miserable way of showing his own excellence of which he is so thoroughly convinced."[27]

Naville's anger was understandable: it had been ruthless to expose him to public ridicule; yet the naïve simile of the raisins should have told Poole that Petrie's alarm was justified: a priceless archive had been needlessly destroyed, and others might be lost by the same ignorance of archaeological method. Miss Edwards would have realized the danger, but she was no longer there to appeal to, and Petrie therefore wrote to Kate Bradbury, who alone among members of the Committee he thought might be able to persuade them to rescue the remaining documents from destruction by illicit diggers. He urged that Carter and Newberry, who were at Beni Hasan, be sent up to Mendes to see the site and assess the situation. Meanwhile, he said, he had heard that Naville and D'Hulst were to be allowed to excavate the beautiful cliff temple of Deir el Bahari in western Thebes. This filled him with foreboding; they would be sure to damage the delicate reliefs for which the temple was celebrated: "Count D'Hulst told me, with superior wisdom, that in order to copy the graffiti at Meydum I ought to have put a wet paper on the wall and beaten it so as to bring the ink away on the paper!!! This would be his way of treating a graffito—a priceless and irreplaceable record."

What was wanted, he insisted, was a man who understood Egyptian architecture, was skilled in facsimile drawing, knew the locality and would study the scale of local prices for objects found: "if too much be paid for finds, things will be brought in from outside; if too little, things will be taken away" (he knew quite well that Naville opposed the "purchase system" and did not intend to pay *bakhshish*); Naville would be much more safely employed in clearing part of the Temple of Karnak, where his learning could be employed to good effect.[28]

Miss Bradbury was obviously alarmed. She replied urging Flinders to write himself to the Chairman of the Committee, Maunde Thompson, making a formal statement of his views. This he did, citing the disastrous neglect at Pithom, the bungled excavation of Saft el Hinna, and other enormities. Naville had insisted on a late date for his finds at Tell el Yehudiya, though Griffith had proved them to be much earlier; at Ahnas the cemetery was cleared, without any record being made of the tombs. Finally, there was the dismal story of Mendes. The Fund had lost immeasurably by the loss of small antiquities from Naville's excavations, and of what had been brought back "there is hardly any published record". It was time that such an obsolete and wasteful system should be discontinued. In a postscript he added: "If you look at Pitt-Rivers' 'Excavations at Bokerley Dyke' you will know what excavating means."

Petrie's letters were not, it seems, read to the Committee till their next meeting on 1 February, by which time Naville was on his way to Egypt. They decided to send him a telegram before it was too late, telling him to defer his application for Deir el Bahari and to ask De Morgan for Karnak instead. Naville received the telegram at Assuan, whither he had followed De Morgan; he had just got his permit for Deir al Bahari. Furious with the Committee, he sent in his resignation on the spot—knowing well that it would not be accepted. "If my work is of so little value, not to say none, as Mr. Petrie thinks, I shall not impose myself any longer on the Society, and it is far better that I should go."[29]

In the end he went to Deir el Bahari and began his excavation of the temple, the Committee only stipulating that in future seasons Howard Carter, or Hogarth, or some other trained excavator should accompany him to ensure that small finds were not ignored. The problem of D'Hulst was soon resolved: he unwisely offended De Morgan in Cairo, and Naville had no alternative but to dispense with his services.

As for Mendes, the Fund agreed to send Howard Carter there in March with a young man called Guthrie Roger, to rescue the papyri. The expedition was a fiasco: they hunted about on the mounds but Naville's directions were imprecise and they could not locate the library; while they waited in vain for De Morgan's permit to dig, they were miserably confined to their tent by the *khamasîn*, and in the end they gave up and left.[30] Guthrie Roger went home and as far as is known, was lost to archaeology; Carter, who had wasted two months, was probably relieved when, in 1896, Grenfell asked the Fund to transfer the concession to him. Unhappily, he never dug there. A few scrolls found their way through dealers to Europe; the rest were lost to the *sebbakhîn*. In 1906 the Antiquities Service cleared three chambers; the mudbrick floors of two of them were covered with "the charred remains of writings."[31]

Naville went on excavating for the Fund until just before the First World War; he never changed his views about the relative unimportance of small objects and the impossibility of using pottery as a criterion for dating. In 1912, when he was digging at Abydos, his proposal to let the *sebbakhîn* clear the surface debris from an area where he proposed to dig was fortunately vetoed by the Committee. He had gone there with the object, it would seem, of proving Petrie wrong. In reviewing *Royal Tombs of the First Dynasty* in 1902,[32] he disagreed strongly with its main conclusions: what Petrie had found were not tombs at all, he declared, but funerary chapels or cult sanctuaries; the tombs had yet to be found. He rejected Petrie's readings of many of the royal names and also his listing of the kings; Narmer and Aha, he argued, must belong to the Second Dynasty, and Merbapa (Merpeba) and Khasekhemui were one and the same. Petrie's retort came swiftly:[33] Naville's conclusions were impossible; there was no doubt that Umm el Qa'ab was a cemetery; his own relative dating of the tombs was based on the incontrovertible evidence of archaeology. Naville was unconvinced; he asked for the Abydos concession; he opened up the tombs of Umm el Qa'ab again, using a light railway to carry away debris which Petrie had already sifted through, and declared that pottery in the other cemeteries which Petrie had shown to be prehistoric, was in reality that of an African tribal population co-existing with the native Egyptians in dynastic times.[34] To the end of his life he maintained that it was impossible to use pottery as a criterion for dating; differences in type were not chronological, he insisted, but regional. By this time his views were received by Egyptologists with an indulgent smile.

Correspondence between Petrie and the Secretary and Officers of the Fund, and a memorandum sent by him to the Committee in 1904,[35] suggest that he was chafing at the restraints laid upon him by having to wait for their decisions (the Committee met but seldom) and also by lack of adequate funds: with the limited amount they could provide, he could not afford to pay his assistants; often their expenses came from his own pocket. At Ahnas he had run out of money and had been forced to dismiss half his workforce early in the season. Naville's new work on the eleventh dynasty temple at Deir el Bahari was proving more costly than had been anticipated, and the Fund was already in low water financially; they had lost many of their American supporters during the past decade and contributions from the other side of the Atlantic were seriously depleted. This was partly due to a natural process of evolution: Americans were taking an increasing interest in the archaeology of the Old World, an interest fostered not only by the publicity given to the Fund's own discoveries, but also to Babylonian expeditions sponsored by universities. Wealthy patrons were now coming forward to finance excavations on their own: Mrs Phoebe Hearst of California was supporting George Reisner's work in Giza; in Philadelphia Mrs Stevenson and her Society were seeking new ways of augmenting the still embryonic collection of the University Museum; Boston supported Reisner and Lythgoe, and in 1903 Breasted had persuaded J. D. Rockefeller to donate 50,000 dollars to the University of Chicago for field work in the Near East, and the Oriental Exploration Society had come into being: the wealthy citizens of Chicago now had a local cause to support and most withdrew their subscriptions to the Egypt Exploration Fund.

The trouble lay deeper than this. Within the ranks of still-loyal supporters there was dissension, brought about by the increasing hostility of the Reverend Copley Winslow. It was to him, it will be remembered, that the early success of the Fund's appeals in America had been almost entirely due. He had campaigned tirelessly for new members, rounded up subscriptions due, distributed members' copies of the annual publication; he had written numerous articles to the Press, interviewed editors, and lectured to learned bodies, more or less managing by these means to silence Cope Whitehouse; and he had masterminded Miss Edwards' tour of the States—though not entirely to her liking. In his copious correspondence with Amelia Edwards[36] it is possible to detect a note of discontent and thwarted ambition: he was easily offended at what he imagined to be the Committee's lack of appreciation of his services; he insisted on the title "Honorary Vice-President" as well as Honorary Treasurer in the U.S.A., and constantly badgered General Loring, the curator of the Boston Museum of Fine Arts, to make it clear that antiquities sent by the E.E.F. had been donated through his agency. He was avid for honorary degrees, and not averse to canvassing for them; several American universities complied, but the "Hon. D.Phil." of the University of St Andrews which Miss Edwards and Poole reluctantly pulled strings to obtain for him was not, he felt, as much as was his due in the United Kingdom: he sighed in vain for an Oxford doctorate. For nearly twenty years his house in Boston was the official address of the Fund, to which treasurers of the different American branches sent their annual subscriptions, to be forwarded through him to London. As time went on, many complaints were received in London of increasing muddle in the Boston office; he was urged to engage secretarial help, but successive secretaries resigned in fury or despair. His long letters to London got more incoherent and more diffuse; the Fund's American subscribers were puzzled to receive printed circulars complaining of the actions of the Committee in London, and without authorization he declared the monthly journal *Biblia*, edited by his friend Davis, to be the official mouthpiece of the Fund in America.

In 1895, at Petrie's suggestion, the Committee in London decided it was time to reorganize the American Branch: they created an Executive Committee for America under Loring's chairmanship. Winslow, who had expected to be asked to fill this office, was disappointed merely to be named as Honorary Secretary, but as Loring was in poor health, he was still able to enjoy the power he craved. An active and able secretary, Mrs Marie Buckman, was appointed to put the office to rights; to begin with Winslow worked well with her but difficulties quickly developed, and Loring had to warn London that Winslow was circulating printed leaflets urging subscribers in the States to withhold their contributions. James Cotton, the Honorary Secretary of the E.E.F., was sent out to Boston to try to sort things out; he was impressed by Mrs Buckman's tact and patience, but the Committee could not bring themselves to dismiss Winslow. The Boston Committee was reorganized in 1902, and Winslow heard from London that he no longer held any office in the Fund and would no longer "represent, control or direct" the interests of the Fund in the United States.[37] His reaction was predictable: in the summer of 1903 he poured out his fury in a book, *The Truth about the Egypt Exploration Fund*, in which he attacked its folly and ingratitude, and made scandalous allegations of a personal nature against a "Mrs. B." whom nobody could have failed to recognize. This unpleasant document was sent to all subscribers in America; some threw it in the wastepaper basket, others took the accusations seriously and withdrew their membership. In 1900 American subscriptions had totalled nearly £2,500; in 1904 they had fallen to £530.

Unable to plan a large-scale excavation for which he knew he would not be granted sufficient funds, Flinders Petrie decided to embark on an enterprise which he had long planned: the exploration of the area in the Sinai peninsula to which the ancient Egyptians had gone to mine turquoise. It was an expedition for which relatively few workmen would be needed, and there was no lack of volunteers: Currelly needed only his expenses, and a bright lad aptly named Button was eager to go; so was another young man, T. K. Frost. Montague Porch, a gentleman of independent means who was anxious to add to his collection of palaeolithic flints, asked to accompany them for part of the time, and somewhat reluctantly, Petrie invited Captain Reymond Weill, a French Egyptologist who had already spent three years collating copies of all previously recorded inscriptions in the peninsula, to join them. Hilda was to go to Saqqara with Lina Eckenstein, Miss Hansard and her friend Miss Kingsford,* to continue the copying of reliefs in the mastabas of the Old Kingdom for the Research Account; they would live in the same house as Miss Murray's party the year before; Currelly was to go ahead to Egypt to collect some Quftis and bring them over. The whole expedition would be run on a shoestring. It would not be without danger, for the Beduin of Sinai had a bad reputation: as late as 1882 the Orientalist Major Palmer and his three companions had been murdered in the Wady Sidr.

Petrie, Button and Frost, with two Quftis (one the stalwart Erfai, six feet tall and of 'Abâbda stock, who had worked for Petrie since he was a lad), met Weill at Suez on 3 December 1904; when they arrived by boat at the quarantine station, they found riding camels so expensive to hire that they decided to take only a water camel, sending the bulk of the stores on by boat to Bardis, the nearest point on the coast to the mines of Wady el Maghara (the Valley of Caves), their first destination. Instead of riding, they would have to walk. The going was rough, and even Flinders suffered from blistered feet; Weill, also lame, tried riding uncomfortably perched on the water camel. For the last two days they were obliged to hire riding camels; by this time they were short of food: boxes wrongly repacked the previous year were found to contain "useless mattresses".

They reached the Wady Maghara, but they had no stores and water was a problem; the old sheikh was absent in Suez and a local rascal insisted on a written agreement before he would send to the coast; Petrie accordingly wrote one out in his very amateur Arabic script.[38] Porch and his Italian manservant joined them, and they set up an enclosure with tents. The Beduin refused to disclose the whereabouts of the nearest well without payment; whereupon Petrie took a bucket, walked straight down the wady, turned up another and went ahead till he came to the well. The onlookers were astonished at this evidence of his magical powers; in fact, he had earlier observed a lone camel walking in that direction, and had assumed that it must be making for water. In three days, all the stores were brought up from the coast and

* Later Mrs Sydney Cockerell.

they were able to start work, but they were plagued by thieving Beduin, sometimes with stealthy arm under the tent flap, sometimes in a whirlwind raid; one day Montague Porch's servant made a snare, and caught two thieves, "So it was a tug of war of Lorenzo and Porch against the two, who succeeded in wrenching away before we could get down in answer to Porch's shots." In one raid, one of the two petroleum stoves was taken; worse, a large roll of newsprint used for copying and taking squeezes was carried off; Petrie sent a messenger by the next post camel to the editor of a Cairo newspaper for a replacement; in due course a roll arrived, but it was not of the same quality as *The Times*.

Two days after the tent incident, having collected his flints, Porch left to look for palaeoliths in the Nile Valley. Meanwhile Currelly had arrived with twenty-seven men from Egypt. He had had difficulty persuading men from Koptos to come with him, for the fellah fears the desert people, and the Beduin of Sinai in particular. In the end one or two came; the rest had to be recruited from the 'Abâbda Beduin of the eastern desert.[39] Now there were thirty-six mouths to feed; Philip Button was given the task of doling out rations of flour, rice, lentils, sugar, oil and onions to the men, while the arrival of fresh stores was anxiously awaited; there had been a muddle in the Supply Stores at Suez and at one time there was only enough flour left for one day.

The return of the old Sheikh Abu Ghaneym was welcome, for his presence put an end to lawlessness; he knew every inch of the rocky valleys and remembered Major Macdonald, who had lived there with his wife, his son and his cat from 1854 to 1866, mining turquoise; he had taken many squeezes of inscriptions left by the ancient mining expeditions in the valley, and had presented them to the British Museum. Petrie found many more, including one unrecorded royal figure, that of Sa-nakht of the third dynasty; he also found that many of these tablets, carved by various missions sent by kings of the Old and Middle Kingdoms to mine turquoise, had been seriously damaged since Macdonald's time. Much of the destruction was due to recent mining expeditions blasting the rock, and to the local Beduin who were still deliberately defacing the figures. While they were copying inscriptions of the twelfth dynasty, "a native came and defaced them with a hammer during the dinner hour". Petrie came to the reluctant conclusion that the only safe course was to remove the remaining sculptures from the rock.

For the best part of a month Petrie planned the area, and explored the settlements in which the ancient miners had lived; in the floors of the huts of the Middle Kingdom miners, tools and nests of pots were found, hidden away when they had left the site at the end of the mining season, for use when they returned the following winter. Most of the workings had been destroyed by subsequent mining, but a few of the old galleries remained to show the methods and implements employed by the ancient Egyptians; Petrie's study added an important chapter to the history of ancient technology.

On 11 January the party moved on to the other ancient mining area, known to travellers since the time of Niebuhr's visit in 1762; the workings here were mostly of the Middle and New Kingdoms and on the hilltop the Egyptians had erected a place of worship for the deities of the region. The site, Serabit al Khadem, was some twenty miles from Maghara as the crow flies over very rugged terrain; twenty-six camel loads were necessary to transfer the tents and stores over three days to the new camp site. To reach the temple high on a hilltop entailed a daily climb of 250 feet up the Wady, and half an hour's walk to the site (**56**). The wind blew mercilessly; to manage a wide sheet of copying paper needed skill and patience, and numb fingers found difficulty in holding a pencil. At night it froze, and they huddled in their blankets. It was a Spartan existence, but a healthy one; in that pure air there were no colds and sore throats; at the same time Petrie confessed to "a fond craving for a land where it should be always afternoon tea". He wrote to Hilda, advising her not to come; but she was not to be put off; leaving Miss Hansard and Miss Kingsford to continue the work at Saqqara, she and Lina Eckenstein set off by train to Suez, and then by boat to El Shatt. She afterwards wrote a lively account of their six-day journey on camel-back: their equipment included rolls of blankets, four waterskins, a stove and kettle and boxes of food; each of the ladies carried a whip, a notebook, a compass, a water flask and a revolver. Beduin drivers accompanied them, and a trusted Qufti was sent by Flinders to escort them. Three days' journeying took them down the coast to the Wady Gharandel, then their track led inland through a mountainous region of red sandstone peaks and precipitous gorges: further south there were cliffs and canyons of granite, barren except for tufts of aromatic herbs and flowering broom and the occasional acacia bush, fuel for their camp fire at night. They pressed on, seldom stopping during the day for food: "pot and spoon are handed across, and the camels trot on interminably." In the winding gorges they passed an occasional goatherd, clad in sheepskin and sandals; the men were usually heavily armed, carrying a large blunderbuss, and girt with a long curved sword and a brass-handled dagger.[40]

The arrival of two extra copyists was very welcome, for there was much to be done: 275 inscribed blocks, statues and stelae had been numbered for recording, and several basketsful of broken pieces of glazed ware, some with royal names, were being brought in every evening. Moreover Captain Weill was anxious to return to Paris; he left the following day, somewhat to Petrie's relief; he had not been a congenial member of the company; a certain arrogance had kept him aloof, and he had been detected deliberately smashing a small stela, in order to be able to boast that he had fitted the pieces together. In the evenings, when the talk turned inevitably to the Biblical narrative of the wanderings of the Children of Israel through Sinai, he had pooh-poohed the whole story, whereas Petrie pondered the problem of the enormous numbers of Israelites said to have been involved in the journey, and reluctant to reject the tradition, sought an explanation: it was impossible that 600,000 people (the figure arrived at by adding the numbers in each tribe according to the census lists in the Book of Numbers) could have been marched by Moses through Sinai—the girl at the well, familiar from a remembered nursery picture, would have to have waited years for her next pitcherful! When he returned to England he consulted Hebrew scholars, and came up with the suggestion that the word *aleph*, "thousand", might have been confused with a word meaning tent, so that with a normal average of people to a family tent, there might have been about six thousand tribespeople in the migration—a reasonable number. This theory he published later, in a small book which came out only after his father was dead:[41] the old man had an unshakeable belief in the Old Testament narrative as he had learnt it in his childhood, and would have been deeply grieved at his son's attempt to modify it in the cause of historical probability.

On 7 February Currelly left the camp with a few men, to explore the rubbish heaps of St Catherine's Monastery in search of discarded manuscripts. It was a bitterly cold ride, and on a high pass it snowed a little, to the astonishment of the 'Ababda, who had never before seen a snowflake: they called it "rice from heaven". The middens outside the monastery walls were sodden with recent rains and it was soon evident that no perishable documents could have survived centuries of saturation.[42] On his way back, Currelly investigated one or two of the strange circular structures known in Sinai as *nawâmîs*, mosquito-houses—Beduin legend attributed their building to the Children of Israel, as a protection against a plague of those insects. Currelly supposed them to be tombs, but he found neither bodies nor grave goods, and not one sherd of pottery inside or out; though more have been examined since, their purpose and date are still an enigma.[43] He then returned to Tor, and went back to Egypt to excavate for the Egyptian Research Account in Naville's old site at Tell el Maskhuta; Petrie remained in Serabit until the middle of March, hard at work. On the basis of the squeezes and copies he sent home from Cairo (by post, for safety) in fourteen great rolls, he hoped to publish a large volume to be entitled *The Egyptians in Sinai*. He had made a complete plan of the temple; unlike a normal Egyptian temple, it had a series of courts in which stood great pillar-like stelae somewhat like the *maṣṣebôth* of a Canaanite place of worship (**58**): it was, as Petrie maintained, a temple of Semitic rather than Egyptian type.

Without doubt his most important discovery at Serabit was that of a new and unknown script: alongside the inscriptions in hieroglyphics left by Egyptian officials who had visited the area with the mining expeditions, others—he supposed them to be natives of Sinai—had left their own records in crudely cut letters on small, roughly-shaped stone figures or in the shafts of the turquoise mines. The script appeared to be alphabetic since only about thirty signs were employed (the Egyptian hieroglyphic system has some seven hundred). One or two of the signs resemble hieroglyphs, most are simple linear shapes. The script became known as Proto-Sinaitic; many attempts have since then been made to translate these short texts usually on the basis that they are early attempts to write a "proto-Canaanite" (i.e. Semitic) language. Petrie's dating of them to the early eighteenth dynasty —once thought too late—is nowadays generally accepted.[44] The most precious find of artistic quality was a little head of Queen Tiy, the wife of Amenophis III, in the realistic Amarna style. Petrie judged it to be "one of the most striking portraits ever carved by an Egyptian" (**53**).

The small stelae and statues, which he had decided to take back with him to Cairo, had each to be lowered by ropes down the cliff, for there was no path by which camels could reach the temple; the large stelae and the bigger blocks he left in position. When Jaroslav Černý worked at the site in 1935, many had disappeared or been broken up, and he regarded the monuments as doomed to destruction,[45] but between 1968 and 1971, the Israeli Department of Antiquities cleared the temple once more and gave some protection to the surviving stones.[46]

The party arrived at Suez with their numerous boxes and drawings on 23 March 1905; on his way to Cairo, Petrie went with Button to visit Currelly's excavation. He had almost finished; Naville had been wrong in both the date and the purpose of his "Store Chambers" and the bricks which were said to have been made without straw showed every sign that there had been organic matter in them. At the Museum, Maspero was much impressed with Petrie's harvest of inscribed stones. It was agreed that the Museum should bear the cost of transporting to Cairo the slabs which Currelly was to cut from the rock; he accomplished this difficult task in May, in great heat and with unskilled labour (though he nearly lost his precious cargo when a sudden storm blew up in the Red Sea).

Meanwhile Flinders set off with Hilda for Athens, to attend the First International Congress of Archaeology, and take her to Corinth, Mycenae and Tiryns; by the end of April he was back in Hampstead. The Committee of the Egypt Exploration Fund met on 2 May to receive his report. That winter, for the first time, they had had to borrow a considerable sum from the bank to tide them over till the new subscriptions came in; Deir al Bahari was still costing too much, but they were committed to Naville and the continuation of his work there. They proposed to Petrie that their present agreement with him should be terminated, and a new one formulated in the light of the current situation; the matter was referred to a sub-committee for negotiation. Alarmed by the cost of publishing the large amount of material he had brought back, they agreed to bring out a book of large format containing all the copies of inscriptions, but would not consider a second volume for the archaeological material. He therefore determined to publish this independently, at his own expense. The sub-committee met a few days later, their suggestion that Petrie should suspend excavation for a while and try to raise money in Egypt for the Fund he rejected outright; "by mutual consent" his employment was at an end. Henceforward he would have to rely solely on the Research Account for all his work in Egypt. He must have felt somewhat bitter when he read, in February 1904, of a sale by auction of Amélineau's loot from Abydos; the Louvre had obtained several items, including the stela of King Djet (Wadji), which had realized 94,000 francs, "the highest amount ever paid by the Louvre for a single hieroglyphic document."[47]

In preferring Naville to Petrie, the Fund were probably wise —Flinders Petrie was too much of an individualist to submit readily to the rule of a committee; but it cannot be denied that by choosing an archaeologist of the old school, they lost their greatest asset. Nevertheless, the young men whom they continued to send out with

Naville, and a number of those who were to excavate for the Fund in years to come, or to contribute their counsels to its Committee, owed their archaeological training to Petrie, and their successors accept today as a matter of course many of the principles which he had striven so persistently to establish.

Village houses

CHAPTER XIII

The British School

(1906–11)

FLINDERS PETRIE NOW took a step which he had been contemplating for some time past. At a lecture given at University College he announced the separation of his work from that of the Egypt Exploration Fund and the formation of a British School of Archaeology in Egypt. This new organization would depend, he said, on the Egyptian Research Account, which would now have to be much larger in order to support all his own work in Egypt as well as those of his students. He sounded a number of his friends in the E.E.F., to see whether they would join his new committee; some were reluctant, but Sayce and Ernest Gardner were willing to serve, and Hilton Price, the Director of the Society of Antiquaries, who was a Vice-President of the Fund, agreed to continue as Treasurer of the E.R.A. Petrie then wrote to a number of influential people including his old patrons, Jesse Haworth and Walter Morrison. He soon had an impressive list of forty-four committee members; Dr Walker and Mrs Petrie were to be the Secretaries of the new organization and Petrie himself the Director. The official announcement appeared in the daily newspapers in June, before the exhibition opened: Professor Petrie's excavations would henceforward be supported entirely by the Research Account, to which contributions were invited from "all those who care for the past glory of Egypt"; it was estimated that £1,000–£1,500 would be needed annually. The School would have its base in University College London; there would be no need for a central building in Egypt, like those of the British Schools in Athens and Rome—the site for excavation would be the students' centre. Subscribers would receive the annual excavation volume, and all antiquities found would, as hitherto, be placed in public museums.[1]

A few days after this, Sir John Evans and Herbert Grueber wrote to *The Times* complaining that in his announcement, Petrie had not once mentioned the Egypt Exploration Fund; they assured past subscribers that the Fund still needed their support.[2] It was clear that the separation of the two excavating bodies would not be effected without misunderstandings and a good deal of bad feeling. Petrie and his helpers wrote to those who had hitherto supported his work, describing his plans for the next season and asking for donations for the new School; some of the Fund's regular subscribers thereupon wrote to tell the E.E.F. that they could not pay twice, and would now prefer to spend their money on Petrie's work; to these Miss Paterson replied that in fact they still owed the Fund their subscription for the year 1904–5. When he heard of this, Petrie wrote to her protesting that the E.E.F. were appropriating money intended for his work: to claim money owed for work already done was, he said, "a rotten system of accounts", and he held himself free to appeal to any and all of the Fund's subscribers to continue to support his excavations. An acrimonious correspondence ensued.[3] On 21 July the first meeting of the School was held and regulations were drawn up; *The Times* reported that they planned to excavate in the winter on the eastern side of the Delta, where it was hoped that traces of the Hyksos and the Israelites might be found. The Old Testament bait was being dangled once more. As Winslow had once observed, there were many Americans who would contribute to a Biblical excavation, but not to that of a heathen temple.[4]

The exhibition at University College attracted unusual interest; Petrie had made a model of the temple at Serabit al Khadem (**59**) and for the first time, showed lantern slides of some of his finds and some general views of the sites. Naville refused to exhibit at the College, where he would be, as he said "under Petrie's protection";[5] henceforward he was to hold his annual exhibitions in King's College London, of which he was an Honorary Fellow. A scathing anonymous review, which one suspects may have been from his pen, denied that the restoration of the "Semitic temple" was correct, or indeed, that it was a Semitic temple at all; Petrie's claims to that effect might however be excused, said the reviewer "in view of the extreme paucity of results from his late unlucky expedition to Sinai".[6]

That summer Flinders and Hilda had no time for a holiday together: she was busy writing hundreds of letters to the prominent and wealthy, seeking support for the work of the School, and he, as soon as the exhibition was packed up, set off on a gruelling round of visits; in five weeks, between late September and early November, he lectured in seventeen different cities in England and Wales; henceforward, the annual round of fund-raising would take him to most of the big cities in the United Kingdom. In each place he reckoned to gain new subscribers; by 1908 a number of Honorary Secretaries, in England and abroad, were making themselves responsible for rounding up local support and publicizing the work of the School. It was hard work, but effective: in, 1905, the first year of the School's existence, subscriptions and donations totalled £1,150; by 1913, four times that amount.

In thus seeking support by their personal efforts, the Petries cannot be said to have been diverting very much from the coffers of the Egypt Exploration Fund. Since Poole's illness and Miss Edwards' death, no member of that organization—with occasional exceptions—had had the time or the energy to go round the country campaigning for new subscribers. America, however, was a different matter. In seeking help for his work from the United States, Petrie was in a real difficulty. Winslow had always stressed the indebtedness of the Fund to Petrie's brilliant work, and in his articles in *Biblia*, he had never associated Petrie with the misdemeanours of the London Committee. Many Americans were now dismayed to hear that he had left the Fund. This was Winslow's opportunity: he declared himself the agent of the Egyptian Research Account in America, through whom those who wished to support the Professor's work could send their contributions: and he put it about that Petrie had resigned from the Fund in disgust with the past behaviour of the Committee towards himself.[7] When this came to Petrie's notice he consulted his supporters at once and Ernest Gardner was asked to inform the E.E.F. that Dr Winslow was "in no way authorized to act as their agent in America or given any official recognition". Nevertheless, considerable sums of money arrived "*per* Dr Winslow", and eventually, when after the First World War an American Branch of the School was formed, he was given the official designations of Honorary Treasurer and Honorary Vice-President. Petrie never made the mistake, however, of allowing the title to be anything other than soothing to his vanity.

In December 1905 the Committee of the E.E.F. reconsidered their promise to publish the Sinai inscriptions: it would have after all to be a *quarto* volume; it must stand over for the present in favour of Naville's latest volume on Deir el Bahari. Petrie washed his hands of the affair; his rolls of drawings were put on one side, and many years later, published by others.[8] *Researches in Sinai* came out in June of the following year, without the Fund's imprimatur; it is one of his most important books.

On 10 November, just before his departure for Egypt, Flinders

Petrie lectured to the Fund for the last time, on his work in Sinai. At a subsequent meeting of the Fund's Committee it was agreed that in printing the Annual Report, "the omission of passages from Professor Petrie's address should be left to the discretion of the Secretary."

The British School of Archaeology in Egypt held its first Annual general meeting at the end of October. An executive committee was formed, and Petrie's cousin Sir Robert Hensley, a distinguished engineer and civil servant, was elected Chairman. A new set of regulations was approved: the executive would meet regularly, the whole committee at least annually; if the Directorship were to fall vacant, it was to pass to the next Edwards Professor provided "that he conduct excavation or teaching in Egypt". All routine business was to be dealt with by the Director; but questions of importance were to be submitted by him for consideration by the executive. In other words, the Director was to run the school with very few restraints on his actions; as one of his students was to put it, some years later, it was the ideal committee: "Petrie only consults it when there is something he doesn't want to do."

Neither of the two students selected this year[9] had had any experience in the field, and Petrie was relieved when his friend Garrow Duncan, who had been with him at Naqada, decided to come out and help once more. To Petrie's regret, Currelly had decided to accept the offer of the Fund to be Naville's archaeological assistant at Deir el Bahari. He was reluctant to leave Petrie, who had shown him much kindness, taken him to stay in his house on more than one occasion, and introduced him to Holman Hunt and other of his Pre-Raphaelite friends; through Petrie, too, he got to know a man he had long wanted to meet: Prince Peter Kropotkin, the gentle anarchist who since 1901 had been a friend and next-door neighbour of William Petrie's in Bromley. The experience he had gained working with Flinders Petrie was to stand Currelly in good stead for the rest of his life; in Egypt he was buying antiquities for the museum of the University of Toronto, and one of the most valuable things Petrie taught him was the importance of packing delicate objects so that they travelled safely—an art requiring not only care, but considerable expertise: when he was in charge of packing the Abydos treasures, Petrie got in a professional packer from Shoolbred's the department store in Tottenham Court Road to instruct him.

Currelly had also benefited from the Professor's long experience in the detection of forgeries. Petrie had an extraordinary instinct for something that was not genuine; his knowledge of ancient techniques and craftsmanship enabled him to detect the work of the modern forger and he could often put a name to the man who had made an object, though he was seldom dogmatic: "I wouldn't like to buy it," he would say.[10] On one occasion however, he was near to staking his reputation on the genuineness of a notable piece which was proved to be a fake by scholars with better linguistic knowledge. This was a large scarab which was offered for sale by the son of the Egyptologist Urbain Bouriant after his death and purporting to come from his collection; the object was remarkable not only for its large size, but because the inscription purported to record the owner's participation in the Phoenician circumnavigation of Africa in the reign of Necho at the end of the seventh century BC, as related by Herodotus.[11] The scarab, and a duplicate of it, were bought by Jean Capart for 20,000 francs, for his museum in Brussels, and he laid the inscription before a congress of Orientalists in Paris under Naville's presidency. Petrie, to whom Capart sent squeezes of the text, declared his conviction that the scarabs were genuine, in spite of not having seen them himself, and jubilant at so dramatic a vindication of Herodotus, prepared a paper in which he commented on details given in the text as translated by Capart; the probable dates of sailing and arrival, the mention of two harvests, and so forth. Meanwhile, however, the authenticity of the scarabs had been challenged in Germany; Schäfer and Erman were able to demonstrate that the text was a clumsy compilation of passages from seven different sources, and where a link passage had been needed, it was full of grammatical mistakes—the forger, in fact, had only superficial knowledge of the language. Petrie heard this verdict in time to alter the text of his article in proof, though he was still reluctant to believe that the philologists were right. Capart, convinced at last, sued the young man for the money he had paid; the matter was settled when a sculptor came forward in court and declared that he had carved and engraved two large scarabs for M. Bouriant a year or so previously.[12] Bouriant went to prison, and the editor of *The Geographical Journal* added a footnote to Petrie's article to the effect that the inscription had now been thoroughly discredited.

The Petries travelled out to Egypt in mid-November; after a few days in Cairo, they took the train to Shibin in the Delta and walked two miles to their destination, a big sandy mound known as Tell el Yehudiya, The Mound of the Jew. Once again Petrie was to excavate a site already dug by Naville: in 1887, with the help of Frank Griffith, the Swiss scholar had explored a number of ruins at this place.[13] One large *tell* covered the ruins of a town with fortifications; a smaller mound, the temple and town tentatively identified with Leontopolis, which as Josephus relates, the exiled Jewish priest Onias was permitted by Ptolemy Philometor to build. Outside the enclosure they had found a Graeco-Jewish cemetery. On the main mound little had been done; a few monuments of the Ramesside period had previously been uncovered here, and Griffith considered the rampart not earlier than the New Kingdom.

It proved an uncomfortable site: they had tents, but only one hut, and the nights were cold and damp; at first they were plagued by mosquitoes and sleep was almost impossible. As winter drew on they built more huts and the mosquitoes left, but the wind howled through the camp. Part of the site was occupied by the brown tents of a Beduin encampment; they looked wild enough, though they were gentle folk compared with the fierce Arabs of Sinai. Their custom of driving their flocks of goats and sheep over the excavation site every evening introduced a new element of anxiety into life on a dig. The *sebbakhîn* had been hard at work plundering the mounds; Petrie felt that he was only just in time to rescue what remained. His excavation of the City of Onias confirmed the identity of this "New Jerusalem"; he planned the temple and the town fortifications noting that the proportions of the former were copied from that of the Temple in Jerusalem.[14] The camp on the main mound he ascribed to the period of the Hyksos invaders of Egypt, on the evidence of scarabs with royal names which he found in graves within the perimeter of the rampart. It was the first time that a site had been dated on the evidence of scarabs alone.[15] With them in these tombs were small black juglets with pricked lines of decoration, and bronze daggers of distinctive shape, and one or two "toggle-pins" used—but not in Egypt—to fasten a cloak or wrap. Tracing a white line in the soil, he found that the sloping outer side of the earthwork had been faced with plaster to form a defensive glacis. All these features he was to encounter once more twenty years later in Palestine, and he took them to be characteristic of the Hyksos, or Shepherd Kings; he was inclined to think that he had found Avaris, the main Hyksos city in the Delta and their last stronghold in Egypt before they were driven out. Avaris is now known to have been further north, near Qantir[16]—but Petrie's discoveries were of great importance at that time, and Tell el Yahudiya became the type-site for this little-known period of Egyptian history.

After about eight weeks the camp was moved further north to the Wadi Tumilât. Naville, at Tell el Maskhuta, had claimed to find Pithom; and Tell el Retaba, half way along the narrow strip of cultivation, where they set up camp in January, Petrie tentatively identified with Raamses, the second of the two "store cities" built by the Israelites before their escape from bondage. In 1885, on a brief visit, Naville had found earlier remains here but had expressed his belief that the mound was Late Roman in date;[17] Petrie's excavations uncovered one or two fine Ramesside blocks, and stone vases of Old Kingdom date in the lower levels showed that the site had had a long period of occupation; it was, he decided, the oldest site known east of Bubastis.

Tell el Retâba was a much pleasanter spot to live in than their previous wet, cold camp at Yehudiya: the desert air was pure and dry, and the Sweet Water canal, fringed with flowering plants and rushes, pleasant to bathe in when work was done. They built huts up against the old wall of the town, using ancient bricks. Local labour was scarce, but they had a number of Quftis; Yusuf and the few others who had been in Sinai with the "Pasha", enjoyed a certain prestige now among their fellows.

A brief entry in Petrie's diary, "squeezing Darius", refers to a great stela weighing several tons and broken into several pieces, which had been found by Currelly the previous year. It commemorated the re-excavation by Darius King of Persia of the old canal linking the Nile with the Red Sea, and it lay in the desert south of Tell el Maskhuta. Later he effected its transport to Cairo, "and now it is invisible in that dim place" was his subsequent comment. He had no use for the new Cairo Museum, completed two years before (**88**); it was, he decided,

> . . . the worst building I ever saw made for such a purpose. Half of it is too dark to be used at all, and much of it is scorched with sun through enormous skylights. The scale of it is far too large, and dwarfs the largest statues, making them look like dolls. And the style is incongruous: great circles and ellipses. Nearly half the site is wasted in spaces left to display the abominable architecture; and if ever there was a case this is one for Ray Lankester's dictum "Begin by hanging the eminent architect."[18]

He was strongly of the opinion that it should never have been built in Cairo at all: both Cairo and Alexandria were far too damp. Luxor, in his view, would have been a far better place in which to conserve delicate relics.

Other sites were being dug by members of his team, under his occasional supervision. Duncan excavated a cemetery of many periods at Saft el Hinna, which Naville had identified with the Biblical Goshen since it commanded the western end of the Wady Tumilat. On the desert edge, at Ghita, he found ruins of a town once under Roman occupation, and a cemetery. On two rough tombstones here were inscriptions in a script unknown to the scholarly Duncan, who suggested that they might be archaic Greek. Petrie, seldom at a loss, guessed them to be Libyan and suggested Tifinan,[19] but they are now identified as Thamudic; the burials were probably those of South Arabian mercenaries serving with the Roman garrison.[20]

On their homeward journey the Petries parted company at Naples, she to tour in Italy, he to Genoa; he had introductions to English residents in several Riviera towns, and in San Remo, Bordighera, Mentone and Nice he gave lectures to audiences of a hundred or more; a collection was taken for the work of the British School at the end of each talk. He was urged to do the same the following year, and kept his promise, stopping also to speak in Marseilles; thereafter, he was generally in too much of a hurry to make this detour. For the summer exhibition he had models made of the mound of Onias and of the Hyksos fortification at Tell el Yehudiya, and gave no less than fifty lectures during the course of July. During September and October, he read Mommsen and Gibbon, and Thomas Hodgkin the historian of the Dark Ages, in preparation for the Huxley Lecture of the Anthropological Institute; his subject was "Migrations" and to illustrate his thesis he prepared a series of charts on lantern slides to illustrate the movement of races from Augustus to Charlemagne. This ambitious excursion from his own field followed an introductory outline of changes of population in Egypt over ten thousand years of history, as he interpreted the evidence of variations in skull measurement. He concluded his talk with the generalization that people become adapted to their environment in about 1,000 years. Migrations are a means of supplanting the less capable by the more capable; "the only way to save a country from immigration is to increase the capabilities of its inhabitants by thorough weeding, so that other races cannot get a footing by competition or by force. The ideals of the present time —equality of wages, maintenance of the incapable by the capable, equal opportunities of life for children of bad stock as well as good stock, and exclusion of more economical labour, are the surest means of national extinction."[21]

These ideas were much influenced by the views of his friend Francis Galton on the "gifted class"—the transmission of intelligence and ability by inheritance, and were developed further by Petrie in a longer excursion into sociology which he published as a short book entitled *Janus in Modern Life*, in the following year. The prevalent inefficiency, waste and muddle, he claimed, are a result of the introduction of undesirable elements into the population. The vacuity of the public mind is shown in the morbid horrors and absence of uplifting thought in our newspapers. The trend is towards conformity; Communism tends to drag everyone down to mediocrity. Watching sport is a degrading and futile occupation, betting an unwholesome craving for excitement and greed of gain; instead of encouraging curiosity, modern education destroys initiative and forces every individual into a mould. In his blueprint for the future, work would be made enjoyable, not shunned; amusements would be solely the resort of those incapable of work. He advocated limitation of the birthrate by the State, by encouraging the "best stocks" to breed by means of grants and privileges and penalizing the "lower class of the unfits" with compulsory work; their women would be encouraged to seek voluntary sterilization. The higher the social organization and reward of ability, the more intense will be the weeding of the less capable, and the more highly sustained will be the general level of ability.

Petrie's views, which today seem shockingly élitist, attracted little notice in the Press. A few reviews were condemnatory: *The Academy* accused him of superficial and contradictory judgements: "Janus, indeed, is a clever double-headed professor, who treats rather amateurishly—that is to say, confidently and assertively—many subjects as to which we suspect that his knowledge is not very profound."[22]

Four years later another small book, based on a lecture he gave to the Royal Institution, appeared in print under the title *The Revolutions of Civilization*; in it he made a remarkable and very characteristic attempt to encompass, in relatively few pages, the wide sweep of human progress and the rise and fall of Mediterranean civilization in its successive phases, beginning with earliest Egypt. Civilization, he argued, is a recurrent phenomenon and can be charted by studying one or other of its aspects, notably sculpture. He divided man's progress into periods of approximately equal length, tracing the growth, glory and decay of each, and linking Egypt with Crete, Greece and Rome and mediaeval Europe. Forms of government, he argued, were of little import compared with "the great formative interests of men's minds"; every new phase of civilization goes through a political development from despotism to oligarchy, then to democracy, and "when democracy has attained full power the majority without capital necessarily eat up the capital of the minority and the civilization steadily decays, until the inferior population is swept away to make room for a later people." The period of greatest ability in a new civilization, he argued, is reached in about eight centuries after an admixture of races caused by immigration or invasion. Once more he came back to his Utopia: in some future civilization, eugenics may "carefully segregate fine races and prohibit continued mixture, until they have a distinct type which will start a new civilization when transplanted. The future progress of man may depend as much on isolation to establish a type, as on fusion of types when established."[23] The little book had its admirers; Bernard Shaw quoted it with approval in a speech,[24] and one American academic wrote to the author: "I have more than once said that I would rather have written it than any book published in the twentieth century,"[25] but it attracted scant attention in academic circles; reviewers in literary journals found it worth study but were in general doubtful of its conclusions. His argument was partially invalidated by his distorted view of early chronology. (See p. 313 ff.)

During the autumn of 1906, Flinders' letters to Hilda when she was away show solicitude for her health; before he left without her for Egypt he wrote to his father:

> You will be surprised to hear that Hilda is not going out with me. But it is certain now that she expects to make you a Grandfather next May.
>
> I should tell you that when we married nine years ago she had a terror of such a result, so much so that the subject was dropped altogether. It was a genuine instinct, which wore away as she became stronger in mind and body, owing to the greater tranquillity of life. The last year or two she has been much better every way, and lost her old dread of maternity. She is now in the best health that she has ever had, and looks forward with happiness to the result. She will stay with different friends for the next few months, which will be cheerful for her, as we have let the house to an old friend till March . . . she is more cheerful in mind, and free from worrying about cares than I have ever known her.[26]

She has a lady doctor, he says, who has prescribed a vegetarian diet and fish; this he is sure his father will approve. Meanwhile four young men are going out with him, "most of whom are solid and promising".

One of the young men was from Edinburgh; having gone up to receive an honorary degree from the University of Aberdeen, Flinders had gone on to Edinburgh and in the Royal Scottish Museum he had met Edwin Ward, who had declared his eagerness for experience of excavation in Egypt. Another recruit was a young graduate of Bristol University named Ernest Mackay; like others of Petrie's recruits, he first came to the Professor's attention when he volunteered to help at the summer exhibition; he was to make a lifelong career in archaeology, and for some years to come would be Petrie's right hand in the field.

Missing his wife already, but in joyful anticipation of parenthood, he wrote to Hilda on the way out from Naples:

> Dear, dear heart, I could not bear to go over our old ground, of all the sweet times we have had in Italy, if I did not know that you were well and happy in your great duty of life, making our two lives literally one for ever, with consequences in the future which no one can foresee. Your work may still be effective in ages to come, when all that I have done is forgotten.[27]

Petrie's choice of sites for his excavations was guided not by the expectation of sensational finds—though these were welcome when they came—but by the need to solve the next problem, to answer the next question. This year he had asked for Giza. Here he hoped to find some remains earlier than the pyramids; though the kings of the Archaic Period had been buried at Abydos, their capital, according to tradition, had been Memphis, and traces of their presence there must surely be found in the great necropolis area; since he was debarred from Saqqara, Giza was his choice. He was offered only a small concession, for most of the area was already being worked: in 1902 three applications for Giza had been made simultaneously to Maspero, by the American Reisner, the Italian Schiaparelli and the German Ludwig Borchardt; at Maspero's suggestion they had met at Mena House and had agreed to share out the area between them; all that was left was a small area to the south, including the ledge of rock facing east above the Arab cemetery, and the desert below it. Quftis were set to work, the Firths came for a week or two, and Petrie with his small team systematically cleared the area; tombs of the second dynasty showed that Giza had been a burial ground before the pyramid period. Then an important find was made in the low ground: a *mastaba* partially excavated by Daressy, one of Maspero's assistants,[28] proved to have been large and important; as in the Royal Tombs at Abydos, the superstructure had been panelled in brick and the burial chamber lined with wood, and surrounded by subsidiary burials. Jar sealings of King Djet (or Wadji) were found and the style of the stonecutting and the form of the funerary vessels were as he had found in Djet's tomb at Umm el Qa'ab; one fine piece was so like a bowl from that tomb that Petrie considered that the same craftsman had made them both.[29] It confirmed his belief that civilization in this early period had been uniform over all Egypt—or at least from Abydos to Memphis, and that there was no local superiority or marked regional difference between the two centres. A late cemetery produced some 1,400 skulls to delight Karl Pearson at University College.

After five weeks Petrie considered his Giza site "worked out", and decided to move south. Before he went he attended Cromer's farewell party; Petrie was sorry to see him go—he had got on well with him in recent years and could usually count on his support; his successor Sir Eldon Gorst was an unknown factor in future plans.

The village of Rifa is about six miles south of Assiut. Behind it in the cliffs are several very large tombs; Petrie made the important observation that they must originally have been quarries for the stone with which the local governors or nomarchs had built their palaces by the Nile—buildings which have vanished, but would have been of imposing size; the cavernous halls excavated in the cliff were then decorated and turned into tombs for these noblemen. From the largest tomb, he reckoned that between four and five thousand tons of stone had been taken. The greatest prize of the season was the untouched burial of two brothers, sons of a nomarch; their painted coffins were admirably preserved and with them were statuettes, and models for their use, including little boats, one rigged for sailing upstream, the other for rowing down the Nile. Maspero permitted the whole find to leave Egypt, and Petrie presented it to the Manchester Museum where it has pride of place in the collection—even the British Museum has no comparable tomb group (**93**).[30]

In the graves of the poorer folk in the plain below, a large number of pottery models known as "soul houses" were found. These, originally simple pottery trays of model offerings placed on the tomb, were elaborated in the Middle Kingdom into crude replicas of the dead man's house; some had a courtyard with a portico, some, stairs to the roof, others furniture. In his careful analysis of the domestic features shown in these models, Petrie could say: "We now have a far clearer view of the arrangements and details of the ordinary Egyptian houses than has hitherto been obtained from any of the actual remains, and we see how closely they resemble in most respects the dwellings of the present time in that land."[31]

Meanwhile Mackay and the two volunteers, Ivo Gregg and Arthur Rhoades, excavated other tombs and explored the site of a Coptic monastery of the eighth century at Deir al Bala'iza, finding some inscriptions and a harvest of manuscript leaves.

On 26 April 1907, not long after Flinders' return from Egypt, Hilda gave birth to a son; they named him John Flinders. Their joy was tempered with anxiety: Hilda's father lay seriously ill, and he died six weeks later. After the funeral Mrs Urlin went down to Rustington, the family affairs were wound up and the house at Stafford Terrace sold. William Petrie came up to London with Celia to see his grandson (**65**), but he, too, was failing and he died, at the age of eighty-seven, in the following March while Petrie was in Egypt. When he heard the news he wrote to Hilda:

> I grieve to think I cannot take John to see him again: but it is a sweet memory that I have of *both* the grandfathers seeing John the last time I saw each. We have just knit the generations together. It is a great blessing that my father kept his mind and body so fit to the last. . . . The next generation will mean all the more to us now that the last is vanishing. Are you not thankful now for John above all things? Do tell me, tell me, all you can about his ways. I long, more than I can say, to see and watch him.[32]

Sir Robert Hensley undertook all the necessary arrangements and Hilda was able to go down for William's funeral; the old man was buried in the cemetery of the church at Plaistow, not far from the house where he had lived for thirty-seven years; Celia moved back to her family in North London, and a last link with the past was broken. Before the house in Crescent Road was finally sold in the summer of 1908, Flinders went down there to take charge of all his mother's papers, the family silver and the Flinders relics.

Although Hilda was unable to go out to Egypt for the second year running, she had been busily occupied with proof-reading, seeing *Gizeh and Rifeh* through the press, and dealing with the School's affairs: her friends Mrs Hope Pinker and Miss Caroline Herford were particularly active in organizing lectures; an organization called E.R.S.A. (the Egyptian Research Students Association) had been started by a learned and energetic enthusiast, Mrs Sefton Jones, who organized lectures and meetings in London and in provincial centres, to increase popular interest and publicize the work of the School.[33] Hilda spent part of the winter at Paignton with John and his nurse and Miss Herford. Flinders urged her to keep him down there till spring, when they were to go to Rustington; mindful of his own sickly childhood, he dreaded the fogs and damp of a London winter for his son.

His main objective that winter was an ambitious one; he had decided to dig at Mit Rahina, the ruined, once-great city of Memphis. The site lay among groves of palm trees and was water-logged for part of the year; when he came to inspect it in November, with Edwin Ward and a young German architect named Schuler, whom von Bissing had sent to Petrie to learn excavation method, it was still partly under water, but they found a dry and shaded mound for their house; the place appeared to be infested with rats and Petrie decided they would have to keep a mongoose.

The first part of the winter would be spent in work near Sohag in Middle Egypt. Mackay had gone ahead to make preparations and as soon as the others arrived, work was started: Gregg and Ward excavated a large ruin near the White Monastery which Flinders and Hilda had noticed on their tenting trip in 1901; it proved to be a settlement of the period of Constantine, of great interest to students of early Christianity. Flinders and Mackay uncovered what was left of a large temple of the Ptolemaic period dedicated to the lion-headed goddess of Athribis, Repyt.[34] It had been as large as Dendara, but only the lower part of the walls remained. Schuler spent much time copying the remarkable painted zodiac on the ceiling of a tomb nearby; then he went off to start building at Mit Rahina. One or two other helpers came and went during December: one was dismissed as "hopeless"; another as "utterly useless"; one who stayed was Gerald Wainwright, a friend of Ernest Mackay whom he had met when they were both attending evening classes in Egyptian and Coptic. Egyptology had fascinated him since he was a schoolboy at Clifton College; he had already been to Egypt once, and Petrie, who met him in Bristol the previous year, had invited him out as his assistant; he was to become another of his most competent and reliable excavators. Just before they moved to Mit Rahina, Petrie heard news of the death of his old friend, Mrs Amos; she had been staying with her son Maurice, who was now practising as a lawyer in Cairo and had recently married the daughter of Sir Colin Scott-Moncrieff.

On their arrival at Mit Rahina, the main party found that in spite of

Herr Schuler's training as an architect he had only managed to complete three rooms of their house and these were sopping wet; they camped in tents for the next week or so while the house (which was to be of the more permanent kind, to accommodate them for several years) was finished, and doors and furniture made. The excavation of Memphis was to occupy them during the second half of every season, from January, when the inundation had subsided, to March or April, for the next six years and was only brought to an end by the outbreak of war. The site is a huge one. Greek authors estimated its circumference as 150 *stadia*; this Petrie calculated as about four miles wide and eight miles long, including suburbs, villas and gardens—"the size of London from Bow to Chelsea, and from the Thames to Hampstead". To embark on its excavation was a formidable and costly undertaking; a large labour force would be required, pumps would be needed (for the subsoil water in parts of the site lay very near the surface) and leases would have to be obtained from private landowners. Yet there was an element of urgency about the work: more and more of the area was being built over or put under cultivation, and both Maspero and Sir William Garstin were urging him to excavate; truth to tell, Petrie was excited by the potentialities of this greatest of all city sites: somewhere, the White Walls—the fortress-palace of the first kings of united Egypt—might yet be discovered; reused blocks of Old Kingdom date and a few Middle Kingdom inscriptions, found in the first season, encouraged this hope.

The initial task was to survey the whole area, and attempt to trace the boundaries of the city; Petrie established the limits of the great temple of Ptah, the god of craftsmen and patron deity of Memphis, next to the village of Mit Rahina among the palm trees; found what he believed to be the "Tyrian camp" described by Herodotus, by the presence of a number of terracotta heads depicting foreigners—Persians, Babylonians, Scythians, Greeks and even Indians (**69**); nothing similar had ever been found in Egypt.[35] On a high mound he identified the citadel, and on it a palace of the sixth century BC.

It is remarkable that by the end of the first season, in spite of exceptionally cold winds, heavy rain and fog and quagmires of mud, he was able to publish a sketch map of the area which remains to this day the basis of all plans of ancient Memphis,[36] though other buildings have since been identified by excavators of several nationalities.*

Earlier excavators, including Lepsius and Mariette, had left little or

* A campaign to map the whole area of the ancient city is now being undertaken by the E.E.S. in celebration of their centenary.

no record. During the ensuing years, with Mackay and Wainwright as his chief helpers and a sprinkling of students who came and went, Petrie gradually filled in the details of his plan, and published them in six volumes. In the great palace of Apries, 400 feet long (**71**), huge capitals of columns were found, some of which must have been 50 feet high. "Little had anyone thought that so great a building remained on top of the grey mud hill which every tourist had passed who goes by the north road to Saqqara." Bronze scale armour and weapons suggested the presence of a military garrison here, and seal-impressions and Aramaic dockets showed that the citadel had been occupied by the army of the successors of Cambyses the Persian. Blocks of a gateway were found, sculptured with scenes of coronation rituals. Petrie thought them Middle Kingdom in date and was disappointed when Maspero refused to order their preservation *in situ*; they are usually nowadays ascribed to the sixth century BC—the time of Apries. Petrie's stylistic judgement was seldom at fault, but the finest Saite work imitates the style of earlier ages and so the mistake was pardonable.[37] Drums and capitals of columns in the temple of Ptah showed the vast size of this building also, and a number of impressive pieces of statuary were found, notably a sphinx carved from a single block of alabaster, twenty-six feet long and weighing over seventy tons (**89**). This impressive monument, found lying on its side in the mud, was righted and still crouches near the colossus of Ramesses II found in 1820, sights familiar to every tourist who passes through Memphis on the road to Saqqara.

Returning to England in May 1908, a little later than usual, Flinders found himself caught up in the duties of teaching, lecturing and conferences. Delighted with his little son—he had chafed during the winter at not being able to observe every change in the baby's mental and physical development—he grudged the time he had to spend in London, or lecturing in the provinces, while Hilda stayed in the country at Rustington. He visited the Harveys in July and was distressed to find Susan failing; her death in October came as no surprise. Late next month he returned to Egypt, this time to Thebes for the first half of the season. Hilda, torn between her child and her husband, decided to accompany him, leaving John with his nurse at Miss Herford's house at Great Missenden. They settled in an uninscribed tomb, at Qurna, building a living-hut below it for Wainwright, Mackay, and a young artist, Brian Hatton, a protégé of their friend, G. F. Watts, who spent his time sketching the surrounding landscape.[38] Flinders started to explore, as he had always wanted to do, the valley behind in search of undiscovered tombs, while Hilda began copying scenes in tombs hitherto unrecorded. Here they had many visitors from Luxor; Arthur Weigall and his wife in the Inspectorate were hospitable, Howard Carter and the Davieses were working nearby and just after Christmas the American artist Joe Lindon Smith found Petrie digging at the mouth of a valley "finding little or nothing, but retaining his enthusiasm".[39] Not long after he struck lucky, and found an undisturbed tomb of the seventeenth dynasty, the mummy decked with jewellery—gold necklaces and bracelets, earrings and girdle—together with tomb furniture, baskets and food; by the coffin were a dozen pots in the string matting in which they had been carried to the tomb;[40] Petrie was able to preserve even the network by hours of careful work, coating it with collodion. Maspero, who came over for the division, agreed that this was too fine a tomb-group to be split up and allowed it to go to Britain provided it was kept together; Petrie offered it to the South Kensington Museum,* but as they would not agree to exhibit the group together it was given to the Royal Scottish Museum in consideration of a generous donation to next year's work.

After seven weeks Hilda, discovering that she was again pregnant, left for England while Flinders spent a little longer excavating a chapel on a hilltop. Their daughter Ann was born the following August. One of the young men employed on the excavation later became well known as a dealer in Luxor, Sayid Molattam; when Ann Petrie visited Egypt for the first time in 1977, she called at his shop near the Luxor Hotel; the old man immediately recognized her likeness to her mother.

During the second season in Memphis, Petrie found he could entrust much of the work to his assistants, and was able to pay more frequent visits to Cairo, to lecture once or twice, and to attend the Second International Congress of Archaeology; he also called on the new British Resident, Sir Eldon Gorst, and discussed with him the problems and the possibilities of archaeological work in the Nile Valley. At Memphis he found himself embroiled in local rivalries between the *omdas* of two villages, one of whom resisted the government order that palm trees must be uprooted if they impeded the work; the Ma'mur (Deputy Governor) had to be called in to adjudicate; it was a foreseeable complication, but it bedevilled the work for several years.

* Now the Victoria and Albert Museum.

Choosing Meydum for his site during the first part of the winter of 1910, Petrie was again obeying a request from Maspero (now Sir Gaston—he had been made an Honorary K.C.M.G.): the third-dynasty tombs, badly plundered since he had copied them in 1890, were to be removed for safety to the Museum. Nothing loth, Petrie undertook to do so, and at the same time investigated further puzzling features in the structure of the pyramid which he had not previously been able to clarify. He tackled the great *mastaba* tomb (No. 17) whose entrance he had failed to find nineteen years before, and by cutting through the superstructure (fifty feet of hard chips) at length found the tomb chamber, which he described as the finest tomb, short of royalty, that he had ever seen (**37**).[41] The burial had been thoroughly plundered and only the body of the great prince, stripped of its ornaments, remained; in the sarcophagus each of his limbs had been separately wrapped in linen bandages. Dismantling the three large decorated tombs proved laborious and expensive but Petrie was rewarded by the grant of all the remaining slabs from the tomb of Atet;[42] blocks with coloured inlay were a notable and novel feature of the summer exhibition in London that year. It was not possible to reconstruct even one of the walls, so a sample of the decoration went to each of sixteen different museums in Europe and in America.

In his letters to Hilda[43], Flinders expressed his satisfaction with his team; the two "B.F.s" proved to be delightful company; the volunteer, Benton Fletcher, was a talented artist and a "thorough gentleman", and Jocelyn Bushe-Fox reliable and competent. At night they watched the passage of Halley's comet. In February Miss Murray sent him news that very much distressed him. A scandal had come to light in the Department of Egyptology: it involved a capable and intelligent young woman who had been helping her, and a married man, Walter Crum, a brilliant scholar of whom Petrie had high hopes. Their liaison had now become public knowledge and a subject of shocked gossip in the College. Flinders was appalled at what he considered to be a tragedy for all concerned; like Miss Murray, however, he took the conventional view of the time on such matters of morality, and he insisted that the culprit's name be removed at once from the list of members of the Committee of the British School; henceforward they would both be banned from using the Edwards Library and deprived of their keys to the Department. In the context of 1910, his reaction was understandable; yet this was no passing liaison: Crum's wife, a Roman Catholic, refused to divorce him, and for the rest of their lives, in the face of social ostracism, Walter and Margaret Crum devotedly laboured together on the *Coptic Dictionary* that was to be his life's work; his debt to her is obliquely but eloquently acknowledged in the preface to that great work of scholarship.

In February Petrie moved to Bedrashen, leaving Wainwright to carry on at Meydum. Long and tedious negotiations with the local *omdas* hindered the purchase of land, but work on the Palace of Apries continued and in March they made a start on the low-lying Ptah temple. "It is mud work all day for the men and boys. Each party digs a pit about 6 ft. deep below water level, bailing it out into our canal which we pump out. After enlarging the pit up to sunset it is left to fill with water, and a new pit dug beside it next day. Thus we work over from 4 to 8 sq. metres each day with a party, and we have 36 such parties (**67**)." They were short-handed: Benton Fletcher had gone back to Cairo to sell his pictures, and Mackay was ill. A volunteer who had behaved strangely at Meydum and was found to be taking drugs, had left them for Luxor and was now in an asylum in Cairo. Only Bushe-Fox saved the situation, though the climate did not agree with him. It was very hot, but Flinders, working stark naked in the storeroom, managed to keep cool.

Maspero now granted Petrie a large concession: for the next few years, he might work all the sites on both sides of the river from Dahshur to Ahnas, excepting only the pyramid field at Lisht which was being excavated by an American team from the Metropolitan Museum of Art. Petrie had his eye on a particularly promising cemetery at Hawara which had recently been much plundered; 'Ali Suefi and a government guard were to "sit on it" during the summer. On his way home Petrie stayed, as he often did, with Dr Ruffer and his wife at Alexandria, and gave his usual lecture in their drawing-room; it went exceptionally well: 120 tickets were sold, making him £20 the richer. "My three lectures, Rome, Cairo and Alex cover most of my expenses," he wrote on the way home.

In the series of essays entitled *Historical Studies* published in 1911, there are several contributions by Flinders Petrie on the subject of chronology, an important and much disputed topic on which his discoveries in Sinai had caused him to change his mind. Hitherto his dating of events in the earlier history of Egypt, as set forth in his own *History*, had been more or less in line with the current views of other Egyptologists. The basis for the calculation of Egyptian dates may be briefly explained. The Egyptians dated by the months and days of the regnal years of their kings. Thus, as we have no complete list of Egyptian kings and their years of reign (as we have for Assyria), it would not be possible to equate Egyptian dates with dates BC were it not for the existence of dated Egyptian records of astronomical events. The framework rests essentially on two facts: one is that the Egyptians had no Leap Year; they invented a calendar year which, though a remarkable achievement for its time, was approximately a quarter of a day shorter than the solar year, with the result that the calendar became increasingly out of step with the seasons through sliding back one day in every four years. The second fact is that according to Censorinus, in AD 139 the Egyptian New Year's Day coincided with a rising of Canicula (Sothis or Sirius, the Dog Star) just before dawn —an astronomical event which had been observed annually by the priests from early times. The number of solar years which elapsed between two occurrences of this (to them) notable event can be calculated as approximately 1,460 years[44]—sometimes called a "Sothic Cycle". When therefore the rising of Sothis is recorded on a particular day and month of a particular year of an Egyptian king, the year BC of this event may be calculated with only a small possible error, providing that it is certain in which "Sothic Cycle", reckoned backwards from AD 137, that king reigned.

One or two records of the calendrical date of a rising of Sothis on papyri of Pharaonic date enabled historians like Borchardt in Germany to give an absolute date of 1546 BC, within a year or so, for the ninth year of King Amenophis I in the eighteenth dynasty, and a Sothic date in the seventh year of King Sesostris III on one of the papyri from Kahun fixed the chronology of the well-documented twelfth dynasty —the end of that dynasty could be put at 1786 BC and the interval between that date and the beginning of the eighteenth dynasty would have been 206 years. Or was it 1,666 years—a whole Sothic Cycle earlier? The number of kings recorded for this "Second Intermediate Period" by the fragmentary Turin King List and by the Ptolemaic historian Manetho, and the multiplicity of royal names on monuments of the period, amount to far more than, in Petrie's view, could be accommodated in only 206 years.[45]

Alternative explanations assumed that the dynasties overlapped and were local and ephemeral, or rejected the evidence of Manetho and the Turin papyrus, or else disbelieved the observations of the ancient astronomers; Petrie had been inclined to accept the last of these alternatives. When he began to study the dates on the later Sinai inscriptions, however, he noted that the high season for mining expeditions was January to March; a few had stayed a little later, none beyond April or May. The dates given on twelfth-dynasty tablets

79 Thebes: the Ramesseum from the north-east

80 Flinders Petrie excavating at the Ramesseum, December 1895, by Henry Wallis, R.A. (in University College, London)

81 Western end of the Ramesseum. In the vaulted magazines beyond, Petrie and his team lived during the excavations of 1895/6

Water-colour drawings by Petrie: *above* **(82)**: tombs of the Caliphs, Cairo; *below left* **(83)**: Dendera: brick arch in the mastaba of Adu (Sixth Dynasty); *below right* **(84)**: Predynastic painted pot from Naqada

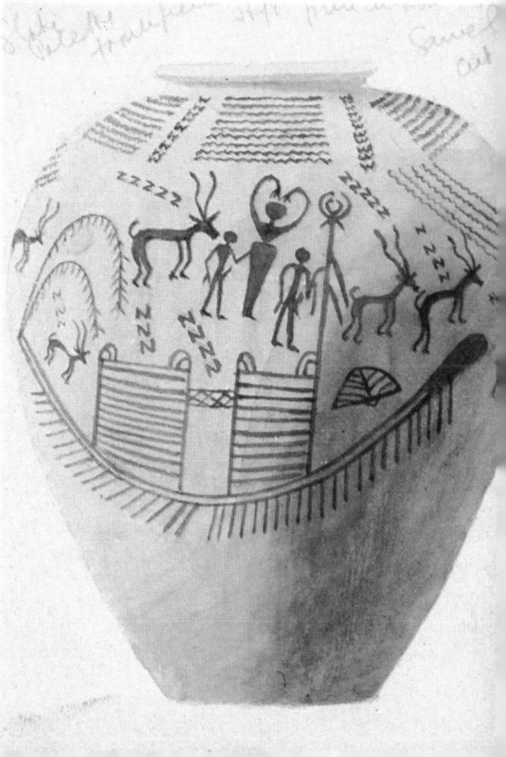

86 The "White Queen" found near the Ramesseum by Petrie in 1896 (Cairo Museum)

85 (*left*) Ann Petrie at Tell el 'Amarna in 1977. Behind her is brickwork excavated by her father in 1892

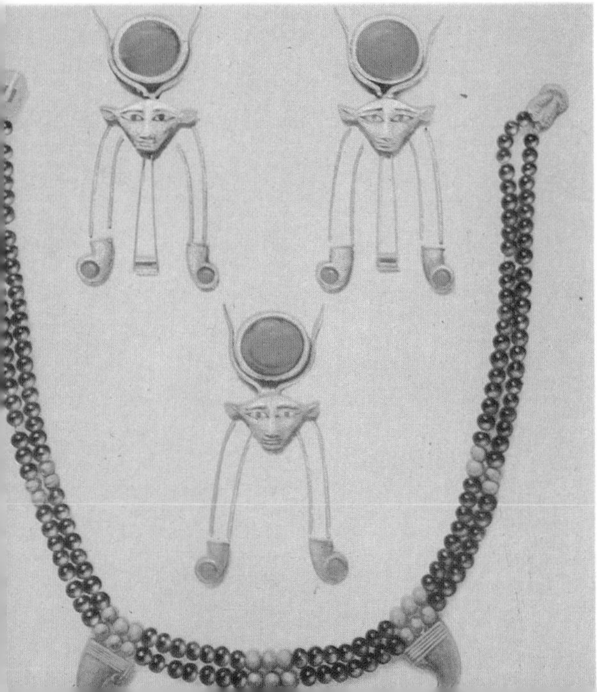

87 Jewels of Princess Sit-Hathor-Iunet found in her tomb in el Lahun in 1914 (reproduced from Guy Brunton, *Lahun I: the Treasure*). The pectoral (*l.*) is in the Cairo Museum; the necklace (*r.*) and other elements are in the Metropolitan Museum of Art, New York, where they have now been differently assembled

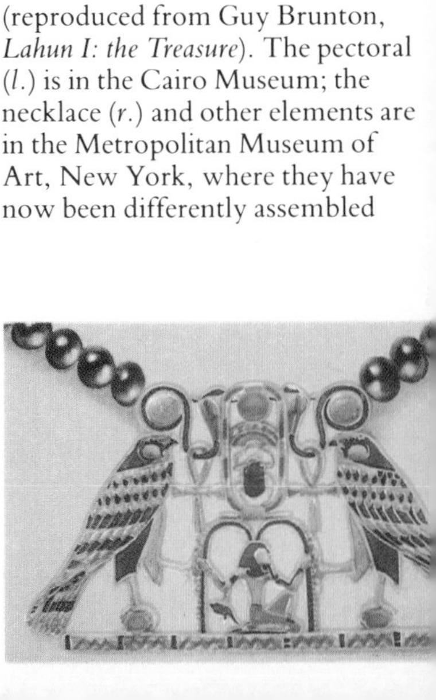

88 The Cairo Museum of Antiquities, opened in 1902

89 The alabaster sphinx of the New Kingdom found by Petrie in 1912. It once stood before the Temple of Ptah

Above left **(90)**: Tell el Hesy: looking south from Petrie's cutting of 1890; *right* **(91)**: Tell el Far'a: the dry Wadi Ghazzeh in summer; *below* **(92)**: Thebes: the Colossi of Memnon

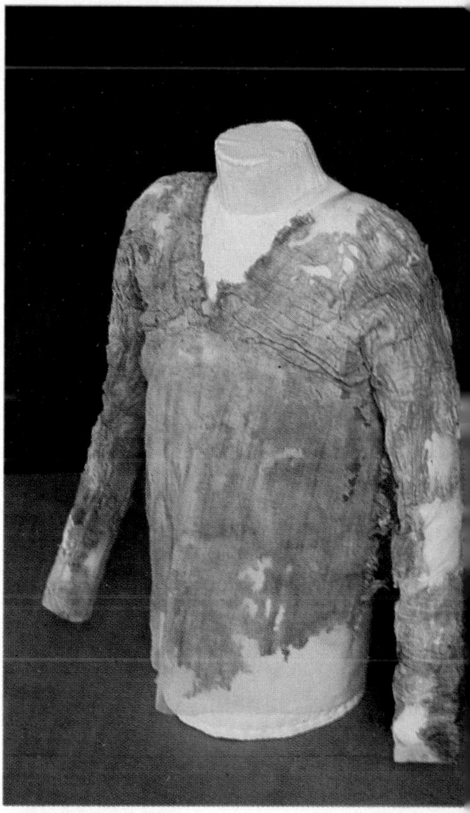

?ainted mummy cases from the Tomb of Two Brothers found at Deir Rifa 1907 (Manchester Museum); *above right* **(94)**: n-tucked linen shirt from a first dynasty grave at Tarkhan (Petrie Museum)

95 (*below*) Fragment of annals known as the ermo Stone (Petrie Museum); *right* **(96)**: Linen ıirt found with others in a tomb at Deshasha in 1897. Fifth dynasty (Petrie Museum)

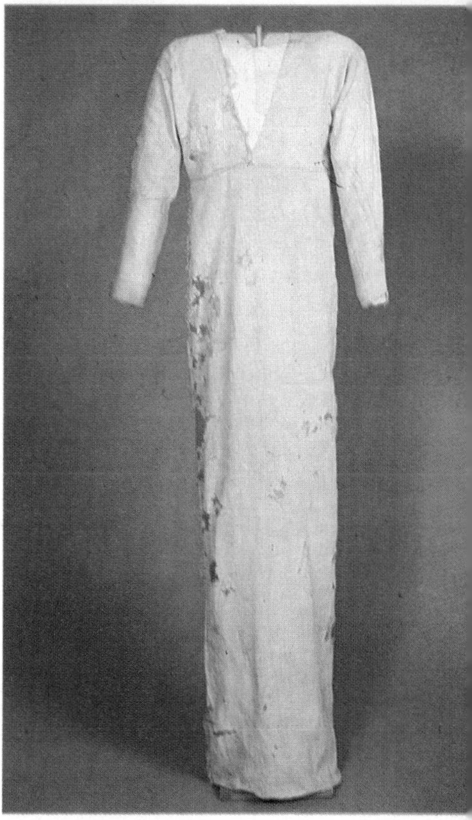

97 Portrait of Sir Flinders Petrie F.R.S., F.B.A., D.C.L., Litt.D., etc., 1934, by Philip de Laszlo R.A. (in University College London)

accorded very well with those of the New Kingdom; the Sirius datings for the Middle Kingdom were vindicated—the ancient astronomers had not erred. Since he had implicit faith in the credibility of Manetho, Petrie decided to adopt the longer interval between the twelfth and eighteenth dynasties and date the beginning of the twelfth to 3246 BC and the beginning of the first dynasty to 5510 BC.

This new chronology, assuming an immense duration of time for early Egyptian civilization, was rejected outright by most historians, though Petrie's friend Arthur Evans welcomed it since it chimed in with his own view that a long interval had elapsed between the link with twelfth dynasty Egypt in the Middle Minoan period, and the later contacts of Crete and Mycenae with the New Kingdom. In this essay in 1911, Petrie put back his dates a little on the basis of Knobel's calculations of Sothic risings, and brought fresh evidence to bear from the casing stones of the Meydum pyramid;[46] on these he had found dated masons' marks showing that the stone had been quarried during the period from March to June (when the harvest was finished and men were free for corvée work) and transported between July and October when the fields would have been under water; the short chronology of the Germans,[47] he claimed, would bring these calendrical months into the wrong season and end the work before the inundation began. Their argument that there are relatively few monuments dated to the Second Intermediate Period he countered by claiming that in other countries and in other ages "the disproportion in the number of monuments proves nothing regarding the length of time they were produced"; their objection that there had been little evolutionary change in the style and manufacture of material objects between the Twelfth and the Eighteenth Dynasties, he refuted by pointing out instances in which there *had* been change; style, he maintained, had little to do with the duration of time. He reaffirmed his unswerving faith in Manetho and his belief in the long chronology; to it, with few modifications, he adhered for the rest of his life. In the eleventh and last edition of his *History of Egypt*, Menes is dated to 5546 BC; Breasted in his *History of Egypt*, published in 1912, began the first dynasty at 3400 BC; nowadays a somewhat lower date is preferred. (See Appendix A.) The scientific procedures now available to determine the age of organic matter by the so-called radio-carbon method, and that of pottery by the process known as thermoluminescence, would certainly have convinced him. As it was, his refusal to conform to accepted opinion in this matter (resulting perhaps partly from his distrust of German "armchair" scholarship) has had the unfortunate effect of misleading some of a younger generation into belittling the value of his work. His contemporaries were not thus mistaken. "No archaeological practitioner of lesser stature could have maintained both his reputation and his chronology."[48]

Next winter (1911–12) Petrie was back in familiar surroundings: illicit digging by dealers and the *sebbakhîn* were wrecking what were left of the Roman tombs at Hawara that had yielded so many fine portraits; Petrie found seventy more, some badly rotted but others as fine as those he previously brought to light. The manner in which some wooden panels had been cut down to fit the mummy suggested to Petrie that they had been painted from life, and had first hung in houses as portraits of the living, and then later taken off the walls and used by the embalmer. Relatively few mummies were so decorated: he reckoned that it took six weeks of work for a digger to find a portrait. Dr Ruffer came down to examine the mummies. The greatest prize was the picture of a woman, "very refined and thoughtful in type", inscribed *Hermione Grammatiké*—the first woman professor, he gleefully suggested, perhaps a classical lecturer in Arsinoë.[49]*

With a large workforce now at his disposal, some of them highly trained excavators, Petrie returned with new confidence to the Labyrinth. By removing a bank of earth and chips along the south face of the Pyramid, the back of the great temple was revealed and several large sculptures came to light, among them statue-busts of the grinning crocodile god, Sobek.[50] The brick pyramids of Mazghuna were investigated: they proved to be of the same plan as Hawara and Petrie dated them to the last rulers of the twelfth dynasty. A prehistoric cemetery at Gerza, four miles north of Meydum, was dug by Wainwright and Mackay before they joined the main party at Memphis for their third season. Petrie boxed up thirty of the best Hawara portraits, and on his way back to England, stopped a few days in Rome and unpacked them all at the British School, where he lectured to an enthralled audience (**55**).

Throughout the winter Petrie's thoughts had been constantly with his children; he longed to be able to superintend John's education, sure that his son was as precocious as he himself had been. He urged Hilda to show him minerals, and start him playing dominoes. She for her part chafed at being left in England; her letters to Flinders were a little petulant in tone and full of small anxieties; she missed him badly, she hated a life of petty domesticities, and felt she was wasting her time.

* It now hangs in Girton College, Cambridge.

Flinders wrote back reassuringly: he missed her too, but it was his duty to be out digging, hers to stay; she must realize that she was doing the greatest work of her life; "keep a brave heart, as you have my second self—John—with you to make a brighter and better boy than his father." She worried too much about the child's little misdeeds: "He will know better when he is older, and he has enough sense to feel whether an objection is reasonable. I would always show him the inconvenience of an act to himself, rather than prohibit it." In each of his letters to her—and he wrote twice a week—he enclosed a little note for John, looking forward already to the day when his son would come to Egypt with him and share the life he loved so much.[51]

The British School was now a flourishing concern; among its most generous contributors—and the greatest to benefit—were the Royal Scottish Museum in Edinburgh, the Ny Carlsberg Glyptothek in Copenhagen, the Metropolitan Museum of Art in New York and the Chicago Society of Egyptian Research (Boston and Philadelphia supported the Fund). There had been some changes in the Committee, and Hayter Lewis had died, to be replaced as Treasurer by the husband of the indefatigable Mrs Sefton-Jones. In the following year, the death of Petrie's cousin Sir Robert Hensley left the Committee without a chairman; thenceforward they appear to have managed without one. Among the crowds who came to admire the mummy portraits one visitor was missing: Holman Hunt, whose admiration of the paintings at the Egyptian Hall in 1888 had begun their long friendship, had not survived to see this second gallery of Roman faces. Hunt's interest in Egypt had been first kindled in 1854, when he had stayed some time in Cairo to paint; in 1893, with his second wife, he determined to make the whole trip up the Nile to Philae; Petrie was not in Egypt that winter, but they invited him to dinner before they went and he, no doubt, briefed them on all that they must see. Later they built a cottage at Sonning-on-Thames, and thither Flinders and Hilda were from time to time invited; the old man loved to entertain and was an excellent raconteur. He had gone almost blind, but he enjoyed riverside walks in Flinders' company; in photographs of the two together they appear to be vying with one another in the length and luxuriance of their beards (**64**). Petrie's last visit was on 27 August 1909; having spent the whole day at Sonning, he arrived home late in Hampstead to find that his daughter had been born. The artist had been failing a little: he died in September of the following year.

CHAPTER XIV

Amulets in the Soup

(1911–14)

WHEN FLINDERS PETRIE left for Egypt in late November 1911 he was tired and a starch-free diet prescribed by his doctor for gout and indigestion had left him weak. Small wonder that he caught a chill waiting on the bank for the ferry boat to take him over to Shurafa, a village on the east bank of the Nile opposite Mazghuna, where Mackay had already pitched tents. He took to his bed, but a persistent pain in his side brought him up to Cairo to consult a specialist, who decreed an operation for hernia. Mackay continued the excavation and planning of Shurafa, a Roman settlement.[1] Engelbach arrived, and tabulated hundreds of Ptolemaic and Roman skulls. In the nursing home Petrie ate properly and read voraciously: Mommsen, Anson's *Voyages* and Gubbio's *Spanish People* (he had never been known to read a modern novel). Early in January Hilda arrived and they stayed for a week or so in a boarding house in Helwan. Here Mackay came to see them with a tale of woe: after Shurafa was finished, they had moved as planned to Atfih (Atfiya), the site of the ancient Aphroditopolis, where they had excavated and started to copy a large Ptolemaic tomb; when however they had been there a few days an indignant message had come from the papyrologist, J. de M. Johnson: he had already applied, he said, for a permit to search for papyrus cartonnage on behalf of the Egypt Exploration Fund. The site was in Petrie's concession, but he judged it unwise to argue and told Mackay to proceed to the next site on the year's programme, Tarkhan, on the west bank of the Nile opposite Shurafa. Clearly there had been some confusion; probably it had been the fault of the Antiquities direction. Johson started on the cemeteries, but on finding that one of his men had bubonic plague he had closed down the work at once and taken quarantine precautions; a health official was called in, the camp was fumigated, and work was resumed nine days later.[2] The small incident did nothing to improve relations between the School and the Fund.

When the Petries arrived at Tarkhan in mid-January, excavations had already begun in the desert west of the village of Kafr 'Ammar; Gerald Wainwright had been there on his own for some time and had built huts for the safekeeping of the finds; the party were to live in tents.

Engelbach arrived with a new assistant; a young classical scholar, T. E. Lawrence, had been sent down by Hogarth from Carchemish, where they were digging, to learn the rudiments of archaeology from the master himself. Lawrence was with Petrie for about six weeks; it was for him one of the most memorable experiences of his adventurous life. Four days after his arrival he sent Hogarth his first impressions: he took to the Professor at once, though the commissariat filled him with alarm:

> He is enormous fun, with systems of opening tins and cleaning his teeth and all that. . . . Why hasn't he died of ptomaine poisoning? It's really rather amusing that they are all in terror of instant death because three people died yesterday in the village, and yet cheerfully eat out of week-opened tins after scraping off the green crust inside. I am going in for it all with great relish and really enjoying it, with the security of being insured.[3]

He assured Hogarth he was learning a lot: he had himself excavated and waxed a skeleton which he would like the Ashmolean Museum to have, as an example of an intact burial. A few days later he wrote to a friend, Mme Rieder:

> Nobody but I would have achieved a letter at all from a Petrie dig. A Petrie dig is a thing with a flavour of its own: tinned kidneys mingle with mummy-corpses and amulets in the soup: my bed is all gritty with prehistoric alabaster jars of unique types—and my feet at night keep the bread-box from rats. For ten mornings in succession I have seen the sun rise as I breakfasted, and we come home at nightfall after lunching at the bottom of a 50-foot shaft, to draw pottery silhouettes or string bead-necklaces. In fact if I hadn't malaria today I could make a pretty story of it all:—only then I wouldn't have time.
>
> To begin with the Professor is the great man of the camp—he's about 5′ 11″ high,* white-haired, grey-bearded, broad and active,

* He was 5 ft 9″ or 10″, according to his mother.

> with a voice that splits when excited and a constant feverish speed of speech; he is a man of ideas and systems, from the right way to dig a temple to the only way to clean one's teeth. Also he only is right in all things: all his subs have to take his number of sugar lumps in their tea, his species of jam with potted tongue, or be dismissed as official-bound unprogressists [*sic*]. Further he is easy-tempered, full of humour, and fickle to a degree that makes him delightfully quaint, and a constant source of joy and amusement in his camp. . . .
>
> About the digging: we have stumbled on what is probably the richest and largest prehistoric cemetery in Egypt, and in our first week have dug out about 100 graves . . . owing to a hitch in his arrangements the Professor has all his workmen here, so twice as many graves are found as we can recover properly; with plenty of time it would be delightful, whereas now we are swamped with the multitude. . . .[4]

Lawrence admired Wainwright's competence, but deplored the fact that the Professor had so little support from most of his students: "all wanting to do independent digs, whereas what P. wants is a pedestrian intelligence to do the hackwork for him, while he does the fine things. Am awfully glad I went to him. But what a life!"

Being accustomed to Syrian workmen, he disliked Egyptians: "Woolley's idea of Kufti men [he had dug with them in Nubia, and was proposing to bring up a team of them to Carchemish] I hope won't come off. Those Egyptians are such worms (though they can dig)."[5]

When he turned up for work on his first morning in camp, dressed as he did in Carchemish in a blazer and football shorts, Petrie had remarked shortly: "We don't play cricket here"; but he soon grew to like this eager, amusing young man and found him hard-working and reliable; he paid him the compliment of suggesting to him that he might go out for the British School and excavate on Bahrein Island in the Persian Gulf: "He told me Best had dug in Bahrein: and when we found some very curious Mesopotamian-like bull's legs of prehistoric beds (one I hope goes to Oxford) he declared that he believed the early dynasties came by sea from Elam or thereabouts to Egypt, and that Bahrein was a stage in their going."[6]

"T.E." did not follow up this offer—he was to be too busy in other fields—but in 1925 Ernest Mackay went to Bahrein for a short season at the expense of the Egyptian Research Account, and excavated about fifty burial mounds there;[7] they had been badly plundered and did not provide the evidence of Persian Gulf trade that Petrie had hoped to find, but his idea, then new, of early contact by sea between Elam or Mesopotamia and Egypt has been proved right by later exploration on that island and elsewhere.

Petrie's work in the winter of 1911–12 was one of his most important, not so much for the Old Kingdom tombs near Kafr 'Ammar as for those in the cemetery near the hamlet of Tarkhan. In these private burials of the latest Predynastic and the Archaic Period the tomb furniture was excellently preserved; in the Royal Tombs of the same date at Abydos, nearly all had been destroyed and burnt. Here, wood and linen and basketry were intact, and Petrie was able to study the weave of rush matting, and mortice and tenon jointing of the beds on which some of the dead had been laid (**54**).[8] There were slate palettes, and copper tools, and Hilda was drawing alabaster pots by the hundred. One of the greatest prizes was a huge jar sealed with the name of King Nar-Mer, the uniter of Egypt. Of the extraordinary preservation of textiles in these graves, Petrie wrote: "The earliest linen is fair and fresh, and some large sheets of the XIth dynasty were as white and sweet as if they had just come off the loom."

Many samples were brought home and studied by a textile expert, W. Midgley of Bolton. Some of the linen garments, folded as they were found, were kept in storage at University College against the day when they might be treated for display and study; one carefully unfolded and mounted by technicians in the Conservation Department of the Victoria and Albert Museum is now exhibited in the Petrie Museum along with the two garments from Deshasha. It is a child's shirt or dress, closely pin-tucked on the sleeves and yoke,[9] and it may claim to be the oldest from Egypt and perhaps the oldest linen garment in the world (**94**).

Though still on his starch-free diet Petrie was in high spirits: as Hilda wrote to her sister:

> Flinders is very well and jolly, much fatter than he was—he was very thin—And I have seen to certain arrangements. . . . I have a good custard-*buduny** made every day, which is for him only, so that he gets more milk and eggs than we do. Also . . . he gets a cup of hot cocoa at bedtime, and I shall get Muhammad thoroughly into this routine before I come away.[10]

* Pudding.

Muhammad Osman el Kreti had ruled their kitchen ever since, as a small Qufti, he had been appointed cook-boy at Dendara in the first year of their marriage. He was to serve them for another twenty-three years; wherever Petrie dug, and even when the work moved to Palestine, Muhammad would be sent for and he would leave his family and come at once. He was something of a buffoon and loved being teased; it was believed that he understood much of what was said at table, and was sometimes detected concealing a tell-tale smile. His sayings were a constant source of amusement. This spring, when there was a storm of unusual violence and very large hailstones fell, Muhammad "thought that someone was throwing stones at him, and said with much disgust that the sky was coming down."

In mid-February the party begain to break up: Lawrence had already gone to Carchemish; Engelbach went off with six Quftis to build huts on the next site, Matariya a little north-east of Cairo. This was the ancient Heliopolis; of the temple, or temples, of the sun-god Rē', one of the greatest of Egypt's deities, little could be seen except a solitary obelisk, still upright—one of the many which had once stood in that city of obelisks. Petrie had high hopes of finding early remains, and planned to spend several spring seasons there; like Memphis, where Mackay and Elverson were to continue work with occasional visits from "the Prof.", the only possible season for work was when the inundation waters had subsided and the site had dried out somewhat. Wainwright was to stay at Kafr 'Ammar until the end of the season. Hilda was not going to Heliopolis—she was anxious to get back to the children—but her departure from Kafr 'Ammar was delayed for a few days by a last-minute surprise: the discovery of an early hieratic inscription on a coffin lid. No one present could read hieratic—the cursive form of hieroglyphic—but Hilda copied accurately; and she knelt on the sand for two days, not daring to touch the powdery surface of the wood.

Matariya, "our wet site", proved something of a disappointment. Flinders began at Tell Hisn in the northern part of the town. Schiaparelli had dug there some seven years before, and had found blocks from a third dynasty temple, which were on display in the Turin Museum but had never been published adequately.[11] He was said to have found a series of concentric brick galleries. Petrie searched but could find no such enigmatic structures; he was forced to the conclusion that Schiaparelli's workmen had tunnelled in circles through a large mud-brick platform, cutting the "galleries" as they went. One more block of the early temple was found; they must have been used, he concluded, as filling for a large embankment in size and shape not unlike the great enclosure at Tell el Yahudiya, and like it, therefore, this had been a Hyksos fortress.[12] Beyond, a section of the great city wall was examined, but of the temple there was little trace, the land behind the spot where the obelisk stood was the Khedive's property, and under cultivation. After long negotiations in Cairo he was permitted to draw up a contract with the tenant of the fields, for the lease of half a *feddan* of land—all he could afford. It was difficult work: as at Memphis, the water had to be baled out constantly, and finds were few; pieces of another obelisk were found—or perhaps of two, for they usually stood in pairs—a few temple blocks and some fine fragments of statuary, badly smashed. Petrie came to the reluctant conclusion that unless the law pronouncing all antiquities on land in private ownership to be government property were to be rescinded, no excavator could afford to hire such land, and afterwards restore it to cultivable condition, without adequate reward in terms of what he had found. Moreover, because the city lay so close to modern Cairo, most of the stone had been removed long ago. He decided to abandon further efforts to dig at Heliopolis, and he was never to return to the site. Other expeditions have made sporadic finds since, but the site is now a suburb of Cairo and no satisfactory plan will ever be made of what was once one of Egypt's greatest and most sacred cities.

Petrie had several visitors during his stay at Heliopolis; one of them was Miss Winifred Crompton, an old friend who had been Honorary Secretary to the Manchester Egyptian Society (of which Jesse Haworth was the patron and President) since 1908; she had attended classes in hieroglyphics and was determined to come out and see Egypt for herself. The Petries were old friends: he often lectured in Manchester and the Museum held many of the outstanding treasures from his excavations; Miss Murray had been cataloguing the collection since 1908, and in that year, 1912, Miss Crompton took over from her as Assistant in charge of Egyptology; she spent two weeks in Petrie's camp, learning about the techniques employed in finding and preserving at their source objects which were destined eventually to come into her care (this is an experience which all museum curators should have, but few are fortunate enough to acquire). In the October following, the Petries were in Manchester for the opening of the Jesse Haworth Building, a handsome extension to the University Museum largely built through his bounty, in token of which he received an honorary Doctorate from the University; Petrie lectured on that occasion, and was present at the opening of the new museum on the following day.

A visit and lecture—"our usual *fantasia* in Manchester" as Hilda called it—became an annual autumn event; in years to come they kept in close touch with Miss Crompton and she often stayed with them in Hampstead when she came up to London.[13]

All that summer Flinders gave daily lessons to his little boy, and in the autumn at the age of five, he went to his first school; he could already read, and was able to understand maps and figures as well as his father had done at that age. It had been an unusually busy summer of lectures and meetings, and Flinders was beginning a catalogue of the various categories of objects in his collection at the College. He stayed with the Griffiths in Oxford. Frank, having inherited a considerable fortune from his father-in-law, had married again; he was now Reader in Egyptology at the University and respected as one of the greatest scholars in his field.

There was still more to be done at Tarkhan, and Petrie decided to return for a second season in 1912–13 with three new students.[14] This year Wainwright was to accompany Sir Henry Wellcome to the Sudan; Mackay, with his new wife, Dorothy, was about to undertake a new project of tomb recording at Thebes; only Rex Engelbach would still be available, and he was to be entrusted with a cemetery of his own at Gerza. Hilda had intended to stay in England, but after less than a month's work Flinders wrote urging her to come out at once: there was a great deal of drawing to do and the new recruits were not able to cope with it to the Professor's satisfaction. He was digging now in the valley, under the sand drift, where he found the ground thick with Archaic tombs; the water table was very near the surface here, and part of the cemetery actually under water, but some hundreds of tombs were excavated, the sodden long bones measured as they lay, and the skulls carefully lifted in a block of sand, and as they dried out, solidified with paraffin wax till they were strong enough to be packed for transport to England, where Professor Karl Pearson eagerly awaited them for his study of racial types. Before they were packed, Petrie photographed each skull in turn, supporting the jawbone on a piece of soap.[15] From time to time he would go over to Gerza to see how Engelbach was getting on; he had confidence in his seasoned students and tried to interfere as little as possible, but sometimes experience suggested a better method of proceeding, or an alternative explanation to some puzzle, and in that case he did not hesitate to explain or advise.

As soon as she arrived, Hilda was almost too busy to write home. The new cemetery, she said, was

> a long straggling area containing several thousand graves. Flinders has already opened 1200 or more since he began work, and he has a complete register of all the contents of these graves, and has made a wonderfully patient and well-covered plan of the whole site. . . . I have not been outside the store room since I arrived, 5 days ago, but as I shunt part of the roof to get sunlight in, the storeroom is as good as out of doors, and there I can work from 7.30 until sunset . . . each of the great pieces of coffin, 6 ft. long, is laid on my bed one by one, and I sit on a box to copy it on great sheets of paper . . . at the head of my bed are 4 great cartonnage heads of mummy cases with staring faces, at the side are collections of alabasters and many bones hard by; at the foot of the bed are 80 skulls.

It was not most people's idea of a cosy bedroom, but Hilda was used to such macabre furnishings and took them as a matter of course.

Among their visitors at Tarkhan that winter were John Crowfoot and his wife; they had been in the Sudan for some years and were now living in Cairo, where he was an Inspector of Education. Grace Crowfoot's interest was in weaving and she was particularly interested to see the Tarkhan cloths. She was to become a leading expert on ancient textiles, and her husband, perhaps inspired by this and subsequent visits to Petrie digs, himself became an archaeologist. Sayce too came to stay, and the MacInneses from the English church in Cairo; he was soon to be the Bishop in Jerusalem.

After Hilda had gone, Flinders spent less than a month at Memphis, then left his assistants to continue the work and went up to Cairo for the division of the Tarkhan material. It was a disaster. There had been changes in the Department resulting from the great change that had taken place recently in the government of Egypt: the policy of Sir Eldon Gorst's regime had been to give the Egyptians wider freedom in administration, but after the assassination of a Prime Minister followed by anti-British demonstrations by the extreme nationalists, Gorst had tendered his resignation (he died within a month), and Lord Kitchener had been sent out to restore order; his Oriental Secretary Sir Ronald Storrs now had authority over the Antiquities Service and it was he who directed Maspero to apply the regulations governing the division of finds *au pied de la lettre*—the finds were to be exactly halved. Maspero may well have been reluctant—none knew the importance of keeping a tomb group together better than he—but he decided to take precisely half of each type of object. Petrie was in despair: he knew that the bulk of what had been kept in Cairo would go into the

Museum shop for sale, and he tried to buy back some of the objects taken, but the prices were above his means: tourists were prepared to pay highly for the guarantee that what they bought was genuine. "Such was the official destruction of the historic value of a unique site," he wrote bitterly later. It increased the dislike he now felt for Maspero; at Memphis that spring he had found him uncooperative in the matter of palm trees which Petrie had planted on ground he had already excavated, in exchange for those which he hoped to uproot; Maspero's order that they must be destroyed was revoked after Petrie had made a strong protest to the Department of the Public Domains.

In the Egypt Exploration Fund, meanwhile, plans were afoot to reform its constitution and widen its activities; a sub-committee recommended that subscribers should now become Members, or Associate Members, of what should henceforward be called the Egypt Exploration Society; an organizing Secretary should be appointed, and the Society should issue a quarterly Journal, the first in England to be devoted to Egyptology and papyrology. During the summer a Journal committee was appointed, including F. G. Walker, the new Organizing Secretary, James Cotton the Honorary Secretary, J. G. Milne representing the Graeco-Roman Branch, and Dr Alan Gardiner, who had been a member of Petrie's committee since the foundation of the British School and in recent years also a member of its Executive Committee. A brilliant philologist, he had spent years studying hieroglyphics in Germany and had assisted in the preparation of the great Berlin Dictionary of the Egyptian Language; while there, he had acted as organizing secretary for contributions to the Egyptian Research Account, and Petrie often asked his advice and help on matters of philology. For the time being he held an academic post in Manchester, but he was often in London and an active member of the E.E.S. Committee also; it may have been he who drew Petrie's attention to the proposed Journal. Petrie wrote in July and suggested that the British School should participate, since they were responsible for much of the archaeological work done in Egypt. In October belated talks were held, and it seemed as if co-operation between the two bodies might be possible; Petrie, however, insisted on joint editorship, and this at the last minute decided the Committee of the Society; they rejected a joint arrangement outright. Milne tried in vain to mediate; Petrie would only come in on his own terms.[16] At once he set about organizing his own quarterly. An editorial board was set up: Petrie was to be the Editor, and Professor Ernest Gardner and Dr Alan Gardiner were to be named as giving their advice and assistance. That same afternoon Macmillan's were approached and agreed to publish the new journal. It was to have short articles, well illustrated by photographs, news of archaeological interest, and reviews of books and periodicals. Petrie postponed his departure for a week or so and wrote to his friends for contributions; Newberry sent a short but important article, Miss Eckenstein had a paper ready on the Moon Cult in Sinai, and Petrie himself contributed the text of a lecture he had recently delivered, and wrote notes and reviews. The first issue of *Ancient Egypt* raced into print in December, a few days before he left for Egypt; two thousand copies were printed and they were soon sold out. The *Journal of Egyptian Archaeology*, the organ of the E.E.S., appeared in January and sold more slowly: Petrie felt he had captured the market.

Rex Engelbach had gone out earlier, and was finding tombs at Haraga four miles from el-Lahun, with the help of a young philologist, Battiscombe Gunn; they were finding tombs of the twelfth and eighteenth dynasties; the site, on an island of desert in the midst of the cultivation, had been spotted the year before by 'Ali es Suefi, and was proving rewarding. Engelbach could be relied on to keep meticulous tomb records; at Riqqa in the previous year he had begun the compilation of a corpus of Middle and New Kingdom pottery; here he was able to add new types to it.[17] When Petrie arrived with the Bruntons, they found huts ready for them at Lahun. Guy Brunton had been a student at University College for the past two years; he had become interested in Egypt at an early age and had haunted Petrie's exhibitions as a schoolboy; at the age of eighteen he had gone to South Africa, but he did not forget his old enthusiasm; returning to England in 1911 with his artist wife Winifred he had joined Miss Murray's language classes, and during the previous winter he had come to Egypt and visited the camp at Tarkhan. They were to prove capable and dedicated fieldworkers.

Petrie's return to Lahun was something that he had long planned: during the twenty-five years that had elapsed since he first entered the pyramid and found the sarcophagus of Sesostris II, pyramids of similar age had been cleared by others, at Dahshur and Lisht, and more was now known about the complex of subsidiary burials of members of the royal family that usually surrounded a twelfth-dynasty pyramid. This one proved to have been surrounded by a wide trench filled with sand and enclosed by a panelled wall; beyond was the wide court containing the rockcut entrances to royal burials. Outside the *temenos*, forty-two trees had been planted on every side. Petrie's task, therefore, was to explore the platform around the pyramid inch by inch, scraping and brushing the rock and examining every fissure and crack in search of stones that might prove to cover pits and tomb shafts. "No site," he wrote "has ever been so thoroughly searched." The work began on 3 January and lasted till early April. Besides the Bruntons there were several students and volunteers.[18] Petrie himself was not very active this year; he was suffering from abdominal pains and twice had to go up to Cairo to see a doctor, but when the big discovery was made he was on the spot and in charge of operations. A number of tombs had been found in the platform, all entered and plundered in antiquity, but in one, the shaft of which actually lay open, patience was rewarded: after clearing the hard mud of centuries from around the sarcophagus, and making sure there was nothing left inside it, the Qufti who had been told to finish emptying the tomb chamber noticed a recess in the wall, also filled with mud; as he started to clear it out, he saw the gleam of gold: first one bead, then another appeared; Brunton was sent for, and for the next week, working through day and part of the night and sleeping in the tomb, he patiently cleared the hiding place of its treasure—the jewellery of the Princess Sit-Hathor-Yunet.[19] As each delicate object was lifted out it was taken back to the huts where Petrie gently detached it from its mud coating and washed it with a camel hair brush, and then photographed it.

> In the midst of the recess lay the crown; the tall plumes of gold lay down flat, with the crown between them. This crown is a broad band of brilliant burnished gold, with fifteen beautifully inlaid rosettes of gold around it, and in front of it the royal cobra of gold inlaid, the head of lapis lazuli. This head was missing when the crown first appeared; some days afterwards, in washing the earth from the recess, the head was found. Then one eye was missing. I washed and searched patiently, preserving the smallest specks of precious stone. Soon a tiny ball of garnet appeared at the bottom of a basin full of mud; this—no larger than a pin's head—was the missing eye. Yet the gold socket of the eye was missing. I remembered having washed out a bead of gold which differed from thousands of others; looking I found it again, and there was the setting of the eye complete.

Besides the crown, there were two pectorals of gold inlaid with a design of cloisonné work in precious stones (**87**), necklaces of gold and amethyst and carnelian, armlets of gold with rows of tiny beads of carnelian and turquoise between, and collars of gold cowries and lions' heads. All these had been in an ivory jewel casket; in another box were toilet objects: the princess's silver mirror, its obsidian handle adorned with a head of the goddess Hathor in gold; razors and knives of bronze, and a set of gold-topped obsidian jars for salves and perfumes. The whole treasure must have been open to view, within arm's reach of the tomb robbers, while they were smashing the granite sarcophagus.

> Slowly the caskets rotted, the vases fell over, the threads decayed, the beads rolled apart, and in perhaps fifty or a hundred years the whole pit was filled with mud and dust, and lost to sight. How such a treasure can possibly have escaped the notice of the men who were zealously searching for it, is one of the mysteries of the inexplicable past.[20]

The utmost secrecy had to be observed; the man who had found the cache was given £30 on the spot and promised a great deal more if he kept his mouth shut: not even his brother could find out how large a reward he finally received. When all was ready, a box was packed with the treasure and Campion took it up to Cairo, to be locked in the Museum safe. A month later, planning finished and the platform exhausted—they had found fourteen tombs, but little else in the way of objects—Petrie and Brunton went up to Cairo for the division. Petrie faced Maspero with some apprehension, but the Director, now applying the half-and-half rule with liberality, took the two unique objects, the crown and the mirror, and one of the two pectorals, but allowed Petrie everything else. It was a remarkably generous division; possibly Maspero felt able to be lenient because Emile Brugsch, who had always jealously watched any grant of objects to Petrie, had retired at last, and also because he himself was about to resign his office and return to France. He was sixty-eight years old and in poor health; he died in Paris two years later.

CHAPTER XV

The War Years

(1914–19)

THE DEPARTMENT OF Egyptology over which Flinders Petrie presided for forty-one years was the first of its kind in the United Kingdom and its museum may still claim to be the finest Egyptological teaching collection in existence. Its growth and organization were accomplished gradually as time and opportunity allowed. Every year part of Petrie's finds and purchases were allocated to the collection. News of his arrival in Cairo spread quickly; on the first day he would generally visit the houses or shops of one or two of the best-known dealers: Cyticas, the Copt Boulos Todros, Farag and Mustafa Agha, and later 'Ali 'Arabi, Maurice Nahman, Tano and the American R. H. Blanchard, whose scarab collection rivalled his own and with whom he would sometimes make an exchange; other dealers would besiege his hotel in the evenings after dinner. When he was excavating, country dealers would sometimes pay him a visit on their way to Cairo, so that he had first pick of their wares. He developed a preference for certain types of objects, not necessarily those in greatest demand: apart from scarabs, he bought tools, weights, stone vases and beads if they were obviously from one necklace and not on a string made up prettily for the tourist. He never bargained nor advanced his offer; he named a price, and the dealers knew that this was his valuation, and they usually accepted it. "The better a man knew me, the more certain we were of doing business." The prices paid were always noted at the back of his pocket diary or in his notebook. In general his purchases were modest enough—he could not afford to buy costly pieces or large statuary—but occasionally he got a real bargain. At Dahshur in 1887 a man from Giza brought him a charming little Greek figurine which he suspected came from Naucratis; he bought a heart scarab of Akhenaten which the dealer from Mallawi "only regarded as being big and having a silver plate"; a gold ring of King Amenophis I was sold to him in Cairo by a dealer who had come up from Luxor soon after the opening of that Pharaoh's tomb.[1]

During the early years, students of Egyptology had had little formal teaching. In 1913, Miss Murray and the Professor put their heads together and devised a two-year Training Course, leading to a diploma which was to be known as the Certificate in Egyptology. A printed prospectus was issued. In the first year students were to study Egyptian history, Egyptian religion and elementary hieroglyphs, attend courses on anthropology in the first and third terms, and on physical anthropology in the second; in the second year Dr Walker took over the language teaching; "Identification of Materials" would be taught by the head of the Geology Department, and Professor Gardner would lecture on Ancient Art. The Professor of Egyptian Archaeology himself took a class on the Dating of Objects in the first term and gave a series of lectures, to which the public were admitted, on his latest discoveries when he returned from Egypt in May. These lectures were already so popular that they had to be repeated, sometimes more than once. Students were expected to help with the arrangement and staffing of the annual exhibition, held in the College, during the summer vacation. "A knowledge of drawing and photography will be required by all students for the purposes of the course," said the Prospectus, and they usually assisted in the preparation of plates for the current excavation report. At the end of the second year they were expected to pass eleven examinations before qualifying for their Certificate.[2]

In 1907 the Yates Library had moved elsewhere, and when Geology was removed to the south wing of the College, the Museum could occupy the whole length of the top floor. One end of it was occupied by the Edwards Library and Petrie's office. New cases were badly needed, for exhibits were crammed together and many were hidden by those on top of them; inscribed stones and large pots were everywhere stacked on the floor, as the time-consuming task of labelling and sorting them went slowly ahead. In 1907 Petrie had written to the Provost, Gregory Foster, suggesting that the College should take over the collection within five years; meanwhile he would continue to add to it. Since it represented almost everything which he had accumulated during his lifetime, he must ask a price for it; if the College could not buy it, he would reluctantly feel obliged to sell it piecemeal to another institution or a private collection. The modest price he set on the collection (£5,685) was based on what he had paid for the objects—the current market value, would have been far higher—but the College had not resources to meet even this expense;

as the five years approached its end, the College Committee finally decided to launch an appeal.[3] The asking price was now a little more, but this included objects acquired by excavation or purchase since the original offer had been made. The appeal went out in May 1913, in the name of the Duke of Connaught, the University's Chancellor; letters were sent first to Egyptologists of means, Alan Gardiner and Percy Newberry among them, and to others like Lord Carnarvon who were known to be interested; Walter Morrison and Dr (later Sir) Robert Mond, already generous patrons of the Research Account, sent £1,000 apiece and smaller sums began to come in. An appeal through the medium of the daily press was planned, but before it could be launched it became unnecessary. Walter Morrison, M.P., was a rich man whose inherited wealth had been augmented by shrewd business, and almost all of his fortune had been donated to learning; many of his benefactions were for archaeology. Since 1905 he had been on the Committee of the British School of Archaeology in Egypt. His modest dislike of publicity was well known, and he now insisted that only his original donation should be credited to him; another £4,000 were to be an anonymous gift, the name of the donor to be known only to Petrie and to the Secretary of the College. The subscription list could at once be closed; a satisfactory margin was left over for future purchases, and for the necessary showcases. At a formal ceremony on 7 November 1913, Petrie finally handed over the collection to University College; it was agreed that in future he would be allowed to spend up to £100 a year on additions to it, and publishers were approached with a view to setting in motion a scheme which he had long had in mind: a series of catalogues of the objects in the collection. The enforced cessation of his excavations during the war years enabled that plan to be at least partially realized.

As soon as Petrie got home, he had gone into hospital for a hernia operation. When he was up and about, he lectured to a very large audience on his recent discoveries, and the splendid jewellery displayed in University College in June drew crowds twice as large as usual; nearly three hundred catalogues were sold on the first two days, and a guard of four police constables was hired by the College authorities to keep an eye on the treasure. A few days after the exhibition closed news came of the sudden death of Dr Walker, Petrie's assistant and colleague for twenty-one years. This was a grievous loss; Petrie wrote of him "I never knew him say or do an unkind thing. He was a single-minded, simple, honest English gentleman, whom it was an honour and pleasure to know."[4] After the funeral the Petries went straight down to Rustington, and it was there, during the next weekend, that they heard the news that war had been declared.

Flinders Petrie hurried back to London. There was much to be done, dismantling the exhibition, and sorting and packing the objects which were to go to the various museums which had contributed to the excavation. The British Museum had first refusal of the jewellery; Petrie was anxious to keep the group together and had written from Egypt suggesting a minimum of £8,000 as a fair price. Budge's reply, that if they thought in the Museum that the hoard was worth it, they "might be able to put hands on a couple of thousand" infuriated Petrie and he withdrew his offer. After the outbreak of war, neither museums nor private collectors in England felt that it would be proper to spend so large a sum, and in the end, after more than two years of correspondence and negotiation, an offer from the Metropolitan Museum of New York was accepted and the exquisite pectoral of the princess (**87**), her girdle of golden cowries, her necklaces of amethyst and gold and turquoise and her cosmetic vases of obsidian and gold are among the greatest treasures of that museum's collections; one of the inlaid ebony caskets in which the jewellery had been placed has been reconstructed and is displayed with its contents, together with a replica of the mirror that stayed in Cairo. The price paid by the Metropolitan Museum for this treasure was, as Petrie pointed out, enough to keep three students in training during the next twenty years: this was his own justification for his reluctant decision to let such pieces leave England.

Within a few days of the outbreak of war Willey, Engelbach and Battiscombe Gunn were off to volunteer for war work or to join the armed forces, and Miss Murray soon left to train as a nursing auxiliary. Guy Brunton stayed to help with the packing, but then he too was called up. Petrie, now sixty-one, offered himself for war work in any capacity: he hoped that long experience of the organization of work gangs might be of use in the war effort. He was told that his services were needed in the College. Though he chafed at inaction, he was not idle. Four years of enforced absence from Egypt, four years when he had time to study and publish the material he had collected over the years—in this sense, the pause from excavation could not have come at a better time for him. He had few students, and none full time, but he gave at least one lecture a week during term time; he sat on a number of professorial committees and several Boards of Studies of the University, and became involved in plans to reform the syllabus of the history school and the teaching of anthropology and classical archaeology. Above all, he was rearranging and cataloguing the Petrie Collection.

The burning of the University Library at Louvain in 1914 during the German advance profoundly shocked him and he feared for the safety of his precious collection, but he kept the Department open and was always ready to welcome volunteers who, like Mrs Georgina Aitken, came to thread beads or help in some other way. For the present there were no Diploma students, but Petrie's lectures were attended by a small but faithful audience, most of them elderly. One was an eccentric lady who kept a marmoset concealed in her muff. It was gleefully remembered by the Petries that at a lecture on some African tribe at the Anthropological Society, the question arose as to whether the tribe in question had been cannibals; she had startled the audience by rising to her feet and declaring "I know they were—they ate my husband!" The Egyptian Research Students' Association (E.R.S.A.) held meetings throughout the war; local Honorary Secretaries roped in not only past students but also members of the public, and papers on Egyptological subjects, often written by Petrie himself, were duplicated and sent round to them. As the war went on the number of active branches diminished and lecturers were more difficult to find, but the London branch maintained its activities (knitting was recommended to everyone but the lecturer at these meetings).[5] Subscriptions to the British School, earmarked for ultimate publication and the eventual resumption of excavation, were meanwhile invested in War Loan; members were encouraged to contribute also to the Scottish Women's Hospitals, an organization of which Hilda Petrie was Honorary Secretary; they maintained hospitals for the Serbian division of the Russian army, for which cause her fund-raising talents were put to use early in the war; later, in uniform, she typed confidential documents.

Almost all Petrie's students were now on active service, and news came of them from time to time: K. T. Frost had fallen in action, gallantly defending a machine-gun post; Lt Philip Button R.N. had been wounded, and so had Sidney Smith, one of the Department's most brilliant students in recent years. Duncan Willey, who spoke fluent Arabic, was a political officer in the Persian Gulf; shortly after the war ended, he was murdered by Kurds in Iraq. Butler-Stoney the artist died of wounds in 1917. Quibell had returned to his post in the Cairo Museum and was busy arranging the galleries; Wainwright was teaching in a boy's school in Cairo. For a time the Egypt Exploration Society were able to carry on their work at Tell el-'Amarna by employing an American excavator and an all-American staff. In 1915

Petrie discovered by accident, through seeing a newspaper cutting, that Americans were digging in Memphis, in the very temple of Merenptah which he had discovered; M. Lacau, the new Director of the Department of Antiquities, had granted the concession to the Museum of Pennsylvania. Since Petrie had intended to resume excavation there after the war he was understandably indignant. Later it became clear that Clarence Fisher, the excavator, had applied for the concession in good faith, assuming that the British School had given up its claim; but the resentment Petrie felt against Lacau did not augur well for their future relationship.

By 1915 the rearrangement of the Petrie Museum was more or less complete and during July, instead of the usual exhibition, Petrie threw it open to the public for the first time. He settled down now to achieve what he had always planned—the production of a series of some twenty monographs on particular groups of artefacts, arranged in typological series. Most of these books were to be based entirely on the material in the Petrie Museum; but in the case of tools and weapons he cast his net more widely, ranging through publications of excavations in the Mediterranean and the Middle East from Spain to Turkestan, in search of comparisons and possible connexions by trade. When, amid a chorus of protest, the Government decided to close the British Museum as a measure of economy in January 1916, he organized a joint letter under the signature of seventeen prominent London academics in an attempt to reverse the decision;[6] it was finally agreed to keep at least the Reading Room open for the use of scholars. Methodically he prepared volume after volume for press, working every weekday, including Saturdays, taking his own photographs, making his own line drawings (Hilda was too busy now to help him in this) and pasting up his own plates; his desk and table were littered with little bits of paper and printed numbers. Amulets were the first to be dealt with, then Scarabs, then Tools and Weapons; two volumes on the predynastic periods had appeared by 1920, others on weights and measures, objects of daily use, and so on, were completed but had to be set aside until restrictions on the supply of paper were relaxed. Fifteen eventually came out, the last posthumously. These volumes, each containing a *corpus* of the objects treated, arranged in series according to type, function and chronological development, together with notes on the technological processes concerned in their production, were the first of their kind and are still indispensable to the field archaeologist and the museum curator, and are reprinted from time to time. In 1915 Petrie could already claim: "When I first went to Egypt,

35 years ago, nothing was known of the technical or industrial history of the country. . . . Now every form, historic and prehistoric, is pretty closely dated, and we know far more of the history of Egyptian products than we do of those of Greece or Italy."[7] The last sentence may have to be modified nowadays, but if it is no longer true of the classical world, this is in no small part due to the example set by Flinders Petrie.

He was nevertheless much exercised in his mind about a problem which had been in the forefront of his thoughts for twenty years: that of the storage of scientific material and in particular, of antiquities. Since the days of his earliest excavations in Egypt he had brought home to England broken stone vases, potsherds, scraps of metal, faience scraps, odd beads, shreds of cloth—material not for display in the glass cases of museums but to be kept available for future study, perhaps in generations to come. "I always keep things I do not understand," he would say, "in order to study them at leisure, and sooner or later I find out what they are." His museum overflowed with them, in drawers and boxes and piles on the floor; the work still being done today with the slender resources of the Department by museum technicians and assistants is a triumphant vindication of this policy—the shirts from Tarkhan and Deshasha and the stone lions of Coptos (pp. 321, 209) are but two recent examples. The problem as he saw it was one which had to be faced by all museum curators and everyone concerned with research. To store everything of whatever kind which might be needed for future study in the conventional museums of the metropolis and elsewhere was manifestly impossible: they were already hard-pressed for storage space and their budgets did not allow for expansion. Moreover, such "study-material", Petrie felt, ought to be available in one spot, and not scattered up and down the country. As early as 1896, in his Presidential Address to the British Association in Liverpool, Petrie had put forward a novel scheme for a huge national repository for all surplus archaeological material, as well as geological specimens and the reserve store of the great ethnographical collection with which the British Museum was bursting at the seams.

The idea was received with some interest and after the meeting a sub-committee was appointed to give it further consideration and draw up a series of proposals. This body did indeed meet a number of times, but the matter went no further until in the summer of 1900 Petrie was invited to read a paper to the Royal Society of Arts.[8] Mankind, he told them, had a duty to conserve every evidence of his past: not merely objects of artistic beauty, but samples of the relics of every age, pottery, flint artefacts, skulls and skeletons, objects of everyday life from every age of past history should be preserved. He looked forward to a great expansion of archaeological exploration during the new century that lay ahead: the mounds of Syria and Mesopotamia were full, he said, of unopened treasure; the ancient civilizations of Cambodia, China and Japan had yet to be studied, the whole continent of America was still untouched; "and yet to get ten square yards of an English museum is a problem."

The repository he proposed should be outside London to save cost; it must be capable of infinite expansion, and therefore planned so that no rearrangement would ever be necessary, with a long gridiron of galleries against which annexes could be attached at any point. It should ideally be near London, in Surrey or Kent perhaps, in an area where land was still available at £50 an acre. A village should be built nearby so that curators and staff, and visiting scholars, could live and work on the spot; ground rents from this land improvement would help to finance the running costs. His paper went on to discuss practical details: alternative designs for the building were suggested, the number of staff required, the probable cost.

This imaginative and far-seeing proposal was well received by the meeting and the Association of Museum Curators recommended further discussion. Not surprisingly, no further action was taken. Petrie sent a copy of his paper to Arthur Balfour, then First Lord of the Treasury, asking for his support and for his advice on how best to present the proposal to the Government. It was essentially, he pointed out, a scheme to save money:

> The whole provision of all the space required for centuries to come could be made by devoting the normal *growth* of the Museum budget to this purpose for only five years and after that letting the museums grow as before. It is not desirable that such a Repository should be a branch of the British Museum; it should be open to all Museums and private persons to deposit a collection approved by its keeper. This elastic constitution would be needed for the new aims, and eventually it might be the great National Museum for Study, while the London museums would be the treasure houses for valuable things needing special safety.[9]

Nothing came of the suggestion; the thinking behind it was far in advance of current concepts of a museum as a treasure house for the rare and beautiful, and it remained one of Petrie's dreams to the end of his life.

A welcome interlude from work came at Whitsun, when Petrie was usually invited for a long weekend to Edward Clodd's house in Aldeburgh, where he was sure of warm hospitality, country walks and stimulating conversation. Clodd, "the Great Magnet of Aldeburgh", had a large circle of friends including many of the latter-day eminent Victorians, many of whom shared his agnostic and rationalist views. He was by profession a banker, but read voraciously and was a keen follower of the latest discoveries in science and anthropology.[10] Thomas Hardy and George Meredith were among his friends, and it was probably Holman Hunt who introduced Flinders Petrie to him; among those whom Petrie met at the "Pentecostal gatherings" in his house at Aldeburgh, beside Hardy and Hunt, were the anthropologist Haddon, Sir Alfred Lyall, and in later years the historian J. B. Bury. Clodd was a genial host who liked to take his guests on little expeditions, sometimes in his yacht *Lotus* on the river Alde, or else by carriage, usually on Whit Sunday (for church was not in the programme) to Orford Castle, Dunwich or Framlingham. In the summer of 1915, when the Petries were in Dorset and visiting Maiden Castle, they took John to call on Thomas Hardy. The Clodds had a house in London at Tufnell Park, and sometimes visited the Petries. Flinders and Hilda visited Aldeburgh for the last time in May 1923; Clodd was then eighty-three and it was almost his last house party; Bury was there, and Professor Haddon, and Lord Clifford, the author of books on science and evolution.

In 1915 news came of the death of Flaxman Spurrell. In a short obituary notice[11] Flinders paid a tribute of gratitude to his old friend, upon whose enthusiastic support he had once relied; although he had never practised as a doctor, he had often given advice and a long-distance diagnosis when Petrie was ill in Egypt. In spite of Spurrell's interest in the Stone Age of the Nile Valley, he was never persuaded to come to Egypt; he was something of a recluse and a pessimist, and during the last twenty years he had withdrawn into melancholia and hardly ever left his Norfolk home. Flinders said of him, "He was almost the only man with whom I was ever familiar, and I owe him more than I can tell."[12]

During the war years, Flinders was able to watch his children grow and get to know them better. At the beginning of the war, John was a sturdy seven-year-old; every Sunday morning his father would take him for a long walk over Child's Hill or Golders Hill, or up the grassy slopes of Hampstead Heath; two years later, Ann joined these Sunday walks. In school holidays they would go down with their mother to Rustington Grange to stay with their grandmother, and Flinders would join them for the weekend and take them down to the beach, or for picnics on the Downs. He liked to visit John at his school, University College Preparatory School in Holly Hill, Hampstead, on such occasions as sports day or prizegiving; during the holidays, he taught him to use carpenter's tools properly and made him a work-bench. The children had very happy memories of the house at Well Road where they were born and where the early part of their child-hood was spent. In the evenings their father would play draughts with them, then he taught them backgammon and chess; he loved to play the piano, very fast and with a liberal sprinkling of wrong notes, and they would dance up and down the passages to the sound of an Irish jig. Bach, Beethoven and Haydn were his favourite composers; he would sometimes sit reading musical scores for enjoyment. Karl Pearson still lived next door, and Ernest Gardner and his wife not far away in Hampstead Square. The house in Well Road showed the influence of the Petries' Pre-Raphaelite and Art Nouveau friends, in furniture and in wall-decoration—pale-olive coloured chairs, lotus patterns in beaten copper, and Botticelli prints. Alma Tadema, Henry Wallis, Holman Hunt and G. F. Watts, at whose houses they used to dine, were now dead, but Ann remembers visiting Henry Holiday in his studio in Hampstead, a little man in a velvet knickerbocker suit, with a bald head and a thin beard.

During the summer, when the College was shut and the schools on holiday, Flinders and Hilda and the two children would take a cottage in the country for two or three weeks, and spend their time surveying the prehistoric hill figures on the chalk downs of Berkshire and Wiltshire; armed with sandwiches and water flasks and a theodolite and tape, they would all troop off in the morning, Flinders' cap "set at a jaunty angle".[13] In the summer of 1917, on the first of these expeditions, they found lodgings in Faringdon and spent three weeks up on the Downs while Flinders planned the White Horse at Uffington and the earthworks of Uffington Castle, to a scale of one in four hundred; next year it was the Long Man of Wilmington, said to be the largest representation of the human figure in the world (it is 231 feet long). The third summer, August 1919, the family took rooms in Cerne Abbas seven miles from Dorchester, above which is the most celebrated of all the hill figures, the Cerne Giant, a Herculean figure club in hand. It was very hot, and planning the figure and the earthworks around it took nearly a month; when they were not holding the end of the tape, the children went for walks over the downs.

Petrie's method in planning these huge figures was to stretch a line from head to feet, then two lines across the shoulders and the legs at right angles to it.

> Standing at the required point, I held two tape measures: the zero of one was held on the long line by my wife, the zero of the other on a cross line by my son, keeping the tapes square with the lines. I then read off the distances to the spot on the ground, and plotted it at once on squared paper. Each of the 160 points was thus fixed. The field plotting was then reduced by photolithography . . . the errors on the plate are probably less than a hundredth of an inch.[14]

These surveys are probably the most accurate ever made, and have abiding value, not least because he recorded details visible in his time, which have since eroded or been cleared away in one of the periodical "cleansings" of the figures. His attempt to date them to the late Stone or early Bronze Age, largely on the basis of some holes near the Cerne Giant which he wrongly took to be ancient flint mines, was not so happy; even less was his—admittedly very tentative—suggestion that there might be a connection with the worship of the Vedic deities of India.[15]

The Petries made other friends in Hampstead through the Hampstead Scientific Society, of which Flinders was invited in 1910 to be President, in succession to Sir Samuel Wilks. This office he held for twenty-three years.[16] He took his duties seriously, inviting the secretary to supper from time to time to discuss the society's business, and making himself available any evening if there were matters to be settled. He presided at many general meetings of the society, and usually lectured himself at least once a year. At the annual *conversazione* in the Town Hall, the President and his lady, in evening dress, received the guests, music was played, refreshments were served, and there was an eminent speaker. On the first of such occasions, the lecturer was the anthropologist Charles Gabriel Seligman; he and his wife had more than once visited the Petries in camp when on their way to the Sudan, when they were living among the Nilotic tribes. Other friends or university colleagues of Petrie's also lectured at these gatherings; the President had a valuable role to play in finding speakers. One of the Society's interests was astronomy, one of Petrie's own hobbies; they owned a small observatory and meteorological station on Hampstead Heath.

The Petries' favourite social events, however, were the *conversaziones* of the Royal Society, of which Petrie had been a Fellow since 1902. His election had not been without controversy, as he heard afterwards: Sir John Evans had wanted to prefer Wallis Budge, but Galton, who was on the Council, had been adamant, and Petrie's name went forward unopposed. He was, with one exception* the last archaeologist to be so honoured; after 1901 the British Academy fulfilled the same role for the Humanities as the Royal Society did for the Sciences; Petrie was one of the very few who were Fellows of both. He often found the lectures too technical for his understanding, but at the soirées, which he made a point of attending with Hilda, he met many of the greatest scientists of the day.

For a time during the war they had a friend and near neighbour in Professor Masaryk, who was staying as a refugee in a boarding house in Holford Road. Two of his girl students from the University of Prague, who had come over for a course in Oxford and been caught by the war, stayed with the Petries; they came for a few days, but stayed for almost a year, and became almost part of the family. In 1929 President Masaryk, as he was by then, invited the Petries to Czechoslovakia to stay with him in his country house, Topolcianky; Flinders could not find time to go, but Hilda and Ann were royally entertained.

Zeppelin raids in the autumn of 1917 gave Flinders grave anxiety for his collection; the skylighted gallery was sadly vulnerable and even stray shrapnel could have done damage; fortunately the building came through the war unscathed. In the following spring, the Petries moved from Well Road to No. 5, Cannon Place, not far away, the house which today bears a commemorative blue plaque. Moving was a formidable undertaking, for the house at Well Road was filled from floor to ceiling with books; books lined the staircase and there were bookshelves even over the door frames. They moved just after Easter; the children were sent off to the seaside and Petrie carried up his precious mineral and coin collections drawer by drawer before the moving men arrived with a cart to move the furniture and books. The Karl Pearsons had already left Well Road and were living in a cottage in the country. The house at Cannon Place had a small lawn and flower garden at the back, but the Petries were no gardeners and the plot

* Mortimer Wheeler in 1968.

became increasingly, and at length entirely devoted to the cultivation of artichokes, of which Flinders was fond.

To his children, Flinders seemed omniscient; confident in his own judgement, he usually had a ready answer for their questions; if not, he knew where to look and would consult a reference book on the spot, even at mealtimes. He had an endless fund of anecdotes and jokes, and a private vocabulary for the amusement of the family. "That's dunded," he would say when he put aside a finished task. There were usually several piles of work on his desk and tables, in various stages of completion. No telephone was permitted in the house—this he regarded as an interruption of work—and he seldom went to concerts, and never to the theatre, which he regarded as mere frivolity; watching sport and reading novels were also wasting time. When Ann, later on, bought herself a small crystal set, he wrote to her, "So you have your longed-for paradise of wireless. Don't let it paralyse your vitality. It is a deadly thing to be a pond instead of a fountain." He was careful of his own money, but generous towards others; "give, never lend," he advised Ann when she discussed with him how she should help a fellow student in difficulties with tuition fees. His own way of life was frugal ("nobody," he would say, "needs more than five inches of water in the bath") and he had few extravagances; when Ann once asked him what he would like for his birthday, his answer was: "Time is all I need."

He built a small laboratory for John against the wall of the house at Cannon Place, and filled it with bottles, hoping that his son had inherited his own childhood's passion for chemistry, but the boy was not really interested. When he was ten, he was sent to St George's, Harpenden, a progressive co-educational boarding-school; Ann joined him there two years later. In the matter of education, as in many other things, their parents had advanced views.

In spite of his preoccupation with the ordering and publication of his collection and the editing of *Ancient Egypt*, Flinders Petrie found time to devote to several organizations in which he had a personal interest, attending their meeting and sometimes speaking; he wrote letters to *The Times* on current political issues and assisted in the drafting of leaflets and petitions. Prominent among his activities was his membership of the Anti-Socialist Society, of which he had been a member for some years; he was the author of at least one of their pamphlets. The views he had so forcibly expressed in *Janus* and in articles in monthly journals had drawn him into the circle of a right-wing body, the British Constitution Association, and in 1914 he was elected their

President in succession to Lord Ritchie.[17] They met several times a year, published leaflets under the title "Constitution Issues" and passed resolutions from time to time opposing constitutional changes proposed by the Liberal Government of the day; in particular they were hostile to the National Insurance Scheme proposed by Lloyd George, and in March 1918 a somewhat startling resolution of theirs, passed at their General Meeting, was published in the daily press, "viewing with alarm the vast and uncontrolled increase of expenditure on public assistance, and supporting the demand for a complete return of all such expenditure by the Central Government and local authorities as an indispensable preliminary to any further expenses."[18] The National Society for Non-Smokers, which was campaigning to secure non-smoking accommodation in teashops and restaurants, and ban smoking in telephone booths, claimed Flinders Petrie as one of their patrons.

In his leisure moments Petrie was reading widely, and he occasionally made forays into print in historical fields remote from his own; in 1918, when invited to address the British Academy, he surprised his audience, who expected a lecture on some aspect of ancient Egyptian civilization, by talking on the sources of early British history,[19] and in a lecture to the Society of Antiquaries for Scotland in Edinburgh he analysed that part of Ptolemy's Geography which treats of Albion.[20] A letter of his to *The Times Literary Supplement* criticized S. R. Gardiner's use of evidence in his account of the English Civil War; the author, he complained, had omitted to cite certain essential documents.[21]

Meanwhile in the Levant the Turks were withdrawing: General Maude occupied Baghdad in March 1917 and in December Allenby entered Jerusalem; it looked as if the war in the Middle East would soon be over. In January 1918 Petrie gave a series of three lectures at the Royal Institution on the subject of *Eastern Exploration, Past and Future*, on which he set out his own vision of what Britain's responsibilities must be towards the antiquities of the countries which were about to come under her mandate.[22] He stressed the need to take "long-sighted and effective measures at once—this year", in order to prevent the destruction of ancient sites and monuments by the rapid development which was sure to follow the establishment of law and order. In particular he stressed the danger to Jerusalem of indiscriminate industrial development: too little was known of its past.

> Whenever free excavation is possible, we may begin really to understand the history of the city in detail. This will never be done if Jerusalem is now left to grow on as a commercial modern town. The site is most unsuitable for business purposes; and much the best course, for practical and for historical reasons, would be to start a modern suburb and then clear ancient Jerusalem down to the Solomonic town, and keep it as a Jewel of the Past, visited by all but appropriated by none.

In Mesopotamia, the cities of the south should be systematically excavated. Sir Stanley Maude's proclamation in Baghdad had gone some way towards laying down principles whereby ancient monuments were to be protected. Ancient sites should now be identified and mapped and travelling inspectors appointed by a Board of Antiquities, who should be authorized to pay small rewards for information leading to the disclosure of accidental discoveries. Excavation by qualified archaeologists of other nationalities would be encouraged, but careful recording and the prompt publication of results should be insisted upon. Local museums were needed; they should not be old houses or palaces converted, but specifically built for the purpose, to simple and suitable designs. It is useless, said Petrie wisely, for any attempt to be made to impose a Government monopoly of antiquities, as Greece and Turkey had done; no prohibitory law can prevent the export of valuable objects. "You may walk through the customs with a priceless vase—if you put a plant in it, and pink paper round it."

One day in May 1918 Petrie went to the British Museum to talk to Dr Leonard King, Assistant Keeper of the Department of Egyptian and Assyrian Antiquities (the Keeper was still Wallis Budge); they formed a committee to discuss the formation of a British School of Archaeology in Jerusalem, on the lines of those in Rome and Athens. An appeal went out that summer,[23] and the British School came into being the following year. John Garstang was appointed its first Director. Meanwhile the Armistice had been signed, and the war was over (KAISER ENDED, wrote Petrie in his diary). The British Academy, at the request of the Government, set up a Joint Archaeological Committee, consisting of representatives of the British Museum, the various archaeological Schools, and the Royal Institute of British Architects; its first task was to draft a Law of Antiquities applicable to Palestine. A small international committee was also set up to draft clauses for inclusion in the peace treaty with Turkey and in the constitutions of the British and French Mandates.[24] The chief points to be clarified were very much along the lines of Petrie's lectures to the Royal Institution.

No mention of Egypt was made in all this, but in March 1919 Sir John Evans wrote a long and eloquent letter to *The Times* pleading the case for a British Institute of Research in Egypt. Other countries, he said—France, Germany, America—had national centres for their students and scholars; the E.E.S. and the B.S.A.E. had been hampered by lack of funds, and had in the past had no support from the British Government; the need now was for a good library, funds for research and publication, and bursaries for the support of students.[25] That day's leading editorial and subsequent letters from Lord Grenfell and Sir John Maxwell endorsed the plea, but Petrie took a more practical view: it was no good, he wrote, sending students to Egypt if subsequently the only jobs that they could get were poorly paid posts in the Antiquities Service "only adequate for bachelor life". Opportunities were now needed for careers in archaeology. "The needful expansion in Egypt can only be properly carried on by some twenty or more new officials. If there were a guarantee that such would be gradually provided for the next few years, the prospects would attract men who would be worthy of the position and of our national reputation."[26]

No action was taken in response to these suggestions, and subsequent representations from time to time, from that day till the present, have met with failure. Though Her Majesty's Government now subsidizes excavation in Egypt, there is still no British Institute of Archaeology in Cairo.

Just after the war Petrie found that he had a new academic colleague, a man with whom he had long been at loggerheads. Grafton Elliot Smith had been Professor of Anatomy in Manchester for the past ten years and before that had held a similar post in the Cairo School of Medicine; he was a leading expert on mummification, having examined the royal mummies in the Cairo Museum and the human remains from Dr Reisner's excavations in Giza and elsewhere in Egypt and Nubia. On his appointment to the Chair of Anthropology at University College he might have been expected to maintain a close liaison with the Department of Egyptology and its Professor. This was far from the case. The antagonism between the two men had begun in October 1910 when, commenting on an article of Petrie's on the recent discoveries at Meydum, Elliot Smith had declared that he was talking nonsense. Petrie had cited Wainwright's discovery of the mummified prince in Mastaba 17, with its defleshed and dismembered limbs, as proof of his larger claim that in Egypt "the disseverance of the skeleton was the custom among the higher classes at the beginning of the Pyramid period". Not so, wrote Elliot Smith; he had examined thousands of mummies, but had never seen a single case of such a practice. He referred to Petrie's other "fantastic speculations": bones at Naqada, he insisted, cannot be assumed to have been "broken to extract the marrow and gnawed" in some cannibalistic ritual; they must have been damaged by rats, or the necrophilic beetle. "The whole evidence afforded by excavations," he declared, "is that this statement is pure fiction."[27]

Petrie replied in the next number of *Nature*: his critic had simply not looked at the evidence. The specimens had been on view at his exhibition in London. "I regret that Prof Elliot Smith did not examine them nor, indeed, honour our excavations by a single inspection during the years when he was in Egypt." The argument continued into November, and was continued thereafter in a very acrimonious private exchange of letters during the following year.[28] In Elliot Smith's view, nothing that Wainwright had found in the Meydum *mastaba*, or that Petrie had observed at Deshasha or at Naqada, was not capable of explanation by the natural processes of decomposition, of which, he said, Petrie and Wainwright appeared to be ignorant. Petrie had one trump card: the bundle of leg bones from Deshasha, of which he had published an X-ray photograph (see p. 229); for this Elliot Smith had no explanation to offer but he declined to be convinced by a single case.

In spite of Petrie's care to observe and record accurately, general opinion has been against his theory of ritual dismemberment and cannibalistic practices, either in predynastic or in dynastic Egypt. It runs counter to the most fundamental beliefs of the ancient Egyptians in corporeal survival in the Afterlife and the concept of the practice of mummification as an attempt to preserve the body whole and complete. There is, however, occasional evidence for the burial of defective or dismembered bodies, of which the Deshasha parcel is one example; it is nowadays assumed that in such cases the body had been disturbed and later reburied, or else imperfectly embalmed and rewrapped later.[29]

Flinders Petrie crossed swords with Elliot Smith on another matter also; in 1915 Smith had written a book entitled *The Ancient Egyptians and the Origins of Civilization*, in which he developed the theory that nothing has been invented more than once, and that therefore all civilization spread from one centre; that centre, he claimed, was the

Nile Valley where, around 4000 BC, the Egyptians evolved an "Archaic Civilization" which they spread over the world as they journeyed by land and sea in search of precious metals. This theory he expounded in 1915 at a meeting of the British Association in Manchester at which Petrie was present; Smith's friend and colleague in the University of Manchester, W. J. Perry, also spoke in the same strain. Petrie noted in his diary "much disgusted". He did not believe a word of it, and his copy of Elliot Smith's book is full of pencilled comments: "No such thing!" "Nonsense!" "No, No!" "No evidence whatsoever".[30] The Diffusionist School attracted many adherents and greatly influenced the Anthropology Department at University College when Smith and Perry joined it; subsequently Perry went even further: his "Children of the Sun" were responsible for introducing into the New World the Egyptian practice of mummification and the building of megalithic monuments. Petrie did not hesitate to say what he thought of the Diffusionists' theories and for some years was barely on speaking terms with Elliot Smith; if Margaret Murray is to be believed, they made it up at last, before they both retired.[31]

The second camp at Abydos, 1901–3

CHAPTER XVI

Egypt over the Border
(1919–30)

FLINDERS PETRIE WAS now sixty-six, an age at which most men might expect to contemplate retirement from active work in the field. His greatest achievements lay behind him; indeed, it might be said that his most important contributions to Egyptology had been made and completed nearly twenty years before. No such thought entered his mind; his one desire was to get back to Egypt and to the life he loved, where there was so much still to be done. Hilda shared his eagerness to be off; they were neither of them so happy as when living the simple life and breathing the desert air. In September 1919 Flinders wrote to M. Lacau asking for permission to return to Lahun, where throughout the war 'Ali Suefi had been sent a regular remittance to guard the site and keep the house in repair. The permit came promptly; the Petries sorted their papers, left the affairs of the British School in the hands of Miss Murray and a young cousin of theirs, Beatrice Rowe, and set off one November morning on the familiar early boat train from Victoria. The children, safely now at boarding school, were judged sensible enough to be given their own bank accounts and shown how to write cheques and pay their own school bills. They would stay with their grandmother in Hampstead for the Christmas holidays.

The familiar pattern of events was repeated; on the evening of their arrival in Cairo, Petrie was off to the dealers to see what had turned up. Lord Allenby, the new High Commissioner, consented to become patron of the British School and professed interest in Petrie's work, and at the Museum they met the Director, M. Pierre Lacau, a handsome and learned man with a flowing white beard and piercing eyes (his nickname among archaeologists was God the Father); Daressy was still there, and James Quibell was now Curator of the Museum. The Petries invited the Sobhys, old friends, to dine, and they met for the first time that eccentric and delightful personality, Captain Archibald Creswell, a leading authority on Moslem architecture.

Captain Brunton and Captain Engelbach went ahead to open up the camp; Petrie conscientiously took his new recruits[1] round the museum and out to Giza. When on 8 December they found themselves sitting in Illahun in the same mess hut, with Muhammad Osman once more beaming at the kitchen door and nearly all the same Quftis ready to begin work, it seemed difficult to believe that so much had happened since their last season. But things were different now: the country was under martial law, and had been so since early in the war; the continued presence of the occupying power was resented and the party of the Wafd were vociferous in demanding independence. Zaghloul Pasha, their leader, had been recalled from exile by Allenby, but unrest continued; there had been riots in the provinces and ugly incidents; only that March a party of seven Englishmen had been dragged from the train at Deirut in Upper Egypt and murdered. A strike of cabmen had hindered the Petries' departure from Cairo and in February an unprecedented entry in Petrie's diary records that the Lahunis, his local workers, went on strike for a day. Not so the Quftis; their unfailing loyalty, and the pleasure they showed at being once more with "the Pasha", gives the lie to opinions apparently current in some arachaeological circles in Egypt today that Petrie "heartily loathed" his Quftis and was hated by them.[2] Nothing could have been further from the truth.

It was not a season for startling discoveries; minute examination of the burial chamber of the pyramid was rewarded with one precious fragment from the royal diadem: the golden uraeus, or cobra, inlaid with carnelian and lapis lazuli, with eyes of garnet set in gold.[3] A cemetery of many periods was dug on the desert edge. In April the work closed; Lacau inspected the finds but for some reason postponed the division; when the boxes finally arrived in London it was too late for an exhibition. There was plenty, however, to be done: *Ancient Egypt* could now be issued again, and Petrie as Editor had the task of assembling the articles and reviews almost single-handed.

In June 1920 he attended a meeting of the Society of Antiquaries at which a report was read on recent work in Stonehenge; during the war the army had carried out manoeuvres on Salisbury Plain; many of the stones were leaning and appeared to be unsafe. It was not the first time he had voiced his concern about England's greatest monument, for which he understandably felt a special responsibility. Long ago, in a storm on New Year's Eve 1900, one of the stones had blown down and others were damaged; it was decided that the site must be fenced in and the stones made secure. As soon as he read this, in camp at

Abydos, Petrie had written to *The Times* in protest, both on aesthetic grounds and because he feared inexpert excavation and injudicious restoration.[4] In fact, a discreet fence was put up—the time was past when such treasures could be left unprotected—and Sir William Garland, who carried out the necessary work, produced a careful report which shed much light on the history of the monument (he deduced 1800 BC as its probable date). Petrie was still of the opinion that Stonehenge had been, as Geoffrey of Monmouth had said, the burial place of British kings. In 1915, when the site was up for sale, he made some attempt to raise enough money to buy it—he would certainly have liked to dig there himself; but it was bought by a local landowner, who then presented it to the nation, and the Society of Antiquaries undertook the work of consolidation and restoration for the Office of Works. Petrie protested in vain[5]; his fears were not without foundation, for the excavation carried out by Col William Hawley dragged on till 1926, was poorly executed and reached few positive conclusions.[6] By that time, Petrie had perforce washed his hands of the matter.

The Petries' holiday was spent in Cornwall; they stayed in a cottage at Camelford, went to Tintagel, and planned hut circles on the western edge of Bodmin moor. During the winter of 1920–21 they were back in the Fayum again; Brunton spent most of the season patiently testing the Queen's pyramid at Lahun, without finding any trace of a burial shaft; it was concluded that it must have been a dummy. Petrie's party camped for a time near Gurob and then, deeming the cemeteries to be thoroughly exhausted, moved on southwards to Sedment, the cemetery of Ahnas. It will be remembered that in 1904, when they were working at Ahnas, Currelly had been sent over to see what Naville had left (for he had brought back little or nothing from the tombs he had opened there). Petrie was convinced that there was yet more to find. He was not disappointed. Here were tombs of the Archaic period and many of the Old Kingdom;[7] one sixth-dynasty tomb chamber contained three fine figures of the owner; one (**74**) he was allowed to take, and it went to the British Museum. Yet there was no sign of what he hoped and expected to find: the tombs of the Herakleiopolitan rulers of the twenty-first and twenty-second dynasties; he was forced to the conclusion that they must have been buried elsewhere.

Sedment was one of their oddest camps: the site, on an isolated ridge divided by cultivation from the desert, was pitted with craters, funnel-shaped pits where large tombs had been opened, and the entrances filled again with sand. In these they found shelter from the howling wind. Their tents were so well concealed that it was possible to walk right past without noticing them, and the party felt safe from prowlers and thieves.[8] The precaution was not without justification: one day Muhammad Osman, returning at dusk from market, was waylaid and brutally beaten by Arabs; he was eventually found by a search party from the camp and carried home unconscious. Petrie summoned the police, who took a statement; after some days a large gathering of sheikhs and guards met to discuss whether the place where the cook had been attacked was in the territory of Beni Suef; they decided it was not. Then a similar assembly was called together in the neighbouring *mudiriya* of Medinet el Fayum, which reached a similar conclusion. Legal formalities thus completed, nobody was arrested and the matter was dropped. Petrie protested to Maurice Amos, now a judge in Cairo, but in vain. "Had every Arab squatter within two miles of us been arrested at once, the cook could have recognised which of them attacked him, and the case would have been settled in twelve hours." Petrie knew his Egypt, however, and was not surprised at the outcome of his attempts to secure justice.

Quibell came down for the division as the Museum's representative, in company with Wainwright who had recently been given the post of Inspector of Antiquities in Middle Egypt, while Engelbach had been appointed Inspector of Monuments in Upper Egypt. Only Mackay was still in Palestine; he had been appointed Custodian of Antiquities, with his headquarters in Jerusalem.

In 1921 Petrie was back in Abydos. The objective was a site in the cemetery area which T. E. Peet had discovered ten years earlier but had had no time to investigate; that it had produced objects of the first dynasty[9] was enough for Petrie. It had been his first priority in his application to Lacau just after the war, but he had been told that the E.E.S. still held the concession. Now they formally relinquished the site to him and offered him the use of the excavation house; this he declined—he intended to pitch tents near the work, in the shelter of the great mud brick "fort" known as Shunet ez Zebib. Here they would be secure against possible raiders or sneak-thieves; from previous experience he knew 'Araba el Madfuna as a village from which trouble might be expected. In the event, there were no untoward incidents.

The excavations, in a low gravel plain behind the ancient town, about a mile from Umm el Qa'ab, proved puzzling: cut into by many later burials were hundreds of small, brick-lined tombs of the first dynasty, similar to those which had surrounded the tombs of the earliest kings; they were ranged in a double line around the sides of three great squares, but instead of a central burial, though he trenched in several directions, Petrie could find nothing. Had the area been used for some ceremony? Each of the groups of graves contained objects with royal names, respectively those of Zer, Zet and Mer Neith; they must, Petrie thought, be some kind of overflow from the crowded site at Umm el Qa'ab. He dubbed them the Tombs of the Courtiers. Their significance is still uncertain; it has been suggested that the occupants were minor palace officials, artisans and craftsmen, buried around some kind of funerary palaces the structures of which have disappeared, and that the other large brick "forts" nearby may have been later, second-dynasty counterparts to these early palaces.[10]

The party excavating with the Petries this year included a young geologist, Gertrude Caton-Thompson, a Cambridge graduate who had been a civil servant during the war, but whose interest was in palaeolithic archaeology. She had come to University College to see the Professor, full of questions about Egyptian flints, and had jumped at the idea of going out with him; she would leave the camp early every morning and go off into the high desert in search of flint implements and likely caves; occasionally Hilda would accompany her. On one of these expeditions they found, in a gorge, the cell of a Coptic hermit who had lived there in the fifth century AD. It was Christmas Eve, and a day of unrest in the province; from the camp the rattle of Lewis guns could be heard, but in this deep valley in the heart of the desert the silence of the anchorite's solitary life could be felt. A Qufti and two boys were taken up to help them clear the cave. The hermit had protected himself from prowling hyenas and foxes with a stone enclosure wall; in the cave mouth was his sitting-room, with a small oratory attached to it, and behind, a rockcut bench for his bed and a pedestal basin cut in the rock. At the back was his cooking bench, a larder furnished with storage jars, his cooking pot with its lid, his pottery soup ladle and his palm fibre brush. The walls were covered, inside and out, with pious *graffiti* and holy symbols in red and black paint; one read: "Jesus Christ, remember Mena."[11]

After two months at Abydos, Petrie moved to Behnesa, the scene of his first probings in 1896 on the mound in which Grenfell and Hunt had subsequently found so rich a harvest of papyri. They had concentrated their work on the city's rubbish heaps, but Oxyrhynchus had been a large town and Petrie wanted to find out more about it. Unfortunately the place had fallen a prey to the *sebbakhîn*, many of whom were still hard at work, unchecked by authority, using a light railway to carry away the earth and take it down to the canal; within a lifetime, Petrie ruefully concluded, there would probably be nothing left but sifted potsherds, over an area of some two square miles. Parts of several colonnades had turned up in the process; in the Roman period there had been some fine public buildings here. A large area of sand and chips turned out to be the site of the theatre; unable to dig it out completely—this would have entailed a workforce much larger than his slender resources could command—he found the general dimensions of the building and enough of the layout to plan it;[12] it had been quite large, with a stage two hundred feet long, a spiral staircase at each end, and an orchestra 100 feet wide. It had held, he calculated, some ten thousand people. As the only Roman theatre found in Egypt* it had considerable importance.

As the season neared its end, news came of the death of Mrs Urlin; Hilda hurried home, but Flinders stayed on a little in Cairo; he wanted to test a theory that the Great Sphinx at Giza might have had a counterpart on the other side of the Nile; he walked from Ma'adi over every foot of the ground opposite the pyramids, examining each outcrop of rock, and decided that there was no evidence for a contra-sphinx.

He was back in London late in April 1922; in May Hilda paid her first visit to Prague, in the company of Mrs Beauchamp Tufnell, the founder and secretary of the Czech Society of Great Britain, who organized tours in Czechoslovakia; Hilda offered to help, and a close and lasting friendship began between the two women; Mrs Tufnell's daughter Olga, fresh from school, became Hilda Petrie's secretary and assistant in the management of the affairs of the British School in Egypt, in place of Beatrice Rowe. It was dull, repetitive work for the most part, writing reminders to defaulting subscribers and begging letters—always by hand, and if possible delivered by hand; no typewriter or telephone was permitted—or invitations to a *conversazione* before the exhibition. The School's office was a couple of chairs and tables tucked away between the show cases in the Petrie Museum. Fraternization with the students was not encouraged; Beatrice, having rashly gone out to lunch with one of them, had been moved up to work in Cannon Place.

In mid-July, just as the exhibition was due to open, Flinders caught a bronchial cold and was confined to bed for nearly a month: Brunton took charge of the exhibition, helped by a new student, James Leslie

* Another has since been dug at Antinoopolis.

Starkey, in whom Petrie at once detected great promise. He had been an aircraftman in the Royal Air Force during the war and afterwards he had set about educating himself; he worked for a time as a lighthouse keeper, in order to have time to read all the books about ancient Egypt he could lay his hands on; then, working as a warehouseman and furniture salesman, he joined Miss Murray's evening class at University College.[13]

John and Ann were doing well at School and were keen on scouting and the Guides. They had spent the previous Christmas holidays with the Crowfoots at Beccles on the Norfolk–Suffolk border and John, bidden by his father to make, as a holiday task, a map of the countryside, had had to borrow a bicycle from one of the four Crowfoot daughters and learn to ride it. That summer, when John was seventeen, Flinders decided to give him his first taste of excavation; he had already taken him several times to meetings of the British Association, and the boy had shown interest; he had high hopes of making an archaeologist of him. In the previous summer they had spent two weeks in the Avebury district, walking over the Downs and planning earthworks and stone circles; it was to be expected that Petrie's curiosity would be aroused by the presence, less than a mile from Avebury, of that stupendous earthwork, Silbury Hill, the largest ancient man-made mound in Europe. Why, and when, this huge conical hill was erected had puzzled antiquarians over the centuries; the Duke of Northumberland had employed Cornish miners to drive a vertical shaft from the top, and in 1849 the Dean of Hereford tunnelled into the mound from the side, but found no burial chamber. In spite of its symmetrical shape and apparently artificial appearance, some considered it a natural formation. Petrie was determined to see whether more scientific excavation could solve the riddle. He had written to Lord Avebury on his return to London, to ask his permission to conduct a small-scale investigation, and in August 1922 he and John packed a tent and surveying equipment and set up camp at the foot of the hill; Hilda and Ann stayed with friends near by. It was bitterly cold and each morning there was ice on the tent. Engaging a few local workmen, they drove a shaft into the base of the mound opposite the eastern causeway, searching for a possible entrance passage; they found neither this nor a burial chamber during the three weeks they worked there, but the work had one important result: they were able to establish that Silbury Hill was indeed man-made and that it had been built in a series of horizontal layers, as a *tell* is formed.[14] Fragments of deer antlers used as picks by the ancient builders suggested an early date: it could not anyway be Roman, said Petrie, because the Roman Road had made a detour to avoid it. Subsequent excavation undertaken in 1966 under the sponsorship of the B.B.C. and watched by large audiences on television found further evidence of how the mound was constructed, and radio-carbon tests established a Neolithic date for the pottery and animal remains, but no burial was found and there was—and still is—no clue to the purpose and function of the earthwork (**72**).[15]

That winter, 1922–23, Flinders Petrie again decided to stay in England. One of the reasons was the need to proceed with a backlog of publications: books long planned had been held up by the paper shortage and increased costs of printing. Four books and seventeen articles and reviews came from his pen that year, and he was also working on his contribution to Herbert Spencer's *Descriptive Sociology*, compiled from the writings of ancient and modern authors; in this, as in some of Petrie's other books written for the general public, his lack of specialist knowledge of the original texts makes the book little used today.

On 26 November 1922 an event occurred which was to have a profound effect on the future of archaeology in Egypt: Howard Carter, with his patron Lord Carnarvon and Lady Evelyn Herbert at his side, peered through a little hole and saw, beyond the blocked doorway, undreamt-of treasures. The official opening of the tomb of Tutankhamun took place three days later; thereafter, to Carter's distraction, sightseers began to arrive in their hundreds, some with introductions, others claiming special privilege. Had Flinders Petrie been there, he would certainly have been one of the few whom Carter, his one-time pupil, would have showed round ungrudgingly. As it was, he regarded himself fortunate not to be involved in the unseemly quarrels and petty jealousies that hindered the work of clearance in the months that followed.[16]

Another reason for his decision not to dig that winter was the uncertainty caused by Lacau's announcement that it was intended to abrogate that provision in the Antiquities Law relating to the division of antiquities found in excavation between the excavator and the government of Egypt; under Maspero the principle had been that of equal shares, except in certain specified areas, notably the Valley of the Tombs of the Kings and Saqqara. Now it was proposed that excavating bodies should only receive what (if anything) the Director chose to give them; he would also be empowered to grant or withhold concessions at his pleasure. On 28 February of that year the British

Protectorate over Egypt had officially ended, and Egypt had become an independent kingdom; there were therefore no English officials to whom appeal could be made. This and other proposed restrictions would mean that museums, who expected to enlarge their collections in return for their patronage, could no longer be relied upon to support excavation in Egypt. Petrie viewed this situation with the utmost alarm; when he heard of it he wrote at once to Lythgoe, Breasted and the officials of other museums in the United States and in Europe, and on 5 December 1922 he summoned a meeting at University College at which the Egypt Exploration Society was represented by its President Sir John Maxwell, the Honorary Secretary H. R. Hall and Alan Gardiner; Lythgoe, Mace and Wace came over for the Metropolitan Museum of New York, and Petrie represented the British School. A formal protest on behalf of the archaeologists of Great Britain and America was drafted by Petrie and Lythgoe, and approved by all the members; the chairman of the Joint Archaeological Committee, together with the President of the Society of Antiquaries and other prominent archaeologists, added their signatures and it was forwarded to the Council of Ministers in Cairo, to Lord Allenby as the High Commissioner, and to M. Lacau.[17]

As a result of this and similar protests from other countries, the passing of the new law was suspended: it would not come into force for two years, they were told: nevertheless the threat hung over all excavating bodies, curtailing their plans for new work. In the case of the treasures from the Tomb of Tutankhamun it was understandable that the Egyptian Government should assert its right to retain everything: the whole contents of the tomb were needed for the national collection. The Egypt Exploration Society and the Americans decided that the best attitude to adopt was "the renunciation of any rights to objects discovered, with an appeal to the generosity of the Government in respect to duplicates and objects not wanted for the National Collections."[18] Petrie had less faith in Lacau's generosity. He decided to confine himself to excavations in which there was little likelihood of finding anything of value; for the next three years the work of the British School was devoted chiefly to the early cemeteries and to the exploration of Stone Age sites. He also decided to explore the possibility of excavating outside Egypt, in Palestine or Syria: in January 1923 he wrote to John Garstang, now the Director of Antiquities for the Government of Palestine, applying for permission to dig in Jerusalem on the Hill of Ophel near the Pool of Siloam, in the following spring.[19] He was told that the concession for this site—a particularly important one, since here remains of the earliest Jerusalem might be expected —had already been promised: R. A. S. Macalister was to go out that year (1923) for the Palestine Exploration Fund.

Petrie then sought Garstang's support for another scheme. Byblos, the modern Jubail on the coast of what is now Lebanon, was a site of prime importance for Egyptian history; Pierre Montet had been finding objects of the finest Egyptian workmanship: a chance fall of the cliff face in 1922 had revealed tombs containing royal treasure, some pieces of which were Egyptian royal objects of the twelfth dynasty; in an article in *Ancient Egypt*[20] Petrie emphasized the importance of the discovery for relations between Syria and Egypt and expressed the hope that a complete record would be made of the find—he was evidently afraid that it would not. He had two alternative proposals: he would either work for the French, free of all cost, if they would provide up to £50 a week for the excavation, or else he would himself find £50 a week from the Research Fund; in the first case, he would have only the right of publication; in the second, he would claim the right to nominate the museums to which his half-share of the objects should be given.[21] This plan came to nothing, Montet (perhaps wisely) preferring independence to the temptation of additional funds. Two years later Petrie asked Newberry, who was intending to visit Byblos, if he could do anything to further his proposal; digging, he had heard, was "scrappy and irregular", and the site was being lamentably plundered whenever the excavators were not there. "It is a scandal that one of the most important places should be thus ruined."[22]

Meanwhile an expedition had gone to Egypt as usual on behalf of the School: the Bruntons were working at a new site, Qau el Kebir on the east bank of the Nile between Asyut and Sohag, the ancient Antaeopolis; with them were Henri Bach and two students, both of whom were to make their names in archaeology: one was Starkey, the other a brilliant young Dutchman, Henri Frankfort, whose studies in the University of Amsterdam had been interrupted by three years in the Netherlands army; after the war he had come to learn Egyptology at University College. This was to be his only season with the British School, so that he never actually dug with Petrie; he was later to conduct several seasons of excavation for the Egypt Exploration Society at Abydos, el 'Amarna and Armant, before becoming the director of the excavations of the Oriental Institute in Iraq. It was Starkey who found, that winter at Qau, a papyrus wrapped in a cloth and buried in a jar, containing the earliest Coptic version of St John's

Gospel; at home Petrie unfolded, flattened and mounted it with Miss Tufnell's help. In July, Flinders Petrie received his knighthood. The citation made no mention of archaeology, but was "for services to Egypt" (this was true enough, for his single-minded devotion to the rescue of their past had put all Egyptians in his debt). His diary reads laconically: *July 25th. 10.30 Buckingham Palace. Knighted. Back by 12.*

One of the Petrie's guests that summer was O. G. S. Crawford, who had been in the Sudan before the war with Reisner. In his autobiography he speaks with gratitude of the encouragement given him by Petrie, "who taught and inspired me".[23] The importance of his innovatory work on the aerial survey of archaeological sites was immediately obvious to Petrie and it was largely due to his encouragement that the journal *Antiquity*, which was to do much to popularize archaeology in England, was started in 1927 by Crawford, its editor till his death in 1957.

In June, in celebration of his seventieth birthday, Petrie's friends and colleagues decided to raise money for a bronze medal, to be called the Petrie Medal; it was to be awarded "for distinguished work in archaeology" and the first recipient was to be Petrie himself. The sculptor took some time to execute the medal, it was presented to Petrie in July 1925 by the Chancellor of the University at a ceremony in the College. Thenceforward the medal was awarded every three or four years until the money ran short; Sir Aurel Stein, the distinguished Austrian explorer, was the recipient in 1928, then Sir Arthur Evans,

G. *The Petrie Medal.* The head on the reverse may be derived from the ivory head of Khufu from Abydos; the ibis denotes Thoth, the Egyptian god of wisdom.

the excavator of Knossos, the great prehistorian the Abbé Breuil, and Professor J. D. Beazley; after the war, Sir Mortimer Wheeler received the award in 1950, Professor A. B. Wace, the excavator of Mycenae, in 1953, and Sir Leonard Woolley in 1957. Thereafter the decision was taken to devote the remaining money to a Petrie Prize to be awarded to a young archaeologist of promise at University College. Petrie seems to have disliked the design of the medal (p. 358). "The first aim of the artist seems to have been his own virtuosity according to modern standards." It was indeed a far cry from the Pre-Raphaelites, but hardly avant-garde. Conservative in art as in music, he was a stern critic of the "new sculpture"; when in 1929 Epstein's "Night and Day", was unveiled on St James's Park Underground Station, he joined the chorus of condemnation in the daily press.[24]

In the winter of 1923–4 Flinders went to Egypt without Hilda. The Bruntons again worked at their cemetery sites; Petrie himself spent most of his time recording the rock cut tombs of the rulers of the tenth Upper Egyptian nome. They were imposing structures, with grand porticoes and causeways leading up to rock-cut chapels and pillared halls, and finally to the burial chambers hewn in the heart of the cliff. With him was a student, Greenlees, Lt Commander Noel Wheeler, for a time Mrs Ethel Benson, an old friend who had proved at Behnesa that she could turn her hand to anything, and two other visitors, Miss Irene Donne* and Mrs Aitken, the patient stringer of beads, out for the first time on a "dig"; they lived snugly in empty rock-tombs and shared the chores of the camp. Unhappily Mrs Benson was taken ill and had to be sent to hospital before she had been there very long. The Bruntons, with another party, were five miles to the north digging cemeteries.

Three great tombs in particular needed recording. Two previous expeditions had worked at Qau; in 1905–6 the Italian Archaeological Mission had excavated the tombs; a great deal of sculpture had been found, including parts of over life-size statues and many fragments of relief from the walls; most were in the Museum in Turin (Petrie spent a day there on his way out, looking at these and a number of photographs), but nothing had ever been published. The Ernst von Siegelin expedition, just before the war, had made a thorough survey and their architect had made elaborate plans and reconstructions of the tombs; these Petrie can hardly have seen or even perhaps known about, since they too awaited publication. It was not a question, then, of excava-

* Later Lady Burton.

tion, but of recording, and though Petrie's plans of the tombs were excelled by Plaumann's, published some years later,[25] his careful copies of what remained on the walls and ceilings were of great value. The walls had been badly wrecked in ancient times and were encrusted with bat droppings; these had to be soaked for an hour or so with wetted pads of cloth propped on poles against the surface; the walls could then be cleaned. To photograph them Petrie used reflectors made of half a dozen biscuit tin lids nailed to a large box; two or more of these, carefully positioned, brought sunlight into the dark interior; a suspended white sheet softened the innermost reflexion. Fixing the focus of the camera outside to the measured distance from floor to ceiling, he could thus photograph the elaborately patterned roofs of the chambers;[26] they were also copied in colour by the artist of the party, Duncan Greenlees.

Unfortunately, though the recording of these tombs was of value, the historical conclusions Petrie drew from them[27] were quite mistaken. Comparing their plan with that of the "speos" type of rock-cut temple which is common in Nubia (though not, it must be added, unknown in Egypt also) he saw in them proof of the southern origin of the owners. Since some of the names found in the tombs were common in the ninth and tenth dynasties, and the name Sesostris also occurs, he assumed that Wah-ka, Ibu and the other nomarchs of Qau were forebears of the royal family of the twelfth dynasty. In their facial appearance he saw a resemblance to the kings of the twelfth dynasty, particularly those on the strange sphinxes and groups found by Mariette at Tanis, which had once been attributed to the Hyksos, but were now thought to represent Ammenemes III. In these Petrie had already some years before seen a facial likeness to the modern Gallas on the Sudanese borders of Abyssinia.[28] The nomarchs of Qau, then, had been invaders from Africa, and their rock-cut tombs confirmed their origin. This was pure fantasy; the nomarchs of Qau were contemporaries, not forerunners, of the twelfth dynasty, and nothing in their tombs was foreign to Egypt.

Earlier that year, Petrie had written an article for *Ancient Egypt* under the title "Current Fallacies about History" in which he pointed out the traps into which historians of early civilizations can fall by drawing false conclusions from superficial similarities, coincidences and misleading physical resemblances.[29] His article was largely aimed at the Diffusionists, but he would have done well to apply the same strictures to his own over-hasty judgments. It was unfortunate that as sole editor of his own journal, Petrie lacked the sober restraints normally imposed on contributors to learned periodicals. Some of his articles in *Ancient Egypt* were factual and informative, but in others his imagination ranged widely in space and time: as when he argued that mythological place-names in the "Book of the Dead" could be paralleled by those of regions, rivers and other geographical features in the Caucasus—the Lakes of Fire, for instance, echoed a memory of petroleum springs—and that therefore the earliest Egyptians must have stemmed from that region.[30] This too was fantasy, and none but a few of his faithful followers would have taken it seriously, but it served to diminish his reputation with those who could not appreciate where his true greatness lay.

Very important discoveries were meanwhile being made by Brunton and his party at Hemamiya. The extensive cemeteries they were digging had been first discovered by the sharp eyes of 'Ali es Suefi, who was with them. Gertrude Caton-Thompson spent part of the time exploring the desert on a camel, but she also undertook the excavation of a small area at Hemamiya. Henri Bach and the archaeologist S. Yeivin participated in the work. At first it had appeared to be an area of predynastic cemeteries of the usual type, but Brunton noticed among the tombs some which had polished red, black-topped pottery of a finer kind, with a rippled surface as if the pot had been combed. Petrie, who came over from time to time to see the progress of the work, named the new pottery, with the accompanying grave goods, "Badarian", after the district Badari in which they were working. Miss Caton-Thompson's excavation, a very careful examination of a small settlement area of circular huts, stripping layer by layer and sieving the earth from hearths and floors, gave the needed stratification: Badarian was earlier than Amratian. Petrie had been right to leave a gap at the beginning of his Sequence Dating, in case one day earlier phases of civilization might be found; in that gap, the Badarians could now be inserted.[31]

For two winters, 1924–5 and 1925–6, Petrie did not go out to Egypt; the tensions between Lacau and the archaeologists had eased somewhat since the final clearance of the Tomb of Tutankhamun, but the Director General was still having to walk delicately, pressed by the militant nationalists to limit all Western enterprise. Brunton, working almost single handed at Hemamiya, fell ill and the dig had to be abandoned. In the second year Miss Caton Thompson and a geologist, Miss Gardner, explored the Fayum as sole representatives of the British School. They sent Petrie regular progress reports: with a few Quftis, and a car that constantly broke down, they surveyed the northern shore of the Birket el Qarun, the shrunken remnant of Lake Moeris, in search of early settlements and found evidence of early farming settlements on the shores of the ancient lake. In the view of Elinor Gardner, on geological evidence, the earliest settlements, in the phase of civilization which they termed Fayum 'A', were those furthest from the present shore-line: the level of the lake had gradually shrunk throughout ancient times. Petrie, though he was not a geologist by training, ventured to disagree with Miss Gardner's report; there was some reason, he suggested, to suppose that the lake shore had fluctuated during historic times; why not then in prehistoric?[32] His warning went unheeded, but forty years later "Carbon 14" tests proved that Petrie had been right: Fayum "A" was indeed later, not earlier, than "B".[33]

In the summer of 1925 John Petrie had left school at the age of eighteen; he was to go to University College London, and read for a degree in maths. The fervent hope of his father that he would decide on archaeology as a career was encouraged by the enjoyment the boy evidently derived from their expeditions into the countryside: the two of them spent a fortnight in Devonshire the previous summer, exploring Dartmoor, and John proved as formidable a long-distance walker as his father. In the Christmas vacation they took rooms in a cottage near Brockenhurst in the New Forest and tramped over miles of moorland in the rain; Flinders noted in his diary: "Much chess with John every day." This close companionship was very precious to him. In the following summer and the next, after the exhibition closed, the whole family spent three weeks on a busman's holiday in Wales, surveying hill forts and stone circles; first to Brecon, then in August 1926 to Cardiganshire, between Cardigan and Fishguard. In Brecon they had company; they stayed in the same lodgings as Tessa and Mortimer Wheeler near the Gaer, a beautiful site on the River Usk where they were excavating a Roman fort. Petrie had known Wheeler for some years; he had first met him when, having read classics with A. E. Housman at University College and attended Ernest Gardner's classes on classical sculpture, the young man worked for a time as secretary to the Provost of the College, Gregory Foster. Now, in 1925, he was a fully fledged archaeologist and Director of the National Museum of Wales. Every day the Petrie family would go off up to the moors round Brecon Beacon. Flinders, at seventy-three, was still vigorous; Wheeler remembered his amused astonishment at discovering that the only equipment the old man took with him on these expeditions was a bamboo peastick and a visiting card: the stick as a marker, and the card, when carefully sighted along two edges, to give him an accurate right-angle.[34] In fact, he would almost certainly have had with him his long surveying tape, and probably a small theodolite as well—such tales grow in the telling.

Mortimer Wheeler had a great admiration for Flinders Petrie; Petrie admired Wheeler's enthusiasm and his efforts, at length successful, to establish the teaching of British archaeology as an academic subject in the University of London. His wife, Tessa Verney Wheeler, also a capable archaeologist, joined the committee of the British School in 1927 and was later to be their chief executive officer in England. During the next few years, John spent a week or two in the summer on Wheeler's digs, at Lydney Park in Gloucestershire, at Richborough in Kent and, in the early 1930s at Verulamium (St. Alban's); these digging holidays, encamped in a small tent near the site, he enjoyed, but his father was greatly disappointed by his disinclination to give serious consideration to a career in archaeology; though he was mathematically gifted and had inherited his father's unusual visual accuracy (it is said by John's daughter that he was able, when concentrating intensely, to visualize a spatial fourth dimension), he failed in Physics and came down from College without a degree; military history interested him, he joined the Territorials and was increasingly drawn towards the Army as a profession, an ambition from which his father tried in vain to dissuade him; in Flinders' view, a soldier's life deadened initiative and destroyed independent thought. He took his son to see Jocelyn Bushe-Fox, now Inspector of Ancient Monuments, and there was some talk of his training as an architect for the Office of Works.

The conditions imposed on excavators in Egypt were becoming increasingly difficult: M. Lacau's policy of stringent control and meagre returns was beginning to have its effect. The paucity of objects accorded to the Egypt Exploration Society in 1925–6 had already caused the withdrawal of promised grants from museums, and the Americans were deciding on epigraphic work rather than excavation. Petrie reluctantly decided the time had come to abandon excavation in Egypt. At a meeting of his committee in June 1926, the decision was taken to transfer the work of the British School to Palestine. As he explained:

> The continuity of the civilisation of Egypt has now been completely traced in recent years, from the Badarian period onwards. The British School in Egypt, therefore, in the coming season will

proceed with the collateral search on the Egyptian remains in the South of Palestine—Egypt over the Border. This is in accordance with the constitution of the School, which was founded to work in any country that has been subject to Egypt, and so to deal with all branches of the Egyptian civilisation. Such research has been cordially accepted by the authorities and the other representatives of British excavation in Palestine."[35]

He chose his team carefully: Starkey, who would bring his wife, had already proved himself outstandingly capable and entirely reliable in the field; since working with Petrie at Qau he had been in charge of the excavations of the University of Michigan at Karanis, a Greek city in the Fayum. Gerald Lankester Harding had no experience of Egypt, though he had helped Petrie with exhibitions in London. He had had little formal education, and had been working in a publisher's office; a visit to one of Petrie's exhibitions had kindled his interest and, encouraged by Petrie, he attended Miss Murray's evening classes; now, on her strong recommendation, he was to start on the career to which he was to devote the rest of his life.[36] He joined the Petries in Wales in August for a short time, to learn surveying, and left England with them in mid-November. Spending a few days in Cairo, they were taken to Saqqara by Quibell to see exciting recent discoveries near the Step Pyramid; then they were off by the evening train for Suez, crossing the canal by ferry at night, boarding the train on the other side, and reaching Gaza in the dark at half-past four next morning.

The first few days were spent in prospecting for a suitable site, but Petrie already had a shrewd idea where he would dig. The Wady Ghazzeh (nowadays called the Wady Besor) is a watercourse which crosses the Negev and debouches in the sea just south of Gaza. In summer it is dry, but in winter after rain it becomes a raging torrent; in ancient times it was a formidable barrier to an advancing army, a natural line of defence, and along it a string of *tells* marks the site of a series of ancient fortresses which were built to keep out marauders from the south; when the Egyptians conquered the country and captured them, they became strong points in the Pharaonic system of occupation. Flinders Petrie decided to dig one of the largest, Tell Jemmeh, about nine miles to the south-east of Gaza. A preliminary probe here had already been made by the Revd Phythian Adams three years earlier; he and others before him had argued that this must be Gerar, the city of Abimelech. Petrie accepted this identification without question. Unfortunately, just as he had wrongly persisted in calling Tell el Hesy Lachish, so now he adopted the name Gerar for his site; it was the same with his later excavations in Palestine. No doubt he sought to emphasize the Biblical aspect of his discoveries, for the School's subscribers in England were anxious to find in archaeology proofs of the literal truth of the Bible. One of them, Sir Charles Marston, had written a book called *The Bible Is True*, in which the results of excavations at ancient Jericho were hailed as proof that the walls besieged by Joshua had really collapsed. "If we can get any tablet letters of Abimelech," Petrie wrote wistfully "the prize will be great." It was too much to hope for, of course, and most modern scholars are agreed that Tell Jemmeh is not the ancient Gerar but probably Yurzaa, named in ancient Egyptian texts as the most southerly city to rebel against the Pharaoh Tuthmosis III, and one of those captured by Sheshonq I in about 920 BC. Tell el Far'a, nine miles further along the wady, Petrie decided, must be Bethpelet. He was reasoning from a false etymology;[37] the identification was accepted by George Adam Smith in later editions of his *Historical Geography of the Holy Land*, but more recent researches favour the theory that this is Sharuhen, the first halting place of the Pharaoh Ahmose's army on their march into Palestine, the ancient land of Retenu, about 1520 BC.

Starkey and Harding were sent ahead to Tell Jemmeh to build a house. It was a lonely site, exposed to wind and weather; they built in the lee of the great mound (**98**), with the aid of the six Quftis whom Petrie had brought up from Egypt. The house, long and low, was built of stones and mud and roofed with sheets of corrugated iron brought from Jaffa by camel. The local wells produced brackish undrinkable water, so a camel had to be sent to Gaza several times a week for a fresh supply. As soon as the house was habitable the Petries moved in; they were joined by the Risdons, he a retired naval commander, she "young and charming", according to Hilda: "she works well, and enjoys this picnic in the wilderness". The camp was completed by an elderly doctor named Parker, who proved a great acquisition; though frail in appearance he was indefatigable on the dig, would get up at four in the morning and thought nothing of walking eighteen miles to Gaza and back in a day; his ministrations were soon in demand for the staff, who found even Gaza water difficult to stomach, and also for the Beduin workers and their families, who flocked to his "clinic" for bandaging and medicines. They were a wild and picturesque lot, these Beduin; almost all the men carried knives or daggers, some swords, from which they would not be parted; under kerchief and headrope their long unkempt locks hung down to their shoulders. Some were very handsome. They came in their hundreds seeking work; Petrie ranged them in rows, squatting on the ground, their faces to the sun; as always, he chose them by their faces, believing that after long experience he could judge character and intelligence at first glance; he was seldom proved wrong. He had been warned that these semi-nomadic Arabs of the Negev, unaccustomed to regular work of any kind, would be useless; with the memory of his experience at Tell el Hesy, he was inclined to believe this; but they took readily and cheerfully to pick-axe work; the best of them proved quick to learn from the Quftis so that in a year or so, Petrie had built up a small team of skilled excavators almost, if not quite, as good as the experts from Egypt, whose services he then no longer needed. When the work was fully organized about ninety men and 180 children were employed; the boys and girls who came from a distance had their own camp in the shelter of the hill.

Flinders Petrie was in his element again; he seemed to have taken on a new lease of life. "Daddy talks astronomy, travel, various sciences, with amazing energy here," wrote Hilda to her son, "and has wielded a hammer and chisel all day. He is in top spirits, always up by 6 a.m. and working hard." Several times a day he climbed the steep path to the top of the 100 foot mound, to superintend the work and suggest the extension of a trench or the taking of a photograph. He himself did most of the photography of objects in the camp, and drew hundreds of them; Hilda and Mrs Risdon helped with drawing and cataloguing, and took their turn on the mound. Great attention was paid to pottery; little had been done, since the days of Tell el Hesy, to compile a Palestinian corpus and most excavators drew only whole pots in their reports. From the beginning of his work at Tell Jemmeh, Petrie planned the compilation of a corpus of dated shapes such as he had made for Egypt. His old friend and erstwhile student, the Revd J. Garrow Duncan, who had been working as an archaeologist for many years in Palestine with Macalister, put the corpus together; it was based largely on the repertory of shapes from Tell Jemmeh and Petrie's next dig, Tell el Far'a, and was for some years an indispensable tool for the field archaeologist in Palestine.[38]

Tell Jemmeh proved to have been a heavily fortified town for something like a thousand years. In the Persian period, great circular granaries had crowned the mound; Petrie concluded that the city had been the main base for the army of Cambyses when he conquered Egypt; he calculated the capacity of the granaries and concluded that they would have held enough grain to feed 70,000 men for two months. A broken red-figure Attic vase found in the rubbish under the floor of one of them fixed the date of their construction to within a few years. There were many other fragments of Greek wares, evidence of trade with the Aegean during the sixth and fifth centuries BC. The earlier, Assyrian occupation of the country was represented by a cylinder seal and broken fragments of fine pottery—the thinnest he had ever seen—which he recognized, from memory of what he had seen in the British Museum, as Assyrian; it was, he supposed, "the dinner service of the Assyrian governor".[39]

Deeper down in the mound, in the level he ascribed to the Solomonic period, large smelting furnaces were found, the first known in Palestine, and a number of iron tools. The earliest level he reached, which he tentatively ascribed to the time of Tuthmosis III from the earliest scarab found, is now thought to be somewhat later. Subsequent excavations have gone deeper and found remains of the Early Bronze Age.[40] It was not Petrie's usual policy to clear a site down to bedrock; he was content to extract the "bones" of history and leave others to complete the picture.

On New Year's Eve 1927, the Starkeys and Harding walked to Gaza for a party, "with their ties and collars and toothbrushes and the ukelele [this was perhaps Gerald Harding's]"; they returned early next morning by lorry. The countryside was in the grip of drought—it had not rained for a year. For two or three days at a time fierce winds covered everything with dust and work was brought to a standstill; drawing and even writing were impossible on grit-covered paper.

On 16 January Petrie wrote:

> The people are nearly all settled Bedawy, who have been here a few years, cultivating the ground, but mostly still living in the open-sided low tent of their ancestors. I am surprised to see how well they work, tho' not equal to Egyptians; also how amenable they are, and ready to be friendly. Raids which used to be common here have died away owing to good police work; there have been four attempts on Beersheba in the year, but none reached out to this region. . . . Three times a week two police come round here to see that all is quiet, either from G[aza] or from B[eersheba]. They also act as our postmen. Our position is all the stronger, owing to the drought. The lateness and scantiness of the rains threaten to stop most of the cultivation so that the people are largely dependent on our wages to keep them for the season. . . .

> Feb. 8th. Famine conditions continue, and hundreds of the Bedawy families with all their possessions are trekking north along this great road from Egypt into Palestine. The trains of loaded camels, flocks of sheep all pass along to find pasture: moving creatures in file appear as in a perpetual cinematograph.

The doctor from the municipal hospital came out from time to time to test the stream for malaria, and in mid-January all the workers were inoculated.

Visitors arrived: in January Yeivin stayed a night or two, and later Humphrey Bowman, the Director of Education for Palestine, came with FitzGerald, the excavator of Beth-Shan; Petrie's old friend Harold Wiener, a frequent contributor to *Ancient Egypt* on Old Testament subjects, arrived in February in the company of Père Vincent of the Dominican Fathers, the *doyen* of archaeologists in Jerusalem, whom they took to instantly; he was to be one of Petrie's advocates against his detractors in the future. Hilda took a few days off to stay as the guest of the Bishop in Jerusalem and Mrs MacInnes, and thence travelled by country bus to Tiberias, where she stayed in the hospice of a Franciscan monastery and explored the Biblical sites around the lake.

In February the rains came with a vengeance: there were violent storms of rain and hail, the wind blew so hard that they had to hold on to the roof, and the Wady Ghazzeh, transformed into a raging torrent, cut them off from Gaza for a week; nobody could ford the stream, and the water camel had no foothold in the slippery mud. Their supplies ran low. Rain filled a Roman cistern and for a day or so they drank that, but when communication with Gaza was restored they were back on the "camel water" that was making them ill. At one time only one member of the party was fit to go up to the *tell*; Petrie himself suffered violent attacks of vomiting and finally went to Jerusalem for consultation; when the doctor saw his emaciated state ("I thinned away until skin hung on my bones like an old cloak; it took three months of milk diet afterwards to set me up again"), he insisted that all drinking water should be either distilled or bottled. The season was coming to an end; P. L. O. Guy, the Director of the Palestine Museum, came down to Tell Jemmeh to make his selection. The antiquities law—half to the excavator, half to the Museum, but all unique pieces to remain—was generously applied and Petrie was able to bring home a representative collection of pottery, flints, weights and other objects. After the exhibition at University College in July, most of this material was stored in boxes in the College, against the day when it could be properly housed and displayed.

On 21 April came the news that Ann lay seriously ill at her school in Harpenden; Hilda left at once and was home within a week. Flinders stopped the work and left Gerar two weeks later. He went up to Beirut; at the American University, where he was given hospitality, someone with a car offered to take him to Byblos. He met M. Dunand who took him round the site, but Petrie was hard put to it to conceal his disapproval of what he saw: there were no day-to-day plans, the excavator "did not know his pottery", and was keeping only inscribed fragments of stone vases, throwing the rest away by the truckload without sorting: "I heard that much had been recovered from the tip heap by a collector waiting in a boat at the bottom of the slope." There had also, he understood, been "scandalous leakages" of gold objects from the site to western museums. Never reluctant to take up the cudgels on behalf of scientific archaeology, he wrote an angry letter to Salomon Reinach, the President of the French Academy, who passed the letter on to the Director of Antiquities for Syria. "Later an account of the work was published by M. Dunand stating what care was given to details of work exactly as I said should be done, and rather later M. Reinach made an inspection of all the Syrian work, and reported that it was as perfect as it could be."

Returning to Haifa, he left for Alexandria, and on the boat gave an impromptu talk to a party of clergymen on his recent discoveries. The same lecture, three times repeated because of its popularity, was given at University College a few days after he arrived home; he only just had time to get slides made. Ann was convalescing after an operation, and he himself was in hospital in August; the operation (another hernia), this time done under local anaesthetic, he watched with great interest. Two particular problems occupied his mind during the summer. One was Stonehenge once more: he was invited by J. C. Squire to join the committee of the Stonehenge Preservation Society, aimed at restoring the downland around the monument to its pre-war condition, free from disfiguring buildings. An appeal was launched and public response, though initially slow, resulted in enough money being raised to buy the surrounding land for the nation. The other concerned the future of his Palestine collections, packed up in crates in the basement of University College. No existing museum was prepared to house and display this unique collection. At a lecture which he gave to the Palestine Exploration Fund in July he stressed the need for a Palestine Museum in London, in which a teaching collection similar to the Petrie Museum of Egyptology could be housed. During that summer, Dr Mortimer Wheeler also was seeking to enlist support for the establishment of a school or institute, preferably within the University of London, where would-be archaeologists could be trained in field work and the technical skills of their profession. In the previous year he had become Curator of the London Museum; now a part-time lectureship in British Archaeology was established for him at University College; Petrie had in his old friend a colleague and an ally.

The Petries did not join the Wheelers on holiday this year, however. Hilda dislocated her hip, and went on a six-week cruise up the Amazon with Mrs Tufnell to recover. Ann was in Italy. Flinders felt in need of a respite from fieldwork; he decided not to go out to Palestine that winter, but to leave Tell el Far'a, the next objective, in the hands of Starkey and Harding, of whose work he already had the highest opinion. The Risdons were going again, and Olga Tufnell, who after five years' dull routine work in the office of the British School, was at last to be given the chance to participate in field work. Again, Petrie's judgment was not at fault: her careful record of tombs of the Solomonic period met with his complete approval and he invited her to contribute her own chapter to the volume in which they were published.[41] The party went out by way of Egypt, and on the way, all save Starkey spent a few weeks at Qau, completing the copying of a few incompletely recorded tombs. One of Miss Murray's former students, Myrtle Broome, who was with them, was later to spend several winters at Abydos with Miss Amice Calverly expertly copying the reliefs in the temple of Sethos I.

Flinders had been told by his doctors that he must on no account spend another winter in England; in the winters of 1924 and 1926 heavy colds had frequently confined him to bed and left him feeling weak and fit for little. He decided to spend the whole winter in Italy, in his beloved Rome. Starkey was to write him weekly reports on the progress of the excavation; in any emergency he could reach Palestine in less than a week. In a quiet and sunny *pensione** in the via Sardegna, less than half an hour's pleasant walk through the park of the Villa Borghese to the British School in Rome, where he had the free run of an excellent library, and the nearby Villa Giulia with its magnificent Etruscan collection, he was in his element; he had many friends in Rome: one was Bernard Ashmole, the Director of the British School;

* Today the Hotel Tea.

old Senator Lanciani ("my revered Lanciani") and his second wife, the Duchess of San Teodoro, invited him frequently to their house and he saw much of David Randall MacIver, his erstwhile student and helper, now a leading authority on early Etruscan archaeology, who lived close by. John joined him for the Christmas vacation and he delighted in showing his son the early churches of Rome which he knew so well. During the five months he spent in Italy that winter, he completed the compilation of a list of Egyptian officials,[42] and worked on a remarkable corpus of decorative patterns, culled from museums and from books; he had been making a collection of drawings for some years past, and now he had amassed some thousands more examples—spirals, concentric circles, plant forms, key patterns—all drawn, dated and classified to show their evolution and development. Nothing similar had been attempted before, and since 1930, when it was published, the book has been a valued source and inspiration for art historians.[43] Petrie was also starting to write his autobiography; he had taken with him his old diaries and bundles of letters, and found that his memory of some incidents was as sharp as the day they had happened.

Tell Far'a ("Beth-Pelet") proved as promising a site as Tell Jemmeh; the excavators, in Petrie's absence, had confined their work mostly to tombs, in one of which a bronze couch of the Persian period had been found, and an attractive silver ladle with a handle in the shape of a swimming girl;[44] a little gold jewellery had turned up and a large number of scarabs, which showed the expected contact with Egypt. The excavators had suffered a good deal from the heat towards the end; Commander Risdon had been so ill that his doctor warned him not to spend another season there. Petrie resolved that in future the excavations would close before the beginning of May. He had decided to go out himself, but to leave Hilda in England to raise funds for the work by lecturing to women's clubs and societies. The family again joined in an August holiday, this time at Bishop's Castle in Shropshire, where they measured stone circles. Ann had left school now, and was about to enter University College to read Italian with Professor Edmund Gardner.

On 14 November 1928, Flinders Petrie again started out for the Levant; this time he had decided to try the overland journey on the Orient Express; it would be quicker than the sea voyage, and would avoid the seasickness he so much dreaded. The experiment was a success; the sleeping cars were comfortable, he was fascinated by the countryside as the train crossed Europe, and he had the opportunity of staying a few days in Constantinople, which he had never seen. He had pleasant travelling companions in Mrs Benson and her friend Lady Agnew who were bound for Baghdad. In Santa Sophia he watched a large group of unveiled Turkish women praying towards Mecca.

> It was not a united party of any kind, but a spontaneous outcome of the new *régime* in which woman at last is allowed a soul. There were a few men, one by one about, but no union though it was Friday. The women formed a congregation of their own, some 20 or 30 together. I must say I would rather see the Publican worshipping Allah thus, than see the Pharisee of a pompous Patriarch back again in possession. There is hope for a new Islam.[45]

In the museum they saw the Hittite sculptures, and the sarcophagi from Sidon particularly interested Flinders, though he lamented the lack of proper labelling in show cases. Then they were off across Anatolia, and through the wild gorges of the Taurus, amazed at the virtuosity of the railway engineers. At Rayak in North Syria they changed trains; from Beirut southwards it was pouring with rain and after Gaza, where one of the Quftis met Petrie, it was doubtful whether they could reach Tell Far'a on the rutted, water-logged road, but Tarazi, the owner of the Gaza taxi, insisted on coming with them and they managed to avoid getting stuck in the mud and sand. The excavation party had already been at work for some days: the Starkeys, Miss Tufnell, Gerald Harding as before, and a new student Oliver Myers, who soon earned the Professor's approval.

The work was divided between the fort at one end, the cemetery, the saddle between the two halves of the *tell*, where Petrie hoped to find a temple, and a ravine at the entrance where a sloping glacis was coming to light and here, in some tombs, were scarabs, daggers and toggle-pins which told him that he had found the Hyksos in their homeland. Each excavator was put in charge of a section, and Petrie drew pottery, planned and photographed; in the evenings he wrote articles and reviews and corrected proofs. Mrs Benson and Lady Agnew arrived: they had been unable to reach Baghdad by car—rain had turned the desert to a sea of mud. Harold Wiener came again, with Dorothy Garrod who was excavating a palaeolithic site in Mount Carmel. Muhammad Osman rose to the occasion: "Mohammed has gone ahead in cookery and does excellent cakes, stews, and there is constant fresh lemonade going." Doubtless Mrs Starkey had been giving him cookery lessons in the previous season. Beduin dogs of all colours and sizes hung around the camp: "There has been pandemonium, or rather pankuneion, going on at night in our courtyard, with every kind of snarl, growl and yelp. . . . Large water-worn palaeoliths are to be picked up in the wady here among the stream-bed flints; half a dozen have come in; in the hills are many little scrapers, and now a delicate arrow-head and another half-made, showing how the form was blocked out before working it down thin. We buy up all we can at ¼d. or ½d. each. Boys and men rake all the bed for 6 or 8 miles both ways." This zeal was later to bring Petrie much trouble.

A hundred and twenty pickmen were taken on, far more than at Tell Jemmeh, in an attempt to speed up the work; some very large tombs were being found and the work on the town was expensive. A new recruit joined them in February: Harris Colt was an American with private means; he came with a warm recommendation from Miss Murray, with whom he had been excavating in Malta. Petrie thought him "quite good, not in the least rich-spoilt." Dr Parker's eventual arrival was welcomed by them all, especially by Olga who had had to do nearly all the doctoring at the end of a long day's tomb digging.

As spring came, the surrounding hills were covered with tufts of asphodels and tiny marigolds; later there were red anemones. In mid-February came excitement: Captain St Barbe Baker, who was in Palestine to found a branch of his Men of the Trees organization, arrived to make a film. It was to be called "Palestine's Lost Cities". Shots were taken of the excavators at work: Sir Flinders examining a basket of potsherds, Dr Parker doctoring the Beduin, a girl sifting for beads, the arrival of the water-camels from Khan Yunis, Gerald Harding riding a camel, and a *fantasia* with Beduin dancing. The expedition staff thoroughly enjoyed this interruption of their daily routine, but Petrie viewed the whole operation somewhat sourly, grudging the loss of time.

The flint hunters were now being paid for finding ancient settlement sites with early pottery; Petrie determined to earmark the area for work next year.

In March, when the dig was nearing its end, the most important find was made in what Petrie named the Governor's Residence: the burnt remains of what had been an ivory box, engraved on each face with court scenes in the Egyptian style but in Palestinian workmanship; it had been badly burnt, but patient work restored the little panels (**100**).[46] The dig ended earlier than Petrie had planned: he had hoped to finish before the onset of heat, but Starkey went down with fever, Colt returned to America, and it was decided to close the camp. E. T. Richmond, the new Director of Antiquities, came down for the division; he was cordial and pressed Petrie to stay a few days with him and his wife in their house outside Jerusalem before going home; this Petrie was glad to do, and they "discussed all kinds of administrative affairs". He had decided, after all, not to go home by Orient Express: it was considerably dearer than the sea route. A slow boat from Haifa, stopping at Larnaca, Constantinople, and the Piraeus would take him to Naples, whence he could finish his journey by train. Though economical, it proved a tedious way to travel, and he did not try it again. Before he left Haifa, he stayed a night with the Americans at Megiddo, and P. L. O. Guy took him over the excavations of the Oriental Institute of Chicago on that huge and impressive site.

During the winter Hilda had worked hard to raise money for the work. She had also hunted out a number of boxes of Coptic textiles, bought by Flinders in the 1880s and washed at that time by Kate Bradbury, and had had them valued; Petrie was surprised to find how much they were now worth. It was the job of Miss Tufnell's successor as Assistant Secretary to wash these grimy scraps again and mount them on card; they could then be sold to members and Associates of the British School. Hilda had written hundreds of letters asking for contributions and now included many churchmen in her mailing-list. Having discovered that the date of the twenty-first Lambeth Conference of bishops was to coincide with that of the exhibition in the summer, she sent every one of them an invitation to the private view, and many of them came.

Petrie judged that he could now form a picture of "Beth-Pelet" as it was in the time of the Hyksos, during its occupation by the Egyptian army in the eighteenth dynasty, and after its capture by Sheshonq (Shishak) at the end of the Solomonic Period; the latest remains on the mound were Roman. The many tombs excavated around the city gave a picture of more or less continuous occupation during the Late Bronze and Early Iron Ages. Some of the tombs had contained the handsome painted pottery known as Philistine—familiar now, but in those days something of a novelty. The great gate of the Hyksos age, flanked by towers, and the glacis and ditch of the Middle Bronze fortification, were the finest examples of the type hitherto found; so too was the plan of the palace of the Egyptian resident, of the late Bronze Age, in which the ivory box had been found.[47] There was still more to be done on the site. Petrie had decided not to go, but Starkey, Harding and Colt would go out again. Oliver Myers would be in Egypt: he was to join Sir Robert Mond's excavation of the Bucheum at Armant; and was later to be given charge of the excavations there; he never again worked for Petrie. A young geologist, Eann Macdonald, who had had experience of excavation in Richborough, was to be given charge of Petrie's eagerly awaited palaeolithic and neolithic survey, under Starkey's direction.

Meanwhile in August 1929 the family went on the last of their holidays together, for three weeks in Caerleon in Monmouthshire, a Roman site which the Wheelers and their helpers had been digging for the past two years; Mortimer Wheeler himself was now excavating in Lydney Park in the Forest of Dean, not far away; the Petries went over to look at his excavations and John worked with him for a time. While they were in Caerleon the Petries met Lord Raglan and other members of the local Archaeological Society, and were invited to their ancient houses. At the end of August Hilda and Ann went off to Czechoslovakia for their visit to the Masaryks. Flinders was working hard, preparing *Beth Pelet* and correcting the proofs of *Gerar*; then, in mid-November when his lectures to the students at University College were done, he set off once more for the sunshine of an Italian winter. His friends in Rome received him warmly and the staff of the *pensione* welcomed him back: "I dropped into my old nest just as I left it." He was very tired—both he and Hilda were suffering from overwork—but he spent the first week or so in relaxation, revisiting museums and early churches and calling on old friends at the Villa San Teodoro and the British School, on the van Burens, and on Mrs Eugenie Strong, an authority on Greek and Roman sculpture. He wrote every few days to his wife, giving her instructions about proofs, stocks of publications, difficulties with the printers in Vienna, and the distribution of copies—the affairs of the British School in Egypt were never far from his mind. She herself had planned another round of lectures, but late in November she was knocked down by a car and had to stay some weeks in bed with an injured foot; then she lectured on crutches. Petrie was working hard to finish his book, *Decorative Patterns of the Ancient World*; he had some 3,000 drawings to make up into plates and was still collecting more examples; besides that of the British School, he had permission to read in several other libraries in Rome.[48] He lectured to the American Academy in Rome on the history of the cross and other symbols, and to the British School in Rome on his excavations at "Beth Pelet". He was introduced to Commander Mangarelli who was excavating at the Etruscan site of Caere; when Hilda and Ann arrived in Rome a little before Easter, they all spent a day there at his invitation. Flinders was in a holiday mood; they visited Albano and Ostia, and he took them to meet his friends, and a round of dinner parties and invitations followed; never in London had the Petries been so sociable.

Letters from Starkey assured him that all was well at Tell Fara, though there had been Arab riots in Gaza and the shop of their favourite greengrocer had been burnt down; he was a Jew. Worse had occurred elsewhere: Arabs had murdered Jews in Hebron and Safad. It was the first rumble of the approaching storm, but Petrie could not yet realize what lay in store for the unhappy land of Palestine: "The Bedawy around our work," he assured readers of *Ancient Egypt*, "are all quiet and pleasant, and officially we are welcomed as helping the cause of peace."[49]

The Pyramid of el-Lahun

CHAPTER XVII

Jubilee

(1930–33)

THE YEAR 1930 was a memorable one for Flinders Petrie: it was just fifty years since he had first gone to Egypt to begin his life's work. His friends determined to celebrate the occasion, and to use it as an excuse for raising money for his future work. A charity matinée was planned; it was to take the form of historical sketches and *tableaux vivants*, the kind of entertainment once popular in Victorian times. Petrie in Rome was let into the secret; he insisted on vetting and partly rewriting the scenario: his wife and her committee had been over-ambitious in some scenes, he thought, and sometimes historically inaccurate. He viewed the whole operation with some misgiving, and after Christmas, wishing her a Happy New Year, added, "But I can't stand being *Jubilated*."[1] The pageant was organized by Lady Newnes, the energetic and forceful wife of Sir Frank Newnes the publisher; seventy-five names appeared in the list of titled and eminent patrons, and the organizing committee numbered 140; Dr Robert Mond, a generous patron of all Egyptological enterprises, acted as Treasurer. The proceeds were to go jointly to Petrie's excavations and to the Friends of the Poor.[2]

"A Vision of the Ages" was performed on the afternoon of 3 June, the Professor's birthday, in the London Hippodrome; numbers of Petrie's students and members of the British School and some of the organizers' friends took silent or speaking parts: the programme listed a cast of eighty-one players and a white pigeon. Lady Newnes cast herself and her friends in leading roles. A collection of Egyptian instruments was loaned for the occasion, and Harding and others drummed on the *dharabouka*. The programme claimed that the accompaniments were "derived from authentic and ancient sources". Some scenes were in silent *tableau*: Badarians with their black-topped pots and flint implements crouched in the desert—the first settled inhabitants of Egypt; against a fresco of ships, the predynastic potters of

Hierakonpolis appeared. In a short play written by Terence Gray, King Khufu ordered the building of his pyramid. Lady Ossulton appeared as a vision of the Princess Sit-Hathor-Yunet, wearing copies of her jewellery, and Sir Frank Newnes made a brief appearance as a Tomb Robber. Prince Galitzine, appearing as Akhenaten, was seen riding in a chariot with Nefertiti. In the second half of the programme a series of moving *tableaux* depicted the story of Cleopatra, with Lady Newnes in the title role: this gave many people an opportunity to appear as Greeks or Egyptians of the court. It was an ambitious programme and not without its hilarious moments: Olga Tufnell, who played Charmian, remembers a moment of suppressed mirth when Cleopatra, with a dramatic gesture, thrust away the asp (by courtesy of Willy Clarkson and made of wood), and it clattered across the floor. During the interval Captain Spencer-Churchill, one of the prime organizers, presented an address to Sir Flinders, signed by a number of eminent scholars. Nearly £900 was raised for the British School, and a like amount for the poor.

That was not the end of the celebrations: on 19 June Dr Robert Mond gave a dinner at the Savoy Hotel in honour of Sir Flinders Petrie, to nearly 180 guests including many of his colleagues and his former students.[3] The tables were decorated with lotuses, and there were congratulatory speeches. The daily papers the following day published an interview which he had given to the Press; he took the occasion to sound a note of warning, drawing parallels between conditions which preceded the fall of the Roman Empire and the present condition of England; the growth of the trade unions he compared with that of the guilds of Constantine's day, leading to the collapse of the empire; taxation then had been exorbitant, it was so now in England. Destructive elements, he complained—officialdom, the rage for speed, the "raucous twaddle" of the gramophone, the reek of tobacco, the ugly mechanism of modern art—have invaded the modern world; it was more and more necessary to seek the quiet and peace of the desert where "the rush of new impressions can be sorted over and built into one's own personality, and where the battle of prejudices and principles can be quietly concluded and a new structure of assumptions accepted."[4]

The summer exhibition displayed some fine pottery from the Tell Far'a tombs and a large collection of the palaeoliths collected from the bed of the Wady Ghuzzeh. These Eann Macdonald had classified in the orthodox way, as Chellean, Aurignacian and so on; Petrie rearranged them according to their purpose, as "pick forms for breaking earth,

98 Tell Jemmeh ("Gerar"): the dig house and the *tell*

99 Workmen assembling after the dinner-hour at the northern end of Tell Jemmeh

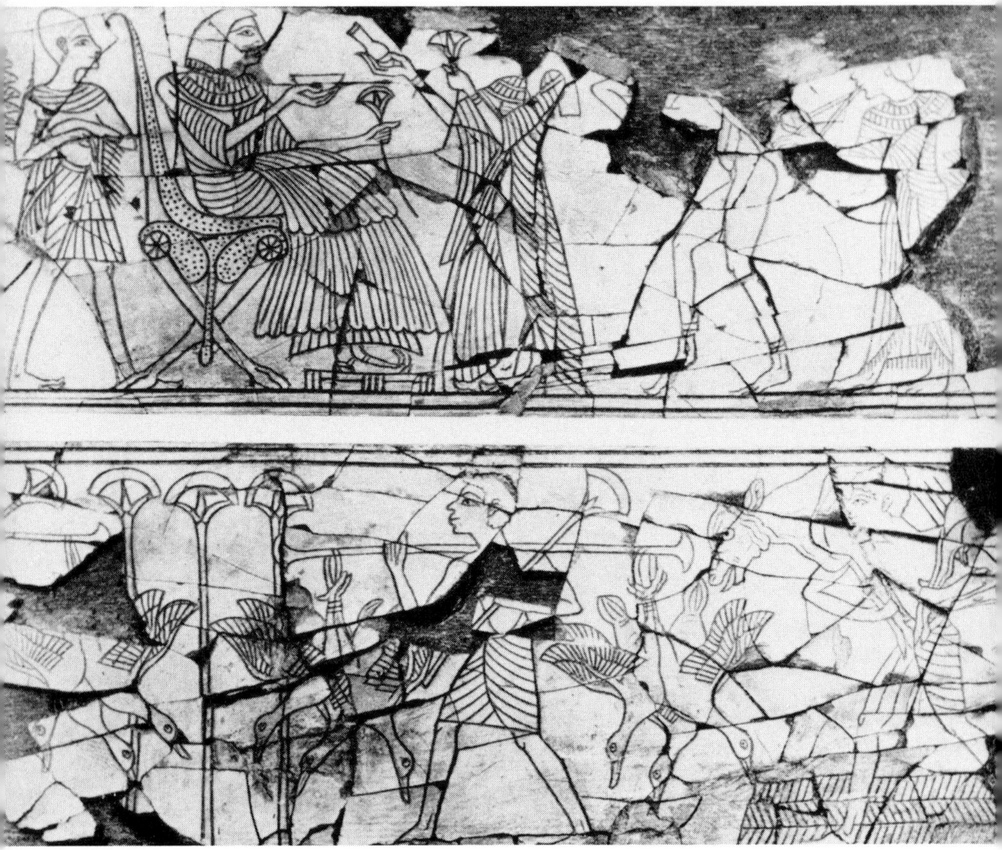

100 Decoration in the Egyptian style, from an ivory box found in the Governor's Palace, Tell el Far'a. Above, an important personage (?the Governor) with attendants; below, fowlers in the papyrus marshes with ducks, and a herdsman carrying a calf through the water (*Beth-Pelet I*, pl. LV)

101 (*left*) "Astarte" pendants and jewellery of sheet gold, Tell el 'Ajjul, 1933–4 (*Ancient Gaza IV*, pl. XIII)

102 Island of Ruad, off the Syrian coast opposite Amrit

103 Tell el 'Ajjul, 1931: Olga Tufnell superintends the excavation of a tomb. The quid, perhaps a horse, one of several found in tombs of the Late Bronze Age here, was associated by Petrie with the Hyksos invaders of Egypt

104 Beduin girls washing pottery, Tell el 'Ajjul

105 Tell el 'Ajjul: hearth from a house in an early level of the *tell* (*Ancient Gaza I*, pl. VI)

106 (*left*) Petrie photographing at Tell el 'Ajjul, 1938. The "biscuit box" camera is hidden by a cloth

107 Muhammad Osman el Kreti, the Petries' cook for thirty-seven years, with the water-camel and its driver at Tell el 'Ajjul, 1933

108 Jack Ellis on the dig, Sheikh Zoweyd

109 Petrie at Buckfastleigh, Dartmoor, August 21, 1934; eight days later, he left England for the last time

110 Petrie at the opening of his first Palestinian exhibition, at University College in July 1930, his jubilee year. Pottery from Tell el Far'a is displayed and he holds a little alabaster vase of Egyptian workmanship

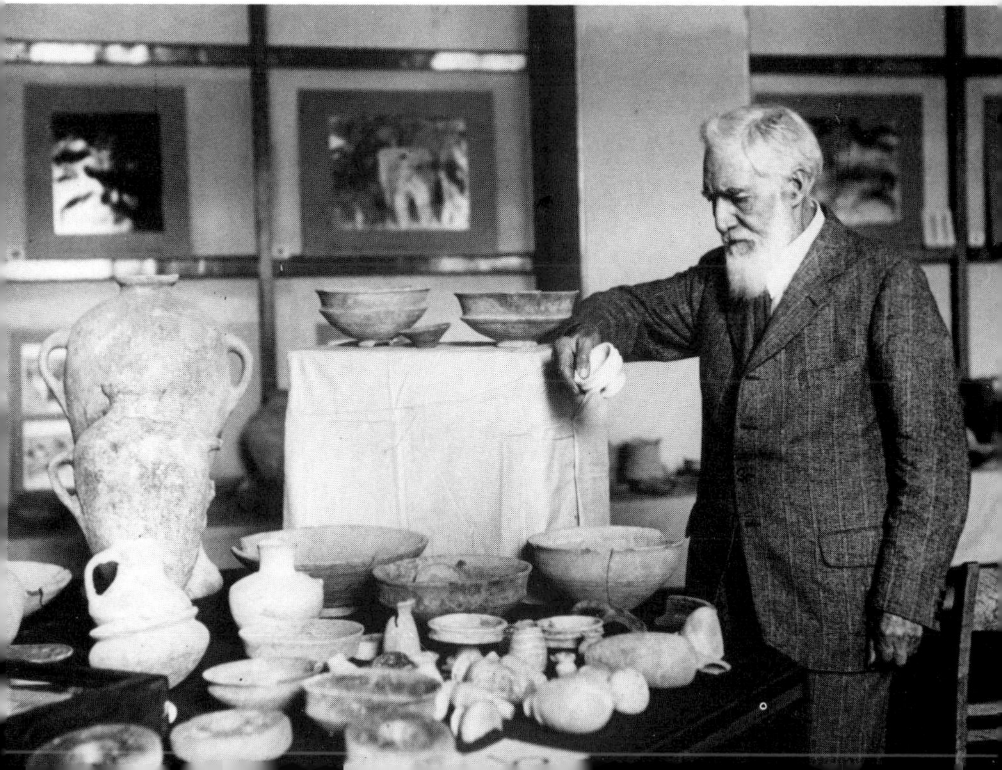

111 Sir Flinders and Lady Petrie about to start on their Syrian tour, with the old bus in which they travelled and slept (October, 1934)

112 (*left*) Children at Tell Ternos, near Safita; Petrie is seated on the extreme right, talking to them

114 (*above right*) The Petries with their staff of excavators at Sheikh Zoweyd, in the winter of 1935-6, (*l.* to *r.*) V. Seton-Williams, C. Pape, J. Waechter, J. C. Ellis, Sir Flinders Petrie, Lady Petrie

113 The harbour at Jebeleh, Syria, looking west

116 Dr Margaret Murray

115 In the garden of the American School of Oriental Research, Jerusalem

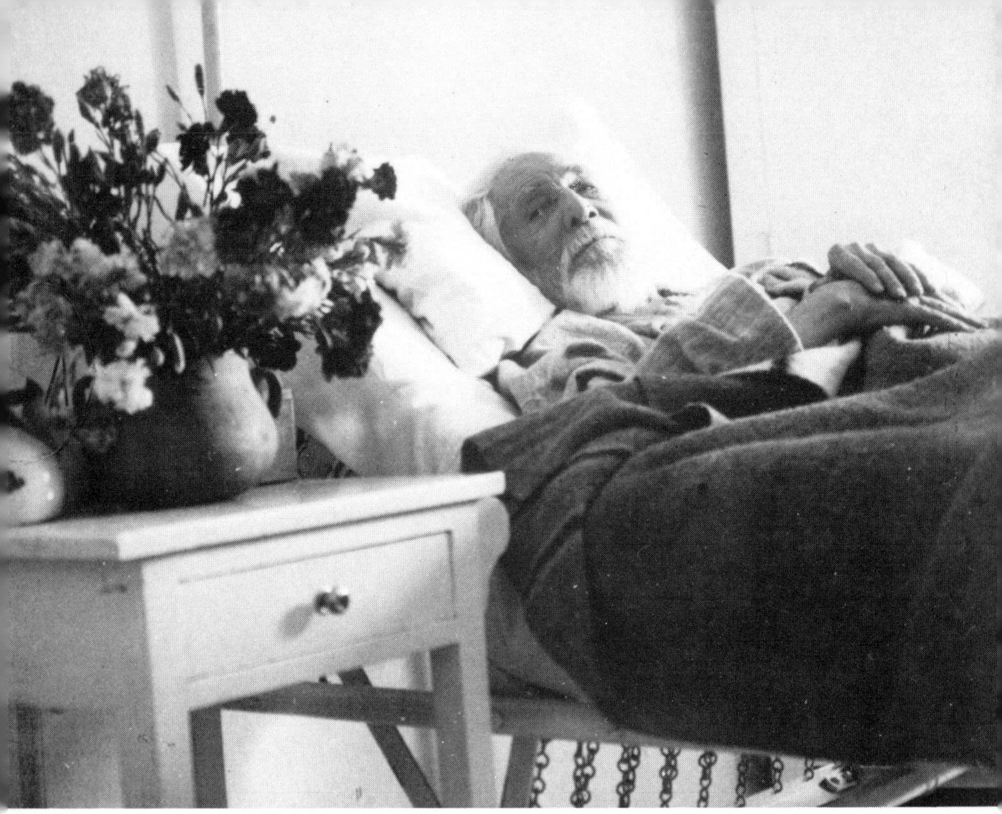

117 In hospital in Jerusalem, spring or early summer 1942

118 At Donington, Lincs (Matthew Flinders' birthplace) for celebrations in connection with the Festival of Britain, 1951 (*l.* to *r.*) Ann Petrie, John Petrie, Lady Petrie, John's wife Anne holding Lisette Flinders Petrie

ovates for cutting food, axes, choppers, borers, pounders, bashers". His classification was unorthodox, but probably of greater interest to the viewing public, and prehistorians nowadays tend to lay more stress on the importance of function (**110**).

It was during this summer that John Petrie decided to make the army his career; he went to a Territorial camp in Dover and loved the life there; when he wrote to his father of his decision, he was dismayed at the vehemence of Flinders' attempts to dissuade him; at length, however, seeing that John's mind was made up, the old man gave way. A sad little entry in his diary reads "Wrote John, renouncing all." Like many eminent men, he was forced to realize that sons do not readily fill the role of heir presumptive.

During this summer he had more than one discussion with the Secretary and Principal of the Senate of the University of London on a problem that continued to exercise his mind: the proper housing of his Palestinian material. It was plain that University College could not spare space for it; but the University had recently taken the decision to move from cramped and unsatisfactory quarters in South Kensington to a new site in Bloomsbury, only a few minutes' walk from University College; in the Senate House, Petrie hoped there might be provision made for a large museum; he began to plan it in his mind, envisaging a gallery running the length of the top floor; he discussed his ideas with Mortimer Wheeler, who since 1927 had been hatching his own plan for an Institute of Archaeology, with teaching collections for British archaeology.[5] The University authorities soon made it clear that all space in the new building was earmarked for administrative offices and for the University Library. Petrie was not without friends, however; he had made his need widely known, and a year or so later an anonymous donor came forward with the very generous promise of £10,000. Petrie's offer to Wheeler that he should make over the money to him for an Institute, on condition that the Palestine collection was housed and displayed in it, was gratefully accepted, and an appeal for further funds was launched in 1932. Two years later a suitable building was found in St John's Lodge, a handsome eighteenth-century house in the middle of Regent's Park, which had once been the home of the Marquess of Bute. It was derelict and needed a great deal of repair and some alteration, but the great drawing-room made an excellent display gallery; a photographic studio and a technical laboratory were incorporated in the plan.[6] By November of that year Petrie's Palestinian collection was being unpacked but the Institute was not formally opened until April 1937. The identity of the anonymous donor was not known, even to him. It was not disclosed until after her death.[7] She was Mrs Mary Woodgate Wharrie, in whose memory a tablet was erected in the Institute. She had been a modest subscriber to the British School for several years.

In late October the Petries went out to Palestine by Orient Express with three new students.[8] They had intended to go straight to Gaza, but Starkey met them in Lydda with the news that malaria was rampant in Tell 'Ajjul, their objective for the year. Starkey had been building a house for the excavators, but a quarter of his labourers were in hospital; it would not be advisable to start work till the winter flood had swept away the mosquitoes. They decided to go instead to Jerusalem. Flinders had business in any case which he wished to attend to, and the new recruits could spend a few days sightseeing. He had some reason to be disturbed: in September he had written Richmond the usual letter requesting permission to dig at Tell 'Ajjul during the coming winter, and to "make soundings from Latitude 31° 29′ southward". He had had a very stiff reply, to the effect that the British School had not carried out its obligations under the Antiquities law last season: Macdonald had excavated sites beyond the limit permitted by the licence, and Starkey's list of objects found had not been complete; in particular pottery models of dogs had not been mentioned.[9] (Unfortunately, though Starkey had seen nothing unusual in these, Petrie had made a great point of them in his lectures in England, associating them with the Calebite tribe.)[10] Moreover, wrote Richmond, Petrie's current application to make soundings was too vague: a specific site must be mentioned; and licences could only be granted for one site at a time. Later he sent a permit for excavation at 'Ajjul, but pointed out another infringement of the law: the purchase of antiquities must stop.[11] This was a bitter blow to Petrie, who relied on such purchases to bring him information about new sites and also to bring in objects which would otherwise be sold to dealers. Richmond had seemed so friendly two years ago, and so ready to be helpful; something was badly wrong now.

He went to talk to the High Commissioner, Sir John Chancellor, at Government House, and put his case; in Egypt, he said, he had been allowed to buy antiquities locally, and a permit to excavate extended two miles around the site: now he was only being allowed to dig on the *tell* itself. He voiced his suspicion that a meeting of archaeologists in London had decided to exclude him from studying prehistoric sites in Palestine and had asked for a monopoly of such work.[12] It is not clear on what this notion was based; Sir John was clearly puzzled but assured him there was no conspiracy against him. Petrie declared that he had a competent staff who were perfectly capable of digging a second site under his supervision, and he vehemently protested against the ban on purchase.

Two days later Petrie went to see Richmond, but receiving little satisfaction, he left saying that he would bring the matter up with the Joint Archaeological Board in London; Macdonald had excavated under his orders, under the impression that his work was covered by the permit for Tell Far'a. So the matter was left for the time being. Tragically, Macdonald himself could not defend his actions; he had been drowned in a sailing accident during the summer.

They moved to Gaza but the malaria had not abated so it was decided to move back to Tell Far'a and excavate there till it was safe to return. A one-ton truck was ordered and Hilda took command: "F.P. and Mrs Benson I seated in the cab of it, and Richmond Brown and I mounted on the summit of the baggage behind—suitcases, boxes of water, 2 mattresses, a vast mousetrap, my Gaza-purchased canteen, garden chairs, a lamp, water jugs, draining boards, medicines, overcoats, tools, a large melon, a bath, tin of petroleum, 6 pails with vegetables in them and hosts of things besides."[13]

They found the house, which had been dismantled at the end of the previous season, ready; Harding and Scott had gone ahead. Hilda had not seen the excavation; she wrote:

> The tell is a grandly precipitous place, most striking as to scenery. The Egyptian governor's residence with the paved courtyard and the great walls of Rameses III and of Shishak are very imposing. I have given 69 lectures on them, and raised about £350 by it, and love to meet them. I find the steep hills and the climate very trying, and of course I am out of practice with all the odd building and carpentering jobs I have to do; yesterday I got hold of a fine-looking Bedawy to make mud-mortaring for me, and together we filled open windows with stones and mudded them in, I inside with trowel and he outside. The shelves are mostly up now.[14]

They spent a couple of weeks on cemetery work. In the evenings Hilda coached the newcomers in Arabic. Then the rains came, and it was time to move back to 'Ajjul.

Tell el 'Ajjul was excavated by Petrie for four consecutive years, and later for a final season; the results were published in five volumes, the last appearing long after his death. The most extensive remains were of the Middle Bronze Age, when it must have been one of the richest and most powerful cities in Canaan. The site covers 33 acres; it was discovered by Starkey, who had a flair for finding good places to excavate, but indeed the place would have been difficult to miss if one followed the line of dunes which fringe the shore; it is shaped like a huge upturned boat, its prow towards the sea, about six miles south of the modern town of Gaza (Ghazzeh). The Wady Ghazzeh skirts the southern side of the mound and the sea can be glimpsed from the top; the city must once have been an estuarine port. Petrie called it the City of the Shepherd Kings, since the great fortifications of the Middle Bronze Age were associated by him, as by others at that time, with the invaders of Egypt, the builders of the fortresses of Tell el Yehudiya and Heliopolis. His theory was that this was Old Gaza, the city which had given its name to the Wady and in the second millennium BC was an important centre of Egyptian rule in Canaan. Later, he suggested, the population had been forced to move, probably because of malaria, to a site six miles further north, in the modern town of Gaza. Since there seemed to him to be no occupation of the site after the end of the Bronze Age, he concluded that it had not been the Philistine city, the site of Samson's imprisonment and Delilah's betrayal; that must have been the second Gaza.[15] The first season showed the importance of 'Ajjul. The excavators found a great ditch around part of the mound, and the great gate; a large cemetery was cleared, and in one of the tombs the bones of an equid, either a horse or a large donkey, were found (**103**), and in another gold jewellery. High on the mound there were houses, some with an oven and a privy[16]; narrow winding alleys ran between them, and in one of these there was a kiln. In houses and tombs, a great deal of pottery was found, adding many new types to the corpus.

The excavators' camp at Tell el 'Ajjul was designed in the usual Petrie tradition. Huts were built round three sides of a courtyard, with a low mud wall and a gate in front; nobody was allowed past the gate except the *khawagas* (Europeans) and the domestic staff, Abdallah the guard and the cook, Muhammad Osman, who still came every year from Quft.[17] Along the courtyard wall stood great pottery jars, filled every day by the man who brought the water-camel (**107**). Milkmen would arrive every morning waiting and chatting while their small contributions were taken and measured, and their cans scalded before being returned to them. The post was brought from Gaza town by a young Beduin who also carried the day's supply of Arab bread in a sack (when, as sometimes happened, it was reduced to crumbs on the journey, there was bread-pudding for supper).

Shopping in Gaza town meant an early start, walking a mile or so along a sandy track bordered with high hedges of prickly pear, and then five miles along a broad sandy road, the main road from Khan Yunis to Gaza. Gaza itself was a sprawling, half-ruined town; it had been besieged and heavily bombarded during the 1914–18 war and had not yet been rebuilt. When Hilda went into town she would stop in a cemetery outside the town walls to slip a skirt or long dress over her breeches, watched by a rapidly-gathering crowd of small boys. English groceries could be bought in the Police canteen; then, hot and dusty, she would repair to the cool garden of the C.M.S. hospital for a glass of lemonade. Then back to 'Ajjul, competing for a foothold at the edge of the road with camels, donkeys, goats, sheep, men, women and children, dogs and chickens, returning in Biblical procession from the fields.

Beyond the camp to the south, the fields stretched away into the distance; camels ploughed, women in long black dresses hung with necklaces tended the flocks, and here and there stood a cluster of black tents; beyond, distant orange groves. Early in the season, a health inspector came from Gaza, and advised the digging of a canal to keep the stagnant water in the wady flowing; Petrie set his men, and some prisoners from the local jail, to work and at a cost of £100 the canal was completed; it had to be cleared afresh every season.

Meal-times were never solemn affairs; the Professor had a fund of humorous anecdotes and was an excellent mimic; he delighted in telling a story, one eye cocked on the listener, and he would join himself in the resulting laughter. He was an accomplished raconteur; often he recalled some comic incident from his years in Egypt, at other times it was some joke or anecdote he had read. As Miss Tufnell remembers: "No one ever laughed with so much of his person. He shook from head to toe, his eyes crinkled up, his hands and arms shook."

In camp he would wake very early, and read for an hour before breakfast; then he would be off to inspect the work.

> Those years were characterised by the usual energy and concentration. Before daybreak he was to be seen striding up the stony path towards the work; as the sun rose he stood for a moment on the summit of the mound, the wind ruffling his hair and beard, his precious measuring rod in his hand. Workmen hurried to their

> places, a whistle blew, and the day's work began. Surveying in wind or rain, planning, drawing, writing, his day was all too short. In the cool hour between dusk and dark, he would sometimes walk over the hills and through the valleys talking of history, philosophy or music. His humour was entirely Celtic and he was aware of his idiosyncrasies.[18]

When the day's work was done, he sometimes read in the evenings in bed. At Tell Jemmeh his bedroom, larger than any of the others, had also been a storeroom for antiquities and had a shelf of reference books. Gerald Harding used later to relate how one evening, wishing to consult a book, he knocked on the wall in the usual way by the Professor's door, and getting no answer, entered the darkened room; in one corner a candle burned dimly. The candle spoke: "What are you looking for, Harding?" and Gerald, peering through the gloom, saw Petrie lying in bed reading, the candlestick balanced on his forehead. Harding's offer to bring a chair to put by the bed was refused: "Always remember, when you are reading you should have the light *behind* your eyes." Tea should always be stirred in one direction, not the other. His ingenious application of scientific principles to practical living was not always successful. When Irene Donne, at Qau, cut her finger he would not let her put sticking plaster on it: it was important, he said to be able to watch the progress of a wound. He produced a piece of clear celluloid film and bound it on, and every day he would peer through the window at the cut; as it did not heal, he was forced to admit that conventional first-aid was probably more efficacious. He preferred to be his own doctor, and believed in the efficacy of the essential oils, eucalyptus and oil of cloves, and often slept with a dab of oil of aniseed across his nose.

A simple diet was what suited him best, and Muhammad knew his preferences: his baked custard was still prepared for him daily, he ate little meat except chicken, and onions were banned from the kitchen. (When Petrie joined the party in camp at Tell el Fara in the second season, Starkey had told the cook to say nothing, but to disregard the prohibition: "What delicious soup!" said Petrie on tasting it.) His fondness for biscuits persisted and he was never without a bar of York chocolate to nibble. Muhammad had become an expert at juggling a meal from two primus stoves; he was not permitted to cook Arab food, but lentil soup, the old favourite, was still frequent on the menu. Hilda left all the catering to him; he would go off to Gaza on market day without a shopping list having memorized the camp's many requirements (he could neither read nor write). A fisherman occasionally brought fresh fish to the camp; on one occasion a note arrived: SEA IS TALL AND FISH NO. At 'Ajjul the staff lived better than at any other Petrie dig; here there was less need to rely on tinned or dried foods, though a packeted shape called Bink Buduny* turned up once a week with terrible regularity.

At the end of March Petrie wrote asking for a division; Richmond replied very formally (beginning his letter "Sir") with a new complaint: the list of pottery which had been sent with the request was incomplete, and no plans or sections had been sent; no division was possible till adequate lists were made.[19] Petrie had followed his usual practice: listed only what he deemed important, and assumed that except in the case of new pottery types, reference to numbers in the Palestinian corpus would suffice; however, he worked hard for three days and sent the revised inventory, with an equally formal letter. Eventually Richmond came down, with the curator of the Museum, J. H. Iliffe, for the division. The Petries closed the dig and went home without passing through Jerusalem. On their journey they stopped in Belgrade and stayed a few days as guests of the University, and Professor Vassitch took them round the Danubian site of Vinča.

That summer Ann got her degree; she was to go on to postgraduate work, choosing as the subject of her thesis an Italian writer of the Risorgimento; her father had hoped that she would choose to study Etruscan. In the summer exhibition plans and photographs explained the new site, pottery and bronze weapons and scarabs were displayed and there were parts of an "ablution bench" of mud, paved with cockle-shells; there had been three of these in houses on the *tell* and Petrie thought them of enough interest to bring one home in pieces; they were, he thought, for washing the feet before entering small domestic shrines. On sale at the exhibition was a camerascope with a set of photographs of "Exploration in Bible Cities"; this, said the catalogue, "is the latest and most direct way of seeing excavation in progress. An after-tea amusement, and instructive." Donations were urgently invited for the continuation of the work; it was suggested that they might be earmarked for one or two scholarships, one in memory of Gertrude Bell, the other to be called the Biblical Research Scholarship; it was also hoped that there might be enough for a Bursary in Ancient Zoology. (Evidently there was not, for it is not mentioned again.) Money was urgently needed, for America was in

* Pink pudding.

the grip of the Depression; the contribution from New York University which in the previous year had provided a quarter of the total raised, was not to be repeated; at this time of economic stringency, archaeology was a luxury few could afford. The committee were forced to dig into their capital reserves; only Sir Charles Marston made his usual generous contribution. The Annual General Meeting in October was attended by all four of the School's patrons, Sir John Chancellor, the retiring High Commissioner, Sir Arthur Wauchope who was to succeed him, Lord Allenby and Lord Lloyd.

The year 1931 saw the publication of Petrie's autobiography. He called it *Seventy Years in Archaeology*, for he reckoned that his career had begun at the age of eight when he first began collecting coins. The narrative is reticent about his personal feelings and family life; "this is only a record of the work, and of what led me up to it, and has nothing otherwise to do with the inner life." Yet the private hopes and fears, the prejudices and enthusiasms peep through, lines from his own poems are quoted and personal anecdotes and incidents lighten the tale. Running through it like a *Leitmotif* is the story of his battles with authority, in particular with the French. It has been said that he was anti-French—Amélineau once made the accusation in print[20]—and it might reasonably be supposed that his mother, whose father had suffered such grievous wrong in French hands, might have influenced him in this; but both she and he were proud of their Chappell ancestry (to this his family attributed his habit of sweeping off his hat and bowing in a near-parody of Gallic politeness). It was rather that he chafed at the petty controls and regulations of an authority which happened, in Egypt, to be exclusively French. Now he was to find that a British administration, too, could frustrate and thwart him.

Richmond granted him a licence to excavate, but complained of an irregularity in the division: he had not, he said, been shown the ablution bench of which there was a photograph in the June number of *Ancient Egypt*. Petrie could only assure him that one of the three found had been pointed out to him, but that he and Iliffe had rejected it.[21] Richmond and Iliffe both denied this. Richmond then demanded that he furnish complete copies of all his records in the form in which they were to be published, adding running numbers to each object; the Department would then consider whether his records fulfilled the conditions set down in his licence. It was an unprecedented request and one which would entail a great deal of work in the coming season, but Petrie had no choice but to agree. He was tired and not feeling well: the journey had been uncomfortable and there was much to do before the main party arrived: six new bedrooms were to be built (for the party was to include an unusual number of volunteers); there was to be a new storeroom for the *antikas*, the dining hut was enlarged and heightened, and the kitchen whitewashed and tiled.

Gradually the team assembled: Royds, Harding, Starkey and Richmond Brown were there from the start, and a newcomer named O'Brien, a tall bearded young man, soon arrived to help with the preparations; three days later Olga Tufnell turned up on a donkey. This year, needing transport for supplies from Gaza and for transfers to hospital, they had a truck, which Hilda, always ready for anything, drove as far as the town outskirts (she had no licence) "spinning along the very twisted rutty roads crossing rail line twice, open ditches on both sides and many camels, donkeys and natives. . . . I was said to steer with consummate skill."[22] Several of the men, fortunately, were taking their driving test. Then the volunteers arrived: Dr Sperrin Johnson, an elderly professor of biology from New Zealand who took charge of the clinic as well as measuring skulls; a retired army colonel named Clarke whose interest was in military fortifications, and a young couple named Warren Hastings; Miss Bentwich, the sister of Norman Bentwich and a gifted musician, stayed with them; Mrs Colt and her sister were there for a time, and so was Gerald Harding's mother. It was the largest camp the Petries had ever had, but it was not one of the happiest: Hilda's letters give some hint of tensions. Small grievances tended to grow into exasperation and resentment. While she and Flinders were in Jerusalem for a few days, staying in Government House with the new High Commissioner, Colt bought a puppy which chased Hilda's cat, gobbled the Quftis' food and made messes everywhere (the living compound had to be surrounded with wire-netting to keep him out).

Some of the team were not pulling their weight: Hilda and Flinders always dressed in the dark and had early breakfast, and O'Brien was always out on the *tell* by sunrise, but most of the others, she complained, got up much later. Someone had been smoking in the dining-room—discipline was getting slack. The camp tended to split into two, the younger members congregating in the evenings in the "Taylorian" a little way from the camp. This was a large room which Harris Colt had built at his own expense; it was wooden, built in sections and it was called after Taylor the carpenter who, during the previous season, had spent some weeks at the camp building it. Furnished with comfortable chairs, it served as a recreation room and a place where the younger members of the party could meet in the evenings for a beer or a cigarette, and there was a portable gramophone; the Petries, who disapproved of alcohol and tobacco and hated jazz, were not invited. It was understandable, indeed inevitable; the stern principles of self-discipline to which Flinders had adhered all his life (he had once told Spurrell: "I would rather do a week's hard work than take part in one day's pleasure") could not be expected to appeal to the younger generation of the 1930s; they worked hard, but they expected some relaxation of austerity at the end of the day.

There was more to it than this, however; the experienced members of the team, in particular Starkey and Lankester Harding, were fully qualified to run their own excavation. Many of Petrie's former apprentices in the past had broken away after a couple of years at most; these had been with him for seven. Perhaps they expected that the "Prof.", now nearly eighty, would hand over control of the work to them, but of this he showed no sign. They felt critical, too, of certain aspects of the running of the dig. In January Harris Colt went up to Jerusalem for a couple of days' leave, and without Petrie's knowledge went to see Richmond; he complained that the part of the *tell* on which they were currently working was not being excavated by layers over the whole area, but in a series of small plots, the earth from each being dumped into the one previously dug; work was being directed by untrained staff, insufficiently supervised by the Professor.[23] Richmond very properly told Colt that he should have addressed his protests to Petrie, not gone behind his back; once the Department had granted a licence, he said, the excavator was left to use his own methods. Nevertheless, the complaint did not improve Petrie's stock in the Museum in Jerusalem.

The truth of the matter was that on this great mound Petrie for the first time was out of his depth. The stratigraphical excavation of a *tell*, layer by layer, had been his own invention when in 1890 at Tell Hesy he had taken vertical sections and noted the level at which each characteristic type of pottery was found; but his "strata" were measured from a datum and bore little or no relation to the floors and foundations of buildings. Since that time, he had had little cause to apply methods of stratigraphical recording to his excavations; he had dug very few settlement sites and when he had excavated a temple, successive levels were dated by the presence of inscriptions with royal names. In the case of the successive Osiris temples at Abydos (p. 265), built one on top of another over a period of more than 2,000 years, he had taken careful measurements of the depth at which objects were found, and attempted to relate structures of each period by their position and by the size of the bricks, but his method made no allowance for differences of floor level within the same building at a given time, nor did it solve the difficulty of distinguishing where the foundations of later buildings were dug below the floors of the earlier. In the publication no sections were drawn and the plans of successive phases of the temple were not related one to another. Stratified records received no mention in his manual of archaeological technique, *Methods and Aims in Archaeology*. Now, confronted with a huge accumulation of the debris of successive centuries of human occupation, he realized his inability to record each level of rebuilding; at Tell Jemmeh and Tell Fara' the buildings he had excavated were of widely differing ages; here at 'Ajjul he had streets of houses continuously occupied over generations, even centuries, the walls repaired and rebuilt on the same plan. Vital evidence from successive floor levels was missed, and those who have later attempted to assign artefacts found in the town to a specific phase in its architectural history have confessed themselves baffled.[24] It must however be borne in mind that techniques of settlement excavation, in 1931, were still in their infancy. Albright at Tell Beit Mersim and Clarence Fisher and P. L. O. Guy at Megiddo were currently attempting to read the riddle of superimposed walls, and Reisner at Samaria, as early as 1909, had drawn a rough section through successive building levels,[25] but it was not until Mortimer Wheeler's excavation of Verulamium and Maiden Castle in England in the early Thirties that the careful labelling of each level and the drawing of sections in each trench was insisted upon; Kathleen Kenyon, who worked with Wheeler on both sites, brought his technique to Palestine just before the war, when first test-trenching (the digging of trenches at right angles to walls) and then, after the war, the use of a grid of baulks of earth, between which successive levels could be excavated down to bedrock, became normal archaeological practice.[26]

In one respect, however, Petrie's work in Palestine set a standard: the meticulous excavation and recording of tombs, on the system developed by him since Negada days in the 1890s. Printed tomb cards were now supplied to each member of the staff supervising cemetery work (p. 391). Each tomb opened had a number, and on sections of the card the size and orientation of the tomb, the attitude of the skeleton, its sex and any unusual features were noted; the pottery in the tomb was listed by corpus numbers and the other contents detailed under separate headings. On the back of the card the recorder would usually sketch the position of the whole contents of the tomb. There was no excuse for any detail to be missed or forgotten, and as each object was removed from the tomb, it was marked with the tomb number.

Whatever the causes, the atmosphere in the camp at Tell el 'Ajjul in the winter of 1931–2 was not a happy one, and Hilda was relieved when, during the Bairam holiday, most of the younger members of the staff went off to Jerusalem for a few days. "We have considerable worries," she wrote to Ann, "most of which have no solution." The division, for which Iliffe came down, went smoothly enough, and the Petries spent a few days at Megiddo on their way home, without going up to Jerusalem. Not long after their return to London, Starkey told Petrie that he would be working on his own next season; he had had discussions with several possible patrons, and had been promised assistance by Sir Charles Marston, Sir Robert Mond and most important, Sir Henry Wellcome, an enthusiast for archaeology who had himself in the past conducted excavations and amassed a large collection of antiquities; they had a promising site in mind, Tell Duweir, in the foothills further north, and hoped to start that autumn. Gerald Harding, the Harris Colts, and Richmond Brown decided to join in this new venture, and Olga Tufnell, torn between her affection and respect for the Professor (with whom over the last five years she had enjoyed many of those evening walks and talks), and her friendship and loyalty to her friends and contemporaries, somewhat unhappily decided to go with them.

It was a bitter blow to Petrie, who saw their defection as ingratitude and worse—such a thing had never happened to him before; nevertheless he probably realized that this was the best, indeed the only, solution to an impossible situation. In the autumn the "Taylorian" was dismantled and removed, with its furniture, to the new site. Except for Mr Royds, the staff at 'Ajjul were all to be new. The summer exhibition again had as its centre-piece a display of gold jewellery, most of it found in or near the palace area in the centre of the mound; gold armlets, earrings and toggle pins were found here, and in a tomb, an earring twisted in a manner somewhat resembling the Bronze Age torques of Ireland; always on the lookout for possible links between cultures, Petrie concluded a trade link with the far west, and referred in the future to the "Irish gold" of Palestine. The toggle pins Petrie derived from the Caucasus, whence, he suggested, the Hyksos had come.[27] Neither archaeologists nor anthropologists would endorse these conclusions today; the frequency of finds of gold jewellery in 'Ajjul is still unexplained, but parallels of many of the pieces have been found elsewhere, in Cyprus and the Near East, and

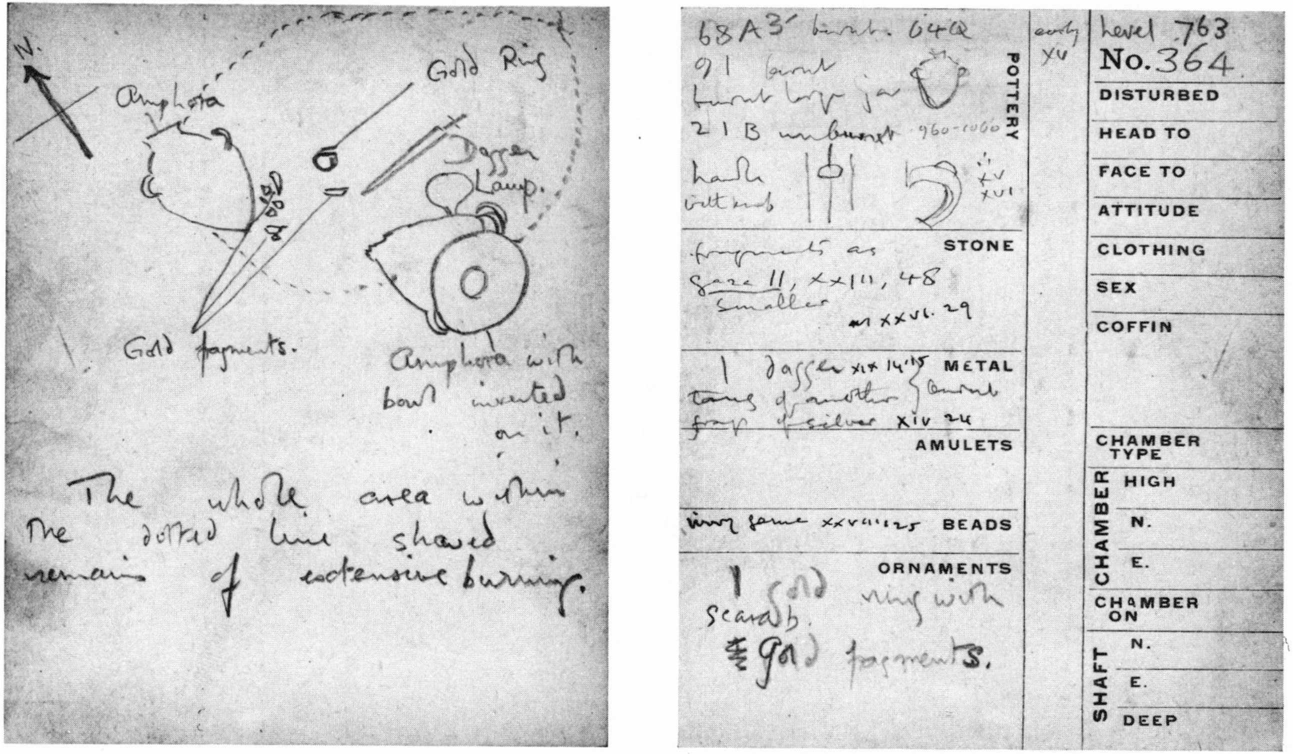

H. *Tomb card used at Tell el ʻAjjul, 1933*; obverse and reverse. The card was filled in by the student supervising the excavation of the tomb; Petrie has added details.

the twisted coils may well have evolved in Palestine itself—perhaps even as a speciality of the inventive goldworkers of Gaza itself.[28] The modern finder of this particular cache was well rewarded—he bought himself a new wife with the proceeds—and rumours flew; a local Arabic newspaper announced the discovery of a golden bull weighing eight cwt, with diamond-studded horns.

During the summer Flinders Petrie met with his Executive Sub-Committee and drew up a new set of rules for students, setting out their duties and responsibilities as members of his expedition.[29] Some of the regulations suggest what causes he and Lady Petrie may have had for dissatisfaction during the past season: no visitor may reside in the camp without the Director's permission, nor stay more than three days; every student in the camp must "take a definite active share in the work"; the hours of rising, meals and work are exactly specified; commissariat arrangements must be subject to the Director's control (i.e. no smuggling in of extra luxuries).

Flinders Petrie was now coming to the end of his long tenure of the Edwards Chair at University College; he was to retire at the end of the next session, in the summer of 1933. The present writer was one of the last three students to take his Diploma course in Egyptology. I first met the Professor when I was still at school; fired by letters from my parents, who lived in Baghdad, describing their visits to ancient sites in Iraq, I had decided that archaeology was what I wanted for my future career. At the British Museum I was advised that instead of going to Oxford to read Greats as I hoped I should take the Diploma course in London, since that offered the only practical training course available at any British University. In the summer of 1929, therefore, I kept my appointment in the Edwards Library and was met at the door by the great man himself; I have a memory of twinkling eyes, an unexpectedly high, light voice, bushy eyebrows and a patriarchal white beard. He questioned me a little, and then agreed to accept me as a student, but strongly advised me, since I had the opportunity, to travel abroad for a year after leaving school; this good advice I was able to take, and in October 1931 I began my course at the College.

The curriculum laid down in 1913 had changed but little, though new subjects had been added. We were taught to draw pottery, using Petrie's simple apparatus; our facsimile drawings of scarabs, if approved, would be included in the next excavation report. The Professor himself gave us little individual attention beyond a beaming encouragement; he delivered one or two lectures before departing for Palestine, and a course of public lectures on his discoveries in the summer term after his return. As always, the audience packed the theatre.

One or two of the young people who frequented the Petrie Museum were going out with him next season. Petrie was always on the lookout for potential helpers, and while his summer exhibitions were on in London, he would require his assistants to act as talent scouts, on the alert for any young people who appeared to be particuarly interested, and bring them to be introduced to him. Lady Burton more than once acted in this capacity; several archaeologists, among them Starkey and Lankester Harding, called her their "Egyptian godmother" because their enthusiasm had first caught her observant eye. If Petrie's first impression was favourable, he would interview the young man again, and might then offer him a place in the next season's team. Hence it came about that few of his recruits during the latter years had any academic background; perhaps there were some grounds for the belief that he preferred them to have no degree, since they were less likely to have preconceived ideas. Legend further has it that there were two more tests: the aspirant was invited to lunch at Petrie's favourite teashop, the Express Dairy near the College, at the corner of Gower Street. If he chose a frugal meal, he met with approbation; if he plumped for meat and two vegetables with a sweet to follow, he scored zero and was unlikely to be accepted. After lunch he was taken back to the Department. There were no lifts in the College in those days; the Professor would skip lightly up the long curving flight of stairs to the door of the museum; no candidate who did not follow close on his heels and arrive at the top without feeling breathless would be considered fit enough to withstand the rigours of life in a Petrie camp.

It was an advantage for a student to be well-off, for then he could contribute to the dig and could also afford to keep himself while training. Towards those enthusiasts, however, who showed real promise but lacked means, Petrie was generous in his encouragement and unsparing of his time and trouble. Starkey used to say that but for the Professor, he would have been a pawnbroker's assistant all his life; Harding, too, had had little education and no money, and had a widowed mother to support. To these and other promising students Petrie would give coaching after working hours, and Miss Murray ran evening classes for them.

Most of our tuition was given round the table in the Edwards Library; Miss Murray believed in informality in teaching; during her classes, a box of chocolates was sometimes passed round. She had been

Assistant Professor since 1924, but her salary was not large; she lived in a bed-sitter near the College, and when in 1927 the University had conferred on her an honorary degree, her old students had subscribed to buy her the gown that she could not herself afford. She lectured on Egyptian History and Religion, Elementary Hieroglyphics and Coptic; a stimulating weekly talk on the Origin and Development of Signs made us familiar with the individual hieroglyphs but also led to dissertations on ancient Egyptian tools and weapons, dress, flora and fauna, and all the manifold objects depicted by that most pictorial of scripts. Sometimes she would digress and talk about her own particular interest, witchcraft; her *Witch Cult in Western Europe* had made something of a stir when it came out in 1927; its frankness had caused raised eyebrows among some of her reviewers. Mrs Aitken came in from time to time but was no longer Honorary Assistant in the Department; this title was accorded to Dr Edith Guest, a physiologist friend of Dr Murray's who taught "Bones for the Archaeologist". One of the Engineering staff taught us Elementary Surveying: with alidade and drawing board we triangulated and plotted the College quadrangle, and we deployed our Dumpy levels up and down the Portico steps. Lectures on Aegean Pottery from Professor Ashmole, and on Anthropology, given by Professor Seligman, were somehow fitted into the curriculum.

Miss May Bonar, now the Assistant Secretary to the British School of Archaeology in Egypt, had her table half-way down the museum; her unfailing good temper and her sense of humour carried her through perennial small panics and occasional crises: she handled all correspondence for the School when the Petries were away, and had to deal with printers, publishers and the despatch of the four annual parts of *Ancient Egypt*;[29] it was not her fault that they were sometimes a month or two late. When Flinders Petrie was in the museum he would never answer the telephone; if it rang when nobody else was about, he would let it ring. Never having possessed this product of the mechanical age himself, he was disapproving and probably a little nervous of it.

Miss Murray's devotion to the Professor, or "Proffy", was plain to see; she left it in no doubt in her best-selling book, *The Wonder that was Egypt*, which first came out in 1949, and in her autobiography, published when she was in her hundredth year. It was commonly believed by her students that she had, in her youth, aspired to marry him. She and Lady Petrie remained on formal terms; since that season at Abydos in 1902, she had never again been invited to join one of the

Petries' expeditions; when they were away, her presence in London with the students had become indispensable.

The British Association met in York that year; Flinders and Margaret Murray went up by train, and Hilda and Ann met them there; Flinders lectured on his recent discoveries, and the next day they all went over to Allerton Mauleverer, the home of Flinders' forebears (ancestors of his great-grandmother Anne Mallison, who had married a Chappell in 1770); Petrie was delighted to find several Mauleverer monuments in the church, oaken effigies of the thirteenth and fourteenth centuries; as the knights were in poor condition he commissioned the diocesan architect to repair and preserve them.

The following winter in camp, 1932–33, must have been one of the happiest for Flinders and Hilda Petrie; the tensions of the previous year were gone, the staff worked in harmony, their new architect Carl Pape proved excellent; besides Royds, they had the welcome help of Lt Commander Noel Wheeler, who had been with Petrie in Qau nine years before and had since been working in Cyprus; Mrs Benson came out to help with the drawing and best of all, Ann, their daughter, came out for her first experience of life on a dig—that life about which she had heard so much since earliest childhood. She had looked forward to the experience, and she was not disappointed. She took her turn in the early morning, supervising the workmen on the *tell*, lent a hand with the drawing and inking in of objects, accompanied her mother into Gaza on occasional expeditions, and assisted Mrs Benson in the "clinic". A room at the back of the camp outside the compound was set aside for this purpose; the workmen and their families would come here during working hours for injuries, and after work for minor ailments; treatment was of the hit-or-miss variety: fever or headache would be treated with quinine or aspirin, stomach ache generally implied castor oil. Cases of serious illness or injury were sent with a note to the hospital; most of the Beduin dreaded this—a hospital was regarded as a place to which you only went to die—but at the clinic in the camp they learned confidence in thermometers, eyedrops and bandages. There were about 100 men at work, none of them now Quftis, each had his small team of three basket-boys, or basket-girls. Some of the local men had learned their craft well and were now expert at following a wall or excavating a tomb (one or two of the best had been "poached" by Starkey for Tell Duweir). Hilda was in charge of the accounts and pay; men received ten piastres a day—about two shillings—big boys five and little ones four. If doubts arose whether a boy was to be classed as big or small, he would be stood up against one particular boy of middling size, known, because of the colour of his shirt, as "the Pink Gauge".

The work was continuing in the lower levels of a large building Petrie called the Palace; in the cemetery area a large tomb was found, roofed with a vault of stone slabs; among the grave goods were a gold ring bearing the name of Tutankhamun, and a scarab of a later Pharaoh, Ramesses II; Petrie called it the Governors' Tomb, and assumed continuous use by governors of Gaza during two centuries of Egyptian occupation.[30] (The ring may have been an heirloom, and the tomb is now thought to be Ramesside in date.)

There was now an Imperial Airways station at Gaza, and pleasant young pilots sometimes came over to visit the camp. It was their suggestion that they might fly Petrie out from England next season. Flinders, always ready to try new ways of travelling, made a trial cross-Channel trip next summer to Le Touquet and back; the gossip column of an evening newspaper declared the experiment to have been a complete success and quoted him as saying, "Eighty times and more have I crossed the Mediterranean by boat, and never enjoyed it. But never again. I shall always fly in future." This was pure imagination: in fact, the vibration of the plane gave him a bad headache and he never again set foot in one.

The time for retirement from University College had come; he was eighty years old and had held the Edwards Chair for forty-one years. He had already decided that he would make his home one day in Jerusalem; the climate suited him perfectly, and he had many friends there. Two years earlier he had registered as an immigrant and was already a Palestinian citizen. Yet he was not ready to pull up his roots completely; he must ensure that the Petrie Collection and the Department which he had built up were in safe hands. It was not easy to find a successor to fill the Chair; few of Petrie's own disciples, however great their archaeological experience, had academic qualifications to satisfy the requirements of the University. A young Assistant Keeper in the Department of Egyptian Antiquities in the British Museum was finally chosen; although primarily a "language man", he had been one of Frankfort's team excavating at Tell el Amarna for two seasons, and his knowledge of Egyptian artefacts stemmed from five years' experience in the British Museum. There had been, it will be remembered, a clause in Miss Edwards' will excluding employees of the British Museum from appointment to the Chair which she had endowed; to get round the difficulty, Stephen Glanville was appointed in the first place Reader in Egyptology; he succeeded to the Chair two years later.

Petrie, who intended to spend the next summer—his last in London—clarifying and improving the labelling of pottery and other objects in the collection, was appointed Honorary Curator. On 29 June 1933 he gave his last lecture in the College. There was no exhibition for he was too busy in Cannon Place packing up his working library: 56 boxes of books especially made to be converted into bookshelves were despatched to Jerusalem, the rest he had to leave behind. Before the end of August he was ready to embark on his new life.

CHAPTER XVIII

Lone Syrian Shore

(1934–8)

AT THE END of August 1933 Ann Petrie saw her parents off at Victoria Station; they consented for once to take a taxi and porters, for they had numerous boxes and suitcases. They went by train to Rome and were filled with a distaste at the vulgarities of Mussolini's new Italy. In Cairo Guy Brunton, now Assistant Curator in the Museum, showed them the new display of Tutankhamun's treasures; then they were off by an evening train, reaching Jerusalem next day. After the "dig" had ended in the previous spring they had stayed there for a time in a pension near St George's, Beaumont House, where the Crowfoots were living. Here they now settled; Flinders was given an extra room for his library and Hilda had a pleasant bedroom with a view towards the hills. The boxes arrived, and Flinders was busy in arranging the books, calling on old friends and making new ones; he was in excellent spirits. Cannon Place was let for the winter, and Ann went to Milan to work on her thesis; John was still in the army, with little prospect of a commission; there were rumours that his regiment might be sent to India. His father worried a great deal about his prospects, but could do little to help or advise him; John never wrote letters, or answered the most urgent enquiries on the subject of his future.

The fourth season's work at Tell el 'Ajjul began in November; Ann joined her parents from Baghdad, where she had spent a brief holiday, and Pape was again there; one of the new recruits was Jack Ellis, small, quiet and reliable, who had served as a fitter in the R.A.F. in Iraq and Palestine, and spoke a little Arabic. For part of the time, an Australian, J. M. Stewart, was there with his wife, and Dr Immanual Ben-Dor came from Jerusalem.[1] Ann enjoyed the company of a cousin from Australia, Patricia Blundell, who stayed in the camp for a time and eventually travelled back to England with her; she and Ann were sometimes asked over to a party in Gaza given by the Palestine Police or the staff of Imperial Airways; Petrie was not altogether approving of these frivolities. It was not the most successful of seasons from his point of view, for Hilda fell and gashed her leg, many of the staff fell sick, so that they were sometimes short of help. They worked at the south-western end of the *tell*, an area hitherto unexplored, where two wide streets were bordered by blocks of houses; the stratification and the plan of successive strata were very complex; in the notes which Petrie wrote for possible additions to his autobiography if a new edition were called for,[2] he referred disparagingly to "stay-at-home critics" who could not follow the complexity of "hundreds of levels". Numerous finds of jewellery were made again this year, including pendants depicting a stylised female figure, perhaps the goddess Astarte (**101**). So much gold had never before been found on any Palestinian site; Petrie believed, probably rightly, that this was because he rewarded the finders by the exact value of the weight of the metal (the most recent edition of *The Times* in camp gave him the current price of gold). On 24 March Ann noted in her diary the annual miracle:

> Storks on migration . . . thousands upon thousands wheeling around the *tell*. Wings sound like the lapping of the sea on the shore. Thousands settle for the night on the wady . . . Abdel Majid like a patriarch invited us into his tent where his *sitt* was cooking flat bread over a heated iron; the little fire lit up the dark inside of the tent; outside were his child, donkey, goat and camel against the red sky. . . . Then there was a pale half moon, with the white and black storks still circling above.

Such treasured moments enrich the excavator's life.

In April Flinders Petrie sent in his documents and asked for a division; Richmond refused: the lists, he said, were again inadequate and must be re-submitted.[3] Once more Petrie tried to meet the requirements by re-copying the register. The division, when it finally took place, was harsh; as if in punishment, all the gold was taken by Iliffe for the Museum. Hilda went home, and Flinders stayed on for a time with Pape, working on the plans for the next publication. Back in England in June, a letter from Richmond awaited him: small gold objects, listed as from Tomb 1532, were missing. Petrie could only reply that he had brought nothing away: they must be in the Museum. (Next year, when Ellis was looking through the Museum's Gaza collection, he saw number 1532 plainly in view . . . it had been their mistake, not his.) During the summer, the Director sent a formal report, by way of the High Commissioner and the Secretary of State for the Colonies, to the Joint Archaeological Committee in London complaining of Petrie's intransigencies and the deficiency of his records. The report was passed to Ernest Gardner, the Chairman of Petrie's Executive Committee; after some debate, it was decided to send out Dr Margaret Murray (who was leaving the College) to help sort out the difficulties, but she fell ill and was not, after all, able to go. Petrie decided that it was hopeless to expect Richmond to grant another season at Tell el 'Ajjul, for some reason or other the Director was hostile to him and likely to remain so. Even if permission were not actually withheld, it would be hedged about with so many restrictions that work would become impossible. He decided to find a fresh field for exploration. In April he had happened to meet, at a dinner in the Residency, a young French archaeologist, M. Jean Schlumberger, a member of the staff of the Antiquities Department in Syria, who urged him to apply to the French authorities for a Syrian site; they would put no obstacles in his way, he was sure, and he would be assured of a fair half-and-half division. Petrie was already convinced that certain of his recent finds—the gold ornaments and the painted pottery in particular, must have been imports from the north: designs of fish, and a palm tree, suggested that "somewhere up the Cilician coast there must have existed a civilisation far ahead of that of Palestine."[4] He decided to prospect there for a likely site. Money would be a problem, for he could scarcely divert the funds of the B.S.A.E. to a site without any Egyptian connections; he even considered offering himself as a volunteer on a dig run by Schlumberger or some other French excavator.

Meanwhile there was much to do in London: Cannon Place was given up, and much of the furniture and remaining books sold, while Ann and John moved into a small half-house in the Vale of Health, which they named Upfleet, because the Fleet river had its source beside it; this was to be the family home—and Hilda's *pied à terre* when she was in England—for the next twenty-one years. Flinders finished the preparation of *Ancient Gaza IV* for the press and spent what time he could in the Petrie Museum, sorting and labelling. In July and August, he sat for his portrait to Philip de Laszlo (**97**). A number of his friends and colleagues, in commemoration of his forty years in the Edwards Chair, presented it to the College for the Professors' Common Room; since the war it has hung in the Old Refectory in company with those of several of his friends and contemporaries, W. P. Ker, Sir Gregory Foster, and Sir Ambrose Fleming, the Professor of Electrical Engineering (who held his Chair even longer than Petrie). A second portrait, done at the same time for the artist's own enjoyment, was given after his death to Stephen Glanville, who in turn donated it to the National Portrait Gallery; a third version, which de Laszlo called a rough sketch, he painted for the family; Lady Petrie lent it to the College at the time of her husband's Centenary and it hangs at present in the Petrie Collection. Immediately after the final sitting, Petrie went off by train with Ann to the West Country on a last, sentimental journey to say farewell to his favourite places: they visited Salisbury and Bemerton, Wells, Glastonbury, Exeter and Buckfastleigh, travelling by bus and local train, and stopping, as always, in homely lodgings rather than hotels; at Glastonbury they stayed with Ann's godmother, Miss Buckton, who was a fervent believer in the legend of the Holy Thorn. It was a journey full of happy memories, but he knew he would never see England again. Five days after his return, having sent off the last proofs of *Ancient Gaza IV*, he was off with Hilda to Jerusalem, his new and future home.

Now the Petries planned a journey of reconnaissance. With Ellis' help they bought an elderly bus and converted it into a caravan (**111**). Flinders and Hilda were to sleep on the benches, Jack Ellis and the chauffeur in a tent. The tent, buckets and other equipment were stacked on the roof of the bus, tins of food were stowed under the benches, and canteen equipment with the blanket-box on the back seat; when opened the box lid served as a table. A hurricane lamp, a trenching tool, and three water canisters completed the outfit; the windows were protected with wire-netting and mosquito nets could be suspended at night. M. Schlumberger had lent them maps. At every stop, Ellis was to tramp the neighbourhood hunting for sites and would bring back a selection of sherds from the surface for the Professor to sort through and date; he also took charge of the cooking, and sometimes took a hand at the wheel to relieve the chauffeur, a Palestinian Christian whose knowledge of the countryside was to prove invaluable. A letter from Lady Petrie appeared in the *Morning Post*: a new fund, she said, had been started, named the Biblical Research Account. "Prospects are favourable in Syria, and nothing lacks except the means. Interest in the early peoples of the Biblical record, and in the alluring problems awaiting investigation, should surely prove an incentive towards sending assistance."[5]

Their journey occupied seven weeks, and took them up the coast to Beirut and on to Latakiyeh and Antioch, then down the Orontes valley; in all they covered over 1,200 miles.[6] When they started Petrie, at eighty-one, was looking very frail and Ellis wondered if he was going to bring the old man back alive; but they took things slowly, often stopping to set up camp in the early afternoon so that he could have a short nap, and the nomadic life seems to have suited him; on his return he declared he felt better than he had done for some time past. They started from Jerusalem on 16 October, and spent the first night encamped at Megiddo, hospitably entertained by the team of the Oriental Institute of Chicago. Crossing the frontier next morning, they continued past Tyre and Sidon, camping in the valley of the Litany river, and next day visiting the caves of Adlūn, where Petrie noticed the characteristic marks of the heavy long-handled picks which he pronounced to be Phoenician rather than Roman. In Beirut they were welcomed by Dr Bayard Dodge, the founder and Principal of the American University of Beirut, and camped in the garden for three nights; they met Dr Ingholt, who showed them early pottery from his site at Hama on the Orontes; they called on the Director of Antiquities, Dr Henri Seyrig, in his museum, and were invited to dinner to meet a party of American archaeologists from Dura Europos, and Comte du Mesnil du Buisson from the expedition at Qatna. On Monday they took to the road again. At Byblos they were disappointed to find that nobody was digging there; after walking over the ravaged site, they continued northwards and pitched camp at lunch-time in an orchard at Kubbeh, a little settlement just south of the Ras esh Shakkeh. Here Petrie hoped to find an occupation mound, but though Ellis explored in either direction he could find no early pottery. Both the Petries were out of sorts the next day, and while Ellis went off up the valley inland they stayed quietly in camp. "We found the peasants very friendly, many saying they hoped to see us return that way. A youth here picks up flint flakes and implements, for which there is a local demand by collectors. . . . Altogether, the M'sallaha, as it is called, is a place strange and notable, which may yet repay close research. . . ."

Leaving by the coastal road which passes through two tunnels in the rock, they halted in Tripoli to buy stores; at Qubbet al Bedawi they could not resist stopping to look at the sacred fish swarming in the large circular pool behind the mosque. Delighted as always to find a survival from ancient times, he compared the holy fishpond with that of Urfa and derived both from the Syrian worship of Atargatis.

Now they were in the plain of the Eleutheros river, the Nahr el Kebir, which divides Lebanon from Syria. At Tell 'Arka, "a great grey mass unlike any other hill" the road took a twist to cross the Arka river on an ancient stone bridge. Petrie found the *tell* larger and finer than any they saw, but could only find Roman pottery. From now on he was looking for sites on or near the coast which might be identified with the cities mentioned in the Amarna letters, as correspondents with the Pharaoh or dependencies of the Egyptian empire. 'Arka itself was probably Irqata, but Petrie did not venture on this identification. He looked in vain for Simyra. Since all the region south of the Eleutheros was part of the Lebanese state "the council of which is jealous about excavation and refuses any share to excavators" they sought no further. Over the bridge and north of the river, however, was another matter; here they were in Syria where the fifty-fifty rule applied, and they set about hunting for promising mounds. The aspect of the country had changed: the black volcanic earth afforded rich grazing for cattle and buffaloes. They noted a different physical type here, which Petrie identified as "Amorite"—good-looking people with long faces and aquiline noses. This, he thought, must have been the type the ancient Egyptians so much admired and which, through intermarriage with the women of their vassals and captives, produced in the eighteenth dynasty "the delicate-featured type which characterised the Egyptians of that age".

For several days they moved about the countryside; several mounds they examined had Middle Bronze Age pottery—what Petrie called Hyksos pottery. They turned eastwards toward the hills, noting a difference again in the physical type of the children who crowded in curiosity round the bus, no doubt to stare at the venerable bearded foreigner in his wide felt hat, and the elderly lady with white bobbed hair, in a pith helmet, breeches and knee-boots. They climbed the road to Safita, where a square Crusading fortress dominates the ridge above deep valleys (**112**); while Hilda and Jack Ellis shopped, Flinders in the bus examined hundreds of coins brought by the local children: coins of all periods "which told the history of the place pretty well", little Phoenician copper coins of Aradus, Roman money from Trajan to Constantine, from Anastasius to Mauricius; Byzantine coins of the Crusading period, some fine Renaissance silver "showing a surprising amount of trade going on then in this inland centre".

It was now 1 November. They approached Amrit, the ancient Marathus; the whole area appeared to have served as a quarry for building the island fortress of Aradus lying opposite. Its Phoenician remains had never been properly recorded, though Renan had described and sketched one or two.[7] Petrie decided that plans and measured elevations must be taken of the chief monuments, the Ma'bed or sanctuary, the two tombs known as the Maghazîî, or

"Spindles", and the "Cubic Tomb". They camped there for four nights, Petrie superintending the survey, while Hilda and Ellis "clambered up and down the masonry to all accessible parts for taping and from these, got the still higher detail by stretching up with measuring pole." Petrie was impressed by the size of these great stone monuments and with the accuracy of their construction . . . the best, he said, had an error of only one per cent—but he could not feel great enthusiasm for the Phoenician civilization. "I confess that I have a prejudice against the Phoenicians. They have had immense credit, as the result of their activity, but they were merely traders seeking new outlets. Their productions are only base commercial copies of the artistic wares of Egypt and Assyria."

Tartus (Antaradus) was visited for supplies and for repairs to the tent. While they waited, they visited the fine Crusading Church; reclaimed from use as a mosque it lay derelict, but it housed a number of statues found at Amrit some years before, which particularly interested Petrie by their distinctive dress. He had strained his knee, so they decided to put off their visit to the island of Ruad till the return journey. After exploring the castle of Markab, they approached Jebeleh, and decided to camp at a small *tell* called Sghabeh, a site with plenty of Bronze Age pottery. Petrie came to the conclusion that this was the Shuarbi of the Amarna Letters: he based his conclusion on the assumption that Jebeleh must be the ancient Gubla (Ribaddi, King of Gubla, in one of the letters says that Shuarbi is the gate of Gubla). This was a curious error: it had long been accepted by German and French scholars that Gubla was the modern Jubeil, known in classical times as Byblos, a city that had had strong connections with Egypt from early times, as the centre of the export trade in coniferous woods from the forests of Lebanon. Evidently no book such as M. René Dussaud's comprehensive *Topographie historique*, published in 1928,[8] was among those Petrie had brought with him for consultation. In fact, Jebeleh is known to have been the ancient Gabala (**113**).

In Latakia, where they camped among olive groves near the sea, they were able to see the important discoveries made by Claude Schaeffer at Ras Shamra since 1929, which were then housed temporarily in the Governorate, but for some reason they did not visit the site, only a few miles away at Minet el Beida, where the French were at that time excavating. Continuing northwards on the main road towards Antioch, the road climbed steadily; twenty-two miles on, they camped at sunset overshadowed by the mighty peak of Mount Casios, the Jebel Aqrā, and next morning crossed the Kizil Dagh pass and on to Antioch, which they found picturesque but "the least attractive city to live in, mostly squalid and with a Turkish flavour" (four years later it passed into Turkish hands). Then they struck west along a very rough and bumpy road towards the coast, for Petrie felt certain that the mouth of the Orontes would prove to be "of great importance as an outlet of central Syria, and a passage for eastern trade at all periods".

Suweidiyeh, the ancient Seleucia Pieria, proved to be little more than a large village on the north bank of the river's mouth. They made enquiries, and were directed to a mound on the north side of the town, called Tell Ruweisseh, where they picked up sherds of many periods from Early Bronze Age to Roman; it seemed to promise well. Returning now to Antioch (it was 18 November) they were shown round the extensive classical remains by M. Lassus, who was working there for the Louvre in partnership with an American team from Princeton. They admired the beauty of the mosaics, but what most interested Petrie was the characteristic pottery of the Seleucid period, none of which he had seen before; he urged the excavators to hasten with the publication of their discoveries.

Two days later, the travellers left Antioch and made their way over the mountains and eastwards to Aleppo, ignoring possible sites on the way and anxious only to reach their destination. Hastened by the autumn chills, they continued southwards over the steppe, glimpsing at intervals distant villages of beehive-domed huts. Crossing the Orontes at Jisr esh-Shogur, they retraced their steps to Jebeleh to take a further look at the port from which Petrie imagined Ribaddi sailing on his last flight from his enemies. When they had been there before, Hilda had bought a plank from the local saw-mill, carried it back to the bus on her shoulder and nailed it into position as an extra shelf. Now the children, recognizing her, called "*Es sitt en Najjâr!*"—"The carpenter-lady!"

A heavy rainstorm warned them to hurry home, but they had further measuring to do at Amrit, and Hilda was determined to visit Ruad. She went with Ellis in the post launch, while Petrie remained in the bus looking across at the silhouette of the distant island (**102**), the schooners of her fishing fleet moving up and down the coast. He meditated on her chequered history, and wrote a poem on the decline of a once prosperous and powerful city. Hilda and Jack Ellis meanwhile spent a day exploring the island, watching the shipbuilders at work and examining the huge blocks which once walled the city. In the account of their travels, entitled *Lone Syrian Shore*, which Petrie wrote but which was never published, Hilda contributed a chapter on Ruad.

Two days' measuring remained at Amrit; by the desolate sea-shore they met the owner of a farmhouse, who offered them the use of an empty room. Their survey completed, they hurried back through the rain, reaching Beirut on 29 November. A full report was made to M. Seyrig, and they finally got to Jerusalem four days later—none too soon, for "the very day after our return, one of the most violent rainstorms recently known burst over all the land".

Petrie sent a formal application for two sites, and in January he appealed in the columns of *The Times* for funds to dig in Syria: "I have now applied for two of the ancient ports which would have been busy centres of the trade plying from 3000 BC. As soon as the rains are over, shortly, and the contributions of the public have come in, I hope to begin excavating with several trained assistants and we look forward to a season of great promise in discovery."[9] It may be surmised that the sites he had in mind were Jebeleh and Tell Ruweisseh. Greatly to his surprise and disappointment, his application was refused. Before deciding, Seyrig had written to Richmond, who had referred him to the Joint Archaeological Committee, and they had refused to recommend his application: North Syria was reserved for Leonard Woolley, who intended to dig there under the auspices of the British Museum. To have encouraged him so far, and then to deny him, was shabby dealing and Petrie may be excused for feeling bitter; but it is just possible that somebody had also drawn the attention of the authorities in Beirut to Petrie's caustic comments in his recently published autobiography: not only were excavators in Syria incompetent, but when objects did reach the Museum they were put "without any mark or source or registration, so that the collection is as intelligible and useful as a dealer's shop. . . . Still, there are pleasant posts for a French and a Syrian Keeper of the Museum."

For the rest of December and the first two months of 1935, Petrie stayed in Jerusalem; but his urge to be out digging again was not to be denied. Palestine and Syria were forbidden ground; there remained two possibilities: Trans-Jordan and Egypt. In Egypt he would feel at home; but his base was in Palestine now and his trained workmen from the Gaza region; it would not be easy to pull up his roots and return to the Nile Valley. The perfect solution occurred to him: he would excavate a site just over the border in Sinai, somewhere along the coastal road beyond El Arish, which the Assyrians had called "the River of Egypt". Major Jarvis, the Governor of Sinai, who had more than once been an interested visitor to the dig at Tell al 'Ajjul, gave him every encouragement, and Brunton and Engelbach facilitated his application to the Antiquities Service in Cairo; permission to excavate was readily granted.

In March the Petries set off from Jerusalem in the rattle-trap bus, with Jack Ellis and their young architect, Carl Pape. In order to avoid the coastal dunes they drove by the Beersheba road, but at El Arish the bus stuck fast in the sand and it became clear that only a car with balloon tyres would be able to negotiate the dunes to the south. Jarvis Bey lent them a police car, and they went prospecting; several *tell*s appeared to be Roman, but on Tell Abu Selima, brickwork could be seen in the side of the dune and pottery of varying dates betrayed its greater antiquity. Petrie decided to dig here, though it was more than twenty miles from El Arish, the nearest town, over a very rough track. Near the *tell* there was a small village, called Sheikh Zowayd after a local saint, a police post and a disused railway station, and a Beduin settlement from which some of the workmen would come. Ellis was sent off to Cairo by train to find a suitable vehicle, while Pape, left in the police post, built a house. Meanwhile Ellis had returned with a Ford Sedan and the baggage and equipment had been brought from 'Ajjul on camels. While Petrie was still in the Rest House in El Arish, Dr Murray arrived, on her way to Jerusalem; she was to go through last year's inventories and clarify them to the satisfaction of the Museum authorities, copying Petrie's closely-written sheets (which Iliffe declared he could not understand) in her own, clear round hand.[10]

Preliminary excavation at Sheikh Zowayd lasted for only a month: by mid-May it was intolerably hot, and high winds raised choking clouds; walking up the slopes of the mound through deep soft sand was laborious, and supplies difficult to obtain; the well water was brackish and they lived out of tins (the chauffeur, who had said he could cook, was barely able to boil a kettle). Petrie commented drily: "The position for excavators was one of the worst I have known. . . . It was not a bad test for a man who had been set aside for a monopoly, as unfit to work in the pleasant fields of Syria."[11] Early in May the Petries returned to Jerusalem leaving Ellis and Pape, who stood the heat well, to close the dig; a larger expedition was planned for the coming winter. Dr Murray, they found, was still working in the Museum, checking and copying; the task took her until the end of June. Then the division, delayed from the previous year, took place and Petrie was sent a document acquitting him of further obligation.

Flinders and Hilda were still at Beaumont House, but they were not happy there: the constant blare of a gramophone, played by a fellow-guest who had nothing better to do all day, drove them to distraction and they decided they must move. A happy solution was found. The American Schools of Oriental Research have a centre in Jerusalem,* a large house on a hill not far from the Cathedral, with accommodation for students and visitors and an excellent library; at the back there is a garden, shady and cool. Professor Albright, the School's Director, and his wife made them very welcome; he was a great admirer of Petrie, whom he called "the greatest archaeological genius of modern times"[12] though he disagreed with many of his conclusions regarding Palestinian archaeology and in 1938 was to write a paper correcting the chronology adopted in *Ancient Gaza*, lowering Petrie's dates by more than a thousand years.[13] The move from Beaumont House was made in June. Petrie now had ample opportunity for study: besides his own library and that of the American School, the books of the British School of Archaeology in Jerusalem were housed downstairs with Crowfoot's office and not far away was the excellent library of the Dominican Fathers. Flinders had a room with a private balcony, and a view over towards the Mount of Olives; visiting scholars constantly came and went, and he was occasionally asked to give a lecture.

For the first time in his life he found time to enjoy listening to music; there were concerts, the Cathedral organist gave Bach recitals and Miss Bentwich played the violin. Occasionally friends took Hilda off with them for an excursion by car, and in August the couple went on what Flinders called a "sheer spree", their first package tour. At the inclusive cost of £1 a day apiece they shared a car with a Syrian couple and stayed at modest hotels; after a day boating at Tabgha on the Sea of Galilee, they stayed two nights in Damascus, then up to Zahleh in the Lebanon—"rushing water and lovely scenery, but too many tea-gardens"—along the coast to Tripoli, and up the precipitous road to Bsharreh and the Cedars of Lebanon. Petrie, who had never before had any trip organized for him, thoroughly enjoyed it.

Ann wrote regularly: she had taken a secretarial course and had now been posted to a small Government unit; her future looked secure. John maintained silence. His mother wrote repeatedly begging him to answer their letters; he had resigned the commission which for a time he had held, and bought himself out to appease his father; now he was doing little but reading and experimenting with ballistics, the subject which most interested him. They had all sorts of suggestions for a career—would he consider the Signals in Palestine? There might be a

* Now the Albright Institute.

job in the new radio station at Jerusalem; there was Chartered Accountancy. Petrie was deeply grieved at his son's failure to communicate, but now he was beginning to accept it as an idiosyncrasy. "John's future is a sore spot in my brain," he wrote to Ann, "which keeps me awake o'nights. . . . I keep a delightful coloured model of 4 intersecting cubes, as a memento of what he *was*." A little later John went back to the army, as a sergeant in the Wiltshire Regiment; he was not commissioned till the outbreak of war.

While Dr Murray was in Jerusalem the Petries had discussed with her a problem which had occupied their thoughts for some time: now that they were based in Jerusalem and no longer came to London every summer, they disliked having to refer to the Executive Committee of the British School of Archaeology for all decisions involving policy or expenditure. Many of the old committee had gone: Tessa Wheeler, now Chairman of the committee, found herself embarrassed at having to answer to the Joint Archaeological Committee for decisions and actions taken by the Petries without her knowledge, and they on their side complained that "London" was acting high-handedly. After much correspondence, the decision was taken to abolish the Executive and set up a new body in Jerusalem. Members of the General Committee (which seldom if ever met) were sent a circular letter and at a meeting in November 1935 the Executive Committee was formally dissolved; the new administrative body consisted of friends of Petrie's in Jerusalem, including Dr Sukenik, a prominent Biblical archaeologist; P. L. O. Guy, Père Vincent, Humphrey Bowman the Director of Education, and as treasurer, the head of a local bank. Mrs McInnes, the widow of the Bishop, was elected as Chairman. It was a most satisfactory solution for Petrie; the money was still collected in England, but Miss Bonar alone was responsible for transferring it to the treasurer in Jerusalem. Subscriptions had dwindled, however, and it was evident that drastic cuts would have to be made; it was decided that *Ancient Egypt*, now edited from London by Dr Murray and Mrs Mackay, would have to be replaced next year by a much smaller publication,[14] and that there would have to be other economies, both on and off the dig.

There was no question of stopping excavation, however; whatever happened Petrie was determined to carry on. The team for the second season at Sheikh Zowayd, in the winter of 1935–6, was, said Petrie, "exceptionally good". Jack Ellis had spent some time in the summer excavating with the Mortimer Wheelers and so too had an Australian girl, Veronica Seton-Williams. John Waechter was fresh from school and only eighteen. Carl Pape was now an A.R.I.B.A. (he was keen to come again); and a married couple, the Teasdales, both doctors, were to join them for part of the time. Ellis went on ahead to build rooms for the extra staff.

On the way down, the main party stopped for two nights at Tell el 'Ajjul to pick up stores and heavy equipment, and here the new recruits had their first taste of the unusual life they were about to embark on.[15] Veronica, sleeping on the kitchen table, was woken during the night by a crashing noise; investigating, she found that it came from a nearby store hut in which skulls were stacked on shelves to the ceiling; large monitor lizards had got into the hut and were knocking the skulls to the floor. Veronica and John were left next day to superintend the loading and despatch of the camels; neither of them knew anything about camels or spoke a word of Arabic.

The camp at Sheikh Zowayd was reduced to basic necessities, for every penny had to be saved. The cook was old and incompetent (Muhammad Osman was no longer sent for) and as in the earliest days in Egypt, the fare was tea and lentil soup, gritty Arab bread, jam, tinned sardines and pilchards. Work followed a strict routine: woken by Hilda's whistle, the staff downed a hasty cup of tea and had to be on the dig by sunrise; breakfast was at ten, when there was a break of half an hour; an hour was allowed for lunch, and some stopped work at teatime, taking it in turns to remain on the site till sunset. Some 400 workmen were employed, a few, picked men from Gaza, the rest the local Beduin who arrived with knives, swords and guns and had to be disarmed before work started; they were very quarrelsome. The daily sick parade was a lengthy affair, for the Beduin came from far and wide, and Veronica and Hilda were kept busy arbitrarily doling out aspirins and Epsom salts, to the disapproval of the Teasdales. It was cold and wet; howling gales and clouds of sand made life a misery, as Hilda described to Ann: "In storms we never speak or meet between meals. Each person has to stick to his room, and it is an effort to reach the dining hut. The roar of the gale almost prevents speaking, and the grinding and groaning of the metal roofing and the fierce metallic thuds are almost unbearable. . . ."

Huddled in all her clothes and wrapped in a shawl, she sat in bed to do the accounts, wearing her pith helmet to protect her head from a shower of small chips of mud from roof and walls. Occasionally a sheet of corrugated iron roofing blew off, with considerable danger to anyone passing. One after another the staff went down with influenza and Veronica was so ill that she had to spend some time in the hospital in Gaza; Jack Ellis suffered from malaria acquired during his service in Iraq. Only Flinders kept tolerably well and as cheerful and active as usual; though he did not now climb to the top of the steep dunes every day he kept a sharp lookout through his telescope, and if he thought that any of the staff were wasting their time talking, he would send up a note of gentle reprimand. Once a week he would be taken by car to the nearest point and assisted up the slope to inspect the progress of the work; he relied on the experience of Ellis and Pape to record as they dug; as each level was completed and planned, and photographed by Pape, it was removed and work began on the level below. Petrie himself undertook the photography of the objects; in the evenings he developed them by the light of a candle, shielded by a piece of red glass.

The ancient name of the site they were digging is not known; Petrie identified it with the classical Anthedon, relying on Ptolemy's itinerary. It was clear that it must once have been a fertile place, before the creeping sands overwhelmed it. In digging the *tell* Petrie resorted to a new method based on an idea which had recently developed in his adventurous mind: statistics, still more or less new in archaeology, had captured his imagination and he determined to experiment. By recording the number of artefacts found in every level on the site, he hoped to be able to gauge the relative prosperity or poverty of the period to which they belonged. Then he drew a prosperity curve, a graph for every five inches' depth of soil excavated, assuming a uniform average accumulation of soil in every century.* The result entirely satisfied him; it was, he said, "a barometer of national welfare".

"Every successful reign of a Jewish king or of a Ptolemy is marked by an increase of material, every invasion by a falling off. By this statistic alone we can estimate the course of history. We have here a method of writing unwritten history in a site of any age, and like the history of seasons in the rings of a great conifer, it may serve as a guide to history otherwise beyond our reach."[16] An innovation then, the concept is a commonplace today.

It was getting hot; the water used for developing tended to melt the emulsion on the plates. The Teasdales had departed long since, finding camp life too Spartan, but the rest of the team worked on till the beginning of April; the Petries, having despatched several boxes to Cairo for the eventual division, got back to Jerusalem by the middle of the month, only just in time: Arab resentment, long smouldering,

* An assumption with which few excavators would agree.

burst into flame and the small disturbances which had made Petrie decide not to attempt, after all, to try for another season at Tell el 'Ajjul were now assuming a more serious aspect.

The worsening political situation in Palestine could not fail to distress him. During the early 1930s the Arabs were in protest against the ever-increasing numbers of Jews entering the country illegally; the Government, committed to the policy of a Jewish National Home, appeared to be turning a blind eye to the influx; once established, the newcomers were buying up arable land from Arab landowners. Petrie himself had divided sympathies. His friend Harold Wiener had been murdered by Arabs in 1928: "the fanaticism of Islam never worked a worse deed," he wrote then; but he knew well that it was not religious fanaticism that lay at the root of the troubles. He had lived among Arabic-speaking peoples for most of his life and understood both their likeable qualities and their failings. The solution, he believed, lay in the proper use of land: the fecklessness of the Palestinian Arab had distressed him in 1890; since 1926 he had seen potentially fertile fields just as stony and neglected as they had been under Turkish rule—trees cut down, the Wady Ghazzeh rushing away to the sea instead of being harnessed for irrigation. In the spring of 1936 there was rioting in Tel Aviv and Jaffa; people were killed; the Arabs declared a general strike; telephone wires were cut, and some Jews were murdered in Jerusalem. In July Petrie sent an appeal to *The Palestine Post*, under the headline "Heal the Land".[17] The Arabs, he argued, have laid waste the fertile land which they inherited 1,300 years ago. They must now be educated to make use of it, not allowed to sell it to the immigrants; there should be an Arab Development Fund, funded by a heavy tax on all land sales. "I appeal to Arabs to help themselves; if they intend to make a claim to be treated as a nation, and not a horde, they must learn the first step in united finances, united training, to make the best of the land which they have so long misused." His letter brought protests from Arab correspondents who accused him of misreading history and ignoring the Islamic contribution to the arts and sciences. He replied, and was accused of having done little but embitter Arab feeling. He then wrote to the London *Times*[18] expressing admiration for the achievement of the Palestinian Jews in bringing progress and improvement to the country, but adding on behalf of the Arabs: "the fellah . . . is a competent and a capable agriculturalist and there is little doubt that were he given the chance of having better methods and the capital which is the necessary preliminary to their employment, he would rapidly improve his position."

Later that year he wrote a pamphlet, which was privately printed, under the title *The Revival in Palestine.* It was a fuller statement of his previous thesis, but put forward suggestions for "the welding of the people". All fresh Jewish settlements, he suggested, should be compelled by law to employ a large proportion of Arabs, who would thus learn their methods; Jewish settlement must be limited for the next thirty years at least, and should be evenly divided between the plains, the hills and the south. Education was urgently needed among Arabs. A feeling of common heritage should be created by a kind of National Trust. To this end, common meeting grounds were needed for all creeds and races: reading rooms, libraries and public gardens like those of Tripoli would humanize Jerusalem, which is "below the level of many villages in England" in its amenities. "In all these ways Jerusalem has inherited a fatal dose of Turkish lethargy, but should now awake, and aim at a state of civic satisfaction, where the mutual rivalries of race and sect are finally laid to rest." Two thousand copies of this pamphlet were circulated by Jews, in Palestine and in America.

The strike made life in Jerusalem difficult and not a little hazardous, and a curfew curtailed social life. Hilda wrote home in September: "The food difficulties during this 5 months' food and transport strike have been great, but we are getting quite used to no traffic on the streets, and no people about, and tin hats and bare bayonets at every street corner; and the sounds of shooting and trench mortars on certain nights."[19]

During the summer, she had returned to London for a couple of months leaving her husband in Jerusalem in the good care of the American School. The new Director, Dr Nelson Glueck, was as hospitable as his predecessor, and the other permanent residents, Dr Clarence Fisher, now retired, and Miss Wambold who had been a missionary in Korea for forty years, were now old friends; John Crowfoot had been replaced by P. L. O. Guy as head of the British School in Jerusalem. The new museum, built by a generous grant from John D. Rockefeller, was now almost finished. It was widely admired but, predictably, Petrie disliked it.

> The new museum is a melancholy place. I call it the whited sepulchre. The galleries have not a tenth of the windows that they should have, and all the walls and roofs are white, so that there is a glare of weak light all round. To add to the ineffectualness there are to be no disfiguring clear labels, only little faint numbers, to be looked up in a catalogue hung by the case. . . . They are proud of

> some horrid creations of tablets by Eric Gill. . . . Altogether a sad bungle over £400,000!!, and a great opportunity thrown away.[20]

His own ideas about the proper design and lighting of a museum were set out in an article published two years later, in 1938, in *The Journal of the Royal Institute of British Architects*. This included an ingenious diagram, placing cases obliquely so that the glass would not reflect light coming from the gallery windows and ensuring, by an arrangement which he called "peak lighting", that both direct and oblique light would fall on the objects displayed.[21]

In mid-November 1936, the Petries went down for a brief, last season in Sinai. For a short time they had their old friend Mr Walker with them, and an elderly retired judge from India named Saunders; energetic and cheerful, he had "a great sense of humour", which he may well have needed, for the cook had been sacked for incompetence and the cooking was being shared between the two chauffeurs. Ellis and Pape undertook most of the site supervision. Jarvis Bey, who had occasionally called on them the previous year with vegetables from his garden, had now retired; the new Governor was too busy to visit them. By early January they had reached sand at the bottom of the trenches and it was evident that the site had not been occupied in early times. After two weeks' measuring, photographing and packing the dig was closed for good; the Petries boarded a train for Cairo with their boxes, and next day Engelbach and Brunton helped them with the division; they found the new Director General, the Abbé Drioton, co-operative and pleasant, and all went smoothly. Rex Engelbach took them out to see W. B. Emery's remarkable discoveries at Saqqara North, where he was finding richly furnished tombs of the first dynasty for the Department of Antiquities. Petrie wrote to him later in the year in a vain attempt to persuade him to come and dig at Tell 'Ajjul; Emery of course replied that he was far too busy.[22]

Back in Jerusalem, Petrie hastened to finish the publication of *Anthedon*, and on 20 March it went to press. In a note to subscribers in *Syro-Egypt*, the small successor to *Ancient Egypt*, which was now the vehicle for announcements concerning his work, he could not refrain from contrasting the speed of his publication with the fact that the excavations at Tell el Duweir and Ras Shamra still remained unpublished.[23] Ellis and Judge Saunders, meanwhile, were engaged on a small excavation with Dr Murray at the Nabataean site of Petra, and Ann, out for a short holiday in March, stayed in Petra for a few days with her mother and thoroughly explored that enchanted valley.

In spite of heightened tension in the countryside and a toll of daily violence in towns and villages and on the roads, Petrie decided to make one more application for Tell el 'Ajjul; in September 1937 he applied through his committee for a permit, not in his own name, but in that of Dr Margaret Murray, and also of Dr Ernest Mackay, whose years as Custodian of Antiquities for the Palestine Government would commend him as director of the dig. Richmond was away, and Robert Hamilton, the Acting Director, proceeded with tact and caution: he replied to Mrs MacInnes, as chairman of the committee, asking for assurances that the excavation was really to be run on new lines; while there could be no objection to visitors staying in the camp he would like assurances that the direction of the work was to be in entirely fresh hands.[24] After some correspondence, a fresh list of requirements for the proper presentation of the catalogue and plans was drawn up; these conditions being accepted, a licence to excavate was granted on 4 January. Ellis and Pape went down at once to open the dig house, but on the 10th, a few days before the main party was due to leave for Gaza, news came of an event so shocking that it might well have deterred them from going altogether: J. L. Starkey, on his way from Tell el Duweir to the official opening of the new Palestine Museum, was ambushed and shot by a bandit at Beit Jibrin on the Jerusalem road. It was not a political murder: Starkey had been popular with his workmen, and around the *tell* he had encouraged the local Arabs to make terraces of the stones and earth he excavated, and to grow tomatoes. It was said that the assassin later expressed regret: the fact that Starkey, unlike most Europeans, wore a beard had caused him to be mistaken for a Jew.[25]

Flinders, confined to bed with a stomach disorder, was unable to go to the funeral next day. Miss Tufnell and her colleagues pluckily went on digging at Tell el Duweir for the rest of the season, and Petrie's plans for 'Ajjul went ahead. At eighty-five he was feeling his age, but he insisted on climbing to the top of the *tell* twice a day. Miss Murray, ten years his junior, spent her time in the camp, drawing and making up the list; Hilda kept the accounts and paid the workmen and Stella van Hollick doctored them, while Mackay, with the assistance of Pape, Jack Ellis and an energetic newcomer, Leon Kiralfy, superintended the work on the mound. One of the finest discoveries of the season was yet another hoard of gold; some of the ornaments were damaged, leading Petrie to suggest that what they had found was the stock-in-trade of some itinerant pedlar or jeweller.[26]

The season lasted four months. March was very wet; as thunder rolled over Gaza, storm clouds of a more sinister kind were rolling over Europe, as Hitler's army marched into Austria. Petrie was tired; as he sat in the car waiting for their luggage to be brought out, he said to Dr Murray: "I begin to find that camp life is becoming too much for me, but [with a sigh] I do love the freedom of it."[27] He had not done with camp life yet. Only four days after returning to Jerusalem, he and Hilda were off with Pape and Kiralfy in the green bus, across the Jordan to 'Amman: Transjordan presented no obstacle, for Gerald Lankester Harding was now Chief Curator of Antiquities in the Amirate, and he readily gave them permission to survey ancient sites in the Malfûf to the west of 'Amman. For a few days they toured the area, Flinders and Hilda guarding the camp while the two young men went off to explore stone towers, villages, dolmens and a small arcaded building, perhaps a church, which Petrie dated by the pottery to the third century AD;[28] but it was scorching in the bus; after a while they returned to the cool shade of the hotel garden from which they had set out, and left Kiralfy and Pape to complete the survey; then the little expedition returned to Jerusalem.

This was Petrie's last piece of fieldwork. He had hoped to return to 'Ajjul, but at the end of September, the camp was attacked. Bandits looted and smashed everything, burning what they could not carry away. Petrie asked permission from the police to go down and view the damage, but was refused—the Gaza area was deemed too unsafe. Four months later there was another attack and a raider burnt and smashed what remained in the wreckage. This time Petrie was allowed to go down with an armed police escort; he slept at the hospital in Gaza and visited the *tell* with British police constables. Everything had gone—domestic furniture, the contents of eighteen rooms and equipment for a dozen members of staff; kitchen and canteen, cases of food, books, instruments, clothes, medical supplies and the Ford car. "I had my trenching tool with me, and I raked among the charred ruins for an hour or two, but I only found, to bring away, a packet of luggage labels and a wooden bracket."[29]

In reporting this disaster to the members of the British School, Petrie sadly admitted that it meant the end of his work in Gaza, but there was no question in his mind that somewhere there would be more digging. It would be necessary, he said, in his annual report, to replace some, though not all, of the lost equipment and probably the car. In admiration of the old man's indomitable optimism, many sent contributions for the continuance of his work; members of the Hampstead Scientific Society clubbed together to send a donation. A week or so after his visit to Gaza Commander Risdon wrote to him: he had been working on the anthropological report of the skulls from Tell el Duweir; now he was anxious to return to field archaeology: could the Professor recommend him a site, perhaps in Egypt? In his long reply, full of suggestions, Petrie said: "Our plans are very vague at present. Certainly not Palestine, as our whole camp has been burnt out and the country is too unsafe. I have two or three people in view for next winter, probably in Egypt, or Cyprus."[30]

During the previous autumn (1938) they had had another visit from Ann; by a stroke of good fortune, because of changes in the organization for which she was now working, she was transferred to another branch of the Foreign Office, and given three months' unpaid leave in the meantime. She and her friend Marian Bowley* set off on a long walking tour through Yugoslavia, and then on horseback through Albania, ending in Northern Greece; from Salonika Ann took a boat to Beirut, where Hilda met her. Her parents had the pleasure of her company in Jerusalem for over two months. When she left for England in December, she had a strong feeling that she had seen her father for the last time; since Munich in mid-September it had been clear to her, as to many others, that war was inevitable.

Gaza: painted pottery

* Later Professor of Political Economy at University College, London.

CHAPTER XIX

Sunset in Jerusalem

FLINDERS PETRIE WAS happy in Jerusalem, and more than once expressed the wish that he might end his days there. He loved the clear light, gleaming on whitewashed walls and piercing the dim alleys of the Old City; he loved the scent of lilacs in the cloistered garden of the American School; he loved to hear the cry of the muezzin from the minaret of the mosque of Sheikh Jarrah, the liquid notes of the *bulbul* and the soothing, monotonous coo of the palm doves; he loved the mingling of creeds and races, the mixture of old and new. Life at the School was pleasant. Meals were taken in the communal dining-room, afternoon tea in the cool shady garden. Apart from the modest boarding fee they had few expenses; when invited to take tea or to dine with some member of the Jerusalem community they usually walked there and back. Petrie's extraordinary energy had still not deserted him, though his once springy step was now a shuffle; slowly, he could still manage the hilly streets of Jerusalem. His diary (in which he recorded little now but the state of his health) reveals that there were days when he suffered from stomach pains or bouts of malaria; but his brain was as active as ever, his industry astonishing. After his birthday he wrote to his daughter:

> Another milestone of life at 86. Happily it is life in good health but only bothered by knees and eyes giving way a little. I am still getting on with finishing up books which are in hand. The Architecture and Making of Egypt are done, the Science of Egypt is at the printers, Gaza V is nearly ready, only Mammy is finishing some drawings. Two or three books are nearly ready. So I am pretty well clearing the decks before the old ship goes down.[1]

In *The Making of Egypt* he attempted something new and ambitious: a survey of the development of Egyptian civilization from the earliest times to the age of the Ptolemies, as shown by the characteristic products—pottery, tools, sculpture, ornament—of each period. The book, written in a highly-compressed style, may have puzzled readers who lacked familiarity with the terms used, and Petrie's own sometimes highly controversial theories are introduced without discussion, as proven facts. This and his outmoded chronology led the book to be more severely criticized than it deserved, and perhaps damaged his reputation among those who failed to appreciate that this was the distillation of a long lifetime of intellectual adventure. In an appendix he set out the results of another of his recent experiments with statistics: he had come to the conclusion that it was useless to consider the mean dimensions of a number of skulls, assuming that the group was homogeneous; one should rather draw diagrams of the whole range of variation, in order to distinguish different ethnic strains. He had recently charted thousands of measurements of skulls from his past publications, in an attempt to distinguish a major or dominant group in each period, from other strains recessive but persisting. As he explained "We do not measure an average feline by mixing together cats and civet cats, still less by averaging tigers in with them. We need to see the sense of our material before we begin to draw statistical conclusions from it."[2]

The Making of Egypt was published in the summer of 1939; in a short postscript Lady Petrie made an urgent appeal for funds, pointing out that the enforced cessation of the annual lectures and exhibitions in London had led to a serious falling-off of subscriptions; they were still thinking of future work in the field.

The outbreak of war in Europe put an end to any such plans. Life in Jerusalem became easier: the Arab revolt was halted and the presence of British troops in Palestine in increasing numbers, as action shifted to North Africa and Egypt, ensured the reality of the truce; the formation of joint units composed of Arabs and Jews cemented it. Social life was curtailed but Hilda found an outlet for her energies in war work and Flinders once or twice lectured to British troops stationed in the area; once he went up to Nathanya to give a talk in the camp on the history of ancient Palestine.

He did not worry about his museum; in the summer vacation of the previous year, after the Germans had invaded Czechoslovakia and it seemed as if war might be imminent, most of the valuable items in the Petrie collection, including the tomb-groups, had been packed in crates by Professor Glanville and a body of students and helpers, and sent to safety in the country. What remained was removed from the top floor in August 1939, in the tense days between Hitler's invasion of Poland and Britain's declaration of war, again by volunteers, the largest pots and stone objects being manhandled down the long stairway to the basement for storage; the library too was evacuated. When, during the bombing raids of 1940 and 1941, the south wing of the College was demolished by a direct hit and conflagration, virtually nothing was in the Petrie Museum but empty cases.

Ann, with her fluent Italian, was busy throughout the war in the Intelligence branch of the Foreign Office; after Rommel's defeat she was for a time in Algiers, then in Naples and Rome. John, now a Second Lieutenant, took part in the retreat to Dunkirk and was reported missing on 25 May 1940; his platoon was leading the company in an attempted withdrawal along the River Scarpe. Later they had news that he was a prisoner-of-war in Germany. The news came, as it did to many parents in like circumstances, as a relief that he was at least removed from the dangers of active service; his commanding officer had written in high praise of his bravery and his qualities of leadership. Very occasionally a brief letter came through from him: he was in a camp with facilities for music and study; he was teaching mathematics and Italian and learning Welsh. They wrote to him regularly, on the brief page allowed, and sent him parcels through the Red Cross.

On 26 October 1940 Flinders was admitted into the Government Hospital in Jerusalem with a serious attack of malaria. He recovered, but the illness left him too weak to walk; it was decided that he should stay in hospital where he could be properly looked after. The realization that his active life was over was at first very bitter; his frustration was expressed in verse:

> No more the running boy in English woods,
> No more to roam the ewe-leaze and the tor,
> No more to delve in pyramids and towns,
> No more to trace the thoughts of man of yore,
> No more, no more.

Soon, however, his resentment at inactivity was replaced with a philosophic acceptance of his present limitations. Enforced immobility did not dim the vigour of his mind or lessen the wide range of his memory. During twenty-one months propped up with pillows in bed or seated in a wheelchair by the bedside, his mind ranged unceasingly over the sights and sounds of his past life—the creak of the waterwheel, the songs of the workers echoing the familiar work-refrains, the magical silence of the desert; he followed the progress of the war, and talked of the future, of the problems peace would bring; he talked often of his children, of his faith in their character and capabilities, the great opportunities he believed lay ahead, for individuals and for the nations of the world. The hospital had a happy and tranquil atmosphere; outside his window the sunlight streamed in through waving palms. He was a great favourite with the nurses and made them laugh. He had constant visitors, and Hilda came every day to see him, and to write letters and poems to his dictation, and discuss the business of the British School, with which he liked to keep in touch, though there was little now to do; subscriptions had ceased and publication was at a standstill. For a time he was still working, still writing. He drafted a brief additional chapter for a second edition of *Seventy Years in Archaeology*; his account of the caravan trip to Syria, *Lone Syrian Shore*, was completed. Three historical studies with a setting in ancient Rome were sent to Jonathan Cape under the title *Truth in Fantasy*: one, "Fragments of a Journal of Cleopatra", had been written years earlier; another which had appeared in 1912 under the title "Three hours; 24 August 410", described with dramatic vividness the sack of Rome by the Goths in the words of an eyewitness (Thomas Hodgkin, to whom Petrie had sent the manuscript then, had given it his approval as "very truly imagined").[3] The third, written in Petrie's own shaky hand, is "The Triumph of Caesar". He had once told his wife that some of the characters in Roman history were more vividly alive to him than any modern personalities.[4] In the last few years he would have liked to write more of these "fantasies" but lacked both the time and the opportunity for research; in Jerusalem one amenity he had missed greatly was the Reading Room of the British Museum. He told Dr Glueck that he contemplated writing a book entitled "Man in the Ice Age".[5]

His mind travelled widely in space as well as in time. Looking back over his life, he must have had regrets for experiences missed and places unvisited. Apart from England and Wales, his horizon had been bounded by the shores of the Mediterranean; France, Malta, Greece and in particular Italy had been his haunts; sea passages had brought him briefly to ports of call in Morocco and Algeria, but he knew nothing of the hinterland of North Africa west of Egypt. In his later years he had travelled by train through the Balkans, spent happy days exploring Istanbul, and traversed the whole length of the Levantine coast, but he had never crossed the desert to Iraq to see the ancient cities of that other great riverine civilization whose history was so closely linked with that of Egypt. More strangely, after one visit to

Assuan and Philae in 1887, he never again went further south than Thebes. Though his mind was always occupied with the problems of the origins of Egyptian civilization, he did not follow in the wake of Pharaonic armies southwards into Nubia and the Sudan, as Griffith had done, nor seek to trace the influences from central Africa which he believed had contributed towards the formation of the dynastic peoples of Egypt. Had he been asked why, he would probably have said that he simply had not had time. Many times he was invited to lecture in the United States; the offer was tempting, it would have meant good publicity for his work and money for excavation, yet he never went. Perhaps he dreaded the Atlantic crossing, and perhaps too he feared the impact of so much in the Brave New World that he considered shallow, superficial and second-rate. Australia must have drawn him, but the long expensive voyage was out of the question, and he was content to keep up a correspondence with his cousin John Flinders Pilgrim, the grandson of Matthew Flinders' sister Susannah, who gave his family news, and he was always glad to see Australian soldiers when they came to Jerusalem.

For a time Swedish massage helped to restore a little strength to his legs and he managed, with support, to walk round his bed. "His incurable optimism," wrote Hilda to Mrs Tufnell, "is standing him in good stead. He always thinks he will be movable shortly, and pursuing work at a desk." In May 1941 came a letter from the High Commissioner, Sir Harold MacMichael: he had been awarded a grant of £250 by the Prime Minister, Sir Winston Churchill, from a fund available for "persons who have given distinguished service to the nation in Arts and Sciences", in recognition of his services to archaeology.

As time went on and his eyes grew dim, he loved to be read to; one of the English officers in the Palestine Police, John Briance, used to read to him from Doughty's *Arabia Deserta* or *The Seven Pillars of Wisdom*; the death of T. E. Lawrence in 1936 had saddened him, though they had had little contact since the days in camp at Tarkhan. It was in hospital that Petrie wrote in a shaky hand: "It is the perpetual struggles of man to acquire abilities, to hold back disorder, to frame a firm civilisation, to climb out of selfish passions into reasonable civic life; that is the theme of our search into these dim ages which have many lessons to teach us in search of the betterment of the world."

On 3 June 1942 his birthday was celebrated in hospital with a cake and many flowers and cards, and some of his friends visited him. On the same day a short notice appeared in the *Palestine Post* inviting people to come and talk to him. "Though he is no longer mobile, his interests are unimpaired." Thenceforward he grew weaker almost imperceptibly, day by day. One of his last visitors was Colonel Mortimer Wheeler, who was at that time with the Eighth Army in the Western Desert.

> One day I heard somehow or other that he was dying. I took twenty-four hours' leave, drove across Sinai to Jerusalem, and made my way to the hospital where Petrie in his eighty-ninth year lay placidly on his death-bed. The picture of him is stamped upon my mind. He was swathed in white sheets, and a sort of turban of white linen was about his head. His grey beard and superb profile gave him the aspect of a biblical patriarch. His mind was running even faster than was its wont, as though it had a great distance still to cover before the approaching end. In the course of ten minutes it ranged without pause over a wide variety of matters, from the copper implements of Mesopotamia to the lethal incidence of the malarial mosquito at Gaza. I left the room quietly, my brain stretched by the immensity and impetus of a mind for which there were no trivialities in life and no place of respite.[6]

On 28 July Hilda telegraphed to Ann: "Father weaker". She was summoned by telephone at four the next morning, walked by moonlight to the hospital, and remained with him as he slumbered fitfully through the day, and in the evening, as she sat by his side, he slipped out of life. "After peaceful hours, peaceful flight." When Ann read this telegram, the funeral must already have taken place.

Flinders Petrie's grave is in the Protestant cemetery on the summit of Mount Zion; his headstone faces the rising sun. Next to it is the grave of his friend Clarence Fisher, the excavator of Beth-Shan and Megiddo; not far away lies J. L. Starkey, his one-time pupil, and around them, under the cypresses, are the graves of British sergeants and men of the Palestine police, most of whom met their deaths at the hands of terrorists during the troubled years of Petrie's sojourn in the Holy Land and the still more violent times that followed the end of hostilities in Europe. "O pray for the peace of Jerusalem" is engraved on one of the gravestones. His own headstone, a rough-hewn monolith, bears only the words *Flinders Petrie* and above them a single sign, the Egyptian hieroglyph *'ankh*, "life". That same symbol lies over the tomb of his friend and benefactor, Amelia Blandford Edwards.

The funeral service was attended by representatives of the Government, the Hebrew University, the Museum of Antiquities, the Dominican Fathers and the various Schools, and by a host of those who had known him. Six constables of the Palestine Police escorted the flag-draped coffin in an open lorry to the cemetery and British and Palestinian police followed in a tender banked with flowers.[7] It had been a hot day, but on the hillside there was a cool breeze. Dr Thompson, the head of the hospital, who had cared for him so long and so kindly, walked with Lady Petrie to the grave.

One last secret they shared. When Flinders Petrie was first admitted to hospital, he expressed the wish that, in the event of his not surviving the malaria attack, his head should be donated to the Royal College of Surgeons in London, as a specimen of a typical British skull. During his stay in hospital he several times reiterated this wish; he hoped also that it might be possible to preserve his brain for scientific investigation. In conformity with his instructions, and with Hilda Petrie's full consent, Dr Thompson and the chief bacteriologist of the hospital removed the head on the night he died and took suitable steps to preserve it. Sir Arthur Keith, on behalf of the College, agreed to receive it, but it was not possible to send it to England during the war, and so the jar was kept for the time being in the hospital laboratory. Dr Thompson was anxious that the brain should be subjected to histological examination as soon as possible; he hoped that it might "reveal some of the reasons for the remarkable capacity and retentive memory he had, even up to the day he died, of the most minute facts". He planned to take the head back to England himself, but before the war was over he was transferred to UNWRA in Albania. After the cessation of hostilities with Germany, arrangements were made with the Director of Antiquities in Jerusalem, Robert Hamilton, to ship the box home as containing an antiquity—as indeed it did. When it finally reached the Royal College of Surgeons, nothing appears to have been done; the museum had been badly bombed and there had been a change of professor in the Anatomy Department; the arrival of the box was not notified until Lady Petrie made an enquiry in December 1948; she then received an assurance that "the brain has been the subject of concentrated study".[8] The jar appears to have lost its label and was only re-identified after enquiries were made in the mid-Seventies; no trace of a report has been found. Flinders Petrie would have frowned on yet one more example of the neglect of scientific evidence.

After Flinders' death, Hilda Petrie stayed on in the American School and busied herself with typing his manuscripts and editing the volumes yet to be published. Like many elderly people she became increasingly obsessed with the need to save every penny; her letters tended to be written on the backs of sheets of paper salvaged from the wastepaper basket. Some of her husband's personal books and belongings were sold, but his working library, by his own wish, was to go to some emergent school or archaeological foundation, preferably in one of the countries of the Arab world, for he was convinced that there would be a rapid growth of interest in their ancient past. It was probably through W. B. Emery that Hilda was put in touch with Anthony Arkell, who at that time had the task of organizing an Antiquities Service in the Sudan; the offer was gratefully accepted by the Sudanese Government and nearly fifteen hundred volumes, with boxes of photographs and pamphlets, were packed and sent off to Khartoum, where they were housed in a special building known as the Flinders Petrie Library; they have now been incorporated into the library of the National Museum of Antiquities, of which they formed the nucleus.

Hilda had many friends in Jerusalem, and continued her busy social life as long as the war lasted; a kind and indefatigable guide, she was a familiar figure in the streets of the Old City, striding along bareheaded in a long embroidered Bethlehem dress and sandals. To those like myself who were fortunate enough to be taken on a guided tour around the Old City, she was generous of her time, and her knowledge and her energies.

On the afternoon of 24 April 1946, while she was still in Palestine, Robert Hamilton organized a meeting in memory of Flinders Petrie in the Archaeological Museum. In his opening address he paid tribute to "the pioneer of what may without exaggeration be called a new field of human knowledge".

> Many of us were privileged, at one time or another, to enjoy his friendship and genial humour, and to learn something from the vast store of knowledge and experience which he was always ready to put at the disposal of younger men. If at times differences appeared, as they did, they were differences which touched on method only, and left undiminished and unaffected our affection and respect for the scientific devotion and energy and for those flashes of insight which so often enabled Sir Flinders to illuminate, in the fewest possible words, the intricacies of a subject and to disentangle from the confusion of evidence the essential truth.[9]

Each of the speakers that followed represented one of the archaeological foundations working in Jerusalem, and each in turn paid their tribute; the longest speech was that of Père Vincent, who claimed to have known him before all the others, twenty years before. He summarized the remarkable career of his friend and colleague, in what was virtually a digest of *Seventy Years*, and ended with Petrie's own: "All work is but an incompleted intention."

Ann Petrie, released from her wartime employment and not intending to return to life in an office, came out to join her mother in September 1946 and found her still busy typing manuscripts, sorting and packing books and papers. Since the end of the war, hostilities had broken out once more in Jerusalem; the Old City was out of bounds, sniping and bombing were back in the streets and the curfew was again in force. The winter of 1946–7 was very severe in England and Ann dared not bring her mother home till the spring; in March they set about booking a passage by sea with all their belongings including several cases of antiquities from the School's last excavations, but the matter was taken out of their hands when, after a military operation —a message delivered in code, and a meeting at a secret rendez-vous —all British women in Jerusalem were evacuated with a single suitcase apiece, under armed escort to Sarafand and thence by plane to Cairo, where they spent a Spartan week or so in a former army camp at Ma'adi, then stayed more comfortably in Heliopolis till, reunited with their cases and crates, they were finally repatriated by sea.

Back in England, Hilda Petrie picked up the threads of her life again and made contact with old friends. She and Ann were again living in Upfleet; Ann was working in a market garden with friends, while her mother prepared outstanding volumes of British School publications for the press. *Ancient Gaza V*, to which she wrote a short introduction, was partly from Flinders' pen; his last catalogue volume, on ceremonial slate palettes, could be published, and her own book, with the copies of tomb reliefs made by her and her friends at Saqqara in 1904 (for which Dr Murray had contributed a chapter on the inscriptions) at last saw the light of day;[10] she had worked on the text with Flinders' help in Jerusalem. Upon her too devolved the running of the British School; the distribution of books and routine correspondence was still dealt with by Miss Bonar (now Lady Thornton), but after Sir Flinders' death Hilda had written to all members of the General Committee to obtain their approval, and thenceforward took over the role of Director. Yet with his death, the role of the School was little more than a publishing concern; it was unlikely that there would ever again be excavation.

The celebrations in connection with the centenary of her husband's birth have already been described; she had played a great part in the organization of the commemoration and in drawing up the list of those to be invited, and she spoke at the dinner with the ease and confidence of one long used to public speaking. She was now eighty-two, somewhat bowed and gaunt, but still a commanding figure; she still enjoyed public occasions, and insisted on going each year to the *conversazione* of the Royal Society; for the last eve-of-exhibition party at the Royal Academy, Ann had to borrow a wheelchair for her.

The British School of Archaeology in Egypt was formally wound up in 1954, and what money remained was put into a fund to be administered by University College, to provide travelling scholarships for students, in memory of Sir Flinders Petrie. His plans of earthworks and stone circles were presented to the Society of Antiquaries; some were rough copies of those given three-quarters of a century before to the British Museum; the rest, the fruits of his holidays in the West Country and in Wales in more recent years. Hilda wrote round to the secretaries of local history societies, informing them of the gift, in the hope that future archaeologists might make use of the plans.

Meanwhile John Petrie, released from prison camp in Germany and demobbed, had gone down to Dartington School to visit a godchild, liked it there, and stayed on, first as odd-job man, then as maths coach; he married another teacher there, Anne Grant, and after a little they moved up to Hampstead. He had at last found his vocation. After six months' work he got his degree in mathematics, then qualified with a teachers' training course, and thereafter taught maths in a school in Godalming; he brought to the Centenary celebration his wife and their small daughter, Anne Lisette Flinders Petrie. Tragically, both parents died within a few days of each other in 1972. Their daughter possesses the mathematical gifts of her father, her grandfather, her great-grandfather William Petrie and her great-great-grandfather Matthew Flinders; at the time of her parents' death she was an undergraduate in the University of Sussex and has since worked in computer science and added three children to the family tree. In 1974 she was invited to Australia to speak at a symposium held at Flinders University to celebrate the bicentenary of the birth of Matthew Flinders.[11]

Ann stayed in Hampstead with her mother, but in 1955 old Lady Petrie was in hospital for a time and thereafter needed constant attention and professional nursing; in 1957 a stroke deprived her of speech, and she died in University College Hospital. Ann left London and settled in the Thames Valley where she has since then followed the outdoor life she loves in her own market garden, and has become an accomplished potter; on many of her pots and dishes may be found a little fish, a favourite symbol of the potters of ancient Gaza.

When news of Flinders Petrie's death first became known, obituary notices in the daily papers dwelt on his role as "proving the truth of the Bible"; it was understandable, since this aspect of his work had been stressed in recent years as more likely to bring in public support. "A doughty warrior for Bible truth," proclaimed the label on one of the wreaths at his funeral. More informed writers stressed his services to archaeology. Yet Petrie had seen himself in another light. Archaeology had been his life, but it was the handmaid of history, and he regarded himself first and foremost as a historian. Convinced that the past has a lesson to teach the present, he had developed a cyclical theory of human development: ancient civilizations teach, he said, that mankind does not continually progress, but rather that each civilization in turn has its phases of excellence, successively in art, in literature, in mechanics, in science and then in material wealth, before it is overwhelmed by another race. In *Revolutions of Civilization*, which he considered his most important book (he believed that it had been for this that he had received his knighthood)[12] he had elaborated this theory and in 1938 he had sent a brief note to *Nature* pointing out that these cycles recur, on his reckoning, every 1,115 years, and that one was almost at its end; "when we know the cause of a cycle's death, we may be able to save our own from destruction".[13]

Preoccupation with the ancient world had not prevented him from expressing his views on modern problems. As late as 1941 he wrote to Lord Stamp urging the adoption of an international currency.[14] Two suggestions made by him to local authorities in London eventually bore fruit (though not necessarily as a result of his urging): one was that all omnibuses and routes should be numbered, and a map issued for the public's use; the other was to introduce traffic roundabouts at busy street crossings. In 1918, with the expansion of London after the First World War, he had urged the need for satellite towns twenty miles out, linked with the City by rapid trains. The answer of the L.C.C. had been that they were in too great a hurry to devise so large a scheme: "it was only hand-to-mouth extension that could be considered, which crowded up all the street connections to jamming point." He also—at what date is not known—proposed the building of a large dam across the Thames at Gravesend, with locks to keep out dangerously high tides and maintain the river level; the gain would be the drying of the Thames marshes as a space for factories to be moved out of crowded areas, and the prevention of flooding in London. On town planning, too, he had ideas of his own: placing houses diagonally to the street, to lower the skyline and reduce echo; building houses with recessed upper storeys to save light, and not confronting each other in a road, but facing the spaces or gardens between.[15] He had strong views on the education of children, partly influenced no doubt by his own unconventional upbringing: it was important, he argued, to make a child think out problems for himself, not bombard him with facts and theories, but provide him with ample material for his voyages of mental discovery. Rural education should follow lines quite different from that of town children; country children should learn subjects relevant to their environment: the elementary anatomy of animals and men, the chemistry of soils and plants, local and biographical history, and boys should be taught carpentry and building; in summer time the classroom should be mainly in the fields.[16] He advocated not only co-educational schools and colleges, but also communal boarding-houses for the after-school vocational training of boys and girls.

Flinders Petrie inherited, from his father and his grandfather, an extraordinary ingenuity and inventive talent which he applied to the problems of everyday life and which enabled him to adapt easily to a Robinson Crusoe existence. Griffith, who had a great admiration for his capabilities, said of him

> It seemed to me at that time that nothing was beyond his powers . . . when suddenly called upon, he could conjure up the plan of a buried city, reproduce the timetables of distant railway stations, or design to a nicety a perfectly balanced book cradle for Lepsius' colossal *Denkmäler*. If there had been any purpose in producing rabbits from a hat, I am certain that he could and would have performed that and many other tricks on request. . . .[17]

One of his inventions was a novel chain balance for weighing quickly and accurately; it is described in his autobiography.

Petrie's best work was done in little more than twenty years—the years between 1880 and 1903. By 1885 he had already set new standards for archaeological work, by insisting on the importance of keeping a full record of everything found, whether broken or not, and of the outstanding value of pottery as an indication of age; he had revolutionized the attitude of an excavator towards his workmen, by insisting on supervising them personally, and substituting for the *kurbash* a sympathetic and personal relationship and a system of rewards for care and vigilance; and he had found Naucratis. In the next five years he had established chronological links between Egypt and Palestine, and between Egypt and the Aegean world, by a brilliant use of potsherds for cross-dating; he had opened a new page in the history of portrait painting, and at Kahun had revealed the intimate trappings of domestic life in the small houses of a workmen's community. By 1895 he had added a fresh chapter to the history of Egyptian art by his discoveries at el 'Amarna, and had discovered a new field of investigation in the cemeteries at Naqada; that discovery was followed by what was perhaps his most triumphant and ingenious contribution to archaeological method: the system known as Sequence Dating, which though it has subsequently needed some modification, still remains the basis of the work of all prehistorians in Egypt. Finally, his years at Abydos, between 1899 and 1903 fixed the sequence of the earliest kings of Egypt and revealed the exquisite craftsmanship of their artisans. By 1903, too, his Qufti workmen—another legacy for future archaeologists—were fully trained and Petrie had perfected his own technological expertise.

Thereafter his work in Egypt was concerned with filling in the picture; neither his methods nor his attitudes changed. It was not given to him to make sensational discoveries such as Carter's in the tomb of Tutankhamun: the Lahun jewellery, the Fayum portraits and the funerary panoply of Horuta at Hawara had perhaps been his most spectacular finds. Yet the sheer volume of all the discoveries he made is astonishing; objects found in his excavations have enriched museums all over the New World and the Old, from Philadelphia and Copenhagen to Sydney and Tokyo; both the great national collections and small local museums in towns and schools benefited from the fruits of his work.

In assessing Flinders Petrie's achievement, comparison with another great personality in Egyptian archaeology, who died only a few weeks before him, is inevitable. The American George Reisner has figured little in this narrative, largely because Petrie seldom visited him in his house at Giza. He is thought by some to have disliked Petrie; certainly his unpublished autobiography gives grounds for supposing this, and one or two of Petrie's assistants were under the impression that the dislike was mutual. It is true they were rivals more than once in applying to Maspero for sites to excavate such as Dahshur, which was granted to neither. Yet Reisner remained a member of Petrie's committee governing the British School of Archaeology in Egypt from its second year (1906) until at least 1935, and Petrie, briefly reviewing Reisner's preliminary publication of one of his greatest finds, the almost intact tomb of the mother of Cheops at Giza, praised the "unbounded care and attention" he had given to the clearing of the tomb.[18] In many ways the two men were disparate in method and in temperament: Reisner, after a linguistic training with Erman in Berlin, entered the archaeological field some twenty years later than Petrie; his employment of workmen from Quft already trained by Petrie as specialists in excavation, and of Arthur Mace, fresh from the work at Abydos in 1901, taught him Petrie's methods and in particular his emphasis on the importance of pottery and small finds. Some of the younger Quftis in Reisner's continuous employment at Giza became highly professional and a few were trained as photographers and clerks, to maintain the object register—a huge ledger, kept in duplicate, in which every object found and every scrap of material which came out of the ground was recorded in detail.[19] Yet, though Petrie admired the care given by Reisner to his discoveries, his voluminous notes and his meticulous research, he deplored—as did many others—his long delay in publishing his results; only a fraction of his work appeared in book form during his lifetime, and some, despite the devoted labours of Dows Dunham, still awaits publication; this, in Petrie's eyes, was unforgivable.

In some respects it must be admitted that Reisner improved upon Petrie's methods; his elaborate recording system was developed while he was living in one place, where year after year he excavated in the *mastaba* field around the Great Pyramid; this permanent base in close proximity to Cairo, and an ample endowment from the University of Harvard and the Boston Museum of Fine Art, greatly assisted him in becoming, as he did, a specialist in the history and archaeology of the Old Kingdom. Petrie's net was cast far more widely: all Egypt and all Egyptian history was his domain. He was constantly moving from site to site, district to district, period to period. For more than half the year he was absent from Egypt, teaching, lecturing, mounting exhibitions, raising money for his work; the excavation report had to be ready for the printer before he left England each autumn. Reisner's books, when they did appear, were voluminous tomes expensively produced; Petrie's could be bought for a few shillings and were deliberately kept within the means of the student and the public.

No archaeologist has equalled Petrie's record for prompt publication. It was a dictum of Pitt-Rivers that "the date of a new discovery is the date of its publication". This Flinders Petrie kept in mind from the beginning. In 1886 he wrote:

> It is a golden principle to let each year see the publication of the year's work, in any research; but the writer places himself thus at the disadvantage of showing how his information may have been defective, or his views requiring change, as year after year goes on. Such a course, however, is the most honest and the most useful, as half a loaf is better than no bread. This volume, therefore, with all its imperfections, its half-gleaned results, its transitory views, comes forth to show what is already ascertained, and to supply a mass of certain facts for the assimilation of scholars, who may accept or not the way in which they are built up.
>
> It may be said that further research in what is already known ought to have been made, before placing results in such a form. I think not. So long as enough study is given to the materials to present them in an intelligible and usable form, it is better to let them be at the disposal of all students, without waiting for a final summing up at the close of the excavations.[20]

Thus Petrie answered his critics. He has been accused of rushing too quickly to conclusions, of inadequate presentation, poorly drawn plates, inaccurate references; not everything he found or bought during a season was illustrated, not everything illustrated was described. Yet records were not destroyed: there were notebooks, tomb registers, distribution lists naming the destination of objects, and work is still being carried on by research students and archaeologists on the basis of these records. Too many excavators sit for years on their material, hoping to cross every T and elucidate every puzzle before they commit themselves to print, while their memory of their fieldwork fades, costs of production rise, and the world waits for the information only they can provide.

Petrie acknowledged his own limitations: he learnt languages with great difficulty, never mastered Latin and Greek, and was hampered all his life by an insufficient knowledge of ancient Egyptian and an inability to read easily books and articles by his German contemporaries. He has been accused of fostering in his pupils "some sort of antithesis between philology and archaeology".[21] His own writings give the lie to this; he was very conscious of the importance of the ancient language and liked to have on his digs someone who, like Griffith in the early days, could supply that deficiency. Yet he maintained that, for a field archaeologist, "scholarship is by no means all that is wanted: the engineering training will really fit an archaeologist better for excavating than bookwork can alone. Best of all is the combination of a scholar and the engineer, the man of physics and mathematics, when such can be found." Alas, such a paragon is rare indeed. Petrie's lack of philological training and academic discipline led him into curious mistakes, some of which have been pointed out in these pages.

Petrie once enumerated the subjects which he felt to be his own special abilities: first, the collection of evidence, of "securing all the requisite information, of realising the importance of everything found and avoiding oversights, of proving and testing hypotheses constantly as work goes on, of acquiring everything of interest not only to myself, but others."[22] Secondly, "The weaving of history out of material evidence." Two of the other three were the outcome of his own childhood training: the chemical analysis of materials, and archaeological surveying. The fifth was metrology; with this he had begun his scientific career; his chapter on Weights and Measures in the tenth edition of the *Encyclopaedia Britannica* was a notable advance in the subject, and *Inductive Metrology* still appears in the bibliography of modern books on the subject.

The sense of mission with which he had gone out to Egypt in December 1883 remained with him for the rest of his life. Utterly dedicated to the work he believed that only he could do, he spared nothing of himself, and endured hardship, deprivation and sometimes danger in pursuit of his goal. Always there was another question to be answered, another riddle to be solved. To-mery, the Beloved Land, had him in thrall. In that ruthless quest he had little time for intimate friendships, and indeed there were few whom he could call close friends. A fearless fighter, he did not spare those whom he believed to have fallen short of his own standards in archaeological method; yet he bore no grudges. His short obituary notice of Edouard Naville, whom he describes as a true gentleman, shows that he bore the old man no personal ill-will.[23]

During his long life of Spartan self-discipline and never-ending toil he was supported by two tremendous assets: one was his remarkably robust constitution: in spite of frequent minor illnesses and accidents, he survived under physical conditions which would have taxed the health of many younger men, and walked prodigious distances oblivious of wind and weather. The other was his wife. In Hilda he found the ideal partner, ready to share every aspect of his labours and to endure every hardship of his ascetic life. Wives of archaeologists seldom get their due, and it is taken for granted that they will run the domestic side of camp life, though they often do far more. Few can have played so active a role in the daily routine of an excavation. We have seen Hilda Petrie descending tomb shafts on a rope ladder, copying all day long lying prone in the dust, accompanying her husband on long desert expeditions with tent and donkey, crossing Sinai by camel to join him in the wilderness. *Es Sitt* Hilda, as she was called by the workmen, learned to speak Arabic as fluently as her husband; often she helped with the weekly payroll, and during the last years she entirely took over this function and all the camp accountancy. Above all, she took from his shoulders the burden of fund-raising, without which he could not dig. For this she had a peculiar talent, pursuing possible donors with ruthless persistence till she had coaxed out of them twice what they had intended to give. Flinders seldom criticized or praised her work, but he did not take it for granted; his autobiography is dedicated "To my Wife, on whose toil most of the work has depended."

Perhaps Petrie over-reacted to the situation in Egypt in the 1920s; perhaps he should have stayed and continued excavating there (to him it was unthinkable that he should stop digging altogether). With the wisdom of hindsight, it might be thought that in doing so he might have spared himself much of the anxiety and disappointment that marred his latter years. Yet Palestine, too, brought its rewards, and there too he had a contribution to make; excavators trained by him went on to make their mark in the archaeology of the Levant.

Nobody in England has excited so much public interest in ancient Egypt, through lectures, exhibitions, popular writings and countless articles in newspapers and encyclopaedias; nobody has trained so many workers for the field. He himself reckoned that about a hundred students had passed through the British School, and that about half of them had continued permanently in the subject. Some, little qualified, joined his expeditions for the adventure, and soon drifted away again. He watched their progress and capabilities carefully; if they proved unsuitable, nothing was said, but they were not invited to join the next expedition. Of those who stayed the course and made archaeology their career, there were a number who, like Grenfell and Hunt, Garstang, Engelbach and Brunton, rose to the top of their profession.

There can be few who excavate in the countries of the Near East today, and in particular in Egypt, who have not in some degree come into contact with Petrie's doctrines and methods, as practised by those who learnt from him.

Archaeology has today taken its rightful place among the sciences; it has many branches, and comprises many different disciplines. The modern archaeologist can call upon a multiplicity of scientific techniques to help him: air photography, photogrammetry and echo-detection help him to locate buried buildings and plan his sites; radio-carbon tests date his bones, thermo-luminescence his pottery and dendrochronology his wooden artefacts; the geomorphologist analyses his soil samples and the palaeobotanist his plant remains; statistical analyses are handed over to the computer. Had they been available, there is no doubt that Petrie would have welcomed and made full use of them. In their absence, his single-handed endeavours to wring the maximum of information from his discoveries achieved extraordinary results. He was a pioneer, exploring untrodden paths, and must be judged in the context of his time. At Tell el Hesy in 1890 he excavated single-handed; at Tell el Hesy in 1979 the American team numbered forty-eight, including site supervisors, two palaeobotanists, a geologist, an osteologist, three photographers, an artist, an architect, two surveyors and consultants in malacology and lithics.[24] Nobody can doubt which of the two expeditions made the greater contribution to history.

It is as the pioneer of scientific archaeology in the Near East that he will always be revered. His many volumes of reports and catalogues will never lose their value: they are his legacy to posterity. In the evening of his life he looked backwards with a sense of mission fulfilled:

> Let there be no regrets, now that this life is past,
> For earth, and friends, and work have all been sweet to me—
> And labour garnered safe has laid the ages clear
> That all may plainly see what none had thought before.

NOTES, BIBLIOGRAPHY, GLOSSARY, APPENDICES & INDEX

NOTES AND REFERENCES

Abbreviations used in the Notes

A.B.E.	Miss Amelia Blandford Edwards
A.E.	*Ancient Egypt* (periodical)
B.S.A.E.	British School of Archaeology in Egypt
E.E.F.	Egypt Exploration Fund
E.E.S.	Egypt Exploration Society
EES	Archive of the E.E.S.
E.R.A.	Egyptian Research Account
E.R.S.A.	Egyptian Research Students' Association
FF	"Family Faculties Book" (see p. 440)
F.P.	Flinders Petrie (later Sir Flinders Petrie)
F.Ll. G.	Francis Llewellyn Griffith
GI	Letters in the Griffith Institute, Oxford
H.P.	(Lady) Hilda Petrie
J.E.A.	*Journal of Egyptian Archaeology*
P.E.F.	Palestine Exploration Fund
P.E.Q.	*Palestine Exploration Fund, Quarterly Statement*
PP	Petrie Papers (see p. xv)
R.S.P.	Dr Reginald Stuart Poole
S.C.O.	Somerville College, Oxford (papers of Amelia Edwards)
S.P.M.A.E.	Society for the Protection of the Monuments of Ancient Egypt
UCL, U.C.L.	University College, London
W.P.	William Petrie

Note Where no other reference is given, quotations in the text are from the relevant Journal which will be listed under Sources.

Chapter I The Flinders and the Petries

Sources

Dictionary of National Biography, arts. *Flinders, Matthew (1774–1814)* and *Petrie, William (1821–1908)*, J. J. Fahie, "Biographical Sketch of Mr William Petrie, with some account of his researches in Electricity, Magnetism and Electric Lighting", reprinted from *The Electrical Engineer*, 6 Feb. 1903. Some volumes of W.P.'s diary have survived (May 1850–Nov. 1858; Jan. 1866–Nov. 1868; Jan. 1870–Dec. 1874) and in a smaller format, most years from 1881 to 1906.

Notes

1. See D.N.B. *Petrie, Martin (1823–1892).*
2. W. Petrie, "Results of some Experiments in Electricity and Magnetism", in *The Philosophical Magazine*, Nov. 1841.
3. *70 Years*, p.4.
4. See further James D. Mack, *Matthew Flinders*, Melbourne, 1966; Ernest Scott, *The Life of Matthew Flinders R.N.*, Sydney, 1914; Joseph Bryant, *Captain Matthew Flinders R.N. His Voyages, Discoveries and Fortunes*, with a Foreword by Sir Flinders Petrie, London, 1928.
5. *A Voyage to Terra Australis: undertaken for the Purpose of Completing the Discovery of that Vast Country, and Prosecuted in the Years 1801, 1802 and 1803. . . .* London, 1814.
6. R. W. Russell, "Flinders Revisited", in *Matthew Flinders: The Ifs of History*, Flinders University of South Australia, 1979, pp.1–20.
7. Matthew Flinders to Ann Chappell, 18.12.1800 (National Maritime Museum Greenwich, 60/ 17. FL I/25).
8. Miss Tyler to W.P., Sept. 1847: *PP* 11(xiv).
9. *Ibid.*
10. *FF*, p.19. The "Family Faculties Book", a questionnaire devised by the geneticist Francis Galton in 1884, in order to trace for statistical purposes the transmission of physical and mental qualities in families through four generations; a prize was offered for the best-compiled. A copy of this book, filled out by Anne Petrie, Flinders' mother, survives in the family records, and is here referred to as *FF*.
11. *Felix de Lisle: an Autobiography*, anon., London, 1840, and *Confessions of an Apostate*, by the Author of Felix de Lisle, London, 1842. *Naboth the Jezreelite*, Bath, 1844, and *The Field of Honour or, Scenes in the Nineteenth Century*, London, 1844.
12. In the library of the Sudan Museum of Antiquities, Khartoum (see p.425).
13. W.P. to his mother, 16.10.1846: *PP* 11(viii).
14. See n.8.
15. J. H. Fahie, "Staite and Petrie's Electric Light, 1846–1853", in *The Electrical Engineer*, 29 Aug. 1902, pp.297–301.
16. *PP* 11(viii).
17. He had been a disciple and friend of Benjamin Wills Newton, the founder of the Plymouth Brethren, but disagreed with them on certain points of dogma.

Chapter II The Making of an Archaeologist (1853–80)

Sources

Flinders Petrie's diary (*UCL* Petrie MSS) begins 12.7.1876 and omits short periods when he was away on survey trips in the country; these are covered by the Journals: 2(i) 1875–1880.

Notes

1. Margaret Petrie to her son W.P., 10.6.1853: *UCL* Petrie MSS.
2. John Cannon, "Samuel Petrie and the Borough of Cricklade", in *Wiltshire Archaeological and Natural History Magazine*, LVI, 1956, p.131ff.
3. *UCL* Petrie MSS.
4. Letters of Isabella Tyler to Anne Petrie: *PP* 11(vi).
5. Anne Petrie, "A sketch of his Life from the Pen of his Mother", quoted in *Biblia* IV, June 1891, no.3, p.61ff.
6. Isabella Tyler's MS account, "Narrative of William Matthew Flinders Petrie, Aged 2 till 12, 1853–1865": *PP* 11(v).
7. See n.5.
8. L. B. Hunt, "George Matthey and the Building of the Platinum Industry", in *Platinum Metals Review*, vol. 23, 1979, p.71.
9. Anne Petrie to Miss Tyler, 6.6.1860: *PP* 11(vi).
10. W.P. to his mother, 11.4.1863: *PP* 11(viii).
11. *Ibid.*, 9.7.1863.
12. *70 Years*, p.9.
13. *Ibid.*
14. *FF*, p.33.
15. *Methods and Aims in Archaeology*, London, 1904, p.58.
16. Christopher Chippindale, *Stonehenge Complete*, London, 1983, p.137.
17. F. Galton, *Inquiries into the Human Faculty*, London, 1883, p.95.
18. F.P. to Spurrell, 8.8.1878: *UCL* Petrie MSS (Spurrell).
19. Spurrell to F.P., 11.8.78: *PP* 9(v).
20. *Inductive Metrology: or the Recovery of Ancient Measures from the Monuments*, London, 1877, p. 143.
21. C. Piazzi Smyth, *Our Inheritance in the Great Pyramid*, 3rd edition, 1874, p.150.
22. No.6680, 3 October 1873.
23. *The Restoration of Israel and Judah; Plain Questions with Plain Answers*, London, 1877.
24. *The Pyramids and Temples of Gizeh*, London, 1883, p.10ff.
25. *Ibid.*, p.18n.
26. J. A. Murray, *An Appeal to the English-speaking Public*, London, 1879; *Transactions of the Philological Society*, 16 May 1884, p.129.
27. BM. Ref. no Add 31333; now in the Manuscript Room; copies were later deposited in the library of the Society of Antiquaries (see p.427).

28. K. M. E. Murray, *Caught in the Web of Words: James A. H. Murray and the "Oxford English Dictionary"*, New Haven and London, 1977.

Chapter III The Pyramid Survey (1880–2)

Sources

Journals: I,i (Gizeh 1880–1881); I,ii (Gizeh 1881–1882).
Pocket diaries: Jan.–May 1881; 1882 missing. Diary: *UCL* Petrie MSS.
Notebooks: 25, 26, 31 (1880–81); 27, 30, 32, 32A, 33, 56, 12 (1881–82).

Notes

1. *UCL* Petrie MSS (Spurrell), 11.2.1881.
2. *Wilbour*, 1936, p.32.
3. T. G. H. James, *The British Museum and Ancient Egypt*, London, 1981, p.20ff.
4. I. E. S. Edwards, *The Pyramids of Egypt*, London, 1961, p.127.
5. Archives of the Oriental Department, British Museum, Vol. for 1868–81, nos. 4711–4715. Birch's book *A History of Ancient Pottery* (2nd edition London, 1873) contained illustrations of Egyptian pottery, but none were given a date.
6. *The Athenaeum*, 23.4.1881, p.566.
7. This was forestalled by *The Times*, 16.6.1881.
8. *Proceedings of the Society for Biblical Archaeology*, June 1881, pp.111–16, with 7 plates.
9. Maspero to A.B.E., 4.8.1881: S.C.O. 154.
10. 18 and 25 March 1881: *PP* 9(i).
11. W.P.'s diary, entry for 15.4.1881.
12. One of Petrie's cameras is now in the possession of the Royal Photographic Society.
13. *PP* 6(i), Oct. 1887.
14. *The Globe*, 26.10.1881: *PP* 4(vii).
15. *The Academy*, 17.12.1881, p.462.
16. W.P. to F.P., 23.12.1881: *PP* 9(i).
17. E. A. Wallis Budge, *The Rise and Progress of Assyriology*, London, 1925, p.185; Charles Breasted, 1948, p.67.
18. O. V. Volkoff, *Comment on visitait la Vallée du Nil*, Cairo, 1967.
19. Thomas Cook, *Up the Nile by Steam*, London, 1875.
20. *The Academy*, 4.2.1882, p.88f.
21. A. B. Edwards, *A Thousand Miles up the Nile*, London, 1887, vol. II, p.519f.
22. See M. S. Drower, "Gaston Maspero and the Birth of the Egypt Exploration Fund (1881–3)", in *J.E.A.*, 68, 1982, pp.299–317 for this correspondence; also *Excavating in Egypt; the Egypt Exploration Society 1882–1982* (ed. T. G. H. James), London, 1982, chapter 1.

23. *Dictionary of American Biography*, vol. xx, pp.132–3, art. "Frederick Cope Whitehouse (1842–1911)".
24. *UCL* Petrie MSS (Spurrell), 1.9.1881.
25. F. Cope Whitehouse, "Lake Moeris and recent explorations in the desert near the Fayoum" in *Proceedings of the Society of Biblical Archaeology*, 1.11.1881, pp.124–35.
26. *The Academy*, 1.4.1882; see n.21 above.
27. *70 Years*, p.42.

Chapter IV "Father of Pots": Delta Explorations (1883–6)

Sources

Journals: I,iii (Dartmoor and Paris, 1883); II,ii (Tanis, 1883–4); II,iii (Naucratis 1884–5); I,iv (Naucratis 1885, Nebesha, Defenna 1886).
Diary: (*UCL* Petrie MSS.)
Pocket diaries: Nov. 1883–July 1884; Nov. 1884–June 1885; Nov. 1885–Nov. 1886.
Notebooks: 98a–h. (Tanis); 51 (Suweilin etc.); 6 73, 74 (Naucratis and other Delta sites); 23, 44, 51 (Nebira, Nabesha, Defenna 1885–6).

Notes

1. *EES* III j.19.
2. *The Times*, 30.3.1882.
3. 1.4.1882, p.462.
4. S.C.O. 165; see ch.3, n.21.
5. H. Brugsch, *Dictionnaire géographique de l'ancienne Egypte*, Leipzig, 1878–80; J. Duemichen, *Geographische Inschriften altaegyptischer Denkmäler*, 1865–85; A. B. Edwards, "The Site of Raamses", in *The Academy*, 24.4.1880, p.307f.
6. *70 Years*, p.33f.
7. *UCL* Petrie MSS (Spurrell), 11.8.1881.
8. *The Archaeological Journal*, vol. 40, 1883.
9. *The Pyramids and Temples of Gizeh*, London, 1883.
10. E. Naville, *The Store City of Pithom and the Route of the Exodus* (E.E.F. first Memoir), London, 1884.
11. *PP* 15(ii).
12. *EES* IV e.1.
13. A.B.E. to R.S.P.: *EES* III a.1.; R.S.P. to A.B.E.: *EES* V d.
14. *The Academy*, 10.11.1883, p.308f.
15. *The Banner of Israel*, 21 Nov. 1883, p. 506ff and 5 Dec. 1885, p.1.
16. *PP* 10(iii) "Memorandum on the Purchase of Antiquities in Egypt. November 1884", and *EES* XVI, f.6.
17. *EES* XVI f.6.

18. W. M. F. Petrie, *Tanis Part I* (E.E.F. Memoir 2), London, 1885, p.1.
19. *EES* XVI f.27.
20. *PP* 9(iv) 1.
21. *The Pyramids and Temples of Gizeh*, revised edition, London, 1885.
22. *PP* 9(i); *EES* XIXa.40,41.
23. *Egypt Exploration Fund, Second Annual Report*, p.4ff.
24. Diary entry for 31.10.1884.
25. *Naukratis Part I. 1884–5*. With chapters by Cecil Smith, Ernest Gardner and Barclay V. Head (E.E.F. Memoir 3), London, 1886, pl.XLIV.
26. "A Digger's Life" in *The English Illustrated Magazine*, March 1886, p.445.
27. *Ibid.*, p.443ff.
28. *Illustrated London News*, 21.11.1885.
29. *The Churchman*, 14.11.1884; *The Critics*, 6.12.1884; *EES* V c.14, IV d.12.
30. *The Athenaeum*, 14.3.1885, p.351f.; Naville to R.S.P.: *EES* V d.4.
31. A.B.E. to Anne Petrie: *PP* 9(i).
32. A. B. Edwards, "My Home Life", in *Arena*, 1891, p.240f.
33. *PP* 9(iv) 26.
34. E. A. Gardiner, *Naukratis Part II* (E.E.F. Memoir 6), London, 1888, p.21ff, Pl.XVI.
35. *EES* XIX b.
36. *Tanis Part II. Nebesheh(Am) and Defenneh(Tahpanhes)* (E.E.F. Memoir 4), London, 1886, p.50f.
37. A. H. Sayce (1923), p.240f.
38. *EES* XVI f.83.
39. *Ibid.*, f.90.
40. For this correspondence and what follows, see the Minute Books of the E.E.F. Sub-Committee 1885–6: *EES* XIX a and b.
41. *EES* XVI c.11.
42. *PP* 9(iv) 6.
43. *EES* XVII c.23.
44. *EES* III b.3.
45. *PP* 9(iv) 12.
46. *Ibid.*, 15.
47. *Ibid.*, 16.

Chapter V Up the Nile (1886–7)

Sources
Journal: I,v (Nile and Dahshur), 1886–7.
The pocket diary for this year is missing.
Notebooks: 46, 94–5, 122–23 (Nile journey); 32 (Dahshur).

Notes

1. Renouf to A.B.E.: *EES* II a.47; III b.76.
2. A.B.E. to F.Ll.G.: *EES* III a.49.
3. A.B.E. to Renouf: *EES* III j.39.
4. A.B.E. to F.P., 19.1.1887: *PP* 10(iv) 19.
5. British Museum, W. Asiatic Department archives, 1886.
6. F.P. to A.B.E., 31.12.1887: *EES* XVII c.47.
7. *UCL* Petrie MSS. (Spurrell), 1.2.1887.
8. W. M. F. Petrie, *A Season in Egypt*, London, 1887. Now Esbeyda is generally known as El Sheikh Said, where there are Old Kingdom tombs; the southern part is Sheikh Zobeida. N. de Garis Davies copied the tombs for the E.E.F. in 1899.
9. N. de Garis Davies, *The Rock Tombs of Deir al Gebrawi*, 2 vols., E.E.F. Archaeological Survey, London, 1902.
10. The incident is described in *Studies presented to F.Ll. Griffith*, ed. S. R. K. Glanville, London, 1932, p.477ff.
11. *A Thousand Miles up the Nile*, p.455ff.
12. A.B.E. to F.P., 30.12.1886: *PP* 9(iv) 18.
13. W.P. to F.P., 10.12.1886: *PP* 9(i).
14. *PP* 9(v) 24.
15. *PP* 9(i) (Benest).
16. *PP* 9(iv) 18, 19.
17. *EES* XVII c.49; Maspero did not incorporate them in his book.
18. *UCL* Petrie MSS. (Spurrell), 1.2.1887.
19. J. Quibell and F. W. Green. See pp.248, 254.
20. R. Engelbach, *The Problem of the Obelisks*, London, 1923.
21. *PP* 9(iv) 19.
22. *Ibid.*, 20. The "throne" is part of a bed (BM no. 21613) and not with certainty to be ascribed to Hatshepsut.
23. *EES* XVI f.162.
24. W. M. F. Petrie, *Ten Years' Digging in Egypt*, London, [1892] p.77ff.; "The Grand Tour in Egypt Three Thousand Years Ago", in *Harper's Magazine*, New York, 1888, p.297ff.
25. *EES* XVI f.162–3.
26. J. A. Wilson (1964), p.78f.
27. *EES* XVI c.50. The tomb of Mermose had in fact been discovered in 1875; see A. Varille in *Annales du Service des Antiquités*, XLV (1945), p.1ff.
28. The stone pyramids of Dahshur are now known to have been built by Snoferu. Their mortuary temples were explored by Ahmed Fakhry in the 1950s.
29. *EES* V e.18.
30. *PP* 9 (iv) 22.
31. *PP* 9(iv) 25.
32. *EES* XVII c.57.

Chapter VI Pyramids and Portraits (1887–9)

Sources

Journals: I,iv (Fayum 1887–8); I,vii (Fayum 1888–9).
Pocket diaries: Nov. 1887–Nov. 1888; Oct. 1888–Oct. 1889.
Notebooks: 36, 37, 38a, 39a (Hawara and Gurob 1887–8); 35, 39b–e, 48, 49, 50, 77, 78 (Illahun, Gurob, Kahun 1888–9).

Notes

1. *PP* 9(iv) 26.
2. *EES* XVII c.53.
3. *Racial Photographs from the Egyptian Monuments*, London, 1887.
4. *PP* 9(iv) 31.
5. *EES* XVII c.72.
6. *PP* 9(iv) 32.
7. *PP* 9(iii).
8. *EES* XVII c.85.
9. Herodotus, Bk.II, ch.149.
10. Diodorus Siculus I,66; Pliny, N. H. 36,13; Strabo, ch.17,1.
11. For recent discussions of the Labyrinth, see K. Michalowski, "The Labyrinth Enigma: Archaeological Suggestions", in *J.E.A.*, 54, 1968, p.219ff; Alan B. Lloyd, "The Egyptian Labyrinth", in *J.E.A.*, 56, 1970, p.81ff.
12. Hartmut Döhl, *Heinrich Schliemann: Mythos und Ärgernis*, Bucher, 1981, p.42. Schliemann's diary for this journey is missing from the archive in the Gennadius Library and so are his letters from that period; see D. F. Easton in *Annual of the British School of Archaeology at Athens*, 77, 1982, p.99.
13. *EES* V f.3.
14. See J. H. Ottaway, "Rudolf Virchow: an Appreciation" in *Antiquity*, XLVII, 1973, p.101ff.
15. *Historical Scarabs: a Series of Drawings from the Principal Collections, arranged Chronologically*, London, 1889.

Chapter VII Interlude in Palestine (1889–90)

Sources

Journal: I, viii (Fayum and Palestine, 1889–90).
Pocket diary: Sept. 1889–Sept. 1890.
Notebooks: 36, 38–9, 48 (Hawara, Gurob, Kahun, 1889); 77, 78 (Palestine).

Notes

1. *70 Years*, p.107.
2. *Illahun, Kahun and Gurob 1889–90* (London, 1890), pp.21–4 and pl.

XXVI, XXVII. For a revision of the dating of the tomb see V. Hankey and O. Tufnell, "The Tomb of Maket and its Mycenaean Import", in *Annual of the British School of Archaeology in Athens*, 68 (1973), p.103ff.

3. *UCL* Petrie MSS. (Spurrell), 17.12.1889.
4. See Angela Thomas, "Gurob. A New Kingdom Town", *Egyptology Today*, no.5, vol. I, Warminster, 1981, where material from Gurob in the Petrie collection is catalogued, with an account of subsequent excavations. Also B. J. Kemp, "The Harim-Palace at Medinet el-Ghurab", in *Zeitschrift für aegyptische Sprache und Altertumskunde*, 105, 1978, p.122f.
5. *Ten Years' Digging in Egypt*, London, 1892.
6. Correspondence in the archives of the P.E.F.: PEF/PET 1–21, 26.
7. *P.E.Q.*, 1875, p.195ff.
8. *Tell el Hesy 1890*, London, 1891, p.50.
9. For an assessment of the importance of Petrie's work at Tell el Hesy, see Roger Moorey, *Excavation in Palestine,* Guildford, 1981, p.24ff.
10. Baron Platon Grigorieivitch d'Ustinov, the grandfather of the actor and writer Peter Ustinov. See I. Skupinska-Lørset, *The Ustinov Collection: The Palestinian Pottery* (Oslo, 1976) for a history of the collection; neither Petrie nor Tell el Hesy are mentioned.
11. *The Academy*, 26.7.1890, p.76f.
12. *P.E.Q.*, 1890, p.329 and 1891, p.68.

Chapter VIII Tussles with M. Grébaut (1890–2)

Sources

Journal: I,ix (Medum 1890–91); I,x (Tell el 'Amarna 1891–2).
Pocket diaries: Sept. 1889–Sept. 1890; Sept. 1890–Sept. 1891.
Notebooks: 57–59 (Medum); 16, 101–103 (Tel el 'Amarna).

Notes

1. The archives of S.P.M.A.E. are in the E.E.S. (*EES* VIII a–e.).
2. *EES* VIII a.3–9.
3. *EES* VIII a.37.
4. *The Academy*, 8.2.90 and 1.3.90; *EES* VIII a–e.
5. *EES* VIII b.17.
6. *EES* VIII b.39: Report of the Annual General Meeting of S.P.M.A.E., 9.7.1890, p.9ff.
7. *The Times*, 15.10.1890. See T. G. H. James, "The Archaeological Survey", in *Excavating in Egypt*, 1982, ch.8.
8. GI/ Newberry 23.
9. F.P. to Newberry: quoted by Professor Glanville in his Centenary lecture at University College (the whereabouts of the original letter is not known).

10. *Ten Years' Digging in Egypt*, London, 1892, p.138.
11. F.P. to Spurrell, quoted in *70 Years*, p.125f.
12. A. F. Mariette, *Monuments divers recueillés en Egypte: les mastabas de l'ancien empire*, Paris, 1872, 1879.
13. F.P. to Newberry, 23.12.1890: letter in Department of Egyptology, School of Oriental Archaeology and Oriental Studies, University of Liverpool.
14. P. E. Newberry, *Beni Hasan Parts I–IV* (E.E.F. Archaeological Survey, Memoirs 1, 2, 5 and 7), 1893–1900.
15. Correspondence on what follows in *PP* 9(i).
16. *The Academy*, 31.1.91, p.120.
17. *UCL* Petrie MSS. (Spurrell), 19.1.1891.
18. *Wilbour*, 1936, p.579.
19. P.E.F. archives 152/11. See O. Tufnell, "Excavator's Progress", in *P.E.Q.*, 1965, p.112ff.
20. *PP* 9(iii).
21. Hardwicke D. Rawnsley, *Notes for the Nile*, London, 1892, pp.19ff., 45.
22. *Medum*, London, 1892, p.11ff and pl.VIII.
23. *UCL* Petrie MSS. (Spurrell), 19.1.1891.
24. *Journal of the Hellenic Society*, 1890, p.271ff.
25. "Notes on the Antiquities of Mykenae", *op.cit.* 12, 1891, p.199ff.
26. In *Archäologischer Anzeiger*, 1892, p.11ff.
27. *The Classical Review*, 1892, p.132.
28. *Ibid.*, p.98. The subsequent debate was summarized by Cecil Smith, p.462ff.
29. *70 Years*, p.132f.
30. A.B.E. to F.P., *PP* 9(iv) 62.
31. *PP* 9(i) and *70 Years*, p.135f.
32. *Tell el Amarna*, London, 1894, p.17.
33. Journal for 2.1.1892, and *EES* XVII d.20.
34. *EES* d.22, 23.
35. *The Academy*, 23.1.92, p.94.
36. *Ibid.*, 7.2.92, p.189f; 9.4.92, p.356f. Howard Carter's sketch of the royal tomb and one of the reliefs in it appeared in the *Daily Graphic*, 23.3.1892.
37. Other such masks were found by later excavators; that some may be death-masks has been argued by some, e.g. H. Schäfer, *Amarna in Religion und Kunst*, Berlin, 1931; E. Bille De Mot, *The Age of Akhenaten*, London, 1966, p.94ff. Others are thought to be casts of clay life sketches.
38. *Tell el Amarna*, ch.VI.
39. N. de G. Davies, *The Rock Tombs of El Amarna*, vol. V (E.E.S. Archaeological Survey Memoirs 17), p.19f.
40. *PP* 9(xii).

41. *EES* VIII c.36; XV 51.
42. GI/ Griffith 201.
43. Griffith: *PP* 9(i); Chester: *PP* 10(iv); Spurrell: *PP* 9(iv).
44. *Tell el Amarna*, Pl.II.
45. Many of the small objects and important fragments in the Petrie Museum, which for reasons of expense Petrie was not able to include in his report, have since been published by Mrs J. Samson in *City of Akhenaton*, III, 1951 (E.E.S. Memoir 44, London, 1951). ch.XI, and in *Amarna, City of Akhenaton and Nefertiti: Key Pieces from the Petrie Collection*, London, 1972.

Chapter IX University College (1892–7)

Sources

Journals: I,xi (Koptos 1893–4); I,xii (Thebes 1895–6); I,xiii (Beni Mazar (for Behnesa) 1895); I,xiv (Bibeh (for Deshasha, Ahnas) 1895–6). The Journal for Naqada 1894–5 is missing.

Pocket diaries: Nov. 1893–Oct. 1894; Nov. 1894–Nov. 1895; Nov. 1895–Nov. 1896; Nov. 1896–Oct. 1897.

Notebooks: 52–4, 93 and 55 (Quibell) Koptos; 69–72, 75 Naqada; 8, 9, 11 Ballas (Quibell and Duncan); 107–111 Thebes; 83–4 Ramesseum (Quibell); 18–22 (Behnesa and Deshasha).

Notes

1. *Pharaohs, Fellahs and Explorers*, London, 1891.
2. *PP* 9(iv) 63.
3. *PP* 9 (v).
4. Extract from Miss Edwards' will, in Kate Bradbury's writing: *PP* 9(v).
5. *The Times*, 7.9.1892.
6. Text of Petrie's inaugural lecture: *PP* 15.
7. F.P. to the Secretary of the College: *UCL Records: Petrie File*.
8. F.P.'s letters from Italy, Spring 1893: *PP* 4.
9. *UCL Records* Mem. II A/6 (F.P.'s note of the history of his Department).
10. *UCL* Petrie MSS. (Spurrell), 22.7.93.
11. F.P. to W.P., 17.8.1893: *PP* 9(i); 2.11.1893: *UCL* Petrie MSS.
12. *Koptos*, London, 1896, pls.II–V and pp.7–9.
13. B. Adams and R. Jaeschke, "The Koptos lions", *Milwaukee Public Museum Contributions to Anthropology and History*, no. 3, Jan. 1984.
14. M. A. Murray, 1962, pp.92ff., 107ff.
15. *EES* VIII d.20, 20a.; Minutes of E.E.F. Committee d.20, 20a.
16. Cope Whitehouse, "The Expansion of Egypt", in *Contemporary Review*, Sept. 1887, pp.415–27.

17. *A History of Egypt. Vol. I. From the Earliest Times to the XVIth Dynasty*, London, 1894.
18. Dows Dunham, *Recollections of an Egyptologist*, Museum of Fine Arts, Boston, 1972, p.24ff.
19. Priscilla Napier, *A Late Beginner*, London, 1966, p.130f.; Mary Rowlatt, *A Family in Egypt*, London, 1956, p.82f.
20. R. E. M. Wheeler, "Adventure and Flinders Petrie" in *Antiquity* XXVII, 1953, p.87ff.
21. For an appraisal of Petrie's work at Naqada, see E. Baumgartel, *Petrie's Naqada Excavation. A Supplement*, London, 1970.
22. *Naqada and Ballas 1895*, London, 1896, p.viiif.
23. Baumgartel, *op.cit.*, p.7.
24. Charles Breasted, 1948, p.75ff.
25. John A. Wilson, 1964, p.93; J. Lindon Smith, 1956, p.211.
26. *Six Temples at Thebes, 1896*, London, 1897, pls.X–XIV.
27. *A.E.*, 1935, p.63.
28. F. Ll. Griffith, *Hieratic Papyri from Kahun and Gurob*, 2 vols., 1897, 1898.
29. M. A. Murray, 1962, p.63.
30. F.Ll.G. to F.P. 17.3.92: *PP* 9(ii).
31. GI/Griffith 202.
32. *EES* Minutes of E.E.F. Committee Meeting, 1.5.1896.
33. J. De Morgan, *Recherches sur les Origines de l'Egypte*, vol. I, Paris, 1896.
34. The boxes continue to yield treasures. Nearly fifty volumes of *The Oxyrhynchus Papyri* have so far been published by the Egypt Exploration Society; since 1966 the British Academy has shared the costs of publication.
35. H. E. Winlock in *Year Book of the American Philosophical Society*, 1942, p.362.
36. *70 Years*, p.142.
37. *Deshasheh*, pl.IV.
38. "Eaten with Honour", *Contemporary Review*, June 1897, p.819ff.
39. *Deshasheh*, pl.XXXVII.
40. Rosalind M. Hall, "Two linen dresses from the fifth dynasty site of Deshasheh now in the Petrie Museum of Egyptian Archaeology, University College London", in *J.E.A.*, 67, 1981, p.168ff., pls.XIX, XX.

Chapter X Hilda (1896–8)

Sources

Journals: I,xiv, I,xv (F.P. and H.P.); *PP* 4(xiii) (H.P.) Dendereh 1897–8.
Pocket diary: Oct. 1897–Oct. 1898 (some weeks missing).
Notebooks: 14, 15, 17a., b., c.; 13 (Mace). Dendereh.

Notes

1. *The Journals and Reminiscences of Denny Urlin*, edited by his wife, Arden Press, 1909.
2. Early Recollections of Hilda Petrie: *PP* 14(vii).
3. Letters between Flinders Petrie and Hilda Urlin between October 1896 and their wedding day, 29 Nov. 1897, now in possession of the family.
4. *Ibid.*
5. *Ibid.*
6. *Ibid.*
7. For correspondence concerning Edith and Alexander Petrie, *UCL* Petrie MSS.
8. Diary of W.P., 13.9.97 and 29.10.97.
9. *E.E.F. Archaeological Report 1896–7*, p.47ff.
10. J. De Morgan, *Recherches sur les Origines de l'Egypte*, vol. II, Paris, 1897, p.147ff. "Tombeau royal de Negadeh". It is nowadays thought that Cemetery T may have been the burial place of the chieftains or kings of the Late Predynastic or Early Dynastic period, and that Nubt (Naqada) may have been Egypt's earliest capital. See M. Humphrey Case and J. Crowfoot Payne in *J.E.A.*, 48, 1962, p.11.
11. W. M. F. Petrie, *Dendereh 1898* (E.E.F. Memoir 18), London, 1900, pp.15–16 and pl.II and frontispiece.
12. Mrs Sara Yorke Stevenson, *Dictionary of American Biography*, vol. 17, p.635f; David O'Connor and David Silverman, "The University Museum in Egypt", in *Expedition*, vol. 21, Winter 1979, p.4ff.
13. *Ibid.*, p.7.
14. F.P. to Spurrell, 22.4.[1898]: *UCL* Petrie MSS (Spurrell).
15. Letters between F.P. and H.P., Summer 1898, in possession of the family.

Chapter XI Most Ancient Egypt (1899–1903)

Sources

Journals: I,xva (Abadiya and Hu 1898–9) F.P. and H.P.; I,xvi (El Arabah 1899–1900) F.P. and H.P.; I,xvii (El Arabah 1900–1903) F.P. and H.P.
Pocket diaries: Nov. 1898–Nov. 1899 (F.P. and H.P.); Nov. 1899–Sept. 1900; Nov. 1900–Nov. 1901; Nov. 1901–April 1902; Nov. 1902–Nov. 1903.
Notebooks: 96 (Sheikh Ali); 40, 40a, 41, 42 (Mace) Hu 1898–9; 2–4 (Abydos 1899–1901); 1 (Abydos 1902–3) H.P.; 5, 5b (Abydos 1902–3).

Notes

1. F.P. to Newberry, 11.1.1899: GI/ Newberry 37/47.
2. *The Making of Egypt*, London, 1939, p.145f.

3. E. Amélineau, *Les nouvelles fouilles d'Abydos, seconde campagne 1896–7*, Paris, 1902, p.11.
4. *EES* Minutes of the E.E.F. Committee, 7.6.1898 and 11.4.1899.
5. *Diospolis Parva. The Cemeteries of Abadiyeh and Hu, 1898–9* (E.E.F. Memoir 20), London, 1901, p.4ff. and "Sequences in Prehistoric Remains", *Journal of the Anthropological Institute*, 29, 1899, p.295ff.
6. D. G. Kendall, "A Statistical Approach to Flinders Petrie's Sequence Dating", in *Bulletin of the International Statistical Institute*, 40 (1963) p.657ff.; "Some problems and methods in statistical archaeology", in *World Archaeology*, I (1969), p.68ff.
7. *Prehistoric Egypt*, London, 1920, and *Corpus of Prehistoric Pottery and Palettes*, B.S.A.E. Publication 32, 1921.
8. *E.E.F. Annual Report for 1899*, p.26f.
9. J. E. Quibell and F. W. Green, *Hierakonpolis*, Part 2 (E.R.A. Memoir 5), pls. LXXV–LXXIX and p.2ff.
10. Fraser to F.P., 11.7.1899: *PP* 9.
11. See n.8.
12. See n.3.
13. In *Zeitschrift für aegyptische Sprache*, 35, 1897, p.1ff.
14. *The Royal Tombs of the First Dynasty, 1900*, Part I (E.E.F. Memoir 18), London, 1900.
15. F.P. to Galton, 15 and 23.12.1899: *UCL* Galton Papers, no.279.
16. (Sir) Francis Galton, *Memories of my Life*, London, 1908, p.97ff.
17. F. Ll. Griffith, in *E.E.F. Archaeological Report 1899–1900*, p.8ff.
18. *The Royal Tombs of the Earliest Dynasties, 1901*, Part II (E.E.F. Memoir 21), London, 1901, p.27 and pl.IX.
19. *70 Years*, p.175.
20. "The Races of Early Egypt", in *Journal of the Royal Anthropological Institute*, 31, 1901, pp.248–55.
21. D. Randall MacIver and Anthony Wilkin, *Libyan Notes*, London, 1901.
22. D. Randall MacIver, A. C. Mace and F. Ll. Griffith, *El Amrah and Abydos* (E.E.F. Memoir 23), London, 1902.
23. J. Garstang, *El Arabah 1900*, E.R.A. Publication no.6, London, 1901; *Mahasna and Beit Khallaf 1901*, E.R.A. Publication no.7, London, 1902.
24. *E.E.F. Annual Report for 1900–1901*, p.31.
25. A. H. Sayce, 1923, p.307.
26. B. J. Kemp, "The Osiris Temple at Abydos", in *Mitteilungen des deutschen archäologischen Instituts*, XXIII, 1968, p.138ff., and "The Early Development of Towns in Egypt", in *Antiquity*, 51, 1977, p.185ff.
27. *Abydos Part II* (E.E.F. Memoir 24), London, 1903, pl.XIV.
28. M. A. Murray, 1963, p.120f.; Currelly (1956), p.55.
29. A. E. Weigall, in *The Glory of the Pharaohs*, New York, 1933, p.124ff., gives reminiscences of life in the Abydos camp.
30. M. A. Murray in *A.E.*, 1916, p.121ff.
31. M. A. Murray, 1963, p.118f.

32. *The Osireion at Abydos*, E.R.A. Publication no.9, London, 1904, p.2.
33. H. Frankfort, *The Cenotaph of Sety I at Abydos* (E.E.F. Memoir 39), London, 1933.
34. Noel Rawnsley, "Sketches of Life and Labour in the Excavators' Camp", in Canon H. Rawnsley, *The Resurrection of Oldest Egypt*, Laleham, 1904.
35. *EES* I e.1, 2; V k.66.
36. *EES* I h.1, 5; V j.
37. *EES* XX g.
38. *EES* V j.28.
39. *EES* I h.13.

Chapter XII Naville and Petrie: A Clash of Personalities (1903–6)

Sources

Journals: I,xviii (Ehnasya, 1903–4) F.P. and H.P.; (Sicily 1904) H.P.; *PP* 4(xiii) (Sinai 1904–5) F.P.; Letters of H.P. to F.P., Saqqara 1904–5, and F.P. to H.P., Sinai 1904–5: *PP* 6(iii).
Pocket diaries: Nov. 1903–Nov. 1904; Nov. 1904–Nov. 1905.
Notebooks: 23 A and B (Ehnasya); 97 A and B and C (Sinai).

Notes

1. E.E.F. Special Extra Report, 1890–1, "The Season's Work at Ahnas and Beni Hasan" (1891), p.10; see E. Naville, *Ahnas el Medineh (Herakleiopolis Magna)* (E.E.F. Memoir 11), 1894.
2. *Roman Ehnasya (Herakleiopolis Magna)*, Plates and Supplementary Text to Ehnasya (E.E.F. Special Extra Publication, Memoir 26), 1905.
3. *Ehnasya 1904* (E.E.F. Memoir 26), 1904, pl.I and p.18f. It is illustrated in colour in W. Stevenson Smith, *Ancient Egypt as represented in the Museum of Fine Art,* Boston, 1960, p.160.
4. *Ehnasya*, p.3ff and pls.IV–VI.
5. L. Loat, *Gurob* and M. A. Murray, *Saqqara Mastabas,* Part I, E.R.A. 10th Year, London, 1904, p.3ff. and pls.VIII–X.
6. M. A. Murray, 1962, pp.125–9.
7. C. T. Currelly, 1956, p.70. Photographs in *Ehnasya*, pl.XLIII.
8. *70 Years*, p.190.
9. Journal I, xviii.
10. "The Flinders Petrie Archaeological Camera", in *British Journal of Photography*, 24 Feb. 1950.
11. "New Portions of the Annals", in *A.E.*, 1916, p.114ff.
12. *Methods and Aims in Archaeology*, London, 1904, p.71 and fig.36.
13. *Ibid.,* p.26.
14. *Ibid.,* p.18f.

15. *Ibid.*, p.7f.
16. *Ibid.*, p.178ff.
17. See W. R. Dawson and E. P. Uphill, 1972, p.214f for a list of his books; he also wrote innumerable articles and reviews.
18. F.P. to A.B.E.: *EES* XVIII c.12, 24.
19. *EES* XVI f.11.
20. Villiers Stuart, *Egypt after the War*, London, 1884, p.83.
21. *The Academy*, 5.1.1884, p.3.
22. *EES* XVII d.2, 4.
23. A.B.E. to F.P.: *PP* 9(iv) 54.
24. *PP* 9(v) 14.
25. *Egypt Exploration Fund Archaeological Report, 1892–1893*, p.4.
26. *The Academy*, 24.12.1892, p.593f.
27. Naville to R.S.P., *EES* V a.3.
28. *EES* I c.1–3 for this correspondence.
29. *EES* VII a.1 and Minutes of the Committee, 1 Feb. 1893.
30. *EES* VI b.1–17.
31. C. C. Edgar, in *Annales du Service des Antiquités*, VIII, 1907, p.154.
32. E. Naville, "Les plus anciens monuments égyptiens", in *Recueil de Travaux relatifs à la Philologie et à l'Archéologie égyptiennes et assyriennes*, p.109ff.
33. *Ibid.*, p.214ff.
34. E. Naville, *The Cemeteries of Abydos* Part I (E.E.F. Memoir 33), 1914, p.8f.
35. *EES* V h.3.
36. Winslow's correspondence with A.B.E.: *EES* III d., e., f.; subsequently, *EES* II a–c., g., h.
37. *EES* Minutes of the Committee of the E.E.F., 27.5.1902.
38. In notebook 97a.
39. C. T. Currelly, 1956, p.91ff.
40. H. Petrie, "On Camel Back to Sinai", in *The Queen*, 25.11.1905. Miss Eckenstein subsequently wrote *A History of Sinai*, London, 1921.
41. *Egypt and Israel*, London, 1911.
42. Currelly, 1956, p.99ff.
43. For *nawamîs*, and some dramatic photographs of Sinai, see Benno Rothenberg, *Sinai: Pharaohs, Miners, Pilgrims and Soldiers*, Berne, 1979.
44. B. J. Isserlin, "The Earliest Alphabetic Writing", in *Cambridge Ancient History*, 2nd edition, vol. III, Part I, 1982, p.794ff.
45. A. H. Gardiner and T. E. Peet, *The Inscriptions of Sinai*, Part I; 2nd edn revised by J. Černy (E.E.S. Memoir 45), London, 1952, p.6f.
46. R. Giveon, *The Stones of Sinai Speak*, Tokyo, 1978, p.20ff.
47. *The Athenaeum*, 20.2.1904, p.249.

Chapter XIII The British School (1906–11)

Sources

Journals: I,xviii (Tell el Retabeh, 1905–6) H.P.; 5,vii (Qurneh 1909); 5,v (Hawara, 1911).
Pocket diaries: Nov. 1905–Nov. 1906; Nov. 1906–Nov. 1907; Nov. 1907–Nov. 1908; Nov. 1908–Nov. 1909; Nov. 1909–Nov. 1910.
Notebooks: 105, 106 (Tell el Yehudiyeh 1906); 91, 92 (Saft el Hinna, Suwa) Duncan; 90, 104 (Gheyta, Shaghanbeh) Duncan; 85, 87–8 (Rifeh and Memphis, 1907); 86 Mackay; 89 Ward; 89a (Bala'iza, Zaraby); 112 (Zaraby); 190; 80–82 (Qurna and Memphis 1908); 38b (Hawara 1911); 58, 60–67 (Meydum 1910); 68 (Memphis 1912).

Notes

1. *The Times*, 14.6.1905.
2. *Ibid.* 17.6.1905.
3. *EES* XXg. 198–9.
4. *EES* II d.132.
5. *EES* V j.45, 47.
6. *PP* 12.
7. EES XX g.246; II c.20.
8. T. E. Peet and A. H. Gardiner, *The Inscriptions of Sinai*, part I (E.E.S. Excavation Memoir 36), London, 1917.
9. C. Gilbart-Smith and a young artist, T. Butler-Stoney.
10. C. T. Currelly, 1956, pp.39, 58.
11. Bk.IV, 42.
12. A. Erman, *Mein Werden und mein Wirken*, Leipzig, 1929, p.245f. "The first Circuit round Africa, and the Supposed Record of it", in *Geographical Journal*, Nov. 1908, p.480ff.
13. E. Naville and F. Ll. Griffith, *The City of Onias and the Mound of the Jew; the Antiquities of Tell el Yehudiyeh* (E.E.F. Excavation Memoir 7), London, 1890.
14. *Hyksos and Israelite Cities*, B.S.A.E. Publication 12, London, 1906 p.24.
15. O. Tufnell, "Graves at Tell el Yehudiyeh reviewed after a lifetime", in *Archaeology in the Levant: Essays for Kathleen Kenyon* (ed. R. Moorey and P. Parr), Warminster, 1978, p.76ff.
16. See M. Bietak, *Tell el-Daba'*, vol. II, Vienna, 1975.
17. E. Naville, *The Shrine of Saft el Henneh and the Land of Goshen* (E.E.F. Memoir 4), London, 1887.
18. Journal I,xvii (Abydos 1902–3), entry for 17.11.1902.
19. In *Gizeh and Rifeh*, p.44 and in *The Formation of the Alphabet*, 1912.
20. W. E. N. Kensdale, "Three Thamudic Inscriptions from the Nile Delta", in *Le Muséon*, 66, 1953, p.133ff.; H. Grimme, *Die altsinaitischen Buchstabeninschriften*, Berlin, 1929, p.127.

21. *Man*, no.104, 1906, p.170; see also *Journal of the Anthropological Institute*, 36, 1906, p.189ff and pls.19–26.
22. *The Academy*, 30.11.1907, p.185f.
23. *The Revolutions of Civilization*, London and New York, 1911, p.131.
24. R. F. Rattray, "A Neglected Prophet" in *Quarterly Review*, Oct. 1945, p.443ff.
25. *PP* 10.
26. *UCL* Petrie MSS.
27. F.P. to H.P., 20.11.06: *PP* 5(iv).
28. *Annales du Service des Antiquités*, vi, 1906, p.99.
29. *Gizeh and Rifeh*, B.S.A.E. Publication 13, London, 1907, p.5.
30. M. A. Murray, *The Tomb of Two Brothers*, Manchester Museum Publications, 68, Manchester, 1910.
31. *Gizeh and Rifeh*, p.20.
32. F.P. to H.P., 23.3.1908: *UCL* Petrie MSS (letters).
33. For the E.R.S.A., see *A.E.*, 1914, p.47.
34. *Athribis*, B.S.A.E. Publication 14, London, 1908, p.4ff and pls.XVff.
35. These are thought nowadays to have been cult figures of Hellenistic and oriental types.
36. *Memphis I*, B.S.A.E. Publication 15, London, 1909, pl.I.
37. See B. J. Kemp, "The Palace of Apries at Memphis", in *Mitteilungen des deutschen archäologischen Instituts, Abt. Kairo*, Bd. 33, 1977, p. 101ff. for a reappraisal of Petrie's results and p.108 for the "coronation" relief.
38. Celia Davies, *Brian Hatton 1887–1916*, Lavenham, 1978, p.118ff.
39. J. Lindon Smith, 1956, p.104.
40. *Qurneh*, B.S.A.E. Publication 16, London, 1909, p.6ff and pls.XXII–XXIX.
41. *Meydum and Memphis III*, B.S.A.E. Publication 18, London, 1910, p.13ff.
42. In *70 Years* wrongly "Rahotep" (p.216).
43. F.P. to H.P.: *PP* 6(v).
44. More accurately 1,457 years.
45. *Historical Studies*, B.S.A.E. Publication 11, 1911, pp.8–22; *Researches in Sinai*, p.163ff.
46. *Historical Studies*, p.10f.
47. See Eduard Meyer, *Aegyptische Chronologie*, Berlin, 1904; "Nachträge zur aegyptischen Chronologie", *Berlin, Akademie der Wissenschaften, Abhandlungen*, 1907; K. Sethe, *Beiträge zur ältesten Geschichte Aegyptens (Untersuchungen zur Geschichte und Altertumskunde Aegyptens)*, 1904.
48. Sir Mortimer Wheeler, in a broadcast talk.
49. *Roman Portraits and Memphis IV*, pl.II., B.S.A.E. Publication 20, 1911.
50. *The Labyrinth, Gerzeh and Mazghuneh*, B.S.A.E. Publication 21, London, 1912, pl.
51. Correspondence between F.P. and H.P., Winter 1911–12: *PP* 6(v).

Chapter XIV Amulets in the Soup (1911–14)

Sources

Journals: I,xix (Kafr 'Ammar 1912–13); 1913–14 (Lahun).
Pocket diaries: Nov. 1911–Nov. 1912; Nov. 1912–Nov. 1913; Nov. 1913–Nov. 1914.
Notebooks: 99–100 (Tarkhan, Memphis, Heliopolis); 43a, 45 (Lahun).

Notes

1. J. de M. Johnson in *E.E.F. Archaeological Report 1910–1911*, p.5ff, "Excavations in Atfieh".
2. *The Letters of T. E. Lawrence* (ed. David Garnett), London and Toronto, 1938, pp.134–7.
3. *Ibid.*
4. Lawrence to Hogarth, 20.2.1912.
5. *T. E. Lawrence to his Biographer, Liddell Hart,* New York, 1938, p.54; Robert Graves, *Lawrence and the Arabs,* London, 1927, p.63.
6. *The Letters of T. E. Lawrence,* p.136.
7. E. Mackay, Lankester Harding and Flinders Petrie, *Bahrein and Hemamiyeh*, B.S.A.E. Publication 47, 1925.
8. *Tarkhan I and Memphis V*, B.S.A.E. Publication 22, 1913, pl.XXVI.
9. S. Landi and Rosalind Hall, "The discovery and conservation of an ancient Egyptian linen tunic", in *Studies in Conservation*, 24, 1979, p.141ff.
10. H.P. to Amy Urlin, 23.2.1912: *PP* 7(ii).
11. R. Weill, "Monuments nouveaux des premières dynasties", in *Sphinx*, xv, 1911, pp.11ff.
12. *Heliopolis, Kafr Ammar and Shurafa*, B.S.A.E. Publication 24, 1915, p.4.
13. Letters from the Petries to Miss Crompton are in the archives of the Manchester Museum's Egyptian Department.
14. Horace Thompson, G. North and the Rev. C. T. Campion, all new to Egypt.
15. *Tarkhan II*, B.S.A.E. Publication 25, 1914, p.14ff.
16. *EES* Minutes of the Committee, 7 Oct.–4 Nov. 1913.
17. R. Engelbach, *Riqqeh and Memphis VI*, B.S.A.E. Publication 19, 1915.
18. Duncan Willey, F. Frost, C. T. Campion and Dr Walter Amsden, who measured the skulls from Engelbach's tombs.
19. Guy Brunton, *Lahun I. The Treasure*, B.S.A.E. Publication 27, 1920, Chs. IV and V.
20. *Illustrated London News*, 20.6.1914, p.1062f. For the jewellery, see also Albert M. Lythgoe, "The Treasure of Lahun", in *Bulletin of the Metropolitan Museum of Art, New York,* December, 1919, p.3ff; H. E. Winlock, *The Treasure of El Lahūn*, Metropolitan Museum, Publications of the Department of Egyptian Art, New York, 1934.

Chapter XV The War Years (1914–19)

Sources

Pocket diaries: Nov. 1914–Nov. 1915; Dec. 1915–Nov. 1916; Dec. 1916–Dec. 1917; Jan.–Dec. 1917, Jan.–Nov. 1918; Nov. 1918–Nov. 1919.

Notes

1. "The Egyptian Museum, University College", in *A.E.*, 1915, p.168ff.
2. Prospectus of the Department of Egyptology, in *UCL Records*.
3. For correspondence and documents relating to the purchase of the Petrie Collection, see *UCL Library Records* file *Flinders Petrie*, and no.521.
4. *A.E.*, 1914, p.190.
5. *E.R.S.A.*: see *A.E.*, 1914, pp.47, 94; 1915, p.47.
6. *The Times*, 30.1.1915.
7. *A.E.*, 1915, p.180.
8. "A National Repository for Science and Art", in *Journal of the Society of Arts*, 18 May 1900, p.525ff.
9. *PP* 4(iv).
10. Joseph McCabe, *Edward Clodd: a Memoir*, London, 1932; Edward Clodd, *Memories*, London, 1916, pp.121, 234.
11. *A.E.*, 1915, p.93f.
12. *70 Years*, p.17.
13. Ann Flinders Petrie in *Matthew Flinders: The Ifs of History*, 1979, p.32.
14. *The Hill Figures of England*, Royal Anthropological Institute of Great Britain and Ireland, 1926, p.7ff.
15. *Ibid.*, p.16.
16. Reports of the Hampstead Scientific Society 1910–34, and *Seventy-Five Years of Popular Science (Record of the H.S.S. 1899–1974)*, London, 1974, pp.4, 11, 32.
17. *The Times*, 27.6.1914.
18. *Ibid.*, 8.3.1918.
19. "Neglected British History", in *Proceedings of the British Academy*, 8, 1918, p.28ff.
20. "Ptolemy's Geography of Albion", in *Proceedings of the Society of Antiquaries of Scotland*, 52, ser.5, vol. 4, 1917–18, p.12ff.
21. *The Times Literary Supplement*, 27.11.1919.
22. *Eastern Exploration, Past and Future: Lectures at the Royal Institution*, London, 1918.
23. *The Times*, 3.6.1918.
24. *Proceedings of the British Academy*, 1919, Presidential Address, p.3ff.
25. *The Times*, 4.3.1919.
26. *Ibid.*, 7.3.1919.
27. Petrie's article, "Early Burial Customs in Egypt", *Man*, 84, 1910,

p.404; Elliot Smith's criticism in *Nature*, vol. 84, 1910, p.461f; Petrie's reply, p.494 and vol. 85, p.41.

28. *PP* 10(i).
29. See the discussion in A. Lucas, *Ancient Egyptian Materials and Industries*, 3rd edn revised J. Harris, London, 1962, p.289ff.
30. Glyn Daniel, "Elliot Smith, Egypt and Diffusionism", in *Symposium on Elliot Smith,* Zoological Society of London, 1973, no.33, p.407ff.
31. M. A. Murray, 1963, p.163.

Chapter XVI Egypt over the Border (1919–30)

Sources

Journals: I,xx, Gaza and Gerar, 1926; 1927 H.P. Gerar.

Pocket diaries: Nov. 1919–Nov. 1920; Nov. 1920–Nov. 1921; Nov. 1921–Nov. 1922; Nov. 1922–Nov. 1923; Nov. 1923–Nov. 1924; Nov. 1924–Nov. 1925; Nov. 1925–Nov. 1926; Nov. 1926–Nov. 1927; Nov. 1928–Nov. 1929; Nov. 1929–Nov. 1930 (1927–8 missing.)

Notebooks: 43a, 45 (Illahun); 95a–c (Sedment); 5a, 76 (Abydos and Behnesa); 79 (Qau).

Notes

1. Captain Miller, Miss Hughes and G. Jefferies.
2. E.g. in Jessica Mitford, *The Making of a Muckraker*, London, 1979, p.243f.
3. *Lahun II,* B.S.A.E. Publication 32, 1921, p.12 and pl.XXV.
4. *The Times*, 18.2.1901.
5. F.P.'s letter to H. Cunnington in the library of the Wiltshire Archaeological and Natural History Society, Jackson Folio 373, dated 6.9.1918, suggests that Hilda should raise £7,000 for this purpose.
6. Christopher Chippindale, *Stonehenge Complete*, London, 1983, p.167f.
7. *Sedment I*, B.S.A.E. Publication 34, 1925, p.1.
8. *PP* 7(ii).
9. T. E. Peet, *Cemeteries of Abydos* (E.E.S. Memoir 34), London, 1914, p.22ff.
10. See B. J. Kemp, "Abydos and the Royal Tombs of the First Dynasty", in *J.E.A.*, 52, 1966, p.15ff; "The Egyptian First Dynasty Royal Cemetery", in *Antiquity*, 41, 1967, p.22ff.
11. *Tombs of the Courtiers*, p.24 and pls.XLIX–LV.
12. *Ibid.*, ch.V and pl.XXXVIII.
13. O. Tufnell, "James Leslie Starkey", in *P.E.Q.*, 1938, p.80ff.
14. W. M. F. Petrie, "Report of Diggings in Silbury Hill, August 1922", in *The Wiltshire Archaeological and Natural History Magazine*, 42, 1922–4, p.215ff.
15. R. J. C. Atkinson, "Silbury Hill", in *Antiquity*, XLI, 1967, p.259ff.
16. F.P. to Newberry, 17.1.1923: GI/ Newberry 37/85.

17. E.E.S. *Report of the 36th Annual General Meeting*, 1922, p.12f.
18. *Ibid., 38th A.G.M.*, 1924, p.23.
19. F.P. to Garstang, 17.1.1923: *PP* 10.
20. *A.E.*, 1923, p.33ff, "The tomb at Byblos".
21. *70 Years*, p.249.
22. F.P. to Newberry: GI/ Newberry 37/88.
23. O. G. S. Crawford, *Said and Done*, London, 1955, pp.93, 173.
24. *Manchester Guardian*, 27.7.1929.
25. Hans Steckeweh, *Die Fürstengräber von Qâw*, Leipzig, 1936.
26. *Antaeopolis, the Tombs of Qau*, B.S.A.E. Publication 43, 1928, p.7.
27. "The Origin of the Twelfth Dynasty", *A.E.*, 1924, p.38ff; *Antaeopolis*, p.12f.
28. "The Sphinxes of Tanis", in *A.E.*, 1920, p.105f.
29. *A.E.*, 1923, p.78ff.
30. "The Caucasian Atlantis and Egypt", in *A.E.*, 1924, p.123ff; "The origins of the Book of the Dead", in *A.E.*, 1926, p.41f.
31. Guy Brunton and Gertrude Caton-Thompson, *The Badarian Civilisation*, B.S.A.E. and E.R.A., 30th Year, London, 1928.
32. E. W. Gardner, "Observations on the Recent Geology of the North Fayum Desert", in *Journal of the Anthropological Institute*, LVI, 1926, p.321ff; Petrie's comment, p.325f.
33. Michael Hoffmann, *Egypt before the Pharaohs*, London and Henley, 1980, p.187f.
34. R. E. M. Wheeler, *Still Digging; Adventures in Archaeology*, London, 1955, p.62.
35. *A.E.*, 1926, p.96.
36. O. Tufnell, "Gerald Lankester Harding", in *Levant*, 1980, p.iii.
37. The equation of Fara with Arabic *falata*, "to escape"; see *Beth Pelet (Tell Fara) I*, B.S.A.E. Publication 48, 1930, p.2.
38. J. G. Duncan, *A Corpus of Dated Palestinian Pottery*, B.S.A.E. Publication 49, 1930.
39. *Gerar*, B.S.A.E. Publication 43, 1928, p.23.
40. Gus W. Van Beek, "Digging up Tell Jemmeh", in *Archaeology*, 36, Jan.–Feb. 1983, pp.12–19.
41. *Beth-Pelet (Tell Fara) I*, chapter 4.
42. In *A.E.*, 1924–1926, Index in *A.E.*, 1927, p.113ff.
43. E. Gombrich, *The Sense of Order*, Oxford, 1979, p.ix.
44. *Beth Pelet I*, pls.XV, XLVIII.
45. F.P. to H.P., 15.11.1928: *PP* 6(x).
46. *Beth Pelet I*, p.19 and pl.LV.
47. *Beth Pelet II*, B.S.A.E. Publication 52, 1931, pls.LXVII, LXVIII.
48. Letters of F.P. to H.P. from Rome, Winter 1929–30: *PP* 6(ix).
49. *A.E.*, 1929, p.128.

Chapter XVII Jubilee (1930–3)

Sources
Pocket diaries: Oct. 1931–Oct. 1932; Nov. 1932–Dec. 1933; Jan.–Dec. 1934.
Letters to Ann and John replace the Journals (*PP* 7.)

Notes

1. F.P. to H.P.: *PP* 6(v).
2. *A.E.*, 1930, p.31; Programme, "A Vision of the Ages", in *PP* 8.
3. *A.E.*, 1930, p.63; list of guests: *PP* 7.
4. *T.P.'s Weekly*, June 1930.
5. R. E. M. Wheeler, *Still Digging*, London, 1958, p.77ff; Jacquetta Hawkes, *Mortimer Wheeler: Adventurer in Archaeology*, London, 1982, p.129ff.
6. Minutes of the Committee of Management of the Institute of Archaeology, 26.7.1934.
7. *Ibid.*, 28.4.1937.
8. Richmond Brown, J. G. Vernon and Norman Scott. C. F. Royds joined them later as surveyor.
9. Correspondence in the files of the Department of Antiquities of Palestine, ATQ/ 17/6, 41/6.
10. *Annual Report of the B.S.A.E., 36th Year*, 1929–30, p.2, and M. J. Stewart, "The Underdog in the Palestine Conquest", in *A.E.*, 1930, p.78.
11. ATQ/ 41/6, 24.10.1930.
12. *Ibid.*, Memorandum from Secretariat, no.4293.
13. H.P. to J.P. and A.P., 2.12.1930: *PP* 7(iii).
14. *Ibid.*
15. *A.E.*, 1931, p.33.
16. *Ancient Gaza Part I. Tell el Ajjūl*, B.S.A.E. Publication 53, 1931, p.5f and pls. VI, VII.
17. The description of camp life that follows owes much to the personal recollections and diaries of Ann Petrie; also to Olga Tufnell, "Reminiscences of a Petrie Pup", in *P.E.Q.*, 1982, p.81ff, and Frances James, "Petrie in the Wadi Ghazzeh and at Gaza: Harris Colt's Candid Camera", in *P.E.Q.*, 1979, p.75ff.
18. O. Tufnell, "Flinders Petrie", in *P.E.Q.*, 1943, p.5ff.
19. E. T. Richmond to F.P., 31.3.1931: ATQ/41/6: F.P. to Richmond, 4.4.1931: ATQ/17/6.
20. In *Les nouvelles fouilles d'Abydos, seconde campagne 1896–7*, Paris, 1905, p.556.
21. F.P. to Richmond, 3.9.1931: ATQ/41/6; Richmond's reply, 4.4.1931: ATQ/17/6.
22. H.P. to A.P.: *PP* 7(iii).
23. Memorandum of interview, 22.1.1932 in ATQ/41/6.

24. O. Tufnell, "The Courtyard Cemetery at Tell el Ajjul, Palestine", *University of London, Institute of Archaeology, Bulletin*, no. 3, 1962, p.1ff; Review by Bruce Williams of J. R. Stewart, "Tell el 'Ajjūl: The Middle Bronze Age Remains", 1974, in *American Journal of Archaeology* 80, 1976, p.199f.; R. E. M. Wheeler, 1954, p.16f.
25. G. A. Reisner, *Harvard Excavations at Samaria 1908–9*, Cambridge, Mass., 1924, fig.14.
26. K. M. Kenyon, "Excavating Methods in Palestine", in *P.E.Q.*, 1939, pp.29–37; Roger Moorey, *Excavation in Palestine*, Guildford, 1981, p.29ff; R. E. M. Wheeler, 1954, p.372.
27. *Ancient Gaza, Part II. Tell el Ajjūl*, B.S.A.E. Publication 54, 1932, pp.7 and 16.
28. K. R. Maxwell Hyslop, *Western Asiatic Jewellery c.3000–612 B.C.*, London, 1971, p.112ff; O. Negbi, *The Hoards of Goldwork from Tell el Ajjul*, Göteborg, 1970.
29. Minutes of the Executive Subcommittee of B.S.A.E., 19.5.1932, in *PP* 8.
30. *Ancient Gaza, Part III*, p.5ff and pls. VII–XIII.

Chapter XVIII Lone Syrian Shore (1934–8)

Sources

Pocket diaries: Jan.–Dec. 1935; Jan.–Dec. 1936; Jan.–Dec. 1937; Jan.–Dec. 1938.

Notes

1. Other volunteers were H. E. Bird, Patricia Hood, Anne Fuller, C. Peckham and the artist Benton Fletcher.
2. Draft of projected additions to F.P.'s autobiography, in *PP* 15.
3. ATQ/ 41/6, 21.4.1934 (see n.9, chapter 17).
4. *Ancient Gaza, Part IV*, B.S.A.E. Publication 56, 1934, p.19.
5. *Morning Post*, 10.10.1934.
6. The account which follows, including the extracts quoted, is from the manuscript of Petrie's unpublished *Lone Syrian Shore* (*PP* 15).
7. E. Renan, *Mission de Phénicie*, Imprimerie impériale, 1864.
8. René Dussaud, *Topographie historique de la Syrie antique et mediévale*, Paris, 1927.
9. *The Times*, 22.1.1935.
10. M. A. Murray, 1963, p.138f.
11. *Syro-Egypt*, I, 1937, p.3.
12. W. F. Albright, *The Archaeology of Palestine*, Harmondsworth, 1949, p.39f.

13. W. F. Albright, "The Chronology of a South Palestinian City, Tell el 'Ajjûl", in *American Journal of Semitic Languages and Literature*, LV, 1938, p.337ff.
14. *Syro-Egypt.* Only four numbers of the new journal were issued.
15. This description of camp life at Sheikh Zoweyd is based on H.P.'s letters (*PP* 7(iv)) and reminiscences of members of the staff.
16. *Syro-Egypt*, II, 1937, p.5; "prosperity curve" in *Anthedon, Sinai*, B.S.A.E. Publication 58, 1937, pl.XVII.
17. *The Palestine Post,* 19.7.1936, reprinted as a leaflet.
18. *The Times,* 10.8.36.
19. *PP* 7(iv).
20. F.P. to A.P., 17.12.1936: *PP* 7.
21. "Museum Plans", in *J.R.I.B.A.*, 45, 1938, p.340f and p.557.
22. W. B. Emery to F.P., 16.4.1936: *PP* 10.
23. *Syro-Egypt*, IV, 1938, p.27.
24. ATQ/41/6, 11.10.1937.
25. Bernard Fergusson, *The Trumpet in the Hall*, London, 1970, p.47f.
26. Ernest J. H. Mackay and Margaret A. Murray, *City of Shepherd Kings, and Ancient Gaza V,* B.S.A.E. Publication 64, London, 1952, chapter IV (by F.P.).
27. M. A. Murray, 1963, p.113.
28. *Ancient Gaza V*, p.41.
29. *Syro-Egypt*, IV, 1939, p.30; *Report of the B.S.A.E., Forty-fourth Year, 1937–1938,* p.3ff.
30. Risdon papers: F.P. to Risdon, 11.2.1939.

Chapter XIX Sunset in Jerusalem

Sources

Pocket diaries: Sparse entries for 1939–40 (ends 30 May); H.P. 1941.

Notes

1. F.P. to A.P., 5.6.1939: *PP* 7(i).
2. F.P. to Risdon, 22.4.41 (Risdon papers).
3. *The Nineteenth Century*, Sept. 1912; Hodgkin to F.P., *PP* 10(iv).
4. From Lady Petrie's speech at the Centenary dinner, 1953: *PP* 12.
5. *The Palestine Post*, 5.7.46.
6. *Still Digging*, London, 1955, p.63; also in *Antiquity*, XXVII, p.87ff.
7. *The Palestine Post*, 30.7.42.
8. See letters in *PP* 12.
9. For a transcript of this and other speeches at the Flinders Petrie Memorial Meeting, see *PP* 12.
10. H. Petrie, *Seven Memphite Tomb Chapels*, B.S.A.E. Publication 65, 1952.

11. See *Matthew Flinders: The Ifs of History*, ed. R. W. Russell, Flinders University of South Australia, 1979.
12. I owe this information to Miss Tufnell, who brought him the letter conveying the news of his knighthood.
13. In *Nature*, 1.10.1938, p.620.
14. Lord Stamp's reply: 23.1.1939 in *UCL* Petrie MSS.
15. Draft additions to F.P.'s autobiography: *PP* 15.
16. *Daily Express*, 14.12.1925.
17. *EES* XVIII, 7, from a lecture given 31.10.1932 at a celebration of the Society's jubilee.
18. *A.E.*, 1930, p.89.
19. Dows Dunham, "The Egyptian Department and its Excavators", Museum of Fine Arts, Boston, 1954, p.24.
20. *Naukratis Part I*, 1886, p.2.
21. A. H. Gardiner in *Nature*, 17.8.1942, p.3.
22. To Spurrell, quoted in *70 Years*, p.105f.
23. *A.E.*, 1926, p.128.
24. K. G. O'Connell and D. Glenn Rose, "Tell el Hesi, 1979", in *P.E.Q.*, 1979, p.75ff.

BIBLIOGRAPHY

Select Bibliography

BAINES, John, and Jaromir MÁLEK, *Atlas of Ancient Egypt*, Oxford, 1978.

BUDGE, E. A. T. W., *By Nile and Tigris* (2 vols.), London, 1920.

BREASTED, Charles, *Pioneer to the Past. The Story of James Henry Breasted, Archaeologist,* New York, 1948.

CAPART, J. (ed.), *Letters of Charles Edwin Wilbour,* Brooklyn, 1936.

CERAM, C. W., *Gods, Graves and Scholars,* 2nd edn., 1967.

CURRELLY, Charles T., *I Brought the Ages Home,* Toronto, 1956.

DANIEL, Glyn, *A Hundred and Fifty Years of Archaeology*, 2nd edn., London, 1975.

DAWSON, W. R. and E. T. UPHILL, *Who Was Who in Egyptology*, 2nd edn., London, 1972, p.228ff.

DEUEL, LEO, *The Treasures of Time*, Ohio, 1961, chapter 5.

KHATER, A., *Le régime juridique des fouilles et des antiquités en Egypte,* Institut français d'archéologie orientale du Caire, Recherches tom. XII, Cairo, 1960.

MURRAY, Margaret A., *My First Hundred Years,* London, 1963.

PETRIE, Ann Flinders, and Ann Lisette Flinders PETRIE, in *Matthew Flinders: The Ifs of History* (ed. R. W. Russell), Flinders University of South Australia, 1979.

SMITH, Joseph Lindon, *Tombs, Temples and Ancient Art,* University of Oklahoma, 1956.

SAYCE, A. H., *Reminiscences*, London, 1923.

UPHILL, Eric, "A Bibliography of Sir William Matthew Flinders Petrie (1853–1942)", in *Journal of Near Eastern Studies,* vol. 31, October 1972, p.356ff.

WHEELER, R. E. M., "Adventure and Flinders Petrie", in *Antiquity*, XXVII (1953), p.87ff.

WHEELER, R. E. M., *Archaeology from the Earth*, Oxford, 1954.

WILBOUR, Charles Edwin, *Travels in Egypt (December 1880 to May 1891)* (ed. Jean Capart), New York, 1936.

WILSON, John A., *Signs and Wonders upon Pharaoh: a History of American Egyptology,* Chicago and London, 1964.

WORTHAM, John David, *British Egyptology 1549–1956*, Newton Abbot, 1972.

WOOLLEY, Sir Leonard, in *Dictionary of National Biography,* 1941–1950, p.666ff.

The Books of Flinders Petrie
(† denotes joint authorship; * excavation reports)

1874 *Researches on the Great Pyramid: or, Fresh Connections: Being a preliminary notice of some Facts*, etc.
1877 *Diagram of the Great Pyramid: to show that the Great Pyramid's Passages are* not *Chronological, as taught in the So-Called Time Passage Theory.*
1877 *Inductive Metrology: or the Recovery of Ancient Measures from the Monuments.*
1880 *Stonehenge: Plans, Descriptions and Theories.*
1883 *The Pyramids and Temples of Gizeh.*
1885 * *Tanis. Part I 1884–5* (E.E.F. Memoir 2).
1885 *The Pyramids and Temples of Gizeh* (second, abridged edition).
1886 *† *Naukratis. Part I 1884–5* (E.E.F. Memoir 3).
1887 *Racial Photographs from the Egyptian Monuments* (on spine, Racial Types from Egypt).
1887 *† *Tanis. Part II. Nebesheh (Am) and Defenneh (Tahpanhes)* (E.E.F. Memoir 4).
1888 *A Season in Egypt, 1887.*
1889 *Two Hieroglyphic Papyri from Tanis, Part 2: the Geographical Papyrus* (E.E.F. Memoir 9).
1889 *† *Hawara, Biahmu and Arsinoe.*
1889 *Historical Scarabs. A Series of Drawings from the Principal Collections, arranged Chronologically.*
1890 *† *Kahun, Gurob and Hawara.*
1891 *† *Illahun, Kahun and Gurob.*
1891 * *Tell el Hesy (Lachish).*
1892 *† *Medum.*
1892 *Ten Years' Digging in Egypt, 1881–1891.*
1894 *† *Tell el-'Amarna.*
1894 *A History of Egypt.* Vol. I. *From the Earliest Times to the XVth Dynasty.*
1895 *Egyptian Decorative Art: a Course of Lectures at the Royal Institution.*
1895 *Egyptian Tales, translated from the Papyri. First Series IVth to XIIth Dynasty.* Illustrated by Tristram Ellis.
1895 *Egyptian Tales, translated from the Papyri: Second series, XVIIIth to XIXth Dynasty.*
1896 *A History of Egypt.* Vol. II. *During the XVIIth and XVIIIth Dynasties.*
1896 *† *Koptos.*
1897 * *Six Temples at Thebes.* 1896.
1898 *† *Deshasheh, 1897* (E.E.F. Memoir 15).
1898 *Syria and Egypt, from the Tell el 'Amarna Letters.*
1900 *† *Dendereh, 1898* (E.E.F. Memoir 17).
1900 * *The Royal Tombs of the First Dynasty, 1900. Part I* (E.E.F. Memoir 18).

1900 *†*Hierakonpolis I* (E.R.A. 4), by J. E. Quibell.
1898 *Religion and Conscience in Ancient Egypt: Lectures delivered at University College, London.*
1901 * *Diospolis Parva: The Cemeteries of Abadiyeh and Hu, 1898–9* (E.E.F. Memoir 20).
1901 * *The Royal Tombs of the Earliest Dynasties, 1901* (E.E.F. Memoir 21).
1902 * *Abydos. Part I* (E.E.F. Memoir 22).
1903 * *Abydos. Part II* (E.E.F. Memoir 24).
1904 *†*Ehnasya, 1904* (E.E.F. Memoir 26).
1904 *Methods and Aims in Archaeology.*
1905 *A History of Egypt.* Vol. III. *From the XIXth to the XXXth Dynasties.*
1905 * *Roman Ehnasya (Herakleiopolis Magna), 1904* (E.E.F. Memoir 26). Supplementary Plates and Text.
1906 * *Hyksos and Israelite Cities* (B.S.A.E. 12).
1906 *The Religion of Ancient Egypt.*
1906 *†*Researches in Sinai.*
1906 *Migrations.*
1907 * *Gizeh and Rifeh* (B.S.A.E. 13).
1907 *Janus in Modern Life.*
1908 *†*Athribis* (B.S.A.E. 14).
1908 *†*Memphis I* (B.S.A.E. 15).
1909 *†*The Palace of Apries (Memphis II)* (B.S.A.E. 17).
1909 *Personal Religion in Egypt before Christianity.*
1909 *†*Qurneh* (B.S.A.E. 16).
1909 *The Arts and Crafts of Ancient Egypt.*
1910 *†*Meydum and Memphis (III)* (B.S.A.E. 18).
1910 *The Growth of the Gospels as Shown by Structural Criticism.*
1911 †*Historical Studies* (B.S.A.E. 11).
1911 * *Roman Portraits and Memphis (IV)* (B.S.A.E. 20).
1911 *The Revolutions of Civilization.*
1911 *Egypt and Israel.*
1912 *The Formation of the Alphabet* (B.S.A.E. Studies 3).
1912 * *The Labyrinth, Gerzeh and Mazghuneh* (B.S.A.E. 21).
1913 *The Hawara Portfolio: Paintings of the Roman Age, found by W. M. Flinders Petrie in 1888 and 1911* (B.S.A.E. 22).
1913 *†*Tarkhan I and Memphis V* (B.S.A.E. 23).
1914 * *Tarkhan II* (B.S.A.E. 25).
1914 *Amulets, illustrated by the Egyptian Collection in University College, London.*
1915 *†*Heliopolis, Kafr Ammar and Shurafa* (B.S.A.E. 24).
1917 *Scarabs and Cylinders with Names, illustrated by the Collection in University College, London* (B.S.A.E. 29).
1917 *Tools and Weapons, illustrated by the Egyptian Collection at University College, London, and 2,000 Outlines from Other Sources* (B.S.A.E. 30).

1917 *Corpus of Prehistoric Pottery and Palettes* (E.R.A.).
1918 *Eastern Exploration, Past and Future. Lectures at the Royal Institution.*
1919 *Some Sources of Human History.*
1921 *Corpus of Prehistoric Pottery and Palettes* (E.R.A.).
1922 *A History of Egypt.* Vol. I (Tenth edition, revised).
1922 *The Status of the Jews in Egypt.*
1923 *Social Life in Ancient Egypt.*
1923 ★†*Lahun II. The Pyramid* (B.S.A.E. 33).
1924 ★ *Sedment I* (B.S.A.E. 34).
1924 ★ *Sedment II* (B.S.A.E. 35).
1924 *Religious Life in Ancient Egypt.*
1924 "Ancient Egyptians", in Herbert Spencer, *Descriptive Sociology*, division I, no. 1.
1925 ★†*Tombs of the Courtiers and Oxyrhynkhos* (B.S.A.E. 37).
1925 *Buttons and Design Scarabs, illustrated by the Egyptian Collection in University College, London* (B.S.A.E. 38).
1926 *Ancient Weights and Measures, illustrated from the Egyptian Collection in University College, London* (B.S.A.E. 39).
1926 *Glass Stamps and Weights, illustrated from the Egyptian Collection in University College, London* (B.S.A.E. 40).
1927 *Objects of Daily Use, with over 1,800 Figures from University College, London* (B.S.A.E. 42).
1928 *Gerar* (B.S.A.E. 43).
1929 †*How to Observe in Archaeology.*
1929 ★†*Bahrein and Hemamiyeh.*
1930 ★†*Beth-Pelet (Tell Fara) I* (B.S.A.E. 48).
1930 ★ *Antaeopolis: the Tombs of Qau* (B.S.A.E. 51).
1930 †*Corpus of Dated Palestinian Pottery.* (By J. G. Duncan) (B.S.A.E. 49).
1930 *Decorative Patterns of the Ancient World* (B.S.A.E.).
1931 ★ *Ancient Gaza I. Tell el Ajjûl* (B.S.A.E. 53).
1931 *Seventy Years in Archaeology.*
1932 ★ *Ancient Gaza II. Tell el Ajjûl* (B.S.A.E. 54).
1932 ★ *Ancient Gaza III. Tell el Ajjûl* (B.S.A.E. 55).
1934 ★ *Ancient Gaza IV. Tell el Ajjûl.* (B.S.A.E. 56).
1934 *Measures and Weights.*
1934 *Palestine and Israel: Historical Notes.*
1935 *Shabtis, illustrated by the Egyptian Collection in University College, London. With a Catalogue of Figures from many other Sources* (B.S.A.E. 57).
1937 ★†*Anthedon, Sinai* (B.S.A.E. 58).
1937 *The Funeral Furniture of Egypt. Stone and Metal Vases* (B.S.A.E. 59).
1938 *Egyptian Architecture* (B.S.A.E. 60).
1939 *The Making of Egypt.*
1940 *Wisdom of the Egyptians* (B.S.A.E. 63).
1952 ★†*City of Shepherd Kings, and Ancient Gaza V* (B.S.A.E. 64).

1953 *Ceremonial Slate Palettes* (B.S.A.E. 66).
1953 *Corpus of Proto-Dynastic Pottery: Thirty Plates of drawings by W. M. Flinders Petrie*. Centenary Double Volume (B.S.A.E. 66 B.)

His pamphlets, articles and reviews are too numerous to list here: he contributed to the *Encyclopaedia Britannica,* Hastings' *Dictionary of the Bible, and Dictionary of Religion and Ethics,* to *Records of the Past,* and to J. A. Hammerton's *Wonders of the Past* and *Universal History of the World.* A bibliography of his writings, compiled by Eric P. Uphill, can be found in *The Journal of Near Eastern Studies* (published by the University of Chicago), volume 31, no.4 (October 1942), pp.356–79. It contains over 1,000 items.

Obituaries and Appreciations

ALBRIGHT, W. F., in *Bulletin of the American Schools of Oriental Research,* 87, 1942.
EMERY, W. B., "The Founder of Egyptian Archaeology: Genius of Flinders Petrie", in *The Times,* 6.8.1953.
GARDINER, A. H., in *Nature*, vol. 50, 15.8.1942, p.204.
GLUECK, Nelson, in *Bulletin of the American Schools of Oriental Research,* 87 1942, p.6f.
GLANVILLE, S. R. K., "Flinders Petrie: the Scientific Classification of Archaeological Material", in *Proceedings of the Royal Institution*, 32, 1942, p.344ff.
HARDEN, D. B., "The Centenary of Sir Flinders Petrie", in *Museums Journal,* 53, no.4, July 1953, p.107ff.
JAMATI, Habib, in *Chronique d'Egypte*, 35, 1943, p.120; 39, 1945, p.120.
MYRES, J. N. L., in *Man*, 43 (1943), no.9, p.20f.
NEWBERRY, P. E., in *Journal of Egyptian Archaeology*, 29, 1943, p.67ff.
O'CONNOR, David, in *Expedition*, Winter 1979, p.17f.
SMITH, Sidney, in *Obituary Notices of Fellows of the Royal Society,* vol. 5, Nov. 1945, p.3ff, reprinted from *Proceedings of the British Academy*, vol. 28, 1942, p.307ff.
TUFNELL, Olga, in *Palestine Exploration Quarterly,* 75, 1942, p.4f.
The Archaeology of Palestine Centenary Exhibition, Institute of Archaeology Occasional Papers, 10, London, 1953.
Museum of Egyptology, University College, London. Flinders Petrie Centenary Exhibition, 1953.

GLOSSARY OF ARABIC AND TECHNICAL WORDS

antika	antiquity, such as dealers sell
aiwa	yes
Bairam	festal holiday marking the end of Ramadan
balad	village
bakhshîsh	gratuity, tip
cartouche	Egyptian royal name, written within an oval of rope
corvée	forced labour
dhahabiya	Nile houseboat
dharabukka	pottery finger drum
Effendi	Sir, gentleman (used of Orientals)
firmân	official permit
fantasiya	entertainment
fellâh pl. *fellahîn*	peasant, countryman
galabîya	long garment of the countryman
gebel	hill, mountain; the high desert
ghafîr	guard, watchman
kham(a)sîn	"fifty"—the hot dusty wind that is said to blow during fifty days of spring
Khawâga	Sir (used of Europeans)
kurbâsh	hide whip
kôm	sim. *tell* in some districts
mastaba	tomb with bench-like rectangular superstructure
mudîr	director, head
mudiriya	administrative district, county
mufattish	inspector
mutasarrif	district governor
nabbût	peasant's heavy staff
nomarch	governor of a nome (administrative district)
omda	mayor of town or village
pylons	tall structures flanking the gateways of temples, usually sculptured in relief
Pasha	term of respect, honorific
Ramadan	the Moslem month of fasting
reis	chief; foreman of a dig
saqia	waterwheel
scarab	amulet seal in the form of a beetle
sebbakhîn	those who carry away decayed brick from ancient sites, as fertilizer for fields
sheikh	headman of tribe, venerable man, saint
shawabti	see ushabti
sitt	lady, wife
tell	ancient mound
temenos	sacred enclosure
turi'a	digging instrument: a wide-bladed hoe
ushabti	figurine placed in tomb to replace the dead when called on by Osiris to work in the Underworld
wady	valley, watercourse
zikr	ecstatic religious exercise (see p. 98)

APPENDIX A

The Chronology of Ancient Egyptian History

(all dates are BC)

	Recently accepted dates[1]	*Petrie 1895–6*[2]	*Petrie 1905*[3]	*Petrie 1939*[4]
The Prehistoric Ages				
Badarian	5000–4000	arrival of dynastic Egyptians about 4500		7500–6500
Amratian (Naqada I)	4000–3500			6500–5500
Gerzean (Naqada II)	3500–3100			5500–4800
Semainian (Late Predynastic)	3100–2920			4800–3838
Archaic Period				
Dynasties 1 and 2	2920–2650		5546–4991	4320–3838
Old Kingdom				
Dynasties 3 and 4	2650–2470	(Dynasty 4) 3998–3721	4991–4493	3838–3510
Dynasties 5 and 6	2470–2323	3721–3348	4493–4077	3510–3127
First Intermediate Period				
Dynasties 7–11	2323–1991	3322–2778	4077–3579	3127–2738
Middle Kingdom				
Dynasties 12 and 13	1991–*c.* 1700	2778–2565	3579–2913	2738–1918
Second Intermediate Period				
Dynasties 14–17 (Hyksos and Theban Kings)	*c.* 1760–1570	2565–1587 (Hyksos 1928–1587)	2913–1587	1918–1583 (Hyksos 2371–1593)
New Kingdom				
Dynasties 18–20	1552–1070	1587–1102		1583–
Third Intermediate Period				
Dynasties 21–24	1070–712	1102–721		
Ethiopian Dynasty (25th)	712–657	748–664		
Saite Dynasty (26th)	664–525	664–525		
Persian Domination and last native kings	525–332	525–332		
Macedonian and Ptolemaic Kings	332–30	332–30		

NOTES

1. Dates vary slightly in different histories; in general, the chronology adopted in the *Cambridge Ancient History* (3rd edition, 1970) is here followed.
2. In *A History of Egypt* 1st edition, 1894–6 (Vol. III, 1906).
3. In *Researches in Sinai*, 1906, ch. xii, "The Revision of Chronology", somewhat modified in *Historical Studies*, 1911, pp. 20–22.
4. In *The Making of Egypt*, 1939.

APPENDIX B

Sites of work done by Flinders Petrie, or under his supervision

1881–3	Giza
1882	Abu Rawash
1884	Tanis*
1885	Naucratis*
1886	Nabesha*, Defenna*
1887	Aswan, Western Thebes, Dahshur
1888	Biahmu, Arsinoë
1888–9	Hawara
1889–90	Kahun, Ghurob
1890	El Lahun
1890	Tell el Hesy
1890–91	Meydum
1891–2	Tell el ʻAmarna
1893–4	Koptos
1894–5	Ballas, Naqada
1895–6	Western Thebes, Ramesseum
1896	Behnesa* (Oxyrhynchus)
1897	Deshasha*
1897–8	Dendara*
1898–9	Abadiya*, Hu*
1899–1904	Abydos*
1900–1	Mahasna, Beit Khallaf, El ʻAmra*
1903–4	Ahnas*, Sedment*, Ghurob*
1904	Buto*
1904–5	Wady Maghara*, Serabit* (Sinai)
1905	Tell el Maskhuta
1905–6	Tell el Yehudiya
1906	Tell el Retaba, Saft el Henna, Ghita
1906–7	Giza, Rifa, Bala'iza, Shaganba
1907	Atrib, Deir el Abyad, Hagarsa
1908	Memphis
1908–9	Qurna
1909	Memphis
1909–10	Meydum
1910	Memphis
1910–11	Hawara, Mazghuna, Gerza
1911	Memphis, Shurafa, Atfih
1911–12	Tarkhan, Kafr ʻAmmar
1912	Memphis, Heliopolis
1912–13	Tarkhan, Riqqa
1913	Memphis
1913–14	el Lahun, Haraga
1919–20	el Lahun, Kahun, Ghurob
1920–1	Ghurob, Sedment
1921–2	Abydos
1922	Behnesa
1923–4	Qau, Hemamiya (Badari)
1926–7	Tell Jemmeh
1928–30	Tell Farʻa
1930–4	Tell el ʻAjjul (Gaza)
1935–7	Shaikh Zoweyd
1937–8	Tell el ʻAjjul
1938	Transjordan survey

* For the Egypt Exploration Society.

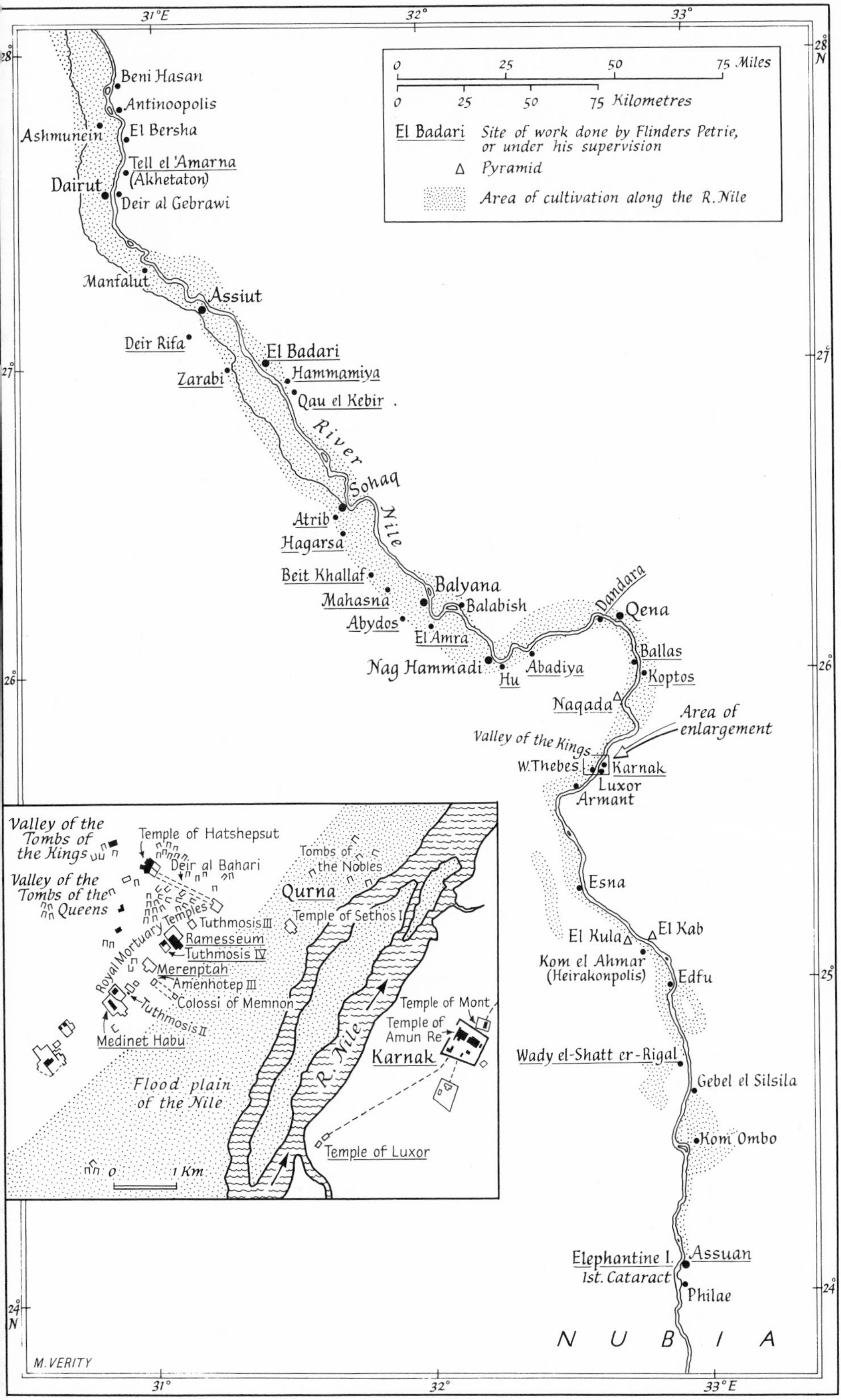
31°E
32°
33°
28° N
27°
26°
25°
24° N
0 25 50 75 Miles
0 25 50 75 Kilometres
El Badari Site of work done by Flinders Petrie, or under his supervision
Pyramid
Area of cultivation along the R. Nile
Beni Hasan
Antinoopolis
Ashmunein
El Bersha
Tell el 'Amarna (Akhetaton)
Dairut
Deir al Gebrawi
Manfalut
Assiut
Deir Rifa
El Badari
Zarabi
Hammamiya
Qau el Kebir
River Nile
Sohaq
Atrib
Hagarsa
Beit Khallaf
Balyana
Mahasna
Balabish
Abydos
El Amra
Nag Hammadi
Hu
Abadiya
Dandara
Qena
Ballas
Koptos
Naqada
Area of enlargement
Valley of the Kings
W. Thebes
Karnak
Luxor
Armant
Esna
El Kula
El Kab
Kom el Ahmar (Heirakonpolis)
Edfu
Wady el-Shatt er-Rigal
Gebel el Silsila
Kom Ombo
Elephantine I.
1st. Cataract
Assuan
Philae
N U B I A
M. VERITY
Valley of the Tombs of the Kings
Valley of the Tombs of the Queens
Temple of Hatshepsut
Deir al Bahari
Tombs of the Nobles
Qurna
Temple of Sethos I
Royal Mortuary Temples
Tuthmosis III
Ramesseum
Tuthmosis IV
Merenptah
Amenhotep III
Colossi of Memnon
Tuthmosis II
Medinet Habu
Flood plain of the Nile
R. Nile
Temple of Mont
Temple of Amun Re
Karnak
Temple of Luxor
0 1 Km

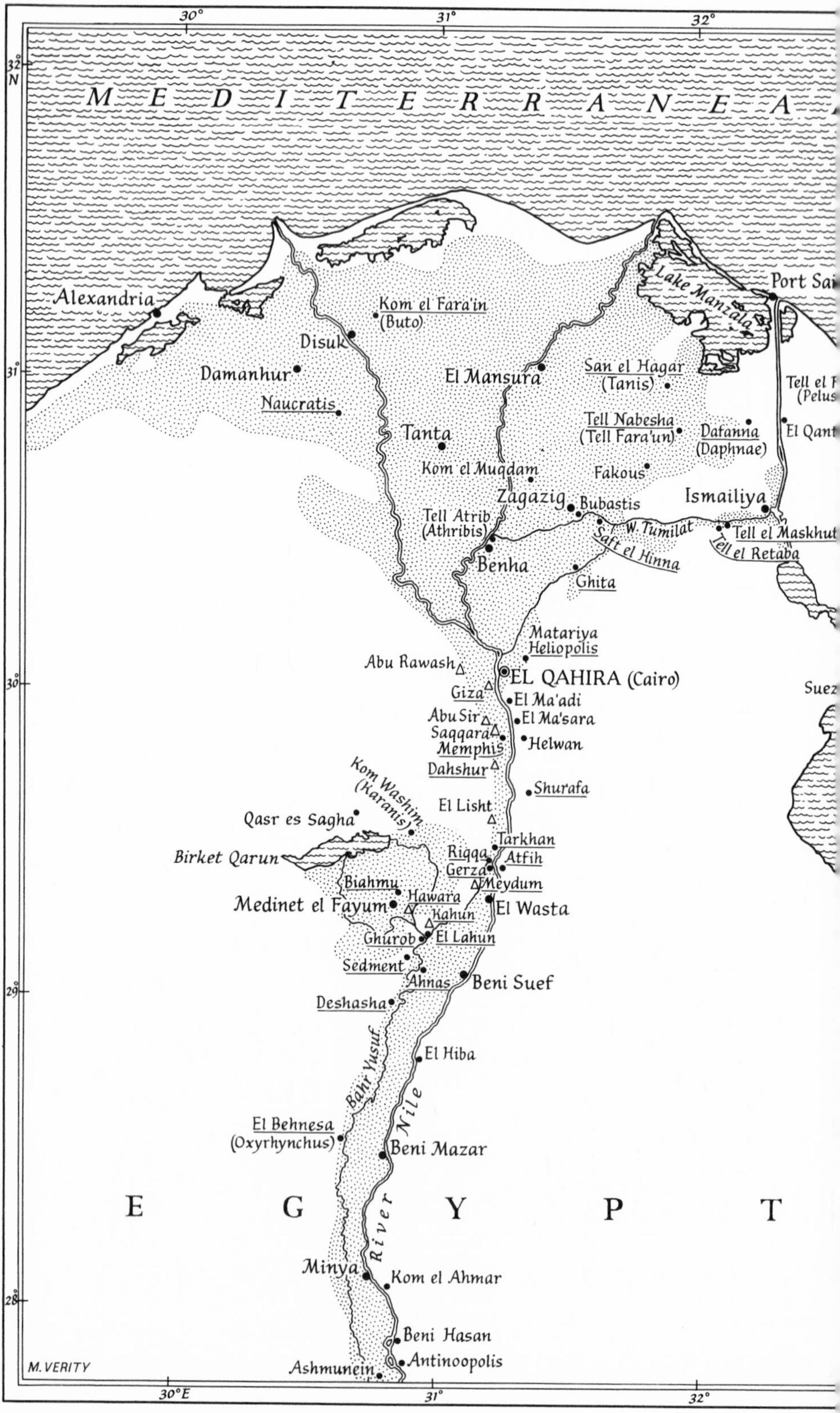

30°
31°
32°
32° N
MEDITERRANEA
Alexandria
Kom el Fara'in
(Buto)
Disuk
Damanhur
Naucratis
Tanta
El Mansura
San el Hagar
(Tanis)
Lake Manzala
Port Sai
Tell el F
(Pelus
Tell Nabesha
(Tell Fara'un)
Dafanna
(Daphnae)
El Qant
Kom el Muqdam
Fakous
Zagazig
Bubastis
Ismailiya
Tell Atrib
(Athribis)
W. Tumilat
Tell el Maskhut
Tell el Retaba
Saft el Hinna
Benha
Ghita
31°
Matariya
Heliopolis
Abu Rawash
EL QAHIRA (Cairo)
30°
Suez
Giza
El Ma'adi
Abu Sir
El Ma'sara
Saqqara
Memphis
Helwan
Dahshur
Kom Washim
(Karanis)
Shurafa
El Lisht
Qasr es Sagha
Tarkhan
Birket Qarun
Riqqa
Atfih
Gerza
Meydum
Biahmu
Hawara
Medinet el Fayum
El Wasta
Kahun
Ghurob
El Lahun
Sedment
Ahnas
Beni Suef
29°
Deshasha
Bahr Yusuf
El Hiba
River Nile
El Behnesa
(Oxyrhynchus)
Beni Mazar
EGYPT
Minya
Kom el Ahmar
28°
Beni Hasan
Antinoopolis
Ashmunein
M. VERITY
30°E
31°
32°

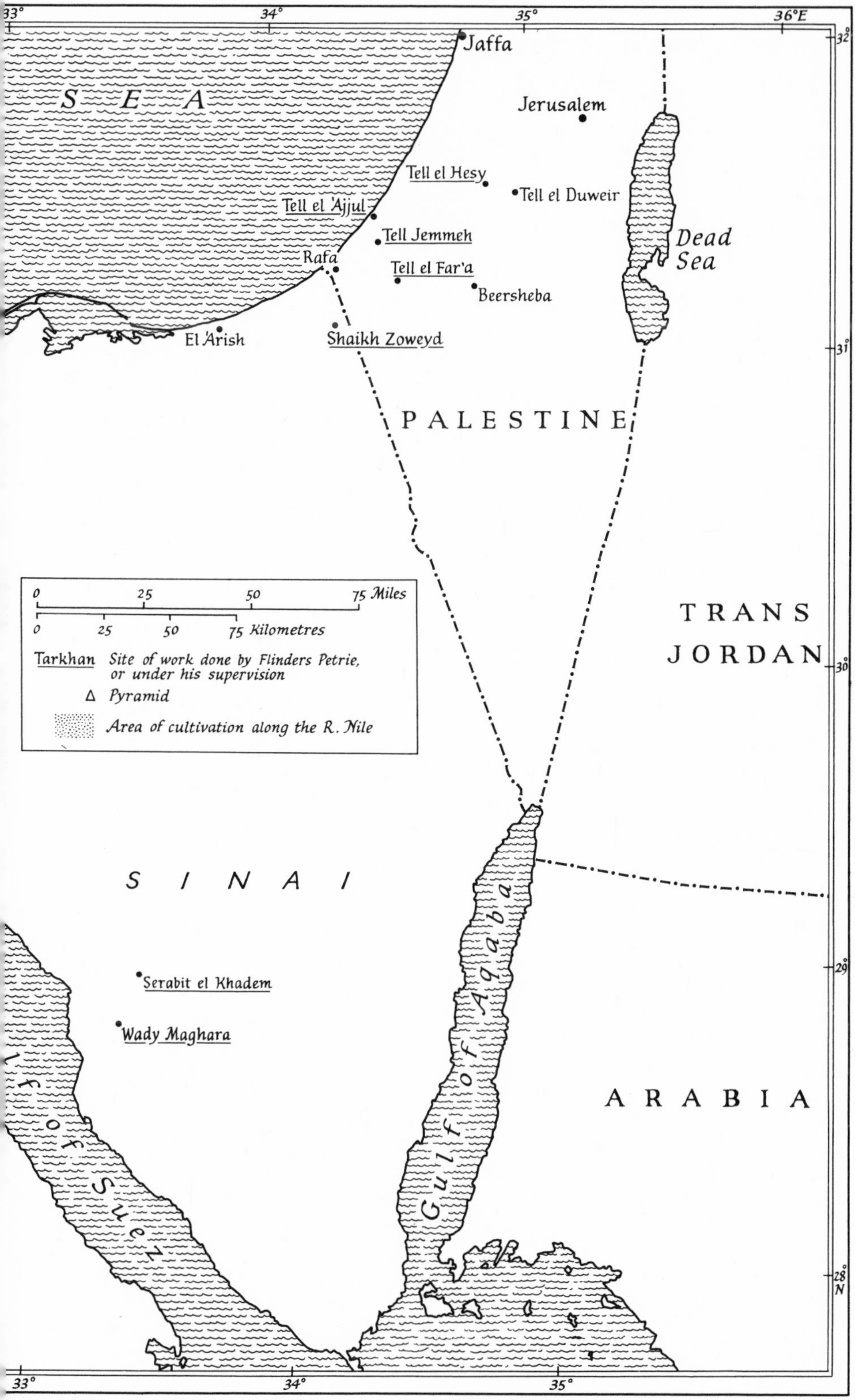

33°
34°
35°
36°E
32°
31°
30°
29°
28° N
S E A
Jaffa
Jerusalem
Tell el Hesy
Tell el Duweir
Tell el 'Ajjul
Tell Jemmeh
Rafa
Tell el Far'a
Beersheba
Dead Sea
El 'Arish
Shaikh Zoweyd
PALESTINE
TRANS JORDAN
0 25 50 75 Miles
0 25 50 75 Kilometres
Tarkhan Site of work done by Flinders Petrie, or under his supervision
Δ Pyramid
Area of cultivation along the R. Nile
SINAI
Gulf of Aqaba
Serabit el Khadem
Wady Maghara
...lf of Suez
ARABIA

APPENDIX C

U.C.L. Galton Papers 152/4

8 Crescent Road,
Bromley, Kent.
17 Feby. 1880

Sir,

Your appeal in Nature for data for your most interesting researches on mental numbers, induces one of the stupid sex to send you the following notes, though they rather shew the force of habit than anything else.

I have no mental tally, nor do I conceive of *numbers* except as written on paper. A large number of units (ie discontinuous quantity) I always conceive as a square, roughly taking the $\sqrt[2]{}$. Quantities to be operated, or continuous quantity, as numbers of dimensions, I either imagine on a scale of equal parts, with each 10 numbered & each 5 a long stroke, like a plotting scale (not necessarily extending to zero); or more usually I think of the number on a slide rule, which I have used more than any other form of scale; in fact complex multiplication (as 27 × 17) I do very roughly (within 1/20 or so) by imagining a slide rule so set.

Decimal fractions I usually conceive as space; but vulgar fractions as the proportion of figures, with an innate sense of *weightiness* more than size. The number of my age is never prominent, in fact I never know it without reckoning. A space is not easily divided mentally into anything but tenths and hundredths. Fractional spaces (as in copying a plan by squares) are carried in the eye and reproduced, without reduction to any expressible standard. + and − are usually conceived of as heights on a uniform scale, *above* and *below* a datum line; not horizontally, though I have done very little levelling.

Mental arithmetic I always do as on paper; though the numbers, beyond the half-dozen or so immediately operated on, are not so much remembered by the mental image, as by the mental speech; going through the will of speech just short of actually using any muscles; except perhaps a slight accenting of the breath.

The limit of mental retention seems to be about a dozen figures in several different ways. Multiplication up to 3 figures by 3 (none of them being 1 or 2), square root to 8 places, Permutations of such words as *Concatenation*, I do without seeing the question; and, with the question on paper to refer to, such algebra as differentiation of tolerably simple fractions as $\frac{x(x+1)}{x^2+x+1}$, $\frac{x^3}{x^2-1} - \frac{x^2}{x-1}$, or $a^x(x^2 - 2x + 2)$, &c.

Connected with mental numbering is the accuracy of estimation of fractions, on which I have tested about a dozen people; part of the results I published in Nature (16 Decr. 1875); and I hope that among your mental statistics you may take it up, as it gives an easy and delicate numerical test of accuracy. The average error of all people tried is 1/55 of the whole space; my own (in later trials than those in Nature) is 1/173.

The retention of colour and sound is a branch well worth working. I do not sharply detect small discords, and am abashed by people complaining of a want of tuning in a piano which I had not observed; perhaps 1/6 or 1/8 of a semitone is the least I can detect; yet *absolute* pitch, without any standard for reference, I can always be certain about (if pure) to the nearest semitone.

Another branch of memory & judgement combined is the accuracy of guessing the ages of books & other things, by their appearance; an estimation employing more complex considerations, but which can be performed with greater accuracy than would be supposed.

I remain, Sir,
yours truly,
W. M. Flinders Petrie

INDEX